Puntsagdash Luvsandorj,
Chuluundorj Khashchuluun,
Namsrai Batnasan (Eds.)

Mongolia at the Market

Global Cultural and Economic Research

Volume 7

LIT

Mongolia at the Market

Dedicated to the 60th Anniversary
of the School of Economic Studies

edited by

Puntsagdash Luvsandorj,
Chuluundorj Khashchuluun,
and Namsrai Batnasan

LIT

Bibliographic information published by the Deutsche Nationalbibliothek
The Deutsche Nationalbibliothek lists this publication in the Deutsche Nationalbibliografie; detailed bibliographic data are available in the Internet at http://dnb.d-nb.de.

ISBN 978-3-643-90213-9

A catalogue record for this book is available from the British Library

Klosbachstr. 107
CH-8032 Zürich
Tel. +41 (0) 44-251 75 05
Fax +41 (0) 44-251 75 06
e-Mail: zuerich@lit-verlag.ch
http://www.lit-verlag.ch

LIT VERLAG Dr. W. Hopf
Berlin 2012
Fresnostr. 2
D-48159 Münster
Tel. +49 (0) 2 51-620 320
Fax +49 (0) 2 51-23 19 72
e-Mail: lit@lit-verlag.de
http://www.lit-verlag.de

Distribution:
In Germany: LIT Verlag Fresnostr. 2, D-48159 Münster
Tel. +49 (0) 2 51-620 32 22, Fax +49 (0) 2 51-922 60 99, e-mail: vertrieb@lit-verlag.de

In Austria: Medienlogistik Pichler-ÖBZ, e-mail: mlo@medien-logistik.at

In Switzerland: B + M Buch- und Medienvertrieb, e-mail: order@buch-medien.ch

In the UK: Global Book Marketing, e-mail: mo@centralbooks.com

CONTENTS

ACKNOWLEDGEMENTS

The authors would like to thank Professor Em. Dr. Dr. h. c. Sung Jo Park, Free University, Berlin, who suggested to translate and publish the book in English and provided invaluable help and support throughout the whole process and everyone at the School of Economic Studies, NUM, for their support, enthusiasm, hard work, in particular associate professor B. Davaasuren, Marketing Department, lecturers of the English Language Centre, who translated the book into English- E. Sainbileg /chapters 1,2, 8/, L. Enkhmend /chapters 3, 7, 9/, Ts. Bayarmaa /chapter 4/, Siilegmaa /chapter 6/, professor D. Dagvadorj from Marketing Department /chapter 5/ and D. Chimgee from Mathematics and Computing department /chapter 4.5/.

PREFACE

The present book *Mongolia at the market*, which summarized economic transition and development process in the years after Mongolia has chosen the market economy at the national level, is the second major work by lecturers and researchers of the School of Economic Studies, NUM.

The book *Mongolian Economy: a handbook of economy in transition* was written in 1999 in cooperation with academics from the University of Manchester, and summarized objectives and policies of the first period of transition. It was published in Ulaanbaatar in Mongolian in 1999, and then in English in the UK and USA in 2000. Although transition and development are interdependent, the new book paid special attention to development issues as well as to the transition ones. Moreover, it is unique as an independent joint work of lecturers and researchers of the National University.

The authors studied the economic transition and development processes at the national level as well as in each sector of the national economy. They examined the general process of the emerging new economic system and each component of the market, so summarized outcomes of their study made a comprehensive research work at national level.

It is good to notice that the book *Mongolia at the market*, a result of comprehensive independent research by lecturers and researchers of the School of Economic Studies, NUM at national level, has become a good present to the academic community on the 60th anniversary of the SES.

Ts. Gantsog	President of National University of Mongolia
Ch. Hashchuluun	Dean of School of Economic Studies

FOREWORD

The book "Mongolia at the market", fruit of collaborative efforts of academics and researchers of the School of Economic Studies, NUM, is a second major study on economic transition and development of Mongolia at the national level in the years since transition of the country to market economy.

The first book on goals and policies of the initial stage of transition, **The Mongolian Economy: A manual of Applied Economics for a Country in Transition** was written in collaboration with academics of the University of Manchester, UK, and was published in Mongolian in Ulaanbaatar, 1999 and then in English, in the USA. Although transition and development are interdependent, the new book offered to your attention is concerned with development issues in equal measure as with transition. Along with it, it is a joint work of the National University academics.

Authors studied economic transition and development processes at the national level by sectors along with the processes of emerging new market economy system in general and by each market component. Study results were consolidated and became a comprehensive national research.

An outcome of comprehensive research carried out by academics and researchers of the School of Economic Studies, NUM, at the national level, the joint work **Mongolia at the market**, became a nice present to the academic community on the 60th anniversary of the school .

The book "Mongolia at the market", written by academics and researchers of the School of Economic Studies, NUM, puts forward an aim to study at the national level in a comprehensive way the process of economic transition and development in the years since Mongolia started the transition to market economy; to describe the new market economic system of Mongolia on the basis of analysis of economic branches, sectors, market components; to examine issues of transition and development, which determine trends of national economic development.

The first chapter on **Outcomes of transition and development trends** describes economic outcomes of transition on a scientific basis, for instance, processes of halting economic crisis and start of recovery, how the national economy became based on the private sector, profound reforms in the structure of its sectors; emergence of elements of the market structures, formation of new relationships; and analyzes unique academic problems of transition economy that took place in transition economies, including Mongolia, which can enrich the modern economic science.

The second chapter on **Human development and labor market** describes changes in demographic situation during the transition process, for instance, changes in the population structure, the birth and mortality rates, migration; changes in the living standards, poverty, inequality and basic social services, for instance, reforms in education, health and social security areas and determines their future trends. Along with it, the process of the labor market formation, numerous issues of employment and unemployment in the frame of regulation and conflicts of labor demand and supply are studied.

The third chapter on the **New banking and finance system and financial markets** examines issues of the state budget, its income and expenditures, local budgets, the state financial policy and financial policies of business enterprises, management reforms; emergence and development of a two-tiered banking system; issues of increasing the role of the financial sector in economy, further improvement of environment for financial market development.

The fourth chapter on **the economic branches and sectors** looks at reforms and development of the basic sectors of the national economic system, for instance, agriculture, industry, construction, transportation, information and communications, domestic trade, tourism industry. Special attention is paid to examination of industrial, information technology and tourism sectors, which have a potential for future development in our country.

The fifth chapter on the **Market and private sector** makes an attempt to apply the theoretical basis of classification of markets by economic contents and regional conditions and by competitive characteristics in Mongolian conditions. The consumer market, which presently is developing in a greater measure in our country, is examined separately and the Mongolian economic business environment is evaluated. A special study is dedicated to emergence and development of the private sector as the market basis, and its role in the market economy.

The sixth chapter on **Business management and organization** includes methodological problems which might be important in management and organization of Mongolian business enterprises, especially companies.

The seventh chapter on **Reform of accounting system** studies methodological and practical issues of the shift of financial reporting to the international standards, formation of the new accounting and auditing system, development of policy coordination, monitoring system, services, information technology related to the shift of national accounting system to international standards and makes conclusions and recommendations in this area.

The eighth chapter on **Economic cooperation and international markets** examines issues of foreign trade, foreign investment, loans and assistance. The process of transition and development, which started with liberalization of foreign trade, is analyzed by the export and import structure, location of countries, main products. Policy and coordination issues are studied and future development trends are determined.

Foreign investment is studied by countries and economic sectors with a special emphasis on the mining sector. Foreign assistance and loans are looked at by donor organizations and countries. Proposals on increasing their effectiveness and role in the national economic transition and development are made.

The ninth chapter on the **Future development perspectives of Mongolian economy** briefly looks at some issues of future development with an aim to add some ideas to the official document called the *Comprehensive policy of national development* where issues of future development of national economy are reflected.

In the end, general conclusions made in each chapter of this book are consolidated.

Editors: N. Batnasan
P. Luvsandorj
Ch. Hashchuluun

CHAPTER ONE

OUTCOMES OF TRANSITION AND DEVELOPMENT TRENDS

Abstract

This article aims to determine Mongolian experience of transition to the market economy on a scientific basis, for instance, to analyze processes of halting economic crisis and starting economic recovery, national economy becoming based on the private sector, deep reforms in the structure of this sector; emergence of elements of the market structure, formation of new relationships, and to sum up some unique scientific issues of transition economy which emerged from the countries with transition economy, Mongolia among them, that can enrich the modern economic science.

1.1 ACADEMIC PROBLEMS OF TRANSITION ECONOMY

The modern economic science has become a great force of knowledge in creating wealth and eliminating poverty. It covers the global community expanding its frame by creating new sectors. However, the academic economic theory schools have national characteristics such as American, British, German, Japanese etc. In developing countries where the majority of humanity lives or in countries in transition development of this science is relatively poor.

Development economics and transition economics may be called a poorly studied "grey stain" in the global economic science and national schools in this direction have not yet been formed. It is related to the fact that new trends in development economics and its mentality in the last half of the 20th century and in transition economics in the brink of the two centuries have appeared recently.

In the end of the 20th century, in the beginning of the 21st century a historic change took place in the global economic system, when former socialist countries with centrally planned economies started a historic transition to the market economy. By its scale, it is a historic process which covered one third of humanity and by its content it is a process which undermines the economic base of the world which was previously divided into two systems. It is also a real basis for implementation of the globalization concept with its declaration of one world, one humanity.

As for Mongolia, only recently a socialist mentality of eliminating poverty on the basis of common property prevailed. At present, following the universal way of humanity, a new mentality of establishing a market economy based on private property is being formed. That is why study of and teaching of modern economic science is a new issue for Mongolia. Especially study of transition economy is a completely new issue. These two together shall become a basis for formation of a national school of economic science in Mongolia. With regard to that there is a need to study the transition economy on a theoretical basis along with study and teaching of modern economic science.

1. **That transition economy is a new branch of science is based on the mixed economy system, and the object of study as well as methods are defined, and certain results are achieved in study of fundamental problems.**

The transition economy science can be imagined as the product of economic theory and the real life practice of countries in transition. Comparative economics research methods need to be used in this case.

In the frame of the transition economy science our object of study is to find answers to such questions as why market laws are not suitable at the moment to the Mongolian economy and how the national economy can be turned into the mainstream.

As our studies show the Mongolian economy in the beginning of transition might be called "not by book"/as it should be/, because the classic market theory was not suitable in the beginning.

Should money supply be increased when the economy faces inflation? According to the theory, the reason of emerging demand inflation is that abundance of money leads to high prices, but if there is short supply of money, inflation will reduce. This is the classical monetarist theory and its common recipe is to reduce supply of money in order to reduce inflation. However, when in our country the currency rate fell down by 5900, the supply of goods reduced by 50% and inflation soared, which worried everyone, there was shortage of cash. Due to objective demand in cash because crisis for agricultural products needed to be increased and crop cultivation activities needed to be financed, money in use were added. It was not very dangerous, because in our country a cost inflation was dominating and did not feel the amount of cash at the same level as the demand inflation. While the demand inflation is stopped by reducing the amount of cash, to stop the cost inflation such methods as support of production and improved goods supply are more appropriate.

Should the prices be higher when production is declining? Decline of production when prices fall is the demand and supply law. According to the same law when prices rise, production should increase too. However, in our country the volume of national production fell by 20-30% when the prices of consumer goods and services soared by 6000%. This is again "not by book".

When the economy is not "by book" can a policy be also "not by book"? When the government defined the main directions of economic and social development in 1992, they put forward an objective to increase the national income production by 8%, but it failed. From this situation we can see a direct answer that if the economy is "not by book" the policy cannot be the same. So is it appropriate to follow policies based on theory when the economy is "not by book"? A strict monetary policy is followed. Such a policy plays a significant role in increasing the interest rate within the country, in attracting foreign capital, in reducing payment balance deficit. However, high interest rates are not in line with the objective of supporting the newly emerging private enterprises. The answer is that policies based on theories should not be directly copied when the economy is not as it should be. It is important to adopt such policies to transition economies. We need to find ways to introduce the economy which is "by book" into the books. In our country a unique process of deliberate transition from the centrally planned economy to the market is taking place, not the process of natural transition from … economy to the commodities economy. It is necessary that policy, decision and law makers always paid attention to this fact as it is the main reason of all problems. It might be that reason for poor implementation of approved laws, policies and decisions is also in this fact.

2. The difference in economic theory schools is the issue of the role of the state in economy. This issue is also related to the transition economies.

One of fundamental problems of transition economics, namely, the role of the state in economy was examined specifically and a conclusion was made that reproducing directly the role played by the state in developed countries in developing countries is hazardous.

The state carries out the following multiple duties in underdeveloped countries with transition economy:

- To create a legal environment for market economy: a double duty of, first, approving new laws, second, approving directives and instructions in order to cover gaps in present laws until the new ones are adopted.
- To be an owner of natural environment and exhaustible resources
- To provide for public health and social security
- To develop education, culture and science
- To provide national security and defense
- To protect the rural population from urban profiteers /speculators?/
- To define a "winning" sector in national economy and privatize it when required
- To participate directly at market as a subject representing the public sector

- To create conditions for competition within the country and abroad to public industries, to protect them and prevent from bankruptcy by developing their competitiveness

In transition and developing economies the role of the state is enormous, but it is very small compared to that in the centrally planned economy, greater than according to the Keynes concept, but the Freedman doctrine is not yet suitable. The state implements unique new duties along with its common responsibilities. For instance, the Mongolian state should take a new responsibility for creating a new sector or a new industry with a future called "the winner", which is necessary to all developing countries. Along with this the Mongolian state should implement such new duties as protecting rural herders from urban traders; protecting the national industry from bankruptcy by improving its competitiveness.

The state of Mongolia coordinates the money of taxpayers, income privatization, assets from the foreign aid, assistance and loans, and owns some of them. In brief, the state is the largest capitalist in Mongolia. One example of it is that the state accumulates over 40% of the net income of economic entities in its budget and uses over 20% of GDP. These two facts are a quantitative proof of the above mentioned theoretical conclusions.

3. **Large structural changes, which can be called fundamental, one due to impact of transition and another one of development process, will take place in the transition economy.**

In the course of transition to the market a surprising conclusion was made that a process of "de-industrialization" took place in Mongolia. Statistical facts and figures show us the following picture. Industry (I) that accounted for 35% of GDP over a decade ago, now has 20%, and agriculture (A), which previously accounted for 15%, now takes up 35%. The service sector (S), which accounted previously for 50%, now takes up 45%, which shows that in over a decade the structure of the national economy moved from the SIA model to the SAI model. This is due to numerous reasons, but the major ones are fundamental changes in the financing system and prices. Along with this, decline of large local and state industries that are not to be recovered should also be included in the de-industrialization process. It is proper to notice here that the sector, which had a capacity to overcome the difficulties of transition in Mongolia, was livestock breeding.

It is astounding that a process of rustication instead of urbanization takes place along with de-industrialization. Urban residents move to the countryside looking for ways of sustaining their livelihood, which leads to decreasing productivity of the sector. This is not a positive process, but obviously this process will turn around at some time. A theoretical formula can be derived here that the structure of the national economy in transition economy will change from the SIA model to the SAI model and back to the SIA model.

Although it may seem similar to the economic structure model of developed countries, it is not with regard to the content and the SIA is a temporary backward model, which will inevitably change to the ISA model. From this a theoretical formula can be derived that the structure of the national economy will be differentiated as the one under impact of transition and the one as a result of development.

4. **If economic sciences are taken as the basis, the Mongolian national economy can be defined as a system with a mix of different economies such as transition economy with elements of the centrally planned and market economy; development economy which is the basis of its development; elements of market economy structure dependent on global economy determining the future of development.**

As for the future space, the transition, development structures which are prominent at present will become slighter in the future and, on the contrary, the market, global structures which are small at present will become clearer in the future. The science will be introduced in real life and Mongolian economy will have a pure economic system.

As for introduction of science into real life, modern economic theories, transition, development, market, global economic theories should be used creatively in accordance with specific conditions of the certain country. For instance, when there is no soil to introduce a developed market theory it should be used gradually as a transition one; if the developing economy theory is outdated, it should be enriched with market and global economic theories; if the global economy theory cannot be introduced directly, it should be used in adaptation to the development and market theories. This is a basis for scientific concept that should be followed in developing and implementing transition and development issues of Mongolian economy.

5. **Experience of counties with transition economy raises unique scientific problems which can enrich the modern economic science and the transition economy. With further expansion of the research frame this knowledge base will grow richer. With use of scientific knowledge in the practice of transition the results of transition will grow.**

Now we can give a new, scientifically based definition of the centrally planned economy.

(1) The macroeconomic balance is under state control. Nominal prices and wages were fixed in the whole of economy. Internal financial activities of

companies were passive, it can be said that only salaries were paid in cash. Purchasing power, level of wages, demand and supply were coordinated forcibly. In the beginning of decline because of loss of balance between wages and prices cash was accumulated in the household economy.

(2) Coordination through plans: economic activity was based on central plan with the number of output targets dictated by the plan. Industry was more dominant compared to services.

(3) Little private ownership: with few exceptions all property belonged to the state and private ownership was not allowed. It denied real efficiency. At that time larger enterprises were more adapted to the plans.

(4) Distorted prices: prices played an accounting role and were reflected in the plan. Prices for housing, power, transportation, education and medical care were kept low and land was free of charge. Costs did not influence changes in prices, low prices were kept in trade and economic activities were conducted in this way.

Let us look briefly at history of development of the centrally planned economic system in Mongolia. Like other people, Mongolian have an ancient history of division and unity, rise and fall. The Great Mongolian Empire founded by Chingis Khan in the 12-13th centuries, is well-known throughout the world. There was also a period when the Mongolian state had lost its independence and had been under the Manchu rule for over 200 years (1691-1911).

As a result of the national liberation movement in 1911 and the People's revolution victory in 1921, Mongolia attained its independence, eliminated the feudal rule and embarked on the new road of free, independent development. **The history of development of the centrally planned economy in Mongolia started from this period.**

(1) The general picture of economic development of Mongolia in 1911-1940 was in many respects similar to the current process of transition to the market economy rather than the centrally planned economy. The main difference is that in the historic period, when the country was at the crossroads of 2 economic development ways, the path of economic development had an orientation not to the market, but to a centrally planned economy. That is why that early period is regarded as a stage which laid prerequisites to the centrally planned economy.

As a result of new economic development such new economic sectors as trade, industry, transportation, communications were established. The turnover of retail trade increased by 21.1 times, and the share of the state trade in 1940 accounted for 30.8%, while cooperatives contributed 59.5% and the private sector- 9.5%. Industrial production, which in 1924 equaled 0.3 million MNT, reached 124.7 million MNT in 1940 and the freight turnover of road transportation increased from 0.3 million ton kilometers to 13.3 million ton kilometers. In the same year the country had 25 post offices, 20 telephone stations, 2.4 thousand telephone points, 16 radio stations, 4.4 thousand wired-radio outlets, 10.9 thousand kilometers of telephone and telegraph lines.

In the process of new cultural development such new sectors of non-material sphere as education, culture, science, arts, healthcare, physical culture and sports were established. It can be said that a "cultural revolution" took place in the country.

A fact that the state had a monopoly for foreign trade can be noted in history as an important phenomenon, which strengthened the political independence of the country by adding economic independence and expelling foreign capital thus providing prerequisites for non-capitalist way of development. History remains history, but a new approach can be used in recording history. Based on the international trade theory and the experience of Mongolia making a transition to the market, it can be concluded that a monopoly of the state to all products of foreign trade, exclusion of all trade partners except for one was a historical mistake related to establishment of the centrally planned economy in the country and orientation towards establishing a socialist system in the world. However, foundation of new economic sectors, national trade and financial system aided greatly to strengthening of the newly attained independence of Mongolia in economic aspect as well.

(2) While in the formative stage of the centrally planned economy there were various forms of property, in the end the state enterprises, state cooperatives or the social sector prevailed. It can be said that with the exception of the last few years, Mongolia at that time had trade and economic relations only with the former Soviet Union.

In 1941-1960 the Gross National Product increased by 3.7 times and the national industrial income grew up by 3.8 times. In 1959 collectivization of the private economy was completed. Along with this, another important objective of agricultural development, namely, cultivation of virgin lands was realized. As a result, the country could meet domestic demand in crops in full measure, and crop cultivation became an independent branch of agriculture.

The Mongolian economy was directed towards further industrialization and the share of other industrialized sectors had been growing continuously. While in 1940 these sectors accounted for about 10% of national income, in 1960 it grew to over 30%.

While in 1950 the state and cooperative sectors accounted for 29.5% of the national income, in 1960 this figure reached nearly 100%. It illustrated that formation of the centrally planned economy in Mongolia had been completed.

(3) In 1961-1990 the country had a centrally planned economy dominated by the state property. At that time over-centralization of economic management on the basis of the state plans led to severe restriction of market relations. Bringing production cooperatives into state forms (1972) eliminated trade of products produced by private enterprises and members of agricultural cooperatives were restricted in sales of some part of produce of farms at the market at free prices. In that period the GNP and the national income grew by 5 and 3.9 times respectively. It was a result of rapid growth of industrialized sectors, especially the prevailing growth of industrial production.

The centrally planned economy had the state subject, nationalized object, planned relationships and mechanisms of enforcement. For instance, Mongolian economy was closed within the frame of the Council of Mutual Economic Assistance /CMEA/, and it was protected by the mechanism of the foreign trade monopoly. Furthermore, the monopoly of the state for foreign trade not only protected the national industry from external forces, but also was an unlimited power to isolate it, which is shown by history. It means that the foreign trade monopoly was one of mechanisms to protect the centrally planned economy and only the centrally planned economy provided such power.

Now we know how to change the centrally planned economy.

(1) A need will arise to recover lost economic stabilization. Stabilization is lost due to liberalization of prices and wages. In general, prices increase, which is related to repressed inflation. The immediate challenge for macroeconomic policy is to slow down the price growth and contain inflation. This change requires transition from the passive to the active monetary policy in economy.

    Persisting inflationary trends are related to a large volume of subsidies given previously to the industrial entities. Liberalization of prices and trade, increasing share and size of the private sector become reasons for reducing subsidies, which in its term reduces inflation.

(2) Production decreases due to breakdown of regulation mechanism. Sudden abolition of comprehensive planning will lead to a need for overall reform of economic regulation. There will be a need to totally change the regulation. This breakdown will influence both efficient and inefficient industries and will continue until an efficient market system evolves. Increasing costs within a short period will bring supply to a halt. After industrial decline and breakdown of planning development of a new market will take place gradually and the process of market liberalization will become stable.

(3) Production will recover due to private ownership and the private sector growth. During market economy with mixed prices profitable industries will be established within the frame of the private sector. In this way economic growth and development will be provided by freedom and growth and development of private sector. Efficient production will be born as a result of competition.

(4) An objective situation of micro-economy and sectors will be provided. This is achieved as a result of price and trade liberalization and elimination of subsidies and will influence change in demand. With elimination of subsidies to centralized industries and decreasing size of industry and agriculture, redistribution of property will take place. This redistribution becomes another indicator providing industrial growth and creates an appropriate mechanism of dependency on demand.

Although these factors reduce production at the first, they improve it in the long run.

In the course of the study it is determined that the stabilization policy including privatization, liberalization, fiscal policy that will reform the command system towards market economy is a new direction, enriching the modern economic science, one of fundamentals of the transition economic science.

In that way, from the experience of countries with transition economies unique academic problems are emerging in transition economy that is enriching the modern economic science. As the frame of study broadens, the knowledge base will grow. With use of scientific knowledge in transition practice results of transition will increase.

1.2 MAJOR OUTCOMES OF THE ECONOMIC TRANSITION

With successful implementation of a comprehensive policy of economic liberalization and stabilization the process of transition in Mongolia is bringing its results.

1. The first major outcome of transition is recovery of declining national economy

In the process of transition from the centrally planned economy to the market reform and changes take place in the whole frame of economy. For instance:

- State property is privatized gradually and the frame of the private sector expands. As for property relations, the basis of common property basis becomes limited and the basis of private property prevails. It means that property in the common frame will be transferred to the private frame. As the owner of the property changes, new relationships emerge.
- A process of price liberalization and bringing them to the international level will take place throughout the country. Due to this a re-distribution of profit and income will take place and the positions of sectors in the national economy, even that of every product will change, too. In the aspect of labor relations it means that the flow of workforce will turn to the most profitable, high-income sector. The prices for all products will not be planned, but will be determined by market laws. Products with low demand would not sell and unprofitable industries will stop.
- In the process of foreign trade liberalization and opening of the national economy reform of labor distribution and industrial and service diversification will take place not only in the national, but also in the international frame. It means that low quality products would not sell not only abroad, but also within the country and industries and services with outdated technologies will cease exist. In a broad sense it means that a great structural change of the national economy will take place in accordance with the international demand.

At that time when a comprehensive policy of economic liberalization and stabilization started to be implemented and processes of reform and changes took place, the national economy entered a deep crisis.

(1) In 1990-1992, at the peak of economic crisis, such main processes of reform and fundamental changes towards market economy relations as price liberalization, privatization of the state property, establishment of the new banking system and foreign trade liberalization started. Agricultural collective farms or negdels were disbanded ad herders acquired private property, the trade and service sector was

privatized with capital investment vouchers and first private enterprises emerged. However, in 1989-1993 the GDP declined by 23%, the volume of foreign trade, export and import decreased twice.

The domestic processing industry went into decline due to lack of working capital and loss of foreign markets. The national currency rate plummeted and the state budget suffered great losses. Loss of the economic balance led to such acute social problems as unemployment and poverty and living standards of population have declined sharply. Although transition to the market is a universal way, an urgent need arose to realize that it is important to study carefully principles of the transition economy in order to adopt them to the unique features of their own country and to take measures on increasing some state coordination and participation.

(2) The government established by MRP as a result of the 1992 elections continued economic liberalization by slowing down industrial decline, correcting distortions made in the course of privatization, increasing efficiency, gradual liberalization of prices, currency rates and foreign trade along with implementation of a strict budget and fiscal policy. As a result, the inflation rate, which reached 325.5% in 1992, decreased twice in 1993, falling down to 183.0% and in 1994 it declined 5 times dropping to 63%. At this stage of transition comprehensive measures were taken in order to decrease budget losses. As a result, the share of total budget deficit in GDP which equaled 15% in 1992 went down to 2.9% in 1995.

Since Mongolia became a member of the IMF, World Bank and ADB and started receiving assistance from them, an external environment for sustainable reform and changes was established. A group of donors and partners supporting reform and changes in Mongolia was founded and nearly 30 countries and over 10 large international organizations became it members.

In that way, due to sound government policy and assistance from international financial organizations and foreign countries, fundamental conditions for economic recovery were created in Mongolia. Operations of some industries were recovered and economy started growing for the first time from the start of transition. In 1994, the volume of GDP increased by 2.3%, in 1995 it went up by 6.3%, the budget balance became positive, the foreign trade deficit declined sharply and the volume of export and import increased. Although some positive changes were observed in economy, the livelihood of population did not experience substantial progress. Real income of population declined, unemployment increased and poverty became widespread. The survey conducted in 1995 together with an international organization made a conclusion that poverty in Mongolia became an objective phenomenon and 36% of total population live in poverty.

In general, at this stage of transition market economic relations emerged and first trends of macro-economic stabilization and recovery were observed, which proved again significance of a sound policy and appropriate coordination from the state in implementing intensive economic changes and reforms.

(3) At the time of the government established by the Democratic party as the result of the 1996 elections, economic reform was represented by such policy measures as liberalization of basic prices and complete transition to the free system of prices and tariffs, intensification of structural reform in the banking sector, elimination of customs tax, acceleration of privatization. Elimination of customs taxes lead to dramatic decline of competitiveness of national industries, which were few in number, had inadequate technical and technological basis and inappropriate structure, so only mining and livestock breeding became a basis for the national economy. Slowdown of economic development since 1996 with an average annual growth of 2.4-3.5% was related to breakdown of the industrial sector and decline of its share in GDP. The unbalanced export structure was too sensitive and vulnerable to fluctuations of prices at the world market. Due to decline of prices for copper, cashmere, skins and hides at the global market the export income of our country fell by over 100.0 million USD in 1998, which affected the national budget income and led to problems in financing some planned activities. On the other hand, an unbalanced economic structure and the economy based basically on livestock breeding was too vulnerable and dependent on natural and climatic conditions. Only in 1999-2000 due to droughts and dzud over 10% of total livestock perished, which caused significant losses to the agricultural sector. In this way because of droughts and dzud the agricultural sector production decreased by nearly 20.0%, the real economic growth slowed down and equaled 1.1% in 2000.

By the way of establishing a 2-tiered banking system with free convertibility of the national currency, which is the fundament of the market economic relations, by implementing a strict fiscal policy the inflation rate was reduced to an ordinary number and the foreign currency reserve increased, which presented an important achievement.

(4) The government established by the MRP as a result of the 2000 parliament elections determined the mid-term development strategy of the country in its Action plan and started its implementation.

Negative effects of difficult weather conditions on economy of our country in 2000 and 2001, sharp decline of prices for the main export products - copper and cashmere at the world market, affected negatively the economic growth. The economic growth in 2000 and 2001 equaled 1.1% and in 2002 it grew to 3.9%, which was provided by growth in mining and processing industries, transportation, communications trade and services sectors. Death of 2.9 million livestock in 2002, which equaled 11.2% of the initial number of livestock, and drought during the crop ripening period in crop cultivation areas made a major impact on the 10.5% decline of the agricultural sector. However, in 2002 the volume of GDP equaled 1231.3 billion MNT by the prices of 2002 and grew by 10.4% compared to the previous year. While GDP per capita in 2000 was 426.6 USD, in 2001 it reached 460.1 USD and in 2002 it rose to 500.7 USD, growing in average by 8.3% in the last 2 years.

(5) The National Unity Government established after 2004 elections is implementing the mid-term program of economic development.

The economic growth in Mongolia is not steady. As economic growth in the last 4 years shows, it grew continuously for several years reaching 4.0% in 2002, 5.6% in 2003 and 10.7% in 2004, then in 2005 it declined to 6.2%. In 2006 the real economic growth in our country is expected to reach 7.5%. With regard to dramatic rise of prices for gold and copper the deflation growth of GDP is 18.6% and it is expected to reach 2891.7 billion MNT by the current prices.

The 7.5% economic growth is expected to be provided by 1.0% growth in agricultural sector, 2.3% in industrial sector and the remaining 4.2%- by the service sector.

Growth of production in knitwear and garment industry and food and beverages industry within the processing sector affected the present stable growth in economy. The number of tourists has grown leading to the growth in the hotel and catering sector. Establishment of the third mobile phone operator, expansion of trade and services activities had a major impact on economic growth. Decline of foreign trade deficit and improving trade conditions have also become one of conditions for economic growth.

The volume of foreign trade has been growing continuously and at present our country has trade relations with 104 countries in the world. The total turnover of foreign trade is expected to increase by 31.9% against 2005. Establishment and operations of the zinc plant in 2006 also affected economic growth.

While in 2005 the average monthly income of a household was 150 thousand MNT, in 2006, by evaluation of the first 6 months, the average monthly income reached 170 thousand MNT.

In the expected performance of the GDP in 2006 capital investment accounts for 26.0%, which is an increase of 25.0% or 156.4 billion MNT compared to the previous year.

The 2007 Basic Directions for Economic development are directed towards unemployment and poverty reduction by improving economic growth, strengthening macro-economic stability, supporting measures implemented in the social sector, improving business environment, increasing foreign and domestic investment and creating workplaces. The real economic growth in 2007 is planned to achieve 8.6%.

Therefore, as the study of development shows, the past decade has been a period of economic decline and recovery.

In the first years of transition economy declined sharply and in 1990-1993 the GDP decreased by over 20%. Since 1994, or as a result of growth in the last decade, the GDP reached the 1989 level only in 2002, i.e. after 13 years.

Figure 1.1 GDP growth acceleration 1981-2003 (%)

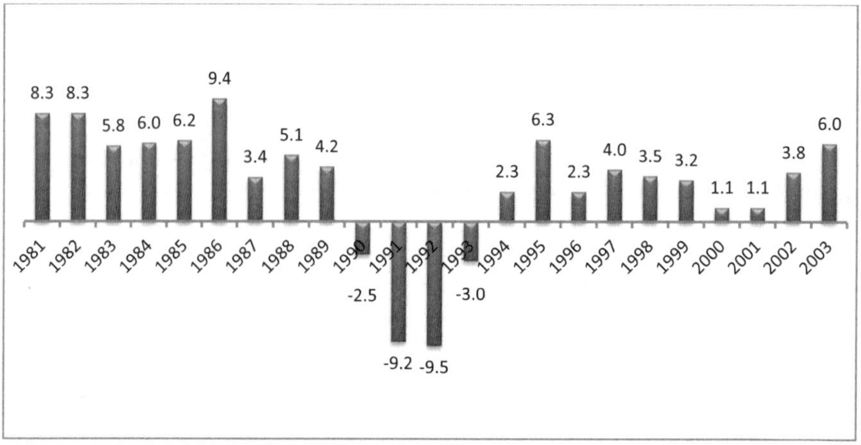

While in 1980-1989 the average economic growth was 8.1% in 1994-2003 it was in average 3.5%.

Table 1. The average and the total growth speed of GDP.

	1980-1989	1990-1993	1993-2002
Average growth speed	8.1	-5.6	3.5
Total growth speed	73.2	-22.3	31.3

Even a slight difference in economic growth speed might create a different situation in the long run.

Figure 1.2. Real GDP (in billion MNT)

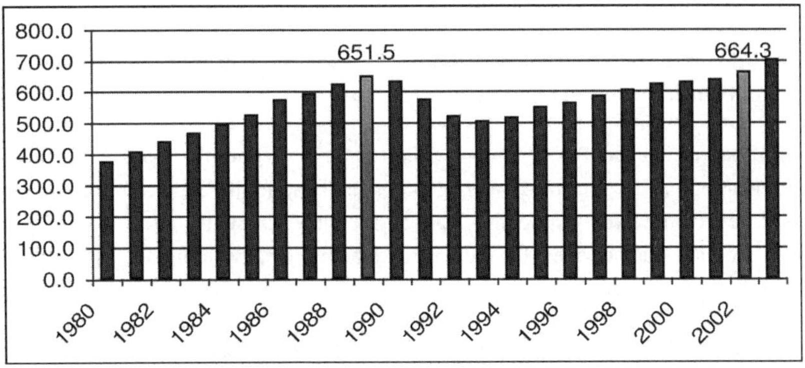

The Human Development Report of Mongolia 2003 noticed that GDP per capita differs considerably in urban vs. rural areas. GDP per capita in urban areas was 2.8 times greater against that in rural areas. While in 2002 GDP per capita in urban areas grew by 38.0 % compared to the 1999 level, there were hardly any changes in rural areas. It shows growing disparities in urban vs. rural living standards. In our country economic growth needs to be not only stable, but fast.

Figure 1.3 Real GDP per capita

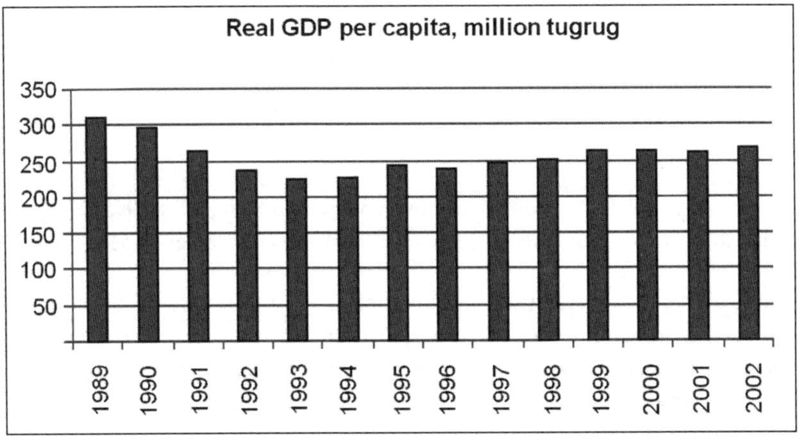

Experience of previously underdeveloped "Asian tigers" shows that at the initial stage economic growth in these countries was steadily high. For instance, economic growth in Singapore, Hong Kong, Taiwan, South Korea, referred to as newly industrialized countries, was at 8-9% in 1980-87. In Mongolia, though, in the last 4 years of relative economic growth, the average was 6.5%. Therefore, there is a need to increase economic growth in our country to no less than 10%.

2. **One important result of the economic transition is a fact that the national economy became based on the private sector.**

Privatization is considered a main condition for economic liberalization, for decentralization of centralized management and administration, for improving economic efficiency, for easing the load of the state financing, for expanding the range of products and services, for increasing demand, for providing an opportunity to compete freely in the market.

Although the goals of privatization include a wide frame of issues, it can be in general divided into main 3 directions as follows:

1. to support and encourage the private sector as the main engine of development;
2. to raise economic efficiency and labor productivity;
3. to encourage competition.

At the first stage of privatization a total of assets valued at 21 billion MNT at prices of that time were privatized to citizen of Mongolia in the form of capital investment vouchers worth 10 thousand MNT each.

In total 1.3 million persons became shareholders and 24.6 million livestock were privatized to members of negdels, their families and some soum officials.

Over 2100 retail trade and catering units, 2500 service points were privatized through auctions.

At the first stage of privatization which covered a period from 1990-1995 the concept of privatization, its program and the basic legal documents were developed.

In 1996-2000, the next stage of privatization, mainly shares of state-owned companies were privatized through auctions and nearly 1000 real estate and business entities were covered by the process. Furthermore, housing of over 87 thousand households was privatized free of charge.

In the new period of privatization, which started since 2000, over 70 industrial entities were privatized and nearly 50 billion MNT were transferred to the national budget. Privatization of valuable business entities, with the aim of trading them at high price, openness with involvement of foreign investors, concern with the future consequences are the main features of the new stage.

The main outcomes of privatization are as follows:

- With regard to property it put a foundation for transition to the market economy
- Although the results were relatively different, a step was made to provide every citizen with their own property to some extent.
- Individual households and large business entities (firms, companies) alike are taught new principles of management, accountability and organization as well as the living skills in the age of market relations.

Although economic growth did not become stable in years of transition, the structure of economic sectors changed favorably to the market. In other words, the position of private sector in the national economy strengthened greatly.

A fact that private sector accounts for over 70% of GDP means that the ground for development of new market relations has been set up.

Table 1.2. Share of the private sector in GDP, by year (percent)

	1999	*2000*	*2001*	*2002*
Share of the private sector	70,3	72,2	75,0	74,5
Share of the private sector, by industries				
Agriculture, hunting, forestry	96,4	98,0	98,3	98,4
Mining and exploration	56,0	56,6	74,9	64,2
Processing industry	75,0	78,7	94,9	87,8
Construction	89,1	89,2	89,5	93,1
Wholesale and retail trade, repair of domestic appliances	80,3	88,8	90,0	98,2
Hotels and catering	84,3	91,7	94,6	100,0
Transport, warehouses, communications	41.1	57.7	58.0	60.1
Financial transaction activities	28.0	31.4	30.6	59.9
Real estate, rent, other business activities	77.6	82.6	78.5	86.0
Education sector activities	12.9	11.0	8.2	9.5
Health and social welfare activities	5.5	6.3	6.5	9.0
Other social and individual services	41.1	45.9	48.4	48.5

Source: Mongolia at the market, 2004, p.97

As the table 1.2 shows, the share of the private sector in Gross Domestic Product went up from 70.3% in 1999 to 74.5% in 2004. This is a consolidated outcome of many qualitative changes and reforms in the wide economic frame, the fertile soil. New market relations should grow on such a soil and there are some results, however small.

However, to cultivate them there is a need for sophisticated methods and technologies, tools and mechanism. The soil also needs a fertilizer. In other words, market relations in our country are at the emerging stage and are low-developed.

The private sector in Mongolia started playing a main role in economic growth and development. While the private sector in 1989 produced only 3.3% of GDP, its share increased every year and reached 75.0% in 2001 and 76.0% in 2004. In the last 4 years growth of the private sector is relatively stable.

However, business entities and companies in the private sector still lack sources of capital and bank loans. That is why the government should support the private sector through loans and an appropriate tax policy. There is a need to develop expert-oriented industries in the private sector and pay attention to their introduction into the world market.

3. **One of main outcomes of transition is a large structural reform in the national economy, which can be called fundamental.**

Let us look at the structure of the national economy in 3 large branches such as services (S), industry (I), agriculture (A) by some years.

Table 1.3. Share of sectors in the national economy.

Years	GDP	A	I	S
1989	100	15,5	38,8	45,7
1995	100	38,0	27,5	34,5
2000	100	29,1	21,9	49,0

Source: calculations by the author

As the table illustrates, agriculture (A) accounted for 15.5% in GDP in 1989 and reached 38.8% in 1995. Industry (I) accounted for 38.8% in 1989 and reached 27.5% in 1995. It can be said that places of these two large economic sectors in the Mongolian economy were switched and a process of de-industrialization took place. In addition, these figures show that in the process of transition from the centrally planned economy to the market economy Mongolian economy moved from the SIA model to the ASI, then to the SAI one. This is a very interesting consolidated conclusion which tells us about a process with a wide frame and rich content.

4. Emergence of the market objects and subjects, acquisition of market features by the national economy is one of the main outcomes of transition.

The real market effectively distributes resources and assets for production of commodities needed by society; strives to earn the highest profit; develops high quality new products and uses the newest technologies in order to compete; quickly adapts to the constantly changing conditions, is flexible; activities and choices of consumers and manufacturers are free. It is common for the market to develop such features in economy. However, due to the degree of the market development these features are unique for every country, in particular, in our country they are only emerging.

Economy that accepts non-centralized decisions is market economy. Those decisions are implemented by means of market. Therefore, market is a form of communication, or relation between businesses that make decisions independently. The history of humanity demonstrates that market is a tested method in resolving a vital problem faced by any society, namely, what, for whom and in what way should be done to meet limitless needs with limited resources.

The market leads to strategic goal of the country to have an effective, productive economy, which easily adopts new scientific and technological achievements and meets the interests of customers. Only with assistance of market relations the mentality of looking for someone's help created by the administrative system can be eliminated and new qualities of free initiative, risk taking and entrepreneurship can be formed. **In this sense, Mongolia made a historic choice of transition to the market economy.**

The unique feature of Mongolian transition to the market is that the country attempts to resolve two major strategic goals at the same time, one of newly forming market subjects, objects and the mechanism of relationships between them and of making this complicated historic transition from planned economy and the other one of recovering the national economy that went into major decline.

In Mongolian conditions creation of a market structure with prevailing free competition is a strategic goal of transition to the market.

The less influence independent companies have on sale conditions, the more competitive is the market. Since in our country there are numerous producers and sellers of food products there is a future for formation of a perfect competitive market. However, in rural areas where customers are located far from producers, the market structure has a distinctive system. In conditions, when there are relatively few customers, without regard to the number of producers a market with competition monopolized by customers, will be formed. It can be called a **remote market**. As a small number of customers will dominate here, their number should be increased.

Although a process of privatization of state property is taking place, due the fact that one product was produced previously only by one or very producers, monopoly is still strong in Mongolia and this affects the unique structure of the emerging market. There is a need to increase the number of producers.

Another unique feature of our country is that an importer, who imports the greatest number of a certain product, has an opportunity to set up a monopoly price for that product and thus has a control over the price of the product in general. In such conditions a structure of monopoly competition will form, so there is a need to increase the number of importers.

As a result competition can become the main coordinating and testing force, which can interfere with personal interests of producers, direct them to the road of producing goods needed by the society, provide an opportunity to make an effective use of limited resources.

The market for goods and services started developing in greater measure in the Mongolian market. Privatization of state-owned trade, procurement and service entities ended. Mongolian consumers now have an opportunity to choose freely food and industrial goods and to sell raw materials at free prices. However, rural population is still isolated from trade and services. One of the ways to come out from this situation is introduction of the trade networks. One or several wholesale units and their clients- retail traders can unite and establish a voluntary wholesale and retail trade network. Retail trade units covered by the network can conduct independent activities and be provided with a guarantee of sustainable activities. Large wholesale trade entities have an opportunity to find new markets in the local areas without making an additional investment by using finance and capital of retail traders-members of the network, thus expanding their service frame and increasing their sales.

Introduction of the trade network will provide an opportunity for business entities to save on their transportation costs, to repay loans in short term, for members of network to work with one trademark and promotion, to conduct trade regionally depending on the geographic location.

Large changes which can be called principal are taking place in the structure of income and expenditure of population.

Table 1.4. Structure of the average monthly income of the household (percent)

	1989			2000			2002		
	National	Urban	Rural	National	Urban	Rural	National	Urban	Rural
Total cash income	100	100	100	100	100	100	100	100	100
Salary, wages	82.4	84.7	75.8	37.4	48.6	22.1	29.4	40.1	18.7
Pensions, allowances	8.2	9.0	6.3	9.6	11.3	7.2	8.6	8.5	8.8
Income from private economy	5.0	1.7	14.2	38.9	24.5	58.7	46.0	32.3	59.6
Other	4.5	4.6	3.9	14.1	15.6	12.0	15.9	19.1	12.9

Source: Mongolia at the market, 2004, p.251

While during the centrally planned economy salaries were the main source of income of population, in transition economy other, different sources of income have emerged. For instance, the share of income of private entities in total income grew from 5.0 % in 1989 to 38.9% in 2000 and 46.0% in 2002 at the national level. In urban areas it increased from 1.7% in 1989 to 24.5% in 2000 and 32.3% in 2002; in rural areas it rose from 14.2% in 1989 to 58.7% in 2000 and 59.6% in 2002, which exceeded salaries. This proves that new labor relations have emerged and are formed on the basis of the private sector. This is a large and profound change taking place in transition economy.

A following picture emerges from research on the present condition of income and expenditure of population:

- The volume of cash expenditure along with income increases at the national level with urban areas exceeding the rural ones;
- Food consumption at the national level increases in greater measure in urban areas, in lesser measure in rural areas similar to the previous indicator;
- Non- food consumption at the national level and in urban areas has grown, but in rural areas it has decreased;
- Services, similar to the first two indicators, have grown at the national level with greater growth in urban areas vs. rural ones.

The consumer market is more formed in urban compared to rural areas. Non-food consumption has grown in urban areas, while in rural areas food consumption has grown in greater measure. The level of savings has grown in rural areas as opposed to its decline in urban areas.

With regard to the above mentioned, steady increase of labor evaluation up to the optimal level is one of the main directions for formation of the consumer market.

Labor market has emerged and is developing. Labor at the market has a free choice and its outcome is evaluated on the basis of quantity and quality. It should have many employers and be provided with freedom of labor to be self-employed.

In conditions when common property dominates in means of production, an individual only sells his labor, while in order to have private property the individual should find himself means of production and a new need to employ labor force will emerge.

Because of changes in property basis of the national economy and dominance of the private sector over the public sector, in place of the state as the only property owner numerous different property owners such as individual households, firms, companies, cooperatives, partnerships, self-employed individuals, associations and groups have emerged.

At the present in our country there are over 500 thousand households, over 250 thousand of which are herder households. In addition, there are over 30 thousand business entities. They are all property owners, household economy.

With regard to emergence of numerous forms of property and increasing share of private property as of 2000 of total workforce 73.0% worked for private business entities, 25.0% worked for public organizations and state-owned industrial entities, the remaining 2.0% worked for community and religious organizations.

If the number of entities conducting real activities in 1998 is compared to that of entities operating in 2002, its total number increased by 50.0%, of it by 9.2% in agriculture; by 8.7% in the mining industry; by 6.1% in the processing industry; by 10.7% in the power industry; by 34.7% in construction; twice in wholesale and retail trade; by 33.0% in hotels and catering industry; by 5.7% in the transportation and communication industry.

Table 1.5. Number of operating businesses- legal entities, by economic sectors

Sector	1998	1999	2000	2001	2002
Total	17008	18328	21085	24954	25523
Agriculture, hunting, forestry, fishing	1557	1647	1675	1743	1701

Sector	1998	1999	2000	2001	2002
Mining exploration industry	172	189	187	212	187
Processing industry	2153	2266	2575	2592	2285
Power and energy industry, water supply	169	186	207	220	199
Construction	513	535	539	542	691
Wholesale and retail trade, services on repair of domestic appliances	4521	5470	6866	9104	9152
Hotels and catering	657	715	773	778	874
Transportation, warehouses, communication	581	594	628	640	614
Financial transaction activities	231	219	220	344	512
Real estate, rental, other business activities	820	761	864	1220	1234
Public administration, defense, mandatory social security activities	1232	1215	1250	1360	1379
Education sector activities	1478	1491	1546	1671	1734
Health and social welfare activities	1087	1233	1355	1568	1630
Other services to the society and individuals	1837	1807	2397	2953	3321
International organizations	-	-	3	7	10

Source: Mongolia at the market 2004, p 133

The share of workers in each sector changed in the following way: in agriculture it increased from 36.5% in 1992 to 41.8% in 2003; in industry it decreased from 16.6% in 1992 to 15.6% in 2003; in trade it grew from 8.4% in 1992 to 14.0% in 2003; in communications and transportation it declined from 6.2% in 1992 to 4.3% in 2003; in construction it reduced from 5.1% in 1992 to 3.8% in 2003.

It is possible to determine productivity of each sector on the basis of economic growth and distribution of workforce by sectors.

Table 1.6 Productivity indicators (by sectors)

	1995			2000		
	GDP (billion MNT)	Workers (thousand p)	Productivity (thousand MNT)	GDP (billion MNT)	Workers (thousand p)	Productivity (thousand MNT)
Total	550.2	767.6	716.8	1018.9	809.0	1259.5
Agriculture, hunting, forestry, fishing	209.1	354.2	590.3	296.5	393.5	753.5
Mining exploration industry	66.0	18.2	3626.4	117.2	18.6	63O1.1
Processing industry	66.4	67.3	986.6	62.5	54.6	1144.7
Power and energy industry, water supply	9.7	22.6	429.2	24.6	17.8	1382.0
Construction	9.2	29.5	311.9	19.3	23.4	824.8
Wholesale and retail trade, services on repair of domestic appliances	93.6	64.8	1444.4	244.6	83.9	2915.4
Hotels and catering	3.8	13.7	277.4	13.6	13.3	1022.6
Transportation, warehouses, communication	35.1	31.6	1110.8	112.2	34.1	3290.3

Source: Author's calculations

As the table shows, the growth of productivity in national economy was 75.7% in 2000 against 1995, of it in agriculture – 27.6%, in mining and exploration -73.8%, in processing industry- 16.0%, in power and energy industry- 22.0%, in construction-164.4%, in wholesale and retail-49.9%, 3.7 times in hotels and catering, and nearly 3 times in transportation.

At the present in Mongolia sectors with most growth are hotels and catering, transportation and communications, construction, mining and exploration industries. Sectors with the highest productivity are mining and exploration, transportation and communications and power industries.

Although the quantitative growth of workforce and productivity growth are in inverse correlation, according to the demand- supply law, the flow of workforce is directed towards highly productive industries. This is an objective evidence of formation of new relations at labor market.

A principle of fair, classified distribution of labor should be implemented at labor market. Since capabilities, talents, labor activity and initiative of people differ, different levels of wages and salaries are justified. Even those who are engaged in the same type of work can receive varying wages. In this way workers will be interested in being more active, in developing themselves, becoming more capable, more professional. This principle, on the one hand, provides an opportunity to the more talented, more capable, more active to improve their lives, to become wealthy, on the other hand, the less talented, less capable, less active might become unemployed and slip into poverty.

A financial market has emerged and a new, two-tiered banking system came into existence. A capital and security markets are forming.

The main outcomes of a financial market establishment and reform of budget income and expenditures on the basis of liberalization of the old financial system in Mongolia are as follows:

- A consolidated system of official taxes that constitute the main part of budget income was established and implemented in economic life and its effects are showing;
- Some changes were made in the budget expenditures structure and steps towards reduction of flow of ineffective financing and clarification of budget capital utilization were taken;
- Current budget deficit declined sharply.

While before 1989 a budget income equivalent to 62% of GDP was accumulated and distributed, it reduced to 60% in 1990 and 47% in 1994. A fact that about 35% of GDP is collected in taxes and public wealth equivalent to 45.2% of GDP is distributed through the budget shows that the role of budget and taxation policy is as important as it was previously. However, the role of budget and taxes has a trend for decline.

With adoption of a Law on Banking in April 1991 a legal basis for a two-tiered banking system with a Central bank /the Mongolbank/ and commercial banks was set up. In 1996 this law was further amended and improved.

In market conditions, the Central bank is the main subject to implement the monetary policy at macrolevel, in other words, to carry out the state coordination of economy by means of money. Commercial banks operate following the Banking Law and their own by-laws and regulations, providing population with financial services and play an important role in implementing the state monetary policy. At present over 10 commercial banks operate in our country.

The above shows that the first step on establishment of financial market, which connects consumers and producers with loans and money, was made.

The price liberalization was conducted in Mongolia gradually. The process of liberalization of fixed state prices started in1991. The first stage of price reform was completed in 1996 with prices for power, heating, energy, petrol products increased since September 1.

According to the inflation theory while initially demand inflation was prevailing due to shortage of goods, then prices of raw materials, fuel, energy, transportation and services fees increased one after another resulting in significant growth of production costs, leading to supply inflation and dramatic price increase. Income growth also added to that.

In the beginning of transition the government introduced a **two- tiered banking** system in the frame of the policy to stabilize the currency rate. However, it was liberated since May 28, 1993. As a result, the rate of MNT dropped sharply and inflation soared. This situation continued until 1992 when it stabilized.

The inflation rate soared in the beginning of transition, reaching 325.5% in 1992 and reduced to 17.5% in 1997.

Table 1.7. Inflation rate, percent

	1991	1992	1993	1994	1995	1996	1997
Annual average	52,7	325,5	183,0	66,3	53,1	53,2	17,5
Monthly average	3,6	12,8	9,1	4,3	3,6	3,6	1,3

The inflation growth was much higher than M1, M2 growth. While in 1992 the inflation rate reached 325%, M1 and M2 grew by 4.3 and 31.6% respectively. When in 1993 the inflation rate dropped to 183%, M1 and M2 increased by 143% and 228% respectively. This situation shows clearly how price liberalization affected growth of prices and supply of money.

Data on money supply illustrates that the government followed a strict fiscal policy after price liberalization. At that time the interest rate was high. Although this situation influenced stabilization of inflation, it affected negatively private capital investment. As a result of the strict monetary policy inflation was halted and reduced, which led to an important outcome of economic stabilization.

In the past period policies and measures implemented in the field of budget and finances were directed towards macro-economic stabilization and its strengthening. In the frame of macro-economic stabilization measures were taken towards provision of transparency and sustainability of the budget, paying of accrued liabilities, improvement of budgetary balance, fiscal and budgetary reform, improvement of budget planning, implementation and control.

In this frame measures were taken to provide transparency and comprehensiveness of budget relations such as development of the mid-term budget instead of short-term planning, coordination of leading economic and social policy directions with the budget income sources and financing, development of the central-local budget relationships, determining optimal norms and standards for budget expenses, introduction of a united public finance account system, improvement of budget reporting.

With implementation of the Law on Management and Financing of Budgetary Organizations transition from a budgeting method based on input (factors) to the budgeting method based on performance and produce was made, which is a major change in the budget management system.

Establishment of a system with an optimal lever directed towards implementation of a dual objective of limiting budget expenses and providing long-term sustainable balance on the one hand, and decentralization of services in order to bring them closer to population, on the other hand, became the main core of the budget sector reform in Mongolia.

With opening of the Mongolian economy development of the international market began. By foreign trade liberalization a strategic objective of enhancing the level of security of the national economy, which was strongly dependent on only a few countries, was achieved.

The volume of foreign trade with the members of CMEA, which previously accounted for 94.2%, declined to 48.9% in 1994, and the total turnover of trade with new partners that accounted for only 5.8% of trade, reached 51.1% in 1994.

A policy of encouraging participation of the private sector in foreign trade operations according to the market conditions is pursued in order to expand foreign trade by finding new markets and new sources for supply of goods.

Development of national economy depends on certain external factors, in particular, foreign assistance and loans. Necessity of an "initial push" for a declining industry is theoretically substantiated. This means that the economy in decline or stagnation will be set into movement with use of external forces. Especially foreign direct investment is the most important, tested means for underdeveloped countries to build new economic structures and find their own place in the international labor division.

Development of export-oriented, import-substitution industry means structural reform of the national economy. In implementing such a reform a problem of shortage of capital will be faced.

According to the **Circle of deprivation** theory due to shortage of capital the level of modern technology usage is limited, the labor productivity remains at a low level, which leads to decline of income per capita, which obstructs growth of savings, so shortage of capital needed for technical equipment of industries becomes chronic in the long-term. The situation in Mongolia is like that.

Foreign countries and international organizations provide aid and loans on favorable terms. Long-term loans on favorable conditions are helpful for gaining time.

New classic models of direct capital investment are widely used in underdeveloped countries. Unfortunately, little attention is paid to this issue in our country. The main importance of these models lies in assistance that direct capital investment gives to developing countries in finding an international trade position that can make the most favorable impact on the national economy of the given country. It is regarded as an international labor division tool that frees economies of developing countries of their outdated structure.

Experience and lessons of other developing countries proves that foreign resources should be utilized very cleverly. First of all, they should be used to develop production of a product with a comparative advantage for the country that could be competitive at the global market. Following the theory of the product life cycle, concentrating capital in an industry that can utilize the final stage of modern production is even better. There is a need for a new state policy for industry.

A constant powerful factor, which is viewed by development economists to be more important than external factors, is economic freedom. By the Economic Freedom Index, determined by the level of economic freedom such as security of private property, freedom of competition, individual choice, voluntary exchange, Mongolia takes the 74th place in the world, which is a rlatively high indicator for our country.

1.3 LESSONS LEARNT, DEVELOPMENT TRENDS

Although Mongolia is an Asian country, it implemented the macro-economic reform before the reform at the micro-level, "top to bottom", following the European method called "the Washington consensus". It suffered substantial damage in the process.

The Asian method of transition started with a micro-economic reform, followed by an organizational reform, an agricultural and industrial reforms, a legal and the price reforms. It can be said that this method used the "bottom to top" approach by implementing these reforms before the macro-economic reforms, namely, the budget, monetary and foreign trade reforms. Researchers view that this order is more efficient, as it is more effective in supporting the market and encouraging supply. It is claimed that along with support of the private sector development, steps taken towards transfer of state-owned enterprises into new conditions have been effective. It is considered that coordination of differentiated prices, money and finances was more advantageous compared with the European method when prices went out of control and a strong inflation exercised its pressure. It cannot be denied that the Asian method can be used in Mongolian reforms.

In the frame of the European method of economic reform, a policy of fast reform was conducted wherever possible. A small social expense is considered to be a useful consequence of such a shock therapy. However, it was very difficult to calculate it. Although a dispute between gradualists and shock therapists is continuing, most European countries followed the first strategy. From their experience it could be seen that a shock therapy should not be used in sectors, which require structural reform in mid- and long term such as a bank reform and privatization. Some other shortcomings were also observed in the process.

Economists such as R. Portes, Nolan and Peter view that following mistakes were made in the process of transition:

- More attention was paid to the macro-economic rather than micro-economic policy.
- The monetary policy was too strict.
- Devaluation was too extreme and the currency rate policy was inappropriate.
- The state-owned enterprises were privatized widely without appropriate policies.
- Rapid disbandment of CMEA affected decline of trade between regions.
- Urgent issues likely to emerge when the old system is changed in a short period were not considered in full measure.

- The role of the government and its responsibilities in providing economic life and guarantee was underestimated.
- The level of measures that should be taken by the state in case "the market" goes wrong in the course of transition was not foreseen.
- Problems in providing a stable political environment were not considered in full measure.

There are grounds to note that all these mistakes were made to some extent in the course of economic transition in Mongolia. National research should be developed in order not to repeat such mistakes in the future. Errors in the public policy are made because of direct copying of experience of countries with developed markets and because of implementing policies following the textbook. It is not a secret that such criticism was made at the international level, too. As CNN reported in one of its reports, the former World Bank economist Joseph Shtiglietz caused quite a commotion saying that: "The IMF and the World Bank, considered the best "doctors" of the world economy, force a ready recipe to the country in transition. While the Western consultants plan to create a mentality of protecting the property by conducting privatization, new owners quickly sell their property and allocate the assets abroad, thus fueling corruption. "

Results of international research on comparative experience prove that the process of democracy and reform is being conducted successfully in Mongolia.

In their research based on the World Bank documents M. De Melo, S. Deniser, A.Gelb included Mongolia in the second group of 26 countries divided into 4 groups by their success in reforms; as they evaluated, Mongolia was the only Asian country, which was combining both the economic and the political reforms, and its experience had an international importance.

It is generally agreed that the key components of the initial stage of the transitional period are liberalization and stabilization. An issue of freeing prices and trade from the state control is liberalization. The objective of stabilization is to maintain stability of the domestic and foreign balances / the state budget and balance-of- payment / and to reduce inflation. These interrelated policies are considered to be the first necessary steps to be made in the process of reform /World Bank, 1996, chapter 2 /. By means of the emerging market mechanism liberalization provides incentives and information and eliminates centralization of production and trade decisions. Stabilization ensures that uncertain situation with rising prices will not take place, savings and investments will not be limited.

The World Bank researchers /World Bank, 1996, chapter 2 De Melo et al/ noticed that countries where liberalization was full and took place early managed to stabilize their economy more quickly and ensure economic growth in shorter time. De Melo, Denizer and Gelb constructed an annual index of liberalization for the transition period beginning in 1989 and then used this index to classify countries into reform groups according to their cumulative experience with economic liberalization as of the end of 1994. /table 1.8/

The liberalization index is the weighted average of the rankings of liberalization in the following three areas:

* Internal markets (I)-liberalization of domestic prices and the abolition of state trading monopolies (weight: 0.3)
* External markets (E)-liberalization of the foreign trade regime, including elimination of export controls and taxes, and substitution of low-to-moderate import duties for import quotas and high import tariffs; current-account convertibility (weight: 0.3)
* Private sector entry (P)-privatization of small-scale and large-scale enterprises and banking reform (weight: 0.4).

De Melo, Denizer and Gelb noticed that economic performance at any given moment is determined not only by the degree of liberalization currently prevailing but also by the structural, institutional, and behavioral changes stimulated by prior policy reforms /WB Economic Review, 10-3, p. 404/. Therefore they defined a cumulative liberalization index (CLI) to represent the duration as well as the intensity of reforms from 1989 onward. The CLI is calculated as the sum of a country's liberalization indexes. Countries are included in one of four reform groups, determined by natural breaks in the CLI values:

* Group 1: Advanced reformers ($CLI > 3$)
* Group 2: High-intermediate reformers ($2 < CLI < 3$)
* Group 3: Low-intermediate reformers ($1.3 < CLI < 2$)
* Group 4: Slow reformers ($CLI < 1.3$)

Table 1.8. Liberalization, Growth, and Inflation in Twenty-Six Countries in Transition, 1989-1994

Country	Cumulative Liberalization index' 1994	Average Liberalization 1993-94	Average annual inflation 1993-94	Annual growth in GDP 1993-94	GDP in 1993-1994 as a percentage of 1989 GDP	Lowest level of GDP as a percent-tage of 1989 GDP
Advanced reformers						
Slovenia	4.16	0.82	26	3.0	84	81
Poland	4.14	0.84	34	4.2	88	82
Hungary	4.11	0.84	21	0.0	81	80
Czech Republic	3.61	0.90	16	0.8	81	80
Slovak Republic	3.47	0.86	19	0.4	79	77
Average	3.90	0.85	23	1.7	83	80
High-intermediate reformers						
Estonia	2.93	0.85	69	0.9	69	67
Bulgaria	2.90	0.68	81	-1.4	73	73
Lithuania	2.72	0.79	231	-7.3	44	44
Latvia	2.45	0.71	73	-4.4	60	59
Albania	2.30	0.70	57	9.5	74	65
Romania	2.29	0.66	194	2.2	69	67
Mongolia	2.27	0.64	164	0.6	84	83
Average	2.55	0.72	124	0.03	67	65
Low-intermediate reformers						
Russian Federation	1.92	0.63	558	-13.5	57	52
Kyrgyz Republic	1.81	0.68	744	-13.2	61	57
Moldova	1.62	0.53	558	-17.0	s3	46
Kazakstan	1.31	0.37	1,870	-18.5	s7	49
Average	1.67	0.55	933	-15.6	57	51
Slow reformers						
Uzbekistan	1.11	0.37	640	-2.5	89	88
Belarus	1.07	0.35	1,694	-16.6	73	64
Ukraine	0.80	0.20	2,789	-18.6	56	48
Turkmenistan	0.63	0.19	2,751	-15.0	69	62
Average	0.90	0.27	1,968	-13.2	72	66
Affected by regional tensions						
Croatia	3.98	0.83	807	-0.7	69	68
Macedonia,FYR	3.92	0.78	157	-10.7	57	55
Armenia	1.44	0.42	4,595	-7.4	38	38
Georgia	1.32	0.35	10,563	-24.6	24	23
Azerbaijan	1.03	0.33	1,167	-17.7	50	44
Tajikistan	0.95	0.28	1,324	-26.3	35	30
Average	2.11	0.50	3,102	-14.5	45	34

The 3 components of CLI are highly correlated, which shows their high percentage in modelling and implementation of various reforms. De Melo, Denizer and Gelb pointed at systematic link between production and reform in each group. As research showed, advanced reformers were stable or growing by 1993-94, and their lowest output levels were about 80 percent of those in 1989. High-intermediate reformers lost about a third of their GDP, but most also stabilized output. Low-intermediate reformers fared the worst, with continuing output losses through 1994. The slowest reformers, excluding Uzbekistan do not differ much from the low-intermediate ones.

By evaluation of the last year's results of the transition in Mongolia are considered successful.

Countries leading in transition

Figure 1.5. 2005 GDP in comparison to 1989 GDP./1989=100/

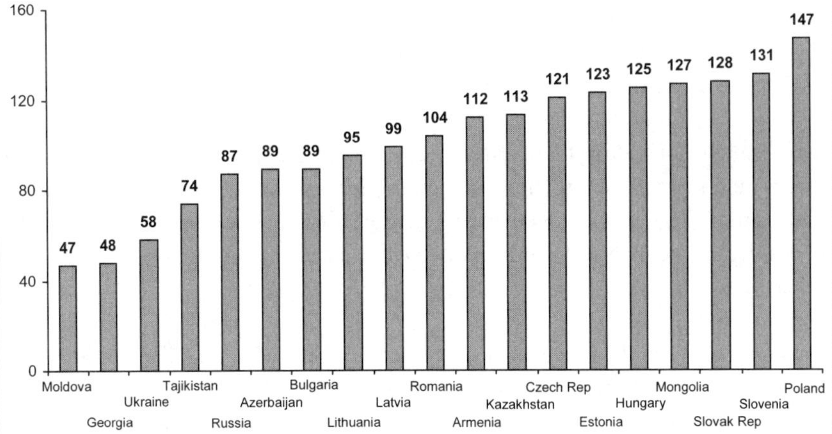

Source: EBRD, Transition report 2005, IMF International Financial Statistics, IMF, World Economic Outlook.

Mongolia reached the pre-transition, 1989 level in 2002 and in 2005 it exceeded it by 27%.

While the transition process in Mongolia is successful, numerous transition and development issues caused by economic backwardness await their resolution.

(1) The power and competitiveness of the national economy is weak.

- Mongolian economy provides for its payment balance with a substantial participation of external sources.

- Mongolian economy has foreign trade deficit, limited export and declining trade conditions.
- Mongolian economy has budget deficit.
- A large part of Mongolian population slipped into poverty.

This is bitter, but truth. We need to find ways to break the repeated circle of depravity, a whirlpool of deficit faced by national economy, business entities, every household: low income due to low productivity, poor technology because of low income, low productivity caused by poor technology which leads to low income and so on. Along with it the united force of the state, business companies, households, every citizen has a decisive role. A slogan we need is high productivity- high income, high income – new technologies, new technologies - high productivity. This is a new issue of public participation in economy.

(2) The issue of strengthening economic capacity of business entities, which are the basic elements of the national economy, can not be left out beyond the frame of the state care, on the mercy of the market.

Kiosks, small shops, drugstores, cafes and gas stations appear like "mushrooms after the rain" and go bankrupt in large numbers, so Mongolian citizen and the Mongolian society suffer. This is a real example of an inadequate performance of the market in the developing economy. Coordination by the state should close the gaps in the market.

Development of rural areas that account for 70-80% of Mongolian territory with population that comprises 60-70% of total population of Mongolia requires special attention. Research shows that over 80% of 250 thousand herder households do not have surplus product. That means they have not entered the market. Another question is how numerous undiversified entities producing similar products from the main five kinds of livestock can enter the market? This question still has not been resolved. Economic capacity of over 30 thousand business entities in our country is weak.

- The percentage of total profit in production costs equals 40-50%. It is not an indicator to ignore, but we need to think about its further preservation and increase.
- The net profit after distribution equals only 5% of production costs. This is an inadequate indicator, so there is a need to decrease the tax burden in the future.

- Over 40% of net income calculated as difference between the sales income of business entities and costs of sold produce are paid to the budget in the form of various taxes.
- Although the tax burden is high, competitiveness of business entities at the national level is weak.

The share of own capital in the capital investment of economic entities equals 30%, external sources account for over 60% and bank loans constitute 6%. The government has an opportunity to manage the bank activities through its monetary policy. There is a need for a comprehensive program in order to increase the role of banks and financial sector in economic development, to bring it to the new, higher level.

(3) It is important to increase public participation in strengthening the capacity and competitiveness of the national economy. Every Mongolian should make the saying "Develop yourself, then develop your home, finally, develop your country" his everyday prayer, the course of his life. This saying has a deep meaning, in economic sense its says that everyone should be hardworking, every household must be a producer, as for the state, it should be a creative force uniting the people.

Mongolia is a developing country with a transition economy. It is obvious that a developing economy cannot become a basis for a developed market. While previously a non-market economy was a barrier to development, at present the developing economy determines the market development and its scope, so it is time to address both transition and development issues.

Development economists determined common characteristics of developing economies as follows:

- Low living standards (low income, inequality, low health and education levels);
- Low level of productivity;
- Fast population growth;
- Increasing or high level of unemployment and underemployment;
- Strong dependence on agricultural production and export of primary products;
- Strong dependence on foreign countries, vulnerability.

As for the national economy:

- Low integration between different sectors of economy (lack of integration).

As for economic supply:

- Domination of oligopoly market in industrial sector, high prices for products.
- Growth of prices for raw materials directly affects the price of the final product.
- Companies take loans from financial organizations in order to pay salaries or purchase raw materials. Production costs grow since they operate on loans.
- Since at the financial market the monetary policy does not work as in developed countries, there are limited opportunities to control money supply.
- The financial dualism (formal and informal monetary markets)- decline of the interest rates for loans does not create growth of investment, but creates flow of money from one market to another. For instance, it is a flow of monetary assets from the formal market to the informal one. Sensitivity to demand and supply at the market is low. In other words, the market operates inadequately.

These common features of developing economies are mostly related to the structure of national economies, they are affected also by their geographic location and territory, the income level, the historic and dependent situation, physical and human resources, relationships between the state and the private sector, the profile of the industrialization structure, foreign economies and political forces.

The above mentioned common features and causes of dependency almost all exist in Mongolian economy. Several examples:

- Underemployment along with unemployment is widespread;
- Agricultural production accounts for 35% of GDP, which is higher than the average of developing countries;
- Like in developing countries, the main export is raw materials, including gold, copper, wool, cashmere, skins and hides;
- In the World development report (World Bank 2000) Mongolia was included in the five countries dependent on the foreign assistance.

The economic and development strategies of developing countries are relevant to Mongolia. It is necessary to resolve transition and development issues in a comprehensive way, in connection to each other.

There is an **imbalanced growth strategy** which aims to limit the influence of the state on economy. It aims to advance the development process under influence of numerous imbalanced factors such as surplus or shortage and especially to create interest of the private sector. There is a need for a policy which allows the state to be in charge of leading major projects on exploitation of large mining deposits, development of large fuel and energy sources and transfer to the private sector implementation of accompanying objects.

Selecting an object of capital investment is not an easy task, because a question of which sector to choose for investment (mining, agriculture, heavy industry, infrastructure) should be resolved. In general, in selecting an object for capital investment it is wise to take into account numerous problems faced by developing countries in a comprehensive way. Emerging production capacity should have following major characteristics:

- Be labor intensive;
- Have highly effective previous and following links;
- Utilize expertly local production methods;
- Use equipment and technologies appropriate to the technical skills of the given population;
- Direct production towards basic needs such as food stuff, clothing, housing, etc;
- The product should substitute the necessary imported product and provide an opportunity to save foreign currency;
- Capital investment should be made in local areas whenever possible;

Based on the above, development and industrialization of agriculture provides for implementation of most of the above requirements. In this way opportunities for creating workplaces in local areas, limiting migration of rural population to urban areas, organizing production at SME in an industrial way will be provided.

For example:

- Plants processing raw materials of livestock origin such as slaughterhouses, dairy products factories, meat and preserves factories, flour mills, wool washing shops, timber processing plants etc.;
- Plants producing means of production required in agriculture such as fodder and fertilizer plants, compact tools shops, cement, construction blocks, brick factories, packaging materials, repair shops etc;
- Plants producing consumer products to be sold at local market such as textile, shoes, clothing, baked goods, soft drinks, soap, kitchen utensils, domestic appliances repair shops. In such conditions industrial development will be introduced in the countryside.

In resolving such questions as whether to establish such plants in each soum, what should be done with present factories, what kind of technology should be used at new SME, where produce should be sold, active support of the government and a new modern attitude will be required.

(2) Most of underdeveloped countries view that industry and agriculture should be possibly developed simultaneously. Agriculture becomes a market for industrial products, meets the demand of urban population in food products, provides workforce and capital for the industry and earns foreign currency required for import of equipment. On the other hand, industry provides industrial products required by agriculture (fodder etc.), produces consumer products needed by rural population, processes food products for domestic consumption and export and in this way a market for some agricultural products is created.

Although such a doctrine of balanced development of two sectors emerged, its value cannot be the same in every developing country. For a country with a large population and scarce agricultural resources developing industry, exporting produced industrial goods and importing food products is the only way. Along with this in conditions of open economy the doctrine of balanced development sometimes looses its meaning.

(3) The goal of industrial development starts with 2 choices, that of exporting produced goods (export oriented production- EOP) or production for domestic market (import substitution production-ISP), but these strategies do not reject each other. If a developing country decides to pursue the ISP policy, several choices related to it should be made:

A. To import equipment (knitwear equipment), raw materials and fuel spending foreign currency on them and produce consumer products (clothing);

B. To purchase means of production (machinery and equipment) using foreign currency and produce industrial equipment (knitwear equipment) used for production of consumer products (clothing), or produce semi-finished products and supply the domestic market with raw materials.

C. To purchase means of production (machinery and equipment) using foreign currency and produce means of production. This classification is necessary to make a choice in different variations. For example, A, B and C versions can start with the stage A then move on to B and further to C stages.

The majority of developing countries choose version A of ISP strategy because of their economic frame and natural resources. In such conditions production equipment is imported and previously imported consumer products are produced in the country for domestic market. Semi-industrialized developing countries choose the C version and a limited number of developing countries (Brazil, India, Mexico) achieved success in production of means of production, but it is quite problematic to make a transition from one stage of ISP to another.

Some developing countries (called newly industrialized countries) such as four Asian tigers- Hong Kong, Singapore, Taiwan, and South Korea have a history of implementing an export-oriented industrialization strategy. Mongolia experienced shortage of export due to implementation of an open economic policy. Foreign currency shortage emerged due to lack of export, which lead to technological backwardness, which in its turn resulted in decline of national productivity. The only decisive way to exit from this situation is increase of Mongolian export. In order to do that it is necessary to increase supply of production factors, for instance, to make a radical reform of the national production structure on the new technological basis. It means that the export supporting policy should be encouraged by foreign trade policy as well as foreign investment, especially direct investment, introduction of equipment and technology via foreign loans and assistance, the policy of introducing new production through industrialization policy.

In developing and implementing development strategies and policies it is necessary to take into account global economic development trends in the era of globalization and their principal effect on transition and developing economies. The need for enrichment of development economic theories on the basis of global economic science is also obvious.

Only recently our world was divided into two conflicting worlds, the capitalist and the socialist ones and the third world became a reserve for these two, so it was more a fight than development. The modern world promotes the slogan of one world - one humanity and the global community started accepting that the road to implementation of this slogan began. The global economy entered the way of globalization. The world socialist system disintegrated and economic reforms have been made in former socialist countries.

An American economist, a renowned researcher Joseph Stiglitz wrote extensively about achievements, shortcomings and issues of concern in countries with transition economies in his book "Globalization and it discontents". He noticed that only lately, 10 years after the beginning, the gradualist method of reform was accepted in the world as the proper one. In conditions when free competition is not operating or has not started operating, privatization of the state monopoly creates an individual monopoly which puts on consumers even heavier load that the state monopoly.

J.Stiglitz emphasized that a proper policy and active state participation was important in providing economic stabilization and growth in countries with transition economies. He observed that creation of an environment favorable for foreign investment was the major factor affecting the national economy. Attention should be paid to this at every level of state administration and conditions with little legal red tape were important as well.

Investors are afraid of corrupted administration. If the state administration can resolve many fundamental problems such as ensuring stable social and economic situation, creating an effective mechanism of tax collection, taking measures on reduction of debt, success can be achieved.

He also emphasized importance of national research and opinions of national consultants. Westerners with little knowledge about the given country can provide little assistance in this question. Their contribution lies in promotion of democratic values such as organization, free media and transparent environment. He pointed that at present, the Western countries were developing, but the East was ridden by poverty and lived in times of social and economic problems. The West confronts other countries with their own interests, conducts a policy in their own interests, negotiates "secretly" under the name of G7 summit and globalization becomes an interest of some countries. Some policies that the West would never try in their own countries were often forced in developing countries. It is important that the USA and other developed countries pay attention to the loan policies of the World Bank and IMF for them to be very accurate and well-considered.

The USA *Foreign policy* magazine and the A.T. Kearney Consulting Company developed a rating of 62 countries that produce 96% of the gross global product by 12 indicators. In *Globalization-2006* among countries that were able to consolidate their efforts and activities in economic and political fields Singapore was leading by economic integration, the USA- by technology, Switzerland- by individual connections and France- by politics.
The increasing level of economic freedom in the world in the process of globalization has also a positive effect. In the Global Economic Freedom Report produced by the Frazer Institute, Canada, countries with a high globalization index such as Singapore, the USA, New Zealand and Switzerland take the leading positions among 130 countries. The last positions were taken by African, Latin American and former communist countries. Economic globalization and economic freedom seem to have a negative correlation at present. In order to make globalization truly global there is a need for a strategy supporting economic freedom.

Figure 1.6. Countries leading globalization

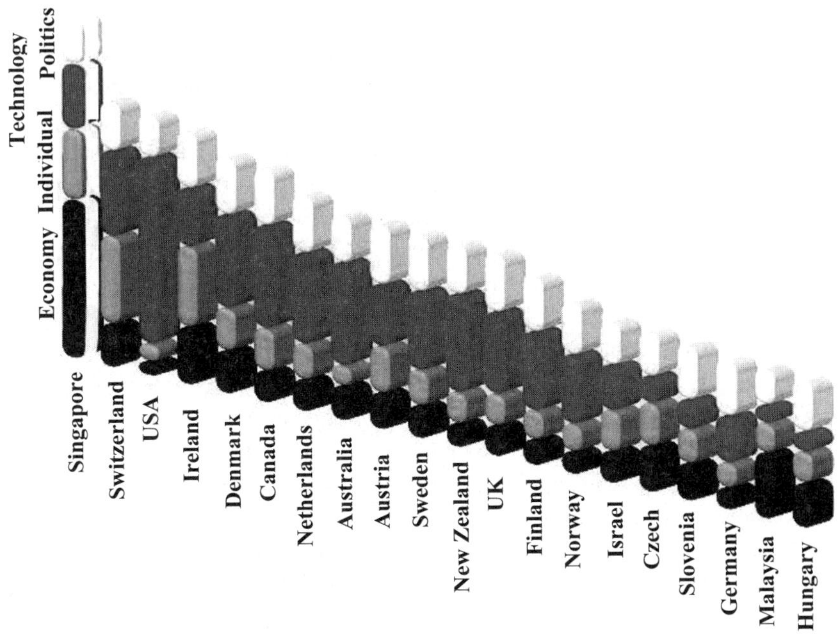

The gap between the poor and the rich is enormous in the modern world. While low-income countries account for 32% of the territory, 60% of population and 21% of NDP, high-income countries account for 24% of the total territory, 15% of population and 56% of NDP. Mongolia is a low-income developing country. Its economic measure is 165, which means that it takes the 165th position among countries in the world, coming in the end. However, as international research shows, our neighbors such as Russia is on the 83th position, China-132nd, our Asian partners as Japan – on the 14th, South Korea- 51st and Vietnam, which was among less developed countries in the frame of CMEA, now is on the 159th position.

When Mongolia is compared to other countries in the world, its territory accounts for 1.2% and the population size and NDP are less than whole numbers. NDP per capita of Mongolia (1.463 USD) is 16 times lower than that of high-income countries, 4.1 times lower compared to average income countries and 1.5 times lower than that of low-income countries. Compared to our neighbors our NDP per capita is 4 times lower than that of Russia, 2 times- than that of China, 16 times lower than that of Japan, 9 times- than that of Korea and by 16% lower than that of Vietnam. These data of comparative international research represent the present capacity of the national economy of Mongolia.

A renown American researcher J.Stiglitz made following suggestions on reform and changes needed in global economy related to countries with transition economies:

1. Acceptance of the dangers of capital market liberalization and that short-term capital flows impose huge externalities, costs borne by those not directly party to the transaction (the lenders and borrowers). Whenever there are such large externalities, interventions through the banking and tax systems are desirable. Rather than resisting these interventions, the international financial institutions should be directing their efforts to making them work better.
2. Bankruptcy reforms and standstills. The appropriate way of addressing problems when private borrowers cannot repay creditors is through bankruptcy, not through an IMF-financed bailout of creditors. On the other hand, a bankruptcy system in which the creditor or his representative is also the bankruptcy judge will never be accepted as fair. At present we can see the example of Argentina on the "brink of bankruptcy".
3. Less reliance on bailouts. A practice of bailout by international institutions when the borrower cannot repay creditors is not a very wise method. The money goes to ensure that western creditors got paid back more than otherwise they would or that the exchange rates were maintained at overvalued levels longer than they otherwise would have been, leaving the country more indebted.
4. Improved banking regulation-both design and implementation. Weak bank regulation in developed countries can lead to bad lending practices and export of instability. For instance, a policy of short-term loans should be paid attention to.
5. Improved risk management. Today countries around the world face enormous risk from the volatility of exchange rates. While the problem is clear the solution is not. IMF experts encouraged to change the local currency to the hard currency, the dollars (for example in Argentina), but it did not solve the problem. As developed countries are better able to handle these risks than the less developed countries, it would make sense for the developed countries to provide loans to developing countries in forms that mitigate the risks, e.g. by having the creditors absorb the risks of large real interest fluctuations.
6. Improved response to crisis. That social and economic factors are closely interlinked should not be overlooked. It is important to prevent from crisis, to do research, to be prepared for it.The IMF should not be concerned only with

protection of foreign investors, but should pay attention to continuing assistance to the country in crisis, provision of loans, stabilization.

7. Poverty alleviation and unemployment reduction policy. When IMF receives a signal in their own statistical research that poverty is on increase in one country, it should revise its own policy and check if their economic model was correct and there were no mistakes in their calculations.
8. Reduce conditionality of loans. When international institutions put numerous conditions in providing loans, the economic situation does not improve. The country has to pay attention not to their own priority issues, but to meeting these conditions. Introduction of a selection system might be more effective in this case. For instance, a developing country might be selected with regard to its achievements and provided with loans and assistance. However, a question of utilizing the loan should be left to the given country.
9. Debt forgiveness. This is a method, which is supported lately by many public organizations. It is understandable that debt forgiveness plays an important role in development of poor countries. This is a policy that should go further than the poorest of the countries, for instance, in countries like Indonesia, which are at a higher level of development, it should be also pursued.

Nowadays, development of the national economy depends in great measure on resolution of global issues of the world economy. Developing countries including Mongolia need to implement an economic policy developed by themselves, which protects their own interests, they need to have a capable public administration machinery, to have an independent court with strong authority and a public and private sectors free of corruption, all of which is very important to development of the country. It is necessary to present their own interests to the international organizations, to discuss openly unique features of their own country, their own interests, to develop projects adapted to their own country instead of copying the previous models.

In summarizing his research J.Stiglitz said: "Development is not about helping a few people get rich… development is about transforming societies, improving the lives of the poor, enabling everyone to have a chance at success and access to health care and education. Making sure that democratic decisions are made means ensuring that the broad range of economists, officials and experts from developing countries are actively involved in the debate. It also means that there must be broad participation that goes well beyond the experts and politicians. Only in this case we can make globalization with a human face". Globalization does not mean that only a few countries get rich. Globalization means such conditions when all over the world every country can provide favorable conditions for lives of their citizen, fundamental economic reforms, elimination of poverty, social welfare. Only in such conditions globalization will become a real force, a common, global development slogan. Strong assistance of developed countries and international institutions and active participation of UN is also very important.

Economic globalization requires from the national industries and services to reach the global level. In other words, the structure of the national economy and its activities need to undergo fundamental changes. This is a perspective strategy which starts today. In order to implement this strategy it is necessary to put forward a new objective of having representatives of world-renown companies and multinational corporations in the national economy.

First of all, there is a need for a national comprehensive policy to implement a structural reform to move from the SAI model (S-services, A- agriculture, I-industry) to the SIA, then to the ISA model by selecting highly effective and productive industries and products.

(1) A policy of agriculture intensification

- Introduction of irrigated crop cultivation
- Increase of livestock productivity, improvement of livestock breeds.

(2) A new industrial policy of developing new industrial sectors, industries and products on the new technological basis.

- Full processing of livestock produce with industrial methods
- Manufacturing a final product in the mining industry by increasing the level of processing.

(3) Policy of "modern services" sector.

- Policy of the "new infrastructure to newly create and develop the economic infrastructure"
- Development of the travel and tourism sector to the level of an independent industry.

Since Mongolia at the present is a low-income, underdeveloped country, **it needs a development strategy to reach the level of middle income countries.**

(1) It is calculated that in 2015 the population of Mongolia will reach 3.0-3.1 million people. If the average annual population growth is 2% as in other developing countries, in 2021 it will reach 4.0 million.

(2) There is a mid-term objective of the government to increase the GDP per capita in Mongolia up to 1066 USD in 2009. If the average annual growth is 10%, in 2015 it will reach 3.5 thousand USD.

(3) The GDP of Mongolia in 2015, when it will have the population of 3 million, will be 3.2 billion USD, in 2024 it will be 14.0 billion USD.

(4)There is some data in the press that in the years following the start of exploitation of Oyu Tolgoi, the GDP will increase in average by 34.3% per year. If these calculations are taken into consideration and additional 30% growth takes place, the GDP in 2015 will reach 4.2 billion USD and in 2021 it will be 18.2 billion USD. The GDP per capita in 2015 and 2021 will be 1400 USD and 4550 USD respectively.

(5)With regard to calculations of GDP per capita equaling 1066 USD in 2009, in 2015 Mongolia will exceed the average of low- and middle income countries and in 2021 it will exceed the average of middle income countries. If this is taken as a basis, a strategic objective can be put forward to bring Mongolia to the ranks of middle income countries by 2021.

Until the long-term strategies are implemented, an objective of choosing and developing priority economic directions of national economy in the frame of long-term strategy should be achieved. In doing so, we need to use theories of utilizing comparative advantages of national economy and creting new comparative advantages.

Conclusions and suggestions.

1. The long-term strategy of economic development in Mongolia should be bringing the national economy to the level of middle income countries.
2. It is important to conduct a visionary policy with a final goal to make fundamental changes in the structure of the national economy; to introduce technological reforms aimed at bringing the quality of production and services to the global level; to have representatives of producers and distributors of global level in the country.
3. It is necessary to combine properly responsibilities of the state and the public in economy; there is a need for a state policy directed towards support of the private sector, when it is weak at the present, and reduce the role of the state, when the private sector becomes stronger.
4. With regard to the mining and power sector and other large projects it is necessary to start implementing a "strategy of unbalanced growth", which was

proved on the experience of developing countries, where the state is leading in the large works and the private sector is in charge of numerous following works.

5. Organizing work on developing national projects and programs and securing assistance of the UN, other international agencies, governments of developed countries, representatives of well-known companies, multinationals, on certain issues of creating new industrial or service sectors, new products that have a decisive role in development of national economy is in line with global trends of economic globalization.

Bibliography

Commander, S. (1992), "Inflation and the Transition to a Market Economy: An overview", The World Bank Economic Review, Vol.6, no.1, January, pp. 3-12

De Melo, M., Denizer, C. and Gelb, A. (1996), "Patterns of Transition from Plan to Market", The World Bank Economic Review, Vol. 10, no.3, pp. 397-424

Lavigne, M. (1995), The Economics of Transition: from Socialist Economy to Market Economy. Macmillan Press Ltd.

Nolan, Peter (1995), China's Rise, Russia's Fall: Politics, Economics and Planning in the Transition from Stalinism, Macmillan.

The Mongolian Economy: A manual of Applied Economics for a Country in Transition 2000EE. Cheltenham, UK. Northampton. MA USA.

Mongolia in a Market system Statistical yearbook 1989-2002 UB. 2004.

Mongolian Statistical yearbook 2005. UB. 2006.

Parker, S., Tritt, G. and Woo, W.T. (1997), "Some Lessons Learned from the Comparison of Transitions in Asia and Eastern Europe" in Woo ew.al./eds./ (1997).

Portes, R. (1994), "Transformation Traps", Economic Journal, Vol. 104, September, pp. 1178-1189.

Rana, Pradumaa B. (1993), Reforms in the Transitional Economies of Asia, Asian Development Bank, Occasional Paper Number 5, Manila.

United Nations Development Programme (1994), Human Development Report 1994, Oxford University Press for the UNDP.

United Nations Development Programme (1997), Human Development Report 1997, Oxford University Press for the UNDP.

Weeks, John (1998), "Open Economy Adjustment and Transition in Vietnam" in Cook, P., Kirkpatrick, CH and Nixson, F. (eds.), Privatization, Enterprise Development and Economic Reform. Experiences of Developing and Transitional Economies, Edward Elgar.

Woo, W.T., Parker, S. and Sachs, J.D. (1997) (eds.), Economies in Transition Comparing Asia and Europe, The MIT Press, Cambridge, Mass.

World Bank (1996), World Development Report, 1996; From Plan to Market, Oxford University Press for the World Bank.

World Bank (1997), World Development Report, 1997, Oxford University Press for the World Bank.

CHAPTER TWO

SOME DEMOGRAPHIC AND HUMAN DEVELOPMENT ISSUES

Abstract

People themselves, i.e. the people of the state are the real wealth of any society. That is why the social and economic system must be directed towards development of human capacities and capabilities and provision of conditions for equal participation and opportunities, i.e. the main goal of development is expanding people's choices.

For instance, free acquisition of knowledge, provision of appropriate food and medical services, having an income required for secure wealthy life, provision of public security conditions for protection from crime and violence, having political and cultural freedom and opportunities for participation in all aspects of social life etc. In order to provide the above mentioned conditions the government should organize well social expenditures, paying special attention to investment in education, health care and development of human capabilities, and direct benefits of economic growth towards human development by fair distribution of capital and income.

The Mongolian history of development shows that the 1990s were the first stage of historic transition to democratic society and market economy system. Although progress as well as decline was observed in human development during the transition period the strategy of overcoming regress and moving towards development has been the chosen strategy.

This chapter will look at changes in the demographic situation of Mongolia, changes in livelihood of population, inequalities, poverty and basic social services as well as the labor market and the employment specifics.

2.1 THE DEMOGRAPHIC SITUATION AND CHANGES IN IT

Population growth and changes

Since 1990 many changes have taken place not only in the political, economic and social life of Mongolia, but also in demographic situation. Even though the Mongolian population has grown quantitatively, the speed of growth declined every year and the growth slowed down. While between the population censuses of 1979 and 1989 the population grew by in average 2.5% annually, between 1989-2000 it slowed down to

1.4%, decreasing by 1.1 points compared to the previous decade[3]. The "Demographic policy of the Government of Mongolia" first approved in 1996 by the State Great Khural put forward a quantitative objective of population growth, namely, the sustainable population growth with an average annual growth of no less than 1.8%. However, a demographic result to provide this level has not been achieved. At the time the real population growth reached an annual average of 1.3%.

Figure 2.1 Population growth, the growth speed, 1990-2005

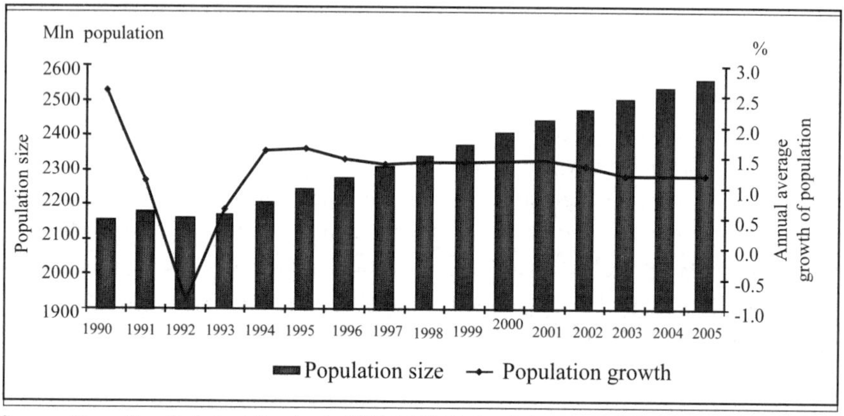

Source: Mongolian Statistical Yearbook, 1995-2005, National Statistical Office, Ulaanbaatar

Since the government realized that the social and economic structure had not developed to the level that can provide population growth by increasing the birth rate, in 2004 the policy document was revised under the name of "The human development policy of the Government of Mongolia" and no concrete quantitative objective was put forward in population growth. The revised policy viewed a complex resolution of the birth rate, the mortality and migration issues that directly affect changes in the population number and structure, as the core problems. In addition, the policy stated that the sustainable growth will be achieved by the way of supporting birth based on free choice of couples and women with respect to their reproductive rights and reduction of morbidity and mortality[4].

The constantly declining birth rate, the flow of out-migration, increasing number of university and college students become the main reasons for slowdown of population growth. In the last 3 years the population growth is relatively sustainable (the average

[3] The National Statistical Office of Mongolia, 2001. Population and housing census 2000: Main results, Ulaanbaatar.
[4] The State Great Khural of Mongolia, 2004. "The human development policy of the Government of Mongolia", Ulaanbaatar.

annual growth speed of 1.2%), which is related to the population momentum, i.e. growth of population by inertia. In particular, in mid 1950s to the end of 1980s the government followed a policy of social and economic development and an active policy of population growth. As a result, a high mortality rate declined, the birth rate increased leading to "the population growth boom" which is the main reason for the present population growth by inertia despite the declining birth rate.

As the population projections show[5], if the present level of population growth remains the same in the future, the growth will be relatively sustainable until 2010, but it will decline quite rapidly after that and by 2025 the growth rate might be less than 1%. If the birth rate is maintained at least at the level of the reproduction, and mortality, especially the infant and child mortality rate is reduced substantially and the average annual population growth is maintained at 1.2%, the population of our country will reach 2.9 million in 2015 and 3.1 million in 2020.

Numerous studies on correlation between such variables as population growth and economic development made different conclusions that there is a positive or negative correlation or denied existence of any correlation between these two. The latest studies viewed that this issue is more questionable at the micro economic level rather than at the macroeconomic level, for instance, such issues as the effect of population growth on poverty, the role of women, the healthcare, human resource development, environmental problems, migration. As for our country where population growth is considered low there is a trend to view that the population number affects greatly economic development and thus it is the main factor which presents an obstacle to achievement of the national goals. Although in some developing countries the pronatalist policy of supporting birth is legalized, it is important to examine its demographic, social and economic, ecological aspects in the frame of policy implementation and have an objective justification. Along with taking into account healthy, high quality population growth rather than looking at the numbers, there is a need to pay attention to protection and maintenance of the present gene pool and the ethnic structure of population which is a priority demographic issue for our country with small population.

The casual net population growth and mechanic growth are the main factors affecting population growth and changes in it. In our country the casual net population, especially declining birth rate make the main impact on decline of population growth.

---

[5] PTRC, MPDA, UNFPA 2004 "Age and sex structure of Mongolian population, future trends", Mongolian demographic journal, volume 10, Ulaanbaatar

Changes in the birth rate

Although during socialist period the government supported natality in a direct and indirect ways and pursued a pro-natalist policy,the birt rate declined substantially in the end of 70s. This decline can be explained by increasing labor participation of women and growing share of women with higher and special technical education. Even though the birth rate has declined since that time, since the absolute population size grew every year, the number of births and that of children born a year has been increasing in the period of 50s until 90s. Sharp decline in birth rate since 1990, when Mongolia started its transition to market, was related to numerous factors such as economic distress and hardships of transition, declining living standards of population, greater use of contraceptives to prevent pregnancy, increasing educational level of women and since late 1989 free access to abortion, which was previously strictly controlled. As a result, the average number of children per woman fell from 6 and over in 80s to 3 and less in 90s[6]. While in 1990 TFK was 4.5, in 2000 it fell down to 2.2 and further down to 1.9 in 2005. The fertility rate today reached a level lower than a fertility rate needed to maintain a stable population[7] and the trend is for further decline of birth rate. Limited economic resources of a family became a majoe economic reason for decline of the birth rate.

Figure 2.2 Natality and mortality rates (per 1000 population), 1990-2005

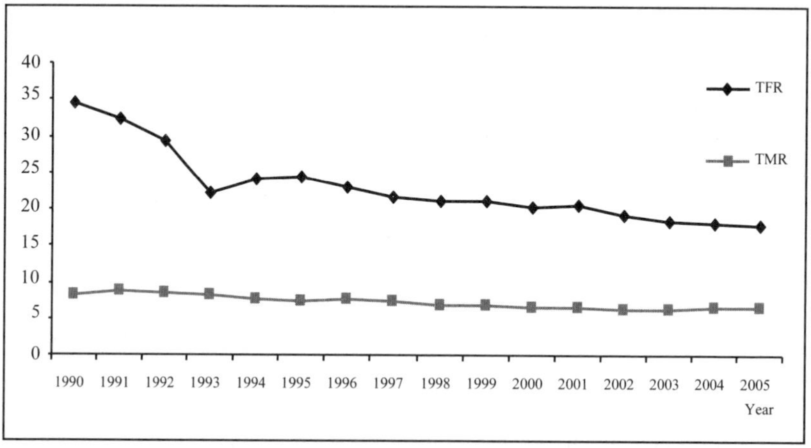

Source:" Mongolia at the market" Mongolian Statistical Yearbook-2003, Mongolian Statistical Yearbook 2005, National Statistical Office, Ulaanbaatar

Although the birt rate has declined, it differs among different social groups.The birt rate is the highest among low-educated women from poor households and adolescent

[6] NSO, 1994. "Mongolian population", Ulaanbaatar

[7] TFK equal to 2.1 or greater is needed to maintain stable population

girls in rural areas. For instance, while in 1996-1998 the birth rate among adolescent women in urban areas declined slightly (from 38 to 33)[8], in rural areas it increased (from 71 to 81)[9]. The higher household income and the educational level of women, the lower the birth rate.

Another important factor affecting natality is the marriage rate. While according to the 1989 population and housing census 65.8% of total population had families, in 2000 it declined to 57.8%[10]. When the 1998[11] and 2003[12] Reproductive Health survey results are compared, the average age of the first marriage among women increased by 0.8 points from 20.8 to 21.6, the average age of first marriage has a significant impact on the birth rate and the average age of the first marriage has increased among urban as well as rural women. The educational level of women affected greatly the older age for marriage, but their employment had no impact. In the years of transition in urban as well as rural areas the share of men who attained education higher than complete secondary became lower than that of women[13]. A gender misbalance in education of young population that took place in the country also affected the marriage level. It might also bring some negative consequences to the future social and family life, for instance, an increasing divorce rate, a growing number of single parents and family conflicts.

While before the economic transition, i.e. during the socialist era the marital status was one of the main criteria to determine the person's social status, it does not have such an importance since 1990s. The divorce rate has been growing every year, and 1622 families divorced in 2005 which is by 42.4% greater compared to 2002. This situation ads to vulnerability of women, in particular women with a large number of young children. Although the number of households with the large number of under age children has declined due to reduced birth rate, the number of women- heads of households, who bring up their children alone and sustain their livelihood themselves reached 70.3 thousand in 2005, which is 4.5 times greater compared to 1990.

On the other hand, although since 2006 the government has spent substantial resources in the frame of the direct policy of supporting young families and natality (by providing cash allowances), such issues as creating new work places, improving access to and supply of housing and housing conditions in order to support creative, proactive state of families and couples have not been resolved.

---

[8] Live births per 1000 women aged 15-19
[9] NSO, UNFPA, 2004. Reproductive Health survey, 2oo3, Ulaanbaatar
[10] NSO 2002, The marriage situation: topic study, Population and housing census 2000, Ulaanbaatar.
[11] NSO, UNFPA, 1999, Reproductive Health survey, 1998, Ulaanbaatar.
[12] NSO, UNFPA, 2004, Reproductive Health survey, 2003, Ulaanbaatar.
[13] NSO 2002, Population and Housing census, 2000: Education, topic study, Ulaanbaatar

Figure 2.3 The share of selected households in total households.

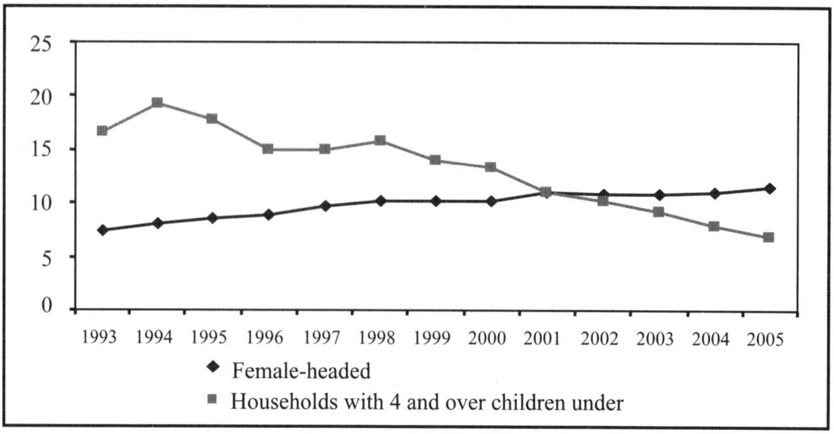

Source: Mongolian Statistical Yearbook, 1995-2005, National Statistical Office, Ulaanbaatar

The new parliament and the coalition government elected in 2004 discussed numerous forms of providing cash allowances for child development and since March 1, 2004 started paying monthly allowances of 3000 MNT to children under 16 years old in poor families with 3 and over children[14], and since July 1, 2006 all children were provided with such allowance. Policy makers should not forget historic experience of other countries with difficult economic situation when similar pro-natalist policies affected increase of birth rate among socially vulnerable groups. A sharp decline in the fertility levels in Mongolia, a phenomenon similar to other former socialist countries, has resulted on the one hand from economic hardships faced by families (household income, unemployment, expenses related to housing and children etc.), and from a substantial improvement in women's education and labor participation on the other. If Mongolian women and families did not put such control and limits to natality in the years of social and economic crisis in transition years, the poverty level might have been even greater than at the present. Since 2006 the government started providing young families with an allowance of 500000 MNT. Even though this measure supports young families and leads to the increase in number of registered families, it is not clear what is their responsibility in case the couple divorces.

Many of our policy makers view that the demographic situation of our country should be at appropriate level to provide economic development[15]. However, the majority of

[14] Children in such families had to answer such criteria as not being engaged in intolerable forms of child labor, attending school and being covered by vaccination.

[15] MPDA, MoH, UNFPA, 2003.Baseline survey on determining knowledge and attitudes of high and mid-level decision-makers on Population, Gender, Development, RH issues, and on development of strategy of advocacy work in this direction

women wish to limit the size of their families and do not wish to have more children (66% of total women, 85% of women with three or more children) as results of reproductive health studies show[16]. The number of rural women who do not wish to have more children increased considerably compared to 1998 and the gap between urban and rural women not wishing to have more children narrowed down. From the nationalistic point of view a small population which is capable, educated and healthy is better than an non-educated large population with poor health. That is why it is more important to pay attention to enhancing the health status of population, to prevent and protect from diseases, to reduce mortality, to alleviate poverty, to "make population high quality", i.e. to have intellectual, creative capable people able to provide for themselves rather than to mobilize resources in order to increase the birth rate.

Changes in the mortality rate

In the last 15 years the mortality rate per 1000 persons has declined from 8.5 down to 6.5 () (Figure 2.4). In the same period the infant mortality per 1000 live births declined from 64.4 to 20.7 (), which might be related to the health care policy and activities in the frame of different programs such as preventive immunization, reduction of malnourishment, increased consumption of vitamin A and iodized salt. Decline of birth rate also made its impact. At present the pattern of mortality in different age groups among population still has characteristics of developing countries with a high infant and child mortality rate. The government put forward a millennium development objective to reduce by 2015 the infant and child mortality by one third compared to 2000[17]. The infant and mortality rate which increased in the first years of transition has declined and reached the level when the MDG can be achieved, as the statistical data show. However, reliability of data on mortality attracts attention. For instance, while according to 2005 health care statistics the infant mortality rate was 20 per 1000 live births, the survey on Children and Development conducted in the same year gave a number twice greater than that. In addition, the infant and child-under-five mortality depends in great measure on geographical location of the household, the educational level of the mother and income poverty of the household. The child mortality is twice higher in rural against urban areas, it is 4 times higher among children, whose mothers have primary education against mothers with college or higher education, child mortality in poor households is twice higher compared to wealthy ones[18]. Since poverty has not declined substantially, food security and daily need for microelements among young children (aged 0-5) of households in vulnerable groups is not provided. Be-

[16] NSO, UNFPA, 2004. Reproductive Health survey 2003, Ulaanbaatar.
[17] The State Great Khural of Mongolia, 2004. "The human development policy of the Government of Mongolia ", Ulaanbaatar
[18] NSO, UNICEF, 2007 Sample survey on multiple indicators groups, Child and development survey, 2005-2006: Main results, Ulaanbaatar

cause of that one in every three children under 5 has deficiency of vitamin D, as researchers determined[19]. It shows uneven access of population groups to general and reproductive services, decline of livelihood, food deficiency, poor housing, access to drinking water, sanitation, hygiene of environment.

As all sources of information show, in general the infant and child mortality has declined and it affects the sustainable increase of the average life expectancy. Although the average life expectancy since birth reached 65 in 2005 there is a substantial gap in life expectancy of men (62.1 years) and women (68.6 years). While in 1993 there were 119 men per 100 dead women, in 2005 the number reached 165 and the mortality rate of men increased sharply. At the same time the share of women- heads of households among total households grew up from 7.4 to 11.5%.

Figure 2.4 Unmarried women with four or over children, 1993-2005

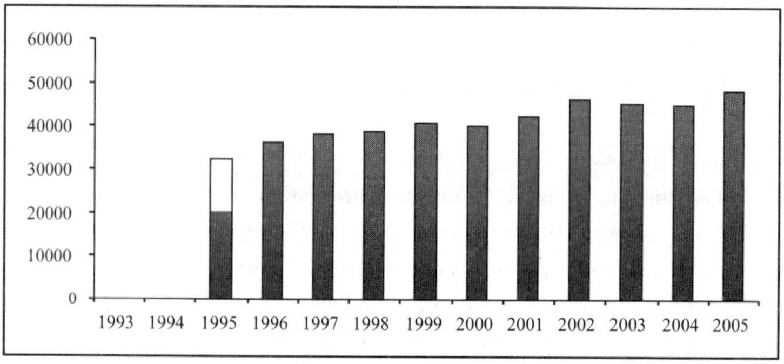

Source: Mongolian Statistical Yearbook, 1995-2005, National Statistical Office, Ulaanbaatar

In this way the increasing share of female headed households (Table 2.4) and semi orphans and orphans increases the risk of the number of poor households to grow further along with the increasing number of beneficiaries form social welfare services.

Since the birth rate in our country has decreased, health and life expectancy of population became the ground for further population growth in Mongolia. Although the life expectancy at birth has been increasing at the national level, it varies substantially among aimags. Therefore, a special attention should be paid to aimags with a high infant mortality rate which is the most important factor affecting the average life expectancy, and use in optimal measure activities of international programs with resources and efforts of the government. As a result, along with increase of the average life expectancy of population at the national level, disparities between aimags will be reduced.

[19] UNICEF, 2002 Report on situational analysis of Mongolian children and women-2000.

Changes in migration levels

Although the sharp decline of the birth rate has a major impact on the net population growth in Mongolia, the increasing internal migration increases the effect of mechanic growth rather than normal population growth in aimags and regions. Since young population predominantly participates in migration it becomes one of conditions for reducing of the birth rate.

At present 32.3% of total population of our country, i.e. one in every three persons lives in the capital city of Ulaanbaatar. The increasing rural urban migration of population not only adds to the effect of mechanic growth on population growth of the city, but also adds to the level of urbanization. For instance, of migrants who participated in migration in the period of 5 years prior to the population census 2000, 8 in every 10 persons moved to Ulaanbaatar and the Central region. Of over 95 thousand migrants in this period 65% moved to Ulaanbaatar, which makes up at present 14% of the capital city population[20]. Rapid growth of population in central regions causes increase of risks to public health due to shortage of safe drinking water, concentration of population in an environment not meeting hygienic demands, decline of natural environment. Rural- urban migration affects urban poverty because migrants are not poor due to migration, but have lower professional and educational levels and lack capacity compared to the non-migrant population. As researchers proved[21], probability of migrant households to slip down into socially vulnerable groups is twice higher against non-migrant households, in other words, apart from income poverty, migrants are poorer and more vulnerable in aspects of access to social services and public participation.

The majority of migrants moved in order to find jobs, improve their livelihood, study and get closer to the market, but although they achieved their main objectives, no progress was observed in their educational level[22]. Living conditions of migrants are poor, they mostly live in ger districts and the school drop-out rate is the highest among children of migrants. The main reason of school drop-out is lack of household registration, so their children are not covered by the medical and educational services in the place of their residence[23]. Among these children the employment level is quite high.

Households who lost their livestock due to natural disasters, drought and dzud and who lack opportunities to move to the aimag centers or cities move from baghs to soum centers, while a well off part of the soum center's population moves to the aimag centers or cities. In relation to this, the poverty level among the soum center

[20] NSO, 2002, Population and Housing Census: Migration and Urbanization, UB
[21] MSWL, PTRC, UNDP, 2004 Poverty and Migration in Ulaanbaatar, Survey report, UB
[22] MSWL, PTRC, UNDP, 2004 Poverty and Migration in Ulaanbaatar, Survey report, UB
[23] MSWL, PTRC, UNDP, 2004 Poverty and Migration in Ulaanbaatar, Survey report, UB

population has become the highest. Although employment opportunities are slightly higher in the aimag centers and cities compared to soum centers, mostly low skilled, physical jobs can be found, and self employment in the informal sector dominates, which does not provide social security to migrants. Furthermore, population that moves from rural to urban areas and to other countries in order to find jobs, to engage in trade, to study, add to spread of HIV/AIDS and STI, which has become another large negative consequence of migration.

As a result of migration to the capital city households living in ger districts are more vulnerable to poverty compared to households from apartment building districts and poverty is widespread in khoroos with the worst environmental conditions, with ditches and ravines, with geographical position least appropriate for housing construction. At present, environmental conditions in the ger district situated in the western part of the capital city contains all characteristics of poor districts in large cities of the world. Large enterprises affecting greatly environment pollution, for instance, the meat processing factory, the city sewage treatment facility, power plants, numerous small brick factories, a large railway station are located in this part, in addition, the city waist point was officially moved here in the late 1990s. Due to this, exhausts, smoke, all kinds of waist, loud noise are worst in this district and it is the worst place for people to live. Of four large roads from and to the capital city, namely the roads passing to the western, the northern and the southern regions are located in the western part of Ulaanbaatar and many industrial plants are concentrated in the district. As the population census and the migration survey show, the majority of migrants to the capital city come from the western, the northern and the southern regions and reside predominantly in the western part of the city. A large part of residents in this district moved here to be closer to markets located and the western part of the city and sustain their livelihood by collecting waist, carrying load on carts, collecting coal and lumber waist, carrying load, engaging in small street trade.

It is important to reduce substantially development disparities between urban and rural areas by weakening the flow of migration by improving quality of and access to basic social services such as rural schools and health clinics, to support small and medium enterprises and self-employment in soum centers, by encouraging capital investment in centers and towns of regional development over-concentration of population in the capital city will be reduced and special attention should be paid to living conditions and livelihood of migrants. With transition to the market economy system and expanding international cooperation at all levels, the number of migrants to foreign countries to study, to work or immigrate has grown in the last years. During the first wave of migration in 1990-1994 population went abroad mostly to engage in border trade, during the second wave or in 1994-1999- people went to work abroad, at the third stage since 1999- to work and live abroad. Shortage of workplaces, unemployment, low salaries and income, low value of labor become the main push factors for migration of population to foreign countries. Although increasing emigration contributes to declining number of unemployed at macro level, decreasing social welfare expenditure from the budget and helps the livelihood of families and relatives of immigrants, there are some negative consequences such as loss of young workforce from the labor market to foreign countries, separation of families and decline of population growth. Furthermore, individuals working abroad illegally are mostly engaged in hard, hazardous, dirty work at small and medium enterprises and often become involved in crime. At the micro level individuals have an opportunity to get acquainted with the foreign culture and civilization, to learn foreign languages, to attain education and a profession, to accumulate monetary savings, to live independently. However, there are also such negative consequences as not working in their professional field, having health problems, delayed marriage and birth, family crisis and problems in child upbringing.

Changes in population structure

If reasons of demographic changes and growth are not realized, the consequences are not fully recognized as well. That is why demographic research is directed towards determining reasons for changes in birth rate, mortality, migration, age and sex structure of population, demographic profile and distribution.

Due to demographic situation of Mongolia substantial changes have taken place in the structure and composition of population in the last 15 years. For the population of our country, which is at the middle stage of demographic transition (with declining natality and mortality), changes in the relative number of children, adolescents and adults are very rapid. The population, which in general had a young age structure, at present is in transition to the adolescent structure (Figure 2.5). While the population pyramid of 1990 represents a period, when the share of children, among them young children, was high and the natality was high, in the 2005 population pyramid the number of population aged 0-4 and 5-9 is lower than that of population aged 10-14. It illustrates that the birth rate has declined substantially, the share of children and adolescents has declined and the share of adults has grown.

As for sex, the number of men per 100 female population has declined slightly compared to 1990. The decline can be explained by the growing out-migration of male population and a high mortality rate of men.

Figure 2.5 Population age-sex pyramis, 1990, 2005, 2010

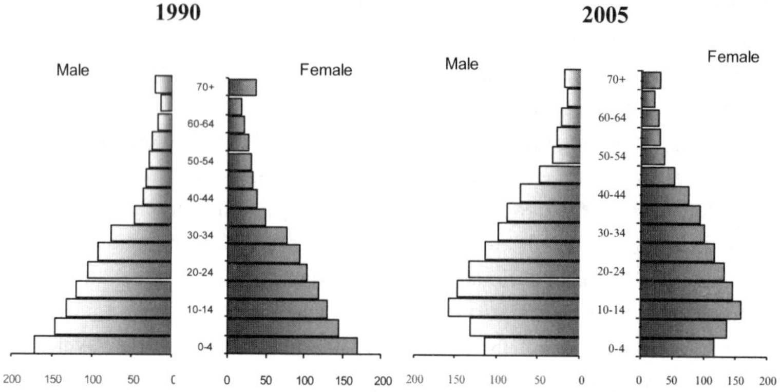

When the 2010 age and sex pyramid of population is examined, although Mongolia has characteristics of transition from the young population to the aged one, the share of children and youth remains relatively high. The share of the population group aged 20-24 in the total population will be the highest.

Source:" Mongolia at the market" Mongolian Statistical Yearbook-2003, Mongolian Statistical Yearbook 2005, National Statistical Office, Ulaanbaatar. Population and Housing Census 2000: population projection in Mongolia, Ulaanbaatar

Even though the population of Mongolia has in general a trend towards young, the medium age has been growing gradually (18.9 in 1990, 22.7 in 2005), which is an outcome of declining natality. Of the total population children aged 0-14 account for 32.6%, and the child load (the number of children aged 0-14 per 100 persons aged 15-64, i.e. of labor age) has been declining. Because of the low average life expectancy level the load of elderly (the number of population aged 65 and over per 100 persons of labor age) is relatively low.

In this way, the declining demographic load or the number of children and elderly per 100 persons of labor age presents a very favorable factor of the population age structure to support Mongolian economy. In demographic science this phenomenon is called "a demographic window". In the conditions of economic development process becoming healthy effective use of "demographic incentive" it is important to realize consciously the present and future trends of labor force and to make appropriate investment in order to support effective and creative employment able to absorb it. Such countries as the Republic of Korea, Taiwan, Singapore and other "Tiger" economies of Eastern and South Eastern Asia, which used their favorable demographic age structure to make an economic development leap, can be mentioned here.

The most significant indicator related to the population age structure is the structure of age groups, which requires special attention from the society of the given country. Although due to reduced natality of previous years the share of population under 18 in total population has declined, it is relatively sustainable. Since supply of young people with high educational demand at the labor market is high, problems of providing them with workplaces and effective use of labor force resources in economic growth need to be resolved. A small population of elderly affects sustainability of the social welfare load.

Table 2.1 Selected target age groups, Mongolia, 1990-2000, 2005, 2010, 2020

Target age groups	Share in total population					
	Real			Projected		
	1990	2000	2005	2010	2015	2020
Children (aged 0-14)	41.5	35.8	32.6	27.5	26.2	24.7
Of labor age (15-64)*	54.4	60.8	63.8	68.5	69.7	70.6
Elder population (64+)	4.1	3.4	3.5	4.0	4.1	4.7
Total population	**2153.4**	**2389.7**	**2562.4**	**2 741.8**	**2918.6**	**3 087.0**

In our country, where natality has declined sharply in the last years, the consequence of changes in the population age structure, i.e. aging is not so high compared to its level in developed countries, but has a trend for more rapidness. The growth speed of population of labor age is greater than the growth speed of total population. There is a trend for even greater increase of the number of population of labor age in 2010. If this growth coincides with growing participation of population in labor and inability to create new workplaces, a high rate of unemployment will be in place, which will increase a danger of increasing demographic pressure at the labor market. The above changes in the population age structure show clearly a need for an appropriate policy in relation to social groups and intensive activities in this field.

Changes in access to and quality of basic social services

Access to and quality of medical services.

With transition to the market economy the social sector faces numerous difficulties and many reforms have been made. In the 1990s the amount of subsidies to the healthcare sector from the state was reduced and the responsibilities were passed from the centralized level to the local administration, which put the foundation for reforms. For instance, the medical services management departments, the regional diagnostic and treatment centers and family doctor services were established in aimags. Unfortunately, as the amount of subsidies to the healthcare sector and financing of the sector declined sharply, provision and supply of medical equipment decreased. Low salaries of medical workers became a reason for many specialists to leave their workplaces, which led to shortage of doctors and medical workers in the countryside, especially in remote regions, and although certain measures have been taken to attract professional human resources to rural areas with economic incentives for their permanent work there, the effect was negligible.

One of the major changes, which took place in the operations of the healthcare sector, its structure and organization, was establishment of family doctor services system. The share of private medical clinics in treatment, services and diagnostics has been growing continuously. Such distinctive structures as paid medical assistance, an insurance system, free medical assistance emerged in medical services. In order to make the financing of medical services more optimal the Medical Insurance Fund was established and over 70% of total population are covered with insurance at present. To provide basic medical assistance family doctor clinics were established at all administrative units and the MIF pays costs for each insurer along with the state financing. The present system of MIF provides financing based on the average number of days patients are treated at hospitals, which creates an interest in increasing the MIF compensation[24] by increasing the number of hospital beds rather than the number of day, domestic or facilitating treatment. Along with it more effort should be made in increasing health education of population.

In the last years attention was paid to development of the private sector in the healthcare sector to lighten the budget load. Although the private healthcare sector is growing rapidly, it does not pay much attention to the health education of population. Due to inappropriate control and coordination of management priority is given to the objective of gaining profit and practice of providing costly services with low guarantee has become widespread. There is a growing trend for solvent individuals to seek treatment abroad as they wish to receive high-quality diagnostic and treatment services in a patient- friendly environment, which is one of indicators of low quality of health services in our country.

While poor and extremely poor households spend 2.3% or 20000 MNT on their health, non-poor households spend 15% or 160000 MNT on their health[25] as the survey results show. Among the population the trend of revering treatment rather than learning methods of health protection and prevention from diseases still prevails. Results of several surveys on activities of healthcare sector showed that[26] additional ser-

[24] MoH, 2005 "Master plan of the healthcare sector", UB

[25] UNFEM, 2001 "The second project on development of healthcare sector in Mongolia". Ppta 3750, Report on Social on social impact, UB

[26] PTRC, UNFPA, 2006. The health sector through the window of corruption, the Mongolian demographic journal, issue 264 (14), p 84, Ulaanbaatar

vices became too dependent on doctors and medical workers, and services provided to patients were unfriendly and discriminatory, medical workers treated their acquaintances differentially and provided them with better services, they accepted bribes, they were irresponsible. It shows that a fair, responsible system is needed in this sector. In the last years special attention is paid to quality management, and measures on creating patient- friendly, pro-poor services, on improvement of legal environment have been taken in order to improve the quality of health services.

Because of poor infrastructure development population of remote areas, among them poor population, is not able to access fully health services. Over – concentration of population in some places, environmental pollution and conditions not meeting hygienic requirements become the major reasons for increasing morbidity among population. In the last 20 years a distribution transition is taking place in our country and contagious diseases related to the lifestyles of people are spreading rapidly. The five leading causes of mortality have changed since 1989 and since 1995 cardiovascular diseases, tumors and accidents have become the leading causes. Incidence of infectious diseases is dominating in morbidity and it does not reduce due to poor social and economic situation, poor access to and quality of public health services. Such infectious diseases as HIV/AIDS, STI, tuberculosis and viral hepatitis associated with risk factors in human behavior, life style, their living environment have a trend for further rise, furthermore, occurrence of mental illnesses and diseases passed from livestock to human has increased, the number of population who uses alcohol and tobacco grows and their age is getting younger. Children, young people, migrants, members of poor and vulnerable groups, that make up the majority of population, are more vulnerable.

For instance, while in 1990 incidents of tuberculosis per 10000 population was 7.5, in 2005 it increased by 10 points reaching 17.5 and morbidity has been increasing since 1997.

Table 2.6 Morbidity among population, by selected indicators, 1990-2005

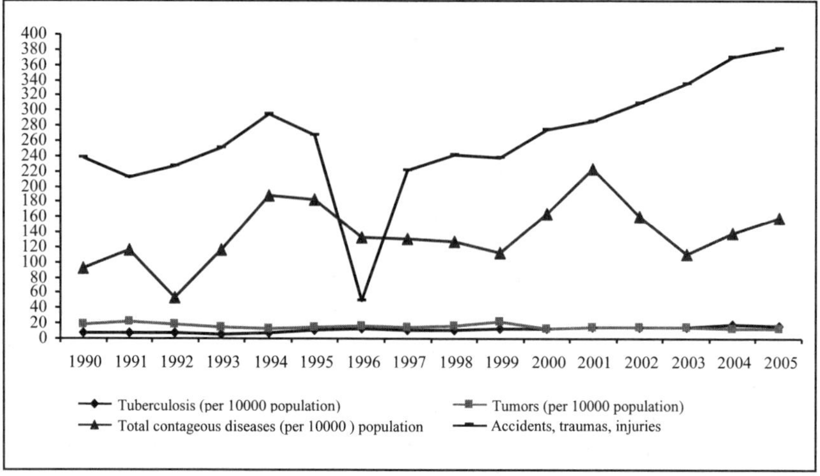

While in 1990 the number of population with infectious diseases was 92.0 thousand, in 1995 it grew twice (182.1 thousand), and in 2001 reached 223.6 thousand.

Maternal mortality is an important indicator representing access to the basic health services, the functioning of the system and gender equality. Due to the fact that work on provision of medical assistance and services to population in general became stagnant in the transition period, maternal mortality increased to 124.6 (per 10000 live births) in 1991, to 199.6 in 1992, and sharply rose to 243.1 in 1993. A fact that a great number of maternal houses in rural areas was closed down made a great impact. In 1993 only 52 out of 287 maternal houses continued their operations. Fewer kinds of medical assistance and services provided to rural population at that period affected negatively a health status of herders. As a result of two national programs on health implemented by the government and programs and projects implemented with technical and economic assistance of UN agencies and other donor organizations, maternal mortality has declined at national level in the last 4 years (Figure 2.7). However, this indicator varies greatly by aimags and regions. For instance, in Bayankhongor, Bayan Ulgii, Khuvsgul, Arkhangai, Khentii, Sukhbaatar aimags maternal mortality remains higher than that of the national average for many years (207-448 per 100000 live births). In Ulaanbaatar as well maternal mortality is higher than that of the national average.

Although the government allocates greater resources in order to make health services more accessible to residents of remote regions, backwardness of health services in rural areas is still in place.

Figure 2.7 Maternal mortality rate (per 100000 live births)

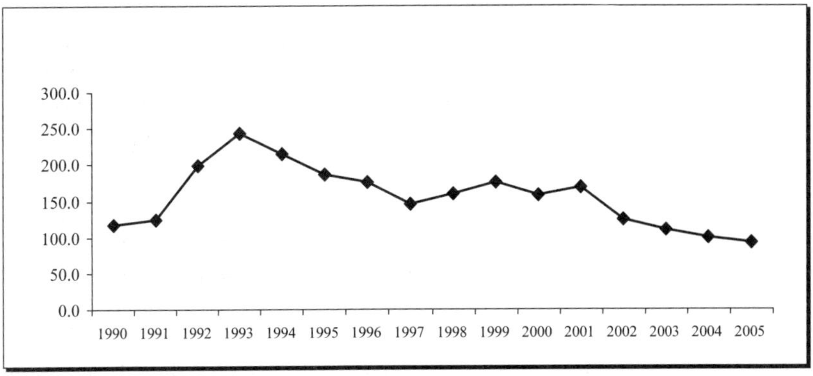

To reduce maternal mortality the government needs to resolve comprehensively such issues as improving quality of medical assistance and services before, during and after delivery, enhancing knowledge and skills of medical doctors and workers, resolving problems of financing bagh clinics, provision of medicines required for emergency assistance during delivery. On the other hand, making the state alone take responsibility for reduction of maternal mortality is a one-sided trend since survey results present other numerous reasons such as lack of attention, care and support from the family, neighbors and co-workers, low attention to their health and low health knowledge of pregnant mothers themselves.

The share of expenditure on healthcare in GDP was 5.5% in 1990, in 1995 it fell sharply to 2.9%, but started increasing again since 1996 and reached 5.2% in 2005. Expenditure on healthcare per capita is increasing steadily (while it was 18.0 million USD in 2000, in 2005 it reached 26.3 million USD). Out of nearly 90 billion of annual expenditure in the healthcare sector over 20% comes from the Medical Insurance Fund, about 70% is financed from the budget and less than 5% is provided by payment of patients. Financing of the healthcare sector by international donor countries has declined in the last years excluding the year 2001 and aid is prevailing in financing of international partners. One third of these resources is spent on the policy making level, about 40% are spent on development of additional health services in selected aimags and districts of the capital city and on infrastructure development.

Changes in the education sector

As a result of special attention paid to the health care and education sectors during the planned economy Mongolia had excellent human resources. As for 1989, 96% of the labor- age population were literate and 7.5% attained higher education. The school attendance rate was very high. In 1989, 98% of primary school age children and 85% of secondary school children were enrolled at school.

The educational reform aimed at purging the educational system from the politicized ideology inherited from the old system, making a curriculum reform, strengthening links between education and industry, improving provision of educational equipment and bringing the quality of education to the international standards.

Since transition of Mongolia to the market economy relations changes in the educational sector required a need to legalize a new environment for development of the educational sector.

Adoption by the Parliament of Mongolia of several laws related to the educational sector in 1995 determined general principles of the system and the main directions of the policy to be followed in education. As a result of gradual activities taken in order to create a legal environment for changes in the educational sector, which took place in the years of transition from the planned to the market economy, a number of important documents on education were developed and approved.

The National Program on Support of Preschool Education (1995), Main directions of reforms to be made in the educational system of Mongolia in 1997-2005 (1997), the National program on development of Informal Education (1996), the National Program on Development of Technical and Vocational Education (1998), the State Policy on Science and Technology (1998), the National Program on Distance Education and other policy documents determined main directions for reforms in the educational sector.

The policy which the Government has followed until the present is the one to maintain the educational sector as a priority sector. However, since 1990 attendance at all levels of school has declined and in 1993, 23%, i.e. about 105000 children that should have studied in 1-8th grades did not attend school as the results of the World Bank study revealed. The DANIDA survey on Reasons of school drop-out showed that the percentage of drop-out was higher among boys compared to girls (DANIDA, School drop-out in Mongolia, 1993).

Capital investment in the educational sector has declined sharply since 1990 and in 1990-1992 the budget expenditure in this sector declined by 69%.

While in 1990 the share of the annual budget of education equaled 11.5% of GDP and 17.6% of the state budget, in 2005 the education expenditure was 3.1% of GDP and

19.3% of the state budget. Although the share of expenditure on education in GDP has declined, the number of private schools has increased and paid education is available, so it lightens the load of expenditure on education.

In the last years the number of colleges and universities, especially private colleges and universities, has increased and the number of college and university students has a trend for sharp increase. As for the 2005-2006 academic year there were 131 non-state owned colleges, institutes and universities.

The former regulations when the number of students was determined by the Government was annulled and since 1993 students of public universities started paying tuition fees.

Reform and organization of tertiary education at the diploma, bachelor's, master's and Ph.D levels, standardization of requirements to the quality of education, especially the quality of teaching staff became an important step in improving the quality of education at the tertiary level. A system of student loans was established in the higher education field.

As it was noticed in the strategic plan of the educational sector development in Mongolia in 2000-2005, 40% of high school graduates enter colleges and universities, which accounts for about 20% of young people aged 18-22. The number of students of technical and vocational schools as well as students of schools at all other levels has grown since the second half of 1990s. The percentage of female students among total students at all levels of schools, including that among college and university students, illustrates changes in the gender ratio of students related to problems faced in the transition economy.

While in the beginning of the 1990s the school drop-out rate increased greatly, the situation changed in the last years and it dropped to 9% in the 2005-2006 academic year. With successful measures on enrollment of children of school age at secondary schools opportunities for implementation of the universal secondary education goal are created.

Compared to years of centrally planned economy the number of vocational schools and centers providing technical education decreased and the number of students has declined. Two major obstacles are faced in development of technical education and vocational training system at the present. First, an ability to foresee the future development of private industries and services which are established at the present and to train workers that can meet the demand for workplaces needed at such enterprises, second, to improve the environment, conditions and technical equipment for training at vocational schools and install new equipment.

Social protection and insurance

Although disbandment of state enterprises and emergence of private ones with beginning of privatization in early 1990s was an appropriate direction for transition to the new economic system, due to weak coordination and control from the government and lack of preparatory and organizational activities unemployment and poverty became widespread and conditions for loss of social security were established. With crisis of industry and services the budget revenue, the state financial reserves and sources reduced and there was lack of resources for implementation of the state social policy.

In connection with transition of Mongolia to the new market economy relations, legal reforms to change the social welfare system to the social insurance system along with the global standards started since 1991. In 1991 a Law on Allowances of Mongolia was approved. According to the law allowances were classified to several kinds such as temporary loss of working ability, pregnancy and delivery, child and child care, unemployment, and the right to receive the above allowances was determined by conditions of having social insurance and payment of duties. Legal coordination was made to pay allowances on temporary loss of working ability, pregnancy and delivery from the Pension Fund of Mongolia, to pay unemployment allowance from the organization the individual has worked previously, and to finance the child and child care allowances from the state budget.

The Law on Social insurance commission of Mongolia approved in 1991 stated that the main source of the Pension Fund shall be the social insurance duties. Along with it the Pension Fund was established in order to provide a source for financing pensions and allowances as well as social measures. According to experts[27] legal reforms of 1991-1994 in social welfare contributed to progress in transition to market relations, but maintained uneconomical situation and added to the state budget load.

In 1990 an amendment was made to the Pension Law and women with four or over children were forced to retire regardless of their age under pretence of social care. Although there was an article in the law stating that women should be willing to do so, in reality it created an opportunity to make women redundant in the first place. In 1994 of women of labor age, but without labor capability, 55.8% were those who retired early on the condition of having four or over children. In the beginning of the 1990s women who worked 27 years and men who worked 32 years were forced on

[27] D.Vandanmagsar,Ts. Sukhbaatar, 2002. Origins, development and reform of social insurance, UB.

retirement regardless of their age. These measures increased sharply the number of pensioners and 1/5 of budget revenue was spent on pensions and allowances. Later they were paid a compensation and a decision was made to pay their social insurance until they were 55 and 60, these years were added to their years of work and all expenditure was taken from the budget. How to accumulate the Social Insurance Fund resources becomes a more important question along with the problem of disparities in the age of retirement.

Table 2.2 Percentage and amount of social insurance in Mongolia

Kind of insurance	Total	From it	
		Paid from wages or other income of the employer	Paid from wages or other income of the insurer
Total amount of social insurance duties	29-30	19-20	10
Pension insurance	19	13.5	5.5
Allowance insurance	2	1.0	1.0
Health insurance	6	3.0	3.0
IAPD insurance	1-2	1.0-2.0	-
Unemployment allowance	1	0.5	0.5

Source: D.Vandanmagsar,Ts. Sukhbaatar, 2002. Origins, development and reform of social insurance, UB.

At the present stage of development the percentage and amount of social insurance to be paid, especially the amount to be paid by the employer, is quite high. For instance, 1/3 of total accumulated duties is to be paid by the insurer and 2/3 are to be paid by the employer. Because of that numerous inappropriate activitiestake place, such as evasion of social insurance payment by employers, establishment of a hidden economic environment with use of illegal methods, purposeful inaccurate reporting, all of which leads to loss of a guarantee by workers to receive pensions in the future.

Since 1995 an old system, when pensions were in general provided from the state budget, was changed, the law on Social Insurance was approved and a new distribution principle of paying pensions from duties paid by employers and insurers was followed. That system, more appropriate to a situation when unemployment is low and relations between insurers and pensioners are favorable, was not suitable for the situation in our country. The Pension Insurance Fund was not able to cover its expenditure with its income and was at deficit, so it has had direct subsidies from the state. The Pension Insurance Fund is the only one from other insurance funds such as the allowances, industrial accidents, professional diseases, unemployment and health insurance funds listed in the Law on Social Insurance, which is at deficit. In order to improve the pension insurance system since 1999 a transition was made to the system of personal accounts and at present the system is in transition to the combined system of distribution-savings. The main principle of that system is accumulation of insurer's fees on a special account and provision of pensions based on total contribution of the insurer. The present personal account system might be called an abstract savings system since a certain part of the insurance fund is spent on pensions for the present pensioners and the rest is entered in the turnover to increase it. In other words, duties paid by the insurer are not in reality kept in the bank on accounts[28].

Since the share of labor-age population in total population of Mongolia has grown at present, this opens a favorable demographic period in the insurance sector. For instance, while in 1990 the labor-age population accounted for 52.6% of total population, in 2005 it grew up to 62%, at the same period the number of insurers per 100 pensioners grew from 144 (1990) to 251 (2005).

The cost of operations of the social insurance institution was 400.0 million MNT in 1995, 1.3 billion MNT in 2000, 4.1 billion MNT in 2004 and reached 4.1 billion in 2005. Unemployment insurance was introduced according to the Social insurance law and an appropriate legal environment was created. In the period between 1995 to 2005 in total 27.4 billion MNT was accumulated in the Insurance Fund, of which 8 billion MNT was spent on unemployment allowances, professional training of over 70 thousand persons and operational costs of the social insurance institution. According to reliable statistical sources of the social insurance institution, of total 200 billion MNT worth of health insurance duties accumulated between 1995-2005, over 160 billion MNT were spent.

At present the government is implementing several programs and activities directed towards retired population and certain other population groups. In the conditions of market relations the main contents of reforms in the social welfare and services system is their direction towards support of socially vulnerable groups. Since 2006 children under 18 receive monthly allowances of 3000 MNT, the new born children-100.0 thousand MNT and the newly married couples receive allowances of 500.0 thousand MNT. Although the social welfare policies and activities are in general directed towards improving living standards of population, different measures cover a large number of recipients, the social and economic effect is not satisfactory and in some aspects might make a negative impact.

---

[28] MSWL, 2005 The present condition of the pension insurance and challenges, Ulaanbaatar

Even though the Law on Social welfare does not have an article on provision of welfare benefits, allowances and services with gender discrimination, some forms are directed towards mothers and women. As research shows in 2002 of total persons covered by welfare benefits and services 44.6% were women and 92.8% of individuals recipients of welfare pensions and allowances were women as well[29].

Since the poor account for one third of population and the poverty level does not decline, the number of pension and allowance recipients is expanding. Since 1990 the number of persons on social welfare has grown twice. While in 1997 total expenditure on social welfare pensions and allowances equaled 7.0 billion MNT, in 2002 it reached 20.0 billion MNT, thus increasing 2.9 times. Due to growing unemployment and poverty along with expanding frame covered by the social insurance and deficit of the state budget puts the social welfare system in a difficult situation. In this way there is a trend for target groups in difficult conditions to be left out resources used for subsistence. On the other hand, pensions and allowances might decrease interest of citizen to work for the well being of their families and children to support the "feed me" mentality, to revere big pensions and allowances, to encourage passive state. Therefore, there is a need to pay attention to finding opportunities for reducing inequalities between large and small families, families with employed members and those with unemployed members, urban and rural households.

Pensions and allowances are being changed with regard to inflation, but they are not related to the minimal living standards and living standards in different regions, so households, women and children, who make their living only with pensions and allowances, are in extremely difficult conditions. In order to increase effectiveness of expenditure in the social services sector there is a need to determine accurately the frame of coverage of any pensions, allowances or services and to link their amount with the minimal living standards at the region.

Livelihood of population, inequality, poverty

Livelihood of population

Before 1990s in the socialist era living standards of population were relatively equal and the gap between the rich and the poor was minimal. With transition of Mongolia to market relations the situation has changed, disparities in living conditions, income and consumption have increased sharply and poverty has become an objective phenomenon.

[29] MSWL, 2004 Gender analysis of the state budget expenditure in the social welfare sector, UB

The human development concept views that growth of the income level is one of the main tools to expand opportunities for wealthy living and improved living standards. In this aspect the income level indicator is used to illustrate material opportunities of the individual. Living standards are determined with regard to the income and consumption levels.

Living standards is an indicator which shows living conditions of the population and income distribution. The livelihood level among population is relatively different so by defining the minimal living standards the government provides opportunities for social security of low income population. As stated in Article 3 of the law of Mongolia on "Determining the minimal living standards of population" …

In 1991-1996 minimal living standards were determined with regard to urban-rural disparities, in 1997-2000 by regions where petrol and fuel prices were defined and since 2001 by the regional development zones. As of 2005 minimal living standards viewed per capita a month present 30000 MNT in Ulaanbaatar, 23200 MNT in the Western region, 25000 MNT in the Eastern region, 22300 in the Central region and 22600 in the Khangai region[30].

To mention some of large surveys to determine minimal living standards of population in our country, the National Statistical Office conducted the first Living Standards Measurement Survey with the World Bank assistance in 1995 and the second Living Standards Measurement Random Survey in 1998 with financial assistance from UNDP. In 2002-2003 the NSO implemented the Survey on the Household income, expenditure and living standards with the World Bank and UNDP assistance. Along with these a Participatory Living Standards Measurement Survey-2000, a Participatory Rural Living Standards Measurement Survey- 2003 were conducted. The above surveys made an important contribution to determining standard indicators illustrating the household profile with a participatory method evaluating indicators showing living standards of population and changes in them.

The results of the livings standards measurement surveys show that living standards of population during the centrally planned economy were relatively even. Since 1990 or with transition to market economy relations income sources of population became multiple and income sources went out of control of registration and statistics, so incomes from the hidden economy, small business, financing from foreign and national organizations, income from projects implemented on commission, remittances from workers abroad were not fully covered. That is why living standards were defined by the way of determining minimal living standards of population.

[30] NSO, The Statistical Yearbook of Mongolia, 2005, 2006.

The difference in living standards of population is represented by consumption per a household member, which is an indicator of livelihood. According to the Household income, expenditure and living standards survey results in 2002 monthly consumption per capita equaled 36750 MNT or approximately 32 USD. The consumption level in urban areas was greater than that of rural areas by 25%, as for regions, consumption in the Central region was the highest and that in the Western region was the lowest or by nearly 20% lower compared to the national average, while in the Khangai and the Eastern regions the levels were similar[31].

As for the structure of consumption, 2/5 of total consumption of rural population is taken up by food, while in rural areas it accounts for over half of total consumption. The main part of non- food consumption is made up by expenditure on clothes and account for 12% of total consumption, with expenditure on education making up 7% and expenditure on health- about 5%.

Figure 2.8 Cash income of households, in rural and urban areas (2005).

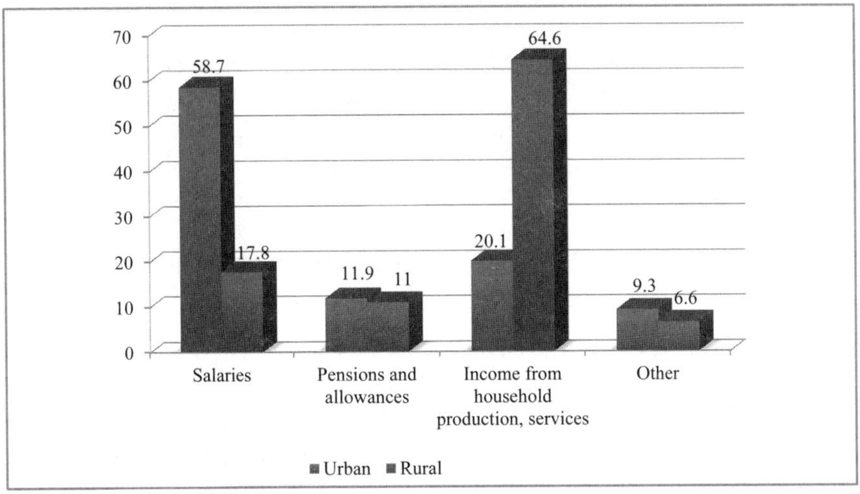

According to calculations by the National Statistical Office of Mongolia the national average of monthly total household income equaled 175017 MNT in 2005 and the cash income grew up to 150208 MNT, i.e. if total income is 100%, cash income accounts for 77.5%, food stuff from household economy- 9%, staff received from others- 3.6%. When average monthly expenditure of a household with such income is examined, in 2005 the average total expenditure of a household equaled 194078 MNT exceeding income by 10.9% and the national average cash expenditure equaled 171865 exceeding income by 14.4%. An indicator, which provides an opportunity to

[31] Household income, expenditure and living standards random survey, 2002-2003

clarify changes in the livelihood of household, is the household expenditure indicator and the structure of expenditure. In 2005 expenditure on non-food goods and services were the greatest accounting for 55.6% of total and expenditure on food made up 30.6% in the cash expenditure structure of the household. Along with this about 8% of household expenditure on food was procured from the individual farm.

As surveys show, the average salary grew by 26% between 1999 and 2002, but the real growth equaled 6%.

As the results of the survey on "Ways to prevent the middle-income families slip into the vulnerable groups" show, the average monthly income of a middle -income household in Mongolia equaled 155.7 thousand MNT and its expenditure made 189.5 thousand MNT. The majority of middle-income households at national average have a summer house and a private house, 2/5 have a car, 2/5 - a truck or a motorcycle. Of total income of the middle-income household 62.1% is basic income and 37.9% is additional income. The main income sources of a middle income household are salaries, income from livestock products, income for sale of livestock and raw materials, pensions and allowances. If middle-income population is classified by their employment, in 2004 26.4% were employed in public service, 30.3%- in education and health sectors, 12.5%- in trade and services, 8.7%- in industry, 6.2%- in agricultural sector, 5.4%- in transport and communications sector. Thus, civil servants, medical doctors and teachers, who are the public service workers, make up the majority of middle-income population.

One of important indicators that represent living standards of population is GDP per capita.

In 1990-1993 this indicator declined by over 30%. When the average income per capita is calculated in USD by 1993 prices, it plummeted from 1245 in 1990 to 374 USD in 1999[32]. While in 1993-2000 the average annual population growth was 1.4%, the annual growth of GDP per capita was only 2.0%. When changes in growth of income per capita between 1990-2001 are examined, in 1990-1995 the growth per capita made -4.3%, in 1996-2001 it grew to 1.2%. While in 1989 the average real income of population was the highest, i.e. 1646 USD, in 2002 the real GDP per capita was lower by 15.8%. As of 2005, when IMF ranked 181 countries, in case GDP per capita in Mongolia was not translated into PPP, our country was at 133rd place, i.e. 735 USD[33].

---

[32] Poverty reduction strategy in Mongolia, 2001 UB.
[33] http://en.wikipedia.org/wiki/list of countries by GDP (PPP) per capita

The National Human Development Report 2003 noticed that GDP per capita differs greatly in urban and rural areas. GDP per capita in urban areas is 2.8 times greater than that in rural areas. By 2002 GDP per capita in urban areas grew by 38.0% compared to the 1999 level, while there were negligible changes in GDP per capita in rural areas. It shows that living standards in urban and rural areas differ even greater at present.

Living conditions directly affect living standards of population. In the last rating of countries by living conditions (2006), which UNDP publishes annually, Mongolia held the 116th position behind Bolivia.

Since 1990s income and useful resources have been distributed unequally and the average income of the majority of population has declined.

Inequality

Inequality is a complex concept with multiple aspects. Inequality can be viewed at the economic, political, social freedom aspects. In order to show inequality in the frame of the whole society there is a need to make a comparative study of different population groups, or aimags and regions.

Economic inequality means that income of an individual or a group of individuals, their assets are different compared to other persons. Income inequality creates further consumption inequality. That is why it is important to pay attention to income, consumption or material inequality.

Origins and causes of economic inequality depend on many different factors. Among them a group of causes including personal characteristics and consumption patterns can be noted, for example, age, sex, education, marital status, consumption patterns of the given individual. Another groups of causes are dependent not on the individual him/herself, but on the society, for instance, income distribution at national level, lack or existence of discrimination by ethnicity, age or sex etc.

Economic inequality makes access to resources unequal. On the basis of all these factors opportunities for human development among different groups of population are relatively different. Poverty is the direct outcome of economic inequality.

In the course of transition from the centrally planned economy to the market economy changes took place in the mechanism of providing social security to population, distribution of income and wealth among different groups of population became unequal and as a result the gap between the rich and the poor has increased sharply.

Table 2.3 Inequality measurements

	Gini coefficient
National average	0.329
Urban	0.331
Rural	0.313

Source: Household income, expenditure and living standards random survey, 2002-2003, Ulaanbaatar

From the table it can be seen that inequality is higher in urban compared to rural areas. When population was divided into five groups by their consumption level total consumption, expenditure of the 20% in the group with the highest living standards was 5.5 times greater compared to the 20% of the poor or those who have the lowest living standards.

According to the National Human Development Report 2003 in 1995-1998 the number of poor in Mongolia increased and the depth of poverty and inequality spread further. Income inequality between larger cities and between cities and aimag centers of remote aimags has become greater. Income disparities between soum center residents and herders- residents of baghs as well as between different soum centers have deepened. Since provision of health and other services to poor people with nomadic lifestyle scattered on the vast territories of Mongolia is costly and faced with many difficulties, it adds to spatial inequality. To overcome this difficulty and to provide equal opportunities for human development it is important to provide population with infrastructure, roads, reliable power and drinking water supply.

As of 2002 the HDI in urban areas (0.723) was higher than that in rural areas (0.636) by 14%. Numerous other examples representing inequality can be mentioned. For instance, the unemployment rate among the poor is twice greater compared to the non-poor population, expenditure on health per capita among the wealthiest part of population (20%) is 7 times greater than that among the poorest part (20%). Children from poor families studying at school have expenditures in average by 60% less than other school children.

While in 1998 the number of bod livestock owned by the wealthiest herder household was twice greater compared to that of the poorest household, in 2002 it increased to

4.7 times[34]. Inequality in ownership of livestock was observed at the time of renewed economic growth as well[35]. Thus, the ever increasing inequality is one of the factors slowing down human development, so eliminating inequality and reducing poverty have become the most urgent issues. To eliminate inequality at birth since different individuals have different talents and capabilities, equal opportunities should be provided to all. If life opportunities are equal, everyone will live using their abilities, which is important for human development.

Poverty

Before 1990s the form of equaled distribution prevailed in Mongolia and the social security system was directed towards making living conditions of all households and individuals as equal as possible.

With transition of Mongolia from the centrally planned economy to the market economy the social security system maintained for many years during the previous political system broke down, which changed the previous situation, when the society supported households and individuals to maintain even level of livelihood and provide favorable living conditions. During the centrally planned economy the state provided households with many children with child allowances and aid. Children were educated in nurseries and kindergartens free of charge, education at all levels of schooling was free, the state also provided free medical assistance and paid attention to providing equal conditions for everyone. Since it has changed, some individuals from vulnerable groups found themselves in difficult conditions as they had to make their living independently, which affected spread of poverty. There are different forms of poverty since poverty is caused by different reasons. In most cases income poverty is examined. Income poverty means lack of possibility to sustain one's livelihood normally due to shortage of income, and living below the minimal livings standards.

However, there is also capability poverty, when one cannot use their sufficient income because they are disabled or bed-ridden due to illness. Lately, capability poverty is on the increase because of school drop-out and school abandonment.

The number of children straying from their home has also increased. Upbringing of street children is inappropriate, they are victims of robbery, they do not follow a basic hygienic and food standard, which makes them ill and leads to decline of their capability. As a result of different infectious diseases some children become mentally disabled and lack an ability to get employment in the society, which is also included in the capability poverty. In other words, poverty is determined from the aspect of the

[34] World Bank 2006
[35] Osmani, 2007

capabilities of an individual. This concept was put forward by the Nobel prize laureate, an economist Amartia Sen. In his definition capabilities include literacy, long and healthy life, freedom of migration, participation in the social life. This concept of capability poverty is more relative compared to that of income poverty and is directly related to the level achieved by the society in the certain historical conditions and commonly accepted. Since capability poverty is a wider concept, the UNDP started calculating indicators reflected in a Human Poverty Index starting from 1997. This has become a first attempt to define poverty based not on income, but human capabilities.

It can be said that the reason for emergence of "social poverty" is capability poverty along with income poverty. Social poverty means lack of opportunity to participate in the social life compared to other members of society, life in inappropriate, humiliating conditions, in other words, living below the minimal standards of the society. The reason for people to find themselves in such situation is having income less than the minimal level or lack of any income, inability to utilize their capabilities due to poor health or missing opportunities because of lack of education. Another reason for becoming poor is abuse of different bad habits, such as alcoholism, drug abuse etc.

Values and objective measures determined by historic, political, social and ethical factors prevailing at given time in the society, are included along with numerous comprehensive problems in the definition of poverty.

Individuals with income less than needed for minimal living standards are classified as poor and those with income less than 40% needed for minimal living standards- as extremely poor. At present 36.1% of population in Mongolia are poor, which means that the monthly consumption per capita is 24743 MNT. The average consumption level of the poor is 11% below the poverty line or the minimal living standards. This indicator is one to measure poverty and is also called a poverty depth index. The poverty sensitivity index represents poverty inequality.

Table 2.4 Basic poverty indicators, national average by cities, the capital city and rural areas, 1995, 1998, 2002.

	Poverty coverage			**Poverty depth index**			**Poverty sensitivity index**		
Location	1995	1998	2002	1995	1998	2002	1995	1998	2002
National average	**36,3**	**35,6**	**36,1**	**10,9**	**11,7**	**11,0**	**4,8**	**5,6**	**4,7**
Urban areas	38,5	39,4	30,3	12,2	13,9	9,2	5,7	7,1	4,0
Of it UB	35,1	34,1	27,3	10,4	13,0	8,1	4,5	7,4	3,3
Rural areas	33,1	32,6	43,4	8,9	9,8	13,2	3,6	4,4	5,6

Source: NSO, World Bank, UNDP, 2004. Household income, expenditure and living standards random survey, 2002-2003, Ulaanbaatar

The poverty sensitivity index in Mongolia equals 4.7, which shows how income and assets distribution is conducted among the poor. Since it shows how low is consumption compared to poverty line, the higher is the indicator, the poorer is the person. When poverty in Mongolia is examined by regions, it is 51.1% in the Western region, 38.7% in the Khangai region, 34.4% in the Central and Eastern regions and 27.3% in Ulaanbaatar.

Table 2.5 Total population and growth of poor population, 1995, 1998, 2002

Location	Total population growth (thousand persons)		Poor population (thousand persons)			Growth of poor population (thousand persons)	
	1995-1998	1998-2002	1995	1998	2002	1995-1998	1998-2002
National average	107	88,4	828	849,8	894,0	21,8	44,2
Urban areas	30,1	119,8	471	493,4	415,3	22,4	-78,1
Of them UB	39,9	97,5	214	221,6	203,8	7,6	-17,8
Aimag centres	-9,8	22,3	257	271,8	211,5	14,8	-60,3
Rural areas	76,9	-31,4	357	369,9	478,7	12,9	108,8

Source: NSO, World Bank, UNDP, 2004. Household income, expenditure and living standards random survey, 2002-2003, Ulaanbaatar

When poverty trends in 2003 were compared to those in 1998, according to the 1998 Living Standards Measurement Survey urban poverty was prevailing, but the 2003 survey results showed that rural poverty had a trend for more rapid growth. One point that should be specifically mentioned here is that results of LSMS studies conducted in 1995, 1998, 2002, 2003 cannot be compared directly. While the sample for the 2002-2003 survey was based on results of the 2000 Population and housing census, samples for 1995 and 1998 surveys were based on the administrative data of that time, not on the census data, so the sampling methodology differs substantially.

Table 2.6 Basic poverty indicators, by regions, 2002

Residence, regions	Poverty coverage	Poverty depth index	Poverty sensitivity index
Residence			
Ulaanbaatar	27,3	8,1	3,3
Aimag centres	33,9	10,0	4,7
Soum centres	44,5	14,4	6,4
Rural areas	42,7	12,6	5,1

Regions			
Western	51,1	14,6	5,7
Khangai	38,7	12,3	5,2
Central	34,4	10,1	4,3
Eastern	34,5	12,4	6,6
Ulaanbaatar	27,3	8,1	3,3
National average	36,1	11,0	4,7

Source: NSO, World Bank, UNDP, 2004. Household income, expenditure and living standards random survey, 2002-2003, Ulaanbaatar

At present poverty in Ulaanbaatar is 22.8%, in aimag centers 23.7%, in soum centers 20.0% and in rural areas 33.6%. Since 44.5% of total soum populations are poor, it equals 20% of the total number of poor in the country. Of households residing in rural baghs 43.7% are poor.

When poverty is viewed by regions, its level is the highest in the Western region and the lowest in the Eastern region. According to LSMS results the poverty coverage was 36.6% in 1995, 35.6% in 1998, 36.1% in 2002, which makes an impression that poverty levels are stable.

According to calculations made by professor Keith Griffin "Incidence of poverty in Mongolia in 1995 equaled 51.1%, reaching 51.7% in 1998"[36]. It shows that poverty in Mongolia became widespread and because a dynamic study to directly compare changes in poverty has not been implemented, results of different studies based on different data, with use of different methods present a picture that poverty size has not increased.

In order to align calculations made in different ways, the World Bank made an attempt to compare the 1998 and 2002-2003 surveys. 9 aimags covered by the 1998 survey were selected and a consumption basket used in both surveys was used. The comparative results show that poverty in Mongolia reached 43% in 1993, but decreased sharply in 2002-2003 down to 36%[37].

[36] Reflecting inequality and poverty reduction issues in the development strategy, report, UB, p31
[37] World Bank, 2006

Figure 2.8 Comparison of urban, rural poverty levels

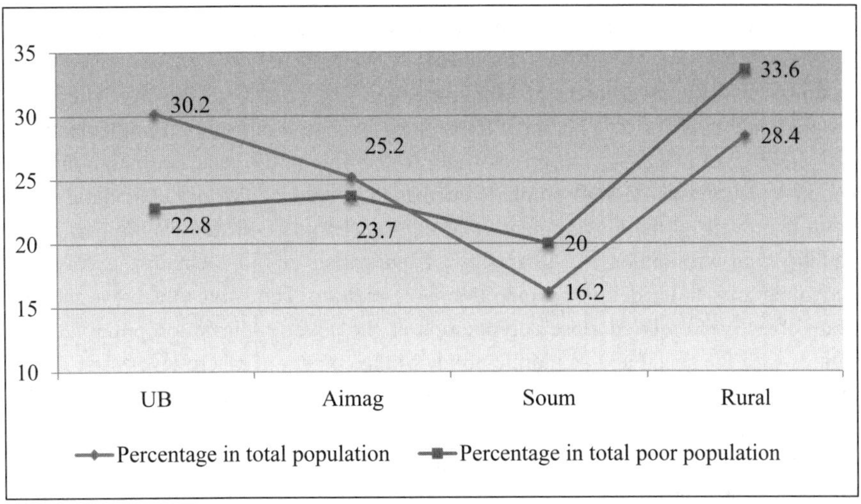

Source: NSO, World Bank, UNDP, 2004. Household income, expenditure and living standards random survey, 2002-2003, Ulaanbaatar

Poverty not only affects the real income of population and decline of living standards, but also has such negative consequences as declining health of poor people due to low calorie nutrition of the poor, loss of normal operations of education and cultural institutions, withdrawal of children from school, their involvement in crime and violations, decline of social morals. Results of Living Standards Measurement Surveys and a Participatory Living Standards Measurement Survey show that households with a single parent and many children, households with less than 100 livestock, unemployed, non-educated people /without basic education/, elderly, disabled, street and orphaned children are often victims of poverty.

There are two ways of poverty alleviation. One is to encourage forms of economic growth that can support the poor or population, who might slip into poverty. Another way is establishment of a social safety network with a specific objective directed towards elimination of some negative consequences of poverty. As the UNDP report noticed, measures against poverty in Mongolia did not put prevention from poverty in the first place, but attempted to treat symptoms of poverty[38].

[38] UNDP, 1997, p35

A fact that poverty has increased compared to the beginning of the 1990s is caused not by slow economic growth, but shows a need to follow an anti-poverty policy along with ensuring economic growth, i. e. support of pro-poor growth.

In mid- 1994 the government of Mongolia approved a National Poverty Alleviation Program and established a National Committee in charge of program implementation and a NPAP Office as its executive office. At the time of the program initiation international institutions, UNDP emphasized that the National Poverty Alleviation Program approved by the Government of Mongolia should be an indivisible part of the country's growth strategy[39]. A strategy of generating employment in the course of economic growth needed to become the main strategy. The ways to achieve the program objectives required close coordination of the poverty alleviation policy and activities with the social and economic policy of the country at macro level, first, alleviating poverty by the way of halting economic decline and providing growth on the basis of generating income sources and workplaces, thus increasing employment. Second, to support and encourage human capital in order to provide active participation of population in economic and social development, third, to develop social welfare system for persons unable to provide for themselves and create conditions for them to provide for their basic needs.

The program included measures on creation of loans and assistance mechanism directed towards provision of basic conditions for increasing employment of population, especially vulnerable groups; generation of labor-intensive workplaces; establishment and strengthening of a system of vocational skills training for poor population and their children; improvement of working conditions of disabled population and rehabilitation of their working capacity. In implementing measures on provision of economic growth and generation of workplaces the objective of enhancing the local infrastructure development was put forward. Along with this a policy of maintaining one of achievements of the socialist era, namely, the high level of human capital or the educational level of population was pursued.

Activation of human factor was considered one of important ways to eliminate a crisis in educational and health care sectors due to economic problems, especially in rural areas, to create conditions for poor population in remote areas to access medical assistance and send their children to school. In relation to this, the government of Mongolia put forward an objective of ensuring sustainable development of health care and education sectors through seeking for and introducing new rational forms of health clinics and schools suitable to rural areas in market conditions.

---

[39] UNDP, 1997, p36

Since in the course of NPAP implementation the government followed a policy of reducing or eliminating numerous subsidies to vulnerable groups of population, it hit hard poor individuals and households at that time. For instance, cutting expenditure on nurseries, kindergartens and other child care institutions, on substantial part of free medical assistance was hard on households with many children, women- heads of households and elderly persons without care givers. Although such problems arose, it was concluded that in the course of project implementation new workplaces were generated, which led to substantial improvement of livelihood of poor households, rural population and herders and income generating projects provided support to poor households in coming out of poverty.

The Government of Mongolia with support from UNDP and World Bank made an independent evaluation of NPAP and determined further versions to be conducted after 2000. In August, 2001 an Interim Poverty Reduction Strategy Paper was developed jointly with IDA and IMF experts. In 2003, the GoM developed an Economic Growth Support and Poverty Reduction Strategy Paper. A two stage National Program on Support of Household Livelihood is being implemented.

The Program has an objective to reduce vulnerability of poor households and individuals and those near the poverty line and to secure and stabilize their livelihood. It is directed towards changing the poverty reduction strategy from its social welfare direction and creating secure stable livelihood for general public.

The main lesson from NPAP implementation is that "poverty alleviation programs - no matter how sound in concept and principles - are unlikely to reduce poverty significantly unless they are supported by broad-based, people-oriented, and labor-intensive growth strategies. In the absence of supportive economic policies and pro-poor expenditure allocation, the gains of targeted poverty alleviation programs are likely to be offset by growing unemployment and economic deterioration. Poverty reduction is not sustainable if - for every person raised above the poverty line - another person falls into poverty to take his or her place" as was noted in the evaluation report before implementation of the project on Sustainable Livelihood.

The outcomes of the presently implemented Sustainable livelihood project will be determined by following basic indicators:

- The poverty level reduced from 36% to 14%;
- The number of livestock lost during dzud reduced twice and the number of herder households losing their livestock reduced by 60%;
- At least 78% of school age children completing secondary education;

- Infant mortality reduced from 32 to 30 per 1000 live births.
- The number of groups and individuals covered by the program and obtaining ability to overcome external effects increased by 100%.

Judging by these indicators importance of Sustainable livelihood project in achieving the Millenium Development Goals is high. In this way the government together with NCPA played an important role in developing and amending the poverty reduction strategy and the policy of control over poverty alleviation, in allocating financial resources to aimags, in monitoring implementation of other project at local level, evaluating their results and disseminating results to total population.

To sum up, the Government of Mongolia paid more attention to social welfare policy directed towards support of vulnerable, poor social groups and left out the economic growth policy directed towards poverty reduction. Imagining that economic growth in itself will reduce poverty did not assist in poverty alleviation, but, on the contrary, affected deepening of poverty. The Economic Growth Support and Poverty Reduction Strategy Paper approved in 2003 specifically directs economic growth towards poverty reduction. In the course of the strategy implementation a need to implement a policy of prevention from poverty has emerged.

Along with implementation of the state policy participation of civil society or NGO, local independent policies, volunteers, cooperatives, international projects and programs implemented in Mongolia play an important role in poverty alleviation. In the past years the government has paid attention to increasing civil society participation in development, implementation and monitoring of policies at all levels of society. Non-government organizations participate actively in poverty reduction activities organizing short- term training in such directions as knitwear, vegetable gardening, crafts, cooking, pargeting, in order to support individuals and households in coming out of poverty, thus assisting poor people in gaining self-confidence and making efforts. In order to provide the poor with opportunities to work, NGOs conduct research and determine needs for directions of work to be conducted, mediate in finding workplaces, distribute food and goods received as aid.

Compared to other developing countries Mongolia has a well developed administrative structure, but due to limited resources to implement the poverty reduction policy, poverty in rural areas has not declined substantially. In order to overcome this obstacle, in the frame of the National Program on Support of Household Livelihood Capacity work on providing micro-loans with financial assistance of the World Bank is conducted in order to strengthen capacity of the poor and provide them with opportunity to engage in small businesses.

It is important to direct individuals in taking care of themselves, in being active, in having a wish to come out of poverty, in teaching skills to mobilize their resources to live independently.

A Mongolian tradition of living together and supporting their relatives and friends, helpful nature, generous assistance is kept at present and proved to be of great help to the poor and elderly. Especially in rural areas households with large herds take the poor as helpers in livestock breeding and provide them with food and clothing, which is a specific feature of nomadic people.

In conclusion, with transition of Mongolia to market economy living standards of population have become substantially different and inequality has deepened in many directions. Poverty has increased and became chronic, with generation to generation poverty.

Although in the last years the economic growth has a trend for stabilization, poverty has not declined. That is why economic growth should be directed towards poverty reduction and human development, then as a result of growth employment will rise and livelihoods will improve and pro- human development growth will prevail.

2.2 LABOR MARKETS

Labor market is created by demand for labor on the one hand and supply of labor on the other hand and it represents labor demand and supply of the country, the region, the sector or the economic entity. The labor market can be understood as a market which buys and sells a special product – the labor force. It does not buy an individual, but rather evaluates, buys and sells professional skills and talents of the individual that are utilized in the process of work, creating the cost. In this sense, as the buyer makes a choice, there is certain workforce that is not sold, persons, who cannot find work, so they join the ranks of unemployed.

Unemployment is a cyclical phenomenon resulting from insufficient demand for goods and service in the economy and excessive supply of labor.

Since positive and negative consequences of labor market directly affect employment, unemployment, productivity, labor evaluation or wages, the process of activisation of laborer, fair distribution of income, tripartite operations of working conditions, labor, social consensus, development of labor relations, study of labor market formation and its future trends is an important need for the science of sound state coordination of the labor market.

In the 1930s John Maynard Keynes established the theory and methodology of the state coordination being necessary in market conditions and this is still one of major concepts of development[40].

The objective of providing economic growth and poverty alleviation at macrolevel is achieved in the frame of effective cooperation of central and local administrative institutions and social partnership. An active labor market policy is an inseparable part of this policy and is implemented on the basis of outcomes of the abovementioned consolidated policy. The active labor market policy should be in accordance with such goals as reduction of unemployment, expansion of the labor market frame, evaluation of labor demand and supply, improving situation of vulnerable social groups, support of appropriate direction of labor force structure – educational, professional or sectoral, and increasing labor productivity.

Main directions of labor market policy accepted at international level are reflected in the International Labor Organization /ILO/conventions. For instance, they are reflected in the Convention 122 on Employment policy, Convention 88 on Employment Service, Convention 142 on Human Resource Development, Convention

[40] Keynes, John Maynard, 1973 a (19360 The General Theory of Employment, Interest and Money in the Collected Writings of J.M. Keynes, vol.7. London: Macmillan

150 on Labor Administration, the Vocational Rehabilitation and Employment Convention 159, the Employment Promotion and Protection against Unemployment Convention 168.

The main directions of labor market policy reflected in the above conventions are unemployment reduction, establishment of a system protecting from unemployment, freedom of choice of employment, support of productive employment with social protection in order to encourage economic growth, generation of additional workplaces, meeting needs of workforce, implementation of active policies directed towards improving living standards through labor evaluation. These policies are determined by articles on providing work for all who are available for and seeking work; providing freedom of choice of employment and the fullest possible opportunity for each worker to qualify for, and to use his skills and endowments in a job; developing methods of unemployment benefit provision that are effective and support freedom of choice of employment; employers offering productive employment to population, creating conditions when individuals are interested in seeking such work; supporting employment issues directed towards generation of workplaces, implementing special programs that are designed to meet the needs for productive employment of categories of persons who have particular problems in the labor market, in particular women, disabled, elderly, unemployed for long time, workers made redundant due to structural reforms.

Following policy directions are related to state coordination of the labor market: to set up advisory committees for the co-operation of representatives of employers and workers in the organization, make agreements, set up the employment service and through it register persons seeking jobs, help them to obtain vocational training and re-training, obtain from employers precise information on vacancies, refer to available employment applicants with suitable skills and physical capacity, help in finding work abroad, collect and analyze available information on the situation of the employment market and its probable evolution; co-operate in the administration of unemployment insurance and assistance and of other measures for the relief of the unemployed; assist other public and private bodies in social and economic planning calculated to ensure a favorable employment situation, provide vocational guidance closely linked with employment; develop, implement, coordinate the national labor policy; together with related institutions make decisions on working and living conditions of informal sector workers and other paid workers not included in the law; provide disabled with work. Although these are main directions at international level, they have been developing in our country as well since 1990s.

The above active policies at labor market are legalized in related laws and implemented with the state participation. With transition of our country to market economy legislative system reflecting the labor market policy has been established. For instance, following laws and regulations can be named: the Constitution of Mongolia, Labor Law, Law on Civil Service, Laws and regulations on Minimal wages, Law on Social Insurance, Law on providing unemployment benefits from the Social Insurance Fund, Trade Union Law, Law on Immigration and travel abroad on private purposes, Law on support of employment, Law on exporting and importing workforce from foreign countries, Laws on vocational education, National program on support of employment, Regulations of the National Employment Council, Regulations on workplace payment, Regulations on establishment of Employment Support Fund, its spending and monitoring, Regulations on providing microloans from the Employment Support Fund, Regulations on organization of public activities, Regulations on establishment of Development Fund for disabled and midgets and Regulations on accredited educational institutions. The above laws, regulations and programs legalized the labor market policy of our country.

Due to reforms and structural changes undertaken with transition of Mongolia to market economy in the 90s a labor supply surplus emerged, principal changes in the structure of workforce took place and the labor market started developing. In the period of 1995 to 2005 the labor-age population increased by 44.8%, the workforce or the economically active population grew by 16.9% and the number of employees went up by 20.7%. In the above period due to privatization and reforms in public sector a large part of workers and civil servants moved to private and informal sectors, and herders and farmers went from industrial, organized forms of labor into household production. The 2005 employment statistics show that of total employees 45.4% are employed in formal sectors, 15.1%- in informal sector, 36.1%- in agriculture.

In2005 compared to the previous year the unemployment rate fell down by 5.7 points to 3.3%, but informal employment is prevailing, labor evaluation in the formal sector is low and working conditions are poor. In the above period unemployment in China was 4.2%, in Russia- 8.3%, in Vietnam- 5.5%, in Bulgaria- 12.7% and in Czeh republic- 8.9%.

Amendments to the Law on employment support were approved and in this frame issues on expanding the range of employment services, introduction of new forms and methods of services to cover informal sector workers and herders, establishment, expenditure and improvement of management system of the Employment Support Fund were reflected. According to 2005 statist disabled accounted for 2.8% of total population or 69.2 thousand persons. Of employed disabled 56.9% are self-employed and only 12.8% work mon contract. With regard to amendments to the Law on

Employment Support the highest level of expenditure per person studying on muniment went up from 50 thousand MNT to 80-120 thousand MNT. In this way, work in the frame of employment policy is expanding.

Figure 2.9. Study of labor demand and supply in 2000-2006 (by quarters)

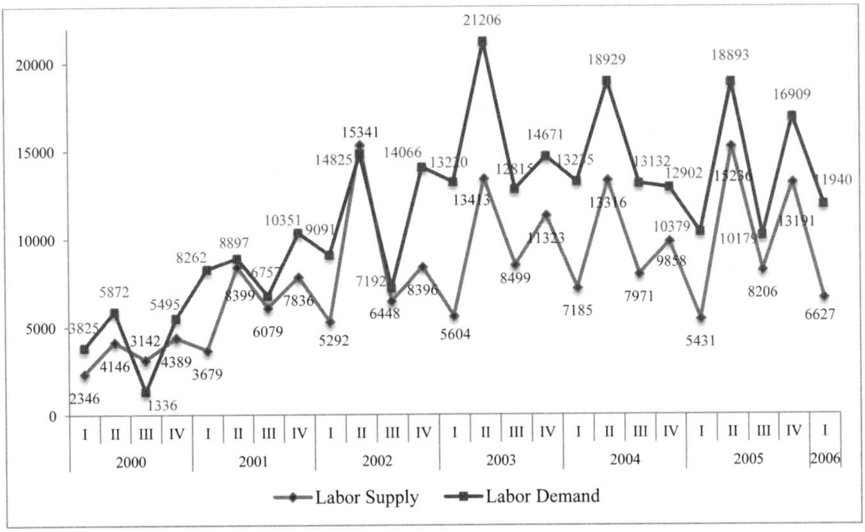

It is especially difficult to conduct a survey and draw conclusions given insufficient data on labor demand and supply in Mongolian statistics. The labor market demand is represented by increase in workplaces, while its supply is measured by the number of registered unemployed willing to work. A survey was conducted on the actual data of 2000-2006 assuming that labor demand is reflected in the fact of the registered unemployed finding employment, while supply is represented by the number of unemployed registered to get a job[41].

The labor market survey illustrates that as a result of economic reforms, especially foreign trade and price liberalization, changes in financing, a demand-led flow of workforce has emerged.

The survey covering 25 quarters over 2000-2006 provides a picture of labor supply increasing after labor demand. The higher the demand and the greater the number of workplaces, the greater increase in supply. For instance, a total of 284379 unemployed were registered to find a job in the above 25 quarters, of which 201353 found employment, and 83026 people remained unemployed. During the survey period

[41] Mongolian Statistical Yearbook 2000- 2006

annually on average 45406 people were registered to find a job, of them 32454 people found employment, and 12952 were left unemployed. In terms of quarters, of 8054 people willing to work 11375 people found employment and 3321 people remained unemployed.

These figures indicate increase of real unemployment with average monthly unemployment of 1107 people, quarterly unemployment of 3321 people, and annual unemployment of 12952 people. In other words, a conclusion can be made that unemployment is on the rise in our country because of the gap between labor demand and supply. If growth of newly generated workplaces does not exceed the labor supply, unemployment from the previous year will add to unemployment of the next year.

Unemployment

According to the Keynes theory of employment unemployment emerges from shortage of labor demand and he viewed that in labor market conditions there is no secure mechanism to ensure full employment[42]. Unemployment is a macroeconomic concept of the market economy and is reflected in shortage of demand and excess supply. This contradiction leads to unemployment. In addition, a need to import and export labor arises.

In 2005, the annual population growth rate was 1.2%, with 3% increase in population of labor age, and 2.6% increase in workers, which shows a 1.8 points faster growth of population of labor age compared to population growth and requires faster generation of new workplaces. However, increase in number of workers lags behind demand for workplaces by 0.4%, which does not influence positively decline of the real unemployment rate caused by previous unemployment and growth of unemployed population.

Unemployment in Mongolia was on the rise in 1992-1993, 1993-1994, 1995-1996, 1996-1997, and 1999-2001 and fell down in 1994-1995 and 1997-2005. The unemployment rate was at 6.5 percent in 1990, 6.3 percent in 1992, 8.5 percent in 1993, 8.6 percent in 1994, 5.4 percent in 1995, 6.5 percent in 1996, 7.5 percent in 1997, 5.8 percent in 1998, 3.6 percent in 2004 and 3.3 percent in 2005. The number of unemployed registered with the Employment office of Mongolia equalled to 54000 in 1992, 45100 in 1995, 55400 in 1996, 63700 in 1997, 49800 in 1998, and 32900 in 2005. The popu-

[42] Keynes, John Maynard, 1973 a (19360 The General Theory of Employment, Interest and Money in the Collected Writings of J.M.Keynes, yol.7. London: Macmillan

lation without employment, which constitutes a reserve of unemployed army, counted 227100 in 1996, 214900 in 1997, and 221400 in 1998 and reached over 200,000 in 2005.

While in 1997 27.2 percent of total employed (214.9/788.3õ100) were not employed in 1997, by 1998 this relative indicator has slightly increased to 27.3 percent, and fallen to 20.7 percent by 2005. This is indicative of underutilization of abundant human resources. Although unemployment in Mongolia has reduced in terms of some indicators, it has some artificial characteristics. The factors at force here are related to the regulation to remove the unemployed from the list if they do not show up for over three months after registration with the Employment office, very limited benefits to the unemployed from getting registered as unemployed, statistical data, especially, labor statistical data fail to be objective and a relatively large number of people without employment.

Unemployment and its consequences were analyzed in a survey on Employment and Unemployment Consequences as we consider that identifying social and economic outcomes of unemployment should facilitate unemployment reduction through state policy. The survey involved 1800 respondents[43], of which 65.5% mentioned limited opportunities for self-development, 58.6% - problems with access to education and health services, 76.5% - unemployment leading to poverty, 61.4% - constant stress, 51.6%- divorce, orphaned children, involvement in crime.

The survey findings indicate that social consequences of unemployment include loss of trust in the future, loosening of discipline, limited self-development, difficulty in access to education, health protection, culture, and other social services, and it can be concluded that unemployment has direct and strong impact on each individual and household. In addition, loss of a job may lead to inclusion in an inactive part of the society, impoverishment, low income, declining living standards, substantial psychological pressure that accompanies unemployment, family separation, crime affiliation, and reduction in health and educational levels.

When asked about economic consequences of unemployment 75.6% of survey participants mentioned under-utilization of laborforce resources, 81.6% - loss of an opportunity to create wealth for the society and for an individual, 71.4% - lack of workplaces, 52.5% - persons were made redundant due to widespread discrimination, 60.5% - inadequate realisation of legislation on coordination of labor relations.

---

[43] Survey on Employment and unemployment consequences, UB, 2005

Figure 2.10 Unemployment (1990-2005, by percent)

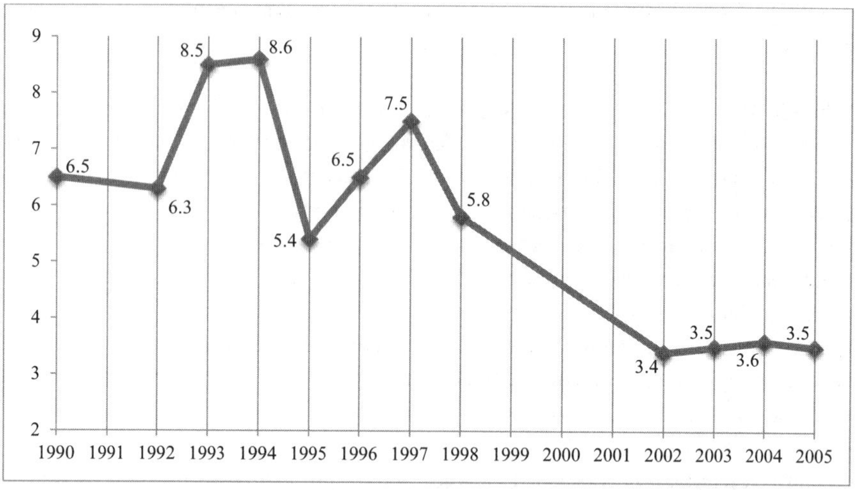

The survey results prove that one economic consequence of unemployment is loss of a potential to create wealth for the society and for oneself as the resources are not fully utilized. Unemployment rises when firings outpace hiring. In some cases, it is appropriate to consider workplace generation, upgrading of professional skills and qualifications, strenghtening of Labor regulation offices, implementation of principles of developing the labor market in its true sense and establishment of legal environment for unemployment reduction. However, leaving out the issue of adequate ratio of firings and hiring, and an appropriate policy in this field is a mistake.

While a laborer produces goods and creates social wealth as well as provides various services to the population, the unemployed get what they need although they do not create anything. Therefore, unemployment causes a significant loss to the society in whole and the household. It can be concluded that it is important to thoroughly analyze negative social and economic consequences of unemployment as well as to understand the importance of reducing unemployment through the state policy.

When asked what should be done in order to reduce unemployment, 72.5% of survey respondents suggested implementation of a national employment policy, 60.8%-improvement of a legal coordination of labor relations, 58.5% - implementation of a national policy on vocational training, 65.4% - increasing labor evaluation, 75.6%-increasing substantially the number of workplacesin urban and rural areas, which are answers expressing opinions of the majority of respondents.

The survey showed that unemployment varies across regions. Unemployment is high in the countryside, especially in the Western and Eastern regions. The Central and Ulaanbaatar regions face relatively low unemployment. In addition, it can be discerned that rural unemployment flows to urban areas. Bayankhongor and Bayan-Ulgiy aimags are leading by unemployment level. In Bayan-Ulgiy aimag unemployment is high because of relatively large population, underdeveloped infrastructure, remoteness, underdeveloped production. Some part of population is involved in the out-migration to Kazakhstan. Bayankhongor faces high unemployment due to undeveloped infrastructure and production, and out-migration of the population to neighboring Uvurkhangai aimag with more developed infrastructure.

Ways to further reduce unemployment and its future perspective:

First of all, to revise the national concept on development of labor market and generation of productive employment and provide its enforcement;

Second, to make amendments in some labor market relation laws and regulations or initiate new regulations in order to create legal and regulatory environment, where labor market can be developed in real terms;

Third, to keep a sustainable structure of a professional ministry in charge of the labor market policy, to create a comprehensive labor management system at national, aimag, capital city, soum and bagh levels, to strengthen employment services, providing them with professional staff and developing them in real terms;

Fourth, to keep a balance between hiring to and firing from employment and implement a policy to increase hiring and reduce firing;

Fifth, to implement a social and economic policy on protection of youth just entering the labor market from unemployment;

Sixth, to promote sole proprietorship, self-employment and small businesses during structural changes;

Seventh, to provide employers with tax and loan incentives if the entities and enterprises create new jobs for those who are made redundant;

Eighth, while implementing a workplace investment policy, to encourage firms and companies that are to deal with industries that can replace export and import products and help them to be independent from own market;

Ninth, to prevent from effect on purchasing power of increasing housing, fuel and electricity prices that have much effect over economy;

Tenth, to keep labor value and taxes at a such level as to attract and encourage people to be employed.

Employment

Employment is activities of an individual to generate income without violation of legal regulations with regard to meeting demand of an individual and the society. It has two basic forms of full employment and free employment. In conditions of full employment everyone has a duty to work, a form of compulsory employment prevails and unemployment does not exist. In conditions of free employment an individual has a right not to be employed, has an opportunity not to engage in unsuitable work, one has a free choice of employment and unemployment is a real phenomenon. Any society is for appropriate, productive employment. According to international standards if an individual is engaged at least in one hour of work per week, he/she is considered employed. However, employees are covered by the tax system and employers have a duty to pay their workers.

The term workforce is used in the same meaning as the economically active population and consists of total employed and unemployed. Workforce in our country was 839.8 thousand in 1995,847.6 thousand in 2000 and 101.2 thousand in 2005.so, in the period of 1995-2005 it grew by 119.2%. The economic and social development level of any country is determined by effective use of its resource and opportunities. Among all kinds of resources, human resources, if well used, are the most infinite, so generation of productive employment is in the center of the social and economic policy and it puts forward an objective of developing a well-considered policy without making mistakes in this field made in other countries.

Generation of productive employment and establishment of the labor market not only brings progress in economic and social aspects, but also becomes a primary factor for poverty reduction and improvement of living standard of population by bringing out the employed people from income poverty. Only when poverty is alleviated, living standards are improved and progress is made in human development, the quality of employees increases, new equipment and technologies are introduced and opportunities for increase of productivity are in place, so that appropriate directions of increasing labor value, coming out of income poverty and poverty reduction in general are set up. Along with this, productive employment will take place in conditions when the state increases the number of workplaces and trains workers and professional staff appropriate for work at such positions. When evaluating the workforce situation, quantitative and qualitative aspects are looked at. The quantitative aspect is related to the population growth and its age structure, while the qualitative aspect is connected with education, professional and special skills and the employment structure of workers.

In 2005 the total population of our country reached 2562.8 thousand and the average annual growth rate was 1.2%. It was a sharp decline compared to the late 1980s when the global annual population growth was 2.0% and the average annual population growth in our country equaled 2.8%. At present, when the population size in our country is only reaching 2.6 million, decline of the average annual population growth from 2.8 to 1.2% will affect gradually the population age structure and cause decline of the work force growth, which will, in its turn, affect negatively economy and national security. Decline of the average annual population growth in the last years may lead to decreasing share of economically active population starting from 2030, graying of population in increasing number of dependents and increasing load of social development. It is explained by the fact that people of 1980s' generation, when the population growth was 2.8%, will retire in 2030s, the population growth will decline and when the present generation is of labor age, the population in general will be old. It means that in the near future unfavorable conditions for growth of workforce are emerging in demographic aspect. In this way the population age structure tend to influence employment through the growth of workforce. If assumed that the employment level is determined by the ratio of employed to the population of labor age, in 1995 the employment level was 67.0%, in 2000- 60.0%, in 2005- 61.4%, which illustrates that in the decade between 1995-200% employment had a trend for decline.

In order to clarify if there is an opportunity to increase further employment in our country, the statistics of the decade between 1995-2005 were used. In the above period the population increased by <u>110.6%,</u> the population of labor age - by <u>132.9%,</u> the population over labor age- by <u>116.8%,</u> the labor resources- by <u>137.8%,</u> the capable population of labor age- by <u>142.8,</u> the number of employed - by <u>121.8%.</u> The number of industry workers declined by 7.5%, the number of the service sector workers increased by <u>208.1%,</u> the number of students of labor age increased by <u>232.4%,</u> the number of working children- by 94.2%, the number of working elderly- by 76.5%, unemployed – by 27.1%, the unemployment level- by 1.9%, the number of the industrial sector workers reduced by 4.2% and the ratio of non-working population against employed declined by 0.5%. However, the non-working population increased by 119.6% and utilization of labor force grew by 1.9%[44] /see Mongolian human resources, their utilization survey/.

A ten-year survey of human resources utilization in Mongolia during 1995-2005 showed that the unemployment rate fell from 5.4 percent to 3.5 percent, labor resources utilization- from 73.1 percent to 64.6 percent, the share of industrial workers

[44] NSO, the Mongolian Statistical Yearbook, 1997-2005
NSO, Employment of population, 1997-2005
GoM National Program on unemployment reduction. Calculations in the annex to the Government Decree 219 of 2005

in the total population - from 25.6 percent to 21.4 percent, the ratio of non-working population to workers - from 27.4 percent to 26.9 percent, respectively, while the labor force utilization increased from 94.6 percent to 96.5 percent.

To sum up, although utilization of human resources increased due to decline of unemployment level, decline of labor resource utilization shows a growing number of the employed in informal sector.

Table 2.7. Human resourses in Mongolia, its utilization study [45]

		End of year results (thousand persons)			Growth decline
		1995	2000	2005	
1	Population	2317.5	2407.5	2562.8	110.6
2	Population of labor age	1186.7	1347.4	1577.0	132.9
3	Population over labor age	156.0	188.0	182.2	116.8
4	Labor resources	1087.4	1283.9	1498.7	137.8
5	Capable population of labor age	1050.5	1269.5	1491.2	142.0
6	Employees	794.7	809.0	968.3	121.8
7	Industrial sector workers	593.2	507.9	549.0	-7.5
8	Service sector workers	201.5	301.1	419.3	208.1
9	Students of labor age	102.0	153.7	237.0	232.4
10	Working children	6.7	1.8	0.4	-94.2
11	Working elderly	30.2	12.6	7.1	76.5
12	Non-working population	217.7	282.7	260.4	119.6
13	Unemployed	45.1	38.6	32.9	-27.1
14	Labor force/Workforce	839.8	847.6	1001.2	119.2
15	Unemployment rate	5.4	4.6	3.5	-1.9
16	Labor resource utilization	73.1	63.0	64.6	-8.5
17	Share of industrial sector workers in population	25.6	21.1	21.4	-4.2
18	Labor force utilization	94.6	95.4	96.5	1.9
19	Non-working population-to- employed ratio	27.4	34.9	26.9	-0.5

According to our estimations, for Mongolia it would be desirable to have a share of industrial sector workers in total population at 33 percent. However, the share has fallen in the above period increasing the load of industrial sector workers. In other words, one individual creating wealth used to feed four individuals including oneself, while now he/she has to feed five. As Adam Smith mentioned, labor producing value

[45] NSO, the Mongolian Statistical Yearbook, 1997-2005
NSO, Employment of population, 1997-2005
Author's calculations. National Statistical Office. Library materials

is "productive", while labor used only at the certain time is "unproductive". He compared labor of a menial servant and a manufacturer and concluded that "A man grows rich by employing a multitude of manufacturers: he grows poor by maintaining a multitude of menial servants. The labor of the menial servant does not fix or realize itself in any particular subject or vendible commodity. His services generally perish in the very instant of their performance"[46].

Therefore, in implementing a policy of productive employment it is important to follow a trend of reducing a load per one producer. The share of non-working population against workers fluctuates around 27.0 percent, which is high. However, we conclude that a slight increase in labor force utilization is related to an artificial reduction in unemployment. Productive employment should be reflected in higher utilization of human resources, higher share of productive workers creating physical wealth, effective reduction of unemployment, and significant decrease in the share of workers in the informal sector. The poor performance of these criteria is a result of insufficient attention paid to the structural aspect of productive employment, which needs to be adjusted.

Assuming that **workforce participation** is determined by ratio of workforce to population of labor age between 1992 and 2005, the labor force participation ratio has fallen by 12.3 points from 75.8 percent to 63.5 percent; the employment ratio by 9.6 points from 71.0 percent to 61.4 percent; the unemployment rate from 6.3 percent to 3.3 percent, which are not good indicators. As long as the workforce participation ratio and employment ratio fall, unemployment should rise, so it can be concluded that unemployment figures are divergent to real situation.

When the employment rate is compared to workforce, the level of workforce participation as well as the employment rate has in general a trend for decline. It illustrates again that unemployment accounts for large part of it. However, it is a good indicator that in some years the employment rate has increased even slightly. When the participation level of workforce is studied, it is interesting that persons aged 30-40 account for the peak of workforce and men and women account for equal share of employees.

The structure of employees has changed with an increasing number of young people, but due to insufficient work experience and lack of capability to generate additional income, they are vulnerable to unemployment, which leads to unstable ratio of demand and supply at labor market. A fact that young people aged 16-29 account for 53% non-working population is related to the Mongolian tradition to support their children. Graduates of secondary and high schools as well as graduates of vocational

[46] A. Smith Wealth of Nations, Volume 2, Chapter 3

school get help from their parents to study further since they cannot find employment and they are not always registered as unemployed. As of 2006 32% of total employees were engaged in animal husbandry sector, of them 50.6% were young people aged 16-35, while of unemployed actively seeking work, registered at employment service, over 60% were unskilled young people, which shows a need to provide rural population, especially young people with jobs.

The unemployment level of young population is relatively higher compared to that of other age groups and of total unemployed registered at national level young people aged 16-34 make up 55.8%. Youth who graduated from secondary schools or vocational institutions do not always have an opportunity to find employment. In order to increase employment among young people it is necessary to implement small projects on improving their professional skills, generating work places suitable to them, creating a business environment and new workplaces, to improve coordination of labor market and to implement a special program directed towards support of young people's employment.

When the share of women among employment indicators of population is studied, in 1992 women accounted for 50.1% of total population of labor age and in 2005 their number grew to 51.4%. In 1992-2005 the share of women among economically active population increased from 48.1% to 49.6%, the share of women among total employees grew from 47.8 to 48.4%, and among unemployed it increased from 53.9 to 54.4%. In relation to the fact that the share of women among total employees has increased, the share of women aged 35-49 is prevailing in labor activities and it is a unique feature of the present development of our country, but there is a trend that women are more vulnerable to unemployment. It is necessary for the state to develop an appropriate strategy in this field.

Structure of employment sectors: Employment restructuring follows economic restructuring. Economic sectors are classified into three groups of primary, secondary, and tertiary, and the share of these groups provides the basis for determining the level of a country's economic development. Primary production covers agriculture, forestry, fishing and hunting, and mining; secondary production - the processing industry, energy production, and construction; tertiary sectors- all service sectors. According to this composition structure, in 2005 of total workers in Mongolia 50.9 percent worked in primary production, 11.8 percent in secondary production, and 37.3 percent in the service sector.

In order to make conclusions from the employment structure survey more understandable, statistics were examined by 3 large sectors, namely, services /S/, industry /I/ and agriculture /A/. The share of agriculture (A) in GDP was 15.5 percent in 1989, grew to 38.8 percent in 1995, and fell to 21.6 percent in 2005. The share of industry (I) was 38.8 percent in 1989, falling to 27.5 percent in 1995, and 27.9 percent in 2005. It can be concluded that the share of these large sectors in the national economy of Mongolia has interchanged, and a process of "S industrialization" has taken place. In addition, these data demonstrate that in its transition from the command economy to a market-oriented economy Mongolian economy moved from the SIA model to the ASI model, and later to the SAI model. This is a very interesting consolidated conclusion about a wide-ranging, deep-context process.

When employment is examined by sectors in 1995-2004 among total workers the share of those employed in agriculture, hunting and forestry reduced from 46.1 to 40.1, the share of mining sector workers grew from 2.4 to 3.5, that in processing declined from 8.8 to 6.0, in power and heating, water supply declined from 2.9 to 2.5%, in construction increased from 3.8 to 4.1, in wholesale and retail, repair of domestic appliances increased from 8.4 to 14.0, in hotels and catering grew from 1.8 to 3.0%, in transportation and warehouses, communication- from 4.1 to 4.4%, in financial activities from 1.1 to 1.7%, in real estate and other renting activities- from 0.9 to 1.2%, in public institutions- from 4.1 to 4.9%, in education it fell from 6.3 to 6.0%, in health care and social welfare – from 5.0 to 4.1%, in social and private services- from 3.5 to 3.6% .

Decline in the number of workers in the industrial sector is related to such factors as outdated equipment and technologies of our factories in the era of globalization and open economy, closing down of some factories during privatization, lack of working capital, changes in direction of production. While in such sectors as agriculture, hunting and forestry, processing, power and electricity, water supply, healthcare and social welfare the employment structure has declined due to slump in demand, that in mining, construction, wholesale and retail, hotels and catering, transportation and warehouses, financial activities, real estate, renting and other business activities, public institutions and social services sectors increased following the demand.

An increasing number of workers in trade and services sector can be explained by total privatization of the sector, emergence of workplaces for numerous people, who were engaged in small and "suitcase" trade. At present people are more interested in working in trade and services, because the national industry has not recovered fully and wages of food processing and light industry workers are not very high.

The private sector has become a large sector of the economy with a 96.6 percent in the total number of enterprises, accounting for 72 percent of GDP. A 2004 survey findings indicated that out of total employees 53.8 percent worked for proprietorship, 17.9 percent- for companies, 15.5 percent- for state budget institutions, 6.0 percent- for state-owned enterprises, 5.7 percent- for partnerships and cooperatives, and 1.2 percent – for non-governmental organizations. This is another employment structure and a fact that employees of private companies account for 71.7% of total employed shows irreversible standing of market economy in Mongolia.

Education factor in employment: Education is a crucial factor in employment and it affects directly the quality of workforce. There is a close link, dependence between educational level of population and employment. Highly productive manufacture activities based on modern scientific and technical progress require educated and skilled workers, and highly qualified technical staff and engineers.

At present, in the era of market economy, the social demand and needs have changed, creating new production and service sectors, qualifications and jobs. New jobs replace old jobs creating a need for training of human resources that meet requirements of new workplaces. In the labor market, the share of unskilled and low-skilled workers has decreased in the light of increased demand for highly educated and skilled workers.

The Mongolian government put forward a goal of universal literacy during the period of 1921-1940, universal primary education since 1941, and universal 8-year schooling or basic education since 1961. When the education structure of workers was studied, in 1990-2005 the share of workers with higher education among total workers increased from 12.8 to 14.5, that of employees with vocational education- from 16.4 to 24.6, that of employees with complete secondary education grew from 22.5 to 23.5, while among total workers the share of those with incomplete secondary education reduced from 31.9 to 26.7 and those with primary and lower education fell from 16.4 to 10.7%.

This is a reflection of the fact that the educational structure of employment is getting higher following the demand. Also a need has emerged to improve the professional and special structure according to the market demand.

Mongolian migrant workers abroad: Due to difficulties and outcomes of poverty and unemployment at labor market, many citizen of our country went abroad to work. The reason why at present 23 thousand Mongolian work in Korea instead of living with their family and working in their own country is directly linked to extremely low labor evaluation in our country. Workers are sent to other countries to acquire production practice or engage in work with an aim to improve specialization of workforce, reduce unemployment and increase income of citizen.

Figure 2.11. Education structure of workers (by percent)

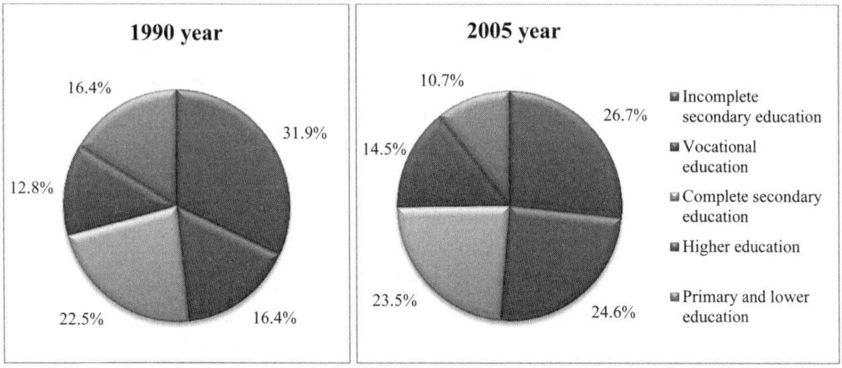

As of 2006, 13 400 Mongolian citizen were sent to DRK, Japan, Czech Republic, Hungary and Taiwan on labor contract or on industrial practice in construction, metal industry, sewing factories, machinery repair, spare parts production, electronics, plastics and decoration. Some calculations show that in total over 30 thousand Mongolian work abroad.

It is necessary to develop a strategy to generate workplaces and create conditions, when emigrant workers will be interested in working in their own country. Only in such conditions emigrant workers will voluntarily return back to work in their own country. Until that time people interested in working abroad should not be restricted in going abroad, but they should be supported until they come back. They create wealth for their country by sending remittances to their families and generating income for themselves.

All workers working abroad with official permission or illegally are called migrant workers, which is different from refugees. However, risks associated with work abroad are true for Mongolian as well. Mongolian migrant workers abroad receive the lowest wages in the given country and are unemployed in difficult, hazardous jobs and a share of women among them is on the increase. While professional workers receive visas and work permissions without any additional fees, non-professionals, who are the most interested in working abroad have to pay official and unofficial fees to get a work permission, so they pawn their assets to cover costs and become more vulnerable to poverty. Moreover, their work, civil and political rights are violated as well. Numerous rights related to labor relations such as rights for an appropriate workplace, wages, recreation, social and health insurance are included in the right for work. Political rights such as participation in presidential or parliament elections and, for illegal workers, even civil rights are often violated. Competition between companies mediating export of workforce is related to the fact that human trafficking next to drugs and arms trade is the most profitable trade in the world. Migrants workers not only trade their professional skills and labor capacity, but also present the main basis and excuse for human trafficking. International practice shows that there is a trend for many migrants to become victims, for instance, going abroad to work as a nurse and becoming a caregiver, a servant without a day of leave.

A fact that young people, who create wealth of the society, go abroad for work makes, to some degree, a negative impact on economic and social development in our country. Due to social situation in our country many young people, who studied abroad and obtained knowledge and profession, refuse to return to our country and contribute to development of Mongolia, preferring to work abroad. That is why it is necessary to implement a strategy of creating a work environment, which is more advantageous compared to that in foreign countries.

Informal sector workers: Informal economy and informal sector is not a production or services sector, which gets an official permission from the state authorities, is registered and is responsible for paying due taxes. Of over 200 thousand persons, who are voluntarily non-employed, in total 126 thousand persons are employed in informal sector as the survey on workforce conducted by NSO shows. It is necessary to evaluate a fact that they meet the demand of their own families as well as various needs of society members and create certain wealth for their country, and draw conclusions. That is why a surveillance study to determine the role and the position of informal sector in national economy, to research forms of care given by the state to workers in this field, to examine how issues of labor and social protection were resolved in this sector[47] was undertaken.

Although this survey can not match the statistical indicators as it did not cover total population, we view that it was conducted at an appropriate level to raise questions about the informal sector and draw attention to them.

Consolidated results of a survey, which covered 800 workers in informal sector in urban and rural areas, showed that of total participants 35.3% were aged 36-45. It can be viewed that they chose the present field of employment 15 years ago, when they were aged 20-25 due to lack of workplaces, because at that time job cuts and bankruptcies were taking place in formal economy and generation of workplaces was

[47] Results of a survey on informal sector workers among 800 persons were used, UB, 2005.

not even mentioned. Of total survey participants persons aged 26-35 accounted for 27%, those aged 46-60 – for 18.5% and youth aged 18-25 –for 14.8%.

Of total informal sector workers women accounted for 60.8%. A question arises whether a high percentage of women working in informal sector was due to their unwillingness to work in formal sector, or whether they were forced to chose informal sector as they were discriminated in labor relations, or whether the sector created favorable environment for women to work there? Since 51.5% of women reported being satisfied with their present jobs, it can be viewed as their own choice.

Since of total informal sector workers 66.3% had complete or incomplete secondary education, they might have chosen to work in informal sector since education attainment of employees is always taken into account in the formal sector. Of workers 42.9% reported working in this sector for 2-4 years, 35.8% - for 2-10 years, nearly 10%- for 11-15 years, which proved again that the workforce moved to this sector in the years of "shock therapy" or privatization and structural reforms. Of informal entities 74.5% had up to 5 workers, of them 22.6 worked alone. It showed that the majority was in the vulnerable group of those working for subsistence. Entities with 6 to 10 workers accounted for 20.4%, those with over 11 workers – for 5.1%, so 25% or one forth of all entities have developed characteristics of organized labor.

Of survey participants 19.8% were paid workers and 47.0% were family members. The survey revealed different levels of income and wages of informal sector workers. 75.8% of them had a monthly income of over 50.0 thousand MNT and 20.5% had a monthly salary of 150 thousand MNT, which is not lower than the average in other sectors. While 75% of informal sector workers reported willingness to work further in the present occupation, 25% answered "no". It shows a continuing trend for employment in informal sector in near future. A conclusion can be made that there is a lack of a state-coordinated policy of merging the informal sector into the formal one.

Labor evaluation

Employment, its structure, utilization of human resources at labor market are directly linked to the level of labor evaluation and the state policy on wages and salaries. Wages that follow a principle of distribution according to the quantity and quality of work is not only a main incentive to activate labor force, increase labor productivity and enhance efficiency of production, but also creates sources of livelihood of workers. Wages is evaluation of labor or, in other words, it is payment for use of one's labor.

Wages affects social and economic development in several ways, as it becomes a primary source for sustaining livelihood, then, if wages is rationally linked to productivity, it can become the best tool to stimulate workers and the size of wages actually determines the consumption level of population. Since wages presents assessment of capacity of labor force, it is a key to development of human resources. Wages is also a main incentive for strenghtening capacity of civil servants andtheir sustainable employment. With increase of labor evaluation, an employee is interested in reducing unproductive hours and increasing work hours. As a result, real income of the workers increases, which leads to increase of their needs and conditions emerge for employees to avoid income poverty.

Market regime labor allocation considers a main principle of inequal or differentiated wages that allows not the equal wages but issue a salary that considered labor productivity that are different in terms of quantity and quality. It becomes a key incentive to activate and specialise the labor force. Even for those who are dealing with the same job, their initiative, productivity and personal skill are different thus allocation of the wages differently based on their productivity is the most fair method.

The Government Decree 112 of 2005 incresed the minimal level of wages by 6.2% and set it at 42500 MNT, which means hourly wages of 251.48 MNT. The Government Decree 12 of 2006 set up the minimal level of wages at 53000 MNT, with hourly wages of 313.61 MNT.

As of 2005 the national average salary was 100.0 thousand MNT with an avrage salary of civil servants at 92.6 thousand MNT, which means the average salary not exceeding 100USD. Therefore, even an employed person falls victim to income poverty. An extremely low minimal level of wages or cost of workforce is one of causes of emerging poverty and unemployment. A low labor evaluation causes loss of the least opportunities for self-development and affects stagnation of human development.

The government has been implementing number of projects and programs, beside it above positive changes couldn't affect and create more income to provide to worker's simple necessity. In the report "Research report to evaluate participation measure for of Mongolian poverty situation" (2005.12.14) was initiated by National Statistical Office and done by from 2004 to 2005 technical assistance for Asian Development Bank and World Bank, it was noted "household's monthly average income is 161.500 tugrik, but monthly average expense is 249.100 tugrik". From this monthly average income can provide 64.8& of total monthly expenses.

215.4 thousands households of total 596.7 households are poor and below standard living. Poverty level is not reduced from 36.1% in country. By theory, if economy grows, poverty will reduce, worker's living standard will get better, and from this side people should be good for the government. If economy grows, there will be no way to worker do not have to be loss, not improving its living standard and if their created output would have dedicated for another thing, it means there is labor unfair allocation was processed. In processing way, each person's ability, physical and vocational capability and active initials are relatively different. That's why salary has to be settled and allocated different and fairly depends on labor productivity. Income based on output was created by proprietors, government and workers, that's why market itself requires labor fair allocation structure. The most manipulation way to promote self-interest, to create intellectual property at highest level, to use their time effectively and to develop him/her, is to give appropriate salary. It means people who work high productivity, they will get much salary and people who work less productivity, and they will get less salary. Like today, if salary is too lower, it is not proper to settle depending on output differentiation. Because of salary differentiation cannot be reached to people promotion level.

CHAPTER THREE

A NEW FINANCIAL AND BANKING STRUCTURE. FINANCIAL MARKETS

Brief introduction.

One of unavoidable conditions of effective development of market relationships is development of financial relationships. They are a main part of market relationships and a source sustaining existence of the market system. Thus, the reform of the financial and money- credit systems was the most important process in transition from the centrally-planned economy to the market economy.

Implementation of a financial reform, along with reform of finance itself, was based on a principle, that only a successful financial reform allows successful reforms in other sectors. The monetary and financial structure in market conditions is an active compound with specific goals and a broad frame. To reform that structure, a comprehensive approach to this problem was needed in the first place. Also, there was a need to create conditions for independent development of corporate and enterprise finance, which is a basis of the public finance and a need to create and form a completely new financial market.

On this basis, the state financial policy and regulations had to change its concept into the one of economic entities, directed towards a clear final result (that of sustainable development of peoples' livelihood). From the present perspective, it is apparent that it is a time-consuming, intricate, complicated process. Although the process of reform of monetary and financial systems in line with market relations has been implemented in general in the last 16 years, and certain achievements have been made, in the aspect of the contents the reform has not yet been fullfilled. Thus, the process of improving the new system, created in the transitional period, enhancing every part and strenghtening links between them are continuing.

3.1 FINANCIAL REFORMS

Finance is an economic relationship, emerging in the process of setting up and utilizing asset funds. It is regarded as an economic category because of this feature. According to the international standard a financial system is regarded as an information system, comprised of one or more applications, that is used for collecting, processing, maintaining, transmitting, and reporting data about financial events; supporting financial planning or budgeting activities; accumulating and reporting cost information; or supporting the preparation of financial statements[1].

---

[1] A. Blogodin, L. Lozovski, B. Raizberg Financial dictionary, Moscow, Infra-M, 1999, p 263

Thus, finance has firstly, the real part, which consists of financial resources, sources and financial instruments, secondly, subject bodies (Ministry of Finance, Bank of Mongolia, Financial Regulatory Committee, affiliate offices, agencies, commercial banks and insurance organizations) with functions to increase the added value (income, revenue), using financial resources and instruments with clear objectives.

In the transitional process from centrally- planned economy to market economy, a goal to establish anew those two parts of the financial system and a real need to improve efficiency have been put forward. This objective had many aspects, covering the economy in whole, involving a process of changing an economic mentality and conscience of individuals, groups, and the society, it was complicated and multifaceted. Moreover, it had inter- sectoral, sector- territorial and inter- territorial features and it required long- and mid-term policies.
The Government of Mongolia, based on the above theoretical and methodological rationale, has achieved certain results in a relatively short time by creating systems of financial resources, sources and instruments, appropriate for market relations, enriching their contents and forms according to Mongolian conditions and introducing new resources, sources and instruments every year. The new objective put forward new, unprecedented requirements to the human factor, the other part of the financial system, which required training of all kinds of new specialists in the financial sector and establishing of new financial organizations and agencies. As a result of the systematical implementation of the above objective, a Mongolian financial system meeting requirements of market relations not only in form, but also in content, has been formed.

Before the transition, in the end of 1980s, 100.0 per cent of Mongolian national revenue was built up by the socialist sector, the country budget had an income of 5743.0 million. tugrik and 5692.0 million tugrik of expenditure /by exchange rate of that period/. Transactions taxes made up 62.7 per cent of the budget revenue, profit commisssions, taxes and fund fees of economic entities accounted for 29.9%[2]. Budget loss was mostly recovered by external sources. By that time in Mongolia there were following economic entities: in total 318 industries, 52 state farms, 255 agricultural farms /negdel/, 17 fodder farms, 17 inter-negdel plants and 17 cooperatives. Among total industries, industries, which produced goods worth 3- 15 mil. Tug, accounted for 39.3 per cent[3].

Financial policy is an inseparable part of economic policy. Taking into consideration a fact that the role and the position of financial policy should increase sharply in market

[2] Economy of MPR in 65 years (1921-1986). Statistical collection. UB, 1986, pp 113, 132-133
[3] Same source

conditions, a reform of financial policy and financial relations was put as a priority among other primary measures during the transitional period. The process of financial reform was implemented at the same time with privatization. The process started in 1991, when the Banking Law was passed and the reform of the money and credit system began and on this basis, a demand for tax and budget reforms arose.

In 1990, price liberalization began, which pushed up the price and inflation levels. Thus, there was shortage of money supply which was mitigated as new banknotes were printed and put into transactions. Because of the decision that prohibited non-cash payment for retail entities, by the third quarter of 1991, the current account balance of entities that accounted for nearly 60. 0 per cent of money supply, decreased to less than 20.0 per cent in 1994. The above mentioned decision, made in conditions when personal savings were small in numbers and inflation went up steeply /the yearly level of inflation was 325.5% in 1992, 193%- in 1993/, was the cause of out-flow of the assets, drawn into the bank. To halt the process, banks took measures to limit the amount of cash that could be withdrawn once from personal savings and current accounts. Besides the cash deficit, the Government resolution # 20, which was passed to decrease the shadow inflation, represented by the shortage of goods and services before the 1990s, became an additional burden. Banks lost their solvency and 11 out of 15 commercial banks, which were set up before 1994, went bankrupt.

Until the end of 1992 real total money changed at the same pace as tugrik accumulation, which might be considered as a consequence of foreign currency loss. In conditions of declining currency reserves, when real shortage of tugrik took place, bank customers started withdrawing foreign currency reserves from their bank accounts; as a result, a dollar supply emerged at the market. Thus, direct influence of physical deficit of tugrik, limitation of non- cash transactions and incapability of drawing cash from the account at first request led to abrupt hardships at monetary market. Commercial banks increased the minimum limit of savings interes, in conditions of lack of credit risk management the effects of data differences worsened and costs of financial intermediary increased sharply because of the assets loss.

All this led to the banking crisis and became the ground for bankruptcy of numerous banks. In 1996 renewed laws such as the " Law on Banking", and the "Law on the Central Bank/Mongol bank/" were enacted and structural changes were made in the monetary sector. Thus, financial intermediation made a recovery, the economy received money and inflation level went down. There has been an upturn in assets of the banking sector since 1999 and the banking sector has recovered. (See Figure 3.1)

Figure 3.1 Changes in inflation and money supply

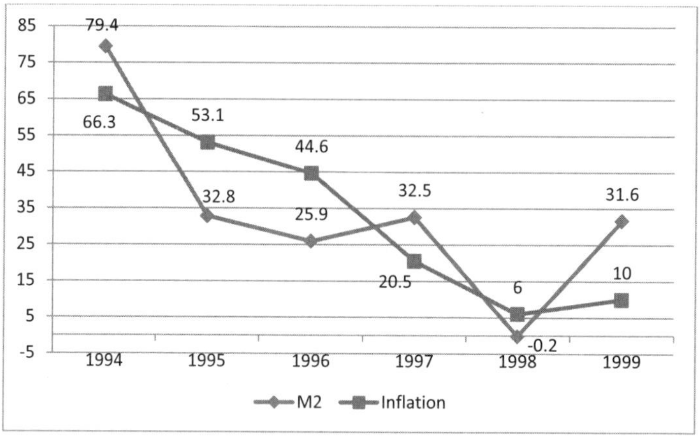

Source: Mongolian Statistical Yearbook, 1999 Ulaanbaatar, 2000 p.72

There are grounds to view that following actions have resulted in such improvement:

1. Concrete steps were made to move to the two-tiered banking structure and adopt financial reserves, sources and financial instruments, that are common in the countries with well- developed market relations with regard to unique local conditions;
2. Due to the impossibility of resolving bankruptcy proceedings of some banks with solvency problems in the frame of the Bankruptcy Law, they were settled in the frame of changes in the banking structure, which was a relatively efficient decision providing a possibility to increase solvency of banks by the way of tax incentives.
3. Money supply (M2) increased by 18.1 times in 1990-1995 following real economic growth and reached 18.5 per cent of Gross Domestic Products (GDP), but as a result of the banking crisis, it went down gradually and reached its lowest point (-2%) in 1998. As a result of structural changes, the amount of real cash increased starting in the end of 1996. However, significant increase was not observed until the first quarter of 1999, when steady growth started. It was a result of recovery of entities, which went bankrupt after the first privatization, of improved money supply of economy following it, stabilization of inflation at the level of 10% and less and a new found direction for improving banking activities;
4. That inflation was reduced in a short time and was held sustainable increased the real interest level and became an economic incentive for deploying assets in banks.

5. As insolvent banks were closed, demand for loans was distributed to other solvent banks, the credit conditions were rationalized and lending practices were facilitated, a lending process has intensified significantly since 1997. Along with this, the ownership capital of banks has increased and the lending technology, rules and regulations have developed from year to year. This had influenced conditions for economy to become free from debt and for financial discipline to improve.
6. There has been an increase in issuance of government bonds and securities of budgetary organizations. As a result, opportunities for deployment of secure assets in banks and flexible management of additional resources have grown.

Thus, a process of supplying economy with money reached a certain level and financial intermediation activities entered a new level since 1999. Figure 3.2 shows needs of total banks for own assets, the situation with and sufficiency of assets.

Figure 3.2 Individual assets of banks (right axis, billion tugrik), sufficiency of individual assets and requirements (both left axis, percentage)

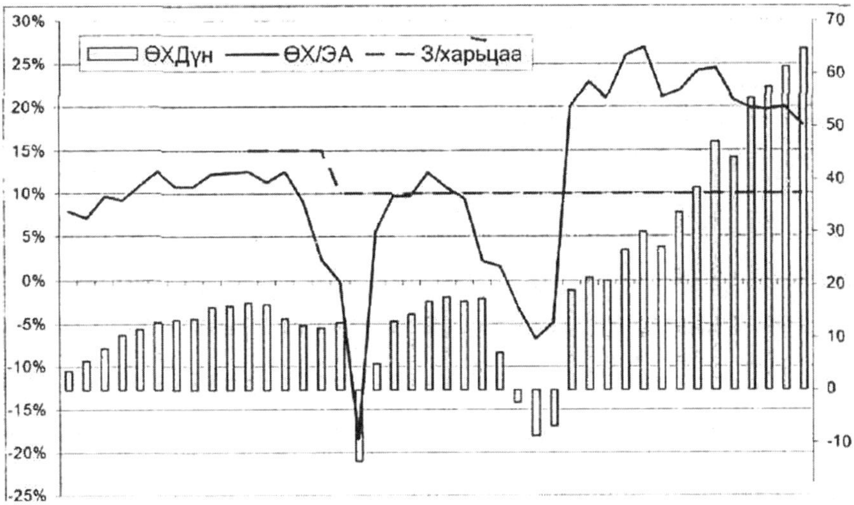

Figure 3.2 shows that individual assets of banks were negative until the beginning of 1999. As a result of abovementioned actions, the amount of individual assets had increased sharply, i.e. banks became interested in investing in business. Sufficiency of individual assets of banks, which was quite high in 2000, declined again. This was an evidence of increasing supply of money in economy and deepening financial intermediation. Research shows that in the future the loan size is likely to increase more quickly than centralized assets.

In the first years of the transition period, along with measures on reform of monetary market to adjust it to market principles, reforms in budget and tax, the main instruments of the state regulation, have been implemented successfully.

Taxation policies of any country are directed at implementing such objectives as accumulating at an appropriate level assets, needed for fulfilling duties and responsibilities of the state, redistributing public income and amending inherited deviations of the market. Accomplishments of establishing a tax system, suited to market economy in Mongolia, can be divided into three periods:

1st period or the period of establishing a basis of the taxation system - 1990-1992
2nd period or the period of establishing a market economy taxation system - 1993-1997
3d period or the period of creating an efficient taxation system - 1998- present

During the initial period of transition in the frame of the budgetary policy following objectives, directed at economic stabilization and provision of future growth were put forward:

- To create a new economic environment and conditions to enable different economic entities, based on different types of property, in economic regions and in the countryside to become fully independent and self-financing;
- To provide the state with necessary financial resources, required to implement important economical and social objectives at the national level and to maintain an appropriate balance at macro- and micro-economic level;
- To support livelihood of people and create expected social security;
- To change the economic structures appropriately, to support and develop traditional national industries and to form a new financial mechanism to support the newly established private sector and small and medium enterprises.

In order to achieve these objectives, the first Taxation Law to set up the basis of the market financial and taxation systems was passed in 1990 and came into force on January 1, 1991.

The law regulated mainly formal tax relations to be collected from personal and corporate income. The historical significance of the law was not only in implementing its main functions, but also in establishing a concept of taxation in conditions of market relations in social psychology.

Since a need to upgrade the first Tax Law, practiced for 2 years, in order to reflect reforms, implemented in the economic sector of the country, to establish in real sense a tax system, appropriate to market economy, to bring the Tax laws and regulations close to world standards arose, a second period of establishing of taxation systems began.

During this period systematic measures were taken to establish a taxation structure, meeting requirements of international standards; to provide budget revenue with sustainable sources; to support production and investment; to broaden the taxation basis and to minimize tax gradation and to set up a skilled tax authority.

In order to upgrade legal environment for taxation, drafts of necessary new tax laws were developed based on experience of countries with high- developed market economies and on recommendations of international financial organizations. In developing laws following principles have been taken into consideration:

1. To bring close tax laws and regulations to common standards of tax laws and regulations of market economy countries;
2. To elaborate an independent law, focused on essential principles of taxation, tax structure and the National Tax Authority system
3. To pass a Tax law, that regulates relations, associated with every type of taxes, fees and commissions.

Thus, the State Ikh Khural approved following five laws, called further as a package of Tax laws that took effect on January 1, 1993:

1. General Law of Taxation of Mongolia
2. Corporate Income Tax of Mongolia
3. Personal Income Tax of Mongolia
4. Trade Income Tax of Mongolia
5. Property Tax on vehicle and movable apparatuses of Mongolia

These laws contained unique aspects of conceptual character. For instance, the package of Tax laws determined main principles of a taxation system, tax types and classification that stayed unchanged until present, which shows that those issues were thoroughly examined.

Although during this period some significant positive changes in the process of implementing the package of Tax Law in the private sector took place, in some aspects they did not reach a sufficient level. Especially, sole proprietorships, which were set up in large numbers, showed unsatisfactory results in delivering tax reports and paying taxes compared to cooperatives and companies, even though they ran business in the same legal environment. For example, while in 1996 of total registered entities

67% were sole proprietorships, they accounted for less than 10% of total taxpayers who paid taxes.

Thus, in order to raise public awareness on tax payment, to collect taxes from unregistered and unreported revenues and to simplify a process of settling accounts with tax agencies, a "Law on Income tax from self-employed persons with revenue, which can not be determined " was passed and came into force. As a result, a trend of paying taxes by patents increased and just within a year or in the years of 1996-1997 the number of sole proprietorships decreased from 22375 to 18856.

In this period a tax system, suited to the market economy system was established completely, the Tax authority strengthened its capacity and taxpayers reached a certain level of development.

As a result of the above measures, in 1998 a total amount of tax revenue increased by 30.3 times compared to 1989 and 3.1 times compared to 1993. A percentage of tax revenue in total budget revenue accounted for 97.0 per cent in 1989, but went down to 90.8 per cent in 1993 and 68.3 per cent in 1998. The budget revenue structure changed following formation of market relations, so the share of corporate income revenue decreased until 1999, but since 1999 it started growing gradually and stabilized.

The budget expenditure also changed in relation to the real market demand. Along with sharp increase in total amount of expenditure (5.6 times in 1998 in comparison with 1993) the current balance of budget has become profitable and asset spending has risen every year. In 1998 GDP went up by 4.2 per cent compared to 1993. In other words, growth of budget expenditure was 1.4 times greater than that of GDP. This is related to a need for the state to mobilize additional resources to fulfill its social responsibilities, to implement policies on implementing structural changes and on increasing investment.

Thus, there was a noticeable economic growth starting from 1997-1998 and a trend for further stabilization was observed.

Actions, taken to improve legal regulations directed towards development of a financial structure, suited to market relations, adjustment of operations of its components, acceleration of the rate of economic growth and increase of investment, gave their results.

Table 3.1 Trends of some macro-economic indicators of Mongolia

Indicators	1998	2000	2004	2005	2006	2007*
Net annual GDP growth (%)	3.5	1.06	10.7	6.2	7.5	8.6
GDP per capita (thousand. Tug.)	351.1	426.2	758.7	889.6	1121.2	1265.2
Total money (M2) (billion tug.)	167.2	258.8	847.0	1170.1	1518.8	1956.2
Annual inflation level (percentage)	6.0	8.1	11.0	9.5	6.3	5.0
Total budget revenue (billion tug.)	225.5	351.0	713.1	837.9	1209.2	1295.6
Total budget expenditure (billion tug.)	342.2	429.6	752.5	764.6	1046.5	1428.0
Unemployment level	5.9	4.6	3.6	3.3	3.3	3.3

Source: Mongolian Statistical Yearbook "Mongolia in the market economy (1989-2002) Ulaanbaatar, 2004, pp. 86, 96, 108, 111, 120-121; Mongolian Statistical Yearbook, 2005, Ulaanbaatar, 2006, pp.105, 115, 125, 132, 146-147; Government News

From table 3.1 it can be seen that in the last years economy has stabilized (although it was estimated without regard to influence of external prices), money supply has risen substantially and there has been a sustainable increase in budget revenue and expenditure. As of 2005, the share of private sector in GDP reached 77.4 per cent and in some sectors it increased to 100 per cent. Consequently, as economy was supplied with money, an average weighted percentage of bank loans has seen a decrease, however small, so loan drawing possibilities of entities have improved. As these possibilities were created and quality changes in economy have emerged, they opened possibilities for implementing comprehensive actions to improve components of the financial structure and to develop financial markets in the last years. New amendments have been made in the Banking Law, Investment Law and Law of Securities and following laws were passed: "Law on Accounting" (2003); "Public Sector Financial Management Law" (2003); "Law on Leasing" (2006) and some principle amendments have been made in the package of tax laws to reduce tax burden and to improve regulatory duties of the code.

So in the whole, there is a tendency for all component parts of the financial structure to be formed in line with the content of actual market relations. Financial resources have increased, sources multiplied, frames of financial instruments have broadened and their effect has improved. The role and position of a human factor, which is considered a driving force of the financial structure, have been advanced and preparedness and skills of financial professionals have improved. From the financial market aspect a monetary market has formed. However, there is a need for intensive development of property and insurance markets.

In conditions, when a financial market becomes a set and there is a competition, the price of financial instruments goes down and actions to support financially economic growth will become systematic. Looking at comprehensive actions, taken for improvement of financial systems, stabilization of the economic growth, improvements in financial sources and resources and increase in efficiency of financial instruments, we can note that a new era of financial system development has begun in Mongolia since 2006.

The specific features of this period are as follows:

1. To upgrade the balanced ratio at micro and macro levels on the basis of speeding up the economic growth and forming an efficient structure of market economy;

2. To change the administrative structure, to improve the internal balance of the budget and to decrease the percentage of budget in GDP by the way of developing new financial standards and increasing efficiency of asset utilization;

3. To implement a policy of equal support of foreign and domestic investment on the basis of increasing efficiency of investment made in previous years, improving the investment capacity of business entities and fully mobilizing all internal financial resources;

4. To create an environment for increasing the number of workplaces and improving productivity and to make the ratio of productivity and income effective on the basis of the state implementing steadfastly policies with an enterprise concept, and supporting activities on improving business environment and introducing modern scientific and technological achievements in production;

5. To organize effectively implementation of new and renewed laws on taxation and economy, to develop intensively the property and insurance markets, which are considered important components of the financial market and to take to a new stage actions, taken to support corporate finance with financial market;

6. To develop small and medium enterprises, to reveal the hidden economy, to create comprehensive economical, financial, legal and organizational environment and to achieve noticeable accomplishments in this frame;

Taking the above objectives as the basis we will talk in the next chapters about upgrading components of the financial system and intensifying their mutual effect.

Corporate finance

Corporate finance is actual relationships of creating costs and a complex of methods and forms for organizing them and reaching results. Since GDP is produced on the enterprise and organizational level and then is distributed through the financial system, it is regarded as the basis of financial system.

The State actions, taken to reform financial systems were definitely a stimulus to renew completely corporate financial relationships along with marketing traditions. Enterprises should be able to work as a main stimulus of developing market relations. This should be the basis of financial reforms in Mongolia. Thus, in the future it is important for enterprises to develop in the production and financial aspects in a short time and to move to a classical market management, on the other side, the state should act as a state with a corporate ideology and it is necessary to develop the content of market relationships by fulfilling its responsibility of upgrading business environment.

Functions of corporate finance should be first determined properly to address reform issues. Corporate finance is fulfilling the following functions in conditions of market relations:

- Investment and development;
- Create a monetary fund with targeted objectives and supplying asset rotation with cash capital;
- Utilize the funds effectively and increase efficiency and productivity;
- Control final results of economic- financial activities of enterprises and encourage efficiency.

Functions of corporate finance condition financial organizational structure, adjusted to them. A common standard of financial organizational structure is established in large companies, operating their businesses along with the market in countries with developed markets. Figure 3.3 shows that the financial organizational structure needs to be in accordance with a requirement to fulfill functions, which determine the content of real financial relationships. The better skills of financiers to determine professional policies, to coordinate, organize, encourage, support, control, the greater productivity and capacity of enterprises and the stronger their position in the market. That is the essence of the above structure.

Consequently, large companies and organizations in our country need to change to this organizational structure. Currently, to evaluate the financial capability of an enterprise one needs to evaluate results of work of financial professionals, who are responsible for constantly increasing income by utilizing proper financial resources, sources and instruments and for maintaining financial stabilization.

Figure 3.3 Model structure of the Financial Department in the market economy

Financial Director/ Manager Financial Department	
Financial Division	Accounting division
▪ Financial Planning (long, medium and short terms) ▪ Investment (real and financial) ▪ Activities on the monetary market (payments , loans) ▪ Activities on the capital market (release securities, buy them etc.) ▪ Activities with suppliers (leasing etc.) ▪ Work with the market (sale on credit, manage debts etc.) ▪ Financial Analysis ▪ Delivering financial information to public, advising etc.)	▪ Cost Accounting ▪ Financial Accounting ▪ Management Accounting ▪ Working out financial norms, normatives and standards ▪ Financial News ▪ Statistical News ▪ Yearly and Quarterly Financial Reports ▪ Internal Auditing ▪ Cooperation with External Auditing ▪ Automation of data ▪ Software

Source: Corporate Finance. Stephen A Pocc, Randolph W Westerfild, Jeffrei Jaffe. London, 1996, p.6

In the future, along with enriching and developing material and real aspects of financial systems, such as financial resources, sources and instruments, it is especially important to upgrade professional and organizational skills of financial professionals, who are considered the main driving force of the system. Currently, almost all enterprises have acoounting divisions, which substitute for financial divisions. When financial divisions are established in their real sense, financial relationships will be carried out at professional level and it will be an important condition for more active development of financial markets.

Another requirement of the market is that enterprises need to reach an appropriate level, suited to the environment and conditions, in terms of sales volume, production capacity and financial management and run sustainable activities, able to withstand competition.

However, introduction of classical management methods and forms is slow and ineffective, because enterprises in Mongolia are too small and there is a small number of shareholding companies, which are not diversified and cooperative. They attempt to justify their small size by narrow frame and low capacity of the market. If they are really interested in being "small", it is, undoubtedly, a factor of influence, however, as a leading Mongolian poet B. Yavuukhulan stated in his poem "... My horse, my verse, we need the world arena...", we need to pursue a goal of increasing substantially our trade with border provinces of our gigantic Northern and Southern neighbors.

It seems that there is no talk about the market being "too small" or "too big" in countries, which produce competitive goods, meeting international standards, where management at global standards is introduced and development in line with time and conditions is under way.

One of numerous indices representing the proper size of enterprises is their grouping by number of employees. In 2005, 78.8 per cent out of 22547 legal entities, running their business in Mongolia had 1-9 employees and only 4.4 per cent of all enterprises employed over 50 people.

In 2006, 32.4 thousand enterprises were counted and in comparison with 1998 there is a tendency of increasing numbers of enterprises in each group by the number of employees. Quantitative increase of enterprises with 1-9 employees was the highest; however, increase in number of big companies with 50 or over people was the lowest (it decreased, actually). Companies with 50 or over employees prevailed in educational, medical and social welfare sectors and in processing industries. However, small entities with 1-9 employees were engaged mostly in wholesale and retail trade, service and agriculture.

Figure 3.2. The number of the enterprises and entities /by number of employees /

Number of employees	1998	2000	2002	2003	2004	2005
Total	17008	21085	25523	26552	25356	22547
1-9	12041	16116	20515	21704	20693	17780
10-19	1973	1982	2052	2016	1913	2001
20-49	1868	1916	1896	1806	1751	1782
50+	1126	1071	1060	1026	999	984

Source: National Statistical Office of Mongolia: "Mongolia in the market" (1989-2002). Ulaanbaatar, 2004, p.133. National Statistical Office of Mongolia 2005- Ulaanbaatar, 2006, p-361

While 36.6 per cent of total enterprises are involved in wholesaling and retailing sectors, only 6.5 per cent run their businesses in the processing industry. This shows that enterprises in Mongolia are too small and they have not reached a proper level to increase efficiency. Furthermore, they have not created labour and production cooperation suited to market conditions and they are not formed in terms of structure.

The above situation is observed clearly when looking at results of the 2006 census of enterprises and entities. For example, 64.0 per cent of all enterprises have 0-4 million tugrik sales revenue. If enterprises (20 per cent) with 5-19 million tugrik sales revenue are added to this list, 84.0 per cent of our enterprises can be regarded as small enterprises. There are only 130 (0.4%) enterprises with 5000.0 million tugrik sales revenue. 42 out of them are in the wholesale and retail sectors, 24 – in processing industry and 18 are in the mining sector.

Thus, an appropriate structure of sectors has not developed yet, and in addition, due to low sales revenue of enterprises, their financial conditions are not stable and profit and accumulation have not increased.

Figure 3.3 Survey of the number of enterprises by sales revenue groups and by economic activity sectors, as of 2005

Sectors	Total	By sales revenue: (million tugrik)					
		0-4	5-19	20-49	50-499	500-4999	5000 or above
A	1	2	3	4	5	6	7
Total	32410	20757	6483	1980	2425	635	130
▪ Agriculture, Hunting, Forestry	1626	1247	225	88	60	5	1
▪ Mining and exploration industry	411	192	56	17	80	48	18
▪ Processing industry	2362	1222	541	215	281	79	24
▪ Supply of electricity, gas and water	234	41	42	38	76	27	10
▪ Construction	1310	562	244	139	282	78	5
▪ Wholesale and retail, home appliances repair services	12134	7636	2733	632	838	253	

▪ Hotel and restaurants	1466	657	534	135	127	12	42
▪ Transportation, warehouse, communication	1178	682	238	87	129	33	1
▪ Financial transaction services	1675	1186	242	121	93	23	9
▪ Real estate, rent, other business activities	2440	1349	630	214	209	33	10
▪ Public administration, defense, compulsory social insurance	1148	1095	34	8	8	2	5
▪ Educational sector	1994	1571	231	76	99	15	1
▪ Health and Social welfare	2010	1444	403	110	45	8	2
▪ Other services to society and individuals	2411	1867	329	99	96	19	1
▪ Other	11	6	1	1	2	-	1

Source: Mongolian National Statistical Office

Asked about reasons of their inability to do business properly, 27.5 per cent of the companies reported shortage of assets and finances. According to the 2005 census, 11.3% out of all 32410 enterprises or 3718, made an investment one way or another.

Figure 3.3 shows the current trend of investment. Most of enterprises (65.1%), which made an investment, have made an investment under 10.0 million tugrik. This shows that small investments in Mongolia prevail over other investments.

If we look at total investments of enterprises by financial sources, direct foreign investment accounts for 31.8%, self-investment – for 31.1%, foreign soft loans – for 17.8%, bank loans – for 13.9%, budget investment – for 2.9%, sales of securities – for 0.1% and other sources account for 2.4%. It shows that a system to support investments by financial market as in the countries with developed markets is not yet in place in Mongolia.

As for investment capacity, mining, exploration, processing industries, construction, wholesaling and retailing, transportation, warehouse and communication sectors surpass others. It might be a correct trend. In the future, the sectoral structure of our country is likely to have a structure, that gives priority to agriculture, mining and processing industries, wholesaling and retailing, financial servicing. This conclusion is being confirmed by other, than the above, research.

Figure 3.4 Number of enterprises, which made investment, by activity sectors and the amount of investment

Sectors	Total	By investment group (thousand tugrik)					
		Up to 500.0	501.0-1000.0	1001.0-10000.0	10001-100000	100001.0 -1000000	1000001.0 or over
A	1	2	3	4	5	6	7
Total	3718	316	426	1678	970	261	67
▪ Agriculture, Hunting, Forestry	272	17	37	147	66	9	1
▪ Mining industry	96	2	2	18	31	34	9
▪ Processing industry	405	23	28	169	139	35	11
▪ Production of electricity and gas, water	71	7	3	16	31	9	5
▪ Construction	186	6	14	52	69	43	2
▪ Wholesaling and Retailing	1357	143	186	678	290	49	11
▪ Hotel and Restaurants	268	20	24	124	81	17	2
▪ Transportation, warehouse, communication	194	11	12	75	64	24	8
▪ Financial transaction services	169	16	27	76	31	11	8
▪ Real estate, rent	232	19	28	85	72	19	9
▪ Educational sector	64	3	5	37	14	5	-
▪ Health and Social Welfare	344	46	57	180	57	3	1
▪ Other services to society and individuals	60	3	3	26	25	3	-

Source: Mongolian Statistical Yearbook

Currently, 61.8 per cent of the enterprises, which made investment, are located in Ulaanbaatar city , Darkhan-Uul and Orkhon provinces, so there is a high location concentration. There are comprehensive benefits of investment initiative in provinces. With further growth of the size of enterprises, their diversification and cooperation, declining tax burden and emerging competition in the financial market, investment possibilities will inevitably improve and increase.

A low level of savings and accumulation along with undeveloped financial market to support investment lead to delay in creation of economic growth, based on fixed capital reforms and increase of labor productivity. The above was said because growth of GDP, based solely on domestic demand growth, will not continue for a long time and there is no possibility for income growth fueled by productivity growth. The main solution is to improve efficiency of a mechanism to change savings and accumulation into investment and make structural changes that will increase investment. Although this is not a new conclusion, it is regarded as the most significant and vital in current situation from the aspect of broadening enterprises and implementing structural reforms leading to the governance of a shareholding company.

A requirement for our enterprises to utilize fully all conditions, factors and possibilities to improve labor productivity along with improving effectiveness of tangible assets utilization is becoming more urgent. As a result of such actions balanced economic relations will be created and an objective basis for income increase will be set up.

The structure of total tangible assets of enterprises in Mongolia, where land accounts for 0.5 per cent, buildings – for 37.9 %, machinery, equipment, vehicles - for 45.7 per cent, and other tangible assets – for 15.9 per cent, is regarded as a reasonable structure for our country. However, a problem of improving effectiveness of its utilization is the most important. The census results showed that 18.3 per cent of enterprises utilized only 50% of the capacity of installed equipment. Our findings showed an even worse situation[4]. The reasons for not utilizing the full capacity were reported as follows: 11.0 per cent – due to shortage of raw materials, 25.7 per cent – due to shortage of financing and current assets, 22.5 per cent – low product demand and needs, 3.2 per cent – power cuts and 37.6 per cent claimed other reasons. These are not reasons that can not be eliminated and overcome. The most important is the human factor. These reasons can be overcome if the proper management is introduced.

Figure 3.5 Ratio between productivity and average remuneration (at the country level, by yearly price)

	2002	2003	2004	2005
Labor productivity (thousand tugrik)	1457.1	1626.0	2036.1	2362.4
Average annual salary and wages of employees of enterprises (thousand tugrik)	71.3	81.5	93.1	101.2

Source: Mongolian Statistical Yearbook 2005-Ulaanbaatar, 2006, p-354-355, 107-108

In the market situation, there is an urgent need to draw proper boundaries between conditions, factors and methods of improving labor productivity and to coordinate them, to create an effective productivity management.

---

[4] N. Bayartsaikhan Mongolia in conditions of globalization, UB, 2003, pp 174-176

If productivity statistics in the last years, when there was an increase in economic growth, are examined, altough labor productivity has gone up, growth is not sufficient for strengthening economic development and increasing average wages of employees. Industry productivity is on relatively higher level in the mining industry (MNT12552.5 thousand), in transportation, warehouse and communication sectors (MNT6513.7 thousand) and in financial transaction activities (MNT5560.0 thousand), however in important sectors such as processing industry (MNT1940.8 thousand) and construction (MNT1192.8 thousand) are on the lower level. By 2005 the average yearly salary of employees was 1214.4 thousand tugrik, which equalled 51.4 per cent of the annual productivity at the national level or higher than the annual productivity of the construction sector. This shows that economic conditions and opportunities for increasing substantially the average salary are very low. Thus, we need to create an environment for improving the productivity to increase steadily average salaries in the future. In other words, there is a need for implementation of an economic development model, based on steadily increasing productivity.
This also shows a need for expanding enterprises to the appropriate level and transforming them to shareholding companies, along with doing reforms in the structure of salaries. Unless the previously mentioned actions are taken, the same pattern of few large companies carrying the main burden for the budget payments and lack of an even growth of income among general population will continue, even if the GDP was increased by setting several large industrial sites.

The following problems should be taken into consideration and implemented in order to strengthen the role of corporate finance in the financial system:

- For the Government to implement policies with enterprisc concepts, to support enterprises with the state financial policies and to develop the financial market;
- To set up financial departments of enterprises in real meaning, to introduce modern classical financial management;
- To expand enterprises and to develop their financial independence and capacity along with upgrading professional skills in vertical and horizontal financial relations;
- To implement the economic growth model, based on industrial productivity growth and, on this basis to conduct activities directed towards increasing income of employees;
- To do the economic and structural reforms directed towards transfer of enterprises to the governance of shareholding companies;
- To improve substantially the quality of financial statements and reports, and to move from "backward- looking" management, based on the balance to the

"forward-looking" management, based on the plan, by acquiring modern methods of financial planning.

Reforms of Governmental Financial policies and regulations

As we mentioned previously, the problem of developing and implementing financial policies of the transition period was a priority issue of the Government; however, it was a complicated one.

During the last 16 years the financial and monetary system of our country saw the worst crisis in 1991-1994, there was a recovery in 1995-1997 and another crisis in 1997-1999. However, it has entered a stable stage since 2000. A financial policy covers all activities, directed towards mobilization, allocation and utilization of financial resources for implementation of programs and objectives put forward by the government for economical and social development. The financial policy of the government has been implemented with regard to times and conditions of the specific period. For instance, financial policies, methods and mechanisms, used in the periods of economic recession or recovery and stabilization had specific features.

The state financial policies are implemented in a comprehensive way in definite directions, including budgetary, taxation, monetary- credit, investment and social policies, along with international financial issues.

The priorities in Mongolian financial policies are as follows:

- To create such a financial environment as to maintain stable economic and social situation and advanced growth;
- To resolve serious social problems and decrease complicated conditions;
- To make the state finance healthy and capable, to maintain financial balance at the micro- and macro- economic level;
- To upgrade monetary and credit systems, to conduct normal professional activities and to increase substantially their role in the economical and social development of the country;
- To provide and improve the balance of commodities and cash flow;
- To increase financial and economic independence and accountability in enterprises, regions and provinces and to create similar conditions in the budget-tax system;
- To improve efficiency of assets utilization in all sectors and subjects and strengthen the financial discipline.

Financial policy and its political administration in the transitional period were represented by three main elements, caused by the conditions of that period.

First: In order to attain the goals, set in the specific period of the economic and social life of our country, there is a need to determine and implement the main objectives of the short-term and long-term financial policies.
Second: In order to achieve efficiently the objectives of the short-term and long-term financial policies, appropriate forms and tools of financial organization are needed to be worked out and utilized appropriately.
Third: To achieve the set goals and organize its implementation; to train, select and place effectively the skilled and highly educated staff.

Financial policy and management often face difficulties and many complicated problems need to be solved. Although in the beginning of the transitional period first steps to put finance into the market ways were taken, shortage of assets due to economic recession put it in a difficult situation. It recovered in the middle of the 90s, when the inflation level and budget losses went down, the current balance had profit and a proper amount of resources was accumulated. However, this positive trend was not maintained for long.

During 1997-1999 due to the distortion of custom and taxation systems and failure of professional financial management, budget losses equalled 12.5% of GDP and the current budget was at loss as well. There was again a budget crisis, which led to financing of wages and salaries, pensions and social activities on credit.

Due to the abovementioned distortion of the budget and financial systems, a debt chain appeared between the private, state-owned and budgetary organizations; budget financing, worth billions of tugriks, could not reach designated organizations, a scope of the shadow economy expanded and bribery and corruption became widespread. A hope of taking financial aid from external parties was lost and the country faced a budgetary and financial disaster. That is why resolute measures have been taken since 2000 the to upgrade the state financial policies and management. In the frame of this work, a prominent objective to "Make the state budgetary and financial systems healthy"was put forward and certain actions were taken to attain financial sustainability; to become free from the internal and external debt burden; to increase steadily sources of budget revenue in order to improve management of the state budget; to plan the budget with regard to the mid-term and long-term macro-economic policies and improve financing; to move to the system of financing outcomes of actions; to improve justification of norms and standards of the budget expenditure management and financing.
To improve rationale of budget planning, a normative method was introduced to budgetary financing and a move from yearly budget planning method to the mid-term continuous budget planning was made. In order to upgrade relationships between the

centralized state budget and local budgets, a shift to a new, inter-budget balance method of revenue allocation was made in 2002, in compliance with international budget standards.

Financial policy reforms are closely connected with the reforms of revenue and expenditure administration, taxation and customs policies. Taxation reforms, which have been made over the last years, are directed towards lightening the overall tax load, avoiding taxation policies, directly dependent on budget expenditure growth, establishing equal and fair taxation, extending the taxation basis, strengthening legislation enforcement, implementing goals of making taxation an incentive to encourage economic growth, activate foreign and domestic investment and support entrepreneurs by the state. Especially, reforms, which went into the force since 2007, have decreased the amount of all taxes, in the future it is intended to cut down tax burden step by step, in particular big tax payers will have reductions and benefits and it is intended to shift to the one-scale tax system, in compliance with the international market standards.

By implementing the "Law of Administration and Financing of Budgetary organizations" since 2003, the Mongolian budgetary relations have changed fundamentally. The budgetary administration reforms contain implementation and results of reforms of the structure and organization of civil service, the cost management and social sectors. The Mongolian Government together with the World Bank have developed in detail the middle-term strategy and program of reforming the civil service and improving the budgetary cost management in Mongolia and started implementing it.

Reforms of budget and statuary fund, directed towards enhancing the state fund systems and increasing statuary fund and treasury are being implemented. The most important direction of the reform is to spend the assets, accumulated in the budget from tax-payers, in the most effective way, under control and only for designated needs. The main components of the reform of the state fund include transition to a united state fund account system, the process of renewing Government accounting in compliance with the international standards, establishment of a debt management system and effective management of cash flow. However, the quality of implementation needs to be improved.

With introduction of the statuary fund system a mechanism has been formed, where the budget is implemented as a law and the government assets management has improved, a responsibility of payment has increased, the budget records, reports and statements have been released on time, the current budget control has improved, the budget discipline has strenghtened and violations of budget and its deficits have decreased over the last years. In establishing the state fund system a goal to introduce an

electronic network for payment, based on advanced modern technology and software was put forward and is being implemented.
Currently Ministry of Finance has connection with all 21 provinces, the capital city Ulaanbaatar and all districts via an electronic network and this gives an opportunity to make payments to all budgetary organizations promptly.

A state financial management and information system was set up for acquiring all budgetary information at any time, controlling budget expenditure and providing financial management with prompt regulations. One of the main problems of financial policy is a problem of domestic and foreign debt. A division in charge of keeping consolidated records of governmental domestic and foreign debt, coordinating payments and accounts, increasing the capacity of paying off the debt and preparing financial statements and reports was set up in the Ministry of Finance. The division has established a central system of debt administration and started using software and systems of debt administration and financial analysis.

With use of a comprehensive system of debt administration, all domestic and foreign debts are recorded and analysis and research works are held. Furthermore, the division works out projections and connects debt demands and needs with the demand for and supply of ODA policy, calculates all alternatives of effects influencing the debt condition and uses the system to make an appropriate decision. International accounting standards are used in budgetary organizations and budget statements and reports are prepared at quality level, on time and disseminated openly. A software to draw up, unite and analyze statements of enterprises activities is installed and the results of analysis are used as a main tool of prompt management.

All these show improvement of the state financial policy and administration, suited to the new market conditions.

Mongolian Budget Reforms

Goals and direction of budget reforms

Over 16 years of transitional period a general model of Mongolian market relations have been formed and procedures have been established. During this period the actions of reforming financial, budgetary and monetary-credit systems have been done and searching, experimental and processing actions of the systems are still carried on. The priority goals were to do the reform in the financial sector from the beginning of transition in direction of conducting suited policy of finance and budget, performing the state with rational and limited participation, utilizing widely the regulatory financial methods /budget, tax, investment, wear and tear, loss/.

There is a tendency of extending resources for accumulate financial reserves and recovering the capacity. The source formation to accumulate financial reserves over the country can be divided into following groups:

1. In the frame of statuary finance the statuary reserves, which are formed by Mongolian Consolidated Budget, state lending, centralized funds of outside budget.
2. Non- centralized funds of all business enterprises /private-owned, including herdsmen household/, all non-industrial organizations /governmental, on- governmental, private, custom etc./ and citizens' . The reserves are spent according to the regulations and laws.
3. In the frame of banking and monetary-credit sector, government foreign currency, cash, gold reserves, savings, accumulation of credit capital, earned profits and fund assets of commercial insurance all have legal basis, specialized resources and specified directions.
4. The most effective and prospective resource of financial reserves is the establishing and developing in Mongolia financial market system, which involves stock, credit, capital, foreign currency and insurance market altogether. All these have been established in Mongolia. Financial additional resources are mobilized to extend the scope of domestic and foreign activities and put the reserves of free assets into circulation.
5. External sources are increasing as loans, aid and investment from donor countries, which support Mongolian development and foreign organizations such as international financial and UNDP branch organizations are regarded as an important source.

In order to distinguish clearly the evolution, changes, results and development boundaries in the financial sector during the transitional period two periods of 1991-1999 and 2000 up to now are clarified:

Finance and Budget in1991-1999

During 1991-1999 major actions to form a financial, budgetary and monetary- credit systems to be functioning in the market, were taken and substantial results were seen. Due to the activities, implemented systematically to set free prices and tariffs, to liberalize foreign trade, to shift currencies to free convertible domestic exchange, to change the banking system and to form a main legal guarantee of cash transactions and insurance relations, macro indicators of economy have stabilized and activities of different subjects, involved in different forms of property, tended to be activated and encouraged.

Financial policy is implemented firstly through the budget system. One of the main problems of regulating economy effectively form the state it was required to improve the correlation between budgetary, taxation and monetary-credit policies. The budget – taxation policy has roles to balance, allocate and control. The Mongolian budget becomes the consolidated indicator of economic policies. Being utilized as the most effective method to reallocate budget, taxation and GDP, it is directed to attain the efficient balance on the micro and macro levels of economy, to develop country's economy and society and to become the financial base of governmental programs. Through the budget and financial policies industrial consumption demand was regulated and furthermore, it started influencing total economic stabilization and growth.

The budget financial policies have been influencing directly and indirectly financial conditions of all enterprises, their accumulation and asset allocation. The budget represents monetary relations, connected with formation and utilization of asset funds, concentrated in the hands of the government by the way of allocating GDP and parts of national wealth for implementing its responsibilities on strategic goals to shift to the market economy and economic and social activities of the state and the country.

The volume of the budget revenue and expenditure of Mongolia has increased and its internal structure has changed in a positive way.

Table 3.6 Mongolian Budget /1991-1999 years, billion tug./

Indicators		**1991**	**1992**	**1993**	**1994**	**1995**	**1996**	**1997**	**1998**	**1999**
Total Revenue		6.5	11.9	54.8	85.4	140.9	159.9	212	225.5	254.8
Total expenditure		8.7	12	61.6	98.9	149.3	176.5	287.6	342.2	361.7
Budget balance	Current	-1.5	-0.1	10.3	7.6	34.2	26.2	13.4	-5.6	56.2
	Total	-2.2	-0.1	-6.8	-13.5	-8.4	-16.6	-75.6	-116.7	-106.9
Percent in GDP	Total revenue	32.1	23.9	33.0	30.4	33.8	30.6	29.2	27.4	27.9
	Total expenditure	47.2	28.7	37.1	35.8	34.9	33.1	38.4	39.1	36.2
	Total loss	-15.1	-4.8	-4.1	-4.2	-1.5	-2.5	-9.1	-14.3	-11.6

The above shows that:

- Although inflation affects the budget revenue and expenditure of Mongolia, it is going up on its basis along with economic recovery. In comparison with the 1996 in 1999 the budget revenue increased by 1.6 times, expenditure – by 2.1 times. However, the expenditure growth was faster than that of the budget revenue. This was the negative phenomenon providing conditions for growth of the budget losses.

- Through the budget revenue and expenditure the role of budget regulation in the economic and financial frame should be provided. Altough this feature of a strong regulator can not be seen yet, there is a trend for it.
- In the centrally planned period 60 per cent of the national revenue was allocated by accumulations in the budget, but by 1999 the share of budget revenue in GDP was 27.9 per cent and expenditure- 36.1 per cent, which was at the average level of the countries with developed market. Furthermore, this indicated democratic activities have developed in financial sector, however, the revenue represented collapse of domestic industry.
- The total budget losses increased by absolute and relative sums and reached 106.9 billion tugrik in 1999 which was 6.4 times greater compared to 1996. Domestic and foreign loans and aid played the main role to sources of compensating the total budget losses,which increases the debt on foreign loans.

The growth and decrease of budget revenue and expenditure, and its structural changes determine the country's economic and social development and changes. In 1991-1999 the budget revenue and expenditure went up in total sum and changed structurally. The budget revenue is made of tax revenue, non-tax revenue, asset revenue, revenue from foreign loans and aid.

As of 1999 tax revenue accounted for 71.1 per cent in the total budget revenue, non-tax revenue- for 26.1 per cent, asset revenue- for 0 per cent and revenue from foreign loans and aids accounted for the rest. An important part of financial policy is to create an effective system of budget revenue and taxation.

In 1991-1999 a transition from the revenue mobilizing system of the centrally planned economy period to the new system of market taxation was completed. In developing the taxation policy, along with following the general theory and trends of developing a taxation policy, it was necessary to take into consideration the special features of Mongolian economic structure, the capacity of paying taxes and the asset revenue level of the population. A set of taxation laws, which was approved in 1992 and later amendments to the law also followed this direction.

In the current situation of the transition period following principles were followed in developing the tax policy:
First, to set the most effective relationships of allocating the resources between the government and enterprises; second, to take steps to mobilize revenue in appropriate measure in order to strengthen the base of the budget revenue in line with increasing demand for financial resources; third, to create favourable conditions for economic independence and self-financing to all enterprises regardless of types of property;

fourth, to encourage production and consumption and to support small and private entities; fifth, to regulate differences in personal incomes of citizens and to create a safety net for poor and vulnerable population.

The influence of the tax system on the economy greatly depends on its types and structure. Currently there are 10 types of taxes and 8 types of duties.

The tax in the budget of Mongolia is divided into two types - direct and non-direct. The direct tax is formed from Income tax of economic entities and organization.

Figure 3.7 The Structure of tax revenue

	1995	**1996**	**1997**	**1998**	**1999**
Total tax revenue Including:	100	100	100	100	100
Income tax	46	37.7	38.2	33.3	21.5
Social Security fee	15	15.3	12.9	17	16.4
Sales tax or VAT	15.5	17.8	23.2	27.9	33
Excise Tax	8.2	9.2	12.4	16.8	14.7
Special service tax	3.1	4.3	2.9	3.9	3.7
Customs duty	9.0	11.5	7.3	1	4.9
Other taxes	3.2	4.2	3.1	5.1	5.1

Source: Statistical Yearbook "Mongolia in the market economy", 1989-2002, Ulaanbaatar, 2004. p-120

Until 1997, 70 per cent of the budget revenue came from tax revenues, however, in 1998 it decreased to 64.2%. It increased again in 1999. Figures over the last years show that the percentage of all tax revenue and income tax went down each year. This resulted from the economic situation of the year, the market formation, the budget, development of the tax law and organization of financial activities.

For example,

- The internal capacity of the budget revenue weakened and it showed a trend for further decline;
- There was a continued decline of national industry and its profits fell down;
- The economic structure, dominated by a few industries (copper, gold, cashmere), that were wholly dependent on the international market prices led to the budget revenue changes depending on the price of raw materials at the world market;

- The phenomenon of taxable income to be wilfully hidden or tax evasion was widespread, while fight against of it was weak. Only 60.0 per cent of all tax were collected.
- Continuous changes to the tax law and tax legislation led to the instability among tax-payers and the loss of budget balance. The VAT, which went into force on July, 1998, suddenly rose by 13% to 30 per cent in September, provoking anger of entrepreneurs. Generally, when the tax was increased and changed, tax evasion and hiding income became widespread.
- When the custom duty was zero-rated, the budget revenue resources decreased by at least 18 billion tugrik. On the other hand, the internal market was filled with imported goods not in demand, which became a barrier to recovery of the national industry and brought great losses to the economy.
- A low level of Income tax and its decrease by comparative indices indicated continuous decline of production of enterprises and their profits. However, enterprises with a revenue over 100 million Tugrik were interested in becoming smaller in order to hide their income and to pay taxes at the lowest rate. This is proved by the fact that the number of enterprises, which had a revenue over 100 mill. Tugrik and paid tax on 40 per cent of the income declined by 50 per cent in 1999 compared to 1996.
- It is important to review the ratio of direct and non-direct tax revenues. In the total sum of tax revenue the direct tax comprised 21 per cent in 1999 and the remaining was from non-direct taxes. The per cent of direct tax tended to decrease further.

Coordination of the budget policy is closely connected to its expenditure and statuary fund policy. The budget expenditure policy was a major tool for implementation of the government programs and concepts for implementing the transition to the market economy and fulfilling its responsibilities to generate financial resources for managing and regulating the economy and society of the country and protecting vital rights and safety of the citizens. The budget spending depends on the one hand, on limited possibilities of revenue in the present conditions of Mongolia, on the other hand, it relies on requirements of demand for financial resources to overcome the economic and social crisis and to maintain further sustainable development.

Budget expenditure is dedicated to finance necessary actions such as developing infrastructure as the basis for economy, providing for the main aspects of human development: education, science, culture, health care, social security, defence of the country and the activities of the statuary administration. As of 1999 the current expenditure accounted for 68.5% of total budget expenditure, 7.8% of asset expenditure, 23.6% accounted for foreign and domestic loan fees. There was a tendency of increasing asset expenditure and foreign and domestic loan repayment. The types of budget expenditure purposes have changed substantially in line with market economy, social structure, government policies and activities.

Figure 3.8 Structure of the budget expenditure /1991-1999, percent/

	1991	1995	1999
Total expenditure	100	100	100
Of it: General Public service	6.3	8.9	9.1
Education	24.2	16.4	17.9
Health care	11.6	11.1	9.9
Insurance, social benefits	12.1	16.3	16.6
Housing, communal service	2.6	1.6	1.3
Leisure, sports, culture	4.6	3.5	3.2
Electricity and heating	4.9	8.6	1.3
Agriculture, Forestry	2.9	2.9	1.4
Minerals, Mining, construction	6.2	1.9	0.3
Transportation and Communication	4.7	3.0	1.9
Other	1.1	2.5	1.2

Source: Statistical Yearbook "Mongolia in the market economy", 1989-2002, Ulaanbaatar, 2004. p-121

Before the transition to the market over 40.0 per cent of the budget expenditure of the country was spent on the material production sector designated for extended reproduction, and the residual method was used for allocation for social actions.

However, according to the budget financing policy during the transition period enterprises of the real economic sectors were directed towards running business on the principle of self-financing, and as of 1999 the process of financing the current expenditure in the economic sectors diminished substantially and fell down to 10%.

In those years the purpose of budget expenditure changed fundamentally. In conditions, when state property was privatized and production sectors shifted almost entirely to the private sector, the main goal was to create an environment and conditions for profitable activities to all enterprises, which ran production and service businesses and were engaged in selling products on the market in order to make profit, regardless of their size or property type.

One of the main parts of the budgetary and financial policy was to make the designation of budget expenditure more efficient, to pay more attention to the problems of human development, to increase expenditure on education, health and social welfare and to allocate the expenditure effectively.

The concept of the "Population policy of Mongolia", approved in 1996 by the State Ikh Khural, states that the basis of the development and progress of Mongolia is a human being, who is a intellectually and physically well-developed, patriotic, hardworking, who has high morals and respects the law. It declared that the population policy is based on a global human-centered development ideology with an aim to respect human rights and freedoms and to develop individuals and families.

Paying more attention to financial resources for priority directions of human development was a pressing problem of budget financing. A need emerged to increase resurces for the core sector of human development in Mongolia /education, health care, supply of drinking water, food supply of households/. As of 1999, 48.9 per cent of budget expenditure was devoted to these activities.

In comparison with 1995, in 1999 expenditure on education increased 2.8 times, on health care – by 2.2 times and on social insurance benefits – by 2.4 times.

However, in 1996-1999 the budget expenditure increased faster than its revenue. Basically because of the continuing recession and financial difficulties on the micro and macro level, the budget losses reached 1000 billion tugrik and occupied 14 per cent in GDP. In this period there were difficulties in the financial sector.

Trends for improvement of budget capacity and stabilization

Since 2000 there has been rapid progress in Mongolian economic and social development, which created the basis for further sustainable growth. Budget revenue and expenditure have increased by the total amount, there have been progressive structural changes and financial capacity has improved substantially.

Table 3.9 The structure of budget revenue, components /billion tugrik, %/

	2000		2001		2002		2003	
	Total	**%**	**Total**	**%**	**Total**	**%**	**Total**	**%**
Sum of total revenue and aid	351.1	100	439.3	100	477.0	100	535.8	100
Current revenue	346.2	98.6	429.9	97.9	469.7	98.5	526.4	98.2
À. Tax revenue	260.6	74.2	328.2	74.7	359.2	75.3	404.4	75.5
Income tax	62.8	17.9	64.5	14.7	72.4	15.2	81.8	15.3
Social security charges	39.3	11.2	54.0	12.3	54.4	11.4	63.6	11.9
VAT	76.2	21.7	104.2	23.7	118.7	24.9	121.7	22.7
Excise tax	41.0	11.7	53.3	12.1	51.3	1.8	58.9	11.0
Special service tax	7.1	2.0	8.9	2.0	8.6	1.8	9.7	1.8
Customs duty	22.3	6.4	27.0	6.1	24.6	5.2	32.7	6.1
Other taxes	11.6	3.3	14.6	3.3	25.8	5.4	31.5	5.9
B. Non-tax revenue	85.6	24.4	101.7	23.2	110.6	23.2	121.9	22.8
C. Asset revenue	0.9	0.02	1.6	0.03	0.4	0.09	0.8	0.1
D. Foreign aid	4.8	1.4	9.2	2.1	6.8	1.4	8.7	1.6

	2004		2005		2006	
	Total	**%**	**Total**	**%**	**Total**	**%**
Sum of total revenue and aid	713.1	100	837.9	100	1209.8	100
Current revenue	706.2	99.0	832.6	99.4	1204.2	99.5
À. Tax revenue	583.1	81.8	692.2	82.6	984.7	81.4
Income tax	144.1	20.2	178.2	21.3	373.5	30.9
Social security charges	82.1	11.5	95.6	11.4	104.4	8.6
VAT	163.1	22.9	181.0	21.6	224.8	18.6
Excise tax	70.3	10.0	79.0	9.4	93.9	7.8
Special service tax	1.9	1.5	11.0	1.3	12.4	1.0
Customs duty	44.7	6.3	57.0	6.8	68.5	5.7
Other taxes	62.1	8.7	83.8	10.0	100.9	8.3
B. Non-tax revenue	123.2	17.3	140.4	16.8	219.5	18.1
C. Asset revenue	0.8	0.1	1.0	0.1	0.8	0.06
D. Foreign aid	6.1	0.9	4.3	0.5	4.1	3.4

Source: Statistical Yearbook "Mongolia in the market economy", 1989-2002, Ulaanbaatar, 2004. p-120, Statistical Yearbook 2005, Ulaanbaatar, p-144. Data taken, from Ministry of Finance

In comparison with 2000, in 2006 total revenue increased 3.4 times, tax revenue – 3.8 times. However, by types of taxes the income tax rose 5.9 times, consumption tax /VAT, excise tax, customs duty/ rose 2.7 times.

It shows that

First: Revenue base has changed substantially;

Second: Rapid increase of income tax shows that production and services of the enterprises of our country have expanded and the volume of sales and profits have gone up.

In 2000-2006 actual improvements in the financial, budgetary and monetary-credit systems of Mongolia took place, the sector stabilized and its capacity improved.

The GDP rose dramatically by 10.6 per cent in 2004. However, it is expected to increase by 8% in 2006 and by 8.6 per cent in 2007. There is improvement in economic balance on the micro and macro levels. Here positive influence of internal and external factors plays a great role. Mutual influence and feedback of the financial, budgetary and monetary- credit sector and economic development have improved. Over the last years the tax revenue plan have been constantly exceeded, it has taken up over 80 per cent of the total revenue and its allotment and organization of tax collection have improved. Besides, the revenue base of tax revenue has been expanding and economic capability for tax paying has increased.

Table 3.10. Structure of tax revenue in 2000-2006 / by per cent/

	2000	**2001**	**2002**	**2003**	**2004**	**2005**	**2006**
Total tax revenue Of it:	100	100	100	100	100	100	100
Income tax	24,1	19,7	20,2	20,2	24,7	25,7	37,9
Social insurance charge	15,1	16,4	15,1	15,7	14,1	13,8	10,6
VAT	29,2	31,7	33	30,1	28	26,1	22,8
Excise tax	15,7	16,2	14,3	14,6	12,1	11,4	9,5
Special service tax	2,7	2,7	2,4	2,4	1,9	1,1	1,3
Customs duty	8,6	8,2	6,8	8,1	7,7	8,2	6,9
Other taxes	4,5	4,4	7,2	7,8	10,6	12,1	10,2

Source: Statistical data of the years and Data taken, from Ministry of Finance

The structure of tax revenue has changed. Although income tax has been increasing every year, in 200-2003 there was a tendency for decrease of its share, making up 20 per cent of the total revenue.

However, since 2004 its share went up and in 2006 it accounted for 37.9 per cent. It was influenced by decrease of the high levels of the income tax allotment scale /from 40 to 30%/ and increasing profit of enterprises. Furthermore, increasing prices of our major export products, copper and gold, at global markets over the last years led to increase in revenue from their export. Although non-direct tax, which is recognized as consumption tax, accounted for 60 per cent, in 2006 it covered only 40.5 per cent. It shows that our budget is still based on the consumption non-direct tax and this is a problem, which needs to be analyzed from theoretical and practical aspects. Besides, the amount of budget expenditure has increased and its structure has changed.

Table 3.11 Budget expenditure of Mongolia /2000-2006, billion tugrik, %/

	2000		**2001**		**2002**		**2003**	
	Total	**%**	**Total**	**%**	**Total**	**%**	**Total**	**%**
The sum of total expenditures and net lending	429.7	100	489.7	100	548.6	100	616.5	100
1. Current expenditure	314.1	73.1	366.7	74.9	413.5	75.4	446.3	72.4
Goods and service expenses	208.5	48.5	254.7	52.0	283.9	51.8	286.9	46.5
Credit service fees	18.2	4.2	16.5	3.4	19.6	3.6	33.6	5.5
Subsidy and current transaction	87.4	20.3	95.5	19.5	109.9	20.0	125.8	20.4
2. Asset expenses	52.6	12.2	59.1	12.1	68.1	12.4	88.8	14.4
3. Capital payment of internal and external loans	63.0	14.7	63.9	13	67.1	12.2	81.43	13.2

	2004		**2005**		**2006**	
	Total	**%**	**Total**	**%**	**Total**	**%**
The sum of total expenditures and net lending	752.5	100	764.6	100	1046.5	100
1. Current expenditure	538.7	71.6	600.3	78.5	795.3	76.0
Goods and service expenses	356.2	66.4	386.7	64.4	506.7	63.7
Credit service fees	22.1	4.1	20.1	3.3	20.2	2.5
Subsidy and current transaction	160.4	29.8	192.9	32.1	268.3	33.7
2. Asset expenses	104.9	13.9	89.8	11.7	177.6	17.0
3. Capital payment of internal and external loans	108.9	14.5	74.5	9.7	73.6	7.0

Source: Statistical data of the years and Data taken, from Ministry of Finance

Over the period the total budget expenditures have risen 2.4 times, current expenditure – 2.5 times and asset expenses have risen 3.4 times. Assets for capital investment have risen rapidly. In 2000-2006 due to increase in investment financing and increasing repayment of internal and external loans, there were changes in the structure of current expenditure.

Since 2003 the new law on "Administration and financing of budgetary organizations" has been implemented and this was the second step of the budget reforms. In spending of budget expenditure ministries of the sectors, or in other words, responsibilities of general budgetary administrators have risen and the contents of expenditure management has changed. In relation to that substantial changes have been made in the types of the budget expenditure.

Table 3.12 The structure of budget expenditure /billion tugrik, %/

	2000		2001		2002	
	Total	**%**	**Total**	**%**	**Total**	**%**
Total expenditure	429.7	100	489.7	100	548.6	100
Of it: General public service	42.2	9.8	50.4	10.3	54.0	9.8
Education	82.1	19.1	98.7	20.2	103.7	18.9
Health care	46.0	10.7	53.1	10.8	58.0	10.7
Insurance, social benefits	76.0	17.7	84.5	17.3	96.0	17.7
Housing, communal services	7.0	1.6	7.1	1.4	7.6	1.4
Leisure, sports, culture	14.3	3.3	15.1	3.1	17.5	3.2
Electricity and heating	8.6	2.0	11.2	2.3	15.0	2.7
Agriculture, Forestry	8.3	1.9	11.7	2.4	13.8	2.5
Minerals, Mining, construction	1.6	0.4	2.1	0.4	3.8	0.7
Transportation and Communication	8.9	2.1	13.3	2.7	16.2	3.0
Other economic	5.6	1.3	6.8	1.4	10.9	1.9

	2003		2004		2005	
	Total	**%**	**Total**	**%**	**Total**	**%**
Total expenditure	616.5	100	752.5	100	764.6	100
Of it: General public service	58.4	9.5	90.6	12.0	113.4	14.8
Education	120.9	19.6	131.7	17.5	153.8	20.1
Health care	57.6	9.3	71.9	9.6	77.8	10.2
Insurance, social benefits	113.9	18.5	146.7	19.5	184.8	24.2

Housing, communal services	7.3	1.2	10.8	1.4	11.1	1.4
Leisure, sports, culture	17.6	2.9	20.7	2.8	18.3	2.4
Electricity and heating	18.0	2.9	27.8	3.7	20.8	2.7
Agriculture, Forestry	12.9	2.1	12.3	1.6	12.8	1.8
Minerals, Mining, construction	3.6	0.5	4.0	0.5	4.0	0.5
Transportation and Communication	21.3	3.5	17.9	2.4	18.4	2.4
Other economic	12.4	2.0	14.3	1.9	14.6	1.9

Source: Statistical data of the years and data provided by Ministry of Finance

The purpose of budget expenditure has changed. As of 2003, 52% of budget expenditure were devoted to social sectors, but in 2006 it increased to 58.3%.

Increase in financing of education, health and science is becoming a development need.

The volume of financing of education rose 1.9 times in 2006 in comparison with 2000, making up 20.1% of the budget expenditure. Furthermore, financing of the health care sector went up 1.7 times accounting for 10.2% of the budget expenditure.

With regard to the goals put forward by the government on development of education and health care sectors and reforms, implemented in these sectors, the volume of budget financing and capital investment tends to increase even more.

By the population growth, its structure and the level of a household and personal income Mongolia is specific and currently there is a trend for some difficulties. Poverty and unemployment levels are still relatively high.

As a result of certain measures, taken by the government to increase pensions and benefits to disabled and poor, vulnerable people, the volume of assets to be paid out of the social insurance and benefit funds is likely to grow. This is the most important requirement of the present period. The total revenue of the social insurance fund reached 10.4 billion tugrik in 2006, increasing 2.7 times compared to 2000. Over 80 per cent of it is composed by the charges, paid by employers- enterprises and employees. Total expenditure of the social insurance fund reached 184.8 billion tugrik, increasing 2.4 times compared to 2000. 90.2% of it was spent on pensions and 3.4% - on benefits.

Over the last years /1999- 2006/ due to measures, taken to eliminate the difference between pensions, set up before and after 1995, additional assets of insurance financing were required. In the future, measures should be taken to make the social insurance fund capable of operating on the principle of self-financing.

Financial assistance and support of the government are vital for intensification of further economic development of Mongolia and for expansion of newly established small and medium enterprises and services. As a result of the government policies to develop infrastructure as a top priority and to support real investment, the volume of investment from the budget to this sector has increased. As of 2006 the amount of centralized budget investment reached 177.6 billion tugrik, twice greater compared to 2003, which makes up 14.7% of budget expenditure.

Changes have been made to the ratios and collection of the state centralized and local budget revenue and expenditure and it is important to raise responsibilities and importance of the budget adjustments in the country, provincial and city economic and social frame. Since 2003 in relation to regulation to manage the budget by the accounts of centralized statuary funds, the revenue, which went to the local budget or the financed spending have been centralized and allocated in the state centralized budget. In relation with this the changes have been made to the ratios of the state centralized budget and local budget.

By the sum of the 2005 budget of Mongolia 91.5% of total revenue and 96.0% of expenditure were implemented by the state centralized budget and the rest - by the local budget. In other words, the share of the local budget revenue and expenditure in the state centralized budget and its absolute amount have decreased since 2003. In the last three years the budget revenue and expenditure of provinces and the capital city have been increasing continuously. In comparison with 2003, in 2005 the net income went up 1.5 times and spending – 1.6 times. Tables 3.13; 3.14 show the budget revenue and expenditure of provinces and city by regions in 2002-2005.

Figure 3.13 Regional budget revenue (Million tugrik)

Provinces, city	2002	2003	2004	2005
Total	104.818.1	52.312.8	68.766.6	78.308.9
Western region				
Total	10.637.6	5117.5	7088.8	7527.7
Bayan- Ulgii	2062.7	887.5	1121.5	1235.0
Govi- Altai	1683.8	1003.4	1437.1	1519.9
Zavkhan	2170.6	974.2	1425.5	1629.5
Uvs	2380.3	1281.6	1603.2	1555.1
Khovd	2340.2	970.8	1501.4	1588.1
Mountainous Region				

Total	18755.6	10171.6	16560.0	17651.7
Arkhangai	2893.4	954.6	1252.9	1406.8
Bayankhongor	2097.4	980.3	1334.5	1507.8
Bulgan	2288.7	876.7	1297.5	2351.0
Orkhon	5344.7	4810.1	9586.4	9120.2
Uvurkhangai	3078.2	1272.4	1590.3	1632.3
Khuvsgul	3053.2	1277.5	1498.5	1633.5
Central region				
Total	19317.2	7846.0	11170.0	12907.8
Govisumber	608.3	536.9	578.0	604.5
Darkhan-Uul	4796.5	1384.7	1627.0	1845.7
Dornogovi	2607.7	1457.8	1856.0	2074.7
Dundgovi	1538.0	895.6	1109.6	1163.6
Umnugovi	1536.3	893.1	1645.9	2254.5
Selenge	4069.8	1264.6	1972.0	2093.0
Tuv	4160.6	1413.3	2381.6	2871.6
Eastern region				
Total	6140.4	2792.6	3539.4	3833.1
Dornod	2155.1	879.3	1147.4	1097.0
Sukhbaatar	1526.2	917.1	1077.2	1288.3
Khentii	2459.1	996.3	1314.8	1447.7
Ulaanbaatar				
Ulaanbaatar	49967.3	26385.0	30408.4	36388.8

As of 2006 Bulgan, Dornogovi, Umnugovi, Darkhan-Uul, Orkhon provinces and Ulaanbaatar city consolidated revenues in the national budget. The budget revenue of other provinces could not recover the expenditure and profits were transferred to give them financial assistance from the state budget.

With regard to the specific time and conditions the names of provinces whose revenues are to be consolidated in the state budget and those to be given financial assistance as well as the amount of the assistance are changing every year. One of determining indicators of macro economy, which determines economic stabilization is budget losses. In the country, where an economic system with the adjustment of the revenue and expenditure ratio is established, the budget does not have any losses or they are low.

Figure 3.14 Regional budget expenditure (MNT million)

Provinces , city	2002	2003	2004	2005
Total	168904.4	50112.1	68802.3	79343.2
Western region				
Total	28307.1	5340.0	6913.6	7568.9
Bayan- Ulgii	5596.0	929.1	1120.3	1237.9
Govi- Altai	5337.5	964.8	1447.2	1583.0
Zavkhan	5965.8	1128.4	1331.0	1619.1
Uvs	5794.6	1277.6	1542.1	1554.7
Khovd	5613.2	1040.0	1473.0	1574.2
Mountainous Region				
Total	34516.2	9777.6	15707.6	18918.6
Arkhangai	5687.2	983.8	1242.5	1356.3
Bayankhongor	5376.1	939.1	1350.7	1449.5
Bulgan	4819.7	917.3	1332.5	2350.2
Orkhon	5621.9	4317.5	8574.5	10448.2
Uvurkhangai	6202.6	1304.8	1727.5	1676.1
Khuvsgul	6808.6	1261.1	1479.8	1638.3
Central region				
Total	37807.3	8078.7	11069.0	12362.3
Govisumber	1521.5	553.5	569.0	601.0
Darkhan-Uul	7655.5	1367.3	1549.9	1855.6
Dornogovi	4965.6	1399.6	1802.4	2121.7
Dundgovi	3573.6	900.2	1110.0	1151.1
Umnugovi	3969.4	883.7	1538.0	1826.5
Selenge	8550.2	1454.8	2063.8	2136.0
Tuv	7571.4	1519.5	2436.0	2670.2
Eastern region				
Total	14589.9	2910.0	3530.3	3722.4
Dornod	4932.3	936.8	1173.7	1077.8
Sukhbaatar	4328.2	970.5	1060.6	1266.3
Khentii	5329.5	1002.6	1296.0	1378.2
Ulaanbaatar				
Ulaanbaatar	53683.8	24005.9	31581.8	36771.1

Source: Statistical Yearbook. 2005, Ulaanbaatar, 2006 p-149-150.

Budget losses are recognized as one of abnormal phenomena that influence negatively economic development, the balance and harmony. There is no principle that the budget of developing countries with small-scale economy should have losses, even in the developed countries there are cases, when there are losses in the budget.

There are several different reasons for budget losses in our country:

- Continuous economic recession;
- Financial deterioration of tax-payer –entities;
- Inevitable increase in demand for expenditure, especially increase in investment financing;
- Excessive increase of non-industrial, non-designated, inefficient expenditure;
- Occurrence of sudden abnormal social and natural phenomena / wars, earthquake, fire, infectious diseases /, loss or damages and catastrophe;
- Occurrence of inappropriate changes with negative effect in foreign economic and political relations.

Table 3.15 Budget losses 1991–1999 / million tugrik /

	1991	**1992**	**1993**	**1994**	**1995**
Current balance	1340.5	741.4	10298.7	9964.0	34176.1
Total balance	-2.160	-106.2	-6783.0	-13471.9	-8447.5
Total losses in GDP /%/	-15.1	-4.8	-4.1	-4.2	-1.5

	1996	**1997**	**1998**	**1999**
Current balance	26150.9	13413.6	-5643.0	8.9
Total balance	-16643.4	-75584.0	-116695.8	-106896.6
Total losses in GDP /%/	-2.6	-9.1	-14.3	-11.6

The current budget balance had not seen any losses since 1993 and revenue had been increasing until it decreased in 1996 and there were losses worth 5.6 billion tugrik in 1998. In general, total budget losses had been increasing each year as it reached 116.7 billion tugrik in 1998 and in 1999 the losses reached 106.9 billion tugrik. The ratio of the losses in GDP had been decreasing, but it went up since 1997, equalling 14.3% in 1998 and 11.6 % in 1999.

A trend for budget loss reduction by absolute and relative amounts was observed in 2000-2006 and the budget total balance has been reported as profitable since 2005.

Table 3.16 Budget losses 2000–2006 /million tugrik ,%/

	2000	**2001**	**2002**	**2003**
Current balance	32086.5	63250.6	56281.5	80089.9
Total balance	-78569.4	-50440.5	-71590.2	-80741.2
Total losses in GDP /%/	-7.7	-4.5	-5.8	-5.9

	2004	2005	2006
Current balance	167593.6	232296.0	408902.6
Total balance	-39372.8	73261.2	162681.8
Total losses in GDP /%/	-2.1	3.2	5.6

The revenue of the current budget balance has been increasing each year and even though the total balance has been at loss, losses have been declining each year from the planned amount and their share in the GDP has been reducing. In 2005 the current budget balance had profits of 232.3 billion tugrik and the total balance – of 73.2 billion tugrik, which made up 3.2 per cent of GDP. In 2006 the revenue of current balance was around 400 billion tugrik.

This indicates that the budget and its financial potential are improving. The important task is to develop the budget capacity and to strengthen the profitability of total balance.

In connection with deepening of market relations, the growth and stabilization of economic and social development, changes in times and conditions, administration and planning of the budget revenue and expenditure and the taxation system need to be upgraded further.

Progress in economic and social development of our country and establishment of further conditions for sustainable growth have good effects on stabilization and capacity of financial, budgetary and monetary credit systems. In 2002 new laws on "Administration and financing of budgetary organizations" and "Consolidated Budget of Mongolia" were passed and have been implemented resolutely. This is recognized as an important stage of budget reforms.

Principal changes have been made to the relations between the centralized budget of Mongolia and local budgets.

The goals of the reform are:

- To improve budget planning, financing and control;
- To shift from a short-term /yearly/ planning system to a medium – term / 3 years'/ planning system;
- To connect economic and social priority directions with asset resources;
- To make budget norms and normatives more effective;
- To introduce a consolidated accounts system of statuary funds, to carry out financing by commodity supply, which is recognized as the real result of activities of budgetary organizations and to improve the control;

In the future, policies on medium-term budget and tax reforms are intended to ensure macro economic stabilization and growth, to improve budget balance, to strengthen the access and quality of public services and to allocate resources effectively.

In that way, following objectives will be implemented:

- Tax reforms are to be implemented by expanding the taxation and budgetary revenue base, reducing the tax burden, improving tax allotment and collection and creating an equal, fair environment. To make taxing a main tool of encouraging capital investment and economic growth and maintaining the efficient ratio between consumption and accumulation;
- To prepare budget planning, utilization and reports by sectors, to connect them closely with results of policy activities of the sectors and to improve duties and responsibilities of budgetary organizations such as ministries and agencies - main budget administrators- in development of the budget, its approval, implementation and reporting;
- To create conditions for control of each revenue and spending of budgetary organizations, to avoid untargeted expenditure by introducing a comprehensive accounting system for public /i.e. budgetary / organizations and installing an accounting data software;
- To upgrade budget cash management, to create possibilities for drawing spare cash in the budget into circulation and to strengthen its accounting control;
- In the frame of the Regional Development concept to upgrade the centralized and local budget relations, to improve responsibilities of local officials and links with local people on the access and quality of public services in order to minimize the difference between urban and rural areas, to intensify social and economic development of provinces and improve livelihood of countryside people.

Comprehensive measures of present budget reforms have been implemented since 2003 and over the last years results of financial and budgetary indicators are improving.

Since 2007 substantial reforms have been made in the budget revenue of Mongolia. Laws of main types of direct and non-direct taxes such as the corporate income tax, income tax, VAT, excise tax have been renewed, the amount of allocated tax has decreased and conditions and regulations have been changed.

To improve the rationale of financial, budgetary and monetary-credit policies it is important to plan the real growth and speed of GDP and its proper distribution ratios in the long and short-term. Hence, working out a 15-20 year- prognostic guidelines of economic and social development of the country on a scientific basis and implementing it in a compulsory way during the rule of any government has many benefits.

In order to upgrade the financial, budgetary administration and management of Mongolia following objectives should be put forward and implemented:

- ✓ To improve financial resources and their supply on the basis of mobilizing internal resources to implement economic and social tasks and to strengthen efficiency of asset utilization;
- ✓ To strengthen the financial and budgetary capacity; to establish a proper ratio of internal and external sources of financial resources and to improve statuary debt management, guided by the principle of mobilizing domestic reserves;
- ✓ To carry out a proper investment policy; to intensify increase of internal resources in its financing and to attract foreign investment;
- ✓ To implement an effective monetary policy of government; to strengthen monetary- credit systems and to make it a reliable and sustainable tool of economic and social development.

Following measures should be taken in order to upgrade the legal basis and administration of taxation and improve the system:

- To reduce the tax burden;
- To extend the tax base, to increase profit and revenue of tax-payers and to provide conditions for self-financing;
- To integrate methods of motivating and encouraging tax-payers, to upgrade its ways and forms and to raise awareness of tax-payers to make them pay and report taxes actively;
- On the basis of improving financial capacity of tax-payers, to raise importance of the direct or income tax and to renew the internal structure of the tax system by improving the rationale for the rate and types of non-direct taxes;
- To carry out all organizational, collection and supervising activities on the basis of creating a financial data network.

To direct budget expenditure towards providing for and improving accesss to common and inevitable needs of sustainable economic and social development, to improve efficiency of asset utilization. To do this there is a need:

- To increase centralized budget resources for financing investment;
- To increase sustainable allocation of budget assets for human development, particularly, education, health care, social benefits and poverty alleviation and

in this frame to combine appropriately internal and external resources of financing;

- To upgrade the current mechanism of reform of budget administration and financing;
- In connection with the regional development trends to take measures to alter the present centralization of budget revenue and expenditure in order to provide conditions for local self-government, independence and self-financing.

To do these:

1) To determine the indicators of economic, social development of the regions (the province, the city) and in line with them to plan demand for financial resources in long and medium terms;
2) On this basis to plan the budget revenue realistically. The main sources of the budget revenue will be comprised of income taxes of individuals and local enterprises, which run their business on the targeted territory, and other commissions and charges;
3) By raising financial duties, rights and responsibilities of provincial and city officials to take comprehensive measures to strengthen the independence of local governments.

In this way, budget reforms are real processes, adjusted to the development of market relations, progress and reforms of monetary financial relations and in this meaning they need to be upgraded continuously.

The top priority issue of economic and financial policy is increase of investment. Attention needs to be paid to appropriate combination of internal and external resources of investment and improvement of efficiency. A goal to increase domestic resources of investment should be put forward. Establishment of realistic demand and directions with regard to the further carrying capacity of liquidity and a capability of absorbing foreign loans and aids, improvement of utilization and adjustment efficiency of assets and enhancement of foreign debt management will be continuous actions.

Social Insurance system

The history of social welfare in our country has long-standing traditions. Its contents and forms have been enriched in the way from 1921, when the state coordinated activities of looking after elders, orphans and poor people, until today and have changed completely. Nowadays, it has developed into an independent system of social insurance and social welfare.

Development of the Mongolian social insurance and social welfare system is divided into 3 periods:

1) 1925-1960 The system of social welfare was established and quality changes in the services of social welfare were made ;
2) 1960-1980 Social welfare in connection with the development of economic and social relations of the country was formed as a consolidated independent system organizationally.
3) 1980-1990 A preparatory period to shift to the social insurance system and to improve social welfare of citizens. For instance, a "Pension Fund" was established in 1990 and sources of the fund were comprised of social insurance premium, paid by owners of entities and self-employed people and the state budget assets. The "Law on social insurance" was passed in 1991 and the premiums have been accumulated in a special state –owned centralized fund. The approval of the "Law on benefits " of Mongolia in 1991 established a legal basis for social welfare.

An inevitable need to reform the system of social welfare arose with transition to the market.

One of the biggest reforms, implemented in the social and economic frame was the change of a social insurance system in line with the market relations standards. In the conditions, when many types of property were established and different forms of entities started their business, not only the state, but also owners of entities and insured people took responsibility for social welfare of the citizens. The system of social insurance and social welfare was changed radically regarding the accumulation of asset resources, legal coordination, organizational forms, its methods and a mechanism. Its legal basis was established with a package of "Laws on Social insurance", which was passed in 1994 by the State Ikh Khural and went into force since 1995.

Following principles were taken into account:

1. Social insurance premium, paid by business entities and their workers, regardless of the type of property, form asset sources of the fund;
2. In case of paying social insurance premium and fulfilling certain conditions persons have a right to be paid out pensions and benefits by the Social Insurance Fund;
3. Each type of insurance had funds with their own sources. Methods of establishing funds, amounts and spending rules were legalized;

4. The previously combined form of social insurance and social welfare was divided and 2 systems were established with regulations for separating asset sources and allocation.

According to the present system social insurance is comprised of five types, namely, a pension insurance, benefits insurance, health insurance, insurance for injury and occupational diseases, unemployment insurance. Each type has its own sources of established premium of its revenue and it is obliged to allocate assets according to its purposes.

The income sources of the Social Insurance Fund are as follows:

1) social insurance premium payable by the insured ;
2) social insurance premium payable by employers;
3) bank deposit interest on the fund's surplus
4) fines imposed for late payment of social insurance premium

   and other sources.

However, certain amounts of assets are transferred to the social insurance from the State general budget and most of it goes to the Pension Insurance fund.

Table 3.17 Income and expenditure of the Social Insurance Fund (1995-2005) (million tugrik)

	1995	**1996**	**1997**	**1998**	**1999**	**2000**
Total income	30664.1	37127.4	45440.9	52832.3	60014.8	80025.0
Of it: Issued from the budget	7352.2	6883.9	5257.9	8560.8	11900.0	14771.0
Total expenditure	24888.3	34008.7	40377.5	51947.8	53722.5	70529.0

	2001	**2002**	**2003**	**2004**	**2005**
Total income	94499.9	107910.9	12127.0	157338.9	176349.8
Of it: Issued from the budget	20958.1	24422.3	24442.3	42008.9	44224.1
Total expenditure	78942.5	90300.4	106832.4	137135.2	155854.2

Source: Reports on Social Insurance

Over the last years the revenue of Social Insurance has increased, it has strengthened financially and designated expenditure has gone up. In comparison with 1995, in 2005 the revenue rose 5.7 times, while expenditure went up 6.3 /3/ times. In this period assets received from the National budget rose 6 times. While in 1995 76 per cent of total assets of Social Insurance came from premium, in 2005 it was 74.9 per cent. In 2006 income of the Social Insurance Fund reached 162.6 billion tugrik and budget financing increased as well.

As the total and share of the charge revenue increases, there is a tendency for decline of financing from the budget.

The structure and growth of the Social Insurance Fund revenue is shown in the following table:

Table 3.18 The structure and growth of Social Insurance Fund revenue

(million tugrik, %)

		1995		**2001**		**2004**		**2005**		**2005/ 1995**	**2005/ 2004**
		Total	%	Total	%	Total	%	Total	%	Times	%
Total		20209.3	100	68174.5	100	109235.8	100	126178.6	100	6.2	115.5
Types	Pension insurance	12623.4	62.5	43618.8	64.0	70458.7	64.5	80341.3	63.4	6.4	114.0
	Benefits insurance	1468.7	7.3	4385.5	6.4	6955.4	6.4	8260.6	6.5	5.6	118.8
	Insurance for employment - related injury and occupa-tion-nal diseases	874.1	4.3	3098.1	4.5	5114.6	4.7	6030.0	4.8	6.9	117.9
	Unemployment insurance	633.8	3.1	2122.5	3.1	3434.9	3.1	4121.2	3.3	6.5	120.0
	Health insurance	4609.3	22.8	14949.6	21.9	23272.2	21.3	27425.5	21.7	6.0	117.8

Source: Data of State Social Insurance General office

As of 2005 premium income of pension fund accounted for 63.4 per cent of total premium income and premium of health insurance fund – 21.7 per cent. The amount of revenue from all types of insurance increased 5.6- 5.9 times during 1995-2005.

Establishment of the health insurance system in our country influenced substantially increase in sources of financing expenditure of health care organizations and development of social insurance.

Table 3.19 The amount of Social Insurance contributions payable by the insured and by the employers

№	Types of Insurances	Amount and weight of premium / by per cent/	
		Social insurance premium payable by employers	Social insurance premium payable by the insured
1	Pension insurance fund	13.5	5.5
2	Benefits insurance fund	1.0	1.0
3	Insurance fund for employment-related injury and occupational diseases	1.0: 2.0: 3	
4	Unemployment insurance fund	0.5	0.5
5	Health insurance fund	3.0	3.0
Total		19.0; 20; 21	10.0

Source: "Law on social insurance"

Before1995 employers paid social insurance premium at 13.5 per cent, however, the premiums of five types of insurance rose in total by 5.5- 7.5% and stayed at 19-21%. The insured were not obliged to pay social insurance premium to the social insurance system before the transition, but now a new rule was set up to pay 10% of their earnings. 80% of health insurance premium of civil servants are paid by the state.

Students of professional schools, self-employed, herders should pay their own social insurance premium themselves. The state is obliged to take responsibility for health insurance premium of children under 16 years old / up to 18 years old if they study in secondary schools /; citizens for whom their pension is the only income source; mothers (fathers) taking care of their babies under the age of 2 years old / 3 if they are twins/, persons, who receive pensions according to the Social Insurance Law, persons on regular military service. Detention centres are responsible for health insurance premium of convicts serving sentence. The number of individuals insured on voluntary coverage has increased.

The minimum of social insurance premium payable monthly by a person on voluntary coverage is at the following rate

1) pension insurance 9.5% of wages or income
2) benefits insurance 1.0%
3) insurance against employment injury and occupational diseases 1.0%

The rate of health insurance premium is determined yearly by the Government. The minimum rate of monthly health insurance premium of persons on voluntary coverage is determined by the related authorities. In case of full payment of health insurance premium for no less than 12 months by persons on voluntary coverage, the privilege is established to have treatment charges from the Health Insurance Fund.

Health Insurance was transferred to the Social insurance since January 1, 1996. Currently it takes up 21.7 per cent of total Social Insurance premium. A subsidy from the state took up 23.0 per cent of the total premium in 1995, it was 22.2% in 2001 and 25.1% - in 2005.

The assets of the Social Insurance Fund is disbursed to persons meeting specific requirements, stipulated in the legislation for the following purposes: paying out pensions and benefits, financing other payments and expenses, stated in the legislation. Furthermore, recovery, prevention and health measures taken for employees are financed by the Social Insurance Fund. Hence, Social Insurance plays an important economic role. On the whole Social Insurance plays an important social role by providing for human development, livelihood, particularly, showing special consideration for the poor and vulnerable.

Total expenditures of the Social Insurance Fund increased 5.9 -6.9 times in 2005 in comparison with 1995 and went up by 13% against previous year. In general such increase is observed each year. In total expenditure the pension expenditure took up 77.7 per cent; the benefits expenditure – 3.3 per cent; and financing of health insurance took up 15.2 per cent. In comparison with the previous year, the expenditure of Social Insurance Fund reached 198.8 billion tugrik and increased by 27.6 per cent.

Table 3.20 The structure and growth of Social Insurance Fund expenditures (million tugrik, %)

		1995		**2001**		**2004**		**2005**		**2005/ 1995**	**2005/ 2004**
		Total	%	Total	%	Total	%	Total	%	Times	%
Total expenditure		24888.4	100	78942.5	100	137135.2	100	155854.2	100	6.3	113.6
Types	Pension insurance fund	17585.0	70.7	58593.6	74.2	106602.3	77.7	121048.1	77.7	6.9	113.6
	Benefits insurance fund	855.0	3.4	2925.3	3.7	4557.4	3.3	5076.5	3.3	5.9	111.4
	Insurance fund for employment injury and occupational diseases	18.1		2232.3	2.8	4034.2	2.9	4760.3	3.1		117.9

	Unemployment insurance fund			561.7	0.7	1039.8	0.7	1280.1	0.8		123.2
	Health insurance fund	6430.3	25.8	14629.4	18.5	20901.3	15.2	23689.3	15.2	3.7	113.3

Source: Data of State Social Insurance General office

According to the Constitution and the "Law on Pension", the insured person, who paid pension insurance premium for not less than 20 years in total is eligible for a retirement pension on attainment of 60 years old. Women who paid pension insurance premium for not less than 20 years can be eligible for a retirement pension on attainment of 55 years old (those who gave birth to 4 and more children – 50). Also persons can get disability pensions and pensions for loss of their breadwinners.

Table 3.21 The structure and growth of Pension Fund expenditures (million tugrik, %)

		1995		**2001**		**2004**		**2005**		**2005/ 1995**	**2005/ 2004**
		Total	%	Total	%	Total	%	Total	%	Times	%
Total expenditure		17584.9	100	60661.2	100	110360.1	100	125413.6	100	7.1	113.6
Types	Retirement pension	13900.0	73.8	41851.5	70.1	73633.1	66.7	8576.0	66.6	6.0	113.5
	Disability pension	1522.3	8.0	6212.9	10.4	14282.7	12.9	16622.0	13.3	10.9	116.8
	Loss of breadwinner's pension	2143.2	11.4	6740.7	11.3	12103.0	9.1	12972.7	10.3	6.1	107.1
	Pension for persons on regular military service	19.3	1.0	3788.5	6.3	6583.5	5.9	7877.4	6.2	414.1	119.6

Source: Yearly repots and data on Social Insurance

Assets for pensions, distributed from the Social Insurance Fund in 2005 increased 6.0 times against 1995. In the sum of assets for pensions the retirement pension accounted for 66.6 per cent; disability pension – for 13.3 per cent; loss of breadwinner's pension-for 10.3 per cent and 6.2 per cent was dedicated to the pension for retired servicemen.

Substantial measures have been taken to increase the amount of pensions and to eliminate the pension difference in 2005-2007. In 2006 pensions, worth 165.2 billion tugrik were received by 287.2 thousand pensioners. Each year the number of pensioners rises by around 3.5-8.0 thousand people, so it rose by 32.8 thousand compared to 2000. Preliminary results show that 11.2 per cent of total population are of working age and 29.7 per cent of active population are covered by pension. The minimum amount of payroll has been set up by the Government 9 times since December 31,

2000 and since January 1, 2007 the minimum amount of full pension reached 51750 tugrik, that of the rate-equalled pension - 34500 tugrik and in comparison with 2000 the increase was 3.2 -3.5 times. The average amount of pension was 18200 tugrik in 2000, however, as of January 1, 2007 it reached 61300 tugrik, i.e. increased 3.4 times.

Substantial measures have been taken to increase the amount of pensions and to eliminate the pension difference in 2005-2007. In 2006 pensions, worth 165.2 billion tugrik were received by 287.2 thousand pensioners. Each year the number of pensioners rises by around 3.5-8.0 thousand people, so it rose by 32.8 thousand compared to 2000. Preliminary results show that 11.2 per cent of total population are of working age and 29.7 per cent of active population are covered by pension. The minimum amount of payroll has been set up by the Government 9 times since December 31, 2000 and since January 1, 2007 the minimum amount of full pension reached 51750 tugrik, that of the rate-equalled pension - 34500 tugrik and in comparison with 2000 the increase was 3.2 -3.5 times. The average amount of pension was 18200 tugrik in 2000, however, as of January 1, 2007 it reached 61300 tugrik, i.e. increased 3.4 times.

With the objective to resolve the problem of eliminating pension differences, reflected in the "The Government Action Plan", the Government issued a resolution (№207) and according to the resolution, the amount of pensions of 291.6 thousand pensioners was renewed since August 1. In order to eliminate pension differences of 44.4 % or 129,5 thousand pensioners altogether 12.4 billion tugrik were spent .

In 2006 165.2 billion tugrik were paid to 287.4 thousand people from the Pension Insurance Fund, 5.8 billion tugrik were paid to 91.6 thousand people from the Benefits Insurance Fund, 6.6 billion tugrik were paid to 9.0 thousand people from the Insurance Fund for employment-related injury and occupational diseases, 1.6 billion tugrik were paid to 9.8 thousand people from the Unemployment Insurance Fund and by duplicated amount 26.0 billion tugrik were paid to 3.8 thousand people from the Health Insurance Fund. In total, 198.8 billion tugrik were paid for pensions, benefits, charges, treatment costs and medicine costs discount.

Social insurance and social security shall be one of the current and prospective problems of the government economic and social development policy. Requirements to upgrade the system of social insurance, particularly, to increase the supply and sufficiency of pensions and benefits are put forward.

There is a need to review thoroughly experiences of other countries of the world, which upgraded their systems for years and adopt a system, which suits the specific conditions of Mongolia.

When practice of other countries is examined, it can be noticed that 3 kinds of after-retirement system are implemented. They are as follows:

- Distributional;
- Semi-accumulative;
- Completely Accumulative

A distributional system is the principle of replacing half of expenditure with revenue by financing pensioners through premium, paid by employers and the insured. Insufficient assets are paid from the state budget.

A semi-accumulative system is a process of transfer from the distribution to a complete accumulative system by using combined distributional and accumulation methods;

An accumulative system uses premium, paid through all life of the insured to the Pension Fund to pay a pension to the person and accumulation of premium is used for self-financing.

In Mongolia a system, when expenditures are compensated by revenue is implemented and the shift from this system to the Complete Accumulation system will certainly face some difficulties because of such problems as instability of economic indicators and monetary rate at the macro level; underdevelopment of infrastructure and stock market; lack of reliable investment environment and a weak financial mechanism.

Considering these circumstances, it is necessary to make a gradual shift from the social insurance distribution system to the Semi-accumulation system and in the future to move to the Complete Accumulation system. In other words, the process of transferring to the Complete Accumulation system on the principle, when pension insurance premium paid by the person for all his working life will return back to him as a pension, shall be the priority goal in the near future.

Opening an individual pension insurance premium account is a tool to attract the interest of insured to accumulate a pension fund and to make a transition from a pension system, paid by the state, to the market relations. Since 2001 a method of an individual pension insurance premium account has been introduced in order to provide preparatory measures to shift to the Semi-accumulation system. An individual pension insurance premium account will provide conditions for establishing pensions for retiring persons on the principle of Semi-accumulation system, thus making a gradual shift from the current distribution system to the accumulation one. Measures are taken to involve contributors born on January 1, 1960 and later to have an individual pension insurance premium account established for them. Over 536.7 thousand persons born on January 1, 1960 and later have opened their individual pension insurance premium accounts and 345.6 billion tugrik has been accumulated in those accounts.

All amounts of premium, paid by the insurer in the individual pension insurance premium account and certain amounts of premium, paid by employers will be registered and the contributions will be kept in the account. It is considered to be paid back not for others' pensions and benefits, but only for the insured. The assets in the account will increase by interest, calculated by yearly inflation and the real growth of payroll. Furthermore, there are possibilities to increase assets of the Insurance Fund and an individual pension insurance premium account by selecting and implementing reliable methods to support economic growth and protect assets from depreciation such as involving certain amounts of asset surplus in government bonds, security market, reliable domestic and foreign investment, purchasing shares of profitable companies, increasing assets by depositing them in commercial banks and lending short-term credits.

Final objectives of the pension reform are as follows:

- To increase economic growth and to improve living standards;
- To protect interests of the senior ctizen, to provide the present insured with appropriate future pension revenues;
- To introduce a fair pension system, which allows to receive a pension according to the amount of premium, paid to the Social Insurance Fund
- To maintain social security by providing a guaranteed minimum pension and providing all pensioners with pensions for the duration of their lives.

Pension reforms will change the system of Pension Insurance to the structure of Semi-accumulation system by replacing expenditures with revenue.

It is important to do a gradual transition to the new system to avoid doing any harm to old people, who have not worked sufficient time to accumulate enough assets for pensions and to set up a stock market, capable of absorbing contributions in the case of implementing an accumulation system.

Persons born on January 1, 1960 and later will be covered by the new system. However, pension issues of persons born before January 1, 1960 will be guided by old regulations. In addition, a question is raised what the persons should do, if they are not covered by the pension system. In this case the person will not have any pension, because they have not accumulated any assets by paying premium for their own pensions.

These reforms are in line with the governmental policy, directed to:

- ✓ Taking care of senior citizen and people, who are nearing the pension age;
- ✓ Creating conditions for persons, who are currently employed, to get a sufficient pension at the retirement age;
- ✓ Maintaining stable asset sources of the Pension Insurance Fund in the long term;
- ✓ Equal treatment of the insured, guided by a fair distribution principle;
- ✓ Implementing economic reforms, based on market economy; developing private property market and intensifying economic development.

Investment policy and financing

While previously investment was regarded only as expenditure, related to accumulating, renewing and fixing fixed assets, in the conditions of market relationships an investment is the current commitment of money and other resources in the hope of reaping future benefits by extending the scopes of production and service and improving the efficiency. This concept expands the understanding and scopes of investment. Investment can be not only assets in the form of money, but also stocks, other securities, shares, conveying technology, machinery and equipment, received as technical assistance, licences, loans, other assets, ownerships rights and intellectual values. One of trends in the market conditions is the concept of regarding intellectual investment as a key to development along with investment in assets.

Investment management is a set of interrelated activities of developing, planning, financing, organizing, encouraging and monitoring an investment policy and it is the hub of financial policies and activities. Investment itself is a complex instrument used to reach the goals of expanding social production, increasing its quality and efficiency and on this basis improving livelihood and living conditions of the citizens. However, it is not the final goal in itself. In the first years of the transition to the market relations, the attitudes were primarily to ignore the efficiency of investment and to worship the increasing foreign investment. This led to negative influence on investment quality and benefits.

Table 3.22 The ratio of investment to GDP

Indicators	1990	1993	1996	2000	2003	2004	2005
Investment by yearly price, billion tugrik	3.4	45.2	135.3	284.7	418.0	501.9	557.3
GDP, by yearly price, billion tugrik	10.4	194.8	646.5	1018.9	1461.2	1910.9	2266.5

Investment profit /tugrik/	3.0	4.31	4.78	3.58	3.49	3.81	4.07

Source: Statistical Yearbook "Mongolia in the market economy", Ulaanbaatar, 2004. p-94,136
Statistical Yearbook 2006, Ulaanbaatar, p-113,156.

This indicator is relatively low in comparison with other countries and it also fluctuates a lot. Furthermore, it is necessary to take into account a fact that in the last years the growth of GDP was caused by the growth of the number of workplaces and the growth of gold and copper prices in the world market rather than by investment. However, there was a leap in volume of investment, when it increased by 163.9 times in 2005 against 1990 and 12.3 times in comparison with 1993. The Incremental Capital-Output Ratio (ICOR) / the amount of GDP equals to 1 investment/ increased each year in the period of 1990-1996 and although there was a decrease in 1999-2000, there is a tendency for increase in recent years. This shows the importance of improving investment efficiency along with expanding investment.

On the other hand, the above indicator is not able to show investment efficiency of the year objectively, because the amount of GDP of the year is the result of investment, made not only in that year, but also in the previous years. Thus, the efficiency of investment is estimated by ICOR in the countries with highly developed markets. The Incremental Capital-Output Ratio (ICOR), is the ratio of investment to growth, which equals to 1 divided by the marginal product of capital.

The ICOR of our country is lower compared to other countries. This indicator is estimated by the Ministry of Finance as GDP and investment have gone up substantially in recent years.

Figure 3.23 The ratio of investment to GDP which equals to 1 / tugrik/

Indicators	**2003**	**2004**	**2006**	**2007 projected**
Total investment by balance payment, billion tugrik	426.6	501.8	782.1	997.7
GDP by yearly prices, billion tugrik	1461.2	1910.9	2891.7	3305.4
The percentage of investment in GDP /%/	29.20	26.26	27.06	29.6
GDP growth, by yearly prices, %	17.77	30.71	27.59	14.3
Economic efficiency of investment /Total investment equals to GDP 1 tugrik /tugrik/	1.65	0.86	0.98	2.1

Source: Government of Mongolia. The planned 2007 overall budget, 2006, p-46

Thus, it is estimated that the investment worth 1.25 tugrik was made to increase GDP by around 1 tugrik in 2003-2006.This indicator is lower 2-3 times against the averages in the Russian Federation, China, the countries in the South-East Asia and most developing countries. It shows a need to increase investment. In the future, it is necessary to determine well the role of investment in the economic and social development of the country and to improve its planning and financing. Technology and the sector structure of investment should also be determined clearly.

While in 1990 in the technological structure of investment the percentage of construction works was 64.9%, the percentage of machinery, equipment and tools was 23.5%, the ratio changed to 45.4; 35.5 in 1996, 25.4; 54.8 in 2000, 35.7; 51.8 in 2004, 35.3; 53.2 in 2005.The relatively high percentage of construction and other works /geology, exploration, cartography etc./ is due to construction and industrialization, which have been a part of reconstruction of our country and it influences specifically the economic efficiency and productivity of investment.

Along with expansion and deepening of market relations, investment resources are becoming diverse. In conditions when cooperation is deepening on the basis of financial market development, expansion of foreign relations and diversification of enterprises, investment resources can be mobilized from anywhere, if we can call for investment management, directed to the future and have trust of investors. However, we should take into consideration that every financial instrument has a price, therefore, any investment should be economically efficient.

Table 3.24 The state of investment financing / billion tugrik/

Resources	1990	1993	1996	2000	2003	2004	2005
Total	3.4	45.2	135.3	284.7	418.0	501.9	557.3
State and regional budget	1.2	0.5	8.4	36.3	55.1	69.0	89.0
Bank loans	0.5	4.4	5.0	22.7	29.8	49.6	74.4
Owner's capital	0.5	11.8	39.4	56.5	67.7	142.8	100.4
Foreign loans and aid	1.2	24.0	82.4	168.0	265.4	240.5	293.5

Source: Statistical Yearbook "Mongolia in the market economy", Ulaanbaatar, 2004. p-136
Statistical Yearbook 2005, Ulaanbaatar 2006, p-156

The survey reveals that in 1989-1992 investment was made through the budget and foreign loans and aid. Gradually there was a tendency of making investment through financing of enterprises` assets and foreign loans and aid. As of 1996 budget assets took up 6.2% of investment resources, bank loans- 3.6%, owner's equity – 2.91%, foreign loans and aids accounted for 61.1% or 82.4 billion tugrik. By 2000 the percentage of owner's equity decreased to 19.8%, bank loans went up a bit to 8.0%. Even though foreign loans and aid rose twice by absolute amount in comparison with 1996, their percentage in the total resources of investment decreased to 59.0%. By the 2005 totals in the total resources of investment the state budget accounted for 16%, bank loans – 13.3%, owner's equity – 18.0% and external resources took up 52.7%. Only in the period from 2000 to 2005 resources, worth 1378.7 billion tugrik were mobilized from outside. The role of bank loans in investment was limited until 2000, because there was not substantial increase of long-term deposits in commercial banks and there were substantial fluctuations each year. However, the loan amount has been increasing gradually since 2000, reaching 74.4 billion tugrik in 2005.

One important comprehensive instrument to increase owner's equity resources in investment, to improve investment efficiency and implement new management is financial leasing. Especially, in conditions, when the unit capacity of equipment has increased and along with it the prices have gone up, any country uses leasing to purchase machinery and equipment. For Mongolia the importance of leasing relations is great and there is a need to organize this relations on a high professional level and access its benefits. Although there is an onset of financial leasing in investment, the survey shows that often it is a just on paper. The "Law on Leasing" passed in 2006 should become a stimulus for conducting and expanding this action in the right course.

In case, when highly- priced, durable industrial machinery and equipment is purchased on financial leasing, the producer and the leasing company require two things from the lessee. First: To maintain high utilization efficiency of the machinery and equipment and depreciate them in the shortest possible period; Second: To have high financial capacity and pay the leasing payment on time. In order to warrant these, the lessee has to work out a long and mid-term / leasing terms/ financial plans and to verify the plan with related contracts. Actually, it is an action to estimate the leasing contract and payment rationale. The higher the leasing payment, the shorter utilization period of the machinery and equipment, which shows that production and financial activities of the leasing company are in good shape.

In the current conditions, when owner's equity resources are limited, it is important to increase the role and significance of the depreciation charge. Only in the industrial sector, in its expenditure structure / by yearly price/ the percentage of depreciation of fixed assets increased from 5.4% to 17.3% in 1995-1999, but decreased from 16.6 to 12.0% in 2000-2005.

In other words, by our approximate estimations, yearly depreciation fees, worth 120.0 billion tugrik are established in the industrial sector. If we add depreciation fees of sectors with a lot of fixed assets, such as construction, transportation and communication, the amount of depreciation fees, which are established every year would reach 300.0 billion tugrik. If these enormous resources were turned into an actual fund even for a short period and utilized to finance investment, there would be possibilities for substantial increase in investment. We complain of insufficient internal accumulation to undertake industrial intensification and lack of own investment resources, but if we are not able to utilize such resources and continue acting as highly developed countries, where the costs of fixed assets are decreased and written off by depreciation amount, it might be a bit early in case of our country. Even the USA used to establish a real fund of depreciation fees and utilized them as actual resources of investment. Thus, it seems wise to utilize depreciation fees by establishing an actual fund and using it to finance investment over certain period.

The real investment and financial investment are tightly connected with each other. Even though everyone understands importance of developing stock market, thus intensifying competitiveness in the financial market and decreasing prices of financial instruments, there have not been any achievements yet. In developed countries in conditions, where shareholding companies are dominating, prices of financial instruments are established in the course of competition in the financial market and choices of financial resources are increasing, the real and financial investment increase steadily, which gives real outcomes. However, in Mongolia there were 475 companies, the securities of which were registered in the stock market in 1995, but this number decreased constantly, reaching 400 in 2000 and 392 in 2005. There were numerous reasons, but the main ones are related to the fact that the state regulatory instruments, including tax laws and regulations were not consistent with economic interests of private sector. However, there is an expectation that amendments, made in the main tax laws in 2006 will give an considerable impetus to investment. It is important that 2007 is announced a year of stock market activation. Currently it is not clear if Mongolia should have the American style financial market with stock market dominance or a European style /German and French/ alternative with monetary market priority. Stock market in Mongolia is in its infant stage of development. The secondary market is not yet formed and is not able to actively support investment. If the world financial market examined, there are countries with strong banks, but a relatively weak stock market, but there are not any countries with a strong stock market and poor banking systems. Thus, Mongolia lacks a certain ideology and models to encourage private sector investment by developing the financial market.

As the possibilities and choices of investment resources increase, utilizing multiple resources, while not giving preference to any of them, has positive influence not only on enterprises, but also on the economic and financial security of the country. In the early period of the transition, in the conditions, when the environment for and management to improve the investment efficiency were poor, the veneration of foreign loans and aid did not give the expected financial results and led to the increase of external debts. In 2002-2005, when investment management improved, investment increased by 69.2%, but total productivity grew from 0.68 tugrik in 2002 to 0.76 tugrik in 2005. However, labor productivity rose by 62.1% during this period. Theoretically, investment of the country is regarded as efficient in case, when the investment index of the state sector equals to the the private sector investment index. Thus, in the future more attention needs to be paid to private sector investment, along with careful planning of investment efficiency of the state sector. Furthermore, domestic and foreign investment need to be encouraged equally.

When the growth correlations of GDP and investment are analyzed with use of a model, the GDP growth was dependent not on foreign and domestic investment coefficient, but more on the growth coefficient of employee numbers./ it was researched by connecting the GDP growth with the Direct Foreign Investment, comparing it with labor and capital growth and reflecting on the function of ordinary production/.The sensitivity of GPD growth, concerned with the growth of employee number is 0.85 and this sensitivity is much higher than sensitivity, concerned with domestic investment /0.18/ and sensitivity, concerned with foreign investment /0.08/. In other words, the survey revealed that the growth of GDP is highly dependent on growth of employee numbers. 74.0% of the changes in GDP are explained by the above 3 factors, taken as independent variables.

Our research revealed that although there was a substantial increase in foreign investment since 1990, its influence on the growth of GDP was low. Theoretically, investment expands production and increases productivity, but it has not been proved in real life. Thus, considering investment as an extreme goal and underestimating final results has been diminishing importance of investment.

Although considerable measures have been taken to attract foreign investments and create a favorable investment and trade environment in Mongolia since 1990, the research hypothesis of Bhagwati /1978/ about dependence of both the amount of direct foreign investment and its efficiency on trade regime of the investment receiveing country was not proved in practice. There might be several reasons to explain this:

- Investing mainly in the mining, textile and knitwear sectors with little technical and technological capacity might not have had great influence on the final productivity. Also, as the survey shows, a relatively small amount of investment from countries with highly developed technology might have affected productivity;

- The growth of GDP during the term of the survey /1990- 2005/ depended greatly on the agriculture, sales and service sectors, which require relatively small investment, but create many workplaces;
- The price fluctuations of raw materials on the world market influence profitability of livestock raw materials' processing industry and mining, which are the sectors with high percentage of DFI /direct foreign investment/.
- A large amount of investment, made in the last few years, has been in the mineral exploration sector and efficiency of such investment can be evaluated only after beginning of mineral mining;
- Because of the geographical position of Mongolia, its continental climate with 4 seasons and underdeveloped infrastructure investment expenses, domestic transportation fees and export and import charges are quite high, which influences profitability of enterprises;
- The percentage of construction work in the technological structure of investment has been much higher /35.3% as of 2005/. As construction work charges are high, this also affects final efficiency of investment.

As Hanson proved, the Income Tax does not have a major influence on attracting DFI /Direct foreign investment/. However, favorable investment environment, especially, a high speed of economic growth, highly qualified staff and well-developed infrastructure play a vital role. To sum up, it is necessary to pay attention to attracting foreign investment, especially, to increasing direct investment to private sectors; however, increasing investment efficiency needs to be emphasized. There is a need to invest in education and technological knowledge and capability. There is an estimation that investment in the intellectual sector has 4-7 times efficiency and the examples of this are South Korea and Israel.

Currently, there is a global transition to the new social and economic era, based on the deep knowledge and substantial changes in attitudes to investment and its management are noticeable. Today, the wealth of knowledge is more powerful than tangible assets and any currency and it is becoming a development factor with a broad scope. In the future competitiveness of any nation of the world will be based only on production systems, based on intellect and there is a tendency of direct dependence on developing abilities to create new knowledge and utilize it. Mongolia can compete with other countries only if it becomes the country of intellectual production, like other countries / there is no possibility of competing with raw materials/. This is the main factor to determine the future investment trends.

The further requirements are as follows:

- In the frame of a long-term, sustainable concept of development of the country it is important to determine and plan the investment goals, directions and the order and to base investment on the country income and expenditure plans. Time is money in the investment sector. That is why "On time" principle is followed in Japan.
- A prerequisite for new investment is to have efficient previous investment. However, this indicator is unsatisfactory in our country and utilization of capacity in use is inadequate. Therefore, there is a need to estimate investment needs well, taking into account the above indicators and to determine clearly efficiency and risks.
- Comprehensive actions on revealing the hidden economy need to be taken by giving official licenses to many small businesses, involved in informal sector and registering them, providing legal assistance and creating for them favorable environment to develop their business. It is necessary to direct a certain amount of foreign investment, that they do not access at present, to them.
- It is important to take into account investment efficiency and management in evaluating the enterprise activities, because the outcome of investment policy and its efficiency is resolved at the certain enterprise.

3.2 A NEW BANKING SYSTEM

Two-tiered banking system

One vital problem of comprehensive measures of reforms in the financial sector, directed towards the shift to market economy, is the reform of monetary-credit systems. In 1991 the "Banking Law" was passed, the old banking system changed and a two-tiered banking system: the Central Bank of Mongolia /Mongol bank/ and commercial banks, which work on the market principle, was created setting up the beginning of further development. Since this period more attention has been paid to development of the financial and banking sectors, which will operate in market conditions; to encouragement of fair competition in the financial market and to creation of legal environment, so measures have been taken to work out the related laws and legal documents, suited to the market principles and requirements and guided by the global standards.

The legal basis for the Central Bank of Mongolia to be the leading core of a new banking system was established by the law. The Mongol bank is in charge of implementing the state monetary policy within the territory of Mongolia. Its primary objectives are to ensure stability of the Mongolian national currency-Togrog and to promote balanced and sustained development of the national economy, through maintaining the stability of financial markets and banking system. The legal regulations were established by law to be the privilege of the State Great Hural to approve the rules and regulations of activities of Mongol bank and its annual reports; to approve and control the revenue allocation and income and expenditure budget; and to appoint the president of Mongol bank.The Bank of Mongolia conducts its activities independently of the government, in a relatively independent environment, and cooperates with the GoM acting as the Government's fiscal intermediary, issuing loans, increasing foreign currencies reserves, if necessary, managing foreign payments and settlement.

Since the middle of 1990s Mongol bank organized and implemented broad-frame activities to create a legal environment for further development of a two-tiered banking system. The State Great Hural approved and enforced the "Law on Currency Settlements" and the "Treasury Law " in 1994, the "Deposit, Loan and Settlement Law" and the Law on Bill in 1995. These laws became the legal basis for forming, regulating and supervising the activities of the Central Bank and commercial banks. However, as the process of structural and organizational reforms, implemented in the banking sector deepened and broadened, a need to renew the "Banking Law" passed in 1991 arose. Numerous issues that needed to be changed have emerged. For instance, it was necessary to settle and regulate many problems such as strengthening the control of banking activities by the Central bank, improving the legal basis for organization of inter-bank payments and settlements, clarifying the conditions of establishing and dismissing banks, using enforcement measures to banks and making banks accountable.

The State Great Hural passed the new "Banking Law of Mongolia" and the "Law of Central Bank" in 1996. These laws became the legal basis for proper development of the newly emerging systems and expanding structural changes in the banking sector in line with the market requirements.

The new laws determined directions for regulation of serious problems:

A commercial bank was defined as a legal for-profit body, which carries out activities to accept deposits, to disburse loans on its own behalf and to provide payment and settlement services and main principles of its activities were established;

- Directions of the commercial bank activities were determined as follows: to accept deposits; to provide transaction services; to disburse loans; to conduct foreign currency transactions, to provide a payment guarantee to the third party on behalf of the bank, to draw up securities and bonds and deal in financial leasing transactions.
- Requirements to and responsibilities of commercial banks activities were defined as follows: to meet the norms and normatives, set up by the Central bank on indicators such as compulsory reserves, the capacity of payment transactions, equity sufficiency and credit – risk fund along with solvency to redeem deposits on the first demand of the personal depositors and clients.

The Central bank requires commercial banks to carry out its activities in compliance with appropriate regulations and ethics and legal norms were set up to take certain enforced actions in case of violation.

Penalties and other enforcement measures against banks, which breach banking laws and regulations such as requirements of Mongol Bank on banking activities and its limitations were determined clearly and include issue of written warnings; passing an order requiring remedial action to be taken by a fixed date; limitting or halting activities of the bank; temporary suspension or dismissal of the executive director from office; imposing a conservatorship; appointing a receiver; revoking the license of the bank.

The Bank of Mongolia has a right to determine the amount of credit given to banks in accordance with an indice of the target for money supply and to determine if the amount of credit given to a particular bank is within the capacity of that bank. Also the Bank of Mongolia has the right to be in contact with commercial banks by providing the requirements of compulsory reserves and to supervise its activities in the frame of the laws not interfering.

Developments periods and stabilization

The period since establishment of a two-tiered banking system can be divided into following three stages:

I. 1991-1993 or the period of establishment of a two-tiered banking system;
II. 1994-1999 or the period of development;
III. Since 2000 or the period of stabilization and capacity strenghtening.

During the last 16 years there have been some serious problems such as bankruptcy and crisis, which become a good lesson to banks, but, indusputably, there have been certain successes. The reforms in the banking sector have not always been direct and successful. Some measures taken to shape market relations, to form a new economic system and to deepen the reform have been slow or have not been completed. As a result, economy faced certain difficulties, the entire banking and financial system was hit by recession and banks have fulfilled their duties of financial intermediaries inadequately.

Since 1991 Mongol Bank has given licenses for conducting banking activities in total to 30 banks, of which currently 16 banks are carrying out their activities in the financial market, and 14 banks were disbanded due to different reasons. Most of disbanded banks or 11 closed down because of insolvency.

There were some factors, which became major conditions and reasons for bankruptcy and insolvency of the entire system:

- Weakness and incapacity of the bank management;
- Risky activities of the initial period;
- Irregular external and internal environment;
- Internal fraud and embezzlement;
- Deficiency of the state regulations at certain periods;
- Difficulties of economic environment or temporary recession of general environment for repayment of loans and investment.

The World Bank survey shows that activities of insolvent banks differ radically from activities of solvent banks. Banks quickly became insolvent because they lost most of their own equity or suffered from bad debts and liability burden.

The period from 1991 to 1994 was the period, when Mongolia faced deep economic and social crisis. The financial and monetary- credit sector also suffered from crisis, it was even more difficult for the sector and the results were long-lasting. Inflation soared, the budget and balance payment were both at loss and financial capacity at micro and macro level declined sharply.

The initial period was hard. The newly established commercial banks just started independent activities and they were not strong financially. Along with it, the Central bank lacked experience to carry out monetary policy in market conditions, and a monitoring system was not yet formed. At its peak inflation reached 325 per cent, money in circulation increased 7.5 times in 1992-1994 and total money (M2) – 5.8 times. Coordination and supervision of banking were chaotic, and generally, monetary management weakened. The amount of off-bank assets went up 10.4 times.

Since 1994 solvency of some commercial banks declined and the recession started. Main reasons were provision of risky loans, inadequate internal information and poor control systems and inability of the enterprises to repay bank loans. Because of these reasons some of first banks such as the " Mongolian Cooperative" and "Selenge" went bankrupt.

The second period was the period from 1994 to 1999. During this period many commercial banks went bankrupt ("Central Asia", "Ediin Tenger", "Ard", "Daatgal", "SBB", "Investment and Reconstruction Bank" and "Export and Import Bank"). There was a continuous recession in the financial and monetary- credit sector. Since bank solvency deteriorated and 10 banks went bankrupt, individuals and enterprises lost their trust in banks. Commercial banks utilized their loan services not to help in recovery of enterprises of the real economic sectors, but served to the elite to privatize property and to repay government loans. The percentage of bad loans accounted for 28-54 per cent of total loans.

Priority objectives at that time were to overcome the crisis and improve solvency of commercial banks. Actions were taken by Mongol Bank and the Government of Mongolia with assistance of the World Bank and Asian Development Bank to implement structural reforms of banks and improve their financial capacity. In the frame of these structural changes the Government of Mongolia drew up bonds, worth 59.4 billion tugrik. The Central bank devoted 12.9 billion tugrik to stop losses. These assets equaled in total to around 7.5 per cent of GDP.

As a result of the actions since 2000 the entire banking sector has stabilized as banking activities improved and possibilities to carry out financial intermediary services in the broad frame were provided.

As activities of the banking sector broadened and results improved, the role played in the economy of the country increased substantially. Their activities moved closer to standards of countries with market economy. If two indicators are compared:

- The ratio of the amount active of the banking system and GDP accounts for in average 50-60% in the countries with market economy. As of 2005 our banking average reached 60.5%;
- The ratio of banking capital and GDP is 5-6% in other countries, meanwhile in our country it equals 9.1%.

Banking capital increases in conditions of stable economic development and increase in growth. It depends in great measure on efficient banking activities.

In relation to banking activities, directed to the service of real economic sectors, a tendency of increasing percentage of loans in total banking actives was observed. It reached 50.9% in 1996; 31.1%- in 2000; 44.45 – in 2001; 51.6%- in 2002 ; 57.6% - in 2003 and 62.6% - in 2005.

Possibilities of basic banking services in economy of the country were restored and viability of the banking system has improved dramatically. There was an increase in bank capital, actives and mobilized assets.

Table 3.25 shows indicators of the banking system. The table shows proper improvement of the ratios of main indicators of the banking sector and GDP, and the ratio between the indicators in 2000- 2005. Asset capacity of banks has improved substantially and their capacity to provide money for economy and loans to the private sector has increased significantly.

The Bank of Mongolia by means of the annual monetary policy regulates money supply and circulation in the economy, and pays special attention to decreasing the inflation level and stabilizing the exchange rate of domestic currency- tugrik. In our country like in other countries, which made a transition to the market economy, financial intermediary and financial markets have been developing and the monetization process of the economy has picked up speed, but there was a decrease in money circulation. In developed countries the ratio of amount of money to GDP is around 60-80%. As of 2005, it equaled 51.6% in our country. This is a major indicator to determine deepening of financial intermediary.

In the last years economic development has stabilized, its growth has increased, along with it banking and financial activities have expanded and a process of monetization of economy is observed. The decrease in speed of money circulation conforms common standards.

One of the major factors, which affects economic growth and development, is lending activities of the banking sector. In the course of their activities commercial banks are contributing to economic growth and development of the country by disbursing loans to individuals and enterprises.

Figure 3.25 Stastical indices of money and credit /1991-2005/ /billion tugrik/

Indices		1991	1992	1993	1994	1995	1996	1997	1998
Current cash	Totals	2.0	2.9	10.3	21.8	29.8	46.1	56.8	61.7
	Outside banks	1.7	1.8	8.7	18.8	25.6	41.7	49.8	56.4
M1		7.3	7.6	18.5	32.9	42.6	64.3	76.1	82.6
Internal deposits	Fixed term deposits	5.6	5.8	9.8	14.1	17.0	22.6	26.3	26.1
	Non-fixed term deposits	1.9	4.4	10.1	28.9	38.5	35.2	44.7	44.8
	Totals	7.5	10.2	19.9	43.0	55.5	57.8	71.0	70.9
Foreign currency deposits		0.6	1.0	14.1	14.9	20.9	28.9	49.3	39.8
Total savings		8.1	11.2	34.0	57.9	76.4	86.7	120.3	110.7
M2		9.9	13.1	42.8	76.8	102.0	128.4	170.1	167.2
Debt Remains of loans	State sector		12.2	21.7	12.2	10.9	9.0	7.8	9.3
	Private sector		6.9	9.9	40.6	51.8	20.3	25.3	39.7
	Totals	12.9	19.1	31.6	52.8	62.7	64.8	50.4	85.6
Of it	Non-performing						8.1	4.6	6.1
	Bad						24.9	9.9	26.6
Own equity		4.8	5.9	8.8	15.8	25.3	1.8	42.1	47.2
Of it	Central Bank's	3.1	3.3	1.5	3.0	8.3	15.3	25	40.1
	Banks'	1.7	2.6	7.3	12.8	17.0	-13.5	16.8	7.1
Total money M2	Totals /trillion tugrik/	9.9	13.1	42.8	76.8	102.0	128.4	170.0	167.2
	Growth %		132.3	326.7	179.4	132.8	125.9	132.5	0.98
	The percentage in GDP/%/	52.4	27.7	25.7	27.1	26.1	24.1	23.1	20.4

Total actives /banks/	Totals /trillion tugrik/	16.4	24.3	55.3	83.4	102.1	127.4	184.7	179.7
	Growth %	100.0	148.2	227.6	150.8	122.4	124.7	114.7	97.3
	The percentage in GDP/%/	86.8	51.4	33.3	29.4	26.1	23.9	25.1	22.0
Total deposits	Totals /trillion tugrik/	8.1	11.2	34.0	57.9	76.4	86.7	120.3	110.7
	Growth %	100.0	138.3	303.6	170.3	131.9	113.5	138.8	92.0
	The percentage in GDP/%/	42.8	23.7	20.4	20.4	19.5	16.3	16.3	13.5
	The percentage in M2	81.8	85.5	79.4	75.4	74.9	67.5	70.7	66.2
The remainders of loans	Totals /trillion tugrik/	12.9	19.1	31.6	52.8	62.7	64.8	50.4	85.6
	Growth %			165.4	167.1	118.7	103.31	0.8	122.1
	The percentage in GDP/%/	68.0	40.4	16.2	16.3	11.5	10.0	6.1	10.5
	The percentage in the actives		78.6	57.1	63.3	61.4	50.9	27.3	47.6
Currency outside banks	Totals /trillion tugrik/	1.7	1.91	8.7	18.8	25.6	41.7	49.8	56.4
	Growth %		111.8	483.3	216.0	136.2	162.9	119.4	113.3
	The percentage in M2		14.1	20.5	24.4	25.1	32.5	29.3	33.7
	The percentage in current currency	85.0	65.5	82.2	86.2	85.9	90.4	87.7	91.4
Own equity of the bank	Totals /trillion tugrik/	1.7	2.6	7.3	12.8	16.9	13.5	16.8	7.1
	Growth %		152.9	280.1	175.3	132.0	79.9	124.4	42.3
	The percentage in GDP/%/	8.9	5.5	4.3	4.5	4.3	2.5	2.3	0.9
	The percentage in the actives	10.3	10.7	13.2	15.3	16.6	10.6	9.1	3.9

Indices		**1999**	**2000**	**2001**	**2002**	**2003**	**2004**	**2005**
Current cash	Totals	91.6	107.4	119.2	134.6	152.8	168.5	191.7
	Outside banks	87.3	100.9	109.2	120.8	131.5	143.5	152.4
M1		114.8	130.8	150.2	187.7	212.8	221.3	269.1
Internal deposits	Fixed term deposits	27.5	29.5	46.9	66.9			
	Non-fixed term deposits	45.0	59.0	87.6	147.2			
Totals		72.5	88.8	134.5	214.1	240.3	300.9	456.0

Foreign currency deposits		62.3	69.1	87.3	135.2	250.2	324.7	445.0
Total savings		134.8	157.9	221.8	349.3	490.5	625.6	901.0
M2		220.2	258.8	331.1	470.1	703.3	847.0	1170.1
Debt Remains of loans	State sector	4.0	5.4	9.5	11.3	15.6	12.6	34.1
	Private sector	29.1	43.3	108.7	194.6	336.0	516.6	742.9
	Totals	77.5	66.8	135.1	231.4	442.2	606.8	859.9
Of it	Non-performing	2.9	1.3	1.8	4.8	15.5	21.5	20.9
	Bad	39.2	14.6	9.1	11.7	21.2	39.1	49.5
Own equity		42.4	72.7	88.4	94.7	151.6	199.1	253.0
Of it	Central Bank's	37.8	42.8	41.2	33.4	41.2	32.0	45.9
	Banks'	4.6	29.9	47.2	61.3	110.4	167.1	207.1
Total money M2	Totals /trillion tugrik/	220.2	258.8	331.1	470.1	703.3	847.0	1170.0
	Growth %	131.7	117.5	127.9	141.9	149.6	120.4	138.1
	The percentage in GDP/%/	23.8	24.8	29.3	37.9	51.8	46.9	51.6
Total actives /banks/	Totals /trillion tugrik/	203.9	214.9	304.4	448.4	766.8	962.0	1371.5
	Growth %	113.5	105.4	141.6	147.3	171.0	125.6	142.5
	The percentage in GDP/%/	22.0	21.1	27.3	36.4	56.2	63.1	60.5
Total deposits	Totals /trillion tugrik/	134.8	157.9	221.8	349.3	490.5	625.6	901.0
	Growth %	121.8	117.1	140.5	157.5	140.4	127.5	144.8
	The percentage in GDP/%/	14.6	15.5	19.9	28.2	35.9	34.6	39.8
	The percentage in M2	61.2	61.0	67.0	74.3	69.7	73.8	77.0
The remainders of loans	Totals /trillion tugrik/	77.5	66.8	135.1	231.4	442.1	606.8	859.9
	Growth %	0.99	0.9	202.2	171.3	191.0	137.3	141.7
	The percentage in GDP/%/	8.4	6.4	11.9	18.7	32.4	33.5	37.9
	The percentage in the actives	38.0	31.1	44.4	51.6	57.6	62.9	62.6
Currency outside banks	Totals /trillion tugrik/	87.3	100.9	109.2	120.8	131.5	143.5	152.4
	Growth %	154.8	115.6	108.2	110.6	108.9	109.2	106.3
	The percentage in M2	39.6	93.0	33.0	25.7	18.7	16.9	13.0
	The percentage in current currency	95.3	93.3	91.3	89.7	86.1	85.1	79.6

Own equity of the bank	Totals /trillion tugrik/	4.6	29.9	47.2	61.3	110.4	167.1	207.1
	Growth %	64.8	6.5	157.8	129.9	180.0	151.8	123.9
	The percentage in GDP/%/	0.5	2.9	4.2	4.9	8.1	9.2	9.1
	The percentage in the actives	2.3	13.9	15.5	13.7	14.4	17.3	15.1

Source: Annual reports of Mongol Bank

However, in the initial development stage many banks went bankrupt because loans were not repaid and turned into bad debts. There were many factors causing bankruptcy such as low capacity of newly established banks, competing with each other in loan disbursement in order to attract customers, bad management of some banks, poor market sensitivity, insufficient knowledge and skills of staff, irresponsibility of borrowers, high interest rates and short terms to repay the loans.

In order to provide reliable banking activities, Mongol bank had taken several measures to strengthen the controls of other banks, to limit loan remainders and to set up and follow the compulsory reserves. Furthermore, amendments made in regulations in the frame of structural reforms halted possibilities and ways to slowdown banking activities. Due to the banking crisis of 1996-1999, the banks, which were declared insolvent closed down, which made the banking sector healthier and became one of the main factors to increase trust of individuals in banks. In addition, banks developed specific regulations on loan disbursement and made the process of accessing loans more stringent, which reduced loan risks and became the beginning of reliable banking activities.

As of November 2006 the debt remainders, given to individuals, enterprises and organizations reached MNT1181.4 billions. The increase of this indicator was 5.1 times against 2002; 2.6 times compared to 2003; 1.9 times against 2004 and 1.4 times against 2005. This increase shows that the frame of banks' intermediation has broadened.

Of total debt remaining private sector loans took up most part or on average 54.1%; individuals – 41.6%; state organizations – 2.7% and foreign organizations, joint companies and community organizations account for the rest. From this it could be concluded that banks offered loans mostly to private companies and individuals. In the last years, for instance the "Agricultural Bank" ("KHAAH"), "KHAS", "Golomt" and "Trade and Development" banks have been successfully implementing micro-loan services in order to encourage small businesses.

Lending is concentrated in a few big banks. The "Trade and Development Bank", "KHAAN", "Golomt Bank" and "Anod " banks are leading in total credit amounts and accounted for 62.6% of of total loan remaining.

Of total loan remaining, the ordinary loans accounted for 91.7%, loans overdue – for 2.7% and bad loans accounted for 5.6%.

In the last years one of the most important changes, which took place in the banking sector, is decrease of poor quality loans and increase in amounts of bank lending. However, it can be noticed that there has been a shortage of investment in the economy, the loan rate is still high and there is lack of mid- and long-term loans.

Decreasing loan rates is one of major issues of the money policy. The banking loan real interest by the amounts of the total banking sector has been 22.05% yearly (monthly 1.84%) on the last 4 year average.

Loan rate is regarded as the price of loans. Asset mobilization by commercial banks and non-banking financial organizations in forms of deposits and currents accounts has been increasing each year, becoming the source of credit supply, which influences slow decrease of loan rates. Loan rates differ with regard to loan types, terms, risks and the characteristics of borrowers and lenders. Furthermore, it depends on macro economic conditions, inflation, tax burden and development of the stock market.

Although there have been some signs of improvement of macro economic environment in our country, decrease of inflation level and tax burden, healthier banking sector and deepening financial intermediation, increasing inter-bank compete-tiveness and along with it, decrease of interest rates of deposits and loans, it is impor-tant to determine the main factors, which slow down decrease of interest rates to the level, sufficient to encourage long-term investment and provide economic growth, as well as measures that should be taken within the policy frame to decrease interest rates.

Insufficient decrease of loan rates is due to poor development of stock market and poor economic environment for long-term investment loans. One of the ways to acquire financial sources is to draw up bonds and sell them in the stock market. Because of underdevelopment of the stock market it is not able to influence the loan demand and supply, which directly affects loan rates.

Currently in Mongolia there are 15 domestic banks, 1 branch of a foreign bank, over 100 non-banking financial organizations, 600 Savings and Credit cooperatives, 17 commercial insurance organizations, over 60 currency exchange centers and 400 pawnshops that are conducting financial intermediary activities.

In considering the importance of the role of banks in the economic and social development of the country, it is necessary to relate the monetary theory with practice. Nowadays, the role of theory in the economic nature of total money, economic coordination and intermediary systems needs to be enhanced.

Two trends are observed:

First trend: Total money tends to be a factor playing a dominant role in providing for the demand and supply as well as budget balance along with price stabilization. Generally, in order to determine the amount of total money properly one needs to be aware of its accumulation factors and relations between them. If the amount of total money is too limited, it will lead to slow down of material valuables turnover and all payment turnover.
Second trend: Money and loans have been independent influential factors to broaden investment, to increase working assets and to activate enterprise turnover. Further there is a need for a reliable and well-organized system of the total money movement (credit, budget and dedicated funds).Thus, total money plays an important role in other systems and tends to become an important regulator in economy.

It is necessary to extend the scope of financial intermediation, to improve its quality and provide the stabilization of banking sector. Moreover, conditions for preventing another crisis in the financial market and a favorable environment, directed to encouraging investment should be created and methods and mechanisms to protect interests of bank customers and deposit owners should be upgraded. To achieve these objectives we need to increase own equity of commercial banks and mobilize free financial resources of individuals and enterprises, to seek proper sources from foreign countries, which will expand collaboration with the real economic sector.

Measures should be taken without delay to speed up payments through banks, to expand efficient forms of non-cash payments, to intensify current cash circulation and to reduce the influence of hidden economy.

In order to improve depositors' trust in banks and prevent from further risks and difficulties in commercial banks, it is necessary to introduce a savings insurance system, to provide banking and financial services to rural areas, to improve operations of non-banking financial organizations and to upgrade control and regulations.

3.3 FINANCIAL MARKET

In current conditions, when at the national level as well as an individual enterprise level proper internal financial accumulations have not been established, it is important to develop a financial market and utilize efficiently intermediary services. Increasing demand for financial resources is an inevitable issue of development. Thus, more attention needs to be paid to utilization of possibilities and conditions of financial market in efficient allocation of financial resources and provision with related assets in short and long terms.

Economic and social environment and factors to activate and develop the financial market in our country are chiefly established. They are as follows:

1. The number of three groups of subjects, namely, households, enterprises and state, engaged in production, service, merchandize and other different kinds of business operations has gone up, and long and short-term demand for assets to conduct ordinary and extended reproduction is continuously increasing. Currently 34.8 thousand households and over 230 thousand herders' families, that raise 34.5 million livestock throughout the country, are engaged in business activities. Obviously, at some time all these subjects face financial surplus or deficit, because of assets circulation.

2. In the course of asset and money transactions circulation in our country short, temporary and long-term monetary resources of certain amounts, accumulation and savings within the frame of economic- financial sectors and individuals have been established and grown. For instance, the total amount of savings in banks is around MNT1.05 trillion, the net reserve of foreign currency amounts to around USD 1 billion. Furthermore, reserves of the budgetary and other cetralized funds as well as those of individuals and business entities have also risen. All of these create opportunities for intermediary services of the financial market.

The scope of financial market is influenced greatly by volume of production and financial situation of real economic sectors of our country, population, and specifical-ly by the employment level. In current situation the financial market in our country is structurally comprised of interdependent and supplementing types, such as:

1. Loan capital market;
2. Stock market;
3. Currency market;
4. Gold market;
5. Insurance market.

Loan capital market

Loan capital market is expanding as the most universal and accessible. The amount of monetary capital disbursed in the form of loans is growing rapidly. Loans are disbursed by 17 commercial banks, around 120 non-banking financial organizations,

Credit and Savings Cooperatives and other business entities with financial capacity. By the economic content, loans are a component of financial reserves, accumulated in our country. A large amount of credit resources, accumulated in the banking and non-banking sector, plays a prominent role in meeting needs of reproduction and economic monetization.

Figure 3.26 Growth of bank loans /2000-2006 / /billion tugrik, %/

Year	2000	2001	2002	2003	2004	2005	2006
Debt remaining of total loan	66.8	135.1	231.4	442.1	606.8	859.9	1586.0
Growth	100	2.0	1.7 times	1.9 times	137.3	141.7	1.8 times

Source: Annual reports of Mongol Bank

The amount of bank loans rose 23.7 times in 2006 against 2000; 3.6 times against 2003 and 1.8 times against 2005. The banking sector takes the dominant position in the market capacity of loan capital and plays an important role in short and long-term investment to contribute to the economic development of the country.

In the last years non-banking financial organizations have conducted loan operations, worth 40-60 billion tugrik, paying more attention to leasing and have taken a certain place in the capital market. Credit and Savings Cooperatives also make certain contribution.

Due to objectives, put to the economic structural changes and growth, a need to position properly and develop national industry, including small and medium enterprises, there is a trend for intensive growth of loan capital market.

Currency market

In our country modern currency market is on the initial stage of its formation. We do not have an opportunity to enter and deal at the international currency market. Currency market is only involved in currency exchange process of commercial banks, non-banking financial organizations, foreign currency exchange centers and individuals.

Currency is a specific instrument, utilized in foreign trade and credit an settlement operations of our country. Furthermore, currency becomes a component of monetary frame in the economy and influences the financial situation of the country and eco-

nomic growth. In addition, it plays an important role in economic relations such as trade, travel, loans and aid.
In 1993 Mongolia introduced floating currency rates. Currency convertibility is:

1. Foreign currency convertibility - Foreign legal bodies and individuals can exchange freely foreign currency into Mongolian National currency.

2. Domestic currency convertibility - Mongolian legal bodies and individuals can exchange national currency - tugrik into foreign currency to purchase goods and conduct activities overseas.

It is inevitable for Mongolia to be involved in certain measure in the process of currency market. However, the following is needed to be taken into account:

- To maintain sustainable currency exchange rates;
- To increase further foreign currency reserves, which accounted for USD 680 million at the end of 2006;
- To pay special attention to profitability of foreign trade balance and balance of payment.

Gold Market

Mongolia has been implementing a "Gold" program since the1990s. Gold market is essential for stabilization of the country's market and increase of currency reserves.

As of the beginning of the 1990s total gold mining equaled approximately 0,6-0,7 tons annually. In 1992-2005 in total 130 tons of gold was mined and MNT108.9 billion was made through the sales of the gold. Currently 134 entities are mining gold from the earth and main deposits.

Table 3.27 Amount of mined gold in 2001-2005 /by кg/

Years	2001	2002	2003	2004	2005
Gold /total/	13674.6	12097.1	11118.6	19417.6	24121.9

Source: Data of Mongol Bank

Sales of gold in the gold market were made mainly through the Mongol Bank, but in 2001 gold mining companies gave gold export rights to commercial banks. A certain amount of foreign currency income has been derived from the gold market each year. The price of gold has increased in the world market over the last three years and in 2006 a price of an ounce (33gr.) of gold reached USD 600, which creates favorable conditions for our country.

Insurance market

Insurance in Mongolia has been developing as one of the most important sectors of the financial market. Insurance relations are regulated by the "Law on Insurance", Civil Code and other legal documents. The " Law on Insurance of Mongolia" was passed by the State Great Hural in 1994 and went into force in 1995. The law has been the first on insurance in the history of our country. During the transitional period private insurance and mixed property companies were established, their activities developed and new forms of insurance relations were formed. Due to these changes there was a need for renewal of the Insurance Law, so a new, amended "Law on Insurance" was passed by the State Great Hural in April 2004. Currently the insurance market con-ducts its activities by the following principles:

- Independence of market subjects;
- Broad delivery of insurance services;
- Cooperation on equal commercial basis;
- Development of a system with vertical and horizontal links;
- Healthy, fair competition.

Insurance market in Mongolia can be divided into following types by its features:

- Life Insurance Market;
- Property Insurance Market;
- Liability Insurance Market.

As of 2006 22 Insurance companies are operating in the Mongolian insurance market providing insurance services to citizens and enterprises. Of them one is a state –owned company /"Ganzam"/, one is a state-incorporated /" UB city Daatgal"/, 2 are foreign-incorporated companies and other are privately –owned companies.

Table 3.28 General indicators of the Insurance Market / million tugrik, %/

№		2001	2002	2003	2004	2005	2005/ 2001
1	Insurance companies	15	18	19	21	22	
2	Total assets	10178.8	11920.4	12863.3	15252.8	15111.6	148.5
3	Total premium	5167.9	6145.5	6318.3	7960.8	9493.4	183.7
4	Net premium	4174.4	4500.0	3740.6	5737.1	7476.9	179.1
5	Claims paid	1766.9	1062.9	1236.2	1395.5	2366.1	134.0

Compared to 2001 in 2005 total assets of Insurance companies increased by 485.0%; total premium – by 83.7%; net premium – by 79.1% and claims paid went up by 34.0 per cent.

As of 2005 insurance premium income reached 9493,4 million tugrik accounting for 0.4% of GDP, which is consioered low compared to other countries with high developed insurance. It represents poor commercial insurance services but, on the other hand, it indicates existence of the market to develop further.

Table 3.29 Insurance premium income structure

	Life, health, interests		Property		Liability		Total
	Total /mln. tugrik/	%	Total /mln. tugrik/	%	Total /mln. tugrik/	%	
2001	327.3	10.2	3213.2	62.2	1427.4	27.6	5167.9
2002	534.1	8.7	3646.1	59.3	1965.3	32.0	6145.5
2003	582.8	9.2	3878.2	61.4	1857.3	29.4	6318.3
2004	670.8	8.4	4919.9	61.8	2370.0	29.8	7960.8
2005	963.1	10.1	6283.5	66.2	2246.8	23.7	9493.4

The Insurance premium income structure shows low percentage of life insurance in total insurance, around 10 per cent. Property insurance took up 60 per cent, however, it went up to 66.2 % over the last year. In 2005 liability Insurance took up 23.7 per cent.

As for insurance premium per capita, that of 3140 tugrik in 2004 and 3700 tugrik in 2005 was 1000 times lower than in highly developed market countries. This low indicator was related to low GDP per capita and low real income of insurees.

Table 3.30 Leading companies by premium income:

№		Amount of premium income /mln. tugrik/	Percentage in the total premium income
1	Mongol Daatgal	5198.8	79.9
2	Bodi Insurance	770.8	4.8
3	Group of Mongolian Daatgal	685.3	5.0
4	Prime Daatgal	474.7	7.2
5	Nomin Daatgal	455.7	8.1
6	Total	7585.2	79.9

The table shows that the above 5 companies account for 80% of the total premium income and other Insurance companies account for 20% of it. By the insurance class, 61.5% of the life insurance premium income came from the accident insurance; 22.2% - from the health insurance of travelers and 14.8%- from temporary disability insurance. This equals to 98.5 per cent of life insurance premium.

As for property Insurance, 34.7% of premium income was from insurance of citizens and entities' property; 26.3 % - from aircraft hull insurance; 22% - from motor vehicle insurance and this equals 83% of total premium.

As for liability insurance, driver's liability insurance accounted for 48.9% of insurance premium; pilots' insurance – for 33.3%; passengers' insurance – for 8.4%. This accounted for 90.6 per cent of liability insurance premium.

To sum up, commercial insurance activities are limited by the above number of insurance types. As for the claims paid, claims paid, worth 2366.1 million tugrik in 2005 took up 24.9% of premium income.

Table 3.31 Claims paid over last 5 years

	Life, health, interests		**Property**		**Liability**		**Total**
	Total /mln. tugrik/	%	Total /mln. tugrik/	%	Total /mln. tugrik/	%	
2001	220.5	12.5	1286.8	72.8	259.6	14.7	1766.9
2002	206.9	19.5	535.6	50.4	320.4	30.1	1062.9
2003	221.6	17.9	669.3	54.1	345.3	27.9	1236.2
2004	267.5	19.2	866.2	62.1	261.8	18.8	1395.5
2005	300.3	12.7	1618.6	68.4	447.2	18.9	2366.1

Of claims paid by insurance types, of claims paid on life insurance 55.9% was spent on claims of the accident insurance; 27.6% - on claims of health insurance of the travelers abroad and 15.9 % - on claims of temporary disability insurance.

As for property insurance, 50.8% of claims paid was on transport accidents; 23.7% - on property insurance of individuals and enterprises; 12.3% - on aircraft hull insurance.

As for liability insurance, 54.5% of claims paid was paid on driver's liability insurance; 40.9 – on aircraft owner's liability.

Claims paid equalling 61.2% out of total claims paid was paid out by "Mongol Daatgal" company; 7.6% - by "Bodi Daatgal" Company; 7.1% - by the Group of "Mongol Daatgal"; 6.9% - by "Nomin Daatgal" and the remaining 17.2% was paid out by other insurance companies. The claims paid level over the last 5 years is as follows:

Table 3.32 Claims paid

2001	2002	2003	2004	2005
34.2%	17.2%	22.1%	17.4%	24.9%

The reserve amount of insurance companies reached 10012.2 million tugrik in 2005. Following measures should be taken in the future:

- To intensify measures on promotion of importance and the role of commercial insurance of the market relations to individuals and entities;
- To introduce new forms and types of commercial insurance and make it accessible to citizens;
- To utilize unused insurance assets by putting them into economic and social circulation /in the forms of short-term loans/ and to consider the possibilities of insurance companies to enter the stock market.

Security market

Establishment of security market in Mongolia and its proper development was naturally determined by transitional economy. As reproduction intensifies and production and commercial activities expand their frame, there is a need for mobilization of a substantial amount of investment and credit assets.

Practice and experience of countries with a developed market economy show that the increasing demand is effectively met by regulating market demand and supply through security market. To stabilize economy and conduct privatization by means of security market it is possible to mobilize the required amount of assets. Thus, the security market is important not only in the macro economic development, but also in determining economic development prospects of Mongolia and to direct the development strategy and the financial- banking system to the proper channel.

The beginning point for operating a security market in Mongolia was connected with privatization of state owned property.

In the first half of 1990 amendments were made to the Constitution and to the Civil Code of Mongolia /in December/. These laws acknowledged private ownership. The government resolution was passed on 18 January 1991 to establish the Mongolian Stock Exchange and temporary rules were approved on March 22.

The State Baga Hural passed the "Law on Economic Entities and Organizations" on 17 May 1991 and the "Law on Privatization" on 22 May 1991. To implement the laws the governmental and local privatization commissions were established and along with these, "Regulations on estimation of properties of enterprises", "Regulations on distribution and utilization of privatization vouchers" and "General rules of organizing and conducting auctions" were enacted.

In June 1991 a list of enterprises to be fully or partially privatized and be privatized was approved. These resolutions had been historic steps towards establishing the basis of market economy. The Mongolian Stock Exchange was established in June 1991 in every city and province and intensive courses for training stockbrokers were conducted. During the period from 30 September and 21 December, a nation-wide network of 29 brokerage houses was established. As of 1 July 1991, inventory of the property of enterprises, which would be listed on the exchange, was conducted. In an attempt to ensure an equitable distribution of assets, the Mongolian government chose to instantiate a voucher-based scheme; one blue voucher worth MNT 7,000 was issued to every citizen born before 31 May 1991 for the purchase of shares in large enterprises.

Auctions officially began on 7 February 1992; shares in three companies were auctioned off. Since then operations of the first stock market were conducted separately until June of 1995, where individuals redeemed their 1989900 blue vouchers, worth MNT 139292 million for shares.

The "Law on Securities" was enacted in September 1994 and the Mongolian Securities and Exchange Commission, which acted as a regulatory and controlling agency, was established in November and December of that year. The Mongolian Great Hural approved the rules of the Mongolian Securities and Exchange Commission in December 1994. The main goal of the commission was to carry out preparatory work for establishment of the secondary market in order to extend stock market in our country and to coordinate and control stock market activities.

Conducting activities of the primary securities market, such as drawing up and distributing shares through the Mongolian Stock Exchange, was an important measure for accumulating experience to develop the secondary market in Mongolia, to further develop the market. Secondary trading began on 28 August 1995, open to both domestic and international investors.

Thus, since that time organizational conditions for the stock exchange market to implement its activities to the whole extent in Mongolia. The " Securities Law of Mongolia" states: "...security market means a primary market where issuers offer securities directly or through underwriters, or a secondary market where securities are traded... ".

The law established the goal and direction of securities market. In the beginning of the secondary security market around 50% of produced goods, most of trade and service and 90 per cent of livestock were allotted to private ownership. Thus, the private sector started taking its proper place and it role was increasing. During the Great privatization 186 majority state-owned shareholding enterprises, 62 partly state-owned shareholding enterprises, 228 fully private enterprises and 400 limited companies were set up. Thus, share- issuing companies were firstly established in the Mongolian security market.

By analyzing processes of the formation of two-scaled: primary and secondary security market during 1991-2000, we can notice some specific features.

Specific features of primary privatization are:

- For the first time many shareholding companies were set up;
- Equity fund was established in only one form, ordinary shares were issued with one type of issued shares and one quoted price;
- A process of distributing company shares and registering them under the owner's names took place;
- Many individuals became shareholders;
- There was a sufficient supply of securities and possibilities and conditions to make a choice were provided;
- The price of stock demand and supply has not been established
- It was not possible to establish a limit to the amount of share supply and demand.

The greatest success in the primary market period was stable activities of Mongolian stock Exchange and beginning of securities registration, and recording share payments of shareholders, savings and shares of the companies.

In 1996 Secondary market began operating and since then possibility opened for shareholders to sell their shares freely in the market. Although the government developed policies to be implemented with regard to stock market, and directions of its development, there were drawbacks in their implementation mainly due to lack of organizational and professional experience.

For a short time stock market activities took place in the frame of the group of people, involved in the security market, brokers, dealers and interested persons. The secondary market started operating at the time, when the stock market had not managed to acquire characteristics of covering the general public.

Specifics of Secondary market are:

- Securities settlement and savings were centralized;
- The number of foreign investors was limited;
- The objectives of domestic investors were to collect controlling portfolios;
- There were no sharp fluctuations in the price of securities;
- Correlation between stock demand and supply was not observed;
- There was no trading of newly issued securities;
- Professional stock organizations, such as stock companies, investment funds were private, but the Mongolian Stock Exchange was state-owned.

Even though underwriting actions were mentioned in the legislation of stock market, those actions have not been implemented successfully. In most foreign countries underwriting actions have been implemented by pension funds, insurance funds, prominent investment funds and investment banks. Social and commercial insurance funds in our country have not been involved in stock market activities yet. The beginning and formation of Stock market in Mongolia /1991-2000/ can be divided into 4 periods:

Ist period: 1991-1994. A period when the role of the state was high in the process of privatization by vouchers and actions of issuing, accumulating and privatization in the primary stock market were implemented.

IInd period: 1994-1995. This was a period of the final stage of primary stock market, when 1.2 million citizens owned shares of the share-holding companies, privatized in the primary stock market and the role of the state was unclear.

IIId period: 1995 – end of 1997. In relation with the beginning of secondary market and cash trade, the Mongolian Securities Committee was established as a state organization to regulate the market. Furthermore, amendments were made in the "Securities Law of Mongolia" and in other related laws on rights and duties of stock-issuers. In this period statuary regulations were not able to cover the general public, but only a few participants and company management.

IVth period: end of 1997 – beginning of 2000. While the shares of companies privatized by vouchers were accumulated in the hands of few people and the issues of state-owned enterprises were settled down by the State Property Commission, the functions and objectives of the Mongolian Securities Commission became unclear. Thus, not only there was not any improvement in the development of stock market, but also there was a tendency for slow down of the stock market. In the attempt of drawing assets into budget by privatization of state-owned enterprises, state-owned enterprises were sold at public auctions and sealed bids.

In that way, stock market in Mongolia has developed as a sub-sector, influencing economic development of the country, with its own unique features, specific structure, legal environment, comprised of statuary regulatory professional organizations, intermediaries, hundreds of stock-issuers, investors and customers. A historical role of establishing a secondary stock market, where shares were traded openly and freely, was played by the Mongolian Stock Exchange and 42 operating broker houses.

In the process of stock market development in Mongolia, certain consequences of transitional character emerged in the economic system and financial structure. For example:

1. The stock market fulfilled the most important duty in changing property relations, which had a decisive role in the shift to a new financial system. Currently private sector accounts for around 80% in the GDP production.
2. Privatization, realized through securities trading, created a new capital market in Mongolia and opened possibilities for further development. In the last 16 years legal documents, laws and regulations to regulate activities of the stock market, securities trade, share-holding companies have been developed. The Mongolian Securities Commission, the Financial Regulatory Commission, the Mongolian Stock Exchange, the Securities Clearing House & Central Depository /SCHCD/ and broker's and dealer's companies have been established and started operations.
3. As stock market developed, in the course of privatization, national specialists to work at the stock market have been trained.

The privatization process, which was realized by means of stock trading became the main condition for transition to the market economy, changed property relations and opened possibilities for development of stock market.

In the beginning of 2000 activities of the Mongolian Stock Exchange were at standstill, but due to proper measures, taken by the Government, a trend for its recovery is observed.

In 2002 a new, amended "Mongolian Law on Stock market" was approved and by the resolution [1] 72 on 26 March 2003 the Mongolian Stock Exchange was re-organized into a State-owned Shareholding company engaged in securities trade and other activities not prohibited by laws. Moreover, according to the resolution, Securities Clearing and Depository Department, which has been conducting its activities within the main operations of MSE, and was in charge of securities clearing and deposits has been transformed into "Securities Clearing House & Central Depository" /SCHCD/" Co.Ltd, which main functions are conducting customers' monetary transactions and security savings. The company has been changed into the state-owned company. All listed securities on the MSE are deposited in dematerialized form with SCHCD.

The mission of MSE is determined as to contribute to the national economy by creating a classical securities market with the purpose of mediating the accumulation of assets in the financial market with lowest possible costs in the long term.

On 1 October 1998 MSE joined the Federation of Euro-Asian Stock Exchange as a full member and in 2003 for the first time a first international memorandum on cooperation between Mongolian Stock Exchange and Taiwan Stock Exchange had been signed. In 2005-2006 the Memorandums of cooperation between Mongolian Stock Exchange and Taiwan GreTai Stock Exchange, Korea Exchange and Istanbul Stock Exchange were signed. Since the beginning of Secondary security market as of the end of 2006, MSE traded 300.2 million securities worth MNT196.7 billion with 2854 trading.

Government bonds trading accounts for 66% of the total trading or MNT 129.1 billion; stock trading accounts for 27% or MNT 54.0 billion and trading of corporate bonds accounts for 7% or MNT 13.6 billion.

Currently, in MSE there are 387 listed companies, which are the property of 483.1 thousand shareholders.

Over the last years new forms of securities likely to attract foreign and domestic investors in the market have emerged and there has been a tendency of increasing trading amount. For instance, shares issued by "Mongol Shiltgeen", "Genco Tour Bureau" and Zoos Bank for investment purpose and bonds issued by construction companies create real investment in the economic sector.

The following figures show stock and bond trading in the stock market.

Table 3.33 Securities Trading / shares/

Trading Days /numbers/		Trading volume /numbers/		Trading Value /MNT mln/	
		Total	Daily average	Total	Daily average
1995	84	6,584.0	78.4	811.5	9.7
1996	236	24,076.6	102.0	4,340.5	18.4
1997	253	33,659.9	133.0	12,165.7	48.1
1998	253	33,073.5	130.7	10,756.0	42.5
1999	252	21,446.7	85.1	3,274.2	13.0
2000	255	35,412.3	138.9	2,973.3	11.7
2001	255	15,877.1	62.3	1,723.3	6.8
2002	255	9,837.9	38.6	1,373.0	5.4
2003	250	8,085.9	32.3	895.9	3.6
2004	255	9,065.8	35.6	654.0	2.6
2005	253	25,948.2	102.6	2,547.3	10.1
2006	253	74,531.7	294.6	12,604.3	49.8
2007	22	13,943.1	633.8	2,962.0	134.6

Source: Data of MSE

Table 3.34 Securities Trading /bonds/

Trading Days /numbers/		Trading volume /numbers/		Trading Value /MNT. mln/	
		Total	Daily average	Total	Daily average
Government Bond					
2000	4	15.8	3.9	144.3	36.1
2001	26	113.1	4.4	11,132.1	428.2
2002	24	343.1	14.3	30,750.2	1,281.3
2003	23	465.0	20.2	41,690.7	1,812.6
2004	9	232.7	25.9	21,722.5	838.7
2005	3	130.0	43.3	12,463.8	4,154.6
2006	1	70.0	70.0	6,767.7	6,767.7
2007	2	47.0	23.5	4,461.5	2,230.8
Corporate Bond					
2001	26	120.4	2.2	1,204.3	21.5
2002	131	317.5	2.4	2,958.0	22.6
2003	70	247.4	3.5	2,988.3	42.7
2004	50	69.2	1.4	2,776.5	55.5
2005	121	305.3	2.5	2,663.7	22.0

Trading Days /numbers/		Trading volume /numbers/		Trading Value /MNT. mln/	
		Total	Daily average	Total	Daily average
2006	84	99.2	1.2	960.9	11.4
2007	10	13.6	1.4	68.2	6.8

Source: Data of MSE

The figures show that stock trading increased until 2000 and decreased in 200-2004, however, there has been a tendency of an increase again. Further the development of stock market sees its flourishing as trading of corporate bonds increases.

An important objective of stock market is to contribute to the national economy by creating a classical securities market with the purpose of mediating assets accumulated in the financial market with lowest possible costs in the long term.

In the global stock market pension funds and insurance companies account for a prominent share of security- buyers through professional organizations. Pension funds, Insurance companies, Investment and other funds and commercial banks are investors of those organizations. Individuals, state organizations and trading and industrial companies are regarded as one group and it is required to increase involvement of this group.

Moreover, in Mongolia it is important to upgrade the structure and organization of investors, to improve asset capacity and to make investors active participants in the stock relationships.

There are some problems to be solved promptly by MSE and they are determined by the Financial Regulatory Commission as follows:

- To analyze privatization results, estimate shareholding companies, listed in MSE, rate them and resolve the issue of companies, that stopped their activities;
- To improve capacities of organizations at stock market and take measures to decrease risks;
- To upgrade the stock market statistics and information system and create a system that promptly provides citizens with fair and transparent information;
- Make mediatory actions accessible in rural areas;

- To issue Government bonds, mortgage securities and shares and securities of mineral exploration companies in the stock market and increase demand and supply of securities;
- To protect investors from risks and support rights of small shareholders.

Conclusions and Recommendations:

The chapter defined the contents and results of actions, taken to reform the monetary-financial system in Mongolia in the first years of the transitional period. Moreover, the process and results of reforms in the course of further development and formation of market relations have been studied and evaluated by every component of the system and conclusions were made. As the scope of market relations expands and deepens, it is obvious that the reform process will continue further.

Following general conclusions emerge from the chapter content :

- The contents and objectives of Mongolian transition to market relations put forward a requirement to conduct a reform of the monetary- financial system and to create a system, new in its contents and forms. Although this was a complicated process in a wide frame, a monetary- financial system, suited to the market relations, was established in Mongolia in a relatively short time. Further, as the scope of market relations expands and deepens, the process of upgrading this monetary- financial system will inevitably continue, it is important to work out principles for complete upgrade of the monetary- financial system, according to the philosophy and long-term sustainable development programs country.
- In order to strengthen further the financial system it is necessary to raise the role of finance of enterprises, which are regarded as the basis of the system. Moreover, it is important to deepen reforms within this framework and to shift promptly to the classical management, suited to market relations;
- Within methods and tools of statuary regulations in the market relations conditions, monetary- financial methods and tools are placed as a priority. Thus, monetary- financial methods and tools of statuary regulations are needed to be upgraded, adjusted to the objectives to improve the business environment, alleviate poverty, speed up the economical development and activate the investment. Especially, it is important to improve further the justification of budget planning, to raise the regulatory role of taxation system and to monitor money supply properly;
- Budget reforms need to be expanded. The role of the budget to speed up the country development does not depend on the budget size, but on its regulatory

and organizational capability. In the future it is more effective for the Mongolian budget to develop in the direction of a human development budget.

- Investment is regarded as a key to development. However, one should not forget that it is not a final goal, but a powerful force to reach this goal. It is important to study the issue of increasing efficiency of investment from every aspect in further investment policies and planning. It is necessary to reduce costs by implementing objectives of equal support of foreign and domestic investment, by increasing the number of financial sources of investment and to by strengthening competitiveness;
- Financial market is needed to be developed intensively. It has specific roles to activate investment; to increase incomes of enterprises and individuals; to strengthen competitiveness in monetary- financial sector and to reduce prices of financial instruments. The main current objective is to create and develop a classical stock market. Governance of shareholding companies needs to be developed.
- The banking system has not yet discovered its resources of power and the prominent role to be accomplished in development of the country. In the future banks are responsible for increasing assets of suppliers, as well as customers and need to be their close assistant and advisor.
- In the market conditions the role of the commercial insurance system is prominent. However, this sector along with the Mongolian stock market is regarded as the weak sector of the current monetary- financial system of the country. Therefore, it is necessary to clarify the state policy on development of insurance system and to work actively for creating the environment and conditions for its active development.

Publications and resources:

1. "Mongolia in the market economy" Statistical Yearbooks (1989-2002), Ulaanbaatar 2004
2. "Financial reforms: studies and problems" D.Tserenpil, Ulaanbaatar 2006
3. Materials of the state census of enterprises. Mongolian National Statistical Agency, Ulaanbaatar 2006
4. "Money, credit, banks" Lavrushina,O Moscow "Finance & Statistics" 2000
5. Economics of the public sector. (Third edition). Joseph E.Stiglitz. 1999
6. "Mongolia in the globalization" Bayartsaikhan, D Ulaanbaatar. 2004
7. Data and reports of Mongolian National Insurance Agency
8. 2007 Mongolian Budget, Mongolian Government Ulaanbaatar.2006
9. Reports and data of Ministry of Finance
10. Mongolian Statistical Yearbook 2005 Ulaanbaatar 2006

11. Mongolian Laws. Brochure Ulaanbaatar 2006
12. Report of Mongol Bank 2003,2004,2005.2006
13. Lectures on public economics. Anthomy B.Atkinson. Joseph E.Stiglitz
14. Money, Credit and Capital. James Tobin, Stephen S.Golub. 2001
15. "Financial Management" Ayurzana, Ts (with "Corporate Finance"), Ulaanbaatar 2007
16. "Investment: policy, legislation, regulation, planning, financing" Ayurzana.Ts, Ulaanbaatar 2005
17. Personal Finance. Jack R. Karoor, Robert. L.Hughes, 2002

CHAPTER FOUR

ECONOMIC SECTORS

Mongolia has faced two historical periods since it declared its independence. During the first period, which lasted until 1990, Mongolia strived to develop a centrally planned command economy with state ownership.

However, since 1990, it has started achieving completely different for Mongolians, political, economic and social changes that led to a market economy. The society got an entire shock facing a number of consequences of the transition such as privatization, shares, pink and blue vouchers, shortage of commodities as well as unemployment, which had not even been dreamt in the old society of centrally planned economy.

A total of 16 years have passed since then. That there have occurred declines, stabilizations and growths in economic sectors during the past 10 years shows how Mongolian people have bravely been experiencing the complexities of the transition to the market economy, learning from their experiences and realizing their perceptions into life. Thus, this chapter aims to describe the problems, achievements, shortcomings, growths and development of the real sector, which is the root of the country's development, during this transitional period.

4.1 AGRICULTURE

Agriculture is a sector that can be developed rapidly in the short to medium term, therefore, is able to become a source for other sectors' recovery and growth as many western and eastern scholars consider. While the growth of other sectors is heavily dependent on the extent, range and rate of investments, the reproduction of agriculture with dominance of using a pastoral and nomadic way of cattle breeding is subject to the reproduction of the nature and the fact that it requires relatively less investments or entirely no investments at all features the sector from others.

However, the quantitative growth and productivity of livestock may vary with favorable and unfavorable weather conditions. This can be characterized by the figures taken from the first years' achievements of the transition; particularly, in 1992- 1998 the number of livestock grew from 25.6 million to 33 million, but in the years of consecutive droughts and dzuds of 1999-2000 it decreased by 10 million animals.

Although that Mongolians have started to use crop land in central and northern parts of the country since 1959 has had both the positive and negative sides, entirely, it is considered a progress made towards the development of the country as it added a brand new branch to the country's agricultural sector. Associated with the rapid emergences of state cooperatives in the agricultural sector in the end of 1950s, there was made a decision in 1958 to establish an institute of agriculture on the basis of faculty of zoology and veterinary science at the National University of Mongolia (NUM) to train various specialists majoring in the sector. As a result, a number of contributions were made to the sector's development as well as to the successful transition of the country to the market economy with the help of these specialists, proving in some senses what Dr. Noil Passel pointed out: 'a formation of a traditional organizational management structure based on skillful professional staff may assist in making some growths even in the early stages of a transition.' (Christopher Ritson 'Agricultural economics principles and policy')

Privatization started in crop and livestock sectors from 1992.

In Mongolia, where the pastoral and nomadic way of animal husbandry is the prevalent practice, the economical transition has set up several trends.

The inconsiderate and disorderly privatization of fixed assets in agriculture has resulted in the still lasting depression of the sector that hinders its recovery to reach the previous level.

Livestock sector

The fluctuations in numbers of households with livestock and herder households are considered an important indicator to detect and measure factors affecting the internal changes in the livestock economy.

The number of herders in the last twenty years is as follows:

Table 4.1 The number of herders

	1985	1990	1995	1999	2000	2001	2002	2003	2004	2005
Number of herders (in thous)	133.4	147.5	390.5	417.7	421.4	407.0	389.8	377.9	369.7	364.4

Source: statistical compilation in agriculture, 1995, Statistical compilation of Mongolia, 2001-2005 editions

The number of livestock in households with livestock and herder households is shown in table 4.2.

Table 4.2 The number of livestock in the grouping of households with livestock and herder households

YEAR	Household	to 10	to 30	31-50	51-100	101-200	201-500	501-999	1000-1499	1500-2000	above 2001	TOTAL
	Households of 1995	43694	50580	40200	61082	53564	31393	3095	280	17	8	283913
1999	Households of 1999	28669	35970	31874	61347	67840	37635	5438	1061	75	41	269950
	1995-1999 changes in households	-15025	-14610	-8326	265	14276	6242	2343	781	58	33	-13963
2000	Households of 2000	31361	40436	35041	63096	59821	33408	4591	893	48	37	268732
	1999-2000 changes in households	2692	4466	3167	1749	-8019	-4227	-847	-168	-27	-4	-1218
2001	Households of 2001	33797	43082	36030	60195	51383	27949	3406	639	38	31	256550
	2000-2001 changes in households	2436	2646	989	-2901	-8438	-5459	-1185	-254	-10	-6	-12182
2002	Households of 2002	33183	42796	36165	55905	46051	25313	3160	601	36	24	243234
	2001-2002 changes in households	-614	-286	135	-4290	-5332	-2636	-246	-38	-2	-7	-13316
2003	Households of 2003	29897	39341	32396	52871	47393	29669	3870	684	61	28	236210
	Changes in households in 2002-2003	-3286	-3455	-3769	-3034	1342	4356	710	83	25	4	-7024
2004	Households of 2004	28010	34295	28930	48860	47946	34941	5367	943	98	47	229437
	Changes in households in 2003-2004	-1887	-5046	-3466	-4011	553	5272	1497	259	37	19	-6773
2005	Households of 2005	24280	32215	26919	46139	49498	38245	6527	1354	142	74	225393
	Changes in households in 2004-2005	-3730	-2080	-2011	-2721	1552	3304	1160	411	44	27	-4044

Sources: statistical compilation in agricultural sectors, UB, 1995, statistical Yearbook MNG, UB, 2001-2005 editions, NSO, 2005

According to the table, the fluctuations of the numbers in herders and households with livestock are occurring in parallel lines simultaneously. While the number of households with 10-100 livestock was decreasing by 36.3-55.6 percent in the given period, the number of households with above 201 livestock increased from 21.8 to 9 percent.

Consequently, although there were some households who managed to increase their number of livestock shifting from the bottom line of the grouping to the top line, there were not a few who remained completely with no livestock. Particularly, due to the droughts and dzuds of 1999-2001, there occurred considerable changes in the numbers of herders and herder households, totally decreasing them year after year.

Table 4.3 The changes in the numbers of herders and herder households

	1999	2000	2001	2002	2003	2004	2005
Decreased number of households in the groupings	37961	13292	18253	13451	13544	14410	10542
Increased number of households in the groupings	23998	12074	6071	135	6720	7637	6498
	-13963	-1218	-12182	-13316	-7024	-6773	-4044

Sources: Sources: statistical compilation in agricultural sectors, UB, 1995, statistical yearbook, NSO UB, 2001-2005 editions,

The main factors affecting the changes were the droughts and dzuds. As the weather conditions worsened, the number of households in the top level of the grouping, regarding the number of the livestock, decreased shifting to the bottom level. During the periods of the droughts and dzuds mentioned earlier, particularly in 2000, the number of households with 10-100 livestock increased by 12074 households but the number of households with above 101 livestock decreased by 13292. The number of households with no livestock was estimated 1218. In 2001 the households with 10-50 livestock increased by 6071, but the households with above 51 livestock decreased by 18253. As a result, 12182 households were estimated with no livestock. Particularly, in 2002, the last year of the droughts and dzuds, the situation worsened even more seriously as a consequence of which in almost every grouping with 10-2000 and above 2001 livestock there occurred decreases in the numbers of households and 13316 households remained with no livestock. In 1999 the number of total livestock was estimated 33.5 million, however, resulting from the successive droughts and dzuds, the number decreased to 23.8 million in 2002. Even though, the number of households with up to 100 livestock has continuously been increasing since 2003, there still exist households remaining with no livestock. However, this tendency is likely to be decreased in the future. The future tendency of the households leaving the bottom level of the grouping is likely to occur in two ways. First, some households are moving from the bottom level to the top, increasing their livestock. Secondly, some households, remaining with no livestock tend to migrate to cities and settled areas, which is considered one of the serious consequences of this phenomenon.

A total of 58520 households with livestock, including cattle- breeding households and 57.1 thousand herders have remained with no livestock and migrated to settled areas such as Ulaanbaatar, Erdenet and Darkhan since 1999. This, in turn, has increased the rate of unemployment, made Social Security services complicated and increased poverty level in the country. However, this has not only been caused by natural disasters like droughts and dzuds, but also, some social factors that should be taken into consideration could have been grounds for the happening to a certain extent. For example, underdeveloped infrastructure, living in long distances away from the markets, running extensive nomadic cattle breeding in harsh conditions, having no access to health and cultural services are considered direct factors affecting the phenomenon.

However, the following survey shows that although the number of herders, households with livestock as well as herder households is decreasing, provided that there is not an emergency natural disaster, the number of livestock tends to increase constantly.

Table 4.4 Increases in the number of livestock (in thousand heads)

	Total	**Camels**	**Horses**	**Cows**	**Sheep**	**Goats**
1990	25856.9	537.5	2262	2848.7	15083	5125.7
1995	28572.3	367.5	2648.4	3317.1	13718.6	8520.7
1999	33568.9	355.6	3163.5	3824.7	15191.3	11033.9
2000	30227.5	322.9	2660.7	3097.6	13876.4	10269.8
2001	26075.3	285.2	2191.8	2069.6	11937.3	9591.3
2002	23897.6	253	1988.9	1884.3	10636.6	9134.8
2003	2525427.7	256.7	1968.9	1792.6	10756.4	10652.9
2004	28027.9	256.6	2005.3	1841.6	11686.4	12238
2005	29901.8	250	2001.2	1940.3	12582.9	13127.4
2006	34802.4	253.5	2114.8	2167.9	14815.1	15451.7

Sources: statistical compilation in agricultural sectors, UB, 1995, statistical yearbook, UB, 2001-2005 editions, news of statistical office, 2005

The fact that in 1992- 1998 the number of livestock grew from 25.8 million to 33.5 million but in the years of successive droughts and zuds of 1999-2000 it decreased to 23.8 million represents that the present Mongolian livestock sector is fully dependent on the nature.

Although the number of livestock tended to increase again from 2003 and reached to 34.8 million in 2006, the number of animals except goats could not reach the 1990 levels. This shows that the harmony of animals is in an inappropriate state. The reason why herders started to 'worship' goats is connected with the growing price of cashmere. Some people deliver a homily that it is an inevitable process according to market laws and it is not worth to try to stop it. However, at present, the theory that states market is manageable and can be regulated by government policies is being exercised worldwide and the examples of this can be seen in experiences of our south neighbor as well as of neighboring countries beyond it.

Researchers are warning that desertification is getting active in some parts of our country due to the global warming. This, to a certain extent, is caused by the intensive expansion in goat numbers. Plants grow passing particular stages: rooting, getting gramineous, getting shrubby, blooming and coming to maturity. But that goats eat only the flowers of any plant stops the reproduction of plants, consequently, activates the process of desertification. By the way, some scholars do not accidently consider that the three powerful empires in the world (Greek, Roman and the empire of two seas) were destroyed by goats. Thus, it is suggestible to make policies at the government level in order to keep the number of goats in an appropriate accordance with other types of livestock as well as with pasture.

While some of our researchers as well as ordinary people relate the growth in livestock numbers to the privatization, there are some people who consider that it just seems to be increased because the livestock privatization stopped the active turnover in Mongolian livestock making it appear a passive growth. They argue that, compared with the active turnover of livestock in the previous years of 1990, the number of livestock decreased but not increased in fact. Besides, people started to criticize that the sector lacked a strong policy to bring the livestock back to the active economic turnover after Aman Tuliev, the Governor of Kemerov province, Russia had exclaimed in 2003: "While in your country the number of livestock was decreasing inefficiently by 10 million animals, we did lack meat in the food supply." That which of the above views is acceptable will be ascertained in further studies.

However, it is worth to indicate that due to the privatization of livestock there were made advanced changes in the structure of total livestock. For example, in 1990, while we had 25 million livestock, a total of 9.6 million young livestock were reared by the same 9.6 million breeding female animals, the total sum of which comprised 19.2 million and adding the number of breeding male animals of 1.1 million to this, a total sum of 20.3 million animals were involved in the reproduction processes. However, while the number of infertile male livestock was estimated 4.7 million and accounted for 18.8 per cent of the livestock, 10 million young livestock were reared by the same amount of breeding female animals and 1.5 million breeding male animals were estimated in 2006. The total sum of these animals altogether comprised 21.5 million animals. Additionally, the number of infertile male animals was estimated 13.3 million and accounted for 38.2 per cent of total livestock according to which it is concluded that there are more opportunities at present to involve the livestock in the active economic turnover compared with the previous years' situation, which favors the herders to accumulate capital and make investments in their livestock.

The number of livestock to be in possession of households with livestock and herder households is relatively different. In 2005, a total of 225391 households were estimated as households with livestock and herder households. 178959 households with 10-2000 animals held a total of 12405.2 million livestock. Accordingly, 79.5 per cent of total households held 41.5 per cent of total livestock. This states that the remaining 20.5 per cent of the total households possessed 17496.6 animals or 58.5 per cent of the total livestock.

According to this statistics, the distinction between the rich and poor tends to be increased. Scholars note that during the Bogd khan's empire, the certain group of population accounting for only 7.8 per cent of the total population owned 49.5 per cent of total livestock, whereas the ordinary people who comprised the remaining 92.2 per cent of the population owned 50.5 per cent of it. As both the history and the present situation suggest, whenever the livestock is privately owned, the majority of the herders tend to be poor while the minority tends to be rich. Accordingly, associated with accumulation of capital, there emerges a danger of distinctions in authority, which entails a just regulation of legal instruments. Otherwise, the vital principal provision of the constitution, which states 'to regard the human right and freedom as superior' is likely to be breached and the majority may occur under an economical oppression. The direction, held by the government towards the livestock economy tends not to strive after the quantitative achievements of the livestock, but to raise a few, highly productive animals using settled or partially settled methods of farming and lastly, to run intensive livestock farming at all levels of the livestock economy. Although the objective is not yet being implemented nationwide, some enterprises are running milk processing industries or specializing in other businesses based on the settlement methods nearby the big cities and settled areas, where the market intercourses are more active. However, the rate of intensity is not adequate enough due to the fact that it is by nature inextricably linked with intellectualized labor and its use in the production processes.

But the current situation cannot provide the necessary agreements of legal, economic and social comprehensive concepts which are supposed to help find out the proper links between science and production; even the approaches of how to determine the links between them are not proposed up yet. However, the fact that it was set up as an objective might give some hope of further development.

The state of consuming livestock products is one of the key indicators of development in agricultural sector including livestock economy and its future trends. In 1992, after the livestock privatization started, the integrated procurement system of livestock produces including other sorts of products was completely removed.

We collected some necessary information about the consumption of livestock products using statistics prepared by statistical office and other sources. First of all, we will consider the cashmere, the main yield from goats. In 1986-1990, on average 1312.3 tons of cashmere was produced annually, in 2005 it was 3649.9 tons accounting for up to 12% of GDP and 17.5 % of total export, which on average equaled 75 million American dollars. Strains (breeds) and clans (tribe) of goats play an important role in producing high quality yields. Currently, there are 2 main breeds and 7 tribes registered. It is important to crossbreed them efficiently by selection in order to rear out a particular best breed.

While the fleece, the byproduct of goat cashmere was produced on average 864.4 tons annually in 1986-1990, currently it is estimated 418.5 tons. Molt wool from big (camel, cattle) livestock was produced 966.7-1329.2 tons in the previous year but currently the number decreased to 298.1- 431.6 tons. Unfortunately, these sources are gradually getting out of the market due to the liquidation of the related industries resulting from the less export demands.

The sheep wool production was on average 19.5 thousand tons in 1986- 1990, but in 2005 it decreased to 16.7 thousand tons. Before 1990, camel wool production was estimated on average 2.7 thousand tons, but currently it is 1.2 thousand tons. During the period, the decrease in camel numbers doubled; consequently, it led to the decline of camel products.

Demands for rawhides of all animals increased. While big livestock rawhides were procured 628.5 thousand annually before the transition to the market economy, now, on average 767.6 thousands are procured annually. As for small cattle (goat, sheep), on average 5.3 million rawhides were procured annually in 1986- 1990; currently the figure reached to 5.8 million.

Cashmere, wool, fleece, molt wool and rawhides are the main yields of livestock economy as well as the chief raw materials for the light industry of the country. However, due to the underdevelopment of these industries they are still being exported unprocessed. Currently we have 85 cashmere processing industries, 4-5 of which produce finished products, but the remainder are engaged to produce only washed and worsted cashmere. These raw materials are exported to over 20 countries in Asia, Europe and North American continent.

Livestock is one of the essential sources to provide the population with food supplies as well as food industries with raw materials- particularly meat and milk are the main supplies.

Mongolia produced 512.1 thousand tons of meat on the hoof (on live weight), 248.9 thousand tons on slaughter weight including camel meat, horse meat, beef, mutton, goat meat, pork and chicken in 1990. In 2005, it procured 403 thousand tons of meat on the hoof and 193.1 thousand tons on slaughter weight of the same animals. Currently, there are 28 industries engaged to produce meat and meat products and 27 of them export these products to some extent.

According to customs office report, on average 17.4 thousand tons of meat, meat products and byproducts are exported to 17 foreign countries annually, which accounts for about 9 per cent of total meat production. Even though the meat production sees certain trends of further increase, some diseases occurring among livestock tend to restrict its potential growth.

Milk is the livestock produce that occupies the highest percentage in food consumption of Mongolians. There were times in Mongolian history when milk and dairy products accounted for 55 per cent of all prices for food stuff. Traditionally, people consume milk of 5 animals in our country. By 1990, 315.7 thousand tons of milk was produced. Currently, 335.1 thousand tons is procured annually - 2.4 thousand tons from she-camels, 33.8- mares, 215.1- cows, 15.8- she-sheep and 68- she goats.

On average 134 liters of milk per capita is consumed annually at present. In terms of dairy products, a similar picture emerges. The milk and dairy product consumption per capita is totally different for urban and rural residents.

In the future milk production sees good prospects to be enhanced. In 2005, as mentioned above, 335.1 thousand tons of milk was produced. But sources say it is viable to milk 7.3 thousand tons of milk from she camels, 59.1- from mares, 305.8-from cows, 30-from she-sheep and 118.3-from she-goats; correspondingly, altogether 520.5 thousand tons of milk is available to be produced. According to this statistics, 185.4 thousand tons of milk is not used due to the fact that Mongolians are not used to consuming milk from small cattle. Consequently, we lack a proper policy to relate milk production to livestock economy and make the intensity consummated.

The problems hindering the livestock economy development are as follows:

1. Dependence of extensive livestock farming on weather;

2. Lack of a policy to relate the market relations to the production methods in the livestock economy;
3. The provision of the constitution 'Livestock in Mongolia is considered to be part of the nation's wealth and is subject to state protection' is not being exercised into practice and we lack a far- sighted and scientifically proven policy on intensive livestock development;
4. The highly contagious diseases such as foot and mouth disease, anthrax and small pox are occurring among livestock due to the poor veterinary and hygienic and sanitation standards, which may lead the situation to a disaster level;
5. The breeds of sheep like 'Orkhon', 'Eroo', 'Khangai' raised for fine- wool, 'Torguud' raised for meat and wool, which were crossbred as a result of multi-year dedicated and hard work of Mongolian scholars became extinct and there is no hope of rebreeding them;
6. It would be a one-sided, prejudiced policy if we tried to develop only intensive livestock farming alone, neglecting the development of national livestock raw material processing industries;
7. As a consequence of the removal of integrated procurement system of livestock yields and raw materials, a great number of raw materials are currently out of utilization or are exported for cheap prices unprocessed; thus, valuable resources of the country continue to be wasted inefficiently.
8. Historically, Mongolian livestock economy has been run in the forms of herder settlements - groups of herder households- cooperatives- household livestock farming; but current situation necessitates an appropriate modern method of labor division of herders.

The above mentioned problems should be placed an emphasis and unless implementing thorough-going measures, they are likely to be accumulated and lead to a crisis. Thus, these measures should be based on the previous researches done in the sector and consistent with the market relations.

Recommendations:

- First of all, rural veterinary services must be run under state control and related service centers should be established in order to improve hygienic conditions for livestock, which will be consistent with the provision of the constitution 'Livestock in Mongolia is considered to be part of the nation's wealth and is subject to state protection''.
- A legal environment must be provided for the merely emerged voluntary groups or cooperatives of herders in order to help them to get an acquisition of legal personality. They have to be provided opportunities to attend training courses or involved in foreign projects, get access to soft loans and utilize

grazing lands and pastures under regulation. All these should be regulated by the government.

- An insurance system for livestock should be started and international double insurance policy must be provided as well.
- In order to develop national industries to process raw materials and yields of livestock, it is vital to outline a policy to set up links between light industry and livestock economy, and start up a livestock product exchange, or restore integrated procurement system over again.
- To facilitate the development of intensive livestock farming, we need legal and economic regulations supporting favorable legal environment for foreign investments and involve national scholars as well as scientific organizations in the policy making.

Crop land sector

Although Mongolians started using crop lands a long time ago, until 1959 it had only been an accompaniment to the animal husbandry. Since 1959, as a result of numerous investments made in the north part of the steppe and forest- steppe regions, agriculture has become an independent sector, which added a new page to the history of Mongolian economy. Owing to the grain farm development, flour and feeding mills were established in Dornod, Undurkhaan, Ulaanbaatar, Darkhan, Selenge, Khar Khorin, Bulgan, Murun and Ulaangom setting up a new branch of light industry in the industrial sector. Mongolia had been one of a few countries which managed to meet the needs of food consumption of its people independently by manufacturing staple foods itself because it developed agriculture as an independent sector.
However, since 1962, according to the entity law and privatization law of assets, more than 70 stately owned entities and companies were privatized; large state owned companies were split into multiple small companies, as a consequence of which most of them could not endure the market competitions and went bankrupt, which was accompanied by a depression of the agricultural sector. The factors affecting the depression are as follows:

1. Lacking knowledge of newly emerging market relations, most of the managers in the sector were nonplussed and got stuck;
2. During the privatization, in place of competent experts who could have led the enterprises efficiently, opportunists took the advantage embezzling the property accumulated from generation to generation.
3. Large scale state enterprises were split into vulnerable small units in the economy.
4. Instead of implementing a more careful managerial policy, the leaders of these small vulnerable entities used the old authoritarian methods of management

precipitating a bankruptcy that resulted from disagreement of production methods with market relations.

5. In the previous practice, the agricultural machinery and equipment were owned by large state owned enterprises and used as a complex in the agricultural processes. But these were dispersed by the privatization. As a consequence, small enterprises as well as individual people who owned the machinery and equipment partially faced a capacity bottleneck which restricted their activities due to the separation. This led to a disorder, which was impossible to overcome and resulted in the depression of the sector.

However, it has only been a depression that possibly will last for a certain period of time, but not a collapse, what the Mongolian agriculture is experiencing at present.

Cropped areas for the past 20 years are shown by plant species.

Table 4.5 Cropped areas (by hectare)

	Total cropped area	**Grain**	**Wheat**	**Potato**	**Vegetables**	**Fodder plants**
1985	789647.8	636239.5	482070.0	10338.1	3330.2	139740.0
1990	787750.7	654090.2	532945.2	12167.0	3649.9	117840.4
1995	372586.7	356465.8	348485.0	6225.7	3243.8	5951.4
2000	209256.2	194734.6	191408.1	7882.6	5373.3	755.8
2001	217598.1	263045.6	193998.4	8859.4	3561.7	1907.8
2002	285719.2	172928.3	259546.6	10232.9	7095.7	2953.7
2003	225874.7	207311.2	202653.2	8421.0	5869.3	3229.6
2004	200498.3	172928.3	168015.2	9078.7	4918.8	5118.6
2005	189548.7	159094.8	153754.4	9757.8	5887.9	5161.1
2006	162040.2	126200.7	117964.7	10723.4	5882.6	3850.5

Source: Agricultural Yearbook, 1995, Statistical Yearbook 2001-2005, Customs statistical yearbook 2005, Statistical yearbook 2004,2005

According to the table 4.5, although since 1990, the cropped areas had been decreasing, 2001 and 2002 saw an increase due to the measures taken by the government towards the recovery of agriculture. However, the sowing of other plants except for potatoes and vegetables has still been declining. The green revolution, which was carried out in the frame of a state policy that aimed to provide rural households and the enterprises engaged in running crop-land farming with a vast opportunity has produced particular outcomes: the production of potatoes and vegetables and cultivation of fruit tended to increase. This attributed to the growing demands for them as well as associated with the possibility of irrigated system. Regrettably, cropped areas for planting grain and fodder plants have still been decreasing and even do not see any progress of recovery.

According to researchers, there are at least 2 million hectares of crop land available in Mongolia. Disappointingly, 162.1 thousand ha crop land was used for planting in 2006. This results from an improper policy that should link market relations with enterprises running planting in crop land areas.

One of the significant indicators representing a crop land sector situation is an amount of gathered harvest.

Table 4.6 Aggregate harvest

	Grain	Wheat	Potato	Vegetables
1985	886171.0	688461.5	113854.4	41187.9
1990	718334.6	596205.9	131053.4	41742.4
1995	261427.6	256741.1	51980.7	27287.8
2000	142066.1	138722.4	58907.2	43999.4
2001	142217.8	138717.4	58033.9	44509.8
2002	125281.0	123064.9	51887.9	39721
2003	165046.7	160362.6	78673.0	59610.2
2004	138412.5	135622.2	801992.1	49175.1
2005	75468.5	73484.7	82841.4	640752
2006	138572.0	127756.5	109069.9	70440.5

Source: Agricultural statistical compilation Ulaanbaatar, 1995, NSO Yearbook

Before 1990, Mongolia was considered one of a few countries in the world that was able to meet their grain demand domestically; even, in some years they exported wheat to foreign countries. However, as the table 4.6 shows, the grain production has been decreasing since 1990 every year. As a result, it hardly meets less than 30 per cent of domestic needs of the country at present. As for potato and vegetables, it approached the previous level compared with the situation prior to 1990; vegetables even increased in relation to the preceding years, which in a sense raises an expectation for a recovery of the sector.

Compared with vegetable planting, grain cultivation requires more arable land, yet produces less harvest. Therefore, for Mongolia, a country with a harsh continental climate and risk to run crop land farming, a medium or over medium- sized enterprise with complex machinery and equipment as well as with technology capable to prevail over the dependence on weather has a tendency to succeed in the sector.

An amount of harvest gathered from a unit hectare area is an indicator representing the development of the crop land sector as well as of an enterprise engaged in it. The table 4.7 shows the amount of harvest gathered from a unit ha area in recent years.

Table 4.7 Harvest from unit ha area.

	Grain	Wheat	Potato	Vegetable
1985	13.9	14.3	110.1	
1990	11.0	11.2	107.7	
1995	7.3	7.4	83.5	84.1
2000	7.3	7.2	74.7	81.9
2001	7.1	7.2	65.6	80.0
2002	5.7	5.9	56.4	55.9
2003	8.0	7.9	93.4	101.6
2004	8.0	8.1	88.3	99.9
2005	4.7	5.8	84.8	108.9
2006	11.0	11.1	101.7	

Source: Agricultural statistical compilation Ulaanbaatar, 1995, NSO Yearbook 2001-2005,Statistical bulletin, 2004,2005

According to the table, the amount of harvest gathered every year is comparatively different and irregular due to perceptions of the given year; consequently, this represents that the crop land economy of our country is fully dependent on weather. It also states the unsatisfactory scientific level of the sector and that agro-technology necessary for producing regular harvest has not still worked out and put into practice yet.

Comparatively, regular harvest from potatoes and vegetables and its tendency for an increase show that the technology used for the sector is superior to the one, which is used in grain sector. However, the crop land economy is not satisfactory to meet the needs of the country. Thus, first of all, the necessary action to take for the regular harvest in the present situation of the country is the development of irrigated crop land farming.

To develop the grain production is a vital strategic issue. Supposed that we produce 360 thousand tons of wheat and not less than 250 thousand tons of flour per annum, we would be able to satisfy the needs of the products domestically as researchers suggest.

This should be regulated by a proper policy based on scientific researches.

Depending on the unique natural conditions of the country, the crop land product needs of the country cannot be satisfied by household crop land farming alone. Instead, we can enhance crop land farming, particularly grain farms with powerful enterprises operating within favorable legal environment and supported by proper state policy.

The issuance of land ownership rights to the Mongolian enterprises running crop land farming should be solved accurately. Historically, in our country, people have had practices to develop cattle breeding on the basis of crop land farming or crop land farming on the basis of cattle breeding, or developed crop land farming separately. It is fully acceptable to apply these practices appropriately in accordance with the current market relations.

Mongolia has abundant resources of fertilizers like animal dung and muck, but it intensely lacks necessary fertilizers for crop land farming. Therefore, to import ecologically friendly minerals, fertilizers and herbicides firstly, to produce them domestically afterwards will contribute to the sustainable development of crop land economy.

Modern crop land farming is hard to imagine without techniques; therefore, in order to make machinery and equipment available for farmers, it is necessary to take the following measures:

- to provide them with soft loans;
- to let enterprises obtain the techniques on leasing;
- to launch maintenance service for agricultural machinery and equipment;
- to produce spare parts domestically;
- to establish a factory to produce the necessary equipment.

The requirements to solve the above mentioned problems in order to recover the crop land farming and develop it until it becomes one of significant economic sectors of the country are rising from life.

Brief conclusion

The section reviewed the policies that have been implemented in the livestock and crop land sectors from the time the country started the transition to a market economy until the present day as well as the future trends and problems that should be solved in the future.

References

1. AGM reports, 'Govi' company Ltd. 2002-2004
2. Christopher Ritson, 'Agricultural Economics Principles and Policy'
3. Customs office statistical news, 2005

4. K. B. Baldin, S.N Vorobiev, 'Risk management', Moscow, 2005
5. M. Tumurjav, 'Pastural livestock of Mongolia', Ulaanbaatar, 2003
6. 'Livestock economy', 2006
7. 'Introduction about meat exports' Ministry of food and agriculture, 2005
8. 'Statistical compilation of Mongolia' Ulaanbaatar, 2001-2005
9. 'Report of Mongolian cashmere and wool association' 2002-2006
10. 'Mongolian economy' Ulaanbaatar, 1997
11. N.Erdenetsogt, 'Mongolian nomadic livestock farming'
12. 'Solongo' magazine, Inner Mongolia, editions of 2004-2005
13. 'News from statistical office' 2004-2005
14. T. Namjim, 'Mongolian Economy' v. I,II,III, Ulaanbaatar, 2004
15. T. Namjim, 'Mongolian husbandry, economy ' vol. I,II Ulaanbaatar, 2000
16. ' Agricultural statistical compilation' Ulaanbaatar, 1995
17. Ts. A. Maiskii, 'Modern Mongolia' Ulaanbaatar, 2001
18. 'Export-oriented management system of production' Ulaanbaatar, 2004

4.2 INDUSTRIAL SECTOR

During the socialist regime, the industrial sector was comparatively large and well organized one, therefore occupied a large percentage of the workforce. In 1990 the sector accounted for a quarter of GDP and of workforce respectively.

Since 1990, the entire links of vertical and horizontal lines of Mongolian economy have been dissolved and faced a collapse. During the transition to society oriented relations based on free economic intercourses, due to the fairly irrational privatization policies of properties, the sector faced a serious shock; consequently, industries went collapsed.

Table 4.8 Percentage of industrial sector accounted for GDP production (1989-2005)

Year	**1989**	**1990**	**1991**	**1992**	**1993**	**1994**	**1995**	**1996**	**1997**
Percentage of industrial sector accounted for GDP production (%)	32,7	35,6	30,2	30,0	26,3	26,6	25,9	18,5	24,0
Year	**1998**	**1999**	**2000**	**2001**	**2002**	**2003**	**2004**	**2005**	
Percentage of industrial sector accounted for GDP production	18,3	18,1	20,0	20,1	20,2	22,3	27,5	27,9	

Source: NSO year books

According to the table 4.8, the percentage of industrial sector accounting for GDP in 2005 could not reach the 1989 level and this represents the future trends of the industrial sector development. Due to the long lasting depression of the sector, a number of industrial enterprises, which were established during the past 70 years, were not able to be recovered resulting in unemployment of 30 thousand employees of the sector, closing the state owned industries worth 3 billion tugrigs by the estimation of that time and leaving some of them just empty buildings. This caused by an abrupt transition policy that did not foresee the future outcomes. On the pretext of privatizing all state owned properties evenly to the people, firstly they aimed to privatize all the industries and enterprises except for more expensive ones; consequently, they left commodities without owners.

The industrial enterprises with complex machinery, equipment and tools, which were established as a result of huge state investments, were all squandered.

As an alternative, had the properties been privatized firstly to professionals or competent persons who could have led the enterprises under a lease agreement supported by government policies with firm control, the properties would not have on one hand, been dissipated this way. On the other hand, it could have produced more outcomes, if the government had regulated the market of raw materials, exercised flexible customs tax policies to restrict particular import goods as well as increased the market awareness of the entrepreneurs.

Dramatic changes that led to a disruption of internal parity among the sectors occurred in the industrial structure in the early 1990s. The market of various domestic woolen and woven, leather and sheepskin and sewn garments was in crisis and stopped their production because of the price boosts, real income decrease of the population as well as import of low quality, cheap and similar goods. For example, the domestic drilling cloth production stopped in 1993 according to the president's initiative that abolished the tax for the drilling cloth import.

The soft leather production stopped and artificial leather as well as leather garments made in China and Korea started to appear everywhere due to the government decision of tax exemption for all imported goods; consequently there have occurred poor purchases for domestically produced woolen blankets, which led to the bankruptcy of the related industries.

Graph 4.1 Production of industrial sector (1989-2005, price estimation of 2000)

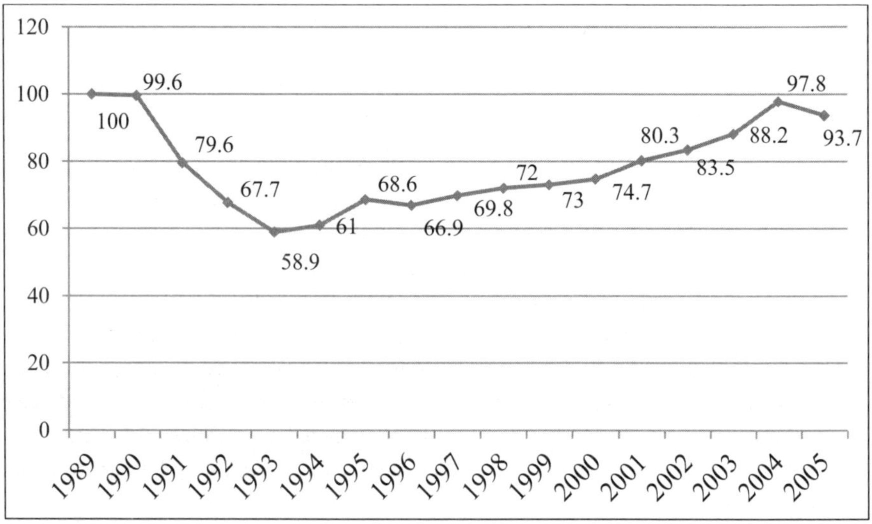

Source: NSO year books

According to the graph, the total production in the sector started to decrease since 1990, which was followed by a steady growth from 1993 to 2004, but it has not reached the 1989 level back yet.

The substantial reduction, which occurred in 1990-1993 in the sector, was due to the misguided privatization policy of state owned industrial enterprises led by the government; as a result, it caused bankruptcies for numerous enterprises.

Table 4.9 Production of staple products of the industrial sector

	measures	1989	1995	2000	2005	1989=1		
						1995	2000	2005
Electricity	mill.sq.km	3568.3	2628.0	2946.0	3418.9	0.736	0.826	0.958
Coal	thous.tons	8044.5	5019.0	5185.0	7517.1	0.624	0.645	0.934
Fluorite	thous.tons	578.2	526.9	733.5	507.9	0.911	1.268	0.878
Red brick	mil.pieces	172.8	21.5	17.3	14.6	0.124	0.100	0.084
Combed cashmere	tons	250.0	420.8	450.9	581.9	1.683	1.804	2.328
Knitwear	thous.pieces	4110.5	522.7	1233.5	3448.5	0.127	0.300	0.839
Hide and skin	thous.metre	1564.3	229.4	5.4	5.9	0.147	0.003	0.0038
Meat	thous.tons	61.7	11.3	6.4	3.6	0.183	0.104	0.058
Milk, milk products	mil.liter	62.0	1.8	1.5	7.1	0.029	0.024	0.114
Alcoholic drinks	thous.lier	4818.8	497.3	111.7	7956.4	0.103	0.023	1.651
Flour	thous.tons	199.7	158.7	40.2	58.3	0.795	0.201	0.292
Gold	kg	...	4504.0	11808	24121.9	6.233*	16.34*	33.38*
Copper concentrate of 35% content	thous. tons	352.9	346.4	357.8	361.6	0.981	1.014	1.025
Cement	thous.tons	512.6	108.8	91.7	111.9	0.212	0.179	0.218

Source: NSO year books

- 722.6 tons of gold were extracted in 1991.
- Percentage compared to figures of 1991.

The production scale of all industries that were operating in the previous economy fell sharply from the first years of the transition to the market economy, which largely resulted in some industries to stop their production. For example, factories such as leather goods, footwear, peltry ware, tannery and carpet factory of Choibalsan city all stopped their production. Previously, they had capacity of producing annually 480 thousand leather goods, 1 million peltry wares and sheepskin coats, 3.5 million pairs of footwear, 650 thousand square meters of carpets of various made, and processing 5 million skins respectively.

However, some of them managed to survive the crisis. For example, 'Knitwear' company started to operate as a sewing factory and the sheepskin garment factory of Darkhan, 'Erdenet carpet', 'Ulaanbaatar carpet' and "Gobi' companies made improvements in their technology and expanded their range and style of products.

As 2005 situation shows, the range of goods except for worsted cashmere (combed down), copper concentrate and alcohol and wine could not reach the 1989 level; as for bricks, skin and meat, they could not achieve even 10 per cent of the 1989 level.

Associated with the internal and external situations of the markets, combed down has increased 2.3 times, alcohol and wine- 1.6 times and gold extraction- 33.4 times since 1989.

Past, present and future prospects of the training system of professional workers in the industrial sector

To provide the reconstructed and newly established factories with professionals as well as to retrain them have become one of crucial issues of the industrial sector since 1960. The vocational training system, which emerged from the mid 1960s in our country, played an exceptional role in the preparation of professional workers.

By 1989, there were 46 vocational schools and 30 technical colleges, which prepared thousands of professional workers and occupational specialists. Besides, hundreds of people were sent to vocational schools in the former Soviet Union. However, the vocational training system principally has fallen into stagnation since 1990s.

Table 4.10 Number of workers in the industrial sector

Years	1989	1990	1991	1992	1993	1994	1995	1996	1997
Total workers in the end of the year /thous.people/	633.2	651.4	665.8	806	772.8	786.5	794.7	791.8	788.3
In industrial sector	107.3	105.9	104.2	133.9	124.1	100.9	108.1	104.6	98.9
Percentage of industrial workers in the total number of workers	0.169	0.162	0.157	0.166	0.160	0.130	0.136	0.132	0.125
Year	**1998**	**1999**	**2000**	**2001**	**2002**	**2003**	**2004**	**2005**	
Total workers in the end of the year /thous.people/	809.5	813.6	809	832.3	870.8	926.5	950.5	968.3	
In industrial sector	97.8	98.8	91.0	93.3	99.2	109.5	114.2	113.9	
Percentage of industrial workers in the total number of workers	0.121	0.121	0.112	0.112	0.114	0.118	0.120	0.118	

Source: NSO year book

Whilst a slight growth was achieved in the number of workers in the last years of the given period as the table shows, it was relatively less growth in terms of special weight compared to the figures in the early years of 1990s. It was associated with the factor that the other sectors such as construction and service sectors started to require more workers.

Even though there have emerged a number of private institutes and universities along-side the state owned ones, the industrial sector still lacks professional workers due to the inadequate numbers of vocational training schools.

In recent years, labour force from other countries tends to occupy work places of Mongolian people as a result of improper policy of the Government on vocational training issues and lack of state regulation.

In fact, instead of preparing a number of professional engineers, it is essential to train professional workers in compliance of the sector's interest, which will definitely have a significant effect on unemployment reduction. Although the existing vocational complex schools offer training, they are not yet able to meet the current demand of the market in terms of quantity and quality of professional workers outpacing the economic development growth; therefore, the issue should be paid more attention.

Thus, it is urgent to open vocational schools that are capable to train professional workers who are competent in all sectors of the economy. Besides the quantity of workers, the market requires their productivity; in other words, the growth of labour productivity is of high importance in the economy.

As for the landlocked country with a weak infrastructure and limited human resource, which has 2.5 million people, half of which are nomads, it is crucial to intensify production in all strength and increase the total productivity; particularly, the labour productivity of the sector is vital to be improved.

It will require a huge investment in order to intensify production, increase productivity and set up a useful structure of economic sector.

The idea of increasing labour productivity is closely connected with the automation and mechanization of production processes; therefore, this relationship is expressed by the proper ratio between labour productivity and means of production. Labour productivity is measured by GDP per capita at macro level and by additional cost per worker at micro level.

As for our country, labour productivity has been estimated by additional cost per worker in recent years, but as we lack appropriate statistics of previous years, the following table shows labour productivity estimated by total production per worker.

Table 4.11. Labour productivity in industrial sector

Year	1989	1990	1991	1992	1993	1994	1995	1996	1997
Industrial production /billion tug./ at price of 2000	92208	919.3	734.7	624.4	543.2	563.2	633.0	617.2	644.2
Annual average number of workers /thous.peopel/	107.3	105.9	104.2	129.0	112.5	104.5	106.35	101.75	98.4
Labour productivity /million tug/	8.6	8.68	7.05	4.84	4.83	5.39	5.95	6.066	6.55
Year	**1998**	**1999**	**2000**	**2001**	**2002**	**2003**	**2004**	**2005**	
Industrial production /billion tug/ at price of 2000	664.9	673.4	689.6	740.9	770.5	814.1	902.1	864.3	
Annual average number of workers /thous.people/	98.35	94.9	92.15	96.25	104.35	111.85	114.5	114.5	
Labor production /million tug/	6.76	7.1	7.48	7.7	7.384	7.28	7.88	7.58	

Source: Statistical Yearbooks of Mongolia

According to the table, the labour productivity of industrial sector decreased until 1993, and then from 1994 it tended to increase furthermore.

It has become a vital and urgent task for any enterprise and business organization to thoroughly seek the possibilities to increase labour productivity and reveal potential resources whenever it is necessary. To facilitate this, it is important to promptly implement scientific and technological advances into production, make sophisticated structural changes, retrain workers, find reasonable managerial and marketing solutions as well as choose an appropriate size of a production site.

Industrial raw material base, its utilization

Natural raw materials, particularly, minerals are the significant resources to develop minerals industry. A country's economy, particularly, the pace of industrial development depends on how the country utilizes its natural resources. The secondary product of processing – the artificial material – is not produced in our country; therefore, we prioritize industrial mineral raw materials. Coal, fluorite, crude petroleum, copper molybdenum ore, iron ore as well as some building materials are considered the main minerals of the sector.

Mining sector plays a significant role in the industrial sector of the country. It accounted for 26.2 per cent of total production of the country in 1989, 44.3 per cent in 2000 and 57 per cent in 2005. However since 1990, exploration of other minerals except for crude petroleum and gold has been substantially declined.

Energy resources

Fossil coal and lignite deposits can be found everywhere in the country and there are over 300 deposits with about 150 billion tons of reserves. Coal has been the major resource of energy for Mongolia, which has not yet started to utilize its crude petroleum and natural gas deposits. Due to the economic depression occurred in the 1990s, coal mining has reduced from 8044.5 million tons in 1989 to 5019 million tons in 1995 and 4.9 million tons in 1999 respectively.

However, as a result of the expansion and reconstruction of larger mines such as Baganuur and Shivee-Ovoo including other regional mines with the assistance of soft loans provided by Japanese Government and ADB as well as other sources, coal mining production got increased and started to meet not only domestic market needs, but also it became possible to export coals to other countries.

Coal mining increased to 5.2 million tons in 2000, 6.865 million tons in 2004 and 8.2 million tons in 2005. The privatization in mining sector has been taking place successfully in recent years and all other mines, except for Baganuur and Shivee-Ovoo have completely been privatized. One of the potential coal deposits in the country is Tavantolgoi, which has 5.0 billion tons of coking coal resources.

It could become a vital source to generate export revenues if the necessary investments for Tavantolgoi deposit are made.

Inset:

Tavan Tolgoi Coking coal Tsogttsutsgiit soum of Umnugovi aimag. 540 km away from UB, 90 km from Dalanzadgad Resource is 5 billion tons out of which 1.6 billion tons is coking coal. It occupies a leading place not only in Asia, but also in the world in terms of its resource and quality.	Nariin Sukhait Gurvan Tes soum of Umnugovi aimag. 849 km away from UB, 296 km from Dalanzadgad, 40 km away from the southern border of Mongolia. Resource is 125.5 million tons, 6435-6935 kcal/kg

Crude petroleum

Mongolia extracted a total of 350 thousand tons of crude petroleum from the Zuunbayan deposit in 1950-1969 and met 20-30 per cent of petroleum consumption of the country at that time. However, from 1969 to 1990, the exploration of petroleum was completely stopped. 'Mongolian Petroleum' company was established under the control of the Government in 1990 and the 'Petroleum law' was released in 1991. In 1991-1993, the companies from the USA, Russia and Great Britain conducted geological and geochemical surveys (prospecting) for crude oil and natural gas in potential 21 contracted sites. Moreover, they started to prospect for crude petroleum in Dornod and Dornogovi aimags. 100 barrels of crude petroleum was extracted from two oil-wells and exported to China in December, 1996. The crude petroleum resource of the country was estimated over 470 million tons. 197.6 thousand barrels of crude petroleum were extracted in 2004.

Table 4.12. Extraction of crude petroleum

Companies	2005		2006	
	Extraction (tons)	Export (tons)	Extraction (tons)	Export (tons)
1. "Petrochina Dachin Tansag Mongolia" Ltd	12.243	1.896	25.355	24.338
2. Donmen crude petroleum (Mongolia) Ltd	14.468	13.067	23.555	20.417

Source: Ministry of Industry and Commerce, 'Complex development program for light and heavy industries'

According to the table, comparing the figures in 2005 to the figures in 2006, the extraction of the first company increased 2.07 times, its export increased 2.03 times and both the extraction and export of the second company increased 1.6 times respectively.

Regarding the petroleum import of the country in 2006, it imported 284.9 thousand tons of diesel fuel, 155.7 thousand tons of A-80 petrol, 99.6 thousand tons of A-92 petrol, 5.6 thousand tons of oil slurry (black oil, fuel oil), 2.2 thousand tons of gas, 1.8 thousand tons of bitumen, 40 thousand tons of TS-1 and 20.9 thousand tons of oil. In relation to the countries, 88 per cent was imported from Russia, 9 per cent from Kazakhstan, 2 per cent from China and 1 per cent from other countries.

Recommendations on the development of crude oil sector:

- Support foreign investments in crude oil sector;
- train and retrain national specialists in the sector;
- commence crude oil extraction, create a fund of foreign currency from the export of crude oil;
- establish a crude oil processing plant and meet the domestic needs to some extent.

Inset:

The project on establishing a crude oil processing factory by 'Vostokneftgaz' Ltd.
- With 100 per cent Russian investment, located 25 km away from UB, near the Rashaant railway station, with capacity of processing 2 million tons of crude oil per annum.
- 41% of which is planned to be diesel fuel, 18%- auto-petrol, 25%- gasoil, (to export to China), 3,6% kerosene, 2%- liquefied burning gas, 0,7%-bitumen and remaining 10%- coking coal.

Forest resource of the country consists of 12 million hectares of land including 140 species of trees and bushes. It accounts for over 9 per cent of all the territory of the country. 2 million cubic meters of trees, 70 per cent of which has been used for heating, are cut annually. The utilization of the remaining 30 per cent of the trees is restricted to the mechanical processing as a result of which 2/3 of the wood becomes a waste product.

It is significant to increase the capacity of utilization of wood by using chemical methods in production in order to produce celluloid, spirit, paper, plastic and tannin. A huge complex factory, which was capable to process 60 thousand cubic meters of wood annually and produce 30 thousand cubic meters of (sawn timber) lumber, 700 pieces of pre-fabricated wooden buildings, 20 thousand doors and windows, 30 million boxes of matches, 5000 cubic meters of boards made of wood shavings, 3000 cubic meters of veneer (plywood) and 3500 tons of various paper annually, was built in 1959 and had worked for over 40 years until it faced the transition, which brought it the same consequences as the other factories. As for Mongolia, wood production has been developing mainly producing woodwork of a yurt and wooden furniture. It has started to produce plastic since the mid 1990s and paper and paper products since 2000. Furthermore, it is vital to protect forests from fires and pests, recover and regenerate forests as well as carry out sensible policies on forestry in order to increase forest resources.

Hydropower (hydroelectricity): The country has a substantial resource of water and the geological formations of rivers and mountains are suitable for producing hydroelectricity. The country's potential resource of current in rivers is estimated approximately 4 billion KWh. Initially, the government made a decision to build a hydropower station in the early 1990s with the intention of using power of larger rivers in the country. Lately, the government has paid more attention to this issue and has commenced building hydropower stations in the western parts (Taishir hydropower station, Durugnii hydropower station ets.) of the country. 'Egiin gol' hydropower station has been agreed to be built with the assistance of the People's Republic of China.

Wind energy (power): The average wind speed in Mongolia is 2-5 meters per second; hence, the midget equipment transforming wind power into electricity has been imported lately with the aim of providing herders in rural areas with cheap electricity. Besides, because most of the days in the country are cloudless, there is a higher opportunity to use the solar energy in Mongolia. Particularly, it is important to produce solar batteries, which converts solar radiation into electricity. Lastly, it is up-and-coming to use solar and wind energies in the country, which has a vast territory, sparse population and pastoral cattle breeding.

Ore and non-metallic fossils

Mongolia is abundant with iron ore, copper, tungsten steel, stannum (tin), molybdenum, gold, fluorite, sodium chloride (cooking salt), phosphorus, crystal, gemstone and semi-gemstone and various building materials. There are a number of gold placer and primary gold deposits. Mongolia occupies the third place in the world for its plentiful resource of fluorite. Also, it has a rich resource of uranium. There is a high demand for uranium worldwide and its market price is increasing steadily every year. The uranium resource in Mongolia is 1.5 million tons and 500 thousand tons of it is located in Dornod, Mardai River, Gurvan Gol and Nemer. Investors are chiefly attracted by the minerals such as gold, copper, uranium and silver. The government of Mongolia is paying attention to the exposed deposits except for above mentioned ones and making an effort to involve them in the market turnover. There was exposed a phosphorus deposit in Mongolia and its resource was estimated 1.4 billion tons, which occupies a high place in the world. Raw materials used in construction such as wall stone (basaltic rocks, granite), mineral pigments, sand gravel mixture and limestone are abundant in most aimags and rural areas.

Gold extraction attracts both the government of Mongolia and investors because it is economically efficient and has a substantial effect to increase the budget revenue. The number of entities with exclusive licenses in gold extraction has been increasing lately, enhancing the gold extraction year by year. 80 entities extracted 5.3 tons of gold in 1996 and 97 entities extracted 6 tons in 1997, which was followed by the increasing number of 137 entities extracting 24 tons of gold by 2005. Currently, the geological reserve of gold has been estimated 3000 tons. The Mongolian- Canadian joint venture in gold extraction, which became the first large industry in the sector, was established in 1997 substantially enhancing the gold mining in the country. According to the minerals law, in case of extracting a chunk of gold above 400 grams or lighter than 400 grams but with an unusual natural shape, or gemstone with a rare shape and color, the exploitation license holder is eligible to sell them to the state treasure fund of the Bank of Mongolia.

Copper industry, its resource: The copper concentrate and copper production of Mongolia account for 1 per cent of the total copper production in the world. There are 11 copper deposits and 86 explored reserves, which contain totally 240 million tons resources of copper nationwide. The Mongolian-Russian joint venture in Erdenet, which mines and concentrates copper ore, was established in 1978. Since its establishment, it has produced a total of 2.5 million tons of copper and 36 thousand tons of molybdenum as concentrate.

Table 4.13 Production of 99 per cent cathodal copper

Year	1997	2000	2001	2002	2003	2004	2005
Cathodal copper 99% /tons/	2702.6	641.6	1475.9	1500	1341.1	2376.1	2474.5

Source: NSO year books

The copper concentrating production fell dramatically in 1991, but it has recovered gradually since 1992 and increased by 2.5 per cent by 2005 in relation to the 1989 situation. Alongside, the 'Erdmin', the Mongolian-American industry, which was established at the 'Erdenet' Mongolian-Russian joint venture, is producing a small amount of 99 per cent of cathodal copper dissolving and concentrating the unbalanced ore produced during the extraction using a specific technology.

Diagram 4.2. Copper concentrate in terms of 35 per cent content /1989=100/

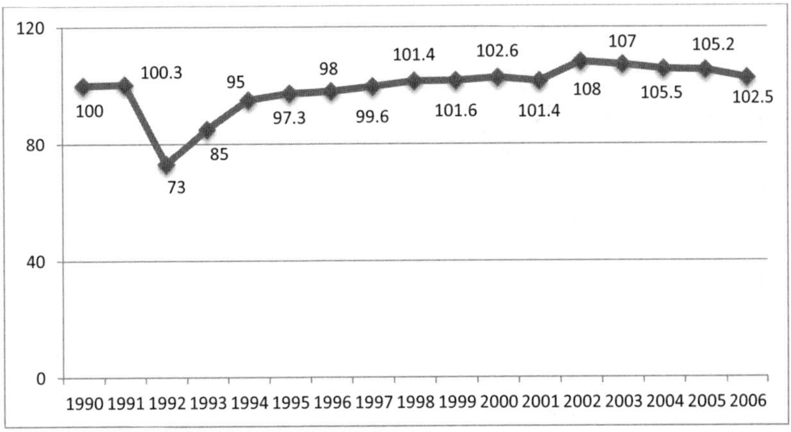

Source: NSO year books

'Erdenet' copper concentrating factory is exporting 584.6 thousand tons of copper concentrate per annum currently. It includes Erdmin factory, which is capable to produce 500 tons of cathodes annually, a workshop with the capacity of casting (rolling) 8 mms of copper wire as well as 'Shim technology' plant with the capacity of producing 1500 tons of molybdenum oxide and other complementary elements. Copper concentrate production has increased recently and accounts for 70 per cent of total exports of the country.

Table 4.14. World consumption of pure copper (2005)

	USA	European Union	Japan	China	Asia /except China/	Other countries	Total
Copper (thousand tons)	2401	4635	1242	3888	3089	1713	16967

Source: Ministry of Industry and Commerce, 'Complex development program for light and heavy industries'

The consumption of pure copper tends to increase in the future. Mongolia exports copper concentrate, cathodal copper and molybdenum to China, Japan and Korea.

Inset:

Oyu-Tolgoi Gold, copper Khanbogd soum of Umnugovi aimag From UB-560 km From Dalanzadgad to the south -220 km From Khanbogd soum to south-west-45 km From Gashuun sukhait border point -85 km Metal resource: -1149,1 million tons of ore -14,6 million tons of copper -600 tons of gold	Tsagaan Suvarga Copper Mandakh soum of Dornogovi aimag From Sainshand city to southwest-220 km Resource at Serven Sukhait: 0,71% of sulfate ore -59,5 million tons 0,57% of oxidized ore -6,5 million tons

Iron production, its resources

Despite the first 'Ironworks', which established in the 1930s to smelt cast-iron for households needs and produce some spare parts for agricultural equipment (harrow etc.), the metallurgical industry was not developed in the country. In the middle of 1990s there was established a Japanese metallurgical plant in Darkhan, which laid the root of the heavy industry in the country.

Fabricated metal, which is a finished product and metal rolls have been produced since1995.

A group of deposits existing in the region of Selenge aimag has 58-61 per cent of metal content and 390 million tons of confirmed resources of high quality iron-ore. The iron-ore deposits exist in the following locations: Hust mountain and Bayangol deposits exist in Eroo sum of Selenge aimag, a group of Tumurtei deposits is in Khuder sum, Selenge and Tumurtolgoi deposits are in Khongor sum of Darkhan-Uul aimag. A group of Bargiltiin deposits is located in Darkhan sum of Khentii aimag. The Tumurtei deposit has 229.3 million tons, the Bayangoliin deposit has 224 million tons, the Bargiltiin deposit has 31 million tons and Khust mountain deposit has 4.4 million tons of iron-ore respectively.

Inset:

Metallurgical factory in Darkhan With capacity of producing 100 thousand tons of casted products using waste iron annually. Established on 4th July, 1994. Processes waste iron and produces reinforced concretes and angle bars.	It produced 56183,4 tons of cast products in 2005 and 54235,6 tons in 2006, which became the highest production after 1994 and its capacity reached 54.2%.

Topical (urgent) issues:

There exist business entities producing construction reinforcing bars without any permission in the country. They do not meet the quality requirements but it was brought to light that they are being sold using the name of the metallurgical plant in Darkhan aimag.

Although Russia is an enormous market for construction reinforcing bars, it is banned to export them from Mongolia.

There arise logical requirements to build a metallurgical complex to process iron-ores of the Tumurtei deposit associated with the substantially reducing resources of irons worldwide.

Fluorites: Mongolia is abundant with fluorites. Fluorite mining reduced from 1991, but since 1995 it has increased and over 500 thousand tons were extracted in 2005. Fluorites and their ores are exported as a main raw material for metallurgical plants – they were exported to only Russia in 1991, but in 2000 they were exported to four, in 2003- to nine and in 2005- to 15 countries respectively. 50 per cent of the export was made to Russia. Besides, they are largely exported to Ukrain, America, China and Korea. The geological resource of fluorite in Mongolia is estimated 30 million tons and occupies the third place in the world. During the privatization, the geological exploration organizations were split into small entities, which resulted in their engagement in only extraction processes due to their incapacity to conduct extensive exploration work. The geological exploration requires a huge investment; therefore, Mongolia, concerning its poor economy, has always paid a considerable attention to foreign investments and they should be increased. Associated with this, there was released the minerals law on 8th July, 2006, which was set up consistent with the international standards. According to this law, the minerals deposits were classified into primary and placer and the deposits affecting the national security and regional economic and social development of the country or the deposits that produce more than 5 per cent of GDP of the country are considered as strategic deposits of the country.

The stability agreement will be made with a foreign investor who invests more than 50 million USA dollars in mineral exploration work for the first five years of the project. According to the agreement, whilst the Mongolian government is liable to provide the investor with a stable tax environment and guarantee him the right to dispose his profits, the special license holder is liable to keep their prices consistent with the international market price, carry out the mining work without harming people's health and environment, protect and rehabilitate the nature, contribute to the development of the region, create new work places as well as compensate for damages. The agreement will last for 10 years if the amount of investment made for the first 5 years of action is more than 50 million, 15 years if the amount is more than 100 million and 30 years if the amount is more than 300 million USA dollars. According to the law, the state involvement can be up to 50 per cent if the strategic deposits, exploration work of which was performed using the state budget revenue, are utilized by the state in cooperation with a private enterprise, and the shares equaling up to 34 per cent of the investment made by the owner in the strategic deposits, exploration work of which was performed without use of the state budget revenue, can be owned by the Mongolian state. A mining license holder shall pay royalties to the treasuries of the central and local administrative bodies on the sales value of all products extracted from the mining claim that are sold, shipped for sale, or used. Royalties paid for the utilization of coal mining and other widespread minerals shall be equal to 2.5 per cent of the sales value of all products extracted from the mining claim that are sold, shipped for sale, or used and 5.0 per cent of the sales value for the utilization of minerals except for coal and other widespread minerals. 10 per cent of the royalties shall be allocated into the budget of the soum or district, 20 per cent of those shall be allocated into the budget of the aimag or capital city, 70 per cent of those shall be allocated into the state budget respectively. The special license holder is eligible to provide citizens of Mongolia with work places and not more than ten (10) per cent of the employees must be foreign citizens. In case the license holder employs more foreign workers than the specified number, he shall monthly pay an amount of payment equaling ten times of the lowest labour rate for each work place to the budget of the soum or district.

The issues of development of industry based on livestock sector

Mongolia occupies a leading place in the world in terms of livestock per capita and is abundant with livestock raw materials. The meat, the main livestock product (on slaughter weight) per capita accounted for 75.4 kg, milk 130.8 liters and eggs 8.3 pieces in 2005. The amount of raw materials come from livestock is estimated depending on the yearly estimations of the livestock census in the country; but, the country has on average a capacity of procuring 15-29 thousand tons of sheep wool, 2600-3300 tons of coat cashmere, 1200-1700 tons of camel wool, 1200-2000 tons of molt hair from big cattle annually. According to the survey conducted on productivity per animal, a sheep produces 1412 grams of wool, a camel - 5034 grams of wool and a coat – 289 grams of cashmere on average. The rate of hide and skin procurement decreased between 1991 and 1995, but increased in 1998-2001 and reached the annual average rate of 1986-1990. The domestic production based on livestock sector decreased substantially in the 1990s and it resulted from the tough competition of Chinese producers who bought the majority of livestock raw materials from Mongolia and supplied consumer goods to the country. The entire livestock of the country belonged to the agricultural cooperatives before 1990, but by the 1990 they were all dispersed and all the livestock was privatized to herders and non herder households. Consequently, the production of livestock based industries fell and they closed their doors.

Cashmere and cashmere products:

Cashmere goods are considered in great demand in European, American and Japanese markets in terms of sumptuous consumption. Mongolia occupies the next place after China that accounts for 70 per cent of the world production of cashmere goods. The production of cashmere goods in the country has increased since the 1990s. However, when the embargo imposed on the export of raw cashmere was taken off in 1996, the domestic industries started to face scarcity of raw cashmere.

According to the graph, because the number of goats increased twice in 1993-1999, the production of raw cashmere increased twice as well from 1.1 tons to 3.2 tons. The cashmere production consists of three types of production. The first production type includes the primary stage processing industries. In this stage raw and dirty cashmere is bought from herders and traders. Combed fine cashmere is produced after it washed up and removed from the coarse hair. There were established joint ventures with China, America, Japan, South Korea and Europe after the embargo on export of raw cashmere was taken off in 1996. The next production type includes the prêt-a-porter industries.

Graph 4.3. Cashmere production

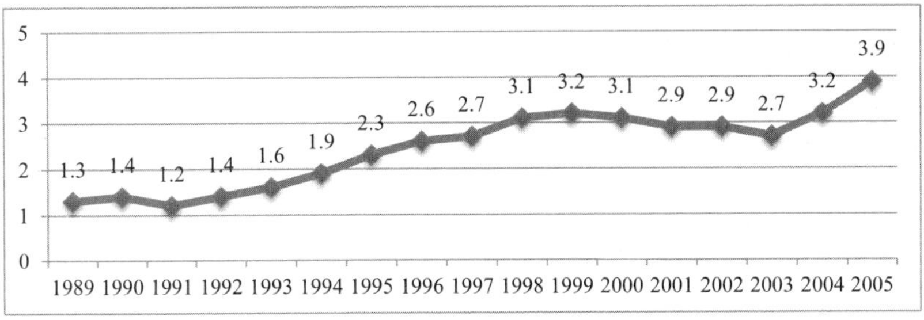

Source: NSO year books

The third production type includes sale of raw cashmere, industries to spin and dye cashmere, produce ready-made clothes and make woven and knitted products. 'Gobi' and 'Byuan' companies are the examples of the third production type.

In spite of the designs and styles of the cashmere products, the colour plays quite an important role on the world market. For instance, white cashmere is more fitting to produce yellowish colour that dominates on the world market of woven apparels for women. But dark colour mainly dominates in Mongolian cashmere and causes to account for lower market shares. Conversely, the length of Mongolian cashmere thread is estimated on average 15 per cent more as much as the Chinese cashmere thread, so the apparels made of it are considered softer, more durable and manageable to spin as well as get less lint (fuzz balls).

In the early 2000, domestic producers were not able to pay 30-40 thousand tugrigs, which was considered a high market price, for a kilo of cashmere because they had to use two kilos of raw cashmere to produce one kilo of combed cashmere and ten thousand tugrigs were spent for processing of cashmere. As a result, several cashmere processing industries in the country were shut up.

Although 3500 tons of cashmere has been produced annually in recent years, about 800 tons of cashmere is shipped to China through customs out of control causing a substantial loss to the state. This should be stopped in the future. On the other hand, the 10 year agreement of export tax on raw cashmere signed in 1997 during the time when Mongolia joined the World Trade organization will expire in 2007. It will result in a decrease of customs revenue.

Carpet and other wool goods:

Mongolia produces a substantial amount of wool every year. The greater part of wool (about 94% according to some sources) is used to produce coarse carpets, felt boots and felt. The remaining part of wool, which is semi coarse or finely fibred, is suitable to produce clothing. There are two big carpet factories (Ulaanbaatar, Erdenet) in Mongolia.

Graph 4.4 Carpet production

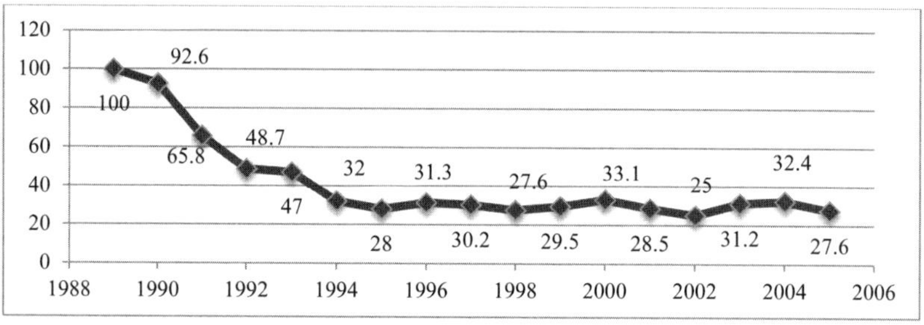

Source: NSO year books

Carpet production fell from 1990 and increased from 2002, but has tended to decrease in recent years even though there are two big markets – Russia and China. There are a number of factors affecting the decrease of the carpet production including outdated technology, rigid policy and the wrong sizes and styles of carpets that cannot meet the demand of modern consumers.

Felt and felt boots production went down substantially from 1990-1991. 2000 saw a slight increase but it started to decrease again in 2004. It tends to increase from 2005.

Graph 4.5 Felt and felt boots production

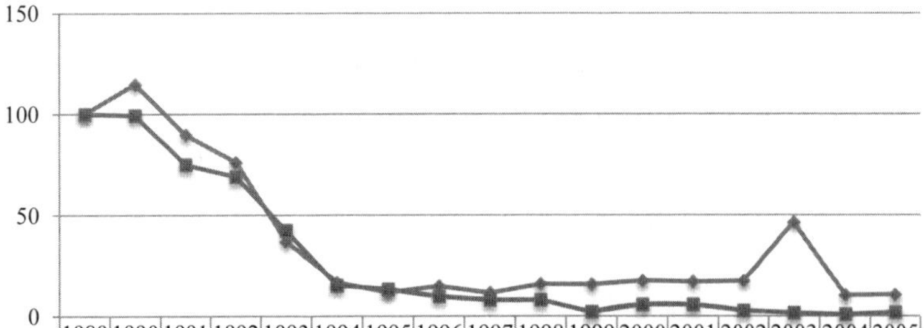

	1989	1990	1991	1992	1993	1994	1995	1996	1997	1998	1999	2000	2001	2002	2003	2004	2005
Felt	100	115	89.8	76.2	37.2	16.6	11.8	14.8	11.5	15.8	15.7	17.5	17	17.4	46.6	10.4	10.6
Felt boots	100	99.3	75	69	42.5	15.2	13.3	9.7	8	8	2	5.7	5.6	2.7	1.5	0.8	1.8

Source: NSO year books

Carpets made of wool of Mongolian sheep are potential to raise the country's market share in the world if carpet industries shall be supplied by coarse wool of Mongolian sheep, and produce woolen carpets of modern design and style that can meet international customers' demand and interests. On the other hand, insistent ads and promotions for the carpets should be made at the international level and the Mongolian carpet producers need to join the international network of well-known carpet producers.

Camel wool is considered scarce in the world with regard to warm quality among the other woolen raw materials; therefore, camel wool industry is regarded as a special type of industry in the sector.

The cashmere, which was produced after the coarse wool of sheep sorted out and washed up thoroughly, can be used to produce threads, woolen cloth, fabric and knitted goods. 30-35 per cent of gross weight of wool of any sheep can produce cashmere; therefore, the prospect of the sector can be determined by increasing the quality of the wool processing in the textile industry.

Hide and skin processing sector

The sound option of tannery industry development in the country is to produce a variety of leather, chrome leather and box-calf materials processing hides and skins of animals using high and green technology in order to make finished goods. Thus, it is potential to develop a unique national technology to process hides and skins of animals, then produce ecologically clean products and enter into the world market. It is vital to procure and process national raw materials domestically and produce various leather garments and boots and learn from the experiences of worldly known industries in Italy, Spain and Turkey and adopt their technologies. One example of rapid depressions of the processing industries after Mongolia stepped in transition is the depression of tannery industry. Prior to 1990, there worked large factories like kid leather and sheepskin leather processing factories in Ulaanbaatar and 'Darkhan sheepskin' factory, which processed the substantial part of hides and skins. In 1990-1995 the production of sheepskin, goat skin, hides and skins of big cattle, footwear, sheepskin coats as well as leather garments decreased by 90 per cent and in 2000 it almost reached a zero point.

Graph 4.6 Production of skin and leather garments /1989=100/

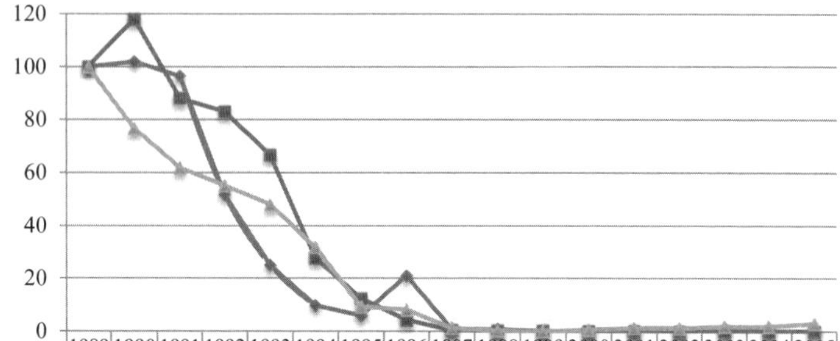

	1989	1990	1991	1992	1993	1994	1995	1996	1997	1998	1999	2000	2001	2002	2003	2004	2005
Footwear	100	102	96.5	51.8	24.9	9.8	5.9	21	1	0.8	0.16	0.13	0.4	0.23	0.1	0.07	0.07
Leather goods	100	118	88	83	66.6	27.6	12.4	4.3	0.5	0.3	0.27	0.08	0.04	0	0.1	0.08	0.1
Sheepskin coats	100	76.6	61.8	55.2	48	31.7	9.3	8.2	1.3	0.3	0,11	0.6	1.3	1.2	1.9	1.9	3

Source: NSO year books

The quality of leather and skin has deteriorated sharply for the last ten years because the raw material processing factories stopped to use baths and chemicals that were used to soak and process hides and skins during the time when livestock was state owned. Moreover, the technologies used to process hides and skins are obsolete and most small and medium size industries producing leather goods have no capacity to export their products. Mongolia has a plentiful resource of hides and skins. Therefore, we should benefit from it promoting leather goods production in order to develop it as a source of foreign currencies. Thus, it is necessary to develop a mutual policy including both the government and representatives of the private sector.

Meat and meat products

Prior to 1990, Mongolia exported its livestock to Russia and other countries in substantial amounts as meat products as well as drove them alive across the borders. However, after the transition to the market economy, the meat export declined substantially; correspondingly the meat and meat product production started to fall from 1990. Yet, tinned meat and sausage production have recovered and increased since 2000.

Only less than 10 per cent of slaughtering takes place in slaughter houses and the remaining part is conducted in households according to some statistics. The slaughtering conducted in households does not meet hygienic requirements and does not undergo through veterinary tests.

Graph 4.7 Production of meat and meat products

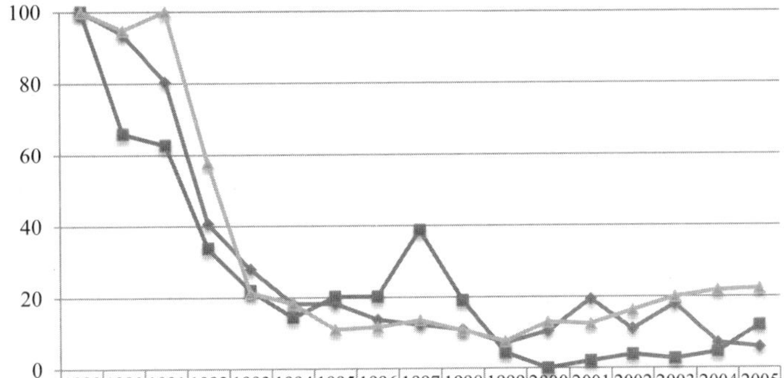

	1989	1990	1991	1992	1993	1994	1995	1996	1997	1998	1999	2000	2001	2002	2003	2004	2005
Livestock meat	100	93.7	80.4	40.7	28	18.3	18.3	13.8	12.2	10.8	7	10.4	19.4	11	18	7	5.8
Tinned meat	100	65.9	62.7	33.8	21.9	14.4	20.2	20.2	38.7	19.1	4.3	0	2	3.8	2.6	4.5	12
Sausage	100	94.8	100	57.7	21.4	18.3	11	11.6	13.6	10.7	7.5	13	12.5	16.3	20	21.8	22.3

Source: NSO year books

Urgent issues:

- make an effort to procure meat in a centralized way, push intermediaries out of the market, create centralized outlets in rural areas. These can help to stop the meat price boosts and let it go down.
- increase meat exports to China and Russia, focus on slaughtering techniques and technologies as well as storage conditions of meat to be consistent with the international standards
- improve breeds of livestock, promote raising and crossbreeding of the finest breed that produces more meat.

Milk and milk products

Mongolia equals many developed countries in the world in terms of milk and milk product consumption per capita. The privatization of most cows and small cattle of finest breed raised for milk in the 1990s resulted in a decline of domestic milk production.

Graph 4.8 Production of milk and milk products* /1989=100/

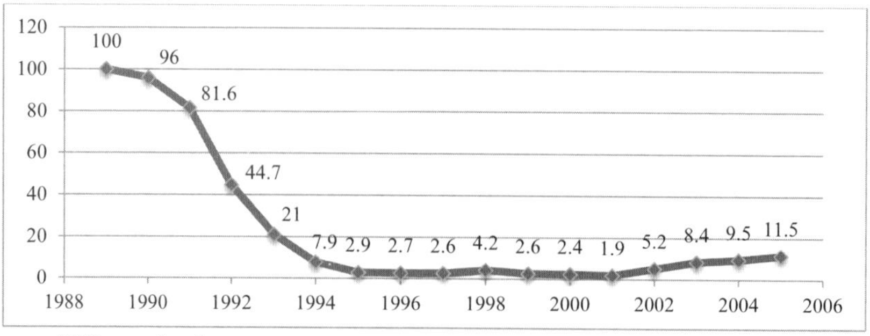

Source: NSO year books
**unboiled milk is not included*

Although the production of milk and milk products recovered and increased from 2002, by 2005 it was estimated 8.7 times less than the 1989 situation.
Prior to 1990, 'Milk factory' of Ulaanbaatar city produced about 40 million liters of milk annually. Since the transition to the market economy the milk supplying system has disappeared, then milk factories closed their doors resulting from the fact that due to the insufficient fodder the number of livestock decreased.

Urgent issues:

1. In order to stop the practice of supplying milk of low quality that does not meet the hygienic requirements to the city dwellers from the suburb districts of the towns and cities, a number of milk outlets should be opened to receive milk from herders and then we need to invite herders to supply their milk on contract.
2. Raise livestock of high productivity that produce more milk;
3. Find solutions to the problems connected with animal fodder

Perspectives of industrial development

The prompt transition into the market economy has continuously caused a number of negative consequences that affected the economy such as bankruptcies of state owned industries that were developing intensively, a collapse of raw material procurement system in the agricultural sector, as well as the quality deterioration of raw materials, hides and skins, wool and cashmere due to the prevalence of livestock diseases resulted from the breakdown of quality control system. However, the national industry has recovered in recent years and the sector now sees a tendency of sustainable development of livestock sector based industries. The Russian market as well as rapidly developing economies of China, Korea and countries in South - East Asia are open for Mongolians. The subject matter of the further strategic policies on development of the country should be based on this opportunity to develop its industrial sector.

I. The issues of development of mining and heavy industries in Mongolia

The adequate conditions for developing heavy industries based on extracted minerals deposits have emerged in the country and the world consumption of ferrous and non ferrous metals and other minerals is increasing and their prices are going up with a jump, too. Particularly, our neighbor -China is in great demand of minerals and this tendency is likely to be maintained in the long term, which favours the landlocked country like Mongolia to penetrate into a substantially efficient market.

It is economically efficient to export semi processed, value added products and avoid exporting minerals in the form of raw materials and ore.

Potential analysis on development of heavy industries in Mongolia[1]	
Strengths	**Weaknesses**
▪ abundant resource of raw materials; ▪ direct interaction with Chinese and Russian markets; ▪ existing favorable legal environment for investors; ▪ high demand for minerals on the international and Chinese markets	▪ weak infrastructure; ▪ a few and sparsely settled population ▪ shortage of professionals; ▪ restricted opportunity of the government investment; ▪ landlocked; ▪ restricted capacity of domestic markets; ▪ dominance of primary processing.
Opportunity	**Threat**
▪ close to Japanese and Korean markets; ▪ tax exemption to markets of European Union.	▪ potential of supplying obsolete, economically inefficient equipment; ▪ risks deriving from political and business policy disputes; ▪ possibility to harm the nature negatively

Complex factories to be built initially in order to develop heavy industries in Mongolia:

1. Complex of mining and metallurgical factories based on iron ore deposits in Tumurtei, Tumur tolgoi, Bayangol and Khustiin that are situated in the region of Darkhan-Selenge aimag;
2. Complex of mining and non-ferrous metallurgical factories based on 'Erdenet mining' factory in Orkhon aimag, 'Tsagaan suvarga' copper deposit in Mandakh soum of Dornogovi aimag, 'Oyu-tolgoi' copper deposit in Khanbogd soum of Umnugovi aimag;
3. Complex factories to 'thoroughly process coal and produce electricity' based upon the coal deposits including 'Tavan tolgoi' in Tsogttsegtsii soum of Umnugovi aimag, 'Nariin Sukhait' in Gurvan Tes soum of Umnugovi aimag.

[1] Source: Ministry of Trade and Industry, 'Complex program on development of light and heavy industries in Mongolia'

II. The issues of development of raw material processing industries [2]

Analysis on development of raw material processing industries	
Strengths	Weaknesses
▪ abundant resource of raw materials ▪ close to Chinese and Russian markets; ▪ long standing experience to run livestock economy	▪ collapse of raw material procurement system ▪ export of unprocessed raw materials ▪ dominance of primary processing in the factories; ▪ low quality livestock raw materials resulting from diseases among livestock.
Opportunity	Threats
▪ opportunity of exporting 7200 ranges of goods on EU markets with import tax exemption; ▪ access to Japanese discount system; ▪ opportunity to penetrate into the USA and Korean markets.	▪ obsolete techniques and technologies; ▪ weak competency in finished goods; ▪ no regulations in imports of similar and substitute goods.

Perspectives of developing industrial complexes

Raw material processing branches to be established in Ulaanbaatar, Erdenet and Darkhan cities and Baganuur district of UB city are as follows:

- Hide and skin processing complex: Foot – wear factory based on hide processing;
- 'Leather goods' factory based on skin processing industry;
- Skin goods factory by expanding 'Darkhan skin coat' factory;
- Complex of woven and knitted goods factories in order to enhance finished goods production and increase quality of wool and cashmere processing;
- Complex of wood processing factories in Darkhan

Some measures have been taken by the Government with regard to supporting small and medium size industries. For instance:

- Create legal environment;
- Support them by tax and financial policy;
- Provide them with open and prompt state service

III. Production of electricity

The level of economic and cultural development of nations substantially depends on the amount of production of electricity. It would be difficult to imagine not only how to run production and service businesses but also how to improve levels of people's

[2] Source : Ministry of Trade and Industry, 'Complex program on development of light and heavy industries in Mongolia'

cultured living without electricity. The following table shows the production of electricity during the transitional period.

Table 4.15 Production of electricity (1989-2005)

Years	**1989**	**1990**	**1991**	**1992**	**1993**	**1994**	**1995**	**1996**	**1997**
Electricity (million kwt/h)	3568.3	3347.9	3228.6	2928.6	2131.7	2122.7	2628.0	2614.0	2662.0
Percentage compared to 1989 situation	100.0	93.8	90.5	82.0	59.7	59.5	73.6	73.3	74.6
Percentage of growth	-	93.8	96.43	87.6	72.8	99.6	123.8	99.5	101.8
Years	**1998**	**1999**	**2000**	**2001**	**2002**	**2003**	**2004**	**2005**	
Electricity (million kwt/h)	2675.0	2842.0	2946.0	3017.0	3111.7	3137.7	3303.4	3418.9	
Percentage compared to 1989 situation	74.9	79.6	82.6	84.5	87.2	88.0	92.6	95.8	
Percentage of growth	110.5	106.2	103.6	102.4	103.1	100.8	105.3	103.5	

Source: NSO year books

According to the table, the production of electricity started to decline from 1990 and in 1994 it barely produced only 59.5 per cent of the 1989 production. The utilization of project capacity in terms of electricity and heat production by 2005 is shown in the following table.

According to the table, utilization of the project capacity is 47.9 per cent with regard to electricity production and 68.7 per cent in terms of heat production.

Table 4.16 Utilization of project capacity

	Project capacity	2005 production	Utilization (%)
Electricity million kwt/h	7135.2	3418.9	47.9
Heat energy thous.g.cal	11367.1	7805.6	68.7

Source: Ministry of Trade and Industry, 'Complex program for development of heavy industries in Mongolia'

Mongolia needs to follow directions of not only to produce electricity domestically, but also export it to foreign countries.

The western region of the country is supplied by electricity from the integrated energy system in Krasnoyarsk, Russia. In Zavkhan and Govi-Altai aimags, a diesel electric power station produces electricity, which is considered of high cost. The herders, who accounts for over 50 per cent of the population in this region need to be provided by electricity. The 'Taishiriin' hydroelectric power station (HPS) that is able to produce 11 mwt of electricity in Govi-Altai aimag, the 'Durgunii' HPS with a capacity of producing 12 mwt of electricity in Khovd aimag are going to be built in 2006-2007, which will enhance the supply of electricity. Moreover, a project to build a HPS with a capacity of producing 10500 mwt is going to be started on the 'Egiin' River with assistance of China and Swetzerland.

Thermal power stations with a capacity of 15000 mwt are planned to be built based on substantial coal deposits. When a thermal power station of 4000 mwt of capacity is built in Tavan Tolgoi, Mongolia can export electricity to China and Russia.

Mongolia has 2250-3300 hours of sunny days throughout the year and the average amount of energy coming from the sun is estimated 1400 kwh/cubic meters. The potential of wind energy resource is estimated 836.8 billion kw/h with a utilization period of 3.5-4.6 thousand hours a year. The average speed of wind in eastern parts of the country is estimated 4-5 meters in second and over 60 per cent of the territory or 947 thousand square km area has wind energy of more than 100 W in square meter. Thus, it is potential to provide consumers with electricity using wind energy power sets with a capacity of 50-100 w.

References:

1. D.Zagasbaldan ' Mongolia in the world development of economy and culture' 1978
2. Mongolia: Research on policy of the development of trade and industry. 2003
3. Sustainable development program of Mongolia in the 21st century. 1999
4. Ministry of Trade and Industry. 'Complex program for the development of light and heavy industries in Mongolia'
5. The development of light industries in Mongolia 2004, vol 1,2.
6. Statistical issues. 2006 N1
7. NSO year books 1989, 1991, 2005

4.3 CONSTRUCTION

The construction sector that collapsed in the early 1990s in line with the transition to a market economy, the construction erection performance of which fell to the 1960 level, has recovered again and accounted for 1.7 per cent of GDP in 1995 and 2.4 per cent of GDP in 2005. The privatization of significant state owned construction trusts in the 1990s resulted in depression of the sector. Alongside, the termination of investments flowed from the state budget caused a sharp decline in the total production of the sector. Like the other sectors in the economy, the construction sector reached today's development level overcoming a number of obstacles. The sector's current situation and some urgent issues are considered herein.

Due to the poor urban planning, haphazard and speculative buildings with disordered streets have resulted in the urban agglomeration. Alongside, the obsolete engineering piping networks and underground engineering construction, which are considered the vital vessels of cities, can hinder the development of the city.

A master plan developed on the implementation of 'Housing for 40000 households' program was approved and is being put into action. In the frame of the program implementation, the government decided to issue bonds worth 60.0 billion tugrigs. That 81 flats were built in 2005 and 113 in 2006 represents the program started to be implemented intensively. In line with the implementation of the program, taxes for some building materials and equipment were exempted. In addition, in the frame of the program, in some aimags and centers of some soums the construction work for housing has already started. What is more, maintenance work for bridges and roads has intensively been started.

Production in construction sector

Currently, 1150 business entities have been given a special lisence to run a construction and erection business and 400 of them are operating actively. Although the number of entities engaged in the construction business is increasing every year, they lack professional skills and the increased number of construction and erection companies that have almost no production basis affects the quality of construction and erection work negatively.

Particularly, the construction technology with cast-in-place concrete frames is being dominantly used at present, therefore concrete mixing standard, technical requirements, casting, maintenance as well as quality control must be paid a particular attention.

The most urgent issue in the construction sector is labour force and its resource. After the privatization, in connection with reduced work performance, the demand for professional workers in the sector went down. However, due to the expansion of construction work, it started to increase; especially, there is a high demand for professional workers of primary and junior levels in the present day.

Graph 4.9. Construction, erection and rehabilitation work 1989 – 2005, million tugrigs

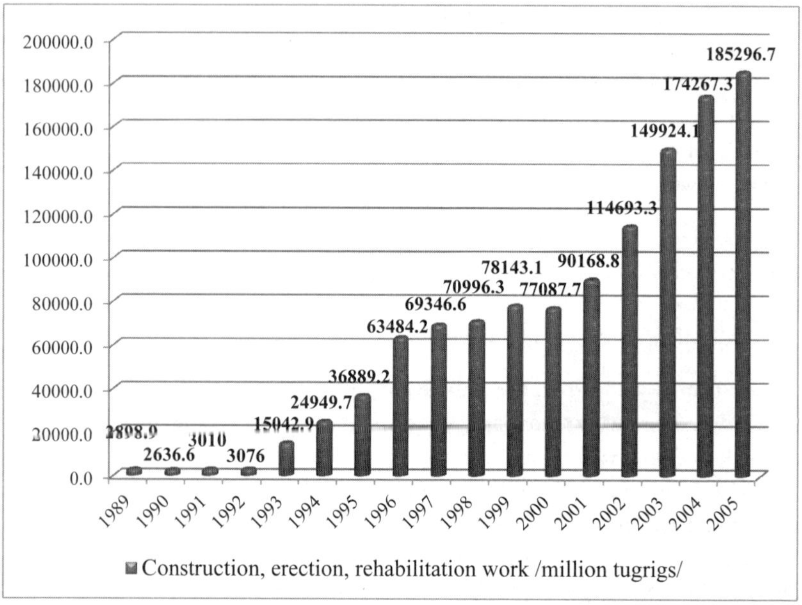

Source: Mongolia in market economy; 1989-2002, NSO year book, Statistical bulletin December, 2006, NSO

However, that some of the professionals previously prepared in the sector moved to another sector, some became old and some lack professionalism or morality caused deficiency in national professional workers, which resulted in imports of professional workers from other countries in order to meet the sector's labour force demand.

There are not a few obstacles in preparation of national professional workers, which are in high demand. Particularly:

- techniques and technologies of the institutes that train specialized workers in construction sector became obsolete;
- construction companies, which were privatized, turned into far too small in size entities, which made it complicated to estimate demand of qualified workers;
- a contemporary mechanism of mutual collaboration between the training institutes and industrial organizations has not set up yet;
- the financing in the training institutes is not appropriate;

- they have almost no investments;
- on the spot training is not provided, even a minimum form of labour training has not set up yet.

'Land law' was released in 1994 and started to regulate the relations associated with possession and use of state-owned land and other related issues. The state policy on land issues, authority of local self-governing organizations regarding land issues, relations associated with possession, use and protection of land, settlement of land related disputes as well as sanctions for violation of legislation are all included in the land law.

Privatization that has been conducted through three stages since 1990 as well as relations of market economy did not leave the land related issues in peace. New land relations tended to develop more increasingly according to the market economy law; (i) the owners of a building, facility and factories wanted to own the land around them in order to take it under their possession in the long term, (ii)people wanted to own a land that has a useful location to run a business in centralized settled areas as well as a land for second holiday homes nearby a settled areas, (iii)herders wanted to take their winter and spring quarters in their possession and (iv)those who are engaged in agricultural business wanted to privatize their crop lands and so forth. This necessitated changes in legal environment of land relations in order to implement the provisions of the Constitution. In 2002, the Parliament passed a 'Law on land' and 'Law on giving land for possession of Mongolian citizen', which were reformed along the lines of the project 'Strengthening land reforms', one of the 11 significant leading directions of the Government.

Enforcement of these two laws favored the development of land market on the basis of a transparent, equal and just competition, closure of underground land economy, decrease of poverty among the population as well as the increase of living standards of people. For example, at present, most people are able to get access to a loan pledging their own lands and run a business.

Construction and erection work

In the early years of the transition, the construction sector was more susceptible to a depression in relation to other sectors and first and foremost, its operation almost stopped even though the rehabilitation and minor erection work accounted for a higher percentage in the total production. This resulted from the privatization of substantial construction trusts, which were split into a number of small entities. Another factor affected the sharp decline of total production in the sector is the termination of investments flowed from the state budget.

However, since the last half of the 1990s, a number of new business entities have emerged stabilizing the situation of the sector and there occurred 2.6 per cent growth in total production of the sector in 1996, which was considered as a high growth at that time.

Nevertheless, in 2000, some substantial construction companies had to stand facing downtimes resulted from insufficient financial sources, which led to the decline of total production. Due to the foreign investments, loans and aids provided from 2001, substantial construction, erection and rehabilitation works were started setting up positive trends in the sector again.

The performance of construction, erection and rehabilitation works reached 185.3 billion tugrigs by 2005 and increased by 6.3 per cent in relation to 2004.That construction, erection and rehabilitation works increased by 5.0 per cent in 1996-2000 and by 19.7 per cent in 2001-2005 every year in that order shows the sector started to recover and see relatively high growth in production.

Table 4.17. Growth of construction, erection, rehabilitation works (by price in given year) (million tugrigs)

Indicators		1996	1997	1998	1999	2000	Annual average growth of 1995-2000, per cent
Construction, erection and rehabilitation works, total		63484	69347	70996	78143	77088	5.0
Out of which:	Work performed by domestic companies	40071	47523	48764	51040	58416	9.9
	Work performed by foreign companies	23413	21824	22233	27103	18672	-5.5
Indicators		**2001**	**2002**	**2003**	**2004**	**2005**	**Annual average growth of 2001-2005, per cent**
Construction, erection and rehabilitation works, total		90169	114693	149924	174267	185297	19.7
Out of which:	Work performed by domestic companies	73617	88314	104922	133862	148055	19.1
	Work performed by foreign companies	16552	26379	45002	40405	37242	22.5

Source: Mongolia in market economy, 1989-2002, NSO, yearbooks 2004, 2005

Although the construction, erection and rehabilitation works performed by foreign companies decreased by up to 31.1 per cent in 2000 against 1990, foreign investments increased in 2002-2005 and annual average growth reached to 22.5 per cent.

Graph 4.10. Structure of construction, erection and rehabilitation work, funds invested in completed buildings (million tugrigs)

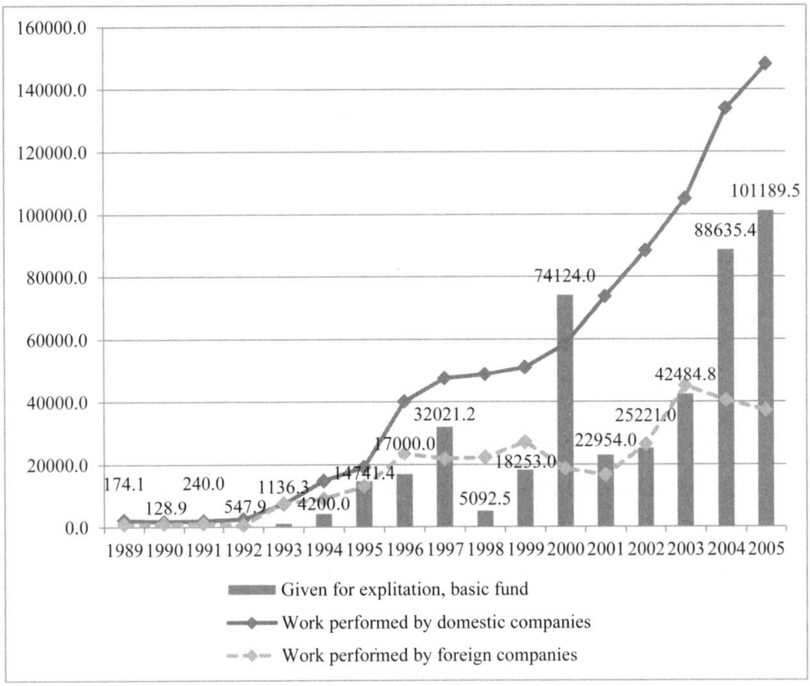

Source: Mongolia in market economy, 1989-2002. NSO yearbooks 2004-2005

In 2005-2006, 5.2 thousand km of road and 90 bridges were rehabilitated. Moreover, programs on ‘Housing for population’ and ‘More work places in construction sector' were elaborated and are getting ready to be submitted to the Parliament.

The implementation of these programs shall facilitate not only to increase the supply of housing and improve the living conditions of people, but also it will help to create a positive atmosphere in the social psychology and motivate people to work.

It is impossible to illustrate the types of construction work by their location, but it is probable to show the aimag where a construction company is operating and the type of construction work that is being performed there. Typically, almost every aimag has one or more construction companies operating on their own territory and cities too, have their construction companies operating in Ulaanbaatar, Darkhan and Erdenet. Besides, rail station and military construction divisions are functioning in the capital city and rural areas.

Graph 4.11. Amount of construction, erection and rehabilitation work, by performance of construction companies, in percentage

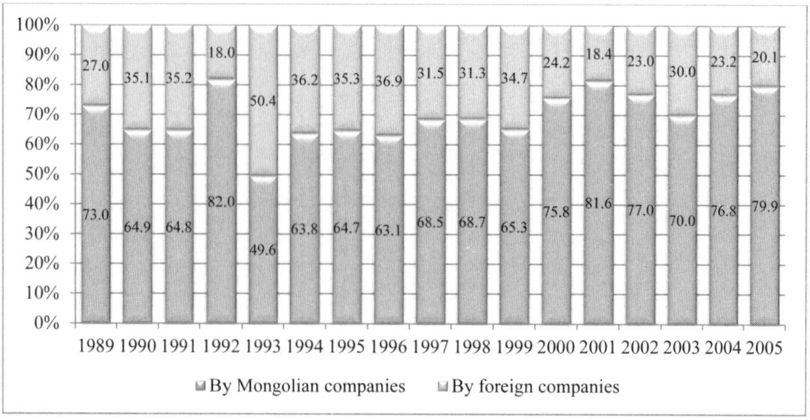

Source: Mongolia in market economy, 1989-2002. NSO yearbooks 2004-2005

Financing for construction sector and investment made in the sector

In 2005, there was made investment worth 208,2 billion tugrigs in the construction sector, which increased it by 16.2 per cent or by 29.0 billion tugrigs compared to the previous year. The construction, erection and rehabilitation work accounts for the certain part of investments made in the sector.

Table 4.18 Investment in construction sector by source (million tugrigs)

Source	2000	2001	2002	2003	2004	2005
Internal source	194609.9	193 291.6	209 146.1	269 446.2	398 732.1	402 644.3
External source	168036.9	200 905.5	210 279.6	274 129.5	240 512.9	394 494.3
Total	362646.8	394197.1	419425.7	543575.7	639245	797138.6
among them: investments in construction and erection work	72387.3	90 727.6	131 362.1	169 848.1	179 105.8	208 153.2

Source: Statistical bulletin December 2006, NSO

26.1 per cent of the total investment made in the sector was made in the construction and erection work in 2005. Although the percentage of the construction and erection work in the investments decreased by 1.9 points in 2004, it increased by 6.1 points in 2005 compared to 2000.

Regarding each financial source, 402.6 billion tugrigs or 50.5 per cent of the investment was made from the internal sources by 2005, 64.8 billion tugrigs or 16.1 per cent of which was made from the state budget, 233.1 billion tugrigs or 57.9 per cent - was made from the owner's equity and 104.0 billion tugrigs or 25.9 per cent - were bank loans. 394.5 billion tugrigs or 49.5 per cent of the investment was made from external sources, 150.5 billion tugrigs or 38.1 per cent of which were foreign loans, 24.2 billion tugrigs or 6.2 per cent - were foreign grants and 219.8 billion tugrigs or 55.7 per cent - were direct investments.

Concerning the technological structure of the investments, the majority part of the investments made in the construction sector was allocated to equipment.

Graph 4.12 Investments by structure, by percentage

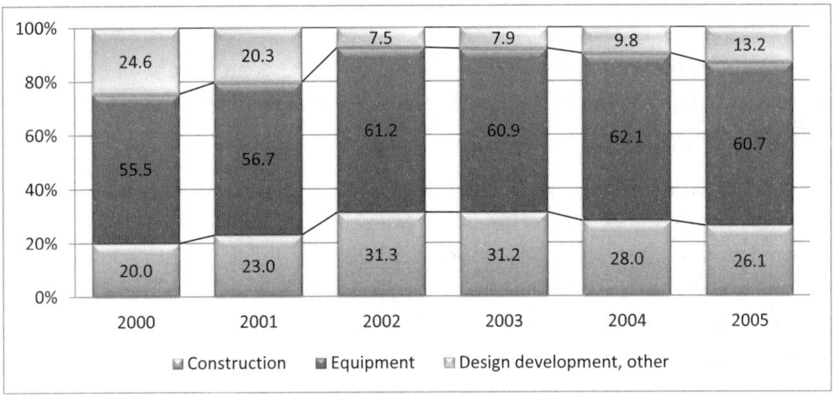

Source: NSO yearbook of 2005

One of the complex social and economic issues of a country has been housing for population. That the number of private housing is increasing every year is pleasing. Particularly, the number of housing increased by 9.1 per cent in 2005 compared to 2004. A number of factors including migration of population, demands of market and locations of housing affect the growth that occurs in numbers of housing.

Obstacles and urgent issues on the implementation of the housing policy:

- Low incomes below the guaranteed living standards (about 36 per cent of Mongolian population);
- Weak development of domestic production of building materials;
- Lack of fixed financial structure for housing;
- Disorder in city planning and land policies;

- Still lacking dwellers' unions in flat districts; weak initiatives and involvement of ger district residents in the improvement of their living environment and their limited awareness of that knowledge;
- Still existing underdeveloped infrastructure and poor living environment in ger as well as flat districts after ineffective partial improvements made due to the limited investments;
- Financial incapacity of the residents as well as the local governing authorities to render full scale supports to improve the infrastructure and living conditions of ger and flat districts.

The engineering structure works include activities such as the power grid changes, wire-laying for communication network, maintenance work for railways and motorways and minor works in bridges, bridge crossings, dams, channels and other types of road and ground works.

The mission of the construction sector is to provide the population with comfortable and secure living conditions by developing land relations, urban development and public utilities.

The sector focuses on the introduction of new materials and technologies, capacity expansion, construction and erection work extension and improvement of housing for the population in 2007-2009. The measures to increase funds for the '40000 housing program' and intensify its implementation work will be taken. In the frame of the project, it is planned to finish housing for 9.3 thousand families in 2007. Moreover, an integrated database with the information related to immovable estates, construction, urban development and land management is planned to be set up.

The following measures are going to be taken urgently in the frame of the development plan of construction and building material industries with modern techniques and technologies:

- Develop a system to prepare and retrain the professional workers and personnel in the construction sector and establish vocational schools in order to fully provide the sector with skilled workers.
- Sophisticate the quality control on both imported and domestically produced building materials and qualify the assertion procedures.
- Support the national building material industries fully and conduct flexible customs and VAT policies in order to protect their products from the negative effects of import.
- Familiarize and use the new world technological advances of science in the construction and urban development sector making them appropriate in the conditions and to raw material features of the country.

- Use prefabricated and cast concretes and structures in order to decrease seasonal affections on construction erection works.
- Direct the innovation of building material industry technologies to the heat loss reduction, weight reduction, energy efficiency and use environmentally friendly materials for construction
- Locate export oriented small and medium size industries that can substitute imports according to the regional development policy.

The implementation of above measures will facilitate (i) to increase the quality and design of buildings through introduction of new sophisticated technologies in the construction, erection and building material industries, (ii) to develop and follow the appropriate norms and standards on the basis of the scientific research of the sector with the aim of building heat and energy efficient housing suitable for weather conditions of the country, (iii) to introduce new technologies of construction and erection work, which will meet the requirements of the development and reflect a new range of material structures in the design, (iv) and to strengthen the national capacity of building tall housing and substantial industries.

Appendix 4.1. Prices of staple materials in construction, (at the end of each year)

Materials, by producing countries	2004	2005	$\frac{2005}{2004}$%
Mongolia			
Concrete mortar M-100,m^2	37 392	51 000	136.4
macadam, m^2	40 000	39 000	97.5
Iron concrete 700,m^3	46 500	56 000	120.4
Brick made from clay M-100, thous.pieces	70 000	80 000	114.3
Cement M-500, kg	270	280	103.7
Sand (unsifted), m^2	12 400	13 000	104.8
Lime (meli), kg	210	210	100.0
Plank for floor, m^2	44 000	103 000	234.1
Palk (30x30) , m^2	47 500	86 500	182.1
Russian Federation			
Glass for window 4mm, m^2	4 500	5 000	111.1
Roofing paper, m^2	850	880	103.5
Spike, 100mm, kg	1 400	1 500	107.1
Drying oil , kg	1 500	1 500	100.0
Wallpaper, m^2	510	520	102.0
Oil paint, kg	3 200	3 150	98.4
Linoleum, m^2	6 500	6 500	100.0
Lime (meli), kg	300	300	100.0
Slab stone (40x40), pieces	550	550	100.0
Ceramic sink, set	35 000	35 000	100.0
Ceramic lavatory pan, pieces	60 000	70 000	116.7
China			
Iron concrete, 700, m^2	45 500	45 500	100.0
Emulsion, (external), kg	440	900	204.5
Brick made from clay M-100, thous.pieces	75 000	82 000	109.3
Cement M-500, kg	260	260	100.0
Glass for window 3mm, m^2	3 000	3 100	103.3
Roofing paper, m^2	300	294	98.0
Spike, 100mm, kg	1 000	1 200	120.0
Oil paint, kg	1 250	1 250	100.0
Drying oil, kg	1 100	1 100	100.0
Wallpaper, m^2	580	849	146.4
Linoleum, m^2	2 500	2 500	100.0
Emulsion, (internal), kg	660	660	100.0
Lime (meli), kg	263	263	100.0

Slab stone (40x40), pieces	600	600	100.0
Ceramic sink, set	55 000	55 000	100.0
Ceramic lavatory pan, pieces	60 000	60 000	100.0
Door,(iron) pieces	120 000	120 000	100.0
Germany			
Emulsion, (external), kg	1 900	2 500	131.6
Emulsion, (internal), kg	1 300	2 500	192.3
South Korea			
Wallpaper, m^2	640	640	100.0

Source: NSO, 'Yearbook of 2005', 2006

Appendix 4.2

Construction, erection, rehabilitation works, funds invested in completed buildings (by the price of the year)

/million tugrigs/

Performance works	1989	1990	1991	1992	1993	1994	1995	1996	1997	1998	1999	2000	2001	2002	2003	2004	2005
Construction, erection capital maintenance works:	2 898.9	2 636.6	3 010.0	3 076.0	15 042.9	24 949.7	36 889.2	63 484.2	69 346.6	70 996.3	78 143.1	77 087.7	90 168.8	114 693.3	149 924.1	174 267.3	185 296. 7
Performed by domestic construction companies:	2 116.9	1 710.0	1 951.7	2 521.0	7 326.0	14 810.3	19 113.4	31 892.6	34 291.9	36 496.5	44 922.4	51 819.0	67 394.6	81 538.4	87 631.1	123 956.2	148 054. 6
Mongolian-foreign joint companies:	-	-	-	-	139.9	1 102.9	4 740.0	8 178.8	13 231.0	12 267.0	6 117.6	6 597.2	6 222.6	6 776.0	17 290.8	9 905.8	-
Performed by foreign companies:	782.0	926.6	1 058.3	555.0	7 577.0	9 036.5	13 035.8	23 412.8	21 823.7	22 232.8	27 103.1	18 671.5	16 551.6	26 378.9	45 002.2	40 405.3	37 242. 1
Fund invested in finished Buildings	174.1	128.9	240.0	547.9	1 136.3	4 200.0	14 741.4	17 000.0	32 021.2	5 092.5	18 253.0	74 124.0	22 954.0	25 221.0	42 484.8	88 635.4	101 189.5

Source: NSO, 'Yearbook of 2005' 2006

4.4 TRANSPORTATION

Road transport occupies a dominating place in the Mongolian economy, which has a wide territory with sparse population and is considered as a logistical force that plays an important role in the economy and social development of settled and rural areas. By 2005, 8.3 per cent of the GDP was created by the transport sector.

Over the transitional periods, associated with the total depression in the country, the transport sector faced unfavorable circumstances and serious consequences of that, as a result of which a number of entities and organizations in the sector experienced a deep slump in production and finance. While the freight, carried by all means of transportation reached 62.0 million tons in 1989, it reached 54.0 million tons in 1990, 36.5 million tons in 1991, 15.2 million tons in 1992 and lastly 8.4 million tons in 1997, which is considered the trough during the last 15 years, as a result of nonstop declines.

Graph 4.13 Transportation of freight and passengers by all means

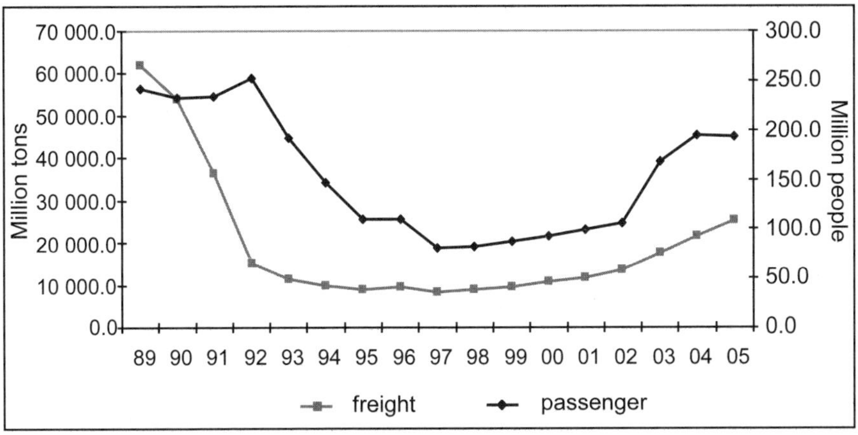

Source: Mongolia in the market economy, 1989-2002, NSO, 2004 он

These declines resulted from (i) the reduced freight transportation due to the slump in the industrial sector, (ii) privatization of agricultural cooperatives, (iii) privatization of state transport entities and of their vehicles to private entities, the performance of which, particularly, the information on a number of indicators including the volume of transportation, number of carried passengers, freight turnover, passenger turnover, total revenue and number of employees stopped to be provided to the statistical data of the country.

1997-2005 saw some growth in the sector and during this period, the annual average growth in freight equaled 14.9 per cent and in passenger transportation - 12.7 per cent respectively. 25.2 million tons of cargo and 192.7 million passengers in repeated numbers were carried by all means of transport and freight turnover reached 10267.1 million tons/km, passenger turnover – 2696.6 million people/km, and total revenue- 308.1 billion tugrigs in 2005.

Table 4.19 Main indicators in transport sector

	1990	1992	1996	2000	2001	2002	2003	2004	2005
Freight turnover mil.ton.km	6971.6	3320.9	2685.4	4418.3	5427.3	6604.4	7504.1	9169.3	10267.1
Freight transportation mil.ton	54.0	15.2	9.5	10.6	11.8	13.5	17.6	21.6	25.2
Passenger turnover mil.peop.km	2056.1	1956.5	1541.1	1946.0	1972.2	2108.3	2246.3	2621.6	2696.6
Passengers mil.peop	232.2	252.2	109.1	93.0	98.5	105.7	167.9	194.2	192.7

Source: 'Mongolia in the market economy', 1989-2002, NSO, 2004, 'Yearbook 2005', NSO, 2006.

14.4 per cent of total revenue in the transport sector generated from road transport, 62.8 per cent - from railway transport, and 22.8 per cent - from air transport respectively.

Although the volume of transport service has been increasing since 1997 every year, the indicator at present is far lower than the indicator that was revealed 16 years ago. Freight carried by all means of transport decreased by 2.1 per cent in 2005 compared to 1990 and passenger transportation – by 17.0 per cent in that order. Also, there has occurred a substantial change in the role of the vehicles.

Whereas auto transport played a dominating role in freight transportation during the centrally planned periods, the railway transport is a main factor of today.

Table 4.20 The structure of main indicators in transport sector, by vehicle types

	1970	1980	1990	1995	2000	2004	2005
Freight transportation:	100.0	100.0	100.0	100.0	100.0	100.0	100.0
of which:							
Motorway	67.1	70.3	73.0	18.4	13.9	35.0	38.2
Railway	32.7	29.6	26.9	81.5	86.1	65.0	61.8
Airway	0.0	0.0	0.0	0.03	0.0	0.0	0.0
water transportation	0.2	0.1	0.1	0.02	0.0	0.0	0.0

Passenger transportation:	100.0	100.0	100.0	100.0	100.0	100.0	100.0
of which:							
Motorway	98.3	98.4	98.5	97.2	95.1	97.6	97.7
Railway	1.3	1.2	1.1	2.6	4.6	2.2	2.2
Airway	0.4	0.4	0.4	0.2	0.3	0.2	0.2

Source: Statistical yearbook of 2005, NSO,2006

The government of Mongolia has laid a particular emphasis on the development of the sector and included the following objectives in the frame of the 'Objectives on intensive development of infrastructure with effect on economic growth', which was the supplement to the 24th Resolution of the Parliament on 'Approval of Government Action Program' released on the 5th November, 2004:

- Continuously implement the programs, which are aimed to develop the integrated data network of energy, motor roads and communication;
- Expand the railway transportation network, extend the capacity of railway and increase the international competitiveness of railway service. Build double-track railway, conduct a research on provision of railways with electricity.
- Increase the number of airplanes and flights to foreign countries, support the projects to build a new international airport.
- Study and implement projects on commencing additional air transport services.

The Ministry of Road, Transport and Tourism (MRTT) as well as organizations engaged in transport sector are carrying out particular actions in line with above objectives. 186 entities engaged in road transportation, seven - in air transportation, one- in railway transportation and one - in water transportation business are involved in additional cost estimation of 2005.

The research on hidden economy in transport sector was carried out in 1999 and 2004 respectively and the additional costs and total production of informal sector have been calculated basing on the outcomes of the research annually since 1999. The estimation of informal sector in the transport sector was carried out in five directions including, automobiles (passenger cars), trucks, buses, warm garages and open garages. The statistics on MOT-test (annual test of motor vehicles) of 2005 as well as transport service index and fuel price index of 2005 are included in the estimation. The total withdrawal of the informal sector was estimated 215.4 billion tugrigs and its additional cost – 84.9 billion tugrigs.

According to the MOT-test of 2005, a total of 131.2 thousand cars of different types were estimated and 87.8 thousand of those were passenger cars, 27.4 thousand – trucks, 11.1 thousand – buses, 3.6 thousand – vehicles with special equipment and 1.3 thousand were tank wagons. 101.6 thousand private cars were estimated and they accounted for 77.4 per cent of total cars involved in the test.

The total length of improved roads was estimated 6126.7 km in the end of 2005, 2278.6 km of which was paved roads. The length of improved roads increased by 1809.8 km, of paved roads by 1035.6 km respectively compared to 1990.

Air transport

Mongolian Civil Aviation transport started operating in 1956 when flights from Ulaanbaatar to Choibalsan, Khuvsgul and Khovd provinces were commenced to provide with regular airmail service. The international air transport root was laid in 1957 when there started an airmail service flight from Ulaanbaatar to Irkutsk. In the early years of transition to the market economy, all operations of Mongolian Civil Aviation were managed by MIAT Company. However, in August of 1993, the company was split into Mongolian Civil Aviation Authority (MCAA), which is responsible for implementing policies and resolutions of the government and MIAT Company Ltd, which was arranged to act as a business entity.

The international relations of civil aviation organizations are expanding more increasingly due to growing activities on domestic as well as international markets and increasing number of flight destinations contribute to it as well. Currently, Mongolian civil aviation organizations are in constant relationship on flight clearance issues with the same organizations in Russia, Germany, China, South Korea and Japan and their representative agents are operating in Berlin, Germany, Moscow and Irkutsk, Russia, Beijing and Khukh Khot, China, Tokyo, Japan and Seoul, Korea providing ticketing, reservation, luggage and passenger services.

Law of Mongolia on Civil Aviation passed in 1999 created legal environment to regulate multilateral relations in the sector. MCAA is managing operations of Mongolian civil aviation organizations pursuing the law.

Six aviation companies including passenger transportation companies with regular operation such as 'MIAT', 'Aero Mongolia', 'Ulgii Air' and 'Ulgii Trans' and companies providing chartered flights such as 'Blue Sky Aviation' and 'Tengeriin Ulaach Shine' and one state owned organization – MCAA operated in the sector in 2005.

Table 4.21. Basic indicators in air transport

	2000	2001	2002	2003	2004	2005	2005/2004 %
Freight transportation,thous.ton	**2.9**	**2.9**	**2.4**	**2.3**	**2.3**	**2.0**	**88.5**
mail	0.5	0.5	0.5	0.5	0.6	0.4	**75.5**
luggage	0.5	0.5	0.3	0.3	0.4	0.4	**88.7**
cargo	1.9	1.9	1.6	1.5	1.2	1.2	**94.6**
Freight turnover, mil.ton.km	**9.4**	**9.5**	**9.0**	**8.5**	**8.9**	**8.3**	**93.0**
mail	0.6	0.6	0.7	1.0	1.2	0.9	**72.7**
luggage	0.6	0.6	0.6	0.6	0.7	0.5	**69.9**
cargo	8.2	8.3	7.7	6.9	7.0	6.9	**98.9**
Passenger transportation,mil.peop	**0.3**	**0.3**	**0.3**	**0.3**	**0.3**	**0.3**	**100.0**
international	0.1	0.2	0.2	0.1	0.2	0.2	**100.0**
domestic	0.2	0.1	0.1	0.1	0.2	0.1	**50.0**
Passenger turnover,mil.peop.km	**514.6**	**538.9**	**661.2**	**651.0**	**758.1**	**822.5**	**108.5**
Transferred mil.ton.km	52.7	53.5	70.9	67.6	78.7	84.8	**107.7**
Transportation revenue mil.tug	39 696.4	41 636.6	48 375.2	51 092.4	63 503.9	70 179.6	**110.5**

Source: Statistical bulletin December, 2006 NSO, 2006

Freight transported by air reached 1991.9 tons; passenger transportation reached 318.1 thousand people in 2005. However, freight transportation decreased by 11.5 per cent; passenger transportation by 6.6 per cent against 2004. Yet, passenger turnover increased by 8.5 per cent, transportation revenue by 10.5 per cent or 6675.6 million tugrigs.

As a result of civil aviation sector development policies, particularly the fleet expansion policy of domestic flights developed and implemented by MRTT, two AN-38 planes and one Fokker-100 plane started to fly additionally. Revenue of 14.5 billion tugrigs from navigation was added to the state budget of the country in 2005 and it increased by 8.0 per cent or by 1068.6 million tugrigs against 2004. 57.5 thousand passengers and 359.7 tons of freight were transported by air in the first quarter of 2005, 79.1 thousand passengers and 574.1 tons freight in the second quarter, 108.0 thousand passengers and 475.4 tons of freight in the third quarter and 73.5 thousand passengers and 616.1 tons freight in the fourth quarter correspondingly.

The rate of passenger transportation tends to increase in June to September according to a study carried out on the monthly rate of passenger transportation.

Knowing what months show increases in the rate of passenger and freight transportation and what months show the decreases in it helps to make a good planning.

Let us calculate the seasonal fluctuations occurring in the rate of passenger and freight transportation by air.

It is required to collect data on quarterly (seasonal) and monthly basis of at least 3-5 years, so we used here the data of 2002-2005. The main method used to calculate the quarterly fluctuation is the phased mean calculation method. (appendix-5) Using this method we can calculate the quarterly (seasonal) index, consequently, the dynamic information discharged from the quarterly effects can be produced.

Table 4.22 Passenger and freight transportation by air, by months

Freight transportation, tons

Months	2001	2002	2003	2004	2005
I	228.9	118.0	172.3	152.5	129.0
II	200.2	152.9	163.3	229.7	121.8
III	224.1	161.0	189.8	137.6	108.9
IV	270.8	370.1	171.1	149.1	120.3
V	244.1	151.2	184.9	411.8	290.9
VI	242.1	420.6	224.8	187.6	163.5
VII	241.3	221.8	207.9	191.8	173.0
VIII	259.2	213.2	220.7	136.9	165.1
IX	271.8	218.0	192.2	184.2	137.3
X	255.6	226.2	161.0	169.3	232.6
XI	208.1	365.0	168.8	142.4	197.5
XII	244.6	194.0	174.0	158.6	186.0

Passenger transportation, persons

Months	2001	2002	2003	2004	2005
I	16801	15460	18499	17418	18902
II	15754	15354	13982	17900	16019
III	16255	17693	18244	16082	22537
IV	16839	18408	18816	16644	20786
V	19043	21670	19247	27487	25015
VI	25072	26827	26285	52974	33551
VII	32655	32327	28097	47198	46091
VIII	32888	36908	32549	50730	31261
IX	23846	25694	22788	22059	30898
X	18584	20928	18707	18519	20671
XI	15913	19329	17143	39302	25813
XII	17127	17359	17358	14323	27037

Source: Statistical bulletin December, 2003-2005, NSO

The quarterly index presents seasonal fluctuations in the dynamic row and is the main indicator to measure them. Using this index we can get rid of the seasonal fluctuations in the dynamic row and furthermore, it gives us to make dynamic trend analysis and precalculate the future rate as well as make plans. The rate of passenger transportation by air increases from January to May and from September to November of the year and decreases in October and December.

Table 4.23 Quarterly index of freight and passenger transportation by air

Months	Quarterly index of passenger transportation	Months	Quarterly index of freight transportation
I	74.6	I	80.6
II	64.5	II	91.6
III	77.2	III	77.8
IY	76.4	IY	79.7
Y	95.6	Y	164.4
YI	146.8	YI	107.0
YII	148.2	YII	104.0
YIII	165.8	YIII	95.2
IX	99.8	IX	100.3
X	82.0	X	94.9
XI	100.7	XI	112.4
XII	68.4	XII	92.1

Source: Statistical bulletin December, 2006, NSO

The passenger transportation reaches its peak in July and august. It overlaps with the peak period of tourism in the country. Yet, the rate of freight transportation increases in May – July and September – November.

Diagram 4.14 Quarterly index of freight and passenger transportation (2001-2005)

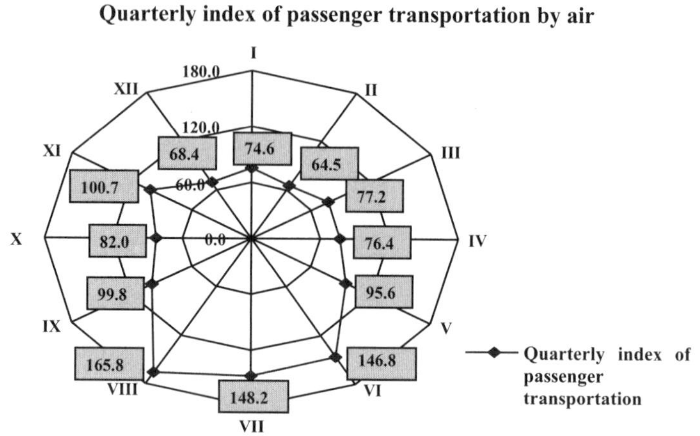

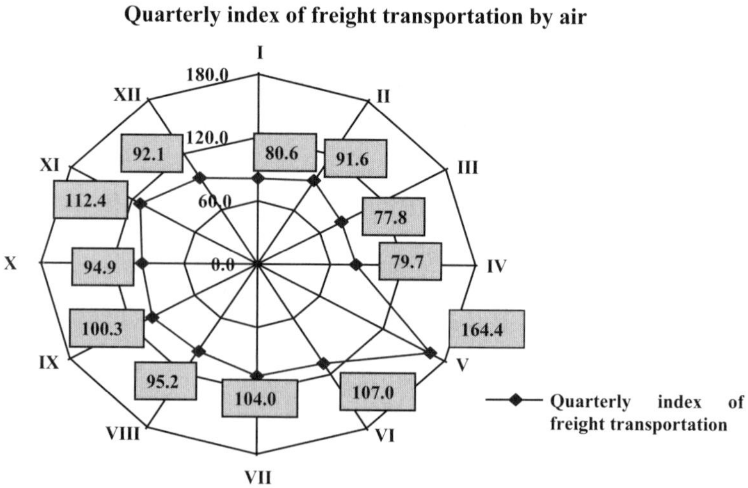

Source: Statistical bulletin December, 2005, NSO, 2006

Railway transport

The substantial decline, which has been occurred in the national income production, industrial and agricultural products and foreign trade turnover since 1989 resulted in the insufficient railway freight transportation. In other words the railway freight transportation and its turnover fell associated with the sharp decline of export and import as well as of transit freight through the country in the early periods of the transition. A number of internal and external factors affected this phenomenon seriously including the collapse of the old foreign trade system of the country, abrupt changes and deep depression in the social and political spheres of the foreign trade partner countries and the downtime and shutting up of domestic industries due to the financial and raw material constraints.

However, the sector started to see some recoveries in the middle of the 1990s due to some measures taken by railway organizations to strengthen the stability of railway operations, improve railway capacity and its utilization and mobilize all available internal resources.

The first train of 6000 tons of weight started its operation in 2005 and six new junctions were built as well as the lengths of railways of receiving and dispatching posts of 18 relay and junction stations were expanded.

The freight transportation by railway reached 15.6 million tons and passenger transportation in repeated numbers reached 4.2 million people in 2005. Compared to the previous year, freight transportation increased by 11.1 per cent or by 1.6 tons, freight turnover – by 12.0 per cent or by 1.1 billion tons/km, passenger turnover – by 1.3 per cent or by 15.4 million people in km, transport revenue – by 43.4 per cent or by 58.6 billion tugrigs respectively, but the passenger transportation fell by 2.3 per cent or by 0.1 million people.

Table 4.24 Basic indicators of railway freight transportation

	2000	2001	2002	2003	2004	2005	$\frac{2005}{2004}$ %
Freight transportation, mil.ton	**9158.5**	**10147.7**	**11637.0**	**12284.7**	**14031.8**	**15586.3**	**111.1**
Domestic	5960.4	6267.7	6643.1	6588.6	6857.3	7558.7	110.2
Outward	769.1	844.5	849.4	975.0	1125.3	1468.3	130.5
Inward	916.8	871.6	1058.4	1080.4	1225.2	1166.0	95.2
Transit	1512.2	2163.9	3086.1	3640.7	4824.0	5393.3	111.8
Freight turnover, mil.ton.km	**4282.5**	**5287.9**	**6461.3**	**7253.3**	**8878.1**	**9947.8**	**112.0**
Domestic	1457.5	1650.4	1774.9	1782.6	1916.0	2160.4	112.8
Outward	736.8	820.6	807.7	961.8	1094.8	1272.0	116.2

Inward	409.7	414.8	453.1	467.2	512.7	528.8	103.1
Transit	1678.5	2402.1	3425.6	4041.7	5354.6	5986.6	111.8
Passenger transportation, mil.peop.	**4.3**	**4.1**	**4.0**	**3.9**	**4.3**	**4.2**	**97.7**
International	0.1	0.2	0.2	0.1	0.2	0.2	106.4
Domestic	4.2	3.9	3.8	3.8	4.2	4.0	97.3
Passenger turnover, mil.peop.km	**1067.2**	**1062.2**	**1066.5**	**1038.8**	**1218.9**	**1234.3**	**101.3**
Transferred ton.km.mil	5349.6	6350.1	7527.8	8292.1	10096.9	11182.0	110.7
Transportation revenue, mil.tug	47838.2	63207.1	86643.8	109853.7	135000.0	193550.6	143.4

Structure of freight transportation, per cent

Freight transportation	**100.0**	**100.0**	**100.0**	**100.0**	**100.0**	**100.0**
Domestic	65.1	61.8	57.1	53.6	48.9	48.5
Outward	8.4	8.3	7.3	7.9	8.0	9.4
Inward	10.0	8.6	9.1	8.8	8.7	7.5
Transit	16.5	21.3	26.5	29.6	34.4	34.6

Source: Statistical yearbook, NSO, 2004, 2005

Domestic railway freight transportation increased by 10.2 per cent, outward cargo by 30.5 per cent and transit freight by 11.8 per cent respectively, but inward cargo decreased by 4.8 per cent. The percentage of transit freight in freight transportation went up by 18.1 points, outward cargo by 1.0 points, but the percentage of domestic freight transportation went down by 16.6 points and inward cargo by 2.5 points correspondingly in 2005 against 2000.

The domestic freight transportation continuously declined from 2000 and inward cargo from 2002 respectively.

A total of 1.0 million passengers and 3.8 million tons of freight were transported by railway in the first quarter of 2005, 1.0 million passengers and 3.7 million tons of freight in the second quarter, 1.2 million passengers and 3.9 million tons of freight in the third quarter and 1.0 million passengers and 4.4 million tons of freight in the fourth quarter of 2005 respectively. Let us calculate the quarterly index of the railway passenger transportation that characterizes the months in which the passenger transportation increases and the months in which it decreases basing on last four years' dynamics. (2001-2005)

Table 4.25 Railway passenger and freight transportation, by months

Freight, tons

Months	2001	2002	2003	2004	2005
I	840.9	1 014.6	1 021.9	1 133.0	1 305.7
II	845.9	978.6	926.3	1 077.9	1 205.6
III	888.9	1 030.7	1 017.0	1 086.2	1 336.6
IV	786.6	910.2	970.8	1 056.3	1 278.9
V	790.3	897.9	1 053.7	1 136.4	1 281.5
VI	761.4	881.4	983.5	1 158.3	1 150.2
VII	769.0	918.2	850.8	1 142.0	1 186.0
VIII	822.7	971.6	937.4	1 074.4	1 321.7
IX	839.9	1 036.1	1 112.5	1 233.8	1 395.1
X	903.3	1 055.8	1 119.1	1 330.8	1 551.9
XI	947.9	912.3	1 095.8	1 299.2	1 329.1
XII	951.0	1 029.6	1 195.9	1 303.5	1 554.5

Passengers, people

Months	2001	2002	2003	2004	2005
I	299.6	307.5	331.9	322.1	346.0
II	369.8	351.8	319.4	391.7	359.5
III	310.9	356.3	286.7	319.5	315.2
IV	303.7	226.3	280.1	344.4	331.9
V	328.9	315.5	263.0	370.4	348.3
VI	356.4	342.0	339.9	331.2	334.3
VII	403.6	412.0	358.1	409.0	392.5
VIII	440.0	369.4	416.2	449.4	443.4
IX	302.5	306.4	312.8	332.4	332.1
X	311.5	322.3	339.8	361.5	352.0
XI	348.7	345.1	372.5	377.9	352.2
XII	307.3	308.0	327.4	316.6	319.8

Source: Statistical bulletin, NSO, December 2005

The passenger transportation by railway increases slightly in February and then decreases in March-June and increases again in July, August and November, then decreases in September, October and December. The passenger transportation index reaches its peak in July and August, which are considered the summer holiday months in the country.

However, freight transportation by railway slightly increases in January, March, May, September, October, November and December and decreases in the remaining months. To our surprise, it increases in all odd months except for July.

Table 4.26 Quarterly index of railway passenger and freight transportation (2001-2005)

Months	Quarterly index of passenger transportation
I	97.2
II	103.5
III	88.9
IY	91.9
Y	93.9
YI	96.7
YII	115.5
YIII	120.6
IX	93.1
X	99.9
XI	106.3
XII	92.4

Months	Quarterly index of freight transportation
I	104.0
II	95.8
III	101.7
IY	96.7
Y	100.8
YI	94.7
YII	91.6
YIII	93.7
IX	105.4
X	108.1
XI	100.6
XII	106.9

Source: Statistical bulletin, NSO, December 2005

Diagram 4.15 Quarterly index of railway passenger and freight transportation (2001-2005)

Quarterly index of passenger transportation by railway

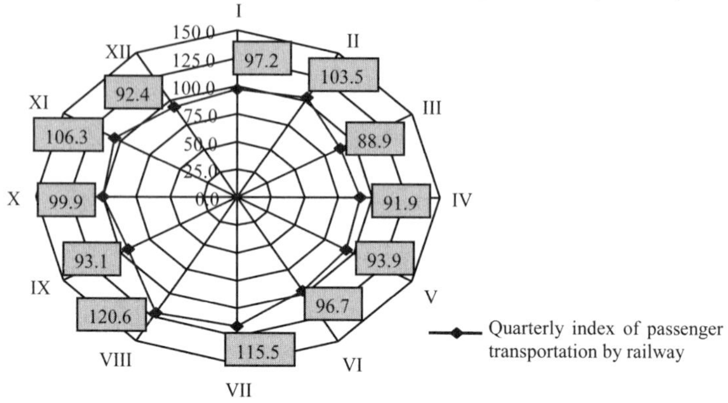

Quarterly index of freight transportation by railway

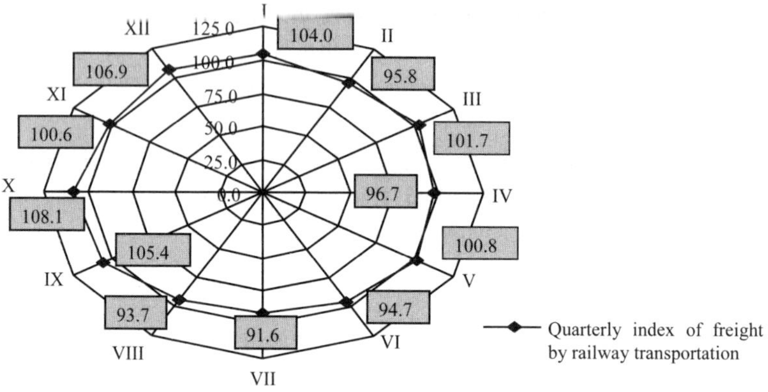

Source: Statistical bulletin, 2004-2005, NSO December 2006

According to the diagram, the rate of railway passenger transportation increases in July and August. Yet, the rate of freight transportation increases from September to January and in May. 8.9 thousand employees worked in the railway sector in 2005, which represents an increase by 8.0 per cent or by 0.7 thousand people against 2004.

Table 4.27 Annual average number of workers in railway transport sector

	2001	2002	2003	2004	2005	2005/2004 %
Annual average number of employees person	7498	7770	7961	8253	8914	108.0

Source: Statistical bulletin, NSO, 2005

Road transport

After Mongolia refused to develop the centrally planned economy in the early 1990s, it started to take considerable measures so as to transit to the market economy including privatization of state assets, development of private sector, promotion and expansion of production through price liberalizations, creation of favorable environment for free competitions and liberalization of foreign exchange rate; as a result, road transport institutions were privatized and private sector started to dominate in the sector.

The structure, organization and management style of the road transport sector, even the supervisory mechanism of prosedures in the sector have entirely changed. When the old management structure of the sector was removed, the sector lost its steering wheel during the first 2-3 years of the market economy because they started the reform with only superficial undenstanding of the market economy when the new mechanism that could have replaced the old one was not set up and actual directions or action plans and programs that would have led the sector to the market economy were not ready. Consequently, the road organizations faced a deep depression, malfanction in operation and recession. Although the privatization in the sector encountered above difficulties, it is coming to the end stepping particular phases. Besides, a number of entities engaged in the transportation, technical maintenance and transport mediation businesses have emerged in the sector expanding its sphere.

In 2005, freight transportation reached 9.6 million tons and passenger transportation 188.2 million passengers in repeated numbers and the freight transportation increased by 27.2 per cent, freight turnover by 10.2 per cent respectively, but passenger transportation decreased by 0.7 per cent and passenger turnover by 0.7 per cent respectively against 2004. Besides, the total revenue in the sector reached 44.3 billion tugrigs by the price of the year and it increased by 0.3 per cent or by 126.2 million tugrigs against 2004.

Table 4.28 Basic indicator in road sector

	1999	2000	2001	2002	2003	2004	2005	$\frac{2005}{2004}$%
Freight trans.thous.tug	1330.4	1480.4	1658.2	1888.7	5335.9	7561.9	9617.4	127.2
Freight turnover, mil.tn.km	123.2	126.1	129.5	133.6	242.4	282.3	311.0	110.2
Passenger trans, mil people	83.3	88.4	94.1	101.4	163.7	189.6	188.2	99.3
Passeng turnover, mil.peop.km	358.4	364.2	371.1	380.6	556.5	644.6	639.8	99.3

Transferred ton.km.mil	246.7	260.6	277.4	300.9	686.6	934.5	1208.0	129.3
Transport revenue,mil.tug	13164.9	14467.3	15972.1	17828.2	32678.8	44124.3	44250.5	100.3

Source: Year book 2002, NSO, 2003, Year book 2005, NSO, 2006

Water transport

Water transport sector was established in 1926 in the country. A ship with a diesel engine named after '10th anniversary of Mongolia' was assembled in 1931 and a ship named 'Sukhbaatar' was assembled in 1943 in Khuvsgul lake. Although the water transport sector faced a depression in the 1990s like other sectors, it has been developing rapidly due to the changes and reforms of the transition relying on the private sector's development. The water transport sector operates in Kuvsgul and Selenge aimags. Over 40 water transport vehicles were estimated in above mentioned aimags according to the MOT test of 2004. The larger ones were 'Sukhbaatar' (with three barges), two 'Yaroslavets', a medium size ship with capacity of carrying 12 people and 'Dalai eej', a passenger ship with capacity of carrying 12 people estimated in Khuvsgul and 'Altanbulag'(with a barge of dry cargo), a ship with 170 horsepower estimated in Selenge aimag.

In 2005, 0.5 thousand tons of freight were transported by water transport and the total outward cargo reached 12.6 million tugrigs, out of which 8.0 per cent or 1.0 million tugrigs were estimated as the additional cost.

Road vehicles

The number of road vehicles

According to the MOT-test of 2005, a total of 131.2 thousand cars of different types were estimated, out of which 87.8 thousand were passenger cars, 27.4 thousand – trucks, 11.1 thousand – buses, 3.6 thousand – vehicles with special equipment and 1.3 thousand were tank wagons. Compared to 2004, passenger cars increased by 10.2 per cent, trucks by 7.9 per cent, buses 4.0 per cent, vehicles for special purposes 10.6 per cent but tank vagons decreased by 7.9 per cent.

Table 4.29 The number of vehicles, its growth

Year	Total (numb.)	Growth (percent)				
		1960=100	1970=100	1980=100	1990=100	2000=100
1960	11565	100.0				
1970	21632	187.0	100.0			

1980	34487	298.2	159.4	100.0		
1990	43792	378.7	202.4	127.0	100.0	
1995	56428	487.9	260.9	163.6	128.9	
1997	70088	606.0	324.0	203.2	160.0	
1999	74840	647.1	346.0	217.0	170.9	
2000	81693	706.4	377.6	236.9	186.5	100.0
2001	93071	804.8	430.2	269.9	212.5	113.9
2002	103805	897.6	479.9	301.0	237.0	127.1
2003	105775	914.6	489.0	306.7	241.5	129.5
2004	120418	1041.2	556.7	349.2	275.0	147.4
2005	131184	1134.3	606.4	380.4	299.6	160.6

Graph 4.16

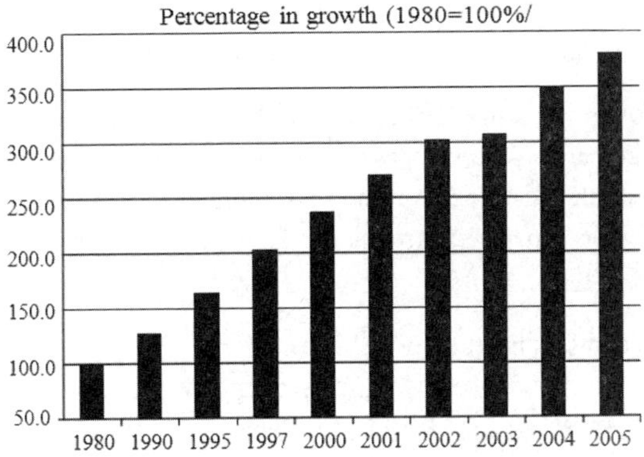

Source: Yearbook 2005, NSO 2006

However, the total number of vehicles increased 11.3 times in relation to 1960, 6.1 times against 1970, 3.8 times against 1980, 3.0 times against 1990 and by 60.6 per cent against 2000. Whereas on average 1.4 cars were allocated in 100 square kilometer area in 1970, 2.8 cars in 1990 and 8.4 cars in 2005 respectively nationwide.

The number of passenger cars and buses has been increasing rapidly in recent years. The number of passenger cars increased 11.0 times and buses 4.3 times but of tank wagons decreased 3.8 times and vehicles of special purposes 1.1 times against 1990.

Table 4.30 The number of vehicles, by types

	1970	1980	1990	2000	2001	2002	2003	2004	2005	$\frac{2005}{1990}$ %
Total	**21632**	**34487**	**43792**	**81693**	**93071**	**103805**	**105775**	**120418**	**131184**	**3.0***
out of which:										
Passenger cars	4343	6887	7962	44051	53198	63224	68458	79691	87792	11.0*
Trucks	14876	20094	24400	24671	24747	24610	22975	25430	27435	112.4
Buses	703	1332	2591	8548	10187	10841	9834	10645	11067	4.3*
Tanks	695	3311	4754	1683	1613	1709	1320	1376	1267	26.7
of special purposes	1015	2863	4085	2740	3326	3421	3188	3276	3623	88.7

* times

Source: Yearbook 2005, NSO 2006, Mongolia in market economy, 1989-2002, NSO 2004

Alongside the growth in numbers of cars, there have occurred considerable changes in the structure of the cars. Whereas passenger cars accounted for 18.2 per cent, trucks for 55.7 per cent and buses for 5.9 in the total number of vehicles in 1990, passenger cars accounted for 66.9 per cent, trucks for 20.9 per cent and buses 8.4 per cent in 2005.

Table 4.31 Types and composition of vehicles

Year	Total	Percentage in total amount				
		Passenger cars	Trucks	Buses	Tanks	Of special purposes
1970	100.0	20.1	68.8	3.2	3.2	4.7
1980	100.0	20.0	58.2	3.9	9.6	8.3
1990	100.0	18.2	55.7	5.9	10.9	9.3
2000	100.0	53.9	30.2	10.5	2.1	3.3
2001	100.0	57.2	26.6	10.9	1.7	3.6
2002	100.0	60.9	23.7	10.4	1.7	3.3
2003	100.0	64.7	21.7	9.3	1.2	3.1
2004	100.0	66.2	21.1	8.8	1.1	2.7
2005	100.0	66.9	20.9	8.4	1.0	2.8

Source: NSO 2006

In 2005, privately owned cars reached 101.6 thousand which shows an increase of 13.2 per cent against 2004, among which passenger cars increased by 14.2 per cent. Privately - owned cars accounts for 77.4 per cent of the total vehicles nationwide, 81.4 per cent of the passenger cars, 71.9 per cent of the trucks and 73.7 per cent of the cars respectively.

Table 4.32 The number of privately-owned cars, percentage in total vehicles

	2001	2002	2003	2004	2005	$\frac{2005}{2004}$%
Total privately owned cars	67448	70816	79045	89730	101563	113.2
out of which:						
Passenger cars	41679	45080	53512	62583	71459	114.2
Percentage of privately owned cars in the total number of vehicles						
Passenger cars	78.3	74.2	78.2	78.5	81.4	
Trucks	68.8	68.5	72.1	69.6	71.9	
Buses	68.3	69	71.1	69.4	73.7	
Tanks	20.5	21.3	25.7	26.9	28.6	
Vehicles of special purposes	43.6	47.6	51.5	51.8	50.9	
Total	72.5	68.2	74.7	74.5	77.4	

Source: yearbook 2005, NSO 2006

In 2005, the number of privately-owned cars increased in aimags and cities except for Arkhangai, Govisumber, Darkhan-Uul, Zavkhan and Selenge against 2004. (Appendix-3). When the number of privately-owned cars compared to the total number of households, one car is allocated in six families in 2005. Out of estimated 5490 trails, 72.0 per cent or 3952 trails are under the possession of households.

Table 4.33 Trails

	2001	2002	2003	2004	2005	$\frac{2005}{2004}$%
Total amount, nationwide	4741	5370	4651	4614	5490	119.0
out of which:						
Privately owned	2633	3398	3039	2986	3952	132.4
Percentage	55.5	53.7	65.3	64.7	72.0	

Source: yearbook 2005, NSO 2006

The number of self propelled mechanisms

According to the 2005 MOT test, a total of 4601 tractors and self propelled mechanisms were estimated, out of which 44.2 per cent are used by individuals. Whilst 68.7 per cent of tractors are utilized in crop areas such as Selenge, Dornod, Tuv, Bulgan and Ulaanbaatar, 37.2 per cent of motorcycles are located in Dornod, Uvurkhangai, Umnugovi and Khuvsgul aimags.

Table 4.34 The number of tractors, self propelled mechanisms and motorcycles estimated in 2005

	Tractor, self propelled mechanisms			motorcycles		
	2004	2005	2005/2004 %	2004	2005	2005/2004 %
Arkhangai	101	106	105.0	2 475	1 410	57.0
Bayan-Ulgii	123	81	65.9	1 468	1 731	117.9
Bayankhongor	29	27	93.1	1 150	1 076	93.6
Bulgan	623	650	104.3	990	996	100.6
Gobi-Altai	6	4	66.7	364	911	250.3
Dornogobi	58	52	89.7	884	723	81.8
Dornod	310	457	147.4	886	2 123	239.6
Dundgobi	52	25	48.1	2 191	1 974	90.1
Zavkhan	83	50	60.2	1 233	774	62.8
Uvurkhangai	34	37	108.8	3 554	2 006	56.4
Umnugobi	42	30	71.4	2 183	2 401	110.0
Sukhbaatar	114	109	95.6	1 484	1 501	101.1
Selenge	1 090	1 062	97.4	314	267	85.0
Tuvi	410	334	81.5	433	304	70.2
Uvs	82	68	82.9	276	805	291.7
Khovd	122	219	179.5	1 451	679	46.8
Khuvsgul	189	156	82.5	1 944	2 102	108.1
Khentii	118	220	186.4	801	839	104.7
Darkhan-Uul	129	113	87.6	50	28	56.0
Ulaanbaatar	730	656	89.9	333	370	111.1
Orkhon	149	126	84.6	96	91	94.8
Govisumber	39	19	48.7	203	204	100.5
Total	4 633	4 601	99.3	24 763	23 315	94.2
Out of which: privately owned	2 182	2 035	93.3	24 333	22 862	94.0
Percentage in total	47.1	44.2		98.3	98.1	

Source: yearbook 2005, NSO 2006

Improved auto roads

The 'Millennium Road', a Government Program has started to be implemented successfully since 2001. This will contribute not only to create a proper network of domestic infrastructure that meets the demand of the population, but also it will provide favorable conditions for the further economic development of the country by developing the international road transport, tourism and passenger transportation sectors. The project will cover four basic regional centers, which are located on the intersection of the horizontal axis of infrastructure that supports the development of the country and the vertical axis of infrastructure that supports the regional development. One third of the total territory, 80 per cent of the population and 72 per cent of the settled areas are included in 200 km areas from the axis of the 'Millennium Road'.

The western route of the 'Millennium Road' covers: Ulaanbaatar-Lun-Bayannuur-Gichgeniin guur-Dashinchilen-Tsahir-Yaruu-Zavkhan teeliin belchir-Khashaatiin davaa-Ulaan baishint and the eastern route covers: Ulaanbaatar-Bayandavaa-Erdene-baganuur-Undurkhaan-Dornod-the border of Sukhbaatar aimag-the border of the country. In the frame of the 'Millennium Road' project, a total of approximately 2600 km of road and two km long reinforced concrete bridges are planned to be built within the recent 8-10 years' period, out of which the work to be implemented in 2001-2005 was approved and is being implemented.

Roads are classified as follows:

- paved roads (Cement, asphaltic roads and roads with slight surface pavement)
- gravel roads (gravel stones are put on the improved earth and toughened)
- improved earth roads (earth roads are reconditioned, leveled and toughened)
- earth roads (country- roads)

Paved road, improved road and gravel roads constitute the improved roads. 6126.7 km of improved roads are utilized nationwide, out of which 2278.6 km of roads are paved roads according to the 2005 statistics, which shows an increase by 19.9 per cent or 377.9 km against 2004. It includes 200 km of paved roads built to the Nalaikh-Choir route, 115 km of paved roads to Kherlen bridge-Undurkhaan route, 65 km of paved roads to Yarant-Khovdiin Bulgan route and 45 km of partial gravel roads built to Arvaikheer-Khovd route.

Table 4.35 The length of improved roads, at the end of a year, km

	2000	2001	2002	2003	2004	2005
Improved roads	5 515.6	5 581.8	5 546.8	5 666.9	5 683.3	6 126.7
out of which:						
Paved roads	1 714.9	1 714.9	1 801.9	1 900.7	1 900.7	2 278.6
Gravel roads	1 877.1	1 943.3	1 871.3	1 892.6	1 937.8	1 980.3
Improved earth roads	1 923.6	1 923.6	1 873.6	1 873.6	1 844.8	1 867.8

Source: Yearbook-2005, NSO, 2006, Yearbook-2003, NSO 2004

In 2005, 10.7 billion tugrigs were spent on roads from the state budget.

Conclusion

The objectives that are reflected in the action program of the government are being implemented effectively with the contribution of business entities and organizations in the transport sector. The most highlighting work performed in the transport sector in 2005 is that the paved roads increased by 19.9 per cent or 377.9 km compared to 2004. The length of paved roads increased by 5.1 per cent or 87.0 km in 2002 against 2001 and 5.5 per cent or 98.9 km in 2003 against 2002 respectively (as for the remaining years there were no changes in it) in the last five years. The principle objectives of MRTT in 2006 include building of 1500 km of paved roads and improvement of 1000 km of earth roads in 2006-2008 and building and completion of 284 km of paved roads in 2006, which signifies the government places a significant emphasis on the transport sector.

The annual average growth that has occurred in the number of vehicles since 2000 is considered about 10.0 per cent; among them the annual average growth in private cars equals 12.0 per cent. According to this estimation, the total number of vehicles in our country tends to reach to 144.3 thousand and privately owned cars to 113.7 thousand in 2006 correspondingly. As indicated by the 2005 MOT test, out of the total vehicles counted nationwide, 56.2 per cent or 73.7 thousand vehicles, out of total privately owned cars, 51.4 per cent or 52.2 thousand cars were belonged to Ulaanbaatar city. In other words, 16 vehicles are allocated to one square km area of Ulaanbaatar city.

The growth of privately owned cars and centralization of the population in Ulaanbaatar city resulted in the decline of domestic passenger transportation by air and railway. However, due to the development of the tourism, the volume of international passenger transportation increased.

One of the urgent issues in the sector is considered that all the information including freight transportation, number of passengers, freight turnover, passenger turnover, total revenue and number of employees of business entities and organizations running business in the sector necessary to be reported officially in the statistical documents and official reports of the country is not still definite. The main reason for that is some private entities engaged in transportation business as well as individuals solely rendering transportation service are not involved in the official reports. Thus, it is important to involve them in the official registration and develop an appropriate policy to regulate their business activities. It will favor to reduce the sphere of informal sector and increase the quality, accuracy and reliability of data and information service in the transport sector.

4.5 INFORMATION AND COMMUNICATIONS SERVICES

It is important to have common understanding about Information and Communication Technology (ICT). Information and Communication Technology is determined in UNDP as:

"a tool to work with the information including different types of product, needs and services for the purpose of collection, storage and archiving, production, distribution and exchange of the information". It includes old information communication technology such as radio, television, telephone as well as new information communication technologies such as personal computers, satellites, wireless communication and internet etc. All these equipments with its required content and demand, working all together establish *world network* which is a huge infrastructure of interconnected telephone lines standard computer hardware, internet, radio and television and which reaches every corner of the world. [1]

Development of the new information communication technologies and establishment of the "Information society" is one of the targets of the National Millennium Development Goals to be achieved by 2015.

Mongolian government determined the sector of information communication technology as an accelerator of the development for the country. It stresses out the importance of the sector and implements many important activities to improve usage and delivery of information and communication technology in all the social sectors.

During the transitional years, foreign and domestic investment, support and assistance of international organizations and donor countries and individuals had shown notable implications in the sector of information and communication technology and demonstrate successful results.

The share of the information and communication sector in the Gross domestic product is shown in the Figure 1.

Figure 1: Percentage Share of the Information and Communication Sector in Gross Domestic Product, 1995-2005

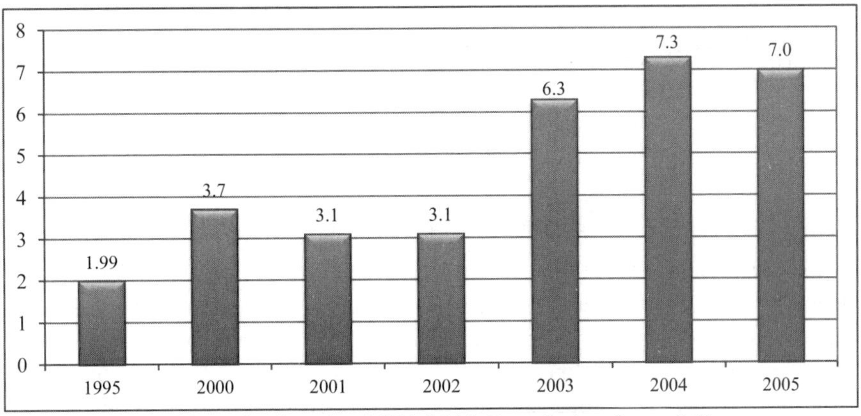

Source: Calculated by author based on ICTA /11/ & Open Society forum /16/.

Percentage of the sector of information and communication technology in gross domestic product was 1.99 in 1995 and increased to 7 percent in 2005, which shows that contribution of the sector in economy has increased.

---

[1] "Open Society" Forum, "Information technology Service deliveries in Rural Areas of Mongolia and faced problems" Study Report, 2006

According to the National Statistical Office, total income growth of the sector of information and communication technology increased from 10 to 43.1 percent and growth of gross domestic product increased from 9.5 to 23.7 percent in the years 2001 and 2004. Income growth of the information and communication technology sector is higher than growth of gross domestic product and it mainly attributable to the increased competitiveness of the sector explained basically by large participation and involvement of the private sector. In addition, it is related to the expansion of the market as a consequence of the introduction of the new mobile phone and information technologies.

Figure 2: Income of the Information and Communication Technology Sector and Gross Domestic product.

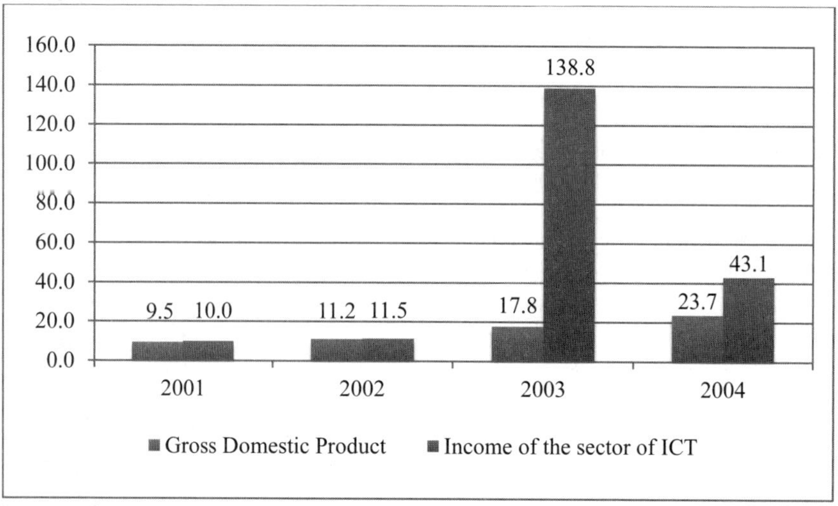

Source: Information and Communication Technology Agency, /10/, 2005

In the recent years, Mongolian information and communication technology sector demonstrate development and progress. As the result of implementing programs of "E-Mongolia" program, "Computerizing all" and "1 tugrug Internet campaign", changing western areas by fiber cable, being possible to utilize new technology with high speed of internet, introducing wireless internet technology and installing CDMA system of moveable internet in rural areas, telephone points to serve to Mongolian population was increased and telephone points of each 1000 people that were 55 in 2002, was reached to 63 in 2005. Number of Personal computer each 1000 people were 18 in 2002 and reached to 33[2] in 2005.

[2] National Statistical Office, Statistical Bulletin of Mongolia, Ulaanbaatar, Mongolia, 2006

In modern time, progresses of information technology quickly introduced in all social sectors are issuing more possibility us. We introduce with intellectual fund and world wealth and exchange information using Internet and local people started to use this possibility. Electronic content of information in Mongolian dramatically increases, high professional specialists of information technology are educated, and the possibility to participate in social and economical life of the country actively increases not concerning with geographical location and new work place and new market are established.

Mongolia is aiming to improve life of population by a way of establishing new economic environment and intellectual ability, increasing competitive skills of the countries and providing stable development according to the program of "E-Mongolia" and to include in first 10 countries in Asia in 2012 by main indexes of information and communications technology. Today's condition of policy regulation of the sector of information and communications technology, legal environment, infrastructure, service and usage, today's development of human resource and faced problems of the sector were considered below.

POLICY REGULATION OF INFORMATION AND COMMUNICATIONS TECHNOLOGY AND LEGAL ENVIRONMENT

As history of Mongolian information and communications regulation, Ministry of Communication, which regulated policy of sector of Information Technology in that time, was changed to Mongolian Communications Committee in 1990.

The first governmental agency responsible all problems of information Communication and Information Agency under the Mongolian Communications Committee was established in 1992. In the result of liberalization in Sector of communication in same year, state owned Mongolian Communications Company was established. Mongolian Communications Company was privatized in 1995 and has been running the activity by name of Telecom Mongolian Co., Ltd with state property to run communications service. In 1995, Additional amendments were made in law of communications and Communications regulation Council was established in structure of Ministry of Infrastructure in same year and worked by ministry to determine the policy of the sector and its executer and approving new amendments of law of communication from The Parliament of Mongolia in 2001, Sector of communication was liberalized, honest competition was established, regulating new and independent structure were established, Communication Regulation Committee was established and All Public Service Responsible Fund (APSRF) was started the activity.

In 2000, Parliament of Mongolia has adopted the "Concept on Information and Communication Technology Development of Mongolia up to 2010" and established National Committee for information and communications technology with purpose of implementing these concepts.

Policy and Regulation Department of information and communications technology was established in structure of Ministry of infrastructure on January 2003 with purpose of implementing the aim, activity and strategy defined by documents of development policy of information and communications technology, organizing sector's investment and producing common policy of information and communications technology that covered all sectors of society and economics, implementing it and intensifying the support work by information technology.

The Parliament and Government pay the attention to Information and communications technology development, implementation of new service and its range and Adaptation Agency of Mongolian Government established Information and Communications Technology Agency (ICTA) with purpose of establishing informed society based on knowledge since October 2004 to unify Policy and Regulation Department of ICT and Post Office.

ICTA works by direction of producing national policy of Information and communications technology, regulating it, managing state property of internal relations and communications and implementing investment program of the sector. Information and Communications Development Center /Post Office/ under the ICTA is responsible to post service. State policy and regulation structure of Sector of ICT Showed on Figure 3.

Figure 3. State policy and regulation structure of the sector of ICT

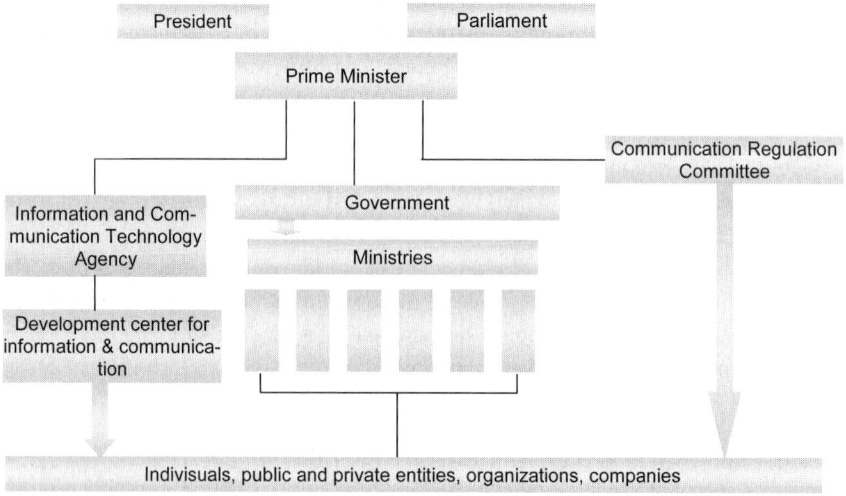

Now the activities of the sector of ICT are regulated by Law of Mongolian telecommunications, Law of radio wave, Law of post, Law of business license, Law of forbidding dishonest competition, Patent law, law of author's right, Law of intellectual property defense, law of technology transfer, law of science and technology and Criminal Law.

The strategy aims such as refining management, policy and regulation of national information and communications technology, supporting and developing all kinds of service based on e-commerce, and information and communication technology, transferring services of tax, custom, insurance, bank and finance in electronic form, being opened state information, developing fruitful information relations between governmental organizations and creating a searching system, state information network and databases, was defined on "Concept on Information and Communication Technology Development of Mongolia up to 2010".

And certain aims to establish legal environment regulating preparation work to transfer in electronic government, and the activity and service in direction of information and communications technology, in order to, the relations related with electronic government, electronic commerce, electronic transaction, and electronic signature in "Strategy of middle term to develop Mongolian Information and Communications Technology".

But now, our country has no legal environment to develop information technology, electronic usage and service and software production.

DOCUMENTS OF DEVELOPMENT POLICY OF INFORMATION AND COMMUNICATIONS TECHNOLOGY:

"Concept on Information and Communication Technology Development of Mongolia up to 2010", Parliament, 2000

Mongolian government determined that development aim of Information and Communications Technology is the first and national economical development key of the activity and way to decrease poverty and close digital division. The goal of the concept was determined that is developing society and increasing life level of the people on the basis of intellectual skill.

Strategy of middle term to develop Mongolian Information and Communications Technology and plan of the activities based on it, Government, 2002

The strategy is main factor of ICT and aims to work fruitfully and determined following basic 4 aims.

1. To establish convenient environment of proper policy, law and regulation.
2. To develop required main infrastructure of communications and information for establishing reliable and cheap connection.
3. To establish economical and business range of utilization of Information and Communication Technology in governance and other usages.
4. To develop human resource for using fruitfully with ICT.

Study of master planning of Mongolian local telecommunications system development, Ministry of Infrastructure, JICA, 2003[3]

In this general planning, the planning with stages of 2008, 2012, 2020 to develop local communications system covered total territories of Mongolia until 2020 was produced and detail study of the firstly implementing project was made.

The proposal to implement with assistance of contribution countries of the firstly implementing project and development, especially Japanese Government was putted.

Plan of governmental activities of 2004-2008, Parliament, 2004

Practice activities related with start of "E-Government" and "E-Mongolia" national programs that are implementing in level of all institutes of government were determined on planning of governmental activities. For example: establishing general code all over the country, establishing united informational system between the hospitals, providing local families and schools by energy reliable resources and computers with purpose of transferring and improving simple communication network to bandwidth technology, establishing common information system.

In the first activities of middle term of governmental ICT:

1. To refine All Public Service Responsible Fund (APSRF) and implement it with purpose of providing local areas and half-urbanized areas of Mongolia by All Public Service Deliveries (APSD).
2. To use ICT in business, social sector and civil society, determine incentive to utilize and implement policy /economical, financial and tax policies/.
3. To strengthen Regulation Committee of Communication and establish competitive development based on private sector of information infrastructure of Mongolia with purpose of well regulating sectors of communications.
4. To implement problems of new service based on internet protocol, data transferring, calling, interconnections, tariffs and improve their wide-using regulation environment.
5. To expand and intensify regulation innovation.
6. Cyber law

[3] Open forum "Open Society" Forum, "Information technology Service deliveries in Rural Areas of Mongolia and faced problems" Study Report, 2006 page 52

7. To improve contents service and deliveries of information technology including e-training, tele-medicine and national databases.
8. To increase of ICT in economic growth /production, financial sector, agriculture, society and economic sectors.
9. To implement e-trade and e-service /usage in all sectors.
10. To consider other general study results those were made in sector of ICT and increase possibilities.
11. To implement digital technology-in house concept and develop it.

E-Government Master Plan, Government, 2005

The most important 22 projects of E-Government were determined in this master plan that produced by Information and Communication Production Support Agency of the Republic of Korea with Information and Communications Technology Agency and following 4 projects was considered to firstly implement.

1. Establish government portal or web site
2. Electronic Identity card, and registration national project
3. Administrative portal
4. Government information center

E-Mongolia, National Program, Government, 2005

In plan of governmental activities of 2004-2012, and E-Mongolia project *t*he requirements to develop new usage of ICT electronic or e-services, innovate basic network between local centers, transfer it to digital form, establish high speed basic network, implement new usages/e-government, e-purchase, e-tax and e-registration/ and decrease digital division between urban and rural areas of Mongolia, was mentioned. This determined that stable sector of Information and Communication Technology was ensured by implementing policy and legal range, establishing infrastructure of reliable information, establishing partnership of state and private sectors, increasing intellectual skill and competition, intensifying foreign and domestic investment, making the investment for development, improving productivity of production, expanding service range and developing human skill.

Mongolian Information and Communication Technology, Mongolian Open Society Institute, 2001

This document values legal documents that are valid now, pays the attention to value institute, infrastructure initiative and donors in this initiative and makes a proposal of advice of Mongolian Open Society Institute about ICT of Mongolia.

Investment of ICT of Mongolia, International Financial Corporation, 2002

Mongolian legal regulation, market of ICT, production, state and private sectors, financial environment, certain business development of ICT, human resource development and supporting ICT were reflected on this document produced by international adviser John Kjelemo for foreign investment and donors.

Today's condition of ICT Development of Mongolia, "Mongolian Development Gateway" Non-governmental organization, InfoCon Co., Ltd, 2003

In the range of study, the more attention was paid in local education and science and the analysis was made in social development strategy, policy of Sector of Information and Communication, legal environment, structure, structure of organization, structure of network, service market, service tariff of Information and Communication Technology and deliveries. Work, service and development trends of daily uses of Information and Communication Technology based on internet were determined.

When Mongolia implements aims defined by principles, strategy and program of Information Technology, the problem to improve law of Information and Communications Technology and legal environment, rendering assistance in policy regulation is considered sharply.

There is a need to approve projects of laws of information technology: General Law of information technology, electronic contract, electronic signature, electronic authority and information security and make additional amendments in laws that are valid related with these laws. Approving these laws, legal law to utilize information technology will be formatted. Moreover, the problems to reach aims and levels in direction of ICT in short time are faced with Mongolian government.

INFRASTRUCTURE OF ICT SECTOR

Network between countries and cities

In modern time, transferring construction of communication between countries, and between cities of Mongolia or generally city's network center transferred each into digital technology with 100% and monopoly service of telecommunication distributed certainly and Telecom Mongolia Co., Ltd, Railway Regulation Office, Mobicom, Skytel and Unitel companies run the telecommunication service in free competition base and price tariff was decreased 3-4 times.

Today, Mongolia communicates with about 150 countries of the world by 7 outsets between countries.

Mongolian state infrastructure of ICT consists of 1800 kilometer fiber cable, about 1700 kilometer analog and 1009 kilometer digital technology radio relay line, television, radio and satellite VSAT station networks connected Ulaanbaatar city with other several aimags. /table 1/

Table 1. Public and mobile telephone services, wireless communication service providers, and basic indicators[4].

Server- Operator	Number of users	Transferring network (km)	Explanation
Telecom Mongolia Co., Ltd	148.500-13.000 WLL CDMA	Fiber cable-1.840.2 Digital Radio relay line-1.009 Analog Radio relay line - 524.7 VSAT-19	Telecom Mongolia Co., Ltd leases from ICTA
Mongolian Railway	13.000+	Fiber cable-1.402	Investment is made from Mongolian Railway
State Communication Department	2.800-800 WLL CDMA	Fiber cable-21	Investment is made and owned by Mongolian Government
Mobicom Corporation	455.100 GSM GPRS 19.000 WLL CDMA	Fiber cable-700 Digital Radio relay line-2076	Investment is made and owned by Mobicom Company
Skytel Company	99.900 CDMA-2001x	Fiber cable-80 Digital Radio relay line-1600	Investment is made and owned by Skytel Company
Total	163.600+455.10 0GSM GPRS 99.900 CDEMA-2001x 32.000 WLL SDMA	Fiber cable-4022.2 Digital Radio relay line-4375.0 Analog Radio relay line-524.7 VSAT-19	

The directions to expand and innovate basic network of telecommunications in level of countries, cities, aimags, soums and settled areas by innovate possibilities of high speed broadband transfer information, and develop usages based on it information technology and remove digital division in rural and urban areas were reflected in pro-

[4] Open forum "Open Society" Forum, "Information technology Service deliveries in Rural Areas of Mongolia and faced problems" Study Report, 2006 page 56

gram of governmental activity and are implementing with purpose of developing new kinds of service and usage of ICT.

Telephone communication

There are total 332 automat station with capacity of 176.8 thousand users in our country and were utilized in 163[5] thousand telephone line service.

Figure 4. Growth of phone and mobile phone users

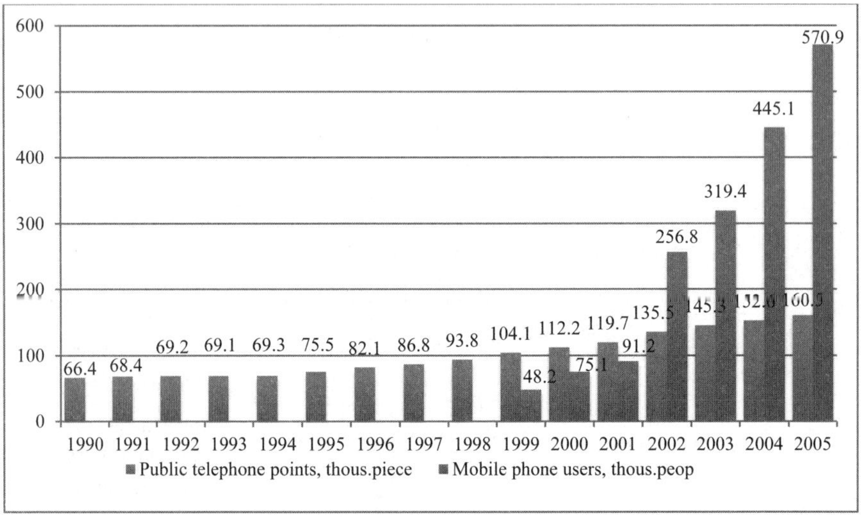

Source: information of USG, 2005

Number of telephone points reached to 160.5 thousand in 2005 and increased 2.4 times more than number of 1990. In recent years, increasing of telephone users related with installing digital technology to increase automated telephone systems in rural areas and expanding capability to install new cable line along railway.

In 2005, cellular telephone users increased 7.5 times more than 2000 and phone users increased 1.4 times more. As this, comparing traditional phone, cellular telephone market is quickly developing in last 5 years.

In, Mongolia, Telecom Mongolia Co., Ltd and Railway run the activity of telephone and Mobicom Corporation and Skytel Company run cellular telephone service and Unitel Company has been running cellular service since 2006.

5 Open forum "Open Society" Forum, "Information technology Service deliveries in Rural Areas of Mongolia and faced problems" Study Report, 2006 page 56

VSAT satellite servers provide different kinds of service with value added cost such as managed network service to issue possibility to utilize Information and Communication Technology in business areas. Mongolian Railway owns infrastructure of fiber cable.

Wireless communication service was started since 1999 with goal to provide communication service in citizens of ger district in Ulaanbaatar city and number of this service user was 14033 in 2002 and increased by 63.9 percent to reach to 23003 in 2005.[6]

Figure 5. Density to share 100 phone and mobile telephone users

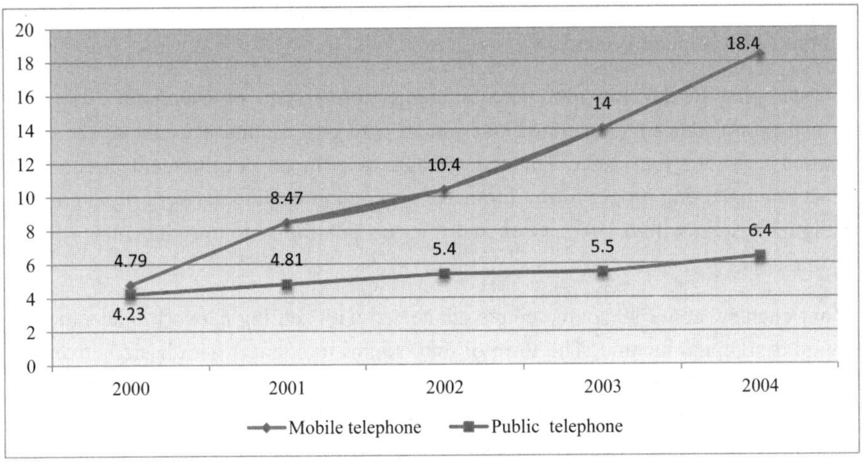

Source: study information of Information and Communication Technology Board, 2005

On December 2004, 6.4 phones and 18.4 mobile telephones were in average 100 people in the range of the country.

In 2004, number of phone and cellular telephone was 21 every 100 people and this amount increased 1.4 times from last year to reach to 30[7] in 2005. In addition to, 3 organization of satellite mobile communication run the activity and their user reached to 300 in 2005.

Rural communication

In the middle of 1990s, the communication was started to transfer from hand connection to automation by certain stages and innovated communication of province and soum centers by automat station with capacity of 50, 100, 200 and 500 users. Now au-

[6] National Statistical Office, Statistical Bulletin of Mongolia, Ulaanbaatar, Mongolia, 2005

[7] National Statistical Office, Statistical Bulletin of Mongolia, Ulaanbaatar, Mongolia, 2005

tomat telephone stations with capacity of average 48-200[8] users work in soums center and it shows certain development of local communication.

Now only Telecom Mongolia Company runs the activity of phone service in local soum centers and this influence with communication quality, type and property capacity issued to rural areas and is one of the conditions to increase difference of urban and rural areas.

In the frame of the project of communication a Bag, in the ending of 2001, 1050 bags established, radio and communication network for special use to connect with soum and province center and started to utilize calling hospital help, facing natural disaster and protecting suddenly accident.

"Master plan to develop rural telecommunication system of Mongolia" was performed by assistance of Japanese Government with goal to innovate rural telecommunication technology in 2003. This master plan determined development direction to finish implementing proper form to transfer telecommunication network of 339 soums to digital system within 10-15 years and it issues possibility to introduce new service to rural areas.

In our country, about 90 soum centers connected with settling network inter-cities by classic design and method. The form of total soums to connect with basic network of information and communication connected by 301 air column lines /steel and /or copper and colored line/, 18 fiber cable, 11 satellite /VSAT/, 46 radio relay lines and 12 radio lines and there are about 60 soum centers with digital telephone automat telephone station and 120 branches installed complete sun battery system. We are planning to utilize VSAT satellite technology until province centers and about 30 soum centers locates at least 150-200 kilometer to improve production, network of communication and deliveries of rural countries isolated from Telecom Mongolia Company and introduce new technology of communication such as internet, distance learning and treatment to soum and bag.

Communication network of railway was established to link Ulaanbaatar city, 5 province centers and 10 larger cities from north border of Mongolia to south border. This issued possibility to reach network service in larger local points locates along Railway connected Russia and China. Information and Communication of Railway Railcom Company constructed communication station with capacity to serve to 14900 users and network of 1600 kilometer long fiber cable along railway since establishment.

---

[8] Open forum "Open Society" Forum, "Information technology Service deliveries in Rural Areas of Mongolia and faced problems" Study Report, 2006 page 69

Content of public service was determined that is problem to reach communication service to the people resides in isolated rural countries in law about Communication of Mongolia. The law defined that is accumulating resource to establish Public Service Charge Fund for installing new network, expanding previous network, innovating and providing required communication service to isolated areas and people to use the resource. But property resource of Public Service Charge Fund was not accumulated now due to not determining in the law definitely and so there is no possible to run the activity.

Difference of digital division of urban and rural areas is in Mongolia due to Infrastructure of communication badly developed in local areas, information service is enough, its cost is high, the activity of Public Service Charge Fund is indefinite and the fund not completed.

Civil Air transportation communication

In the result of project of "Development Air Navigation" implemented in 1998, 21 provinces and cities were networks connected by VSAT satellite station. There is air transportation communication with about 1000 telephone users in zone of "Chinggis" Airport of Ulaanbaatar city and connected by fiber cable with air transportation communication for public use of Ulaanbaatar city.

Radio, television

Wide broadcast of Mongolian National Television is reached transmitting in city, rural areas and soum by Intelsat satellite. Installing digital system in satellite television transmitting construction in 2004, the technical possibility was issued to distribute 4 televisions without increasing the payment.

The first cable network was installed in 1996, television activity was run in about 20 enterprises, total 20 cities and provinces in 2005 and more than 77.3[9] thousand users were connected with it in the country.

Total 37[10] radio and broadcasting stations work in the province centers and settle areas and 26 short waves /FM/ stations of them were put into utilization by domestic investment. Putting short wave radio stations into utilization in Ulaanbaatar, Altai and Murun cities in 2003, there was possible to listen to radio of 2 programs all over the country, its capacity was increased and listening quality was improved.

Radio of the country was 443.2[11] thousand in 1990 and it decreased 6 times in 2005. This related with innovating technique and technology in radio communication, increasing stations to introduce short wave radio in urban and rural areas to the possibil-

[9] National Statistical Office, Statistical Bulletin of Mongolia, Ulaanbaatar, Mongolia, 2006

ity to listen to radio and FM increased. 150000[10] families have radio in our country in 2003.

Post communication

"Mongolian Post Company", main organization of activity of utilization of post communication and service, runs activity with 1050 employers leading 21 provinces, post office of Baganuur district, 30[10] branches of capital city, and post offices of 356 soums. They transport the post from Ulaanbaatar to province center in a week 2-5 times and run the traditional and new postal productions and service. In recent years, private companies have been working in postal service and it started competition of market.

There were 4288 document, letter and packing each 1000 people and this index decreased 13.3[11] times in 2005 and it relates with increasing possibility to utilize internet and electron mail.

Service and usages of ICT sector

Intensifying privatization of sector of information and communications technology and issuing permission to run the activity of internet and cellular service by private and foreign investment to private forms, the market of general service such as telephone service and cellular telephone service inter-countries and cities was opened in 1999.

Internet service

Electron mail network /PCmail/ was introduced all over Mongolia in 1992 and customers of network reached to about 150[12] in 1994. Many progressive services have been quickly introducing in society since Datacom Company established Mongolian first Internet Gateway with assistance of Embassy of USA in Mongolia, American National Scientific Foundation and International Development Research Center /IDRC/ of Canada.

Number of internet service organization was 5 in 2002 and this number reached to 26[9] in 2005. Subscribed Internet users reached to 22.0 thousand in 2005 and increased 4.3 times than 2000.

Figure 6. Number of subscribed internet users

[10] E-Mongolia National Programme 2005

[11] National Statistical Office, Statistical Bulletin of Mongolia, Ulaanbaatar, Mongolia, 2007

[12] UNDP project, *Feasibility study on the Use of Internet for Sustainable Development Network Programme in Mongolia*, 1997, p14

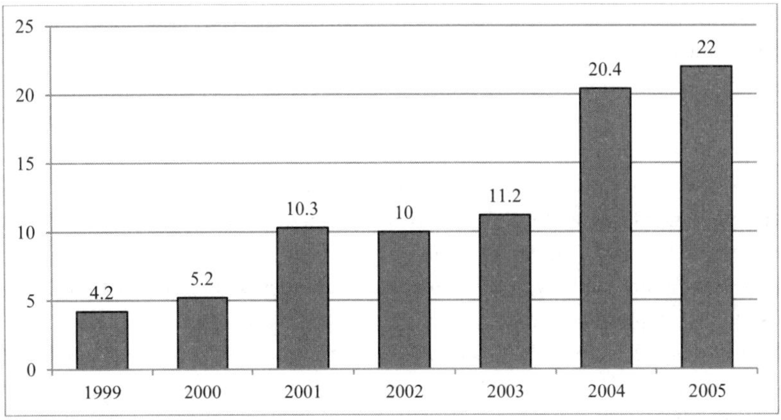

Source: Information of NSO, 2006

Firstly installing internet automat station in Mongolia in 2001 was significant in domestic exchange of internet. Today 8 companies run the internet service by high speed leasing line, dial-up and high speed line with converter. There are internet market and free competitive environment in Mongolia and bandwidth of external gateway of Mongolian internet is 78 mb/s and receiving is 44mb/s and transmitting is 34 [13]mb/s.

As a study of Infocon Company, 32% limited their usage relating with high cost of internet service, 28% have no enough computer facilities and 30% regarded that use of internet of their business partners and users was limited.

Most internet users connect with dial-up technology with server companies. The highest speed of this technology connection is 56 kbit/s and it can not provide requires delivering services with high speed to users. For this, there is possible to connect with internet by high speed using ISDN, xDSL, cable modem, wireless connection and connection technology of local network. Now Mobicom, MCS and SkyC&C companies run service of wireless connection and started cable modem service cooperating with Sansar KATV and Magicnet companies.

DSL technology is very significant to connect users with network by high speed. This technology has high speed to transfer information and characteristics to utilize previously established and well distributed telephone network. This technology was started to implement in our country, but could not introduce well. It relates with high cost and tariff. And having possibility to connect more than 20000 families with internet with monthly cost of 20$ by DSL technology in the range of "Internet to each family" project since 2006 is larger success in this network.

[13] E-Mongolia National Programme 2005

Now internet service of our country directs to network service. In order to, the internet service mainly directs to connect users with Internet and information service is run distributing information contents which are located in foreign countries. Service of information content of internet in Mongolian language is very significant. Introduction and web site with purpose of giving information dominates. For this, there is requirement to improve information content in Mongolian language and increase quantity. Having no content to run multimedia service of high speed by online form is related with connection speed of users not provided the requirements. As a study of Infocon Company, there are actively 1500 Mongolian web sites and 73.6% of these locate in web server of domestic internet servers under the domain name of ".mn". 50.4% of total web sites are under subsidiary of private sectors, 30.7% are under public non-profit organizations, 9.8% are under the individuals and 9.1 are under the governmental-organization.

In the result of innovating communication basic network, Public internet Center, Internet service center and internet cafe are working in Ulaanbaatar city and province centers. In 2005, number of Internet cafe reached to 115 and increased 1.3 times /88/ than 2002. Internet cafe is performing important role to deliver internet service to the people who have no computer and no possible to connect with internet and improve public computer education.

Therefore there is a fact that 87 computer game centers works in Ulaanbaatar city and although these centers positively influences to children and youths to spend their free-time and study to work on computer, but it brings negative consequences in society such as influencing in child health badly and not being at home due to working for profit and playing the children for long time.

Service costs and tariff today

Telephone tariff in city was 7 turgug in 2001 and decided to calculate it by payment unit and has been 0.0085 payment unit since September 2004. the Changes was not made in tariffs of service including callings in cities, callings inter-cities and basic payment of telephone point of foundation telephone service from 1997 to 2004 and it relates with having the state policy to stabilize costs considering life level of people. The condition to serve different tariff in two areas was had because of these tariffs of foundation telephone server is determined lower than expense, callings inter-cities are not more profits and tariffs of Telecom Mongolia Co., Ltd is followed when someone calls to urban and rural user along railway from local areas. They work with loss of these services and has compensated for a loss from income of callings inter-cities and comparing connection. Only two servers that are Telecom Mongolia Co., Ltd and Railway run the activity in calling market in cities and inter-cities of foundation telephone and competition is limited and in cities and settles along railway, but influence of this competition is not in tariff, service quality and adequacy.

The service tariff was intensively decreased relating with calling tariff inter-countries was decreased with certain stages since 1998 and calling monopoly inter-countries was officially broken down in 2002 and competition introduced in this market. When the monopoly was broken down, it relates with technology based on internet was introduced in this service, many internet telephone servers run the activity and they decreased costs to find market firstly due to being free market without certain direction and study about policy. Foreign calling costs was 0.14 in 2001 and now tariff of a minutes is 0.02-0.06 USD.

This costs falling dramatically decreased income of foreign calling exchange and calling loading and total income is not increased before competition and it shows that market is dividing by way to only transfer loading. It influences to business interest of servers and economics negatively and makes unfruitful competition.

Most internet users of our country connects with Internet by dial-up and a minutes cost of this service is 4 tugrug in day and 1 tugrug in night in the range of Electron approximately 10[14] tugrug now.

More than 20000 families started to connect with Internet with 20$ cost a month by DSL technology since 2006 is important step to increase internet users.

About calling tariff of mobile telephone user, observed decreasing in last a year is the reason that the servers introduce new kinds of service and issue possibility to cheaply speak among group users and in network and the third mobile operator started to run the activity newly is a reason to decrease tariff each unit. Now, Mobicon and Skytel servers run the activity by different technology, but service cost is in same level, especially, tariff of a minute in a network is 75 tugrug and this index is 70 tugrug about 3rd operator Unitel Company.

Although, mobile telephone server companies introduced many kinds of additional services provided needs of users, had their advantages by service quality and marketing new policy and run some activity such declaring incentive and sales regularly, but these sales can not be obvious sales to users and calling tariff is stable cost is observed. Limited competition of mobile telephone service influences in this condition.

When doing dial-up connection to internet service companies in Ulaanbaatar city, tariff connection of a minute is 12 tugrug and when doing connection to Micom Company from local countries, tariff of a minute is 20 tugrug and when doing connection to other internet service companies, it is connected by calling tariff inter-cities to call

[14] http://www.mongoliatelecom.net, 2007

from local areas to Ulaanbaatar city[15]. There is need to establish discount of tariff and develop infrastructure decreasing tariff of internet service and doing internet connection to rural people. Deciding this problem positively, we are regarding that technology solution to establish information high speed network, start to introduce IP telephone technology in little settles and establish united information network of Mongolia from Telecom Mongolia Co., Ltd perform important role. Internet service capacity is comparatively low in local countries. It related with high internet service costs and bad infrastructure development. In the document of "Strategy of middle term to develop Mongolian Information and Communications Technology", shall determine state policy, introduce liberalization and competition of basic direction of state policy, control tariffs of service dominated in market and other cost shall be determined by market with purpose to establish fruitful structure of liberalization regulation of telecommunication. But certain result has no in implementation of this policy. But the policy to follow what principle and how regulate about competitive basic factor and /or comparative connection payment was not determined.

Electronic Service

Mongolian government works to pay the attention to furnish the possibility to transfer information by internet, connect with e-service and e-commerce. Life use payment, insurance and salary of banking service, citizens, housing, and communication attended in this firstly and now these activities are running intensively. Skytel and Mobicom companies are proposing WAP service and YoWAP services. Now there is possible to take e-mail service and daily information, receive bank account service, schedule of airport and train station, toys, moon calendar, sound information service, download pictures and signs, utilize dictionary and receive information from Yahoo and Hotmail.

In recent years, certain progresses are being by direction of e-commerce and e-banking in Mongolia in recent years. Introducing card system in services by commercial banks, the progress became in e-commerce and e-business development. Now credit and debit card services are implemented in about 300 shores, hotels, restaurants, larger service organizations, petrol station, tourism and airplane ticket agency.

In Mongolia, e-commerce /B2C/ serves certain users and runs the activity of electronic payment and credit card payment and flows from business to user. E-commerce /B2B/ is very low level and in load transportation companies in low level from busi-

[15] Information and Communications technology Board, Information and Communications service and connection Tariff Today and further principles /convention/, 2005

ness to business. Moreover, e-trade and /or subscription and sales of goods and products including flower, some food products and book is expanding.

In 2001, Infocon company is implementing project of "Distance learning based on the Internet" with assistance of IDRC of Canada in direction of implementing internet in educational sector since 2001.

Following stages of governmental program direct to providing web site to publics and developing professional software.

The government pays the attention to establish new progressive network of communication to improve Internet usage and service quality in Mongolia. It is establishing high speed basic network of Mongolia, being permanent and reliable electric supply of province and soums, improving content measure and quality of Internet in Mongolia and increasing work to run state service by electron type and it is an important factor to be internet usage of people.

There is need to increase use of Information and Communications technology in all range of society and economics to establish new environment and new capacity of economics, increase competitive skill of the country, provide stable development and improve life level of the people.

Software production

In the beginning of transition, computer centers with large machines of united system for atomization of work and reaches little result to spend more property and first personal computer started to introduce, but these works in MS.DOS operation system environment and is complicated to completely program detail service. Thus, composed programs in this time is only works in measure of registration and report and not adjust with international standards requirements.

In 1993, Windows operation system, Microsoft Office programs and programming progressive technologies started to introduce in the countries. Establishing technologies such as object oriented programming and client-server and powerful equipments to work with databases is main factor to develop production of software and study of this direction intensively.

In the result of implemented activities and support of government, enterprises and organization which run the activity by direction of Information and Communications Technology were 51 in 2000 and increased 4 times to reach to 205 in 2006. As number of employers of the organization, there were 213 employers in 2000 and increased 4.6 times in 2006. Software production enterprise and organization are 72 in 2006 and its employer reached to 496 and increased 4 and 10.3 times than 2000. /Figure 7, 8/

Figure 7. Number of enterprises and organizations, which run the activity by direction of ICT

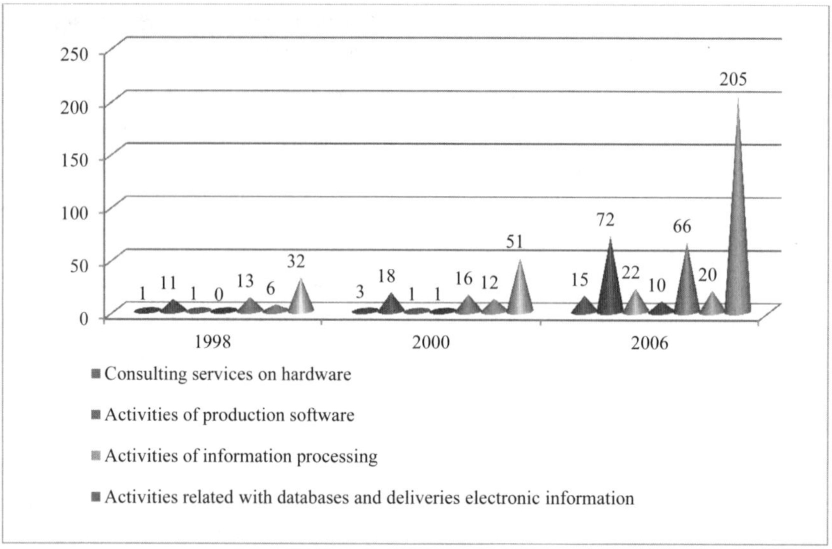

Source: Information of NSO, 2007

In 2003, National Information Technology Park of Mongolia was established in 2003. National Information Technology Park of Mongolia run the activity to implement aims to support companies based on information technology, render assistance to run business with more risk and intellectual high capacity, information technology export developing sector of software and support cooperating expansion of information technology companies. As activity direction of companies attended in National Information Technology Park of Mongolia, their main activity is software, digital content, geo information and web processing.

Mainly private companies run the activity by direction of software production and service. These companies run following activity.

- Bank, finance and accounting
- Statistical accounting
- Securities and stock exchange
- Engineering calculation
- Databases system
- Manufacturing atomization
- Public using reference system
- Driver of Mongolian letter
- Dictionary

ESM Mongolia, Grapesity, Starsoft and Interactive companies had certain standing by software supplies in the market such as bank, finance, accounting, custom, civil registration and information, social insurance, working place atomization and information system of Universities and Institutes.

For Mongolian software companies there is small software market and their main problem is finding subscriptions. Thus, there is important to support these companies from the state with certain policy and give subscriptions. The state implements large project including E-Government and give required subscription of software to software companies. There is need to put control in software of foreign countries, attend it in tax system and reach quality of software production in world standard. And there is need to produce national standard reflected requirements to prepare software, software quality, document and requirements of reliable activity.

In sector of information technology, software production based on good engineering education is future and possible to go to a foreign market. General information of business and trade exchange, marketing, costs, investment study, e-business based on the internet and other business service software influenced with economical growth is very significant in economic development.

Figure 8. Number of employees in enterprises and organizations, which run the activity by direction of ICT

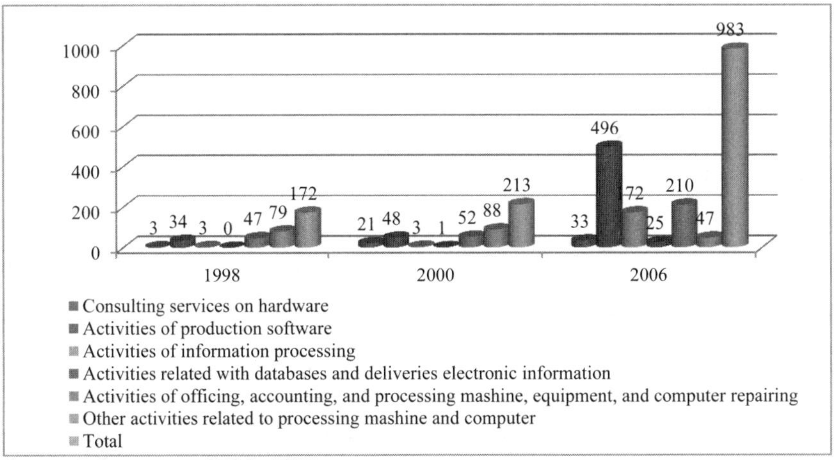

Source: Information of NSO, 2007

Human Resource Development

Today, about 3000 students study in 12 Universities and Institutes that prepare specialist in sector of Information and Communications Technology and are prepared by specialists with bachelor, master and doctor's degree of software, hardware, information system, information system management, information network, tele and radio communication, television technique and information technology. There is a study that about 1600 people graduated from these universities by profession of communication engineers and 1500 people graduated by software engineers.[16] Moreover, Mongolian government is keeping policy to training students in courses of master and doctorate degrees in developed Countries by direction of Information and Communications Technology.

In 2000, UNDP established Cisco Local Academia in the Computer Science and Management Institute with Cisco Company and the Academia run the service to prepare specialist with certificate of Microsoft and Cisco and study retraining.

In the range of Governmental Assistance of Republic of India, establishing "Information Technology Training Center" in School of Information and Communication under Mongolian University of Science and Technology and "Information Center to Serve to citizens" in Arkhangai, Gobi-Altai, Khentii, Umnugobi and Selenge provinces in 2002 is very significant step to study and repeatedly study information technology cadres and furnish capacity.

Establishing National Information Technology Park in 2002 is very significant step to develop sector's human resource, furnish capacity and support newly established company and enterprise.

An example of Mongolia pays the attention to prepare specialist of Information technology is establishing system structure to improve education and knowledge of cadres by way of including lesson of Information technology in public basic educational system, providing specialist – teacher and establishing training centers.

Faced problems to sector of ICT Development

Following difficult factors to consistently introduce information and Communication Technology in sectors of policy and economics were considered in "Development program of Information and Communication Technology" document produced by Mongolian government and Information band Communications Technology Agency.

- The environment of legal regulation was not formed.
- Understandings about Information and Communications technology is disordered, utilization is not well and united structure is not formed in all level of management.

[16] E-Mongolia National Program, 2005

- Tried to put the resource of policy to follow in the sector, but implementing way and property and finance is indefinite and united policy of investment is not formed.
- Paid little attention to prepare cadres of Sector of Information and communications Technology.
- Market competition is closed, network management and organization are lacked and hinds occur in new kinds of service and uses due to company with the state property participation owns basic network of Communications.
- Basic network of communication are still not international gateway.
- Speed and capacity of basic network of communication not provides needs of today.
- Legal and organizing activity to provide security of information was not run.
- Deliveries of information, culture, education and service of information and communications technology and its covered range is not provided well, problem about equality of infrastructure development and digital division has been faced.
- Information and Communications Technology was badly developed in sector of education, health, social defense, labor study, science, art and culture.
- The activity to support private and governmental organizations, support, initiative and cooperation was not run.
- Information and Communications technology was not introduced all over the country equally and technique supply of Information and Communications technology developed badly in rural areas.
- Average education and knowledge level of Information and Communications technology is not enough.
- Uses of Information and Communications technology badly developed among population. Digital index of computer each 1000 people is lower than world level.

Conclusion:

In the transitional period, the sector has been developed successfully in the result of foreign and domestic investment and support, contribution and assistance of international organizations and individuals. Contribution of Information and Communications technology is increasing in development of economics.

Introducing free competition in sector of Information and Communications technology, service engagers of private sector were include in market and introducing new technology in sector of Telephone and Information market, Sector's income is quickly increasing in recent years.

Progress of Information and Communications technology introduces in all sectors quickly and issuing many new possibilities. Using internet, information deliveries are improving in cities, isolated soum and local people. Electron content of information in Mongolian is dramatically increased and internet users are increasing related it. Despite of geographical situation of the countries, the possibility to participate in society and economics is increased and new work place and new market are expanding day by day. High skillful specialists of Information and Communications technology are prepared.

Although, many successes are in sector of Information and Communications technology, but difference of digital division has been in rural areas due to many reasons including infrastructure developed badly, information service deliveries is not enough, its costs is high, activity of duty fund of public service is indefinite.

Certain result is not in tariff policy implementation in sectors of Information and Communications technology, service tariff is high and cost decreasing is not observed in recent years.

Economical index based on knowledge to estimate knowledge and information attended 121 countries of the world was determined in 2002-2003. Mongolian Index is 4.23[17] shows that it is lower than world average.

There have to put the needs to introduce Information and Communications technology creatively, improve influence and quality of administrative, establish reliable information structure, reach state structure to publics, improve activities of state and private sector, establish informed society, decrease backwardness of information, develop infrastructure of Information and Communications technology, clear inequality of information and digital division and form enjoyable legal environment in all range of society and economics.

Process to transit in informed age is intensifying in countries of the world, society establishment based on knowledge, social wealth and valuable things that are knowledge and information are accepted and communication technology was introduced widely.

Mongolia approved principles to introduce world development and establish leading direction of sector of Information and Communications technology and informed society and has to pay the attention to human development, incentive of economics, support, innovation system and information infrastructure development and cooperate with international organizations actively. And expanding cooperation of international

[17] MonTSEME 2006-02-25

organization in sector of Information and Communications technology, studying experience of foreign country by this direction and supporting their assistance and investment is very important.

Bibliography

1. The Parliament of Mongolia, Concept of Information and Communications Technology Development of Mongolia until 2010, Mongolia, 2000
2. Open Society Institute, Information and Communications Technology policy of Mongolia, 2001
3. Mongolian Government, Development strategy of Information and Communication Technology in middle term, strategy based on it, Mongolia, 2002
4. The Parliament of Mongolia, plan of Governmental activity of 2004-2008, Mongolia, 2004
5. International Finance Corporation, ICT of Mongolia, Ulaanbaatar, Mongolia, 2002
6. Mongolian Development Gateway, Non-Governmental organization, Infocon Company, Information and Communications Technology Development of Mongolia Today, Mongolia, 2003
7. Information and Communications Technology Agency of Mongolia, Korean Agency for Information and Communications Production Support, "E-Government of Mongolia" master Planning, Ulaanbaatar, Mongolia, 2005
8. Information and Communications Technology Agency, Information and Communications Coordination Committee "Development Convention of sector of Information and Communications technology", Ulaanbaatar, Mongolia, 2005
9. Information and Communications Technology Agency "Information Technology Today and further aim", 2005
10. Information and Communications Technology Agency, Information and Communications service and connection tariff today and further principles /convention/, 2005
11. Mongolian Government, E-Mongolia Program, 2005
12. The Parliament of Mongolia, Law of Communications, additional amendments of 2001, 2003 and 2005
13. The Parliament of Mongolia, Law of Radio relay, additional amendments of 1999 and 2001
14. The Parliament of Mongolia, Law of Post, additional amendments of 2003 and 2005.
15. "A packet of law of information technology" project, Ulaanbaatar, Mongolia, 2005

16. "Open Society" Forum, "Information technology Service deliveries in Rural Areas of Mongolia and faced problems" Study Report, 2006
17. National Statistical Office, Statistical Bulletin of Mongolia, Ulaanbaatar, Mongolia, 2006

4.6. DOMESTIC TRADE

Overview of trade development

Consumer and industrial durable goods and services produced in the economy reach their ultimate consumers meeting their demands through the trade sector, which acts as the intermediary. The Mongolian trade sector has been making valuable contributions to the economic and social development of the country as the provider of the population with consumer goods and services, the regulator of continuous sales activities for producers as well as the supplier of raw materials, services and inputs of the market to businesses; yet, like other sectors, it too, faced depression in the first years of the transition.

When contributions of the trade sector to economic development are examined, according to the statistics, whereas in 1989 - the year prior to the transition, the added costs of the 'wholesale and retail trade and home appliances repair sector'[1] accounted for 19 per cent of GDP, in 1991 - the early period of the transition, it increased by 27 per cent, but in the following 1993-1996 it decreased steadily by about 2 points on average per annum. In 1997-2000 the percentage of added costs of the sector in the GDP accounted regularly for over 20 per cent, but since 2000 it started to go up, arriving at 27.7 per cent in 2002. However, it started to go down again on average by 2 points per annum and attained the 1999 level in 2005. (See figure 4.25). That 1/5 of GDP is constituted of added costs made in the trade sector illustrates an important position the sector occupies in the economy of the country.

Figure 4.25. Percentage of added costs of the trade sector in GDP, 1989-2005

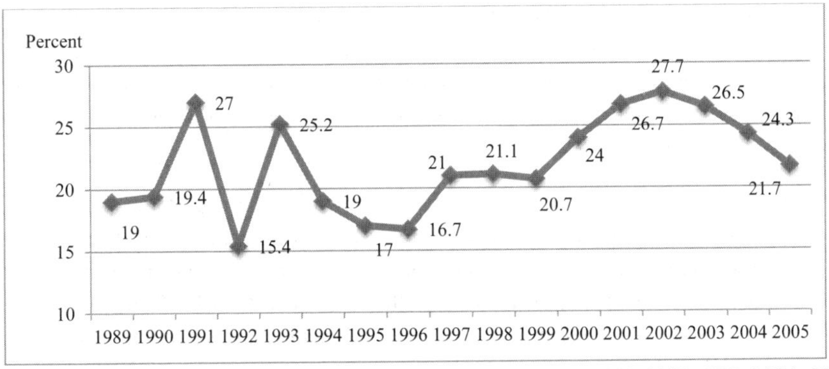

Source: Statistical data 'Mongolia in the market economy', 1989-2002, UB, 2004, NSO, Yearbook, 2005, UB, 2006

[1] Since 1997 the National Statistical Office started applying the UN 'Standardized categories for all sectors of economic activities'; according to these categories, the trade sector is in the 'wholesale, retail and home appliances repair sector' category.

Additionally, the trade sector is one of the sectors playing an exclusive role in the labor force market. While in the first years of the transition the labor force in the trade sector accounted for 6.6 per cent of total labor force, in the middle of the transition (in 1994-1997) it rose by 2 points and achieved 8.6 per cent. Since 1999, the figure had arrived at a decimal number and by 2005 the total percentage of the labor force in the sector equaled 14.5 per cent. (See table 4.36)

Table 4.36. Total labor force including labor force in the trade sector, 1992-2005

Year	**1992**	**1993**	**1994**	**1995**	**1996**	**1997**	**1998**
Total workers /thousand persons/	806	772.8	786.5	794.7	791.8	788.3	809.5
Workers in trade sector	53.8	50.5	67.4	64.8	68.5	67.9	74.5
Percentage of trade sector workers in total labor force	6.67	6.53	8.57	8.15	8.65	8.61	9.20
Year	**1999**	**2000**	**2001**	**2002**	**2003**	**2004**	**2005**
Total workers /thousand persons/	813.6	809	832.3	870.8	926.5	950.5	968.3
Workers in trade sector	83.1	83.9	90.3	104.5	129.7	133.7	140.4
Percentage of trade sector workers in total labor force	10.21	10.37	10.85	12.00	14.00	14.07	14.50

Source: 'Mongolia in the market economy', statistical compilation, 1989-2002, UB 2004
NSO yearbook, 2005, UB, 2006

In the last thirteen years the percentage of the trade sector workers in total labor force has increased by 7.8 points or 2.6 times. When the average annual growth of the employees in the trade sector is compared with the average growth of total labor force, the figure 4.26 illustrates that the former has always exceeded the latter except for 1995 and 1997.

Particularly, in 1994, 1998-1999 and 2002-2003 the number of employees in the sector rose swiftly. During the last thirteen years, the number of total labor force increased by 20.1 per cent; among them, the labor force in the trade sector increased by 16 per cent, which signifies the expansion of the sector as well as attests to its importance in the economy of the country.

However, in 1992 it went down by 22.7 percent in relation to the previous year, and it is considered the trough of the slump the sector faced during the transitional period. In 1993-1996, the rate of added costs stood comparatively at the same point, but since 1997 it tended to go up. That the annual growth of added costs in 1997 and 2000 were 17.08 and 26.08 per cent respectively can be considered the highest abrupt growth occurred in the last 16 years.

Figure 4.26. The average annual growth of total labor force including labor force in the trade sector.

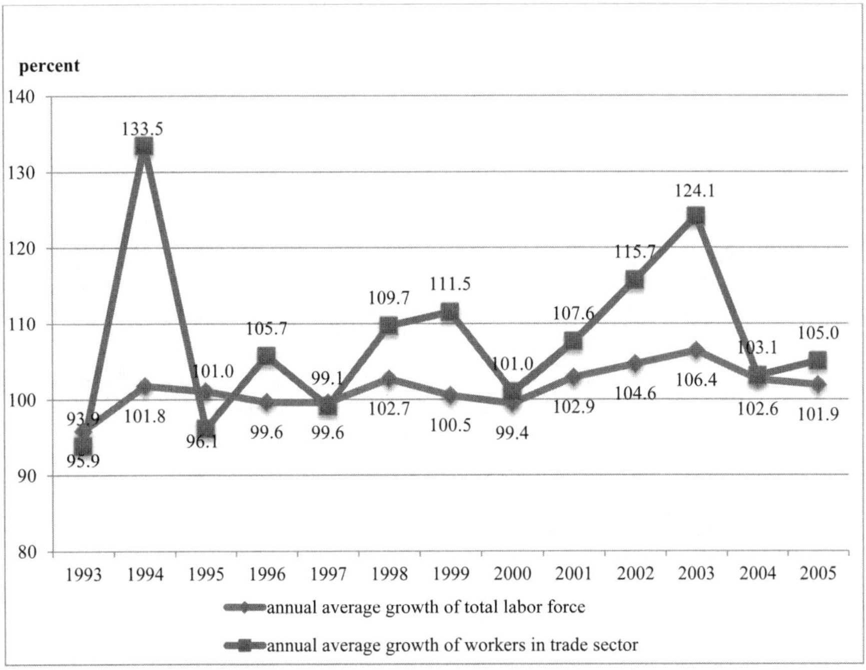

Source: 'Mongolia in the market economy', statistical compilation, 1989-2002, UB 2004
NSO yearbook, 2005, UB, 2006

Although the annual average growth of added costs created in the trade sector has been going down from a decimal number to a one valued number since 2000, a fact that its absolute value has been going up steadily allows us to conclude that the trade sector is on its growth stage.

The absolute rate of added costs in the trade sector reached the 1989 rate of added costs only in 2000, 11 years after the country started a transition into a new economic and social system. (figure 4.27) During those 11 years, the Mongolian population increased by 329400 people or by 16.1 per cent. Since 2000, development of the trade sector has intensified, exceeding the GDP growth. As of 2005, added costs in the trade sector increased by 50 per cent compared to the rate in the period before transition, exceeding the growth of GDP by 23.3 points or nearly twice. The fact shows that market relations have already become well-established in the trade sector and its development is intensifying.

Figure 4.27. Trade added costs, its annual average growth, 1989-2005 (by the 1995 price)

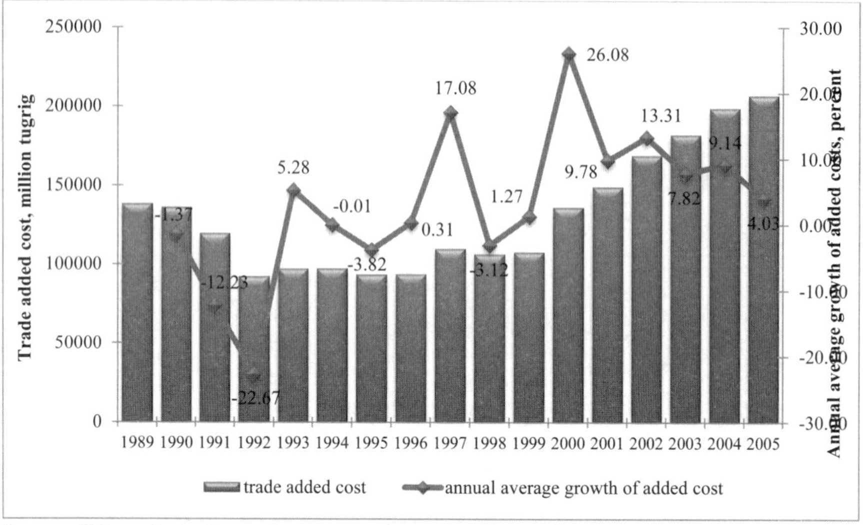

Source: 'Mongolia in the market economy', statistical compilation, 1989-2002, UB 2004 NSO yearbook, 2005, UB, 2006

Figure 4.28. The GDP growth, growth of added costs in trade sector

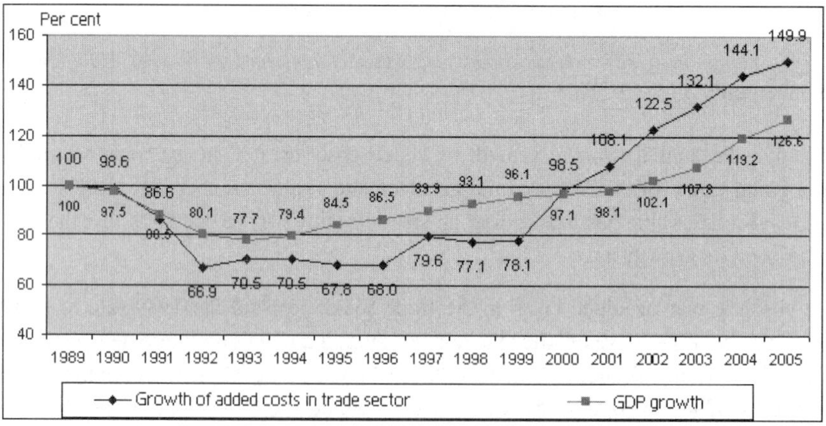

Comment: the growth was estimated on the 1989 basis.

The development of the sector can be divided into two historical periods according to the results of the above review of the trade sector development during the 16 years of the transition to the market economy:

The structural changes in the trade sector, the transitional period (1989-1999);

- The stabilization period of the trade sector development (since 2000).

The structural changes in the trade sector, transitional period

Trade prior to the transition

During the periods of the centrally planned economy, under the supervision of related agencies and ministries there functioned an integrated national system of trading, on the one hand, and of procurement on the other, which was based on the state ownership. According to previously developed comprehensive plans within the 'production-trade, procurement- consumption' scheme, domestically produced commodities as well as consumer and industrial goods and services imported from the external market were distributed to the appropriate consumers, on the one hand, and primary, secondary and waste raw materials necessary for producers and exporters were procured from the suppliers, on the other. The basic functions of this integrated trade and procurement system is shown in the following chart:

Chart 1. The national trade and integrated procurement system in the period before transition

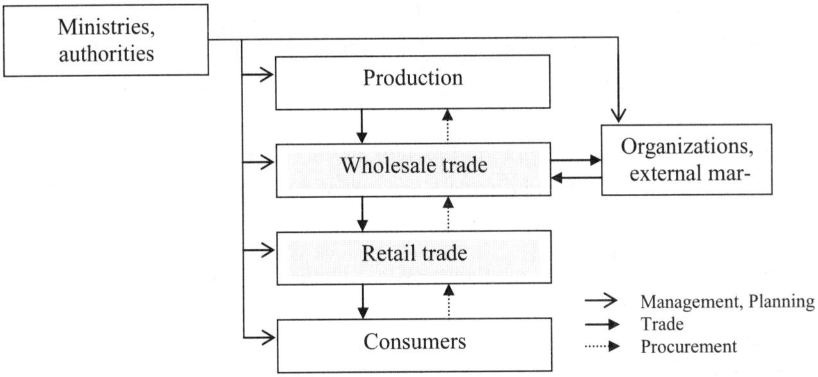

Wholesale trade prior to the transition

As of 1990, i.e. during the centrally planned economy, 10 wholesale co-operatives specialized in goods and services were engaged in wholesale trade in the country. There were, particularly, four co-operatives engaged in domestic trade such as the Food stuff wholesale co-operative, the Wholesale co-operative, the Agricultural supply co-operative, the Border trade barter co-operative and six co-operatives engaged in foreign trade such as the Technical import co-operative, the Auto and petroleum import co-operative, the Mongolian export co-operative, the Mongolian import co-operative, the Materials import and export and the Assorted goods import supplying co-operative that operated in the intermediary market each having precise duties. The four co-operatives engaged in domestic trade were supervised by the Ministry of

Trade and Procurement and the six co-operatives in foreign trade - by the State Committee of Foreign Economic Relations. The domestic wholesale co-operatives were organized so that they could continuously provide industries with raw materials and the population - with consumer goods through retail trade.

The four domestic co-operatives ran their trade activities in urban and rural areas through 'Trade and procurement authorities' located in 18 aimags and cities with the partaking of wholesale bases, trade and procurement units and trusts which were under the jurisdiction of related aimag and city authorities. In other words, trade was conducted via an integrated structure with horizontal pattern of management directed from the top to the bottom. In the years, prior to the transition, within the Ministry of Trade and Procurement system there were 22 wholesale trade co-operatives and bases, 33 trade and procurement units and 28 trusts[2] in operation.

The major responsibilities of wholesale trade of that time to be highlighted are as follows:

- To continuously provide a total of 4726[3] retail units and branches located in cities, aimags and soums with particular nominated goods in accordance with fixed prices approved by the Price Committee;
- To procure livestock raw materials in a centralized way in order to supply producers and exporters with them;
- To supervise achievement of targets and product quality;
- To conduct a research on product demands of the population, to plan and coordinate the supplies based on research.

Wholesale trade - one of the components of the 'wholesale and retail trade and home appliances repair sector', which accounted for 19 per cent or 1/5 of GDP by 1989 - accounted for about 17 per cent or 3.2 per cent of GDP in terms of added costs made in the trade sector[4].

Retail trade situation prior to the transition

Retail activities, which are the continuation of wholesaling, and which main functions are to provide the population with consumer goods as well as to collect primary, secondary and waste raw materials for industries from herders and population were supervised directly by The Ministry of Trade and Procurement and over 10 ministries and special agencies were involved in the activities in direct and indirect ways. By 1990, 1453 stores with 1432 thousand square meter space (574 of which were grocery stores, 549- consumer goods shops and 330- mixed stores) and about 2820 sales ki-

[2] Cited from 1985 statistics. T.Namjim, 'Mongolian Economy', V-2, 2004, p-638.

[3] Cited from 1989 statistics. Source: ' Justification and approaches to set up a new marketing structure for wholesaling' project report, 2003, UB, p-9

[4] Source: "Mongolia in the market' statistical compilation, 1989-2002, 2004, UB.

osks and agents[5] were registered in the Mongolian retail sector. At that time, in every sum and brigade of the aimags there were retail trade units and branches specialized in food, non-food and mixed goods providing people with goods at the fixed prices approved by the Price Committee. Sales agents provided a mobile retail service in scarcely populated areas as well as in herders' settlements. Although it was of high importance in terms of the policy aimed to maintain living standards of rural population at the level similar to that of the urban people as well as to provide conditions for long-term stable settlement of population in rural areas, it clearly was not an economically efficient practice. The retail trade before transition played the following roles:

- To continuously meet the demands of population which dispersed in urban and rural areas providing them with commodities of the same fixed price rates;
- To conduct research on population demands, give orders to wholesalers and take part in the development of production programs;
- To supervise achievements of targets by producers and wholesalers as well as the quality of the products and services supplied;
- To collect primary, secondary and waste raw materials for production from population and supply wholesalers with them.

As the 1989 situation suggests, added costs created in the retail trade accounted for 82.6 per cent of the added costs in the 'wholesale and retail trade and home appliances repair services' sector or 15.7 per cent of GDP.

Trade during the transitional period

In 1990 Mongolia irrevocably chose a way to a market economy in order to join the common realm of other countries in the world. To achieve the very responsible, historical objective of setting up new, market relations and orders, the rulers of that time, as we know, took a number of consecutive, proper as well as miscalculated measures.

The government pursued a policy to liberalize trade; in the first place, in the framework of the policy implementation, it freed up fixed prices with the aim of setting up free trade prices. On 15th January, 1991, when the Government passed a resolution[1] #20 on 'Some measures to transfer economy to the market regulations', which regarded the price liberalization, the wholesale price of most goods increased by 34-45 per cent, and the retail price of all kinds of goods as well as the tariffs of services increased twice as well, which led to a number of negative consequences in the society; yet, it necessitated business entities to make their decisions on price of purchased and sold goods and services independently in accordance with the market demand and supply. Thus, a basis for service at free price in the intermediary market was laid,

[5] T.Namjim, 'Mongolian Economy', vol-2, 2004, UB, p-638

which was a significant step towards the formation of market relations in the trade sector.

One of the major reforms of the economic structure started since 1990 was implementation of an objective concerning privatization issues aimed to change property relations through privatization of state assets. In the framework of the objective, at the first stage of privatization, there was made estimation to privatize 44 per cent of all state assets including trade, public catering, services, food, garment and woodworking industry, construction, livestock and agriculture. First privatization made in the trade sector was privatization of an industrial goods shop #31 in the Sukhe-Bator district, which was sold at an auction in June, 1991. Privatization, made in trade and service sectors was not only a novel process directed towards acquisition of private property by population, support of their aspirations to run private enterprises, elimination of shortage of goods at the time as well as reducing the burden carried by the state. As a result of this, private enterprises emerged and shaped up in the trade sector and most importantly, they acquired an economic freedom to run their business independently.

Besides, with an aim to provide a competitive market environment, and furthermore, to support competition, basic economic laws including the Law on business entity, a package of tax laws, the Law against unfair competition, the accounting and insurance laws were passed, which facilitated to create a legal environment for new enterprises to start and run their operations. In addition, business entities, which were interested in running business in the trade sector, were given an opportunity to enter and leave the sector freely.

Consecutive measures aimed to facilitate the transition to the market economy led to such conditions, where collapse of the earlier mentioned national trade and procurement system, based totally on the state property with unified management structure directed from the top to the bottom, was inevitable; consequently, the system disintegrated. As statistics show, the trade sector faced a deep depression in the first years of the transition, like other sectors. Particularly, the annual average growth of added costs of trade sector went down by 12.2 per cent in 1991 and by 22.7 per cent in 1992, which was lower than the annual average growth of GDP by 3 and 13.2 points respectively.

The depression lasted until 1996; however, in 1997 growth was observed in the sector and the added costs of the sector remained almost at the same level until 2000.

By 1995, 66.1 per cent of added costs of the trade sector in the GDP was created in the private sector, so trade occupied the second place among the GDP sectors after the agricultural sector (88.2 per cent). By 2000, the percentage of the private sector had increased and accounted for 90 per cent of the total added costs in the trade sector. Chart

2 shows the major distinction of the trade sector in the market economy from the pre-transitional period situation of the sector.

Chart 2. Trade sector in the market economy

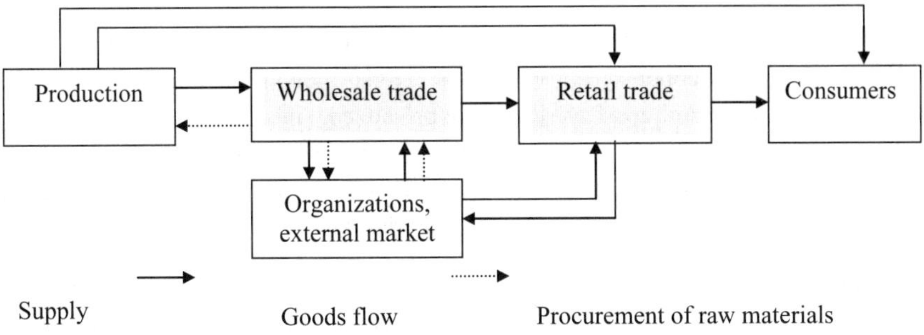

Wholesale trade during the transitional period

Due to the privatization program put into action since 1991, the state property, which was owned by the chief partners of wholesale co-operatives including dozens of retail co-operatives, industrial plants, livestock co-operatives and state farms was transferred to the private sector, completely changing the economic relations, which strongly resulted in the collapse of the trade system. In 1993-1994 most co-operatives running wholesale business were reorganized as shareholding companies with state assets dominating with a ratio of 49:51; since then, the state involvement has noticeably reduced.

The role that wholesalers played in the economy has lessened since the trade sector faced severe depression followed by a collapse of the integrated trade system, after which the state lost its power to regulate the market relations. Particularly, the main role of wholesalers to continuously provide retailers with consumer goods and services has diminished due to the various internal and external factors including the economic crisis of the country, shortage of goods at the market as well as high instability of currencies. Consequently, the living standards of population substantially fell down resulting from the shortage of goods, staples and services necessary for their everyday lives as well as a sharp decline of consumption supplies which followed by a price boom. On the other hand, due to privatization, most of industrial organizations, herders and farmers, which were previously the main partners of trade organizations, started to act independently organizing sale of their products, livestock raw materials, grains, potatoes and vegetables themselves, ignoring the wholesalers. Consequently, collaboration between the wholesalers and their partners started to weaken. In other words, they found it unnecessary to receive services from intermediate merchants like wholesalers; instead, they started to utilize marketing in their sales activities independently. Accordingly, the main function of wholesalers to provide producers with livestock raw materials as well as other necessary goods and materials started to fell short, which produced negative effects on the normal operations of national industries in the first years of the transition.

The other negative factor that affected the decline of production of the trade sector was the improperly conducted privatization. Even though the wholesale bases and trusts in cities and rural areas were already privatized, since the state did not control their operations after privatization, and most of them had limited opportunities to operate as wholesalers, particularly, in outlying rural areas, a huge amount of assets including warehouses, vaults, buildings, raw materials and stocks were wasted.

Regular operations of shareholding companies with prevailing state assets, established on the basis of wholesalers of the previous system started to fail; therefore, most of them had to limit their work by only storing state reserved goods, redistributing them, distributing relief goods including food and non-food goods rendered from countries such as Japan, America, Italy and Taiwan to retailers as well as to the population. According to a government resolution, the state-owned shares of all wholesale limited companies except for the 'Food stuff wholesaler' Ltd. were mainly sold at sealed auctions between 1996 and 1998. Privatized wholesalers failed their main functions, as a result of which the number of professional wholesalers decreased.

Particularly, they almost disappeared in rural areas; alternatively, the era of backpack trade (hucksterism) started in 1993, which is an informal sector with a subsistence character, with an aim to gain a profit sufficient just for tomorrow. This trade performed the role of both the wholesale and retail trade and according to some researchers in unofficial sources, they accounted for about 30-50 per cent of total trade turnover in 1995-1998.

The wholesale production rate accounted for a regular 17 per cent of total production in the trade sector between 1995 and 2000.

Table 4. 38. Total production in trade sector, by prices of the given years

year	Total (mil.T)	Whereas		Structure (%)			Absolute growth (mil.T)			Relative growth (%)		
		Wholesale	Retail	total	wholesale	retail	Total	wholesale	retail	total	wholesale	retail
1995	106.5	18.5	88	100	17	82.6	-	-	-	-	-	-
1996	121.2	21.1	100.1	100	17	82.6	14.7	2.6	12.1	113.8	114.1	113.8
1997	198	34.4	163.6	100	17	82.6	76.8	13.3	63.5	163.4	163	163.4
1998	172.1	29.9	142.2	100	17	82.6	-25.9	-4.5	-21.4	86.9	86.9	86.9
1999	173.8	30.2	143.6	100	17	82.6	1.7	0.3	1.4	101	101	101
2000	189.1	31.9	157.2	100	17	83.1	15.3	1.7	13.6	108.8	105.6	109.5

2001	234.2	60	174.3	100	26	74.4	45.1	28.1	17.1	123.8	188.1	110.9
2002	278.9	84.5	194.4	100	30	69.7	44.7	24.5	20.1	119.1	140.8	111.5
2003	320.9	101	220.4	100	31	68.7	42	16.5	26	115.1	119.5	113.4
2004	345.2	125	219.8	100	36	63.7	24.3	24	-0.6	107.6	123.8	99.7
2005	383.8	139	244.4	100	36	63.7	38.6	14	24.6	111.2	111.2	111.2

Source: 'Mongolia in the market economy', statistical compilation, 1989-2002,UB, 2004
NSO yearbook, 2005, UB, 2006

Retail trade during the transitional period

Implementation of privatization policy started from privatization of retailers. At that time, retailers and small service providers with a rental agreement were privatized by investment vouchers with preferential right of the staff, and retailers without a rental agreement were privatized at an auction. Thus, in the framework of small privatization or by pink vouchers, a total of 3046 small entities with assets worth 2.1 billion tugrigs and stocks worth 385 million tugrigs were privatized[6]. As a result of prompt privatization, in the end of 1992, most of the retailer shops and service entities were privatized and they performed approximately 70 per cent of total retail sale of goods and transactions. Furthermore, over 90 per cent of retailers were privatized by 1995. As it was stated in the report of the State Property Committee, privatized shops and entities changed their primary functions in a relatively lesser degree compared to wholesalers and other sectors. During the severe economic crisis, retailers played the key role in distributing scarce staple commodities to people on ration cards.

With the acquired opportunity to visit other countries freely thanks to the transition to the market economy, a certain part of population started to import essential commodities in certain quantities to meet the needs of population, when there was a shortage of goods. This was called hucksterism or backpack trade and it facilitated provision of scant commodities to people, supplied producers and exporters with raw materials collected from herders and furthermore, reduced the state burden. With the emergence of backpack trade, open markets for various commodities appeared in urban and rural areas, expanding their activities. Since then, the number of non-professionals engaged in the trade business has increased; as a result, the problems associated with trade technology as well as food safety have arisen in the sector. Although backpack trade produced numerous negative consequences including failure to provide people with safe, high quality commodities and services, opportunities for engaging in inequitable exchanges and running trade in inappropriate places by non-professionals, it played a significant role in development of the trade sector.

The percentage of retail trade in total production of the trade sector in1995-2000 was regularly about 83 per cent and its annual average growth in 1996 and 1997 was 13.8

[6] State Property Commission, 'Report on small privatization'

and 6.4 per cent respectively, which are considered the highest years of the growth. (Table 2).

Stabilization of trade sector development

Gradually, the situation of the sector has improved, depression was overthrown in the course of development of the country and a trend for recovery emerged. The frame of activities of backpack traders expanded, and with accumulation of certain experience and practice they started to establish formal, registered entities with a legal status. Various groups of consumers with different purchasing powers have emerged in the society; the expanding buying power of some consumers has had a positive effect on the consumer market profile, which resulted in an establishment of numerous wholesale and retail entities; some of them merged forming trade chains in order to expand their activities. Like in developed countries, wholesale trade representatives such as agencies, brokers, authorized distributors and specialist wholesale centers, retail trade representatives such as department stores, supermarkets, shopping centers, small wholesale centers and specialist retail shops have continuously been developing in Mongolia in line with needs and demand of consumers, owing to already formed market relations in the sector. For example, a number of global brand distributors including the Mercedes Benz, BMW, Nissan, Ford, Wrigley's, IBM, Lenovo, Sony, Panasonic, LG, Samsung, Adidas, Nike, Lipton and Dove, retail chain supermarkets including Nomin, My market, My shop and City shop run their business with an aim to provide services meeting international trade standards. Moreover, a brand new business sector in Mongolia – cyber electronics wholesale trade B2B and retail trade B2C has been established making their first steps of development.

At present, the trade sector is rightfully recognized as one of the markets with strong competition; in order to win competition and furthermore, become the leader of the market, the trade entities are making an effort to not only use management based on practical experience, but also try to adopt modern marketing and business administration methods to formulate their development policy. In other words, they have realized that only professional trade enterprises with competent staff and marketing management, prioritizing their customers' needs are able to strengthen their positions in the market.

However, the market still lacks modern professional trade organizations; particularly, in rural areas, there is shortage of traders who are able to meet food safety requirements, to provide consumers with whatever goods they wish, whenever they want.

Trade has started to increase substantially since 2000 when the sector reached the 1989 level in terms of added costs. In 2005, added costs, calculated at comparative prices of the trade sector, increased by 51.4 per cent in relation to the 2000 figures owing to the growth of the population, their increasing buying powers as well as the economic recovery of partner entities. While the percentage of private sector in total added costs of the trade sector was 90 per cent in 2000, it increased to 99.9 per cent in 2003.

The trade sector occupies a significant place in the informal sector. Total sales in the trade sector increased 2.7 times in 2005 in relation to the 2000 figures. When shares of the formal and informal sectors in sales were calculated, the informal sector, which accounted for 47.6 per cent of the total sales in 2002, started to go down reaching 31.3 per cent in 2005, i.e. decreasing by 16.1 points. It clearly denotes that the role of the informal sector is getting lesser in the trade sector as well as in the economy in whole. It resulted from a fact that workers in the informal sector started to establish entities with a legal status, which enables them to obtain a number of opportunities including access to loans and to a professional guidance.

Table 4.39. Total sales in trade sector, by years

year	total (mil.T)	Formal sector	Informal sector	Percentage in total (%)					
				Total	Formal sector	Informal sector	absolute	relative	
2000	660.6	-	-	-	-	-	-	-	-
2001	992.8	-	-	-	-	-	332.2	150.3	150.3
2002	1103.8	578.5	525.3	100	52.4	47.6	111.0	111.2	167.1
2003	1328.0	749.3	578.5	100	56.4	43.6	224.2	120.3	201.0
2004	1585.0	1032.7	552.3	100	65.2	34.8	257.0	119.3	239.9
2005	1782.7	1221.4	561.3	100	68.5	31.5	197.7	112.5	269.9

Source: Statistical data, UB, 2006

Another indicator, representing expansion of the trade sector is the growing number of business entities. According to the 2006 economic entities census held by the National Statistical Office (NSO), a total of 6046 wholesale entities were registered exceeding the number of entities eight years ago, i.e. in 1998, 5.3 times and a total of 5552 retail entities were counted exceeding that in 1998 by 39.9 per cent; altogether, a total of 12134 entities were estimated in 2006, which exceeded 2.3 times the same number eight years prior. The percentage of trade entities in total entities of the country was 28.4 per cent in 1998 and got to 37.4 per cent in 2006 increasing by 9 points.

Table 4.40. The number of trade entities, 1998-2000

Categories for economic activities	1998	2006	Growth of entities (1998-2006) %
Trade and service of automobiles, motorcycles and petroleum	274	536	95.6
Wholesale and commission trade of goods except automobiles and motorcycles	1135	6046	532.7

Retail trade and home appliances repair service except automobiles and motorcycles	3969	5552	39.9
Percentage in the number of total entities	28.4%	37.4%	-
Total	5378	12134	225.6

Source: the 2006 business entity census, NSO, UB, 2006

Moreover, in 2002, 7953 trade entities were registered in the business registration database, in 2003 the number increased by 27 per cent reaching 101138 entities; further, 9605 entities were registered in 2004 and 9874 in 2005 respectively. The statistics attest to the fact that the trade sector has become a competitive market allowing the entities in and out freely without constraints.

The percentage of wholesalers, accounting for a regular 17 per cent in the trade sector until 2000, started to increase since 2001 and arrived at 36 per cent in 2005. In other words, during the past five years, the wholesale trade went up intensively, and its percentage in the total production of trade sector increased by 19 points; its annual average growth increased by 88.1 per cent in 2001, 40.8 per cent in 2002 and 23.8 per cent in 2004, which displays that it beats growth in the retail sector.

In conclusion, since 2000, market relations have been set up in the trade sector facilitating both stabilization and further growth of the sector.

State policies towards the trade development

Although trade has been intensively expanding and diversifying in urban areas, it has still been weak in remote areas, which lack infrastructure and have tiny market capacity. Because they lack information and optimal trade chains, rural consumers purchase necessary commodities at prices 1.3-2.5 times higher compared to those in urban areas, and sell their agricultural and livestock products at lower prices, sometimes twice lower than the market price[7]; consequently, it not only affects their living standards negatively but also becomes one of main reasons for their migration to urban areas. The Government has started implementing a 'Wholesale network' program aiming to support regional development, provide rural population and herders with high quality food and commodities, approximate prices of commodities in rural areas with those in urban areas as well as continuously provide national processing industries with raw materials of livestock origin.

Initially, the 'Wholesale network' program was approved by a government resolution N98 in 1999. However, due to failure of its implementation, it was approved again by the government resolution N219 in 2001, since it was seen as a priority in the action plan of a new government appointed by the third election of the Parliament in 2000. This time it is included in the frame of activities of the Minister of Trade and Industry.

[7] Findings from the consumer market marketing survey conducted in Bayankhongor, Uvurkhangai, Khovd and Khentii aimags.

According to the directive commended by the Ministry of Trade and Industry sub-programs, which reflected the social, economic and infrastructural features of the aimags, approved by the Governor's Administration Office were developed in each aimag in line with the 'Wholesale network' national program. In order to implement these programs, they activated functions of shopping centers and markets and chose larger entities and co-operatives as the key entities to operate in the aimag or sum. As the Implementation Committee of the program stressed, following real outcomes were produced in the course of 5 years of the 'Wholesale network' program implementation:

- Wholesale trade centers and their branches were established in 86 sums of 14 aimags where the program was implemented, prices for staple foods and commodities for rural population decreased by 3-11 per cent on average and about 500 new work places were created;
- Quality and range of products have improved, supplies became regular, traders started to use appropriate containers for transportation of goods, certain progress in terms of food safety was made;
- Raw materials undergo basic processing before they are supplied to the market.

In the framework of the program, a 'Sales network', an information network was launched. The website provides consumers with information about the range, amount and price offers of products sold by wholesalers and project implementing entities in Ulaanbaatar; it also enabled customers to make purchases and give orders thus facilitating development of B2B, the wholesale electronic trade. The website contains data on 31 large importers of staple foods and commodities, 44 hides and skins processing shops, 67 wool and cashmere processing factories as well as 30 freight forwarding agencies operating in Ulaanbaatar.

Although the program is being carried out effectively, many NGOs claim that by supporting only a few large entities granting them exclusive rights to operate in the market, it restrains free competition creating conditions where rights of other trade units are violated.

The trade sector is closely linked with other economic sectors, particularly with transport, industry and agriculture. A 'National Committee on facilitation of trade and transport' was established according to a government resolution N245 of 2006 with an aim to reduce a number of internal and external obstacles that the trade sector faces and rationalize trade logistics and transport sector functions. The Committee developed a project on the 'National Logistics Program' in the first quarter of 2007 and held discussions on the project among related organizations; now the draft project is getting ready to be submitted to the Government.

In addition, a Council of Retailers, established at the Mongolian Chamber of Commerce and Industry with an aim to support retailers, now carries out a number of activities, introducing Mongolian retailers to the international market, facilitating their participation in trade fairs, enabling economic and trade collaboration and establishing information channels among international retailers.

International organizations too, are increasing their involvement to support the state policy on trade development. Particularly, in the frame of EU assistance the 'ABG', Germany and the 'Backakis', Greece, companies, who won a tender for a project to be implemented in Sukhbaatar, Dornogovi and Govisumber aimags have started the 'Procurement and Supply network' project since 2004. In the framework of the project, a livestock raw materials procurement unit is to be set up in Eastern aimags, which is further going to be a basis for establishment of a model raw materials procurement exchange.

While both national and international programs and projects are being implemented to facilitate trade development, a sound trade network as well as a regular raw materials procurement system have not yet been established so far at the national level. Thus, it is necessary to pay attention to further refinement of the state policy on trade development and its implementation, and creation of conditions for regular operations of the trade network that has been already established in the sector.

Conclusions and recommendations

- An objective, which would lead the trade sector development to the world level, needs to be formulated; in the framework of the objective, development perspectives, policies and strategic directions of the sector should be clearly determined and reflected in the comprehensive policies and development programs of the sector. A research team with representatives involving policy makers, policy implementing agencies, scholars, researchers, foreign experts and consultants as well as representatives of business entities engaged in trade and industry is necessary to work in collaboration with the aim of achieving the above mentioned goal;
- A legal environment, which would provide favorable conditions to support sound and just competition and reduce the hurdles and obstacles in the trade sector, should be created;
- A trade and logistics center, which should integrate all trade activities involving procurement, production, storage, transportation, and distribution of raw materials is needed to be established at national, regional, aimag and soum levels in connection with the infrastructure and an appropriate system for the product and service flows should be set up. Achievements of above goals would result in continuous supply of the national industries with raw materials and the provision of population, particularly, the rural population, with goods and services of high standards.
- Modern marketing management techniques (methods) that prioritize consumer interests and demands and are based on consumer behavior should be introduced

to the enterprises engaged in the trade sector; human resources in the trade sector are needed to be specialized, qualified and made convertible in the market with the help of universities, colleges and training centers;

- New types of economically efficient trade, which are increasingly exploited in industrial countries, where market relations are well-developed, should be adopted in the country; particularly; a legal environment and conditions needed for the further development of wholesale electronic trade B2B and retail electronic trade B2C as well as the raw materials exchange should be properly provided.

References

1. "Report on implementation of the 'Wholesale trade' program", Ministry of Trade and Industry, 2006, UB;
2. "Justification and approaches to set up a new marketing structure for wholesaling' project report, 2003, UB;
3. "Mongolia in the market", statistical compilation of 1989-2002, UB, 2004;
4. "Mongolia: Research on trade and industry development policies" Ministry of Trade and Industry, 2002, UB;
5. Anne T.Coughlan, Erin Anderson, Louis W.Stern. and Adel I.El-Ansary, "Marketing channels" 6th edition, Prentice Hall, 2001;
6. Theodore N.Beckman, Nathanael H.Engle, and Robert D.Buzzell, "Wholesaling" 3rd edition, The Ronald Press, New York, 1957;
7. "The 2006 business entity census", NSO, UB, 2006;
8. NSO year books, 2000-2005, UB;
9. Mongolian Chamber of Trade and Industry, http://www.mongolchamber.mn/ ;
10. T.Namjim, "Mongolian Economy" Vol- 2, 2004, UB;
11. State Property Committee "Report on small privatization";
12. The 'Wholesale trade program' Ministry of Trade and Industry;
13. http://www.salesnetwork.mn

4.7. TOURISM

Development trends

Since ancient times, particularly since the legendary Silk Road period, Mongolia has been one of the countries that have attracted various tourists from all corners of the world, as the history narrates. However, according to some scholars, today's development of tourism started over 50 years ago. Until 1990, the sector's activities were very restricted and all the activities of the sector were led solely by a state-owned company called 'Tourist'. Majority of the tourists of that time were mainly from former Soviet Union and some Central and Eastern European countries and many Mongolian tourists headed to these countries as well.

However, the socio-economic reforms made in this sector have brought a completely new era to the development of the sector; as a result, the number of entities engaged in this sector has reached 534. It dramatically increased the number of foreign and Mongolian tourists entering the national border and the travel routes started to exceed the above mentioned countries. Particularly, in 1990, the number of foreign tourists crossed the national border was 147200; in 2005 it reached 344688 increasing the number 2.3 times. Today, not a few tourists from various countries including China, Russia, Korea, Japan, USA and Germany visit our country being attracted by the beautiful countryside with less overgrazed land and polite hospitality of the people.

Although by and large, the number of foreign tourists tended to increase in 1990-2005, it decreased in 1996-1997 (in 1997 it decreased to 82000) and in the early 2000. It was caused not only by internal factors, but also external factors such as Asian financial depression and prevalence of SARS disease affected it.

Basically, at the same time, despite the natural factors such as geographical location and variable weather conditions, while the demand for tourism based services tended to decrease on the one hand, the supply tended to increase sharply on the other, which resulted in emergence of more than 300 small size tour companies with licenses by 1998. Although such unbalanced state of demand and supply intensified competitions in the sector, it could not reduce the number of business entities as well as individuals engaged in tourism. Over 160 tourist camps and about 300 hotels of different ranks, altogether employing a total of 12000 people were running a business in the sector by 2005 nationwide.

The purposes of tours of domestic and international tourists have substantially changed and expanded over the years as well: the number of tourists traveling on private purpose tended to prevail among the tourists.

While the revenue generated from international tourism reached 42.5 million dollars in 1996, it increased to 181 million dollars by 2004. (graph 4.29)

Graph 4.29 Revenue from tourism, million dollars

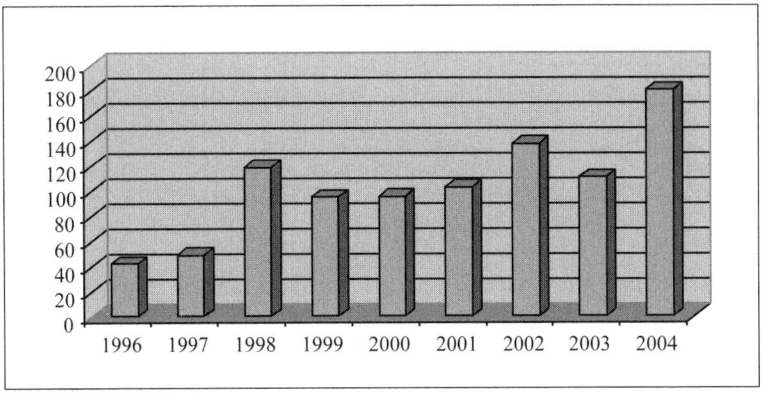

Source: MRTT, Statistical yearbook of Mongolian Tourism, UB, 2005

Alongside, NSO joins the indicators of additional costs of business entities with state registration (incorporated) that send their annual reports regularly to the related authorities together and reflects them in the calculations of GDP. According to this statistics, the state of additional costs of above mentioned entities seems to be quite fluctuating over the last 15 years, yet it is not that disappointing according to the graph 4.30, as you see some increases in recent years.

Graph 4.30. Additional costs of business entities with state registration engaged in tourism, million tugrigs, 1995-2005

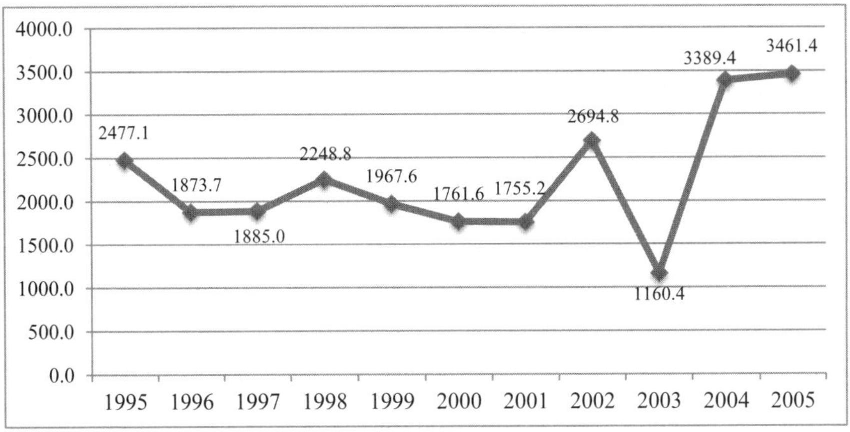

Source:NSO

When the changes in percentage of additional costs of business entities with state registration engaged in tourism in GDP are examined, while it was 0.08 per cent in 1995, it increased to 0.42 in 1999, but it decreased again to 0.17 per cent and to 0.09 per cent in 2005 respectively

Graph 4.3. Percentage of additional costs of business entities with state registration in the GDP, 1995-2005

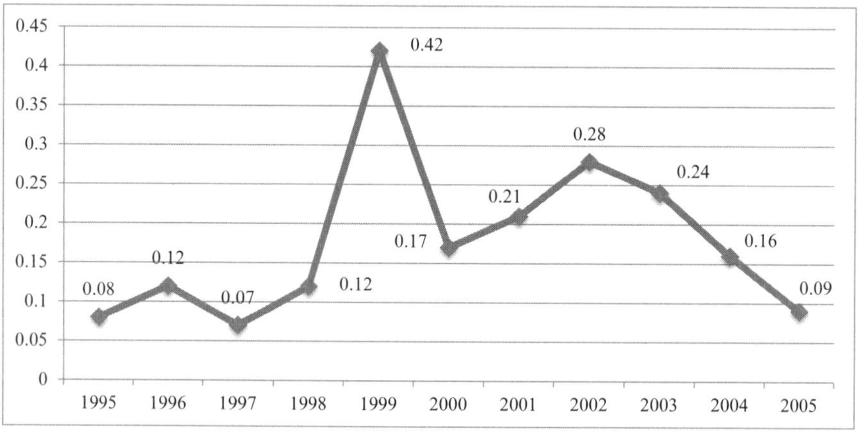

Source: NSO

State policy on tourism, its implementation

Principally, there had been no single state organization that was responsible for the strategies on tourism and their implementation until 1992 and as it was stated above, all the tourism related activities were run by 'Juulchin', which was the sole state owned company in the sector. An 'Authority of Tourism', which was established at the Ministry of Natural Environment in March, 1992 expanded as an 'Administration of Reserved Areas, Authority of Ecotourism' later. When the state regarded the tourism sector as one of the promising sectors to expedite economic growth and reduce poverty, with the aim of renovating the strategies and policies of the sector, the Authority, which acted under the jurisdiction of Ministry of Natural Environment was changed as 'Authority of Policy and Regulation of Tourism' at the Ministry of Trade and Industry in 1995. Soon after, the department started to act under the jurisdiction of Ministry of Infrastructure after the 1996 election. An 'Authority of Tourism', a Government Implementing Agency was established in 1999 and later, it was expanded as 'Authority of Tourism' and started to operate under the jurisdiction of Ministry of Road, Transport and Tourism in 2004.

At present, the tourism related operations run in the territory of Mongolia are regulated and supplied with policies by the MRTT, 'National Policy Regulatory Council of Tourism' at the Prime Minister Office and aimag and capital city units, which are responsible for tourism issues.

The Government passed 'General Directions to Develop Tourism' in 1995 and a 'Master Plan to Develop National Tourism in Mongolia' in 1999. The Parliament released the 'Law on Tourism' on 5th May, 2000, which aimed to support tourism and regulate the relations between the government and business entities and individuals engaged in tourism. Besides, that 2003 was announced as a year of 'Visiting Mongolia', 2004- a year of 'Inspiring Mongolia' and 2006 – a year of '800th anniversary of Great Mongolian State' affirms the Government made a considerable effort on the development of the sector during the transitional period.

The tourism development issues were not left out of the 'Regional Development Concepts' program and its implementation. They were extensively included in 'The Program of Regional Development', which is the supplement to the Government Resolution #54 of 2006. For instance, 'The Program on Tourism Development in Western Regions of Mongolia' prioritized to properly develop tourism as an independent economic sector in western regions of the country.

The Government pursues a policy to attract investors, expand the range of investments and increase their efficiency as it considers private sector and NGO development and investment as a source of the development of the sector. In the frame of this policy, the Government organized the 'Forum of Investors in Mongolia', which discussed the current situations of investment, urgent issues to be solved in the sector as well as solutions to them. Moreover, the Government took a number of effective measures on the development of the sector: (i) the related authorities has terminated to issue a special license on running tourism business since 2002; (ii) 'J' type visa started to be issued on the border ports to tourists from countries where there is not a Mongolian Embassy or Consulate or Honorary Consul in operation and a shared (collective) visa to groups of tourists; (iii) the Tax Office decided to render a tax relief to the business entities that invested in construction of a tourist complex of world standard with multipart services; (iv) the services rendered to foreign tourists by the entities with foreign or domestic investments decided to be exempted from VAT; (v) the imports of winter or of special interest tour equipment decided to be exempted from customs tax and VAT.

One example of considerable attempts made in recent years by government organizations towards the systematic planning of tourism sector development involving all parts is the proposal of 'Mid-term Strategies of Tourism Sector in 2001-2011' formulated by MRTT and discussed three times by the government, non-government and international organizations and representatives from the universities and institutes in Mongolia. After the third discussion, the proposal was adopted in cooperation with the team 'Soyombo 21', which had won the competition 'Development of Complex National Policy'. However, it was not the first attempt to develop a policy and strategy in sector level; a master plan of tourism sector was formulated in cooperation with an international tourism organization in 1989. Since 2002, consistent with the 'Law of Management and Financing of Budget Organizations', related state administrative organizations have started to develop their mid-term action plans within the space of three years.

The Government of Mongolia has been executing policies to increase the number of border points, prolong their working hours and stabilize their operations with the aim of improving the convenience of foreign and domestic passengers traveling in and out of the border. Except for the operations of border points with permanent and regular functions like Zamiin Uud, Buyant-Ukhaa and Altanbulag, the functions of border points such as Shiveekhuren, Sukhbaatar, Tsagaannuur, Gashuunsukhait, Bulgan and Khavirgiin are considered to be run effectively, according to the statistics of passengers entered through the border points. Over 50 per cent of the all domestic and foreign passengers entered the country through Zamiin-Uud border point and over 15 per cent – entered through Byuant-Ukhaa border point in 2005.

The security of tourists was considered as the issue of considerable emphasis, according to the findings of the survey jointly carried out in 2002 by the Mongolian Tourism Association and the 'Initiatives of Competence' project implemented by the Development Agency of USA on the international tourism issues. In the frame of this issue, a feasibility study is being carried out by the 'Authority of Tourism' at MRTT on the possibilities of establishing 'Tourist Police' section under the jurisdiction of 'Metropolitan Police Office'.

The foreign relations of the sector have substantially expanded over the past years and contracts on collaboration with over ten foreign countries were signed by the Government as well as the ministries of Mongolia. Besides, information centers on tourism have been established in Ulaanbaatar, Tokyo and Beijing. Mongolia joined the World Organization of Tourism in 1991 and started to actively participate in activities of numerous international tourism organizations. Alongside, a number of government and non government organizations are making an effort to promote the country in the world arena participating in international trade fairs and exhibitions.

However, a proper policy to provide the sector with professionals has not still rationally exercised, yet. Although there are not a few universities and institutes training professionals in the sector, they are not that competent to prepare personnel of world standard.

Involvement of other parts in the development of the sector

The involvement of non-governmental and international organizations in the development of the tourism sector was tremendous over the past years. A numerous NGOs including National Council of Tourism, Union of Mongolian Tourism, Association of Mongolian National Ecotourism, Association of Mongolian Guides, Association of Mongolian Tourism Organizations have been contributing their efforts to the development of the sector sharing the government burden by exercising the following actions: (i) to conduct necessary researches and surveys; (ii) protect the rights and interests of business entities and individuals running activities in the sector and act as a go between them and the government (for example, according to their efforts road vehicles with right steering wheel are permitted to be utilized in tourism services.); (iii) render necessary business development services such as training, promotion and provision of information.

However, the NGOs are working with only significant entities running business in the sector leaving the smaller in size entities, some of which are merely emerging in the sector out of their activities. Basically, majority of these entities are not able to conduct continuous and efficient activities due to their financial and personnel constraints as well as inadequate experiences.

Besides, international organizations are playing a significant part in the development of the sector. It is worth to note that the international organizations such as Tourism Organization, UNDP, DANIDA, American International Collaboration Agency, World Bank, European Community, Japan International Collaboration Organization and GTZ have been contributing to the government policy realizations implementing a numerous projects including 'Development of Tourism in Mongolia', 'Personnel Development in Tourism Sector' and 'Road of Adventurous Journey'.

Urgent issues of the sector and solutions to them

The following issues should be paid more attention to expedite the development of the sector, when the above mentioned review of tourism sector development of the country during the last 15 years as well as the state policies on tourism development and their implementations are examined proportionate to the world development of tourism:

1. Provide the tourism sector with sustainable and proper policies and strategies;
   The major documents of general development policies in the sector are not coherent with each other, some of which even outdated in terms of importance and could not reflect the sector's long term development planning and future tendencies in a complex way.

2. Create favorable infrastructure to facilitate the development of the sector and support the development of entities providing subsidiary tourism services in the sector like hotels and cafes. Reduce the underdevelopment of infrastructure, which has always been behind the development of the tourism sector and increase the use of modern techniques and technologies, which is considered a vital factor to expedite the development of the sector. Expand investments in the complex services of tourism and encourage the collaborative operations of entities running tour operator, hotel and café business as well as other necessary services.
3. Pay a particular attention to the development of personnel in the sector and train professionals competent in the world market. The transition from the centrally planned economy to the market one caused a number of professionals in various sectors to remain unemployed. Not a few of them counted on the tourism business considering it a viable way to earn their living effortlessly; however, due to the lack of the necessary knowledge, skills and experience, their business was not a success which influenced on the dissatisfaction of foreign tourists, reputation of the country as well as the development of the sector negatively. In addition, even though there are sufficient numbers of state and private universities and institutes in the country (about 54, statistical yearbook of tourism, MRTT, 2005), the sector still lacks skilled and worldly competent personnel.
4. The issues on the development of Ecotourism:
   The country suffers from the deterioration of the environment resulted from a number of factors including the air and water pollution, misuse of wood recourses and soil degradation. Findings of surveys state that it caused by tourism based activities to a certain extent. Therefore, all related parts should lay an enormous emphasis on the development of ecotourism and run environmentally secure activities.
5. Activate the collaboration of government, non-government and international organizations working in the sector.
6. Develop the tourism distinctly by regions counting on the different features of each region.
7. Expand the tourism related activities and reduce their seasonal dependence.
8. Create a reliable database of information and research work on tourism sector activities. Build up a close cooperation between the Statistical Office and the State Administrative Authority on Tourism. Although it is praiseworthy to note that a statistical yearbook on tourism has been compiled by and located in the website of the Authority of Tourism at MRTT in 2006, some sources and estimation techniques of the data are not fully definite.

References

1. Asia policy research Co.Ltd, Tourism and related services background brief, October 2006
2. Helmut Weber, "Travel to the land of Chinggis Khaan: Tourism development in Mongolia"
3. www.investmongolia.com
4. www.mongoliatourism.gov.mn
5. B.Zorigt, 'Ecotourism in Mongolia'
6. Mid-term strategies on the tourism development', MRTT, 2007-2011, UB, 2006
7. Statistical Tourism Yearbook, MRTT, UB, 2005
8. Statistical Yearbook 2003, NSO, UB, 2004
9. Statistical Yearbook 2004, NSO, UB, 2005
10. Statistical Yearbook 2005, NSO, UB, 2006

CHAPTER FIVE

MARKET AND THE PRIVATE SECTOR

Brief contents

In this chapter, a process of market development in Mongolia is analyzed and different forms and kinds of market are studied. Along with this main changes in the Mongolian busines environment, conditions of competition and challenges that are faced are studied. This includes an analysis of the Mongolian private sector development process, which emerged as a result of introduction of market relations in the country, and a definition of new trends and future perspectives.

5.1 MARKET FORMATION

5.1.1. Main Features of Market and multiple forms of its development. Mongolia has been facing difficulties and harsh periods in terms of market economy development during these 16 years since transition to market economy. There is a definition, which defines the market as space and location where produce or money is being sold[1]. In broader meaning, it can be viewed as a social and economic system of buy-and-sell relationships between traders and customers.

In practical aspects market is often described as following:

A place / market to sell goods
Businessmen who produce and sell goods and services
Organisations and individuals who buy or are able to buy goods and services

In fact, market is a mechanism for distribution of goods and services, financial resources according to the demand and supply law, a phenomenon with multiple aspects and structure.

Actually, a market is many sides happening of financial resource is allocated mechanism, good service by demand and supply. An effect of market mechanism identifies by complicated action and that identifies a siduation of market, its development frame, a rate, suitable pricing , a market relation.

Mongolian GPD in 2005 was 2524 billion tugrug and per capita was 984.9 thousand tugrug. This statistic increased upto 1222.9 thousand tugrug in 2006. The economic growth rate is 6.2% since 2002 and the real GPD growth has became 8.4%. Foreign Trade Total turnover in 2005 became 2249.2 million USD and from that export was estimated as 1064.9 million USD and import as1184.3 million USD. In 2006 Foreign

[1] Dictionary of economic and management terms

Trade total turnover became 3018.0 million USD as of 1528.8 million USD for export and 1489.2 million USD for import. This is the first time that the trade balance was positive. The rate of processing industry development has become higher. This can show that Mongolian market has been strengthening and developing.

The market content divide into 2 parts as the comsumers and the business in terms of its sphere of coverage.
The aim of and conditions of purchasement even the decision making process is different.
Consumer market is consisted of the one's purchase for own and for own families and domestic usage needs.
Most of the business secotrs are supplying the needs of consumers into market.

Business market

Reselling goods and services, renting to others, utilize organization`s activity, reproducing product s in the manufactured are the merger of organizations and individual persons. In the generation of centralized economy, the process of delivery goods was used by material techniques supplying system that was behind history. Nowadays the goods circulation between organizations of goods are reaching by thousands billions tugrugs.
Mongolian government has adopted budget` s income by 708.2 tugrugs its expenditure defined by 775.1 billion tugrugs in 2005. The expenditure of purchased state ownership goods has been reached by 27.6 % of the total budget or 222.8 billion tugrugs. It is very important to regulate market economy relations to organizations by legal mechanism. As the legal mechanism has been not implemented over 10 years in the market economy , it caused by unsystematic situation .In 2000 Mongolian Parliament has adopted and implemented the law on " The selecting order of Executor purchase goods and service by state and local ownership property "and was established Purchase Policy and Regulation Department at Ministry of Finance and Economy of Mongolian. In December , 2005 The law on "The selecting order of Executor purchase goods and service by state and local ownership property" was amend by Mongolian Parliament . There are big purchasers such as Mongolian Railway and Erdenet factory. The Mongolian Railway has been operating for activity about 80 billion tugrugs per year. In the framework of survey by Opening Society Forum , The Social Science Department at National University of Mongolia made a survey on statistical and its quality. The survey` s report has been shown that 3475 budget organizations have been operated and 116 thousand staffs have been working in the territory of Mongolia in 2005.After the adoption the law on Purchase , Mongolian government has advertized 2500 tenders and many tenders had imposture and occurred corruption an 4 % of tender bidders submitted complaints. It has shown that the tender partici-

pants `s skills are weaken. Such as perversion came in the first step of market economy relations but purchasing goods and services of state ownership are increasing and buildings and real states.

As classified by economical relations for Mongolian market:

- Consumer goods market
- Service market
- Manufacturing equipments market
- Labor market
- Investment market
- Finance , monetary market
- Bond ,security market

Consumer goods market and service are the part of component of market economy general system, one is element. Consumer goods market is directly connected other market, manufacturing equipments, labor, finance, monetary market, stock, real state, and investment markets. The growing of the retail and wholesale are expressed in the dynamic growing of consumer goods market. In the consumer goods of market includes buying and selling goods and human labor and natural goods. The consumer goods and service are dedicated for the final consumers. The consumer goods and service are absorbent the value which entitled by the opportunely trading for money and it is become one of selling and buying object. Adam and Smith emphasized that the purpose of final manufacture is utility. This is specified main features by goods market. If goods and service are not quality, it is not used and that could not become goods.

Table.5.1 growing for economical branches and the compared price of 2000 year.

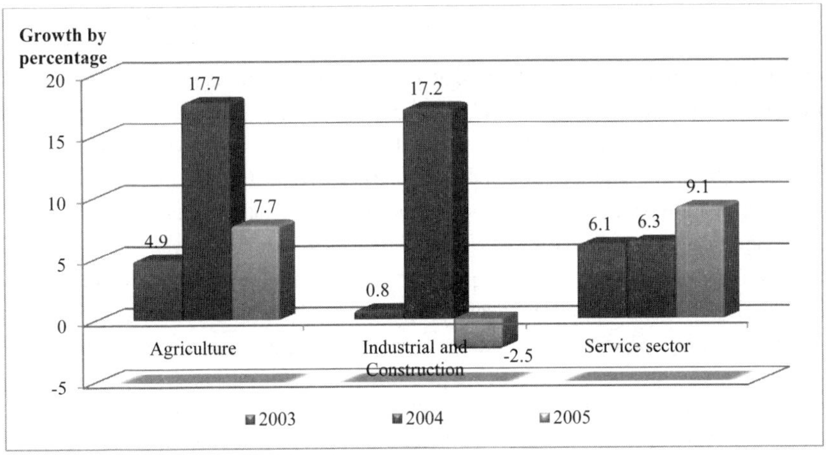

Resource: Institute for National Developemet

The consumer goods shall be specifying by goods items. For example: Sewing and knitted products are one of preoccupied issues for Mongolian. Before 1990, there were operated only 4 big sewing factories and small tailor making workshop each provinces of Mongolia compared by 2004 it is developed dynamically. The peak of manufacturing year was in 2004 there were produced 45.9 million clothes and 25.9 million dollars has been involved in the state budget. But in January, 2005 International trade agreement is expired the duration due to the number restriction of subscriber were shortage, some factory closed. In March, 2005 Mongolian government had resolution the number 32 on providing for rebate to sewing and knitted factories.

There are specified some specifications on the content of market economy, its features:

Specify market economy by geographical location.

- Local community market
- Regional market
- National region market
- Local regional market
- World economy

Mongolia consists of 21 provinces and capital city , and Capital city Ulaanbaatar has 9 district, 121-khoroo , the provinces have 331 soums and 1543 units /bag/ , the market economy has developing all this territory. But there have a few populations in local country, the electric power has not satisfactory supplied and there are also restricted food and retail of consumer goods, the barter of livestock animal productions as poor developing the small and medium business.

It is very important to develop market economy relations to Mongolia and implement the policy of regional development as reason of pasture animal husbandry, wide territory and few populations. So Mongolian Parliament has implementing some projects and policy. Such as "Concepts on Mongolian regional development " in 2001, " Middle term strategy for regional development till 2010" in 2003, " the law on Management, regulation for regional development", 2005 "West ,East and Central region ,in 2006 "the program on regional development of Ulaanbaatar. There are made up a good condition of legal status on regional development. These measures are compound to develop regional market opportunity. But There are caused some difficult for develop classic market relations according to dominate pasture animal husbandry to regional economy, poor developing infrastructure, industry community branches.

We see the following table 5.2 of the capacity of regional market economy, general features of Mongolian DNB. Nowadays the capital city of Ulaanbaatar is big market economy. There are developing speedily some items of market economy such as consumer goods and services, industry equipments, labor, finance and information markets.

The national economy has formulated to reach good result of business market and consumer goods .As developing the national market is increasing the involvement of Mongolian market to Asia and East Northern Asia Regional market.

It is clear that Mongolian market economy is deeply connected the market economy of East Northern Asia survey on "the compared research of consumer goods " of the Department of Marketing –International Trade in National University of Mongolia in 2004-2005...

Pircture 5.2 Regional rate for GDP as of 2005

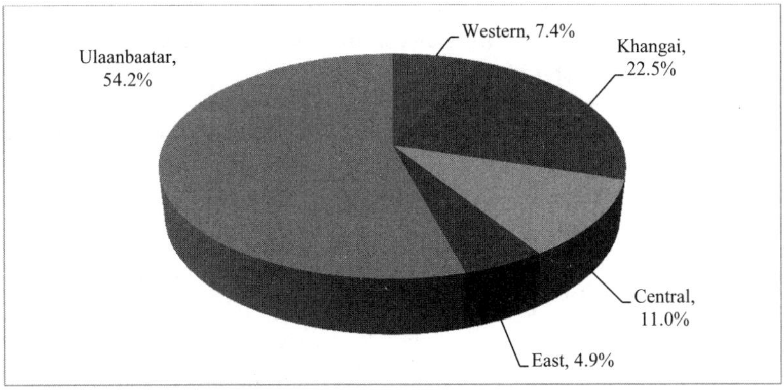

Resource: Institute for National Developemet

As of 2004, 55.9% of export, 85.8 import %, over 70% of foreign investment occurred the East Northern Asian countries. For foreign trade partners , Russian Federation was leaded till 1996, China was leaded last 10 years , since 2000 USA was leaded the second place. Since 2005 European Union has entitled duty free in export goods of over 7000, it is developing the relations of trading with European countries. It is main result of the last 15 years of market economy relations which is introducing Mongolian productions and service to World market.

The competitive of market economy is increasing in the many types of market:

- Monopoly market
- Oligopoly market
- Monopoly competitive market
- Free competitive market

The oligopoly is compound with many buyers and a few big seller. Nowadays the consumer of auto-car complained that fuel oil companies such as "Petrovis" are fuel pump price. These complain is one of compound oligopoly features.

By number of participants are increasing and development of relation's frame. A difference of independent types from others becomes more identify. A net monopoly is a structure of market found and opportunity to influence in service price and goods and brings under control the all and majority production. / in some case, there is a purchaser's monopoly/. A few number of monopoly industries dominated during the socialism / before 1990 / and industry dominating unilateral in a sector disappeared basically in relation of market.

A monopolistic rivalry in different between and identified by many numbers of traders interested to sell a kind of goods. Many kind of juice, bread, fine pastry's market contains this feature. Recently a market of construction and material of construction is possible to include in this type.

Table 5.1 A main difference of market types are sorted by condition of competition

Main features of mood of market	A free competition market	Net monopoly	Oligopoly	Monopolistic rivalry
A number of firms process the product	Too many	Just one big	Several big	Enough many
A type of product	Standardized	No placement	Standardized	Different
To control the price	A market identifies the price	Actually enough controlled	Any influence to lead it	Influence is limited
A difficulty to enter newly in sector	Relative few	Very serious	serious	Possible to enter and come

During the free competition market companies didn't influence in the price level of market. To come and to enter freely onto the market. By base quality free competition market is classic sample of market. Clothes and shoes etc..... a majority of consumer goods are sold by competition market. Type of markets transit in each other by deepening of market relation and a frame of free competition market is attitude to wide. Last time a frame of participants in market relation is widened.

Participants in market relation.

A: A salesperson

- State and personal property production, entity and organizations.
- Agriculture, building and science organizations are including in it.
- Intermediators, sellers
- Non production of state and personal property organizations (by sell the goods owning)
- A communal servic3e organizations to serve the toll service population.
- Communications and non governmental organizations serving to toll service to population are to sell the owning goods.
- Population / a owner sells personal effect, to sell conductivity the goods.

An income of entities and organization organizing an activity is sorted by region and focused in table 5.2.

If to show from it majority of organizations organizing service and production in market and imposing in UB and central region.

Table 5.2. A sales income of entities, by region, 2005.

A regional name	All entities accounting percent in number	0-4 million Tg	5-19 million Tg	20-49 million Tg	50-499 million Tg	500-4999 million Tg	More than 5000 million Tg
West	8.3	10.3	5.7	3.5	4.3	3.3	0.0
Hangain	10.8	12.2	9.8	8.0	5.7	2.7	5.4
Central	13.9	15.0	14.4	11.3	7.9	4.7	8.5
East	4.3	4.7	4.7	2.7	1.9	1.7	0.8
UB	62.7	57.9	65.3	74.4	80.1	87.6	85.4
Total	100	100	100	100	100	100	100

Resource : Research of national development institute

B. A purchaser

* Consumer of production it includes goods producers processes product

* Trade brokers are buying by not to resell and use

* Final user organization

* User population

* There is a many kind of trade mediators outside from producers of consumer's market. Includes:

* A wholesale's

* A small-wholesale's

* A retailing's

* A restaurant's or public catering's.

The property form are the developing all kinds of private organization and financial share. And market's second part is studied that : to be concrete of products rotation and significance to be gainful between participants.
On the 5.3th table seen for last year:
In market to supply with goods other products' increase and reform.

Table 5.3. /comparison with the last year/ Increase of the main products of agriculture

	Products	2003	2004	2005
1	Meat and mass of kill butcher	-27.1	8.5	4.1
2	Leather and hides	-10.6	0.7	20.3
3	Sheep wool	-6.9	18.5	21.9
4	Soft wool	5.7	12.4	2.0
5	Milk	69.0	125.4	33.1
6	egg	31.1	-16.1	-45.4
7	Grains	30.3	-15.5	-45.8
8	Wheat	51.6	1.9	3.2
9	Potatoes	50.1	-17.4	30.3
10	vegetables	59.6	49.2	64.1

Source: National Statistic Center

Agriculture sector's main manufacture products are leather, hides, sheep wool, soft wool, potatoes and vegetables, these are increased stability.
So, coal mining increased by 16.2% more than last year, and metal mining increased by 24.8%.
In this way, may to sum up 'market participants activity is afforded sold these products.

Table 5.4. Unit of economy, organizations good, kind of service and income condition.

	Sectors	Unit o economy and organization number		Sales income	
		Quantity (thousand)	Percent	Quantity (million)	Percent
1	Agriculture, hunting, forest economy, to fish	1.6	6.1	26.3	0.6
2	Mining, manufacture of produce	0.4	1.5	992.6	22.7
3	Manufacture of process raw materials	2.4	8.8	419.3	9.6
4	Electricity, to pro-	0.2	0.9	295.2	6.8

	vide with water and air				
5	Buildings	1.3	4.9	208.1	4.8
6	Whole sale and retail a service to repair the household goods	12.3	45.5	1298.6	29.8
7	Hotel, cafe	1.4	5.4	61.9	1.4
8	Transport, warehouse forming, communication	1.2	4.4	636.5	14.6
9	An activity to carry out a financial transaction	1.6	6.3	243.7	5.6
10	An activity of, business, immovable's, rent	1.8	7.1	138.9	3.2
11	An activity of educational sector	0.5	1.7	8.6	0.2
12	An activity of health and social care	1.5	5.7	15.7	0.4
13	A service to render to individual, social	0.4	1.7	17.0	0.3
	Total	**26.6**	**100.0**	**4362.3**	**100.0**

A Source by National statistical center

A span amount of market identifies a quantity of organization; company becomes purchaser, a quantity of sold goods and salesperson. So, to oversee the main features, a group of goods and its assortment. An indicator of satiety of market accounted for a bigger position an analysis of situation. If entities and organization are considered by sector wholesale and retailing is account for 45.5 percent of total entities but a sales income accounted for 29.8 percent. But a mining sector accounts for only 1.5 percent in total entities and accounted for 22.7 percent of sales income. If entity and organizations are considered by aimag and capital 51.89 percent of total entities are being in UB and 5.85 percent is entities, 41.61 percent budgeted and non-governmental organization, 41.78 percent is self employed people. If seen from it, self employed people accounted for a bigger part of participants of relation of market. A developmental promising new type of market of Mongolia is becoming a capital market credit.

A market of securities developing to become a part by inextricably linked with all sectors of financial market of international and no matter country. A market of bank is other part of financial market and a market of securities interacts with market of bank. Researchers identify "the securities is adapted for devoted to public, a document can to express to guarantee capital. Also the identified that security is financial active which is guaranteed to owning the property of its owner.
/ D. Dulamsuren. Development and formation of securities

This market adapts similar with other markets by the relation of demand and supply. At the beginning in 1991, in which a relation of market starts to develop a pink and blue tickets were used 476 state's industrial places transferred to the type of incorporated company. But a content of share and incorporated company didn't make people understand, in other words, either stockholders, industrial place became incorporated company can not reach to goal by no marketing of business and state and this action gets a bad name and Mongolian stock exchange's activity fell fully into stagnation. But in last 2 years an activity of stock exchange became active and a stock starts to sold by intrinsic content.

A sale of stock of "Mongol shiltgeen" company, "Zoos bank" showed it. Recently Zoos bank floated 2million piece shares sales a piece by 1000-1200tugrug and could accumulated 2 billion tugrugs. An activity of stock exchange and capital market credit grew accustomed and left many decide in the market relation formed countries. Mongolian underground wealth entered pull back and forth in its demand. An action shows that "Ivenhou Mines" company would invest many billion tugrugs to Oyu Tolgoi and it centralized the capital by exchange of New York and Canada. Thus, incorporated company attracts many numbers of stockholders and to open up a possibility to invest in useful stock of air railway of transport of China is bought by considerable account a greeting the Olympic game in Beijing 2008.

A demand of stock of travel companies may increase in our country. "Mongol shiltgeen" "Jenko Tour Bureau" companies realized it and floated a stock and sold successfully.

Thus, a capital market credit starts to consist of condition to develop by classic meaning. A settlement, "savings of securities" "factor age of securities" "a service of anterior is developing in the capital market credit of Mongolia.

As of 2006, 30 companies distributed about four billion tugrugs dividend.

The securities is produce of product produce the securities in demand, an element assumes obligation by own property on behalf of own name. Mongolian investment's market complete for finance that:

1. floated share
2. to submit share

Now Mongolian investment's market has 362 floated share organization. Last 2 years, Companies of "Mongol shiltgeen" company, " Zoos bank" company, 'Jenko Tour Buro" company, " B D Sek" company are sell by own share and participated of big investors to investment market. It is Mongolian market's best activity.

Thus, "Barilga Corporation", "Niislel Urguu" company, "Puma group "company," MCS electronics "company," Anod bank are loaned bond since 2001. But due to by valid reason's capital market credit's activity is not complete. Today, relation of Mongolian capital market credit's is coordinated by 2 rules that "Securities act" and "law about company"(1999) "civil law" "government and property of locality law" and tax's packet of law's instruction are sourced of legal regulation. In development of capital market credit is deficiencied by the first need one: organization status investment found, faithfulness, project of securities act's business and property's value and to establish position. We are seeing that Mongolia is complete system. Let's make to Mongolian market's establishment seen analysis that the possibility and danger, power and powerless: We have a power for the development Mongolia.

Table 5.5 Made in TOWS analysis to Mongolian market's establishment

Possibility	Hurdle
- Ecology's fresh products are increasing of the world market. - Neighbor countries, north and north-eastern Asia's big markets are situated near our country. - Mining products are increasing.	- Just the worldwide to starting feel that Mongolians products and services. - To change economy, international trade and government
Power side	Powerless side
Place, source, historical tradition, culture of people, tradition, establishment of law and democrat ion.	- Small population - The geographic location - Weak infrastructure development - Weak for business development and marketing management.

5.2 A CONSUMER MARKET

A market is classified producer's or organization's and consumer's or population's. A considerable interesting role – picture shows to research and to more pay attention to consumer's market in the frame of general classification of marketing.

David Ricardo /1772-1823/ a bigger representative of classic economists wrote "... useful quality is important as cost but not gauge of commercial cost. In profits this absorbed good commercial cost gets depletely from it's uncomparable quality and spent labour quantity to produce that in the named treation Economics of politics and the first levying of taxes".

An uncomparable quality is the main factor to identifier of commercial costs which is detecting by a research of market and conuber and it becomes extremely popular attitude in modern times.

A population is consisting the market of consumer of Mongolia that reached 2562.4 thousands in 2005 and it increased 2.7 times from 1960 which is viewed as one of the leader country by the growth of range of consamer's market.

As of 2005 62.3 percents of total population live in countryside, soum, and aimag and a bigger part of consumer's market located with very perculiar characteristic in a little part of wide area. In Khuvsgul 121.7 thousands, in Uvurkhangai 113.8 thousands, In Bayan-Ulgii 100.0 thousands, In Selenge 99.8 thousands population reside from aimags and in Gobi-Sumber 12.2 thousands, in Umnugobi 46.1 thousands, in Dundgobi 49.6 thousand, population live and location of consumers is radical different in the countryside.

If you observe a kinematics of structure and study to the consumer market by structure of age of the population the result would be an interesting role picture.

If sees at graphic, from now in 36 years infants /until 9/ accounted for one thirds of consumer's market and in 2005 specific gravity decreased up to one fifth but an addescent together with youth 10-19 are accounting for nearly 44% of total market.

If add specitic gravity of 20-29 ages youth 64.2% youth accounts for total market. It is more identity the sorted feature of mongolian market from other countries. In income of population and indicator and purchasing power are essential significant to identify a mood of consumer's market. In 2005 a fact of state statistical place shows that a cash income accounts average 87.4 percents in a structure a family income, 9.0 percent accounts foods prepared from private farming.

Picture 5.3. A structure of consumer's market

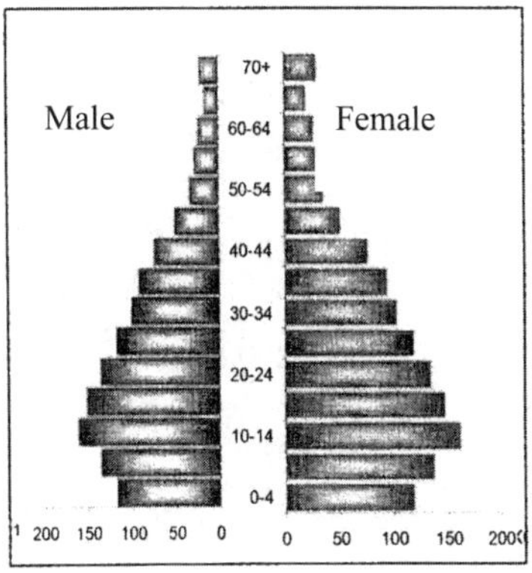

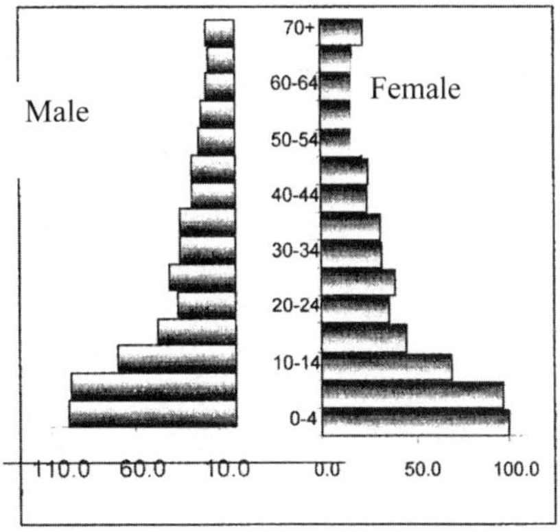

87.4% structure of income become total cash income it is divided into 38.8% salary, 10.3% pension, 38.8% production and service income of family , 7.8% other incomes are accounting.

This fact shosis that a family incame consisted the solary income during the centralised ecomonic structure and compare with that period family production and business developed and radical changes entered in structure of family in come from expanded the relations of market.

But a capital and bigger cities, income, expenditure consumptions are feature of quality from income of countryside population.

Our counry's population's feature of structure of consumpiton shows clearly in consumption of herder family.

Table 5.6. A family's structure of total and cash income of a month. 2000

	City	Countryside
Total income – in all	100.0	100.0
Cash in come – in all	94.8	80.8
A salary	55.6	14.4
A pension	11.3	8.9
A production and service income of a family	19.0	52.3
Other	8.8	5.3
For free took from other	3.7	2.5
Foods prepored from private farming	1.5	16.7

Source: A national statistical place

A herdsman family is not only considered a producer of cattle product but also to consider consumption cum consumer contained, specific feature which ins't in other countries of world.

Herders are viewed as attitude samely and not consider to study in aimed parts the specific feature consumer.

Table 5.7. A number of population, by region of economy, thousand person

	2002	2003	2004	2005
West	301.2	292.1	290.8	289.0
Khangai's	374.2	364.8	361.1	360.0
Central	256.1	258.8	261.2	250.7
East	123.1	124.1	121.9	119.4
Total	1054.5	1039.8	1034.9	1019.0

Source: A research of National Development institute.

When looked at table 5.7 A number of population of every region decreased from increased a number of population who transit to city in 2002.

To say in a different way, a frame of market of consumer of countriside was furled relatively in all regions.

During the transit in relations of market, profound alteration is appearing in all frame of culture, life, society, environment of life of herders and which becomes main reason of purchasing mood of them.

11200 herders had electric source and herders hadn't any TV and automobiles in 1990.

By 1996 11.8 percents or 19100 herder families were provided by electric source and 2300 families had an electric source with wind engine.

If so, there are total 168344 herder families in our country 67701 families that had elecric lights, 60136 families had TV, 23228 families had all kind of automobiles, 2372 families had tractors and 37411 families had a motocycles.

35.4-59.4 percents herder families of population centrelized relatively and near the line of energy Darkhan-Uul, Selenge, Orkhon aimags and UB city have electric lights.

As of 2005 or 10 years later 35.9-74.8 percents have electric lights.

An athtude is increase to produce the food clothes and household products by themselves which is the high priority consumption of living of nomads by productivity of cattle.

But today mongolian, majority of herder's life is poor and far from service of culture education and hospital alongside 56.9 percents or in to 100 head cattle total herder families were become a commercial equipment by sheep, cattle and increases to change by tea tobacco rices, clotheses a every year.

As poor family foods and clothes are identifing the level of demand and request.

About these families a programme is needed to implement to study, to work in the existing market and to coddle creative labour in frame of development of region.

A purchase abiloty of lower income families of center of soum, aimag and UB, not exceeded from daily needs things and it is consisting to the specific and wide range part of consumer's market.

A mood of consumer's market is closely attributable to it's environment.

5.3 COMPETITION AND BUSINESS SITUATION

Change of the macro situation, competition

Our country's business situation is always changing. Having a high price of the world market of the strategy's important products is becoming an important factor of business external situation. There was the high price of copper and gold in the world market becomes export's income of 2006 in the high level and for end of the year trade balance reached in equally level. Even though inflation was 9.2% in august of 2005 and this period of 2006 5.2% is decreased. Balance of state budget is appearing beneficially in succession last two years. Main reason of the increased state budget links with mineral row materials which is reaching special high level, increasing income tax to take from price growth of copper and gold in the world market and getting broader business of service and construction's sector. Having reinforced competition in the all business sectors becomes distinguishing features now.

-Through the condition of the competition:

A. business range which competition is appearing strongly. Here includes in many building- accommodation, production of food, production of intoxicating drink and non-intoxicating drinks in including them, retail and wholesale trade, mineral resource reconnaissance, mining, production of public eating, tourism, communication, and information business.

B.business range which competition is appearing. Here includes in production of materials, sewn, knitted, skins and hides production, trade of domestic goods, hairdresser, and service of photograph. C. in the business range which is beginning action of competition includes in new kinds of service such as road and plumbing construction, manufacturing of mining, babysitting, doing chores

In the having the most strongly competition sectors is gotten in private sectors and this is very good which Mongolian business develop is many-sided and great in content.

Business situation valuation

Also changes are taking unceasing in the business situation. Any country's competition quality depends on considerably how the business situation.

The survey of the international development agency of the USA shows that there were five main factors such as bureaucratic of the Government, undeveloped infrastructure, tax level, corruption, tax code aggravate for held business in Mongolia. It is an advanced action that Serial surveys which are Mongolian economy and business situation are held by Chamber of Commerce and Industry of Mongolia /CCIM/. The department held such surveys in 2002, 2004 and tried to define that how the economy and business situation in Mongolia are available for business people and what problems face to their successful activities

The ministry of trade and industry held the open discussion in first half of 2005 in 7aimags 3 towns and over 700 business people involved and express the views to define the problems that face to business people and small and middle industry. A member and not member of CCIM 159 entities, organization, small and middle-scale enterprises and private retailers took part in the research of "An environment of economy and business of Mongolia". 28.3 percent is commercial, 22.6 percent engages in production, 18.9 percent is service, 9.4 percent is other activities and 5.7 percent engages production, service, trade 3.8 percent is production and service, 1.9 percent engages production and trade. So try to include every kind of entities.

For example: Many works of to improve the service of customs from government it .

For example: To improve the service of customs from a government but the research shows that the service of costumes are not enough enjoy to entities.

In activities of entities and organizations the check-up of customs how to cause difficult and 62.2 percents participants said that difficult by any level. This indicator is compared with the research of 2002 there is no alteration in it. 50.0 percent of participants hoped to improve the service of customs and 28.9 percent participants answered unknown, 21.1 percent participants expressed that it doesn't improve on present form. The participants caused to come many kind of opinions about what services introduce in documents and check-up of customs. Including:

• to decrease many stages and to introduce one-stop service.

• to improve technique and technology and to introduce in network of computer by wide scope.

• to work an oblique supervisor.

Also, opinions about to set a price and it is based on documents of agreement , to use the means of price, to become brief and clear the legislations, rules, resolutions, to implement rightly a law and to become calmly and quickly the officer's character.

Generally, entrepreneurs considered the service of customs is improving and documents, check-up, to cast tax evaluation are difficulty.. Also the research shows that to pay attention to the character of officers. Also what kind of issues related with tax to causes the difficult to entrepreneurs. Participants of research 87.8 percents answered tax fee is high, 83.9 percents answered the check-up of tax is too a lot, 75.0 percents answered the character of officers is bad and the most difficult things are the tax fee is high (29.3), the character of officers is bad (22.7), the tax check-up is a lot (19.4).

According to the new tax law to constituted more comfortable environment to the entrepreneurs and started to serve new system of tax from the1th of January 2007 and it is triumph over the pre-downsides and became very important law condition. From the services of bank and finance the difficult problems are the interest of credit , problem of time and a majority of entities which included in the research or 92.9 percents said the interest of credit is too high , 88.9 percents said the time of credit is too short and this problems are difficult to entrepreneurs but participants of research called a little bit difficulty issues. It includes:

An information about market of credit finance is scanty (36,4%) banks can not secret private information of company (25,0%) a possible is scanty to interact with non-bank financial source or investors (24,2%).

Moreover bank, financial institutions view as important pledge mortgage and moveable property in the credit pledge during grant the credit. So far the small and middle entities became difficulty to grant the credit.

Thus if the bank and financial institutions establish the class of credit and guarantee of third party , mechanism to grant a credit by evaluation of project to start implement correctly in the development of bank and financial institutions and private sector make a headway .

By the current situation to obtain an information about legislation and rules related business is not difficulty and channels to obtain an information is not much popular. Because 4.3 percent of participants answered very easy to gain legislation attributable to run a business 23.4 percent answered it was average level. But 38.3 percent answered it was very difficult in majority happening. But 7.1 percent participants have fully-possible to participate conductivity by yourself and relating representatives and 23.8 percents have possible to participate conductively by relating organization.

An evaluation of factor

Entities were wanted to give evaluation to the current business situation and a result of the research and inquiries shows that majority of it or 40.4 percents viewed our country's business situation improved from the last year and 34.0 percents answered that it didn't change. But 19.2 percents concluded it got worse than pre-year and 6.4 percents said that unknown.

Thus , the situation of business is going to improve generally and entrepreneurs hope to improve the situation of business.

The positive changes of the Business Environment

The above the result of survey is shown that the general assessment of improvement on Mongolian business environment, but it is not complex assessment. In the future it is important to comprise the evaluation system on business environment and to survey and define reasons of these.

In the last year The Mongolian government has been providing many intensive measurements and implementing on the improvement of business environment.

For example the work of the joint Consulting Committee of the Government and private business is reaching a good result. The fist The Business Enterprise Forum held In April, 2004, the businessmen and the government were exchanged their opinions as considering that was very importance event. Thanks to the Forum, The government is issued the resolution 143 on the improvement business environment and adopted its plan and implementing. And they are made "To develop Small and Medium enterprise Project "which grounded the expert`s survey of Ministry of Industry and Trade and The Development Agency of USA and adopted it in April, 2005. According to the project they are implementing the following measures to develop small and medium enterprise, improve their competitive ability, from informal businessmen involved into form of formal condition of business enterprise, set up working accommodation. The fist domestic investor business entrepreneurs were organized In September, 2006. The Japan government had granted two steps loan to development small and medium entrepreneur and are issued $26USD million loan through commercial banks. The fund of to develop of small and middle entrepreneurs of Ministry of Industry and Trade has issued loan to business entrepreneurs.

In the framework of the project of "Let`s develop industry in Mongolia" which reconcilement with a project "One settlement, one product" will produced the brand products, service in local province, soum ,give advises , professional training and selected from 140 business entities are supported them.

We are collaborating with state and business organizations using possibility on supply the export goods are not imposed the tax , its quantity to development countries and the advantages of current agreement and contract of membership of World Trade Organization .

Mongolian government have adopted the amendments and reedited of the Mongolian laws on "Income tax on Business Entities", "Tax on VAT" and law on "Specific Tax" on 29 June,2006.

These laws have enter forced on 1 January, 2007. As implementing the above laws are constituted the positive business environment on tax in the new situations.

But it has shown necessary the current economics, business environment situations that to make amendments and changes in the reedited laws. If we are defined the main tendency is a long development economics which includes export` s planned produces and service, it should make the amendments into these tax laws. Otherwise in the above laws are necessary to make amendments depending on development levels, specific situation of Mongolian.

These laws are not specified the articles of local region`s development progress. The 50% of World Cross Productions, the part of majority of the products are manufactured in Ulaanbaatar. In this case it is very important for Mongolian development` of market economy to support by tax policy in the local region` s development.

As concluded, the forming business environment , the cooperation of state, non-government organization and business entities is sustained year by year ,it is opening a new opportunities in the market economy of Mongolia.

5.4 PRIVATIZATION

After 16 years of Mongolian transformation into market economy, Economy has privatizing and developing open market relations.

Ways and means that developed privatization and individual property:
World history has showing that individual property is the important beginning. Individual property may mean that individual investment majored business.
Scientists and researchers have done studies on Privatization in terms of theoretical and practices. In economics theory, in order to estimate privatization, it often included many subjects such as households, all types companies as well as industries and service houses.
As if consider privatization as dependent complex system of social industries relations, the property of businessman would be element of that system. On the other hand, this property would be a part of market relations.

Development of privatization clearly depends on political and economical structure. Only where established privatization sector could be suitable environment for developing this sector.

There may are 3 means on development privatizations in Mongolia:

1. The mean of privatizing state property
2. Individual business activities by civil and organizations
3. Not by the mean of market ot marketing. However this mean is not common in Mongolia and basically covers people of doing unfair trade, no repaying for bank loan or any action similar to.

1st mean of privatizing property was one of the fundamental one.

During 1980s, Mongolia had started taking actions regarding improvement of economic administration and reduction of economic controlling, so since reforming processing 1990s, privatizing state property environment externally and internally has developed.

First 1991, the privatizing process was started selling the first voucher to public. This programme began in October 1991 and within the programme every person who was born before date of 31 may 1991 received yellow voucher costs 1000 tugrug each for.

It was worth for small state or joint industries which had fewer than 50 staffs. The pink voucher was able to purchase at the second market.

Between October 1991 and July 1992, created blue voucher worth for 7000 tugrug that could build purchase or usage possibilities to the people. We still remember that the blue voucher was provided to the people listed.

Mongolian Stock Exchange was established in January 1991 and then focused to locate its branches into provinces and other cities as federation purpose.

While adopting Mongolian Constitution in January 1992, privatization right was approved so that man can have several properties.

After the constitution adoption, law on security developed and as of August 1995 second trade on voucher started.

Relating to the price control releasing, privatization was strengthening and possibilities and freedom of market relations for businessmen were tightened.

Just seeing the period of 1992-1995, statics shows that 446 large and small industries became privatized. Beside the voucher, the government used to co-use auction sale.

In agricultural sector, the process started by privatizing the livestock to those herders. This had advantages and disadvantages in terms of free of charge. Had collapse of co-operative herds system 30 years history moved into private protection. At that time, the policy started to implement which might be variability to care each of if free of livestock and market economy.

Family business runners faced difficulties to carry along the risky on their own as the collapse was not well planned and no understanding of marketing, finance, price presence and industrial.

So herders carried responsibilities and assumptions on their own and needed to manage to sell and settling in different location as well as solve their social and education demands. This means that they are facing more difficulty to transfer from herder to businessman.

However, new approaches and better understanding are developing nowadays in countryside and that is influencing to herder-businessman actions such as selling milk and meat production. Surely it does depend on the location and what kind of livestock feeding. The ones located nearly to cities or centres, tourist camps, boundary area are more availability to market and its becoming comparable richer and to move into farmer sector.

I have discussed about preparation of marketers able to work countryside and to coordinate marketing management in one of my studies titled " Mongolian Marketing Management " in 1998.

The movement of state property privatizing still continues even passed 2000 and to name a few of those successful companies : Trade and Development Bank of Mongolia, Mongolian Telecom Company.

The second means of privatizing

Its been interesting history that civil started becoming bosses of companies and industries by working dependently at market. Also this can show by the development history of comsumers and producers agencies and self operated business.

The third one – not by mean of marketing

This is the level of difficulty which to be formed in environment of privatized social / steal in financial way, corruption, and to hold by estimating in lower price and so on/. This has shown its disadvantages and no future in arena of Mongolian nomadic culture and social. That business which running in honest and fairness would develop further is the Fate of Mongolians whom named under Great King, Chingiss.

Formation of privatizing

As a fact, agreement on self laboring for civil start was from 1980s. Other words, the reforming movement that developed in Soviet Russia had influenced Mongolia and innovations were creating all over the country. The current successful leaders might be one of those pioneers.

By adopting Mongolian Constitutional Law in 1992, the legal environment of all types property holder was developed and stated that " Mongolia will have different routine economy that meet world economic development approaches which hold its countries perspectives".

Also in 5th article of 1st chapter of the Constitutional Law, it highlighted that " The State will agree and to protect public and private properties by its relative laws" and "The ownership types only limited by means of Law and Legislation".

The property issues are considered into numerous laws such as Civil Law, Criminal Law, Company Law, Law on Patent and Good symbols, Taxation law and so on.

Private sector companies are holding 80 percent of market in current Mongolian business and becoming one of the power of economic growth.

That analyzing the development of private sector and their actions might be significant for reforming or strengthening state polices and strategies towards supportive reason.

So that to make studies in market development process as below periods would be interesting and sufficient:

1. Beginning of Transformation /1990-1995/
2. Accelerating economic structure reforming /1996-2000/
3. Sustaining macro economic

1) Beginning of Transformation /1990-1995/

Mongolia has started its transformation first steps into market economy from 1991. The common difficulties those happened for transforming countries had come to Mongolia.

For instance, GDP has decreased by 20 percentage, import rate declined by 549.5 Million USD from 1990-1993 and reached 374.5 million USD, also investment for GDP reduced rapidly, foreign trade deficit was increasing at the mean time lost the balance of internal and external economic.

During this time, state has taken following actions and policies regarding:

- Released good and service price by stage
- In order to realizing national currency freely at all over the country, state has taken policies on national currency realization towards and in connection of foreign currency since 1993.
- In framework of state property privatizing, investment voucher holding process was taken and as a result each Mongolian civil have had a right to hold equally. This motivated trade and restaurants, and public service places to be privatized. And Livestock privatizing , as Mongolian economic basic foundation, started from 1991-1992 by those vouchers which mentioned above.
- Transformed into 2 staged banking system.
- The government has taken tuff currency policies and paid attention to macro level management administration and coordination.
- In purpose of implementing projects with International Monetary fund, in collaboration with World Bank, Asian Development Bankm and many other donor countries and organizations in direction of sustaining economy of Mongolia have started implementing medium term programmes and projects
- The main resource of coordinating market economy, Taxation Laws, Laws on protection from unfair competent, and Foreign Direct investment, Law and Monetary related Laws, Statistic as well as Social Insurance Laws began to formulated and implemented.

These actions mainly focused on strengthening economic management system, and its mechanism reforming and development of the legal environment.

It was significant for balancing economic situation and sustaining growth and building capacities as a result of implementing projects and programmes under IMF collaboration and cooperation with WB, ADB and donors countries and organizations.

Since 1994 with achievements by those projects, Mongolian economic situation has strengthening and even showed by statistic reports that indicated positive results.

During that time, economic decline has slowed and GDP increased by 2.3 percentage in 1994, 6.3 % in 1995, and 2.4% in 1996 so the per capita GDP became 239.9 thousand tugrug; and the inflation that of 325% in 1992 positively decreased to 66.3% in 1994 and 53.1% in 1995 and sectors maintaining for GDP has changed by the influence of mining and agriculture.

Private sectors are established by replacing state properties and ownership as time changing of economic and social transformation and this actions could maintain successfully so that became main reason of Mongolian economic structural changes. In 1989, the percent of privatization used to hold only 3.3 and this percentage had increasing contentiously that as of 1995 it was 52.6%.

The positive influences were:

- As a result of privatizing properties to people It could gain economic freedom from state and developed environment for changes and reforming at all sectors and level.
- Private sector became one of the important sector for the nation's fundamental resource.
- The persons started to work fort their own lives effectively and actively. Maintaining such actions, the state burden had become positively and erased the common person's thinking which count on that state responsibility and support.

It is clear indeed that privatizing process could help to develop and establish multi relations of property ownership and empowering the role of private sector for nation's economy. Even though, it was still difficult to maintain such effort during the beginning of transformation period. And also economic growth has decreased with industrial production became fewer.

Cattle production sector was one of increasing sector as the privatizing could show its significant. However, the main objective to privatizing the civil in equal condition still remains not successful till now.

As the main result of State policy regarding privatization its property to private sector, In GDP those private sectors used to hold that the private agricultural sector 88.2%, construction sector 63.2%, trade sector 66.1%. transportation sector 21.3% and industrial sector 20.0% each as of 1995.

Recently, these became as of agriculture 55.7%, industrial 9.6%, construction sector 3.1% and trade sector 24.2 in GDP.

Table 5.8. Private sector rate at economy

No	Sector	Private sector rate at National GDP	Sector rate for private sector GDP
1	Agriculture	88.2	55.7
2	Industry	20.0	9.6
3	Construction	63.2	3.1
4	Trade	66.1	24.2
5	Transportation	21.3	3.3
6	Service	24.8	5.9
	Total	52.6	100.0

Resource: Institution for National Development "Extended study on private sector of Mongolia"-scientific study report, UB. 2005.

2) Accelerating economic structure reforming /1996-2000/

Between 1996-2000, the government of Mongolia took actions with purpose of quick reformation process in social and economic sector in collaboration with International level banks, financial organizations and donor countries in order to sustain macro economic, to strengthen structural changes, to minimize state sectors and to support private sectors. As a result of these actions, much positive impact has been showing.

At that time, GDP annual growth reached 2.4 in 1996, 4.0 in 1997, 3.5 in 1998, 3.2 in 1999, 1.1 in 2000 (picture 1) and inflation rate decreased from 53 to 6-10 %, unemployment 4.6%, foreign currency official reserves gained 191 million USD which able for 14 weeks, that 3% on running balance benefit in GDP and the amount of foreign trade total turnover became 1 billion USD.

Picture 5.4 the growth of real sector

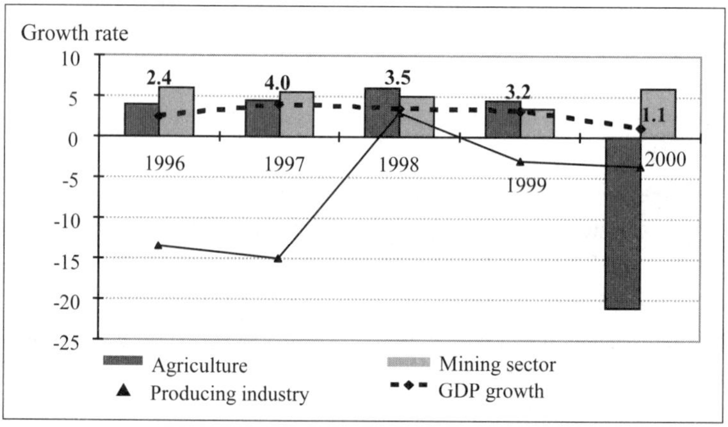

Resource: Institute for National development

As in 1996 GDP per capita was 241.2 thousand tugrug, It became 264.6 thousand tugrug in 2000.

Picture 5.5 GDP per capita and economic real growth (1996-2000)

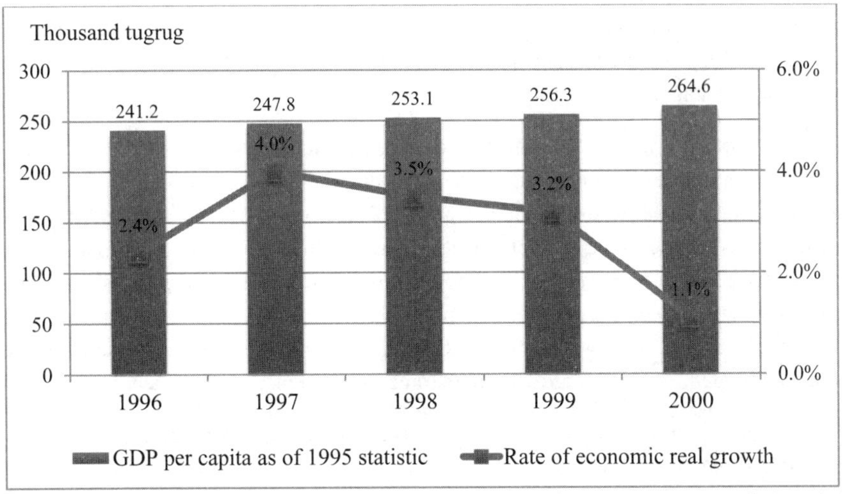

Resource: Institution for National Development "Extended study on private sector of Mongolia"-scientific study report, UB. 2005.

Since 1990, the Governments had paid attention on privatizing process and in their term of office, they formulated policies and concepts, and started to implement step by step. For instance, in 1996, whilst the Government of Mongolia adopted "Law on State and local property", the duty of privatizing was transformed into State property Committee so then the new programme of privatizing started to implement.

In framework of the No160 act of the Government of Mongolia in 1997 "Programme for privatizing state property between 1997- 2000" started. The overall aim of this programme was "to transform state property into private sector, to give the ownership right to civil, to develop environment for national production outcome and to major private sectors for national economy by molding their responsibilities and duties under laws".

As of 1996, the rate of private sector for national GDP was 57.1%, it has been increasing gradually so then reached 72.2% in 2000. Between 1996-2000, GDP in private sector increased by 11.1% as of 1996 and by 15.1% in 1998 from 1996 but decreased after then.

5.5. ORGANIZATION MARKETING PROCESS

Business progress during centralized economy could not directed to the willingness of consumer need and that supplier used to provide producers then from producer to traders for supplement of consumers which was one way trade market with not responsibility of producers in terms of final selling. In this point of view, there was no other way to buy production and services for individual and organizations but limited choices without any resources of.

However, since Mongolia has transformed into open market economy 1990s, have developed competence between producers and so that the direction of market has started into the right and as a result, producers and coordinators had faced the importance of research on consumer demands and wishes, therefore the responsibility of final selling process for relative subjects was developed. In other words, that established many companies with possibilities to compete with others in market as a result of privatizing was change for producers whose progress was first to produce then supply and was the main challenge to move towards world market enriched marketing concept.

It is agreeable with development field of marketing theory and practice as researcher Dagvadorj D studies following:

- Scientific and researching field
- Business sector
- Social, politics and cultural field

As briefly seen the scientific and researching field of development:

Since the importance of marketing in business became high, to develop and to study marketing subject in our country, to aware this subject to business companies and also to educate and to prepare human resource who meet modern standard has become main priority for universities and academies where scientists and researchers experienced in. So that since 1990s, the lectures and subjects of marketing had started at university level and translation of sector pioneers books and studies.

Soon after that, narrative studies such as marketing administration, costumer behavior, organization and service marketing are developed at university education purposes at the same time research works as well. That from 1995, started preparing qualified specialists with degrees of bachelor, master and doctorate successfully was main achievement on skilled human resource supplement for Mongolian business companies.

Business sector marketing development:

The progress on business sector marketing process was running at various level depending on each sector competences.

Industry sector marketing: As seen from the background of marketing science development, because of the competence created by over supplement than demand, means of marketing has processed at industrial sector strongly and leading position, but in Mongolia its started slower compare to other sectors.

By the content and seize of total business organizations at industrial sector following is the types of marketing processing level:

- Large industries that less flexible in terms of marketing environment and its rapid changes for technology and techniques renewing.
- Foreign directed or joint invested Mining and Light, Food industries with differences on finance resources, easily accustom able to changes
- Small and medium enterprises that are trying to positioning at the market in terms of finance capacity and administration management

Most of the national level companies faced transformation difficulties regarding techniques and technology backwardness which made challenges for marketing development. That those industries could gain effective results, however, can shown by experience and reforming of light and food industries current situation, to name a few: APU, Uguuj, Talkh chiher, Gobi, Ulaanbaatar Hivs and Darhan Nehii. Nowadays, It is showing the importance and success as those companies have establishing marketing departments basing on own characters.

As Gobi, one of the major companies, started hiring marketing specialized since 1992 and developing related departments; and nowadays many market leading companies have becoming membership for Mongolian Marketing Association which established in 1994 and successfully participating on its activities covering both theory and practice.

Foreign direct and indirect investment companies are mostly light and food industries those has understanding and experience about market economy, flexible organized and enough budgeted for advertisement from the beginning and processing marketing successfully.

Among sector internal competence, such industries are mainly successors. On the other hand, as mining companies have its characters, the background shows different.

Private small and medium enterprises are mostly intend to position at the market arena, and those are flexible organized, compact administrated and have lack of understanding of marketing. The reason could be the wrong understanding that marketing processing pay much money and that might face challenges in terms of this market demands.

Agricultural sector marketing:

Its been backwardness on competence in this sector compare to other sectors even many types of companies established already. Most of main well functioning companies of the sector are located in outside of city and operating to provide local communities demand at the same time to supply raw materials and food production for the center ones. However, as those companies have lack of skilled and qualified leaders and managers, the competence ability and market policy are lower than such type companies located in central areas.

So it needs to have state level complex policies to support and to encourage in terms of loans and investment including industrialism and service which demands strong organization marketing policy ever.

Service sector marketing:

As the service one of the important sector for the people, its developing rapidly especially in sectors as trade, hospitality, transportation, finance, property, education, health and social since 1990 and in a result marketing is been successfully implementing. The trade development is connected with market economy and as of today, there are around 8.000 selling points functioning well since that time.

During the crisis of economic transition period, due to trade policy has stopped, market economy faced challenges on losing sector system and style, and lack on supplement.

Nowadays, small shops started progressing marketing more effective that becoming exemplary of its sector. Its been new approach of the sector in becoming official distribution of foreign famous brand warehouse. We can concern them as a result of privatizing and market competence.

Generally, that the situation of Mongolian trade organizations has moving in its right way towards developed countries exemption could develop background of distribution channel system between consumers and producers.

Seen at recent promotion and advertisement activities of small shops such making sale, promoted and lottery prize selling and awarding lucky buyer are clear impact of successful market activation and establishment of marketing departments.

Bank and finance loan is becoming higher as time goes as well as enriching sector service by creating types of loans, mortgages, money transfers, credit cards and extended hours and one point service. These reforming is bringing up the honest market competence and mostly good point is developing bank marketing. Same time with insurance of finance market, Non bank financial institution is developing as a brand new sub-sector and this makes the competence more strained.

Other service sector marketing named below are remaining in its requirements, those transportation, hotel, law advice, pub and restaurant, education and health and tourism and so on. Among these sub-sector, IT and restaurant competence is raising rapidly and easily can see from the process of UNITEL, MOBICOM and SKYTEL companies services in telecommunication sector; and also Mongolian, Chinese and Korean restaurants.

Tourism and legal advice centres are establishing enormously. Apparently, except public purposed, transportation service clearly choose methodology and approaches of marketing and under means of market development. This is obvious from managers implementing tasks who works in above business companies marketing departments.

Scientists concerned about the marketing development period which comes close connection with Mongolian business market relations as 3 levels showing below:

1. Period of limited business by trade /1990-1995/
2. Period of developing market research based business /1996- /
3. Modern period of ecology orientation business / 2003- /

However marketing is taking its position within business framework, still there are common lack of understanding.

First. Still marketing remains consumers market

There is common drawback that main focus of companies marketing leads to the final consumers as study of current business market relations. It means that marketing is developing slowly which for producers and traders as a consumers at one side and for purchasers those work to meet the needs of personal and final consumer on the other hand. As the movement from one time negotiation marketing towards long term relations marketing is becoming business development tendency in these days, its becoming necessity for businessmen to make policy including partners from producers to final consumers. Even though, marketing activity for final consumers still have only advertising and few types of promoted selling which remains limited and not exact tendency for.

Two. Company and marketing remain separately

Companies are operating and experiencing marketing departments in various structures, however, as the administration, management, and implementing activities are running in different ways, there seems to have 3 types of relations between company and marketing. /Picture 5.12/

Picture 5.12. Types of relations between company and marketing.

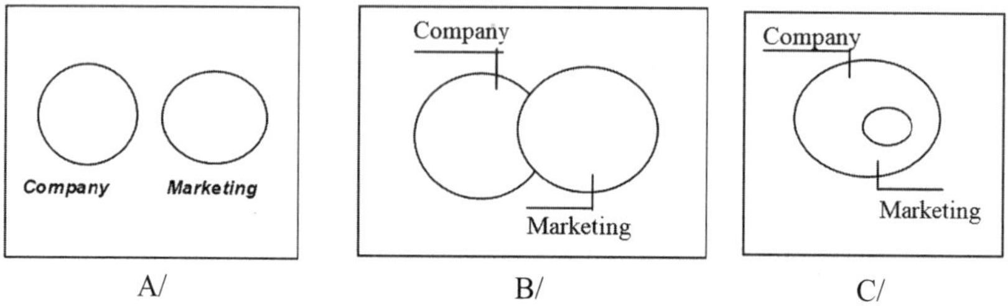

In first type of relations: due to separated relations and lack of inter-communications between company administration and marketing department, marketing department operates by their own and no efficient outcome.

In second type of relations: because of new market cooperation establishing, company administration and marketing department has creating understanding of each other in some activities. Most of the companies in Mongolia have the 1st and 2nd types in terms of the relation between company and marketing departments.

In 3rd type of relations: company administration and marketing department become a unit and have one main purpose of business. This type of relations has not established in Mongolia yet.

Marketing would establish in its means as if the 3rd types which gained close coordination of administration and marketing department.

However, if seen at current experience, most of the organizations have lack on establishment of marketing department structure, its professional staffs, identifying their role and responsibilities and inter-department communications; and importantly problems occurred relating understanding and communication among marketing departments and heads of companies usually influence business success, shows many studies.

it is common that if company reached success it meant a result of collective, but in case of failure it usually counts as the fault of marketing department.

While discussed with young marketers, It brings them down and becomes dis-encouragement for them

As can see from leading business companies experience in worldwide, there is requirement that to have understanding and knowledge of marketing from top administrative to lowest level staffs. What does it influence us?

It is obviously clear that the planning which formulated by professional and skilled marketer, would not be successful if those managers and service officers, who should implement, have no understanding of marketing.

Three. Marketing administration remains not sufficient outcome

In 2000, some experts and researchers made study among 10 leading companies those concerned as if good management capacity than others. The study showed marketing implementation was not efficient enough as comparison of business, duties, and result of total demand functions.

For example, that the medium percentage of proposed functions was 57.7 explains the reasons that company administrations have lack of understanding, decision making process that based on previous experience, and not ready for risky business. Therefore, that functional medium percentage was 61 means active less on human resource policy, insufficient communication between marketing and other departments, and staff skill is poor, maybe no connection between human and organization interest.

But that demand functioning medium percentage was 55 explains of insignificant usage of marketing researches, cost policy usually have poor background and poor distribution channel administrative.

When defining the result of marketing administrative form participated companies, it was directly connected with leaders knowledge of market, long term relationships, complex marketing system.

If sees at social, political, and cultural field of marketing, that State organizations like Taxation and Customs as one of the most important object of state service, have started implementing services such as one point service centres and internet communications, shows the pleasant beginning of marketing progress. Nevertheless, scientists claim that progress of marketing in generally remains slower in governmental organizations and NGOs.

Its been important to answer to the question of How to improve the result seeing organization marketing tendency?

Successful marketing administration implementation does not only relevant in terms of well structured department or qualified staffs, but also to inter-communication and connection of all department actions so that improvement of company function quality means complex actions.

Moreover, we are comparing organization marketing tendency with communication marketing which developed during 1990s . Communication marketing is different from negotiation marketing by its principle that to develop communication among supplier, human resource, trader and influencer, at the mean time of creating capacity for keeping long term consumers.

CHAPTER SIX

MANAGEMENT AND ORGANIZATION OF BUSINESS ENTITIES

Brief contents

There was an urgent need to change management of business entities employed in previous social system as Mongolia has undergone a transition to market economy. During the transition period property relations have been formed and flexible management with long-term policy for business entities is the basis of their survival and growth. Therefore, success of present business entities results from their management and competition that is proceeding in accordance with market-related laws and regulations and international business activities. As for Mongolian business entities, their survival in international competition is directly connected to their management and capacity.

6.1 PROPERTY DIVERSIFICATION OF BUSINESS ENTITIES

Economic content and nature of property relations: Researchers regard property as a defining concept of an economic system. There have been different socio-economic systems with specific features such as capitalism with private property, socialism with state property and a market system, combining multi-property forms in history of mankind. The distinguishing and defining factor of their development is property. In philosophy, influence of private and common property (state property) on social development was described using the growth curve. (Figure – 6.1). It was proven that dominance of one of them cannot lead to social development.

Capitalist economy with single private property that existed until the last decade of XIX century was not the best society for development of mankind since property was centralized in few people's hands and economy was driven for their private interests, which led to poverty and deprivation among masses and plunged countries into economic and political crisis. As a result, a powerful interest in establishment of society and economy with common property was prompted. (Figure – 6.1. Point 3) During this explosion of social aspiration, a theory on management of market economy through state coordination was developed by Keines and his followers, and expansion of production and services for the society and ascertaining responsibilities and activities of public and private sectors have produced correction of capitalist society's slip-up and brought great development success (Figure 6.1. Point 2).

In the early XX century, some countries followed a centrally planned economic system with common property as a result of revolutionary movement. However, economy in those countries became stagnant after a certain period due to restriction of individual freedoms, total control and limitation of free thinking and free competition (Figure 6.1. Point 1). In the late 1980s, socialist countries carried out reforms in order to put to right shortcomings in their society and strived to introduce market mechanisms and establish a society with private property and a private sector. It shows that development based on combination of private and public property is our present choice.

Figure – 6.1 Interdependence of property

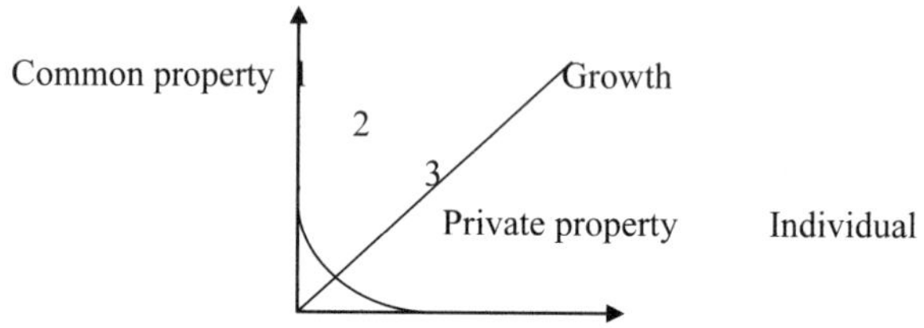

As for Mongolia, it is advisable to take into account experience of developed countries in rational coordination of public and private sectors in the course of implementing reform policies to create a private sector, to introduce market mechanism and develop production and services in a competitive way.

In history, Property has been one of the most important concepts of economics and it is understood as owning, managing and using property.

Property is a legal interaction of one or more people with any tangible items for a period of time or permanently.

The owner is an active side of property relations and they are people who have a right to possess property. They are as follows:

1. Individuals
2. Joint entity
3. State.

Property items are the other side of property relations and are natural and production resources, energy, information, capital, skills and talent, intellectual and psychological values and services etc. Nature of property is shown in figure 2.

Property relations are relationships that emerge between owners and property items. Actions of property relations are ownership, management and use of property.

Regulations between owners and property items create economic and legal concepts of owning, managing and using property. Contents of property relations is shown in figure 6.2.

Ownership is a basic concept of property and is the right of an owner to own property items legally. Ownership is a major defining factor of property relations and the right of ownership is realized when property items are certified by legal documents to be those of owners'. Owners do not have to utilize their property items.

Figure – 6.2. Nature of property

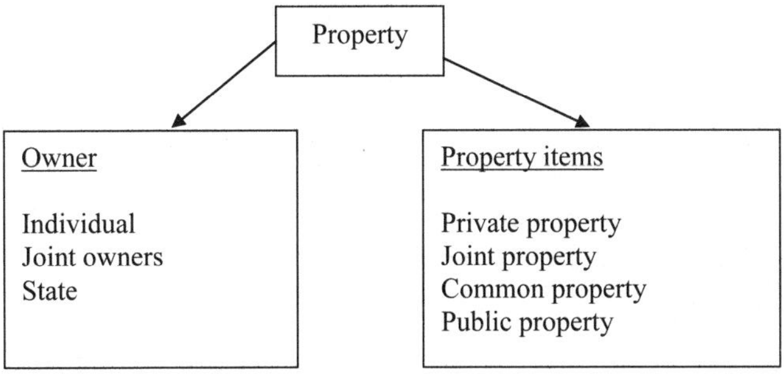

There are cases when some of many owners of one property item do not manage it as long as he/she derives profit from it. Public institutions automatically receive ownership rights to social property items.

Use of property is when a user utilizes property items for certain purpose for his/her own interest. The owner can use and own property items at the same time, as well as different parties/bodies can use them separately, i.e. there is no need to be an owner to use property items.

Control over property is the most important relation to coordinate the owner and property items and is the legal basis for property items to be movable. The controlling body has rights to expend, sell, present, pledge and inherit property items. The owner's controlling right can be a basis for management of entities and production. A body that owns, controls and uses property is called an owner in many countries' constitutions.

Figure - 6.3. Property relations

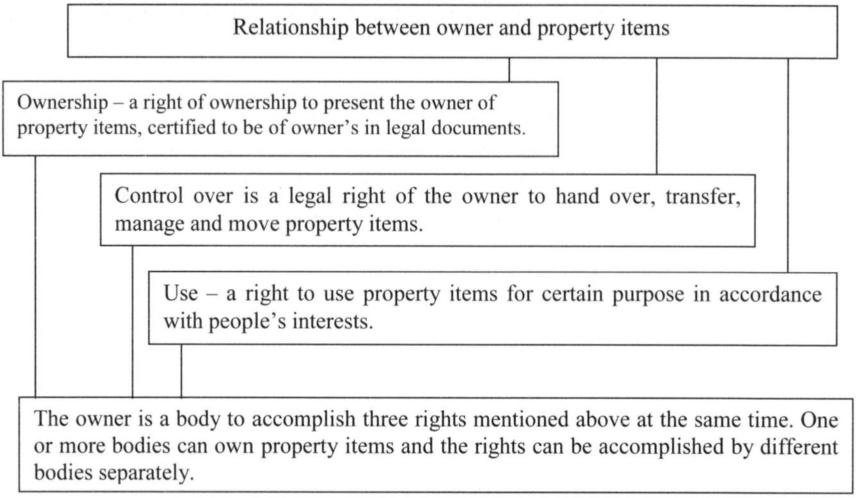

Three property rights can be accomplished separately and it is usual in practice. To identify entities and manufacturers with such relations, a term "sector" is used and it is shown in table 6.1.

Table 6.1. Change of property relations, formation of private and public sectors

Forms of property relations			Production sector
Own	Control	Use	
1. State	State	State	Simple private structure and state-owned enterprises. Public sector
2. State	Individual	State	An organization with an agreement to control property used for public service. Public sector
3. State	Individual	Individual	An entity with an agreement to control and use. Private sector
4. State	State	Individual	A state-owned enterprise that rents its property to others. Public sector
5. Individual	State	State	A state-owned enterprise with leasing of equipment and production tools. Public sector
6. Individual	Individual	State	Use of patents to others. Private sector
7. Individual	State	Individual	Social office with an administrator appointed by the state. Private sector
8. Individual	Individual	Individual	Simple private structure. Private sector

An owner can be one or several entities. There are two opportunities to clarify their interdependence. First, the owner possesses previously created property items for a certain period of time, i.e. within limits of expiration of the right. In this case, coordination is done by the law on joint ownership. Second, people create new property items. In this case, an investor in the new object has the ownership right. Although he may not be directly involved in production and service, he participates in distribution of earnings and profit, i.e. an ownership structure of new property items may be expressed in money.

When one looks at the above two possibilities, a question 'What does the owner own and how?' arises. To answer this, let's define what are assets that are a direct reflection of property items.

<u>Assets:</u> Assets are related to someone and he/she makes a decision to use it for some purposes. For instance, land, water, forest of Mongolia and their resources are under jurisdiction of the country, and the state, representing the people of Mongolia, decides how and what they are used for.

The above relation is expressed as *management* in theoretical terminology. In figure 6.4 *majority* means the people of the country, who manage together the given property. *Minority* means that one or more individuals manage the property. The limit of the number of governing bodies is defined by related laws and regulations. For instance, public management is interpreted by law as "in public authority" or 'parliament that represents the people" or "in power of the all people" etc. It is also interpreted as "the managing body will be the state". If a number of individuals established a joint company combining their assets, they have a right to manage according to the amount of their incorporated assets (Figure 4). Entities established with both state and individual participation are called a shareholding company and management opportunities also depend on the share of property. A growing number of entities with multiple owners have been established for the last few years in many countries.

Figure – 6.4. Orientation to forms of assets

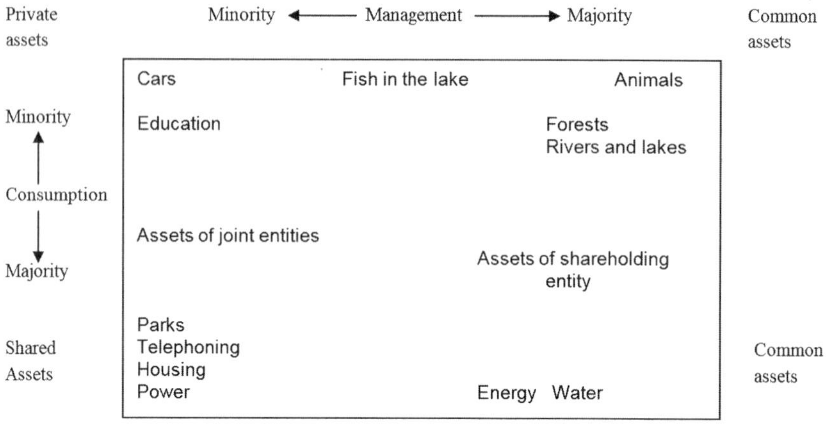

When assets is used for production and livelihood, it acquires economic features, so there is consumption. When property is used by many people at the same time, it is called common consumption and when it is used by one or two people, it forms private consumption. Common consumption is called in law "Public" and "For common purpose". Property is categorized in several forms depending on its use and management (Figure 6.4). Interpretation from figure 6.4 is as follows:

1. When property is used and managed by an individual it will be private property, and when it is used and managed by the public it will be common property.
2. There can be forms close to either of above or including features of both of the above forms.
3. When property is used by an individual and managed by many, it will be public property, and when property is managed by one body and is used by many it will be common property. Water supply sector is taken as an example of this in figure 6.5.

When an individual purchases packed water, it will be his/her private property. People drill wells to use underground water and the wells will be used by an individual or many people, so the water has features of joint/shared property. A group of people builds water channels for public consumption, so it contains features of both shared and common property, thus it will be in-between. One of distinctive features of commom against public property is that common property is created by people.

Figure –6. 5. Water supply

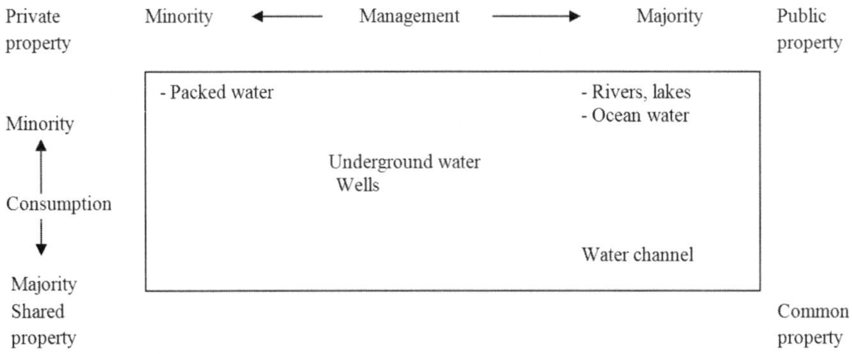

While the general concept of property is interpreted by the above methodology, there are various terms of property used in practice. Property is classified as immovable /real estate/ and movable property in relation to land ownership, and as securities, intellectual, copyright, investment and financial property associated with its usage.

Economy with various forms of property as mentioned above is called a mixed economy and is adopted by many countries in the world. It is apparent that in each country the state intervention is different due to specifics of property in mixed economy and the coordination mechanism of enterprises with various property is unique.

Differently named properties like public, state, common, collective, private, personal, cooperative and community property are used in practice. These names confuse the theoretical terminology on forms of property.

Forms of property is classification of property items depending on the owner, i.e forms of property are named after various owners who possess property items. Theoretically, there are three major forms of property as follows: a) property items with many owners are common property; b) property items that are owned by an individual or citizens are called private property; and c) property items that are owned by more than one owners jointly are called joint property. These forms have their own significance in economy and have specific features accordingly.

Private property is considered very important in socio-economic context and it becomes a solution of many vital issues of social development. Production yield of private sector is viewed to be created with support of common property. Moreover, property of state-owned enterprises, shareholding companies and associations is created as a result of joint investment, so it is helpful for development policy of industry.

The state is the owner of common property and it undertakes obligations to protect common property for the benefit of social development, to render financial support to create common assets and to create a required environment for the government, army and court. Apart from being a political structure, the state is an owner in economic activities, a powerful manufacturer and service provider. That is why the state itself forms a public sector with bodies that make laws and regulations, implementing agencies and court. In other words, the public sector becomes a consumer, a producer, an income-seeker and a sector participating in national economy activities. From the very beginning a man has used natural resources for personal needs and the state had to protect and control natural resources against effects of civilization, population density and industrialization. The subject of this classical form of private property is an individual or a free citizen and the object is public property – the nature and environment in whole. Public property that becomes private property items is owned and used by individuals and they manage it under contract, i.e. sale, rent and inheriting is coordinated in accordance with related laws and regulations.

All assets (small, medium and large) and all kinds (production, service and consumption) of property items may be owned by individual people and private assets are the most influential in economic aspect to promote production, to maintain goods-money ratio and to supply private consumption in order to develop market relations. A private owner is a legal body thus it becomes a tax payer. Difference between common and private properties is shown in table 6.2.

Table 6.2. Comparison between private and common properties

Defining factor	Private property	Common property
Consumer	Individual	Collective or many people at the same time
Consumption fee	One consumer's fee	Common fee
Qualitative and quantitive measurement of property	easy	difficult
Assessment of productional activity of property	easy	difficult
Personal choice	good	bad
Environment to make decision	Market mechanism	Political mechanism

In constitutions of most countries common property is defined as state property. State property is inseparable from state governance and it controls state intervention and forms an administrative structure. Therefore, it expresses many aspects of state activities towards state property as follows:

1. Manage public organizations and provide financing from the state budget
2. Manage national and local governments

3. Coordinate and control productional activities of state-owned enterprises

Although state property has some features against private one, its share in economy was different in different historic periods.

There is a good reason for the state to keep in its property an object that is in all people's interest. Theoretically, state property used for common purpose can be related to private sector, but legal acts are against it, which means that old society attitudes are still in place. It is obvious that such political documents are not for all people's interests and wishes. So there is a need to change property relations in order to improve production yield of state-owned production and ensure consistent consumers' satisfaction.

The state can own property jointly with other legal bodies and that is called a shareholding company. For the last ten years, numerous shareholding companies were established and their production, goods and money capital became joint/shareholding property. Associations and cooperatives are also considered shareholding property owners.

Ownership, regulation and use of shareholding property is decided by shareholders' meeting. Shareholders or legal bodies are registered as one legal body. Entities and enterprises with state participation are created when the state owns properties jointly with various legal bodies and individuals. In this case, the state participates in management through its share of property. Shareholding property can be formed also by private sectors' entities only. Current economy and legal environment allow to become a shareholder of a previously established production and service or refuse from its share.

There is a need to use different forms of property in practice in order to resolve a question of supplying human consumption. But only interests of legal bodies and strategic and procedural results of socio-economic productivity decide what kind of property forms are used in each production, service and sector. In each stage of development, the share of different forms of property was diverse. Before 1930s in Werstern Europe economic productivity was low and there was an economic crisis, although the private sector was dominant in production and trade.

The number of public sector enterprises was raised in order to provide for economic growth. Since 1990's in some countries of Eastern Europe a policy of encouraging establishment of new private businesses and supporting the private sector was followed to meet social and economic demand. As for our country, in order to make a transition to a new, market economy system, to abolish dominance of the state property, privatization was started to foster the private sector and to create a sound market mechanism.

Change of property is when rights of ownership, use and management are given to an individual or the state. A activity to make such a change is called restructuring. Property restructuring is shown in figure 6.6.

Figure 6.6. Restucturing of property.

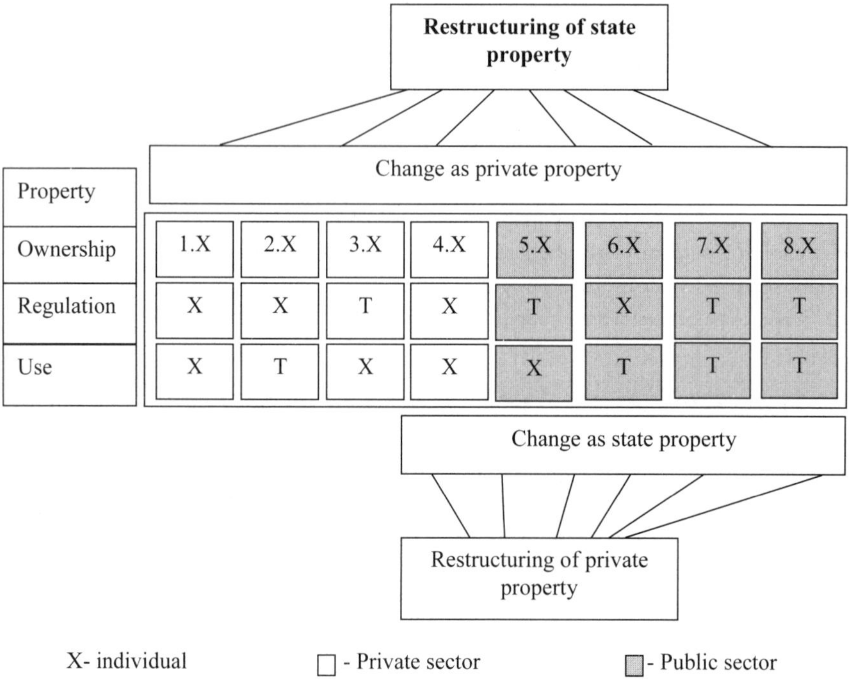

To engage in any production or service provision, if an individual enjoys all or two out of three rights, a private sector entity will be formed, i.e. privatization.

Table 6.3 Restructuring of state property (Formation of private sector)

Variations of property relations			Privatization
Possess	Manage	Use	
1.State	Individual	Individual	Privatization of management and use Private sector is formed.
2. Individual	Individual	State	Privatization of management and use Private sector is formed.
3 Individual	State	Individual	Privatization of ownership and use. Private sector is formed.
4. Individual	Individual	Individual	Privatization: private property is formed.

In the first variation some property relations such as management and utilization rights are enjoyed by individuals and privatization is conducted by the way of making a contract regarding property management and use. Such privatization is called management privatization.

In the second version some property relations such as ownership and management rights are enjoyed by individuals and privatization is conducted by the way of making a contract regarding property ownership and management. This privatization is associated with management privatization.

Private sector is formed when third version of property relations such as ownership and use rights are enjoyed by individuals. Such privatization is carried out through concluding agreement on ownership and use of property.

Private sector is formed when fourth version of property relations, such as ownership, use and regulation rights, are enjoyed by individuals. This is the full "privatization".

Globally, privatization is interpreted "change as private". Currently, privatization contains broad ranges of concepts. Privatization is used to expand human consumption through reducing framework of state actions and increasing private production and service. But change as public means to form public production and service with state and common property. These two undertakings are both directed to maintain economic development.

These two undertakings are carried out under influences of several factors in different countries depending on their peculiarities and this was interpreted by American scientist Savas as follows. Reconstruction of property is affected by several factors such as consumption, idealogical, commercial and community factors (Table 6.4) and this is shown below:

- Consumption factor on improvement of economic productivity of state-owned enterprises and provision of working condition for private sector;
- Ideological factor on rationalizing state intervention and national level management;
- Commercial factor on expansion of production and service framework and appication of profitable methodology;
- Community factor on provision of social demand in order to improve people's wellbeing.

Table 6.4. Influencing factors to change property.

Factors	Goal	Justification
Consumption social	Improve state management system	Increase economic effectiveness of service
Ideological administration	Enhance state management	Eliminate red tapes of state raise confidence on state policy, promote free market relations
Commercial	Create appropriate economic environment and expenditure with mechanism to run production	Spend state bugdet for right sectors, reduce state support of private sector
Community	Create enabling environment of consumption	People have broad range of choices for common services, provide possibility on for people collective consumption, eliminate red tapes

In Mongolia, aforementioned four factors had an effect on provatization of state property. The key factor was directed to create private sector entities in production and service. American scientist Savas noted that 'Privatization is carried out to form mechanism with private sector participation for widening scope of production and service and increasing profitability and productivity'.

Means and mechanism to combine various forms of property in economy: In preceding chapter property, property relations, economic nature of forms of property and reconstruction of property are interpreted. One of key responsibilities of property is it defines economic structure. In accordance with classical economic theory, manufacturers with private property are fully employed running production and service according to free market mechanism but in Marxist economic theory, employment is fully addressed when state runs production and service on the basis of state property. But global economy has been developing under coordinated market economic structure or mixed economy. In mixed economy there are many forms of property as well as economic mechanism is of various types. In line with mixed economy theory, state-owned enterprises have to be run through state productional mechanism and private sector enterprises have to be run through market mechanism but in fact, several mechanisms including both private and public sectors' participation are followed.

Various forms of property lead to creation of entities and other legal bodies that participate in economy, and economic structure with manufacturers with such various forms of property is developed with support of many mechnisms. As mentioned in previous chapter, manufacturers are divided into public or orivate sector depending on forms of property and this helps to set production mechanism. As noted by American scientist S.E.Savas organizational cycle connecting production and consumption is conducted through manufacturers make goods and deliver them to customers and customers finance needed production paying for goods. For instance, coordinating body to rehabilitate city streets is city governor's house, executing body is service company and customers are the people. Service company can either be private or public. As for bread production, manufacturer can either be public or private company. Bread production is coordinated by customers' demand so customers can be considered as coordinating body. As seen in these two examples, identical production can be run by different mechanisms and this is shown in figure 6.7. In this figure every part has its own responsibility. Coordinator is project initiator that chooses, represents and makes proposal. Manufacturer is creator of goods and service and preparer. Customer is financier paying to manufacturer for receiving goods or service or production supporter.

Figure 6.7. Composition of mechanisms of production

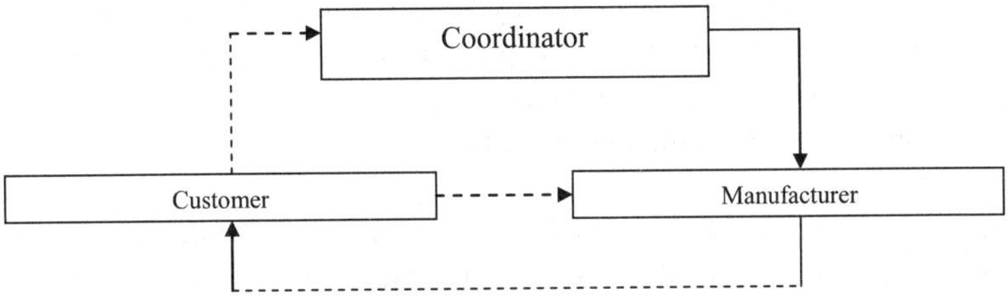

There are 10 production mechanisms depending on sector. There is market mechanism in which private sector prevails (market mechanism), 7 mechanisms including both private and public sectors (coordinated market mechanism) and 2 mechanisms where public sector prevails (public mechanism). Diagram figure on consistency of mechanisms is shown in annex 1. As explained by Dr. Savas, production mechanisms are 1) state production and service, 2) production and service of public organizations, 3) consensus among companies, 4) agreement, 5) special right, 6) allowance, 7) guarantee, 8) market, 9) voluntary service and 10) self-service and they are shown in next page.

1.State production and service. Coordinator of service is state and the people consume the service free of charge. For instance, education and army is provided free of charge by state. This mechanism is called state service (figure 6.8). Although manufacturer is state customers pay for goods and service to state (figure 2). For instance, health service is provided by state but people pay for treatment. This mechanism is called state paid service.

2. Production and service of public organizations. Through this mechanism provider of production and service is state and customers pay for production and service to state so production is coordinated by customers (figure 3). For instance, state service such as energy and water is provided by state and customers pay for consumption to state so customers coordinate supply and production of energy and water service.

3.Consensus among companies. Central higher level organization coordinates and finances local organization's activities and they in turn provide service.

(Figure 4) For instance, aimag and district police departments are financed by Central Police Office. In such mechanism, tax, court, environment conservation, road safety and fire stations are included.

4.Agreement. Private sector delivers substantial production and service to customers but
coordination and financing are done by state (figure 5). Public organization and private sector enter into agreement and provide production and service. For instance, buildings are built by private sector but coordinated and financed by state. Price tariff of freight and flight services is coordinated by state.

5.Special right. Private sector's production and service is coordinated by state and customers pay for that production and service (figure 7). Telecommunication sector's licences are given by state and price tariff is adjusted by state. Here customers are coordinator. But in this mechanism, customers are not always coordinator. For instance, programs of radios and televisions are broadcast irrespective of customer i.e customers can not influence the service.

Figure 6.8. Means and mechanisms to combine various forms of property in economy

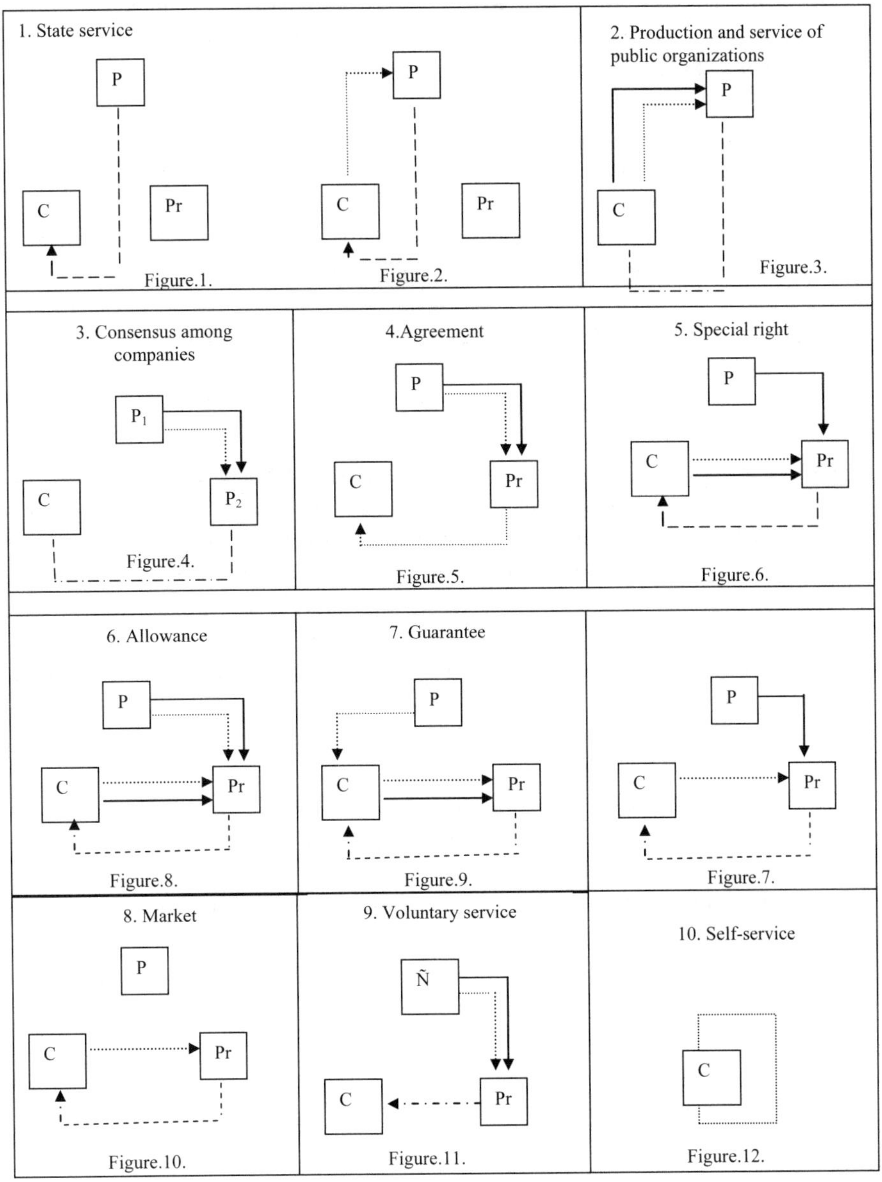

PS: Coordinator, P – Public sector, Manufacturer, Pr – Private sector, Financier C - Customer

6.Allowance. Private sector can be supported financially by state in order to run production and service (figure 8). Agricultural production is supported by state granting tax and credit incentives. Customers purchase ready-made goods so they become one of the coordinators.

7.Guarantee. Customers are granted capital and financial support by state and this is called guarantee (figure 9). For instance, students are granted free bus ride concession.

Blue licence that is given to the people during privatization of state enterprises and food concession tickets are also financial support of state.

8.Market. Private production and service is directed to customers' needs because customers pay for them (figure 10). In free trade, customers choose and and buy goods for their needs so they become coordinators.

9.Voluntary service. It is when people run production and service through their interest and initiatives (figure 11). In many countries there are fire stations that were established voluntarily. In Mongolia, voluntary funds for kids like 'Tsetseg' and 'Oyuntulkhuur' work through this mechanism. Voluntary service is performed concluding an agreement with private sector. Nationwide activities are carried out by voluntarists' initiatives and financing. For instance, Olympic Games in Los Angeles and Statue of Liberty were realized by private sector and voluntary financing and coordination successfully. In Mongolia this mechanism was used to build statue of Janraiseg burkhan and wrestlers' palace.

10.Self-service. Domestic services such as driving own car, growing up children, reading books and newspapers and making food are included in this mechanism.

State coordination and policy are of great importance what mechanism is used in each production and service. Because there is no perfect solution of mechanism in each production and service. Following questions are used to create property newly or change property.

1) Is it specialised service?
2) Is manufacturer multi-sided?
3) Is productivity efficient?
4) What is scope of production?
5) What is ratio between expense and profit?
6) Is it open to customers?
7) Are there any possibilities to cheat?

8) Is there equal economic relations?
9) Does it serve minorities equally?
10) Is there any commandism?
11)Is state inspection effective?

Considering these questions, mechanism is chosen. Mechanisms that accord with the questions are shown in table 6.5.

Table 6.5. Criteria used for choosing mechanism for running production and service

	Mechanism										
Criteria	State service	Production and service of public organization	Consensus among companies	Agreement	Special right	Subsidy	Guarantee	Market	Voluntary service	Self-service
Specialised service	+						+	+	+	+
Multi-sided manufacturer				+			+	+		
Effective productivity				+	+	+	+	+	+	
Broad production scope			+	+	+	+	+	+	+	
Low expense		+	+	+	+	+	+	+	+	+
Open to customers		+			+	+	+	+	+	+
Possibility to cheat	+		+	+		+	+		+	
Equal economic relations										
Serve minorities equally	+		+	+		+	+		+	
Commandism	+	+	+		+					
Low state inspection				+	+	+	+	+	+	+

Productional mechanisms are shown in table 6.6 depending on establishment of public and private sectors. As seen on the table, one version to create private sector is running production and service through market mechanism.

Table 6.6 Creation of private sector, mechanism of activities

Forms of property relations				Mechanism to run production and servcie
№	Ownerhip	Regulation	Use	
1	State	Individual	Individual	Allowance, Agreement, Special right

2	Private	Individual	Individual	Agreement, special right
3	Private	State	Individual	Agreement, special right, allowance, guarantee
4	Private	Individual	Individual	Market, voluntary service, guarantee

In each country running production and service through market mechanism is different and this is expressed in next chapter.

6.2. MANAGEMENT AND ORGANIZATION OF COMPANY

In Mongolia state property reform started in 1990 and this was confirmed by new Constitution and civil law. In the framework of the reform, there has been legal environment for creating private property. In 1991 new law on business entities was adopted and this had an effect on change running business. According to this law, people have right to run entities not only privately but also they can establish company or cooperative jointly. This law enables people to choose and run business through their interest. In line with the Law on Business Entities, there are two types of cooperatives with full and infull liabilities. People run business joining their properties and members are responsible for related activities through their share of property and this is called cooperative with full liability.

Different kinds of entities operate in Mongolia in the framework of existing laws and regulations (figure 6.8). A company was first emerged in England in the late XIX century when trade was done among countries. As global concept, company is a legal body that operates when invested capital of shareholders are divided in shares.

Figure 6.8 Forms of entities in Mongolia

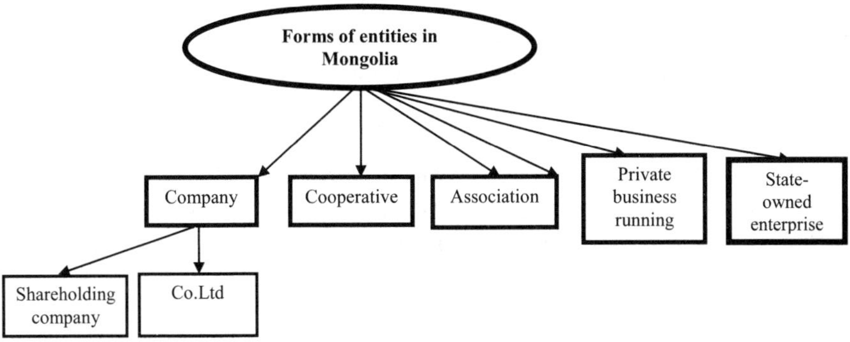

Company is the most common form of entities and this plays key role in economic development of many countries. It is divided into several types according to its forms:

- Shareholding company
- Company with limited liability
- Company with extra liability
- State-owned enterprise

Company with limited liability (Co.Ltd). This was first established in Germany in XIX century due to inflexibility of shareholding company and eradicating limited features of fully responsible cooperatives. Its key distinguishing features are:

- Its property is formed with properties invested by members
- Members have responsibility through amount of their invested capital
- There is possibility to combine and use resources and human skills as following:
    1) Joining property is preferred to joining work force
    2) Shareholders do not have to work for a company
    3) Shareholder can be several companies' shareholder
    4) Any legal body can be a shareholder (can be not professional)

- It is easy to increase and reduce shared capital (minimal amount is fixed)
- Few shareholders (there is tendency to limit numbers according to law)
- Basic document to set up company is an agreement and rules of establishment
- Not compulsory to inform financial and activity reports
- Liquidation is decided by shareholders' proposal

Except for these, it is not easy to quit or enter a company for shareholders. At first shareholder has to make a proposal to sell her/his own shares to other shareholders and if they do not intend to purchase, shares can be sold to others now lower price proposed to the shareholders. Shareholders' permission is needed to give a share as present.

Company with limited liability can have one shareholder. As for our country this type was quite common but it was not always appropriate to mobilize capital and money to expand business so recently joint forms have prevailed.

Shareholding company. Shareholding company is shared capital is divided into certain numbers of shares, and shareholders have responsibility through their amount of shares. In Mongolia first shareholding companies were established when state-owned enterprises were transferred into forms of shareholding company, and their shares were sold as Investment certificate through stock exchange. Through this way therewere about 470 shareholding companies between 1992 and 1995 and since then some of them have become company with limited liability due to various reasons. There are about 390 shareholding companies according to the most recent census of entities.

Specific characteristics of shareholding company are:

- Shared capital is divided into shares that define percentage of invested capital
- Shares can be transferred to others
- Shareholders' registration has to be always kept
- Shareholder has responsibility through his/her invested capital
- Management structure is large, and it has to be independent and professional
- Number of shareholders is not limited by the company's rules

Shareholders of shareholding company can conclude a contract to mutually limit their regulating right of shares on the basis of agreement.

Company with extra liability. It is similar to company with limited liability as for structure and organization. It incorporates extra (subsidy) capital from shareholders during shortage of capital. This is described in detail in the establishment contract and rules. Members have extra responsibility. For instance, when one of shareholders goes bankrupt other shareholders take responsibility equal to their number of shares. This is the advantage of such company to attract other financiers and investors' interest. This form is quite common in Russia and other countries recently. In Mongolia, there is no such company currently. Extra responsibility is incorporated in company's name.

In the Law on Company "A legal body of which main objective is for making profit, and has its own property, and shared capital of a shareholder is divided into certain numbers of shares is called a company".

In civil law of Mongolia (2002) it is stated that legal body is organized one that runs stable activities to reach certain goals, has responsibility for consequences of its activities through the property and has separate capital. Company governance is a system of management and control for activities of a company. Company governance structure defines division of duties and rights, terms of references and rules of decision making of the participants in company's actions like councils, departments, managers, shareholders and others.

Equivalent of a company in Mongolia is named a corporation in the USA. There was certain difficilties in development of company. For example, when company 'British East India' was set up, British parliament gave permission for it. There have always been efforts to make a company with legal status similar with as human. Thus in western countries corporate social responsibility is followed now. There is strong public view that any decision of company may cause any consequences in society so it must be considered well. This is because society became company dominant. From medieval period company played important role in society and at present our society became corpoarte society. For instance, as for the USA, company was basic form to run business in the early period of the independence movement. Development history of the USA is inseparable from companies' activities.

In Mongolia, centralization of shares of shareholding companies became intense and companies were privatized in real way since start of second security market or cash transactions. First transaction of shares of state-owned enterprises that were later changed into 'Shareholding companies' was conducted through investment certificate at stock exchange of Mongolia on 7 February, 1992. Since then 1989.9 thousand shares and dividends with nominal price of ₮ 13.9 billion are sold by investment certificate until August of 1995. As a result, over 50 percent of manufactured products, 90 percent of livestock and production and service were transferred into private property. During the period, 475 state-owned enterprises were changed as Shareholding companies of which 241 enterprises were fully privatized and 5-90 percent of shares of 234 companies were left in state authority.

Before selling shares of privatized shareholding companies, law on "Securities" was adopted in September 1994 and Committee for Securities was established in order to take organizational measures such as forming legal environment of security market and operating independent companies etc. At that time, laws on cooperatives and associations that regulated activities of shareholding companies did not meet the requirements of the time so the law on company was newly adopted in 1999 and amended in 2002.

1. Company – a legal body. Process of formation of companies in Mongolia is related to its choice of transition to multi-sector economy i.e. it is directly connected to the economic theory that society develops on the basis of individuals' initiatives became stronger. There might have been incorrect view that company and founder of company are the same thing. On the other hand, formation of current companies especially shareholding companies is inseparable from privatization process.

In view of Mr. J. Batkhuyag, researcher of privatization, Mongolia's first companies were established in 1991 with a form of a shareholding company. Relations associated with all forms of entities were coordinated by the Law on Entities adopted at that time and this led to emergence of "contemporary forms of company and limited liability" in Mongolia.

As a result of 3 years' intensive privatization, second stock market was launched in Mongolia. In connection with this, law on cooperative and company was adopted in

1995. This law was based on European and North American models and had more detailed organization than the previous one. Previous law had some characteristics of state inspection but the new one tried to make complex coordination and preferred structure of shareholders' responsibility in company's actions.

Three-tier system was changed into two-tier by the new law thus there was structure with shareholders' meeting or board of representatives as we understand now. Company has following forms:

- Open or shareholding company that shareholders' capital is divided into shares and shares are sold to community freely;
- Close or company with limited liability of which shareholders' capital is divided into shares and their regulation right is limited by company's rules. A company's right and activities are coordinated by a shareholding company's legal environment and it is as follows:
- Shareholder of a shareholding company has right to regulate and sell his/her own shares irrespective of other shareholders' view;
- Number of shareholders is not limited by company's rules;
- Shareholding company can issue shares and securities on the basis of open and close order if it is not stated differently in company's rules. Purchaser of added shares issued on the basis of close order has right to regulate and sell them further freely.

2.Setting up a company and its activities. A company can run all activities that are not prohibited by law and it takes up rights and duties to implement those activities. A company which will carry out actions that require special rights operates its activity after getting written permission from related organization. A company is operated for uncertain period of time if it is not stated differently in company's rule.

Responsibilities of a company and shareholders are:

- Property of a company is made up of owned property and rights of property and a company takes responsibility for the whole property;
- A company is not responsible for the shareholders' duties;
- Shareholder is not responsible for the company's duties, and he/she takes responsibility as his/her amount of shares;
- Loss that is occurred as a result of wrong action of single or collective owner of more than 10 percent of company's shares will be compensated by his/her own capital;

- Shareholder takes responsibility together with company for company's liability with his/her own capital and right of capital if his/her invested capital and right of capital is not restricted from private capital and right of capital.

A company can be established newly and reformed (uniting, dividing, spin-off, changing). In case of establishing a company through privatization, state is responsible for duties of founder, and order, sale and transfer of shares is performed according to law of state and local property. Founder of a company can be a citizen of Mongolia, a citizen of foreign nationals and stateless person. Shares of company can be owned by a citizen of Mongolia, a citizen of foreign nationals and stateless person.

Rule of company. Rule of company is a company's internal legal document about company's management and organization and coordination of basic issues of its activities.

3.Securities of company. Taking order of shares intended to community during establishment of a shareholding company is carried out under rules and regulations of the Committee for Securities. To issue shares, following things have to be considered:

1. Shareholding company does not refund capital that is used to purchase shares to investors. When investors purchase shares they finance expenses for a long period of time.
2. Company tries to pay dividend without guarantee.
3. Company will try to set amount of dividend not considering net profit that will be earned. Although there is net profit, a shareholding company can spend it for expanding production and service not paying dividend. A company earns money issuing securities through depositing shares and uses the earned money to form circulating capital and production and non-production capital.

Purchaser of shares has to pay attention on following things:

- Shareholder has possibility to manage the company;
- He/she has right to get profit. He/she gets profit as dividend from company's profit.
- Pay attention to net increase of assets in connection with possible price rise of shares at market. This is key point to get shares.
- To seek possibility to receive any service or products of a shareholding company.
- He/she has preference to get new or added shares.

Share is representation of owner. Shareholder is a co-owner of company and enjoys rights arising from shares. Share is security without a fixed term and shareholder's right is kept during existence of a shareholding company. Co-owners are one legal body regardless of right's dividing among owners. When share is concentrated number of shares goes down and market value of shares goes up and equity capital stays constant.

Types and characteristics of shares. Shares can be named, declared and authorized depending on ownership. In Mongolia only named shares are sold at stock exchange. Shareholder of an open company sells his/her own shares without other shareholders' permission. As for close company, shareholders have preference to sell shares. Shares are divided into issued and announced depending on issuance.

Shares can be ordinary and preferred depending on share's right. Due to privatization of state-owned enterprises, ordinary shares were issued. Ordinary shareholder has right to attend and vote in shareholders' meeting. A shareholder has right to get appropriate property for his/her shares when dividend is allocated and the company closed down. Preferred shareholder does not have right to vote in shareholders' meeting but he/she has right to get dividend and property suitable for his/her shares when the company closed down and dividend is allocated.

Dividend. It is allocated profit of a shareholding company suitable for a nominal price of shareholder's shares from net profit earned throughout a year. A shareholding company has to decide whether to allocate dividend or not. A shareholding company that announced to allocate dividend has to pay the same dividend for similar type of share for a given period.

Dividend can be paid cash, securities and in a form of property of the company and other bodies. In case of not paying dividend on time, a company pays fine through shareholders' claim and the company's administration is responsible for the loss related to this.

Some negotiations are of great importance for a company so to conclude important contracts permission from Board of Representatives and Shareholders' meeting is needed. Herein, agreements worth more than 25 percent of company's ordinary shares that issued previously, or securities equal to it, are included in this type of contract.

4.Financing of a company. Bigger companies find financing with support of share capital, accrued profit, credit and security market. They are as follows:

1. All companies have shareholders and they purchase the company's shares and pay for them. This money is not refunded except it closes down so this becomes long term financing for a company.

2. Accrued profit is increased capital as a result of company's activities of which some or all of it is spent on working capital and other financing. It is earned capital. It is not money.

Accrued capital=net profit-dividend

3. Company's financing is made up of share property and accrued capital but they do not fully provide company's needs. Share property is not increased constantly. Only shareholding company has right to sell shares to community. So financing with credit is flexible and "reliable".

4. Bigger companies issue and sell bonds to get financing from investors. In article 42 of Law on Company "Company can issue bonds with condition of taking back pledging its own property and paying fixed interest after certain period". Among above four means, financing of share's and accrued profit seems least risky since there is no need to pay back and pay interest.

5.Management of company. Some scientists tend to compare management structure of a company with political structure. It is understood that for instance, shareholders' meeting is "the people", elected "king" is "Athens" (company with limited liability) a small town; or shareholding company that is not possible to directly elect by "the people" (large population), parliament i.e. Board of Representatives is set up by contemporary country (shareholding company).

There are several forms of management of a company according to the Law on Company:

1. Shareholders' meeting (company's governing body is a shareholders' meeting)
2. Executive director or group (day-to-day activities are coordinated)
3. Inspection council or inspector (Shareholding company shall have inspection council)
4. Board of Directors (company's governing body will be Board of Directors in absence of shareholders' meeting)

Shareholders' meeting is consisted of all shareholders and it has right to decide all issues except from some issues related with existence of the company.

Executive management. This includes executive body and its group. Salary of executive body is fixed by shareholders' meeting or Board of Directors concluding contract. Executive body's rights and duties shall be in the framework of company's rule and contract concluded with Shareholders' meeting or Board of Directors.

Requirements for executive body: It can not be chair of Board of Directors and in accordance with the law Executive body and its members can not work in management unit of other companies at the same time.

Duties and responsibilities: According to the Law on Company, officers have to work faithfully for a company's interest and perform his/her duties stated in internal rules and regulations of a company. In case of failure, he/she takes responsibility for it in accordance with the contract and article 10 of the Law on Company.

Inspection council has right to monitor performance of decisions made by Shareholders' meeting and company's rule, draw a conclusion on management activity and financial reports and introduce it at Shareholders' meeting, inspect business and financial activities of company on the basis of customers' complaint i.e. its main responsibility is to protect shareholders' interests.

Shareholding company has to have a Board of Directors and company with limited liability can have it and Board of Directors is responsible for following things:

1) Define key objective of company's activities
2) Convene regular and irregular meetings
3) Decide on agendas at Shareholders' meeting, define shareholders who have right to vote and other things related with the meeting;
4) Issue shares within the limit of amount and type of announced share;
5) Issue securities;
6) Set market value of property and property right;
7) Elect, change executive body of company and define its responsibility;
8) Define conditions of contract that will conclude with executive body of a company and arrange amount of bonus, incentives and responsibility for it;
9) Select auditor of a company and decide provisions of its contract ;
10) Review annual financial and activity reports of a company;
11) Ratify terms of reference of a Board of Directors and Executive body;
12) Set amount of dividend and decide its rules;
13) Demand to conduct irregular auditing in accordance with the article 91.2 of the Law on Company.

Summary and comments

1. Combination of private and public properties has been developing in Mongolia and global experiences regarding this unique structure especially characteristics of various forms of property, state ownership or co-ownership of property, transfer of rights of ownership, regulation and use to others have been studied thus new concept is being introduced suitable for Mongolia's situation.
2. There might be several versions of property change when state transfers its right to own, regulate and use its property to others:
   - Transfer of these three rights to individuals is called privatization of property;
   - Transfer of rights of ownership and regulation to individuals is called privatization of management ownership;
   - Transfer of rights of use and regulation to individuals is called privatization of management use;
   - Transfer of rights of ownership and use to individuals is called privatization of management ownership and use.
3. To transfer state right of property ownership to individuals, coordination can be done by leasing contract:
   - Transfer of state right of property ownership to individuals is coordinated by management contract;
   - Transfer of state right of property use to individuals is coordinated by renting contract.
4. According to comparative study of main differences of current "Proprietorship", "Cooperative", "Association" and company, there are several differences on concentration of required resources and investment to carry out activities, its legal environment and responsibility adjusted to their equity amount. It is apparent that the basis to form corporation is shareholding company with legal environment.
5. In order to strengthen corporation, laws on company and securities have to be improved approaching similar international laws suitable for ever-changing environment.

List of used books:

1. " OSSK" Rules of Company with Limited Liability 2006
2. Chistopher D.Stone, Where the Law Ends, 1975
3. Deyeloping Mongolia s Legal Framework ; A Needs Analysis ADB, 1995 t.8
4. John.T.Marlin, Contracting municipal seryies, New York, 1984
5. Lipton and Sachs, Priyatization in Eastern Europe, 1991
6. Madsen Pirie, Priyatization; Theory, Practice and choice, England, 1988

7. Modern Business Law and the regulatory enyironment,3 ed , McGraw-Hill, Inc, t, 728
8. R.W. Hamilton The Law of Corporations in a Nutshell, 5 ed t 1
9. Steye.H.hanke The Theory of Priyatization Washington 1985
10. Witold Wolkowiak, Priyate Sektor and Priyatization in Poland 1990
11. Alexeev.M.Yu Securities market Moscow 1992
12. Anderson.J, Korsun.J, Murrill.P Report of Study on Post-privatization Mongolia 1997.05.20
13. Ayush.B "Development of legal environment of Securities Market" Presentation on conference of 15th anniversary of MSE
14. Маккониелл. К.Р Брю.С.Л Economics Moscow 1992
15. Presentations of seminar called "Privatization and Private Sector" 1996.10.01
16. Civil Law of Mongolia 2002
17. Law on Company of Mongolia 2002
18. Law on Cooperative of Mongolia 2002
19. Statistical compilation of Mongolia 1998
20. Law on Association of Mongolia 1997
21. Privatization UB 1998
22. P.Luvsandorj Key issues of development of People's Republic of Mongolia, UB 1980
23. Савас.Э.С Ключ к рынку Москва 1992
24. Reference of State Committee of Property UB 1998
25. Tuvshintulga. A " Securities, products of property market, economic growth of service" UB 2006
26. Шупыро.М.Т Преобразование государственной собственности Москва 1997

CHAPTER SEVEN

REFORMS OF ACCOUNTING SYSTEMS

Brief Introduction

It has been over 15 years when National Project "Accounting and Financial Information System Reform", suited to the market transition in Mongolia and information globalization has been implemented. During this period in the frame of the development of accounting, reporting and controlling system, a number of projects have been implemented, the Accounting Law, Auditing Law and Law of Statistics have been enacted and substantial progress has been made in financial data processing.

Although reforms of information system have been introduced in Mongolia and there has been a progress among the countries, where market has been formed, in evitable requirements have emerged to the further development of national accounting, financial reporting, and auditing and analysis systems and to accomplish professional policy and controlling system.

This chapter summarizes development processes of Accounting, Analysis and Auditing systems, which have been formed in Mongolia and raises the issues of the national features and specifics of the systems, financial reporting evolution of business and state-sectors and the directions of mid-term issues of the national survey. Development review and trends of financial analysis have been combined and some research, conclusions of financial capacity of business entities has been reviewed.

We have tried to reveal the global tendency of accounting development, environmental changes, the problems of regional and national reforms, features of information supplier and consumers and current problems of national accounting and financial reporting, suited to the transitional economy.

7.1 REFORMS OF ACCOUNTING

Previously Mongolia lacked of data transforming and models of measurement study, different from simple entry, since 1920 basis of double entry and data base; in 1930 financial statement of memorial based nominal price; since 1940s cost budget and basis of accounting were established. Journal entry has been utilized sine 1960; the establishment of mechanization of accounting has been emerged since 1970s and in the 1980s thrift, check account and normative cost accounting have been implemented since 1980.

During this historical development period the centralized accounting system, compatible with the planned economic model, hard price and monopoly structure, had been effected and because the system had not reflected world standards, trends and there were differences, the formation of market system had met evident obstacles. Thus, since 1990 the system was released and information globalization has been merged.

First period of the reforms (1993-2006): The period was directed to accept international standards of financial statement in the national frame and to form the ideology of transforming to world standards. The goal was successfully implemented through series of projects and actions. Financial assistance and free grants from World Bank, Asian Development Bank, UNDP, Australian Government and other donors were played prominent roles. In order to create accounting and auditing systems, the requirements were emerged to create proper legislation environment and to produce qualified staff and upgrade the staff. With this goal "Mongolian Accounting Law ", "Statistical Law" and "Auditing Law" were enacted and National Strategy of developing accounting and auditing capacity was developed and number of projected were implemented.

Since the enact of "Accounting Law" (1993) governmental, public and private organizations and entities such as: Department of Accounting Policy and Methodology, Professional Body of Accounting, Institute of Certified Public Accountants, National Auditing Agency and Independent Auditing Organization were established and Mongolia became the member of the International Accounting Union.

In the frame of development policy of accounting and auditing, more attention was considered to upgrading the skills of professional staff and the national system of renewing curriculum and programs of universities and institutes; training, upgrading and selecting certified public accountants- auditors was created. The governance, control and legal environment of certified public accountants were established at the proper level and the programs of training and upgrading the staff were renewed. The title of "Certified Public Accountant" was awarded those, who attain specific theoretical, practical and professional requirements of accountancy and auditing. A number of professional textbooks, International Accounting and Auditing Standards, brochures, methodological materials, explanatory dictionaries of financial and accounting terminology were translated into Mongolian. The process of adjusting financial statements to the world standards has began since 1995and the process of creating national instructions and regulations and experimenting in business and budget environment was the turning point in the reform of accounting system.

In the frame of good governance, the start of information reforms was set up successfully in our country and we have made considerable progress among the countries, where market economy has been established. However, accounting and auditing system, suited to world standards has not been formed completely and the information reform, professional policy and controlling structures are in outset.

Second period (2007-2020): The main goal of the period will the completion of accrual basis of estimation, statements of nominal (constant) price and models of profit valuation and the improvements of Mongolian National Accounting System and extraction of base parameters of taxation system to the world standards. The requirements are put to develop accounting information technology and professional service.

The requirement – 1: Developing accounting services, policy regulations and controlling system with national specifics, not cheating foreign models and reaching to the world standards.

The requirement – 2: In terms of International Standards of Financial Statements (ISFS) and Declaration of International Public Sector Accounting Standards (DIPSAS), due to many reasons such as: development differences, national features and banking loan traditions, there are many issues that do not suit to the conditions of our country. Moreover, it is common to raise relations not formed yet.

The requirement –3: Security and stock market has not developed properly in Mongolia and derivative stocks and fund compound structures such as exceptional shares, floating stock, options and share rights have not formed yet.

The requirement – 4: Due to the imperfection of financial valuation models and indicators, the classical development theories (Keins theory of Government regulation; E. Fisher, M. Freedman, L. Mizes. R. Mandell's theory of money supply and fund policy; P. Samuelson, J. Hiks's theory of economic phase) do not suit to Mongolian ground, but there are other images appear for us.

Targeted results: Accrual –based, fixed- priced accounting and information service will be created in its actual interpretation and national accounting system and footnotes of the basic parameters of taxation system will be improved to the world standards.

At the moment in the frame of good governance, International Standards of Financial Statements (ISFS) and Declaration of International Public Sector Accounting Standards (DIPSAS) are needed to be utilized directly and enriched with national specifics, amendments should be proposed; some standards are needed to be clarified and each standard should be clarified in the national frame. It is required to consider all above potential alternatives the countries, which are in the market economy and enter the globalization.

In terms of our condition, the experiences and alternatives of the countries such as Cyprus, Kuwait, Latvia, Pakistan, Trinidad, Tobago, Horiatis, which copied foreign models directly, will not suit, but those of Australia, Hong Kong, Denmark, Italy, New Zealand, which approve International Financial Reporting Standards (IFRS) and Declaration of International Public Sector Accounting Standards (DIPSAS), where each standard was selected by comparing and clarifying in the national level, will be perfectly suited in Mongolia.
The policy regulation scheme of national financial reporting in our assumption can be the following:

- Legislation environment;
- IFRS, DIPSAS: national selection, provisions and interpretations;
- Policy regulations, control: (instruction, regulation, guidelines);
- Accounting policy regulations of organizations and enterprises.

To approve IFRS, DIPSAS it is required to study and determine national patterns, compatibility and correlations; to formulate main provisions to be utilized in Mongolia; to prepare the interpretations for enterprises and to move to the final utilization.

The models of national provisions and interpretations of each standard are needed to:
First: make fewer the offered alternatives / main or possible/; *second:* add articles, exercises and samples, suited to certain condition; *third:* focus national specifics and development distinction.

The goals of parameter modeling of selection, provision and interpretations:

a) Maintaining compatibility and harmony of IFRS ISFS and national standards and eliminate differences;
b) Supporting professional entities to prepare national instructions, guidelines, to record similar function and to shorten the alternatives
c) Assisting financial statement – providers to analyze actions and make conclusions;
d) Assisting auditors to make professional conclusions on compatibility of measurement models and statements with ISFS.

Our survey reveals besides the documentation of National declaration, parameters of IFRS, DIPSAS selection, provision and interpretations concern 5 chapters and 55 standards (of it 35- business environment, 20- state sectors), concerning financial statement, assets, property, liabilities, income measurement and financial outputs.

Examples of national selection and provision and interpretation parameters in terms of the standards in compliance with financial statements (IFRS- 1, IFRS - 7, IFRS -10, IFRS - 14, IFRS - 15, IFRS - 24, IFRS - 29, IFRS - 30, IFRS - 32, IFRS - 33, IFRS - 39) it is required to concern accounting policies and procedures, financial measurement and statement scopes, provisions, segment, interim financial statements, monetary transaction, financial instruments and reporting over inflation.

Standards of property, assets and liabilities (IFRS-2, IFRS -16, IFRS -17, IFRS -19, IFRS -20, IFRS -28, IFRS -31, IFRS -37, IFRS - 38, IFRS-40, IFRS-41) concern inventories, tangible and intangible assets, leases, investment, employee benefit and retirement benefit plan and individual pension insurance contribution accounts, government subsidy, guarantee, compensation, borrowing requirements, assessment, measurement, control and management issues.

In terms of the standards, related to the consolidated financial statements (IFRS-1, IFRS 7, IFRS -14, IFRS -15, IFRS-21, IFRS - 22, IFRS - 27, IFRS - 31, IFRS - 32, IFRS - 39) it is needed to consider measurement and statement scopes, provision, business cooperation, financial statement consolidation and minority interest statement, foreign currency, interests in joint ventures and financial measurement.

As we see, the items those need to be focused on the information models:

- Structure, tradition and specifics of the national market;
- Business structure, assets, resources, property structure, amount;
- Knowledge and skills of certified accountants;
- Procedures of information transform (manual, computerized, integrated etc.)
- Information consumer demands.

7.2 FINANCIAL STATEMENTS

Reviewing closely the experiences of the countries with good governance and the countries, where market is being formed, DIPSAS compliance and national specifics, the following alternatives with broad choices in the Public Sector financial statements occur:

- Disclosure budget financing and fund statement in cash base;
- Disclosure budget financing in cash base and fund statement in adjusted accrual base;
- Disclosure budget financing in cash base and fund statement in accrual base;
- Disclosure budget financing and fund statement in accrual base.

However, in any country Public Sector fund statements is presented in fixed (nominal) price market price movement and influence is focused.

Possible utilization and outputs of the bases to be followed in fund statement with popular specification of fixed price and historical cost measurement centered- public sector is compared:

Figure 7.1 Basis of fund statement: utilization, outputs

	Cash-based		**Accrual-based**	
	Cash based	Adjusted cash based	Adjusted accrual based	Accrual based
The legislation goal to be regulated by the Budget Law	Yes	Yes	Yes	Yes
Law and legislation requirements with limited spending	Cash demand and restrictional correlation	Cash equivalent demand and restriction	Cash and fund resources demand and restriction	Cash and economic resources demand and restriction
Resource allocation, financial resource utilization	Cash reserve,resource	Cash equivalent resource	Cash, fund reserve resource	Cash and economic reserve resource
Financing and cash demand	Cash reserve,resource	Cash equivalent resource	Cash, other fund reserve resource	Cash and other financial reserve resource
Accountability and financial capacity	Cash	Cash equivalent	Fund reserves	Economic reserve

Financial state and its changes	Cash state	Cash equivalent state	Financial reserves	Financial aneconomic reserves
Service Cost Financial performance	Data is not recorded	Data is not recorded	Recorded data is limited	Performance data needs to be evaluated is provided

Source: "Governmental Accounting, Reporting" Erdenebileg.S, Ulaanbaatar 2004

Experiences of foreign countries show accrual based accounting and fund statement is utilized widely for accumulation governmental petition, models of governmental regulation, its use and tax income and re-allocation. Cash base shows perfectly cash flow data of budget environment in the frame of legislation environment.

In terms of the complement, adjusted accrual statement comprises of financial position (remainder's balance), financial completion (Income Statement) and Cash Flow Statement. Here measurable income packs, implemented actually in financial disclosure and if measurable fund liabilities occur, all liabilities, expect long-term loan interest charges, should be recognized.

However, Public Sector funds reporting "Governmental Codes and Financial Reporting Standards" of Public Sector Committee of International Federation of Accountants (PSCIFA) of Declaration of International Public Sector Accounting Standards (DIPSAS) and Governmental Sector Accounting Committee have chosen to utilize accrual base. It has been implemented successfully by many countries, which have taken parts in the project "Good Governance and Budget Reforms" such as: Local Authority of Health and Welfare Services of Great Britain, Federal Government of the USA, Public Sectors of New Zealand, Sweden and Canada, Governmental Agency of Finland, Netherlands and Iceland, some public sectors of Germany and Ireland, local governance units of France, Italy, Switzerland, Malaysia and Tanzania.

New Zealand, Australia, Canada, Malaysia, Tanzania have measured driving parameters of long-term financial ratios, taken up in external loans, GDP of credit services (transaction, interest charges), export income and currency reserves and have revealed average indicators, which takes great interests for us. By developing completely the loan service funds management and information networks of monitoring these countries have decreased substantially external loans and public increased debt burden and increased national income, savings and productivity.

New Zealand has developed the management of the state funds and credit service funds and monitoring service and the country implemented successfully the objectives to reach the unit percentage of total credit in GDP to 30%, the unit percentage of total liabilities to 20% in 2000 and the unit percentage of total credit to 28%; the unit percentage of total liabilities to 16, 5% in 2004. New Zealand is considered as one of the few countries, which implemented accrual base in public sector funds accounting.

Mongolia, Russia and the countries of Eastern Europe, Central and East Asia, which were in centralized regime lacked of proper procedures of accounting policies, suited to sophisticated procedures of transaction, the declaration of utilization of generally accepted basis, proper procedures and regulations of accounting policies, suited to adjustment ideology and historically governmental utilization, budget accumulation and budget expenditures were recorded by cash base. In Mongolia legal environment of good governance, a budget reform has been formed and numbers of units of public sector organizations have implemented successfully the project. By developing data network and renewing recommendations of funds accounting appropriate progress has been made and the environment of fair reporting has been formed. Funds accounting with general specification, recorded well has always encouraged budget reform project and the capacity of good governance.

In order to formulate funds accounting system it is required first to study the connection scopes of public sector, the structure of the government. The structure of public sector comprised of two-scaled government unit, primary stage of budget unit and state owned enterprises.

The upper stage of public sector involves the Governance of Presidency, the parliament, Supreme Court, the Government, ministries, agencies; the middle stage involves local government, State Fund, Office of Fire Prevention, Transport Service Center, Fuel and Electricity and Bureau of Apartments and the primary budget units involve around 3500 entities as schools and kindergartens.

The establishment of the consolidate account of state fund is needed for careful investigation on the suitability of the good governance and budget reforms in order to deliver one- point service in the relevance circle.

In the relevance frame, in order to supply goods with minimum expenses and utilize efficiently assets flow, accumulated by tax and loan channels and economic reserves public sector funds reporting and monitoring environment should be made healthy. Here the importance of budget monitoring and independent control rises significantly.

Fund accounting environment is specific because of the recognition of relevance scopes:

- It is not engaged in conducting profit- making actions;

- Main income channel is tax, donations, loans and aids;
- Policies and decisions are based on the agreement of the subjects;
- Budget utilization and allocation is implemented public supervision.

Fund is asset separation action within the ratio, limitation, established by the laws, agreement and special goal. We consider it as a complicated concept of information technology and professional understanding, arisen from specific structures within the public sector relevance circle. In the frame of the concept it is needed to draw boundaries between governmental and public sector funds or equity and private ownerships.

Government fund is the package, which rights are limited by the specified norms and game rules that are with non-profitable goal and no sophisticated regulations and closed. For instance, Consolidated Income Fund, Governmental Reserves Fund and other funds are related. We have considered it to be correct to regulate and report the grant income and credit service funds to be created by foreign loan flows with government reserves funds.
Equity ownership fund is the package, which is profitable, without any limitations, with sophisticated regulations, open and free convertible. Finally, we have agreed to the concept that in order to create specific relevance scopes with the fund data packages the following requirements:

- Operational organization and game rules should be clear;
- There should be separated unit, which has rights to own and spend the fund;
- There should be approved double entry accounting system

In terms of complement, information technology of government reserves fund comprises of *credit service fund* – retained payable, transaction, interest payable, possible liabilities accounting: *assistance income fund* – agreement promise (income brans) and free (spending rights are limited) income accounting.

The important channel, the supporter of national economic capacity is free grant income, accumulated by the agreements to centralized budget grant income fund. It is required to consider all legislation environment of information network, which influences on the data fund transforming in the relevance circle, measurement model, possible alternative selection and procedures.

The data packages of free grant inventories comprises of agreement promise (income brans) accounting, grant income data with limited spending rights and centralized budget (governmental) grant income fund reporting. It is needed to create the suggested fund reporting experimental models by designing data transforming of grant in-

come with limited spending rights / receivable, non-performing receivables, expenditure, loss, fines, transaction, remainders, income brancing / and making closing entry and checking balance.
In current period, when absorbing capacity of foreign loan packages in Mongolian economy is becoming narrow and there is an increase in national economic burden, it is required to develop fund accounting data information network, suited to modern liner operational engineering, project management models by changing completely foreign loan and grant administration, monitoring and policy systems.

The specific feature of the debt administration, monitoring and policy transformation is the active implementation action of the modern project management model. Project management broadens the knowledge of development and creates new possibilities because it implements any changes and projects and based on the organization of main instrument to approve financing, liner operational engineering and the project team / analyst , coordinator, members/.

In this frame, Mongolia needs the public sector fund accounting / standards/ policy document "Basic principles of public debt service, grant income fund data transforming and reporting". The importance of the document is:

- Maintaining the compatibility of International Fund Reporting Standards and national data and eliminate the differences;
- Preparing fund reporting, according to the International Public Sector Accounting Standards and assisting to develop national regulations, rules and methodology;
- Developing information environment and network and improving macro economic driving parameters' extraction.

For this it is needed to study the following problems and formulate basic principles of fixed priced accrual based fund reporting:

a) The goals of fund reporting, consumers;
b) Features and trends of data utilization;
c) Financial element: concept, features, requirements;
d) Fund measurement, adjustment model.

In the case, when single and comparative fund reports of audited fixed price total, involving all relevance circles, regions and units, indicated in International Public Sector Accounting Standards, in the frame of foreign loan, absorbed by the government and centralized grant income fund, financial ratios are analyzed and the possibilities are formed to create driving parameters by the standards, established international organization "Moodes Standards".

It is required here to do the experimental measurement in 10 types of financial ratio indicators or driving parameters such as: the percentage of debt service per person or in nominal price of assets, interest payment- bond income, operational drives- business fund, regional income per person, operational expenses / total expense, ownership, reserve fund/, total income, debt service /total income, retained fund balance/, budgeted expenses of grant income.

To make perfect regional indicators meaning, it is needed to conduct surveillance to additional sources and parameters such as: population movements, asset market valuation, budget expectation, hypothesis of uncertain condition, income- business fund cycle, tax, customs condition, debt burden, fund administration, prospectus study of infrastructure development, probability of possible liabilities, requirements and compatibility level.

Globalization, environment changes create diversification in regions, national features of the country, tradition, ethics, culture and characters and began influencing on the developments of information technology, professional policies and regulations, controls and research. With the assistance of Asian Development Bank and other donor countries in Mongolia series of projects such as "Capability building of accounting and auditing professionals of Mongolia", "Governance Reform – Capacity building of accounting professionals of budgetary organizations" (1993- 2006); with the financial assistance of Science and Technology Fund the contract project "The structure of Accounting and Auditing of Mongolian business and non-profit organizations" and with the financial assistance of Asian Research Center /ARC/ "The Concepts of reporting Financial Statements " (2005) were implemented.

With the projects, which have been implemented by the efforts of domestic scientists and accounting staff, establishment, reform review and trends of national accounting and auditing were studied; the concepts of the developments of accounting and auditing profession and the guidelines of governmental policies were formulated; the amendments of Governmental controls and Auditing laws on Accounting were presented to the appropriate standing committee and were approved by the Great Hural and the utilization of International Financial Reporting Standards (IFRS) and International Public Sector Accounting Standards (IPSAS) were legally confirmed in the national frame.

With the results of the research Batjargal.P (on the theme: "The structure of Mongolian finance and accounting: the examples of industry" 1996); Jaavaa.T (on the theme: "Problems of the reforms of national accounting", 2003) and Gungaanyambuu. Ts (on the theme: "The theoretical problems of national standards of financial reporting",

2006) pursued scientific degrees. Moreover, a great number of publications, presentations, articles were presented and first attempts of modeling of national features, compatibility and correlations of International Financial Reporting Standards (IFRS) and International Public Sector Accounting Standards (IPSAS) have been done.

Research project reports: "Accounting and Auditing system of Mongolian business and non-profit organizations" (2001), "Framework for preparation financial statements" (2005) and monographs such as:" Current Problems of formation and reforms of Financial, Cost and Managerial Accounting" (2002), "History of double- entry accounting" (2004) and "The theoretical and practical problems of Financial Reporting, Managerial Accounting" (2006) were published for public access.

All the research works were based on the study of International Accounting Federation, the model of American researchers Hoffsted Geert, Grane. C.G., who studied the influences of ethnics and cultural variables in professional development and the research of environmental changes of Australian Institute of Public Certified Accountants. The influences of legislations, economy and culture of 28 countries were studied thoroughly and national features, compatibility and correlations were modeled, which takes great interest.

It is considered that there were no relations between legislation and economic variable, however, cultural variable influenced greatly on economic variables by grouping cultural variables with distant influences, legislation variables with civil and social laws and economic variables with industrialized and transitional. According to this, Dr. Jaavaa.T studied the conditions of our country and included Mongolia in the group of the countries, which have no influences of nomadic civilization and distance, the country with civil code, migration and small-sized economy. He concluded that the choice of national features is the state regulations in this development strip and the process of gradual movement to non-governmental and private sector is suited well to world standards. There is an interesting point in the model of the researchers to standardize the financial measurement studies and reporting culture of any country by 4 indications, such as: professionalism, uniformity, conservatism and secrecy.

Due to the positive influence of professional capacity and one –modeled tendency, the preference of conservatism to traditional practices and the risks to strangle reforms but the negative influences of secrecy to encourage hidden economy and illegality, the above mentioned features have much influence on International Standards of Financial Statements (ISFS), national features, the correlation model and the research.

Dr. Jaavaa developed the model and the features in the national frame and concluded that the standards of the reporting accomplishment are below the level (advanced training system and the growth of professional skills is low; there is a insufficient policy and regulation; the reforms are not ready yet; preference to the traditional practices; there is a widespread process of hidden economy and illegality). The studies and the national amendment and selection, the provision parameters and the interpretations, which have been done for the international standards "The concepts of providing financial statements" in the frame of "The principles of the concepts of providing financial statements" (2005) would be utilized as the main source of the further research cycle.

The 2001 alternatives of the national amendment and selection, the provision parameters (6 chapter, 150 article) of the basis standards documentation were discussed widespread (in the paper "Financial News" № 22 /58/, № 23 /59/,№ 24 /60/) and they were renewed with the financial assistance of ARS Centre / South Korea/ in 2005 and transferred for final utilization.

Governmental reforms, ideology of globalization, Anglo-Saxon accrual based fixed-priced (nominal) accounting, measurement studies of tax (accounting) profits, financial ratio indicator of macro economy, selection of driving parameters, national features are focused and the contents are directed to demolish neutral systems of centralized accounting and renew it. The mentioned provision parameters are:

1. Although there are a number of models and measuring in financial statements of business, government sectors and non-governmental organizations, Anglo-Saxon fixed-priced (nominal) accounting and historical cost measurement model is in dominance. However, creative searching has been done in the direction to convert data base to value added measurement; to coordinate financial ratio indicators of macro economy and parameters of national accounting system and to utilize financial reports for solving social issues (ecology and unemployment);
2. Transforming the completion of mentioned data base by marginal profit and economic parameters is encouraged by regional models of management accounting. Data base changes are done with the market with management procedures of budgeting, controlling and resources sand the market to observe the action, consumers and competitors such as: present value (PV); current cost (CC); market price (MP); net price value (NPV); capital accumulation price model (CAPM); based financial measurement and absorption costs (AC); direct cost (DC); job order cost (JC); period cost (PC); standards cost (SC) activity-based cost (ABC), flexible budget, accountability reporting, fluctuation

analysis, efficiency order quantity (EOQ); just in time (JIT) and marketing data packages with value segment basis;

3. A financial statement is a structured instrument with the goal of delivering information and comprises of balance, profit and outcome, the changes of financial state (cash flow, asset movement) and disclosure. The main procedure of the disclosure is notes of sources, third- party inquiries, encouraging tables and explanation. It is not necessary to notify additional clarification numerically, but it can be partially and wholly narrated. Moreover, additional sources, data, graphics and encouraging tables can be attached. The examples of such data are data of business and geographic segments, influences of value changes etc. However, reports of Board Meetings, executive debates and analysis, publications, concerning financial periods are not included.
4. National measurement features and differences are revealed in the following way. 2 principles of ISFS (accrual base and continuous processes) and Financial Accounting Standards Agency (the USA) announce generally accepted 10 principles or hypothesis. However, 7 basic principles such as: historical cost, revenue realization, accumulation realization, consistent, additional clarification, conservatism and material specifics and 5 hypothesis and assumptions such as economic separate unit, continuous process, cash unit, periodically stable, sector practice are formulated in the national business world, the value of public sector economy, accounting of fixed price and financial statements.
5. Financial element for accounting profession is general type and group package that connects the influences of financial processes with economic features. The important tendency to develop theoretical structure is to establish the frames of the element and concept in the package frame. 5 in ISFS (assets, liabilities, property, revenue and expenditures) and 10 components in the American Financial Accounting Concept Declaration are mentioned. The assumption, the features and requirements of 9 connected components such as: assets, liabilities, property, owner's investment and utilization, profit, expenditure and loss, which are concerned more in the budget, value measurement and the reports of business and economy of Mongolia, are being installed with the accrual base utilization.
6. The sketch formula of revenue and expenditure in the "The concepts of providing financial statements" is carefully investigated with the following components within the national frame:
   - Internal flow that will be created by the budget and business normal transformation such as: revenue, stock, production and service. Asset of the organization and owner's equity is increased but liability is decreased.

- Expenditure is the external cash flow, which is related with the budget and business transformation and continuous processes such as stock delivery, production of stock and servicing. It has consequences of decreasing assets and owner's equity of the organization and increasing liabilities.
- The principal formulas such as: the growth and decrease, created due to the non-continuous, occasional transaction: gains and losses; owner's usage; transactions expect investment; processes and circumstances in the property and net assets of the organization, are being put in the Mongolian accounting technology.

However, in this development strip it is the time to put the national studies and discussions in the new step and to put the science into social circulation and movement theoretically and practically. We are facing inevitable social demand and order of the development.

The followings are the modules of the current, middle-term research direction and thesis:

Module-A: Theoretical and experimental research to improve the measurement model of accrual based fixed priced accounting and tax accounting:

- The aspects of financial and tax accounting, financial analysis, auditing of financial statements;
- International Standards of Financial Statements, International Standards of Public Sector Accounting: national correlation analysis, modeling;
- Presentation and solutions of accounting of public sector and business environment;
- Improvements of financial indicators of macro economy and driving parameters etc.

Module-B: From the data usage tendency theoretical model, empirical study and management accounting aspect to create the data fund network with more perfect scaling:

Requirement 1- It is time to solve the changes of dynamic scaling of management accounting and competitive outcome in the current budget and business world

Requirement 2- Due to insufficient formation of the perfect value scaling of economy in our country, millions of dollars are lost in every second from national turnover.

Requirement 3- It is required for national corporations and companies to have the data fund and driving parameters with perfect scaling in order to do responding action in the globalization and to enter the world and regional market.

Purposed outcome: Modeling in the profit scaling of economy and driving parameters are improved, external cash flow expectations are demolished and economic value is absorbed wholly within itself.

- It is necessary to study carefully management accounting regional models (Asian. American and European) and react the evolutions;
- To raise the data network (dynamic) setting to support national marketing strategy, management philosophy, its solution and the procedural proposal;
- To improve the absolute modeling and system network such as: liner operation, expenditure flow engineering and ABC cost system.

Module-C: There is a possibility of try our strength in the following most interesting topics of international research and to contribute national decision.

- The aspects of professional history and chronology (coin, cave painting etc.);
- Scaling model of corporation reports and added value;
- Scaling of human resource, intelligence management and intellectual property;
- Scaling model of economic value;
- Paradigms of micro scaling and data fund transformation

Not only data taxation, citizen's rights, ethic features, but also mentality personal and behavioral movement, which touch consumer's behavior, emotion and psychology mentality personal and behavioral movement and correlation influences are needed for further careful study.

To conclude, many issues are needed to be solved in the development of the study of accounting reform.

7.3 FINANCIAL CONTROL

With the start of the transition of socialist countries with centralized planned economy to market relationship, in all frames of social lives many new assumptions were created and one of the practical utilizations of them was the new form of financial control – auditing, an independent form of control. According to the principle, auditing, as an independent controlling form was created in Mongolia and it was an inevitable social demand.

Previously, for the country with any auditing tradition and in the country, where auditing has been created newly, there is following real needs for auditing to be created:

1. Financial activities of an enterprise have many sides and difficulties are created to verify in documents and disclose in accounting. On the other hand, there is a possibility of containing financial statements the errors, concerned with a number of objective and subjective factors. To reveal the errors and make a conclusion there is a need of utilizing independent controlling system for the management of an organization.
2. Due to the impossibility for users of the data of financial statement to control the accuracy of financial statements, the need of an auditing expert and requirements of their use are created;
3. One of the bases for management decision to be accurate depends on the accuracy and reality of the used data. Thus, specialized, independent control is needed.

Comparing to audit, economic and financial control in Mongolia has a long tradition and the traditional form of controlling is still in use. Along with this, the origin of financial independent control is related with the certain circumstances in the society. Formation of these situations was the base of establishment of auditing. For instance, there were 3 attempts of creating auditing in 1831, 1909, and 1928 by establishing professional auditing organizations, but the attempts fell down. However, by demolishing old system and transferring to the market society, the current auditing base was formed and the auditing is developing along with its natural laws.

The main reasons of unsuccessful attempts of auditing establishment was the underdevelopment of the asset market, more precisely, stockholder's asset market and on the other hand, it is related with the unavailability of formation of legislation roots of auditing activities.

The above mentioned example shows the possibility of audit establishment, which is regarded as a form of outside independent form of financial control on the basis of creating certain circumstances, however, for Mongolia the following are thought to be the preliminary conditions for audit establishment:

1. The start of transition to market economy, formation of democratic system and the start of the process of globalization in social, especially, in economic lives;
2. The dominant property form split up and the establishment of private property began;
3. Creation of stockholders and stock market;
4. Establishment of commercial banks and creation of new roles of the commercial banks in the market and lenders;
5. Splitting up financial independent controlling system of branch ministries and special agencies and most of them were demolished;
6. The increase of users of financial data and in comparison with the previous social system the priority goal of consumers have changed significantly;
7. The condition of unrealistic and inaccurate information supply from officials of organization has been still maintained;
8. Due to the reforms of accounting system and the enact of the accounting standards, which were completely new, the possibilities of inaccuracy in the process of accounting and financial statements and internal controlling have been increased

Due to the conditions of creating these demands, there has been over 15 years of the development of auditing in Mongolia. Although it is certain of independency of auditing, during the development process auditing has had a number of types and forms because of the certain requirements. Private auditing companies have been established and independent (general) auditing was created, however, by the establishment of state auditing there was the start of auditing system.

In the frame of globalization, the big historical changes have been made in the tendency of international auditing development and auditing theories and practices have been enriched and these are considered as one of the main factors of providing auditing development. Over the last years independent control has crossed over financial frames and the auditing, which controls and concludes the services for governmental and public organizations has been established.

As for auditing types, along with the dominance of financial statement auditing, the efficiency and compatibility auditing are done and in the last years internal auditing has played a prominent role in relation with the issues of increasing the efficiency of internal auditing.

The issues of getting introduced and giving conclusions to the current state of auditing system, its structure and development level are considered as the issues of the management of auditing process, the formation of auditing legislation environment and the issues of auditing staff, the structures and organizations of auditing companies, there is a necessity of considering all types of auditing.

Management of Auditing process

There is a common standard of other countries in the world that the governmental and professional organization to take responsibilities of conducting auditing processes throughout the country, organizing and supervising. Along with that, auditing activities are conducted by the central administrative organization in charge of financial policies and the Mongolian Institute of Certified Public Accountants, a non-governmental and professional organization.

Generally, looking at the experiences of the countries around the world, for the country with sufficient experience of auditing process there is a tendency of the dominance of the professional public organization in the administration of auditing processes, however, in other countries like in Mongolia, where auditing has been newly established, there is a dominance of administration of governmental organization.

By the shift to the new system of reporting accounting and financial statements according to the international standards, "Accounting Professional Committee" was established under the supervision of the Minister of Finance in 1993 to maintain accounting and auditing processes with professional administration and the establishment of the committee has played an important role to setting up the auditing foundation from the state and the development of auditing.

Considering that the responsibilities and objectives of this non-governmental organization coincided with the professional public organization, "Accounting Professional Committee" was abolished by the amendments, made in the "Law on Auditing" of 2006, however the committee contributed greatly to enact the international accounting and auditing standards, to train certified accountants and auditors, to create auditing organizations newly, to do control in auditing processes, to create auditing legislation environment and to form auditing system.

The activities, directed to providing approvals of certified actions and abolishing them and enacting related laws, regulations and standards are being done by the governmental organization.

Along with common standards of market society, the Mongolian Institute of Certified Public Accountants (MonICPA) was established on 9 March 1996. MonICPA was the first professional public organization which is conducting its activities in direction to developing and enhancing accounting and auditing systems; creating its legislation foundation and the established training system; extending foreign relationships; implementing international accounting and auditing standards in Mongolia and developing national standards.

Auditing legislation environment and its formation:

We have mentioned the importance of creating auditing environment to develop auditing. To create the legislation environment of auditing processes "Accounting Law of Mongolia", which was passed in 1993; "Rule of Accounting and Trusted controlling organization's activities" and "Auditing Law", which was passed in 1997 played important roles. By the amendments, made in 2006 the law has been the main legislation document of auditing process.
Another important document for formation the legislation foundation of auditing process is the auditing standard. As Mongolian Law on Auditing states: "...in auditing process international standards are followed..." and auditing processes are conducted according to the international auditing standards. In the frame of this action International Auditing Standards were published in 1999 and 2005 in Mongolian language. Internal standards of auditing companies are considered in this document and it is considered as a confidential documentation because it determines the activity policies, directions of auditing companies and the methods of audit assignments. The law states of providing internal standards of the company as one of the required documentations for applying for the approval of establishing an auditing company. In relation with actual demands to develop and follow the national auditing standards, special (sector) standards and internal auditing standards, the related organizations are engaged in the activity in this direction.

Certified Accountants and Auditors

At the beginning of the transition to the market economy with the goal of giving advanced training of accountants and auditors, the actions have started to provide licenses of Certified Public Accountants since 1993 and the licenses of Certified Public Auditors since 1996. Nowadays, there are over 1600 CPA s and over 540 Certified Public Auditors.
The table shows the number of Certified Public Accountants and Certified Public Auditors.

Figure 7.2 Number of Certified Public Accountants and Certified Public Auditors

Years		1993	1994	1995	1996	1997	1998	1999	2000	2001	2002	2003	2004	2005	2006
1. Certified Public Accountants Number		16	16	105	129	187	251	323	468	637	888	1068	1167	1377	1620
Growth	Total	-	-	89	24	58	64	72	145	169	251	180	99	210	243
	%	-	-	6.5*	22.8	44.9	34.2	28.5	45.0	36.1	39.4	20.2	9.2	18.0	17.6
2. Auditors Number		-	-	-	-	39	72	113	229	273	316	398	438	490	537
Growth	Toal	-	-	-	-	-	33	41	116	44	43	82	40	52	47
	%	-	-	-	-	-	84.6	56.9	2.6 *	19.2	15.7	25.9	10.0	11.9	9.6
3. Auditors organizations Number		2	2	3	6	11	20	33	42	43	44	53	58	52	51
Growth	Total	-	-	1	3	5	9	3	9	1	1	9	5	-6	-1
	%	-	-	1.5*	2.0*	83.3	81.8	65.0	27.2	2.3	2.3	20.4	9.4	-10.3	-1.9

Source: Data of Accounting and Control Department of Ministry of Finance of Mongolia

Over the last 14 years the growth of average number of CPA in a year has increased by 133 or 80,5 per cent. In addition the number of auditors has risen to 500.

<u>*The structure and organization of auditing companies*</u>

In the development of auditing in Mongolia the important period was 1993. The establishment of 2 trusted organizations in 1993 was the start of the development of auditing companies. Currently there are 52 auditing companies are conducting their activities. The main indicators of presenting the activity growth of an auditing company are the number of the staff and customers; types of services; its structure and amount of its profit. The indicators are increasing each year and there are changes in the service types and the customers' structure.

The development and formation of independent financial control in Mongolia has the following specifics:

1. Auditing has developed newly in Mongolia. In other words, all processes to manage and organize auditing processes and train staff have been done for the first time because the tradition of independent auditing control was lacked.
2. Considering the experiences of the countries, where auditing established first, auditing is established through the activities of foreign investors by setting up the branches of a large auditing company, however, in Mongolia the establishment of national auditing regarded as a specific process. The example of this is that national auditing companies conducted their activities until 1999.
3. One of the factors of auditing establishment was the changes in property relations. Along with the privatization the preliminary condition for the establishment of auditing was set up and since 1993 (in 1991-1996 the first phase of privatization was conducted) auditing companies have been established.
4. The establishment of auditing started along with economic recession and banking and financial crisis of the country, which is the specific situation of Mongolia.

Considering the auditing system, created in Mongolia, it is now in the phase of acquiring certain development form and in the phase of further development and the following tendency is inevitable:

1. <u>National standardized auditing</u>: It is established in the frame of International Auditing Standards by establishing legislation environment of auditing and developing national auditing standards. It is closely related with the development of national accounting standards. Internal auditing and internal auditing standards of an auditing company is also related with the standardization policy. Although there are internal standards of an auditing company, these standards do not meet the requirements of general auditing standards.
2. <u>Complete auditing:</u> The content of auditing activities is determined by the practical utilization of a number of auditing types and forms. Currently, in Mongolia the service types, provided by an auditing company and profit amounts show that auditing processes are limited by only financial statements. For instance, in the condition of market competition efficiency auditing is in demand from customers. On the other hand, along with the world auditing tendency it is the important to develop the internal auditing.
3. <u>Scientific based Auditing:</u> At present it is important to create auditing based on the theoretical research to develop auditing. Developing the auditing standards with national specifics; creating auditing methodology and determining the development tendency of auditing should be done on the research base. In other words, the most important tendency of auditing development is creating auditing with the scientific basis.

7.4 FINANCIAL ANALYSIS

The implementation of the constitution ideology, which states: "...Mongolia's economy is based on different forms of property following both universal trends of world economic development and national specifics..." into lives and there is a dominance of private sector in business and the increase of its responsibility creates requirements of reforming accounting, its reporting, the organization's internal and independent, further, social or public control (auditing) system. In order to implement these requirements there is a need of the guidance of the generally accepted accounting principles and forming the accounting system, which met the international standards and suited to the national historical tradition and the specifics for the activities of the newly established business sectors and entities with different forms of property.

To consider the issues of the formation the national accounting and auditing system it is important to take consideration into not only reporting and drawing up financial statements but also into the utilization attitude towards accounting statements.

With direction of the " Accounting Law of Mongolia", which states: "...The forms and methodology of accounting reports shall be organized to develop the main economic sectors of the country, to give possibilities for property owners to analyze the actions, to make management decisions and to control..." the requirements have risen to maintain accounting record and prepare the financial statements and information fairly and properly, to do analysis and research to the reports and information and make conclusions, to develop the methodology and organization of financial analysis and to develop and comply with the analysis indication system, suited to the specifics of the activities and business sector.

The methodology and organization of the financial analysis, used previously, was fully tied up with centrally planned economic system and the accounting model.

Reforms of methodology and organization of the Analysis

To implement the reforms it is necessary to be guided with the indicators, widely used in the countries with market economy. Furthermore, the methodology of their estimation and the historical traditions and the current and future trends of financial analysis development, suited to the specifics and condition of the country should also be taken into consideration. In this frame, a number of monographs and research works have been published and PhD and Science Doctor Degrees have been pursued on the themes: establishment and development states of financial and entity activity analysis in Mongolia: establishing the analysis' position, connected with other sciences in the latest information system; determining the systems of analysis indicators, suite to the newly implementing accounting model etc.

As a result of the research we have concluded it is required to classify the financial economic analysis organization of an enterprise into internal and external analysis of an organization and to consider as important the usage issues the research result and evaluation in making management decision, to conduct the analysis systematically with the stage from general to more advanced study by connecting the research with the specifics of the activities of the organization, the forms of property and management direction and duties.

To select the indicators' system and methodology, involved in the study, it is correct to consider the research goal, the interests of research data consumers and their attitude; however, the followings are common indicators to determine financial states of business enterprises:

1. Asset of the enterprise, capital structure, components and growth;
2. Financial stability, liquidity;
3. Payment perspectives, preliminary signal of possible financial recession:
4. Utilization of the assets and capital, invested to the business, productivity and the factors, affected on them;
5. Total and net revenue of the enterprise, its allocation and cost analysis;
6. Business productivity , return on total asset;
7. Financial expenditure and leverage analysis;
8. Market (business) standards of the enterprise.

Above main chapters are involved and each of them has subsystems.

The principles that are needed to be guided to choose the indicators, suited to the research goal:

1. To choose the indicator capable of expressing financial sketches of the research object clearly and entirely;
2. The chosen indicators can be estimated using financial statements and other information;
3. The data should involve clear, required indicators to make decisions
4. Conclusions recommendations of leading researchers and scholars and progressive ideology and methodology should be taken into consideration.

Development Tendency of Financial Analysis

Development of business sector of Mongolia, distribution of financial data, and perspectives of decision-making are at the improper level. Therefore, there is a need of increasing the responsibilities of financial analysis to extend the scopes of consumers of accounting and financial statements; improving data processing and upgrading management decision-making process, its actual rationale and final results.

Since the ancient times, analysis have been used to in the process of cognitive and practical activities and it is recognized as one of the common methods of science to get to know natural and social facts, processes, their effects and consequences.

Economic analysis is done firstly at micro level, which is considered as the main economic basis of the country, or at the specific industry, corporation or in units and it determines the development trends of macro level, reasons of growth and decline and direct and indirect effects.

Researchers have concluded that feudalist accounting of XII century contained elements of analysis and auditing, however, Savary, Jacques /1622-1690/, French scholar, was the first person who studied economic analysis as the one component of accounting and gave an idea of the main assumption of brief and detailed reporting, which is regarded as the basis of modern management accounting – analysis.

In the end of XIX and the beginning of XX century financial statement analysis or publications of balance studies were printed.

To conclude, financial analysis saw its start with the simplest form of the business completion control, detailed reporting and at the certain level of the social development it became a tool of analyzing balance and financial states and the source of new types and directions of financial analysis.

Russian scholars such as Vaitsman N.R; Tatur,S.K; Bakanov,M.I and Sheremet,A.D contributed greatly on developing the position and theoretical basis of economic analysis in the data processing and economic science. Furthermore, the scholars published a great number of works on balance study, theoretical basis of economic analysis, systematic and complex tendency of analysis and factorial analysis.

For Mongolia, since the late 1930s analysis has been taught at finance-economic special; professional schools and "Business Analysis of Industrial sectors" was published by Tumen, Ch /Honored Teacher/ in 1957.

In the late of 1960s and the beginning of 1970 partial and complex analysis were done in the plan fulfillment of factories and organizations and the causes of fulfillment fluctuations were analyzed. With this goal attachment forms of financial statements of industries and organizations and indication systems were added and in some sectors there were over 60 attached forms and hundreds indicators were put in financial statements.

Since the middle of 1990 when centrally- planned economic system was demolished and International Accounting Standards have been implemented, data capacity and abundance was limited and financial statement analysis have been limited to determine some insufficient ratios because there was simplification of financial statements.

However, as a result of the studies and debate of accounting reforms in 2001 "Standardized methods of analyzing financial statement of enterprises" were developed and since 2004 regulations of financial statement interpretations and disclosures were passed out and consolidation of financial reports has been done officially. As a result the contents and scopes of financial analysis have been developed and organizational changes have been made.

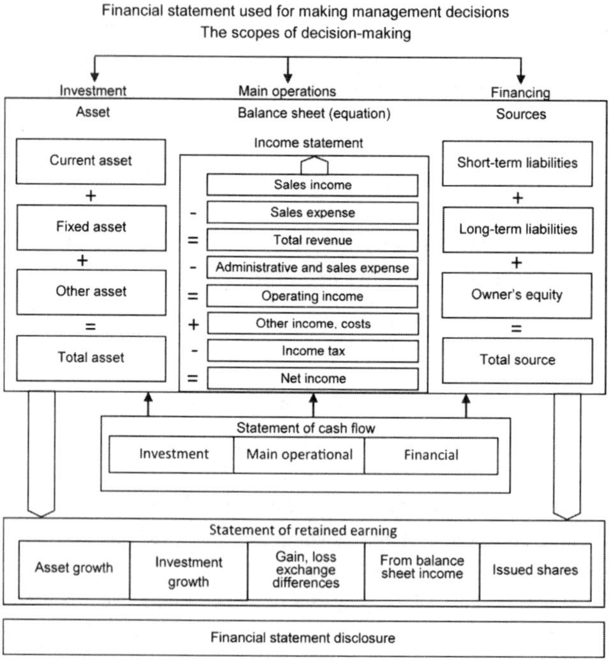

Source: Prof. Sainjargal, B

In relation with the goal, scopes of contents and directions of analysis a nimber of types and directions of analysis such as: Economic Analysis (EA); Financial and Ecoomic Analysis (FEA); Technical Economic Analysis (TEA); Operational Analysis of enterprises (OAE); Financial Analysis (FA); Financial Statement Analysis

(FSA); Management Accounting Analysis (MAA); Investment Analysis (IA) have been developed. The dominance of the types of analysis depends on management system of business, demands and needs of consumers of data, methods of analysis and organizational development.

Since the middle of the last century in relation with financial market and demands of evaluating the stock batch analysis and economic efficiency, discounted analysis of cash flow, operational analysis of enterprises, directed to determine the rationale of planned goals in the countries with centrally planned economic system and fulfillment fluctuation analysis by the factors, influenced were in dominance.

Looking at the current tendency of accounting- information system development of the countries with market economy, as a result of the dominance of financial direction of analysis since the middle of 1990s in Mongolia in the business frame " Fiancial Analysis", however, in the regional and at the sector macrolevel " Financial-Econimic Analysis" have been done mostly.

Figure 7.2

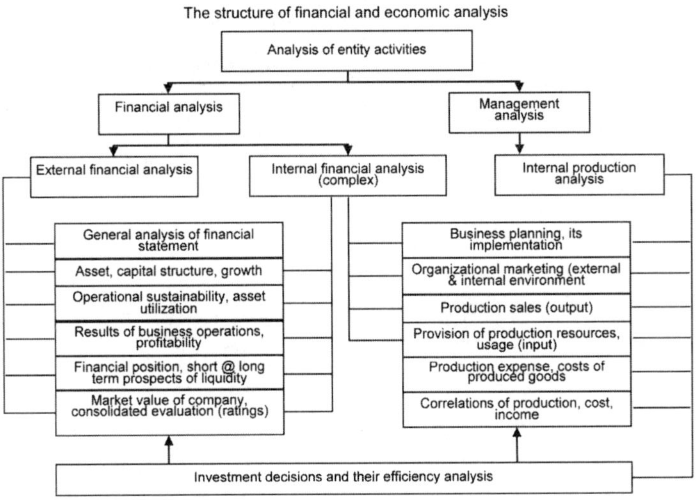

Thus, the dominance of financial direction of analysis is related with the recognition and approval of International Standards of Financial Reporting and Financial Statements worldwide and utilization and implementation of the standarts every country, considering its national specifics, on the other hand, business is flourishing and financial market is developing and globlaization is extending and as a result the responsibilities of financial management expands greatly.

For business enterprises, fiancial resources and long and short-term external finanial instruments sre regognized as the connecting nucleus of not only accounting object, but also financial reporting and financial statement and financial management, based on the fianalcial reporting and statement. One of the most important responsibilities of any business administration is to place the resources efficiently and allocate them flexible in required situations. Therefore, the importance is put to the financial direction of the economic analysis in the countries with market economy and there is a case, when economic analysis is called financial analysis. Because of this financial analysis is a component of financial management and currently, its scopes extend greatly and it is related with many issues such as:investment efficiency, estimated regarding not only finance and liquidity of the business enterprise, but also asset and business appraisal , stock and capital market and the factors of time and business risk.

7.5 STUDIES ON FINANCIAL CAPACITY

One of the main requirements of evaluating business organizations is financial capacity. Financial capacity is one of the components of ewconomic capacity of enterprises and it is a broad concept regarding the possibilities of organization's ability to absorb losses with its own funds or borrowed funds and use effectively not only liquidity but also their own equity, put into business in short period; maintaining continuous business operations and extending business.

For this reason financial capacity of a business organization can be defined as " the capacity with sufficient own equity which relates closely with economic- financial credit systems and which actively takes a part in the stock market and which financial operations have set up sustainable and the capacity, which has full accountability to utilize and incorporate efficiently financial instruments and take all financial responsibilities"

In the current practices of Mongolia there is a possibility of evaluating the financial capacity of a business organization by the following indication systems:

1. The amount of total and own equity, their structure and components;
2. Financial sustainability and liquidity;
3. Utilization of invested assets and turnover;
4. Return on investment and profitability.

We have tried to estimate the states of financial capacity development by calculating the general average of business entities and organizationg of Mongolia of the last decade (1996-2005) with main economic sectors and business entities. The sources we have used are: the research monograph, done in 2000 to determine financial capacity of business entity; "Census -2006 of business entities and organizations", done by National Statistics Authority; "Consolidated Financial Statement of 2005" of Accounting and Auditing Departemnt of the Ministry of Finance.

Facts of the Census -2006 of business entities and organizations

32,4 thousand independent business entities; 2,4 thousand subsidary companies and representatives were involved in the census of 2006 of business entities and organizations and 82,3 per cent or 26,7 thousand of total enterprises and 17,7 per cent or 5,7 thousand – budgetary and non-government organizations were involved in the census.

In the last 7 years of the 1998 Census the number of business enterprises reached 39,7 thousand and it showed 2 times increase and there were considerable changes in the structure, scopes and activity directions of the enterprises.

Looking at the structure as the end of 2005 out of total enterprises, registered in the register fund: 62,3 per cent of limited liability companies; 9,2 per cent- partnerships; 7,6 per cent - cooperatives and 0,9 per cent -shareholding companies and since 1998 unit weight of limited liability companies increased by 34,9 per cent, whilst the number of shareholding companies decreased by 1,1 per cent. 98,2 per cent of enterprises took up private-owned entities, which showed as 2005 77,4 per cent of GDP were done by them.

In 1998 the growth of GDP was 3,5%, whilst in 2005 reached 6,3% and in 2006 – 8% and total investment increased 2 times. Moreover, totally 381,4 thousand employees were engaged in business activities and the enterprises owned fixed assets worth 3468,8 billion tugrugs and made sales worth 436,3 billion tugrugs.

77,1 per cent of 26679 entities, involved in the census led active business operations, whilst others, which were not engaged in active business saw their failure as 57,1 per cent - business activities had not started or quit operations; 27,5 per cent – lack of money and finance; 4,9 per cent – lack of proper work places and skills and experiences.

Looking at the economic activity, state-owned enterprises are engaged in educational, health and social sectors, however, private enterprises are engaged in sales, finance, real estate and business service sectors. Furthermore, 90 per cent of total entities are small and medium entities, which employ 1-19 people and 84 per cent make yearly sales worth 19 million tugrugs and there is a tendency of their growth.

The followings are the main indicators of study totals, done in the above Census -2006 of business entities and organizations, the statistics of the financial statements of 1996-2005:

Total asset, financial structure

In the first years of the transition period financial states of business enterprises were poor, generally, they conducted business operations with own assets, external resources were scarce. Furthermore, due to the irresponsibility of the borrowers and non-performing loans there were bank crisis and bankruptcy.

As a scopes of business extend and financial needs increase, there is a tendency of improving management of actives and increasing the percentage of current or convertilble assests and long and short-term loan payment over the last years. It shows the improvements in business administration and financial market environment to place scarce resources, to utilize them when required and to finance sustainable growth of total business turnover, not only with own financing, but also with external resources, mobilized from others.

For instance, considering the statistics of the decade, estimated by the totals of enterprises and organizations of Mongolia (Figure 7.3) the unit weight of current assets was 27% in 1996-2000, however, it reached 38,4% in 2003-2005 and in 2006 – 40%.

In 1996-2000 68 per cent of total financing was done by own assets or owner's equity, however, in 2005 it decreased to 43,6% and the involment of external resources increased to 56,4%.

Figure 7.3 The structure of assets and financing, estimated by the totals of enterprises and organizations.

Indicators		General trends	Average of 2003-2005	Last 3 years			Average of 1996-2000
				2005	2004	2003	
1	**Asset**						
	Current asset	increase	38.4	39.7	39.3	34.6	27.0
	Fixed asset (net)	decrease	56.2	51.8	57.4	62.2	70.0
	Other asset	increase	5.4	8.5	3.3	3.2	3.0
	Total		100	100	100	100	100
2	**Current asset**						
	Short-term liability	increase	29.6	31.3	31.3	26.3	14.0
	Long-term liability	increase	26.1	25.1	25.1	27.6	18.0
	Owner's equity	decrease	44.3	43.6	43.6	46.1	68.0
	Total		100	100	100	100	100

It is needless to worry for banking and financial organizations (lenders) when there is an increase in loan payment involment in financing and loan ratio, taken up in the owm equity unit exceeds 1. The countries with market economy has the same pattern. For example, it is considered as normal index when the percentage of loan payment in the USA is 60-70%, even in Japan it reaches 70-80%. However, it is important for both sides to form guarantee of business operations and business environment to pay the loans.

It is certain that the structure of assets and financing differs by economic sectors and the types of enterprises connected with the total turnover of operations, conducted by business organizations and times of production cycles. Considering the comparative studies over the last 3 years the percentage of current asset in the construction sector is 56,8%, which is the highest and most material capacity, however, the percentage of fixed asset is the highest in the energy sector, then agricultural, mining sectors and processing industry sector (66,0-61,7%). As the demands for assets with long turnover increase the fixed expense of depreciation increases and flexibility of assets decreases. Thus, the financial administration policies and methods and mechanisms are required.

As for financial structure, 61,4% of total assets in the construction sector ans 60,2% in the sales sector are financed by loan payment of external resources, however, 52,4% of agriculrural sector and 51,9% of processing sector are financed by the owner's equity and this is the highest indicator.

For sustainable business operation the provision of current asset and sufficient resources to finance are essential. Considerin this, short-term liability is 16-29 per cent more than current asset totals of agricultural sector and nearly 100% of stock reserves of sales sector and around 85-95% of current assets in the energy and construction sectors were financed by short-term loans.

It is interesting and it needs for further study the facts that asset and financing structure differs by the types of entities. For example, the average of 2002-2005 shows that 78,4-82,5% 0f total assets of state and regional owned companies fell to fixed assets with slow turnover and this indicator is 66,2 per cent for shareholding companies and 51,5 per cent for limited liability companies. Furthermore, in state-owned companies own resources (50,8-81,5%) dominate, whilst for limited liability companies 53 per cent of total assets and for shareholding companies 62,4 per cent were financed by loans.

Financial Capacity Ratio

The main goal of business operations is to increase competitiveness and total turnover by providing customers with quality products and services, suited to their demand and needs and make profitability and as a result of this, to expand the scopes of business service (market) and improve constantly market standards of the company.

With the goal to show financial capacity growth of business organizations we have tried to determine general tendency (Figure 7.4) by estimating as we consider the most important 4 chapters and 14 indicators by business sectors and types of entities.

Figure 7.4 Main financial indicators, estimated by the totals of business enterprises and organizations

Indicators	General tendency	Average of 2003-2005	Last 3 years			Average of 1996-2000
			2005	2004	2003	
1. Financial stabilization						
Coefficient of independency (Own capital/ Total asset)	decrease	0.443	0.436	0.439	0.461	0.674
Own current asset (billion tugrug)	increase	419.4	504.4	468.6	285.2	
Debt ratio (External capital/Own capital)	increase	1.257	1.292	1.279	1.16	0.483
2. Liquidity						
Current ratio (Current asset / Short-term liability)	constant	1.297	1.270	1.319	1.318	1.92
Quick ratio	constant	0.712	0.721	0.711	0.693	0.86
3. Asset utilization, turnover						
Capacity of total asset	increase	0.635	0.674	0.614	0.595	0.48
Debt turnover (by days)	slow	84	82	90	79	75
Reserve turnover (by days)	slow	102	92	114	101	94
Liability turnover (by days)	slow	132	137	141	120	
Production cycle	slow	186	174	204	180	169
Financial cycle	quick	54	37	63	60	
4. Return on assets (%)						
Return on total assets (Net profit/ Total assets)	increase	2.77	4.41	1.65	1.52	2.48
Return on owners' equity (Net profit/Owner's capital)	increase	6.25	10.10	3.76	3.30	2.52
Sales profitability (Net profit/Sales profit)	increase	4.36	6.54	2.68	2.56	4.54

Financial stabilization

Production and financial environment of enterprises and organizations has been improved each year and business scopes and competitiveness have been increased. The net sum of sales revenue of the enterprises, involved in the research, increased every year by 40,7 per cent in 2003-2005 and the financial statement states of its completion with 4020,8 billion tugrug in 2005.

There is a common economic standard of the market to evaluate the results of business operations with stability and sufficiency of the reserves to provide those activities. Considering that the amount of own financing of the current assets, devoted to provide sustainable operations of production and sales of all Mongolian enterprises rose to

50,4 billion tugrug in 2005 and reached the amount, sufficient to provide the sales of 45 days, which showed the increase by 33 per cent each year. The study shows that there is a deficiency (negative) in current assets by 10,2 billion tugrug in the agricultural sector, however, the highest amount of current assets in mining, transportation and communication sectors. Although, current assets are negative in state and regional owned enterprises and they are highest in limited liability companies and shareholding companies.

The independency coefficient of enterprises was 0,674 in 1996-2000, however there was a decrease each year and it showed 0,436 in 2005 and the increase of debt ratio, allotted to the units of own equity reveals that the additional financing, related to the growth of total turnover was financed by external resources such as: loans. Further, as the service scopes of banking and financing sector extend and interest expenses decrease, the above trends would be stabilized. Since the asset financing is poor in construction and sales sectors, debt ratio is highest 1,59-1,51, however, in agricultural and processing sectors is the lowest 0,91-0,93. By the types of enterprises: public-owned enterprises the debt ratio is the lowest 0,97-0,23, however, it is the highest or 1,66 in shareholding companies.

Liquidity

Liquidity is the degree to which an asset or security can be bought or sold in the market without affecting the asset's price. Liquidity is characterized by the sufficiency of financial resources and payment instruments, required for paying expected liabilities on time. Covering coefficient was 1,92 in 1996-2000 and it decreased in the last 3 years and stayed at 1,3. Compared with the common standard of the countries with market economy (2,1) even though it is the lower indicator, in Mongolia, where short-term loans and liability financing are dominated, such a general average is possible. However, considering the average of 2003-2005 by operational sectors, the highest is 2,36 in mining and transportation and communication sectors, however, the lowest is 0,82 in agricultural sector. By the types of enterprises, the lowest is 0,95 in public-owned enterprises, however, it is the highest 1,60-1,55 in budgetary organizations and shareholding companies.

The ratio of 0,8-1,0 is considered proper, when current payment possibility is estimated by the ratio of quick convertible assets, however, the average of our country was 0,86 in 1996-2000 and the ratio in 2000 was 0,72 and the average of the last 3 years 0,71 shows the trends of moderate decrease. The average of the last 3 years in transportation and communication sector is 1,12, in mining sector it is 0,99, however, in agricultural sector it shows the lowest or 0,82, in construction sector – 0,46, in processing industries – 0,54 and in sales sector it is 0,53, which shows low rates of liquidity in most sectors below 40-60 per cent of the proper level. It is determined by the fact that liquidity of enterprises and organizations depends on a number of factors such as: business operations, the continuous period of production cycle, profit level etc.

The issue should be taken into account to estimate liquidity is to consider the structure and components of payment instruments, to have the possibilities of converting into cash at the comparable level with expected liabilities, on the other hand, to consider the fluctuation of the remainders of financial statement and actual average of financial period.

Asset utilization, turnover

Total asset utilization, estimated by the sales revenue was 48 mungu as the average of 1996-2000 and there was a continuous increase of 67,4 mungu until 2005 and 2003-2005 average reached 63,5. Although it is not satisfactory, there is a sustainable growth. Looking at business sectors, the asset utilization is the highest or 2,31 tugrugs in energy sector, however, the lowest or 43,4 mungu in agricultural sector and the difference is 5,3 times. It is estimated 79 mungu in limited liability companies, public-owned companies 34 mungu or 2,3 times lower. It needs to indicate that the factors: such as specifics of operational sector and property and management initiatives influence on asset utilization, invested in business.

Current assets, especially debt collection and reserve cycle period of stocks are not only the most common indicator of asset utilization, but also they are used to calculate production and financial cycle period and capital demands. Furthermore, financial capacity estimation is summarized.

Our research show by enterprises and organizations totals, the average period of production cycle, calculated by the sum of liabilities and reserve turnover in 1996-2000 was 168 days. Then there was gradual increase and in 2003-2005 it reached 186 days and then it slowed by 18 days. Here 84 days of average debt collection period and around10 day- slowness influenced greatly. Moreover, the calculation revealed that the liabilities of credit purchase are collected after 130 days. By the statistics of 2006 census of enterprises and organizations 82,7 per cent of total liabilities and 81,1 per cent of creditors are allotted to private sectors. Furthermore, by the totals of the enterprises and organizations, involved in the census, the average debt collection period is 219 days; however, the liabilities are collected within 229 days and only in energy sector and financial service sector debt collection period are longer than liabilities. Thus, it is required for business development to have reliable business partners, who are responsible for the short-term debts, according to the agreements.

By the 2003-2005 financial cycle period was 53 days and it speeded up more than 20 days before the period of 3 years. This acceleration made the provision of 3 months reserve of current asset is acceptable for normal business operation.

By sectors, the slowest production cycle period of 390 days in construction sector; 275 days in agricultural sector, however, the shortest period or 72 days in transportation and communication sector. Furthermore, the liability collection period in agriculture, construction and other sectors were slowed down by 15,4-55,6 per cent, which made working capital negative. By the types of enterprises, reserve turnover was the slowest in state-owned industries (240 days), the shortest production cycle or 170 days in limited liability companies, which show the influence of not only actual factors such as: specifics of seasonal operation, other differences, sales channels and customers' payment capacity, but also financial administration.

Return on total asset

To calculate return on assets, invested in business it is necessary for the net profit, allotted to asset unit and dividends are regarded as the base, and the growth and decline of stock market price of invested assets should be also calculated, however, because the specifics of stock market in Mongolia and lack of proper information we are not able to have this as calculation index.

By the totals of the enterprises, involved in the study, the profit, allotted to asset unit was around 2,5 per cent in 1996-2000 and in 2003-2005 it increased to 2,8 per cent. Furthermore, in the previous 5 years the revenue was earned 3,5 percent from the unit of owners' equity and there was an increase of 6,3 per cent in 2003-2005, which shows the increase by 2 times. Due to this, the share demands of big companies were arisen and a number of companies released additional shares and others started selling obligations.

Total sales revenue has been around 30 per cent over the last 3 years and 80 per cent of it have been spent on cover sales and general administration expenses and 4,4 per cent of profit form 1 revenue tugrug, which shows the average of 19960-2000 was saved. The highest percentage of total revenue was 52,7 per cent in mining sector and 62,0 per cent in public-owned companies, however, other sectors have 17,6-23,9 per cent. Companies of enegry sector have a loss by selling products with only 5,1 per cent of additional price over the actual cost.

By the totals of enterprises and organizations, the invesrtment worth 750,0 billion tugrug, made in 2005 was 2 times higher that those made in 1998 and due to the totals of the investment 50,4 per cent of internal financing, especially 31,2 per cent of internal financing of the organization (by own assets and by releasing securities) business capacity has been improving. The sectors, where investments are made substantially, are mining and exploring industry (37,9%), transprotaion, communication sectors and warehousing (15,8) and wholesaling and retail sailing (14,1).

Looking at the return on investment by business sectors, mining sector, which has more investment expenses make the most net profit or 13% from per unit, however, processing industries, agriculture, energy, and sailing sectors have a loss of 1,7-8,5 per cent. By the types of enterprises and organizations shareholding companies and public-owned enterprises had losses, however, limited liability companies made profir.

Thus, the revenue level, the factors, influnced on it and policies and regulations on total revenue differ in industrial sectors and types of enterprises and organizations, which influence on the general level of profitability of business organization.

To sum up, considering the research, done over the last 10 years, as business and economic environment of the country has been improved, financial stability and payment capacity ratios have been increased, however, due to the incapacity of the revenue accumulation growth overtake the investment growth asset utilization (productivity) and return on investment, made are not increased substantially and most sectors are having losses. The reason of the loss depend on the factors of sectors and organization, however, influences of financial factors are in great importance too.

The census of enterprises and organizations reveals that in 2006 over 6100 entities were not involved in business operations and the main reasons were: 27,5 per cent of them see as shortage of assets and finance, however, based capacity utilization was 76,9 per cent and 35,7 per cent they see the shortage of raw materials, financing and current asset and 22,5 per cent –of insufficient production demands and needs.

Ways of preventing financial difficulties and some recommendations

Analyzing enterprises and organizations, especially financial capacity of business organizations not only on the country level but also by the types of regions, operation sectors and organizations and determining the level, achieved by the enterprise and positions are necessary for evaluating really the business, engaged in and determining long-term objectives and directions. Furthermore, the importance lies on choosing partners by evaluating correctly investment and credit risks and determinig the factors, influencing on profitability of the business directly and indirectly. Researchers revealed that 35-40 per cent of the profitability fluctuations of the company depend on the economy of the country, 15-20 per cent on the average of the sector and the remainig 40-50 per cent on the company activities. For our country the sector and general influence of economic environment is at above level.

Determining the company's, partners', regular customers' and the creditors' financial capacity and summarizing the data, comparing with the sector and economic average is regarded as the foundation of preventing the business risks and making the decisions, suited to the certain situations. To achieve this it is required for business people to be aware of the causes, influencing negatively on financial capacity and the prevention measures.

The reasons of deteriotating financial capacity are:

- Poor management;
- Poor financial internal, external and independent control system and inefficient organization;
- Cost structure (fixed and variable, direct and overhead and their leverage level) and the cost, arisen from increasing price of products;
- Market operations;
- Creating inappropriate merge of small companies by bigger ones.

Preliminary signal of financial capacity weakening is disclosed by many forms. Although western European countries have not had any financial crisis yet, auditing organizations have named 9 indicators to be the signals of possible situation and 15 indicators to be the signals of possible crisis in the near future. Russian researchers determined unpleasant situations of the main operation and finance and the indicators of the signal of such a situation and called "painful" issues of a financial statement.

5 factors, the signal of possible situation of financial capacity crisis of creditors, which is estimated by Z index have been in practice for more than 100 years. The index, which was named after the name of a scholar Altmann has been studied and reached positive conclusion.

A number of factors with objective and subjective specifics influence on financial crisis and the influence effect differs. The research revealed that the influence effect depends on the economic, especially, financial and legislation environment of the country, capacity of the company, specifics of the business, engaged in, the skills of the management to forecast the signal and react to it.

Specialists of the countries with market economy have revealed the factors, influenced on the deterioration of business capacity, which are:

	Influencing factors	Percentage of influence
1	Economic factors	47.4
2	Financial factors	38.4
3	Lack of skills and experience	7.1
4	Negligence and fraudulence	6.0
5	Other factors	1.1
	Total	100

Looking at the conclusion, we have made, most influences of business risks have been the factors, related with economic and financial environment, which should be taken into consideration. Moreover, it is necessary of considering common recommendations and requirements of business people to make business legislation regulations and dicisions for business organizations and provision of economic growth of the country.

For research roganizations and researchers in order to encourage business growth and development and to decrease financial risks:

1. Collecting data fund of financial statement and make the fund open for business people. With this goal it is required to implement the standards of the countries with market economy to publish the consolidated statements and the results of the survey, done based on the studies quaterly for public;
2. Analyzing financial capacity of the business, investment profitability and financial statements; developing the methods and guidance of index system, used for the analysis and creating the service to provide necessary information for investors and business people;
3. Developing methods and guidance to provide information public about financial capacity of the companies, which had permission of releasing special drawing rights, obligations and shares and capability of the companies to pay debts. If evaluation index would be issued even in draft outline, it will be for preventing business risks, palcing public capital accumulation effectively and improving life standards of citizens;
4. Increasing knowledge, skills and experiences of financial specialists of business sectosr, state and public organizations at the level of current requirements and producing qualified specialists in this field in higher educational institutions.

Conclusions:

1. Although reforms in financial sector have been made since 1990 in Mongolia and it has achieved substantial changes, it is necessary to develop further the national accounting, auditing and analyze system of financial statements and profit and loss statements, suited to the world standards and improve professional policies, methodology and organizations.
2. During this period with the assistance of Asian Development Bank and other donor countries a number of projects and advanced research such as: "Capability building of accounting and auditing professionals of Mongolia", "Governance Reforms- Capability building of accountants of budgetary organizations " (1993-2006); with the financial assistance of the Science and Technology Fund " Reporting and Auditing System of Business and Non-profit Organizations of Mongolia" (2001); with the financial assistance of Asian Research Centre "Framework for preparing financial statements" (2005) have been implemented.
3. It is required to study the specifics, adjustments and correlations of International Declaration of Financial Statements, Auditing and Public Sector Accounting and publish the guidances for enterprises, organizations and public. The main content of the recommendations is to decrease the number of recommended aletrnatives, to add reports, explanations, exercises and examples, suited to the cert5ain circumstances and to focus on the national specifics and development differences.
4. Monographs, which were released on the issues of the methodology of economic and financial analysis, organization and financial capacity of business entities were surveyd and combined and analysis of index system, data base and organization (Figure 7.1 and 7.2) were estimated. We conclude that although the scopes of operations of business sector, results and financial capacity have been improving constantly, economic and financial influences of the sector and business have remained great. The research concluded that the factors such as: company's executive management, improper internal and external control and skills to reach to the signals are in great importance.
5. There are needs of improvining research and debates on accounting reforms and for theoretical and practical demands the science should be put in circulation and movement. For this goal the current middle-term research directions and theme moduls are:

Module-A: Theoretical and test research to make complete accrual based fixed priced accounting and model of taxation (accounting) revenue measurement: financial, tax accounting, financial analysis, auditing direction of financial statement

Module-B: From the tendency of information usage theoretical model of creating data base network with the most precise measurements amd empirical research: management accounting direction

Module-C: There are the most interesting research themes in the international frame to be studied:

- Professional history, chronology aspect (coins, cave painting etc.)
- Corporation report, measurement model of value added
- Human resource, knowledge amnagement, measurement of intellectual property
- Measurement model of economic value
- Micro measurement, paradigms of data fund transforming.

References:

1. Basic Concepts and Accounting Policies Underlying Financial Statements of Business Enterprises", *Statement of the Accounting Principles Board No. 4,* New York: AICPA, 1970
2. Diagnostic Stady of Accounting and Auditing Arrangements. Mongolio. 2005.
3. Donald E. Kieso, Jerry J. Weygandt Intermediate accounting, Seventh edition: Mongolian Translation , Volume-II, Ulaanbaatar- 2000
4. International Accounting Standards - 2001, IASC, p. 1528
5. Standards of Ethical Conduct, New York: National Association of Accountants, 1989.
6. "Brochure of accounting regulations and instructions for enterprises and organizations", Ministry of Finance and Economy, "Ekimto" Co. Ltd. Ulaanbaatar, 2001
7. " Problems of determining financial capacity of business organizations" Bat-Ulzii, J, Ulaanbaatar- 2001
8. "Theory of economic Analysis" M. I. Ваkanov, A. D. Sheremet Moscow- 1998, 2000, 2005
9. "Methodology of economic analysis of business activities" S. B. Barngolts, M. V. Melnik Moscow -2003
10. "Auditing" I.N. Bogataya, N. T. Labintsev, N. N. Hahonova 2005.
11. "International Standards of Accounting reports" Dimova I, A, M, 2000, 153 p.
12. " Problems of reforms of accounting reports" T. Jaavaa, (Sc. D) Dissertaion Ulaanbaatar- 2003, 28 p.
13. "Auditing" T. V. Mirgorodskaya 2007.
14. Д. Моломжамц" Theoretical and practical problems of Financial Analysis" Ulaanbaatar- 2000

15. "Analysis of Financial Statements" Sainjargal,B Ulaanbaatar- 1999
16. "Analysis of financial capacity of business organizations" Sianjargal, B, Bat-Ulzii. J, 1996-2000
17. "Accounting - Auditing System of buiness and non-profitable organizations of Mongolia" Project Report, Ulaanbaatar- 2002, p.160
18. "Principles of preparing Financial Statements" Research Paper SES, NUM, Ulaanbaatar- 2005

CHAPTER EIGHT

ECONOMIC COOPERATION AND INTERNATIONAL MARKET

Brief contents

As Mongolia made a transition to market economy relations, total turnover of foreign trade have increased continuously and foreign investment and assistance have been growing.

As a result of economic cooperation of our country with developed countries, the volume of export and import have increased and their structure has changed.

Foreign investment has poured mainly in mining, energy and tourism sectors. Foreign investment in these sectors is a basic factor in increasing the volume of export and developing certain manufacturing sectors in our country.

Continuous increase of loans and assistance by donor countries has a positive effect on such activities as stabilization of energy sector, improvement of living standards of population and development of small and medium enterprises. It is undisputable that if Mongolia could boost its economic activities, and utilize them effectively, there are abundant opportunities to accelerate development.

8.1 FOREIGN TRADE

Period before joining the World Trade Organization

Foreign trade statistics and records had emerged in Mongolia before revolution, thus forming a basis for future development. Mongolia had trade relations with Russia, China and other countries from ancient times. The centre of Russian-Mongolian trade was located in Omsk, Russia from 1640 to 1653, then moved into Khiagt in 1854. Russian-Mongolian trade developed rapidly, and while in 1854 there were fifty eight trade firms in Khiahgt, in 4 years, the number grew to a hundred. While in 1860s there had been only a few large and medium trading houses in Mongolia, at the beginning of the 20th century, their number reached five hundred.

In this way, as trade developed, the role of trade records and statistics grew, but it did not develop appropriately. The situation with statistics and its development depends on economic development of the country, so foreign trade statistics system was very underdeveloped.

In 1923 a Trade agreement between Mongolian and Russian governments was signed. From this period records and statistics were kept and reports were developed in Mongolia. Especially when the Soviet Union trade statistics system was introduced, specialists from the Soviet Union helped personally in this work and produced foreign trade statistics and reports.

Customs records were introduced in 1921-1924. On a basis of a decision by the People's provisional government to establish trade relations with the Soviet Union, the Ministry of Finance of Mongolia signed a trade agreement with related organizations of the Far Eastern Republic and started exchange of commodities and raw materials. Since then total exported and imported goods were recorded.

Trade specialists from Soviet Union, working in Mongolia, made a significant contribution to development of trade and its records and statistics. Until 1930s only a few data, including the number of private traders, taxes paid by them to the state, the volume of export and import werereflected and consolidated in the accounting balance report.

National monopoly of foreign trade set up in 1930 and expulsion of foreign traders played a decisive role in further development of trade in our country. After that trade houses in Mongolia expanded even more, and the share of state and cooperative trade became dominant in transactions. Rules were drawn up to submit quarterly foreign trade data including its total turnover, exported goods in detail, by names and data on 20 kinds of imported consumer goods.

As Mongolia developed, relations with foreign countries expanded further, the range of imported and exported goods expanded and data indicators changed. From that time foreign trade statistics had been consolidated even in more detail compared to previous years.

Before 1993, entreprises and industries that carried out export and import activities, submitted their statistical reports to the Foreign Trade organization, then the Ministry for Foreign Trade consolidated the statistics and sent them to the Central Statistical Organization.

Foreign trade statistical methodology in Mongolia has been reformed since 1995. In 1993-1994, along with the abovementioned methodology, the Customs consolidated declarations of goods passing through the Mongolian border, determining export and import volume, which gave an opportunity to compare both reports.

Member countries of the Council for Mutual Economic Assistance /COMECON/ took a major position in foreign trade of Mongolia before 1990 and trade with market economy countries accounted for only two percent. During this period, 80 percent of total foreign trade turnover was occupied solely by the Soviet Union.

Table 8.1 Foreign trade indicators /mln tugruks/

Year	Total turnover	Export	Import	Foreign trade balance /+,-/
1960	676.7	289.6	387.1	-97.5
1970	820.6	337.6	482.8	-145.2
1980	2830.7	1199.5	1631.2	-431.7
1985	5314.2	2052.0	3262.2	-1210.2

Source: Statistical yearbooks, National Statistical Organization

Such factors as collapse of the market for Mongolian export production in the beginning of 1990s, sharp fall of production volume of processing factories due to crisis, technological backwardness and lack of management to switch to production of competitive products led to decrease of export.

Judging from above table, before transition to market economy, Mongolia had deficit in the balance of foreign trade.

Period after joining WTO

The Mongolian government made a request to join the World Trade Organization in 1991. As a result of 6 years negotiations, in 19997 Mongolia became the 134th member country of WTO and a new environment for foreign trade activities emerged. In other words, while before 1997 Mongolia could trade with 14 countries on favorable conditions, after joining WTO it had an opportunity to trade with 140 countries on favorable conditions.

WTO is an international organization that keeps and coordinates established trade rules between countries in the world. By becoming a WTO member, new opportunities opened up for our country to enjoy favorable trade conditions from member countries and to negotiate customs duties established by neighboring countries in order to alleviate difficulties in foreign trade. The main purpose of the WTO is to regulate business relations between manufacturers, customers, exporters and importers.

There was no united customs tariff in Mongolia before 1991. A special permission or a license was required to export meat, crops, spiritus, livestock fodder, and alcohol and export of non-processed cashmere was forbidden. As Mongolia became a member of WTO, it took up a responsibility to keep the highest tariff level under 20%, imposed taxes for export of non-processed cashmere and benefitted from favorable conditions to sell many kinds of sewn and knitted products. As estimated by International Monetary Fund, Mongolia is among countries with fewest sanctions in foreign trade and import tariffs of our country are the lowest in Asia.

Along with WTO, Mongolia cooperates with the UN and its specialized agencies and other international economic organizations. Our country pays great attention to such issues as increasing the volume of export, expanding its range, increasing its efficiency and strengthening human resources. Due to lack of appropriate environment for production and trade in rural areas, individuals and entreprises waste natural resources and provide conditions for sale of raw materials of livestock origin to foreign countries at cheap price.

In order to implement the objective of promoting structural changes based on export-oriented private entreprises the government of Mongolia pays attention to increasing investment, creating favorable legal environment and raising export of products, which absorbed investment, workplaces and costs. In order to reduce the number of goods with a license to cross the national border under state supervision and decrease the red tape, "one stop shop principles" are followed, so the related ministries will grant export and import licenses, as well as work out a coded list of goods to be passed through the border with a license and goods forbidden to bring to the country. Development and approval of laws on legal status of trade zones including an Altanbulag free trade zone, a Zamiin uud free economic zone and Tsagaan nuur trade free trade zone opened possibilities for increasing investment in our country, industrial development and increasing the number of workplaces, and will make an important contribution to economic growth.

Since 1998, five percent customs tax was imposed on most imported goods and some goods, particularly machinery, equipment and materials related to foreign investment in sectors that are especially important in development of the country, were freed from import tax.

Although Mongolia liberalized its foreign trade and is implementing an open policy, foreign trade conditions in Mongolia have declined because of one-sided structure of export and price fluctuations of goods in the world.

Table 8.2 Foreign trade statistics

Year	Million US dollars				By percent		
	Total turnover	Export	Import	Foreign trade equilibrium	Total turnover %	Export %	Import %
1980	950.6	402.8	547.8	-145.0.	100.0	42.4	57.6
1985	1748.6	689.1	1095.5	-406.4	100.0	38.9	61.4
1986	1855.8	716.1	1139.7	-423.6	100.0	38.6	61.4
1987	1822.5	717.9	1104.6	-386.7	100.0	39.4	60.6
1988	1852.7	739.1	1113.6	-374.5	100.0	39.9	60.1
1989	1684.5	721.5	963.0	-241.5	100.0	42.8	57.2
1990	1584.7	660.7	924.0	-263.3	100.0	41.7	58.3
1991	708.9	348.0	360.9	-12.9	100.0	49.1	50.9

1992	806.7	388.4	418.3	-29.9	100.0	48.1	51.9
1993	761.6	382.6	379.0	3.6	100.0	50.2	49.8
1994	614..5	356.1	258.4	97.7	100.0	57.9	42.1
1995	888.6	473.3	415.3	58.0	100.0	53.3	46.7
1996	875.2	424.3	450.9	-26.6	100.0	48.5	51.5
1997	919.8	451.5	468.3	-16.8	100.0	49.1	50.9
1998	848.5	345.2	503.3	-158.1	100.0	40.7	59.3
2000	1150.3	535.8	614.5	-78.7	100.0	41.1	58.9
2001	1159.2	521.5	637.7	-116.2	100.0	46.6	53.4
2002	1214.8	524.0	690.8	-166.8	100.0	43.1	55.0
2003	1416.9	615.9	801.0	-185.1	100.0	43.5	56.9
2004	1890.8	869.7	1021.1	-151.4	100.0	46.0	56.5
2005	2249.2	1064.9	1184.3	-119.4	100.0	47.3	54.0

Statistical yearbooks, National Statistical Office

Foreign trade deficit has declined relatively over the last years. There are certain factors that affect foreign trade deficit of our country.
As a result of great increase of foreign investment in Mongolia in the beginning of 2000s and elimination of import tax for machinery and equipment for enterprises, the volume of production and services increased and a trend of increasing prices for some imported goods at the world market is observed, which is the reason for slow decrease of foreign trade deficit.

Total turnover of foreign trade

In recent years total turnover of foreign trade reached 2.2 billion dollars, which shows that foreign trade is expanding in Mongolia. Compared to 1980, total turnover increased by 236.6 percent, compared to 1985 it increased by 126.0 percent, compared to 1990 it increased by 141.9%, compared to 1995 - by 253.1%, compared to 2000 - by 194.0% and compared to 2004 it increased 118.9 percent.

As a result of a policy of foreign trade expansion and finding new markets as of 2005, total turnover of the foreign trade reached 2.2 billion dollars and increased by 19.0 percent compared to 2004. Export reached 1064.8 million dollars, increasing by 22.4 percent and import reached 1184.4 million dollars, increasing by 16.0 percent.

Figure 8.1 Foreign trade turnover/mln US dollars/

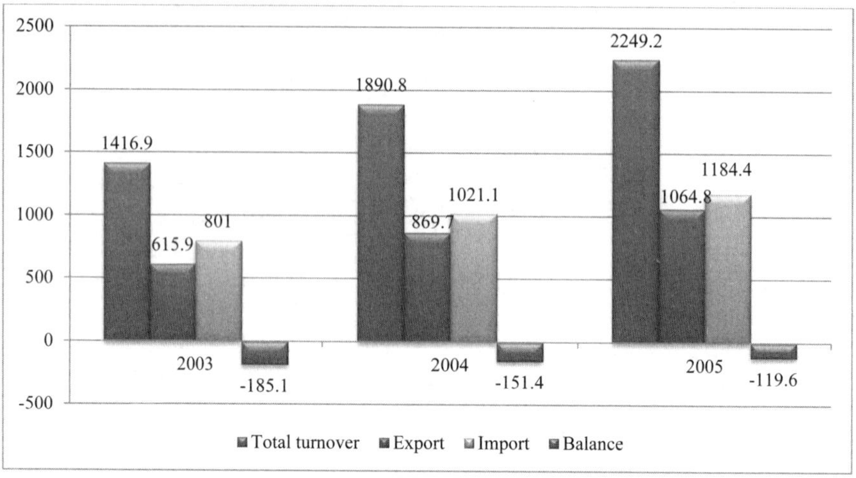

The foreign trade balance had 95.0 million dollars losses, compared to 2004 it decreased by 37.3 percent or 56.4 million dollars. In 2005 Mongolia traded with 96 countries, of which with 24 it had gained trade profit.

Table 8.3 Total turnover of the foreign trade /continent, million, dollar/

Region	2001	2002	2003	2004	2005
Asia	573.9	583.6	702.5	944.9	1130.4
Europe	411.1	406.3	484.1	699.8	748.2
America	162.8	194.8	172.3	228.5	340.2
Africa	0.1	0.1	2.9	0.1	0.4
Australia	11.4	29.9	55.0	17.5	30.0
Total	1159.2	1214.8	1416.9	1890.8	2249.2

Statistical yearbooks, National Statistical Office

When the export and import structure is examined at the country level, primary products account for most of the export goods in underdeveloped countries, but developed countries exported mostly industrially processed products.

Export

In the last years our country exported products to 60 countries. Of them the People's Republic of China accounts for percent 48.1%, the USA – for 14.2 percent, Canada –

for 11.6 percent, Great Britain – for 8.3 percent and Republic of Korea – for 6.2 percent. Export with abovementioned countries accounts for 88.4% of the total export.

Table 8.4 Export /by continents, million US dollars/

Region	2001	2002	2003	2004	2005
Asia	278.5	252.8	344.0	484.4	603.9
Europe	86.3	85.5	91.8	213.6	171.1
America	146.7	167.9	143.9	171.4	275.5
Africa	0.1	0.0	1.7	0.1	0.1
Australia	10.0	17.7	34.5	0.1	14.3
Total	521.5	524.0	615.9	869.7	1064.9

Statistical yearbooks, National Statistical Office

Compared to 2004 total export to the People's Republic China and the Russian Federation, our main trade partners, increased by 22.5-26.0 percent, export to Canada increased 8.3 times, but total export to the USA and Great Britain decreased by 4.0-36.6 percent.

Copper concentrate, gold and cashmere are our chief export products. A few products including garments and knitwear had been manufactured for export. Export income of our country depends on income derived from a few products and it depends directly on the world market prices.

Year 2005 year was favorable for our country because prices for our chief export products including copper, gold and cashmere, increased at the global market. As a result, export income increased, export growth exceeded import growth by 6.4 points, which influenced the fall of the foreign trade losses by 32.0 million US dollars against 2004. Compared to 2004, the average price of 1 ton of raw petrol rose by 41.0%, that of non-processed or semi-processed g old rose by 10.4%, that of fluorspar concentrate- increased by 9.1 percent, and that of cashmere increased by 8.2 percent relatively.

31.5 percent of the total export is taken up by semi-processed and non- processed gold, 30.8 percent - by copper concentrate, 4.9 percent - by combed cashmere and 4.8 percent - by knitwear.

Although total export of garments and knitwear decreased by 31.6 million dollar in 2005 compared to the previous year, Mongolia joined the special EU system of GSP, thanks to which export of garments and knitwear to Germany, Italy, and France increased 26.1 times against 2004.

Figure 8.2 Export structure /by product type/

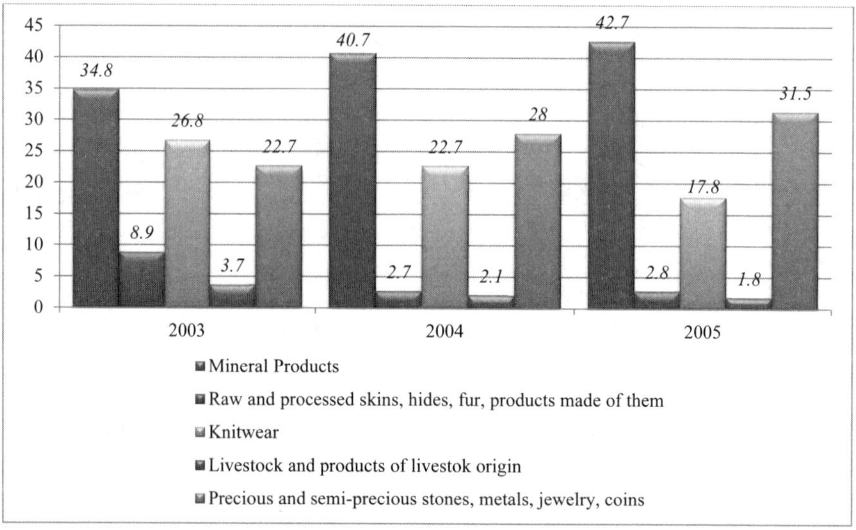

Precious and semi-precious stones, precious metals, jewelries, coins, mineral products, knitwear, raw and processed skins and hides, furs and fur products account for 94.7 of the export.

Table 8.5 Export structure /by goods types, percent/

	1997	**1998**	**1999**	**2000**	**2001**	**2002**	**2003**	**2004**	**2005**
Mineral products	44.2	33.8	32.3	35.2	33.6	33.1	34.6	40.7	42.7
Raw and processed skins and hides, fur and products made of it	4.7	6.0	6.6	7.9	11.3	8.8	8.6	2.7	2.9
Knitwear	17.0	16.8	28.0	35.9	32.9	27.7	26.9	22.7	18.0
Precious, semi-precious stones and metals, jewellery	20.6	26.8	21.8	14.1	14.5	22.8	23.3	28.0	31.1
Total	86.5	83.4	88.8	93.1	92.3	92.4	93.4	94.0	94.7

Statistical yearbooks, National Statistical Office

Import

As of 2005, Mongolia imported goods from total 89 countries, 34.8 percent of the total sum accounts for Russian Federation, 27.7 percent - People's Republic China, 60 percent - Japan, 5.3 percent - Republic of Korea and 3.1 percent - the USA. 77.0 percent of total import is importing the abovementioned countries.

Table 8.6 Import / by continents, million US dollars/

Region	2001	2002	2003	2004	2005
Asia	295.4	330.8	358.5	460.5	526.5
Europe	324.8	320.8	392.3	486.2	577.1
America	16.1	26.9	28.4	57.1	64.7
Africa	0.0	0.1	1.2	0.0	0.3
Australia	1.4	12.2	20.6	17.4	15.7
Total	637.7	690.8	801.0	1021.1	1184.3

Statistical yearbooks, National Statistical Office

Compared to 2004, import from Russia and China rose by 17-23.6 percent, but import from Japan and the USA decreased by 8.1-22.5 percent.
Judging by situation in the last years, the import structure has not changed significantly. Petrol products, machinery, equipment, vehicles and aircraft, their spare parts, knitted goods, main metals and products made of it occupies highest percentage in the import structure.

Table 8.7 Import structure, by groups of goods, percent

	1997	1998	1999	2000	2001	2002	2003	2004	2005
Products of plant origin	6.8	5.3	3.5	7.6	8.0	8.4	4.6	6.9	4.7
Finished food products	8.2	9.3	7.0	7.7	8.3	8.2	7.6	7.2	6.6
Mineral products	19.5	18.1	16.6	19.6	22.8	19.2	20.5	23.2	27.6
Chemical and chemical industry products	5.6	5.8	3.9	4.6	5.3	5.0	5.4	4.6	4.6
Textiles and knitted products	5.7	6.3	9.0	13.0	9.9	12.2	10.4	10.0	6.4

Main metals and metallic products	7.0	5.6	3.8	3.7	4.7	4.5	5.5	6.9	7.2
Machinery, equipment, electric appliances, tape recorders, TV and their spare parts	26.7	25.2	34.5	21.7	17.8	19.5	21.0	19.7	21.6
Cars, air and water transport, their components	9.6	13.5	10.6	10.9	10.8	10.9	10.8	10.2	9.8
Total	89.1	89.1	88.9	88.7	87.7	88.0	85.8	88.7	88.6

Statistical yearbooks, National Statistical Office

Judging from above table, mineral products, including petrol products, machinery, equipment, electric appliances, tape recorders, TV and their spare parts prevail in import products of our country. As of 2005, the import structure examined by product types shows that import of finished food products, products of plant origin, and knitted products decreased by 0.8-3.5 points, while import of machinery, equipment, electric appliances, tape recorders, TV, their spare parts and mineral products rose by 0.6-4.2 points.

Import growth is connected with activation of domestic business environment, in particular, growth of national industry, especially, in processing sector production. Although it can be said that domestic industry has developed and some new sectors have emerged thanks to introduction of best global technologies, it is necessary to supprt domestic production that can substitute for imported products. Prices of finished products rise faster than that of raw materials at the world market.

Products of plant origin, that occupied a large share in total import, decreased by 17.1 million US dollars against 2004 and textiles and knitwear decreased by 26.6 million US dollars. However, import of machinery, equipment, electric appliances, tape recorders, TV, and their spare parts rose by 43.6 million dollars and import of mineral products rose by 78.1 million dollars.

In particular, import of petroleum products worth 291.8 million dollars accounted for 25.4 percent of total import. Of it 85.4% or petroleum products worth 249.1 million US dollars was imported from Russian Federation.

Picture 8.3 Import structure / by types of goods/

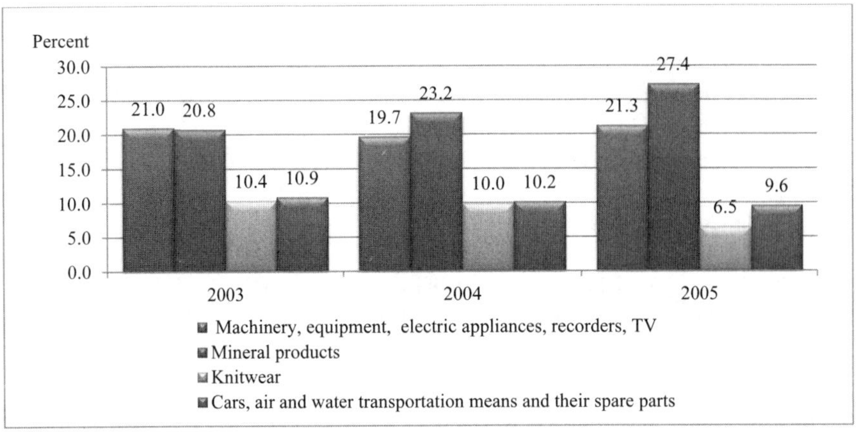

Electric energy import decreased by 0.9 million US dollars against 2004, petrol import increased by 20.9 million US dollars, import of flour increased by 1.9 million US dollars and car import increased by 0.1 million dollars respectively. If export and import structure are shown by continent, most of the export goes to Asia and most of import comes from Europe.

Figure 8.4 Export Import

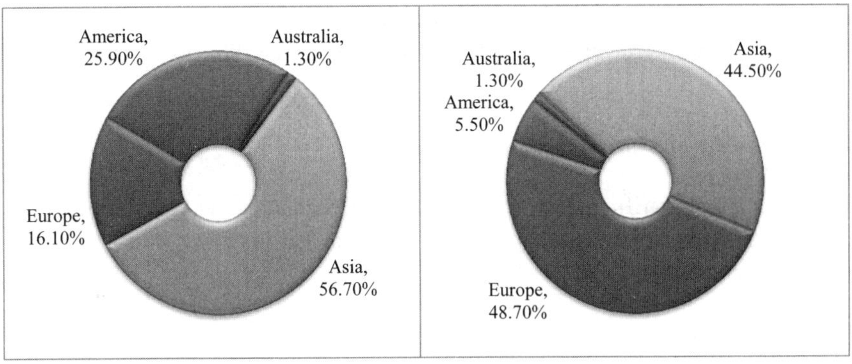

Index of the trade factor

In order to evaluate foreign trade situation, we estimate trade conditions. It is determined by the ratio of an average export price index to the average import price index and if it exceeds 1, we view that trade conditions are favorable.

For our country the index equaled 0.612 in 2001, which shows that conditions for foreign trade in our country are unfavorable.
Decline of trade conditions is directly connected with foreign currency reserves that could be gained from export or saved from import. For instance, it is clear that our country lost 107.0 million dollars in 2001 because of price increase of several above-mentioned export products along with decrease in their volume.
The following tables shows trade conditions rate in the last five years

Table 8.8 Trade conditions coefficient

2001	2002	2003	2004	2005
1.732	0.614	0.683	0.831	0.877

Source: Statistical yearbooks, National Statistical Office

In 2005 the export purchasing power was by 22.3 percent lower than that of import. Most countries take measures against foreign trade deficit by promoting export and decreasing import by means of the tariff and tax policy and raise export by increasing processing industry output. Because of weak economy, raw and semi-processed materials account for the most of export products of our country. Therefore, it is possible to improve trade conditions by processing raw materials into end products. To promote foreign trade on the basis of comprehensive market research, not leaving it by itself, is the basic condition increasing its efficiency. It is necessary to do research of the world market, and to raise requirements to each exporter entity with regard to improving the quality of the export product, changing and processing it.
International trade regulation is implemented in two basic directions, namely, tariff and non-tariff.

International trade tariff regulation

International trade tariff regulation is based on united standards and principles regulating international trade process. The regulation originated from activity of the following organizations:

- World Customs Organization
- European Economic Commission
- United Nations Organization
- World Trade Organization
- UN Conference on Trade and development

Law on customs tax and customs codex are the main legal source of the tariff regulations for many countries. The Customs codex, as a national legal document, does is not covered by international negotiation. However, customs tax is regulated by international regulations and that issue is raised regularly in international negotiations. These negotiations list tariffs imposed on goods, their structure, levels, volumes, amounts imposed in export and import.

The Customs tax sets up a correlation between economic development of the country and the import tax level of the tariff. The more developed the country, the lower amount of the tax. /in other words, there is enough production competitiveness in the country, so tax protection is not that necessary/. Customs tax in Hungary, Australia and Switzerland is 16.8-3.0 percent at average.

Although it is possible that the tax for luxury goods is much higher than for average goods, it depends on financial interest rates of the country. While the average tariff for goods in European Union does not reach 4 percent, the import tax on alcohol exceeds 20 percent and the tariff for caviar is 30 percent.

There is a trend for gradual decrease of import customs tax in present tariff regulations. The average tax for industrial products does not reach 5 percent. The tax decrease will continue in the future. Customs taxes can be divided into two groups.

Import tariff

-It is basis for regulating the foreign trade volume. About 100 countries use it.
-It raises the price of imported goods, so it influences negatively competition in the domestic market of the importer country.
-Manufacturers gain profit because own goods increase due to consumer goods market expansion as a result of products protected by import tariff.

Export tariff

-A few countries use export tariff for natural resources
-Developing countries, rich in natural resources, use export tariff to keep sustainable cheap prices in domestic market and high prices in foreign markets.
-Export tariff is used to increase state denomination stocks
-Export tariff might lead to negative economic consequences to export structure and volumes /by weakening export resources and opportunities of the given country, creating conflicts in foreign trade volume, leading to inflation/

International non-tariff trade regulations

International non-tariff trade regulations play an important role in present trade and political mechanism.

It is unclear how non-tariff regulations affect international trade. It is impossible to make quantative conclusions. While tariff regulations are established by laws and regulations, non-tariff limitations can be made by executive authority centre and its local branches. Experts of the UN conference on Trade and Development concluded that total amount of non-tariff limitations takes up 20 percent of the domestic tax measures and 20 percent of approved regulations. The USA, Japan, European Union have leading positions in use of foreign trade non-tariff limitations.

Non-tariff regulations are used in international practice in following cases:

-To protect national economy

-To provide international security

-To protect health and lives of people

-To fulfill the duty to the international community

-To stabilize the international trade system

An international legal system in the course of using mutually accepted non-tariff regulations in international trade

The international legal system of trade regulation in the frame of the GATT and World Trade Organization is based on non-discrimination and influential market situation. Use of non-tariff instruments may be determined in a following way:

1. Non-tariff regulation is used according to following international principles:
    - Presence of goods of the country at the domestic market of the importer country
    - The status of goods at the domestic market of the importer country
    - Existence of transparent legal grounds for non-tariff regulation
    - Freedom of transit
2. To limit use of non-tariff regulation only by a form of quantative limitation
3. To limit non-tariff regulation by international rules, by the way of prohibiting possible and future discriminatory and protectionist regulations and non-tariff regulation. /For example: special customs and borders rules, technical barriers, and use of sanitary measures etc./
4. To provide following comprehensive factors by means of a finely regulated mechanism in order to balance non-tariff regulation.
    - To protect the importer party from unfair trade practice
    - Sudden changes in the market /anti-demping and protection measures, a balancing tax, measures taken by both sides/
    - Emergency situation in national industry
    - Natural and disaster factors
    - Requirements for people's safety
    - Following local morals and norms

Present situation of foreign trade policy and regulation

An effective foreign trade policy and regulation plays an important role in economic development of the country.

From methodological and theoretical point of view, there are two basic instruments of foreign trade policy regulation, namely, customs tariff and non-tariff regulation. Mongolia uses both instruments of trade regulation in its present practice. Customs tariff, which is an important type of state regulation of foreign trade, is used widely in our country. Customs tariff is a tax imposed on exported and imported goods. By using the tax, Mongolia aims to resolve such issues as regulating the amount of imported and exported goods, protecting national manufacturers from foreign competition and providing economic security.

Customs tariff is a legal document, which includes a goods list, a methodology of determining customs duty, a method of calculating the tax, rules defining the origins and the mechanism related to tax use, changing and decreasing it, and showing the frame of executive governance power in customs regulation.

Customs tariff is an important instrument for the state to regulate foreign trade and provides an opportunity to protect interests of national manufacturers from foreign competitors.

Since the Parliament of Mongolia approved the Law on customs, the Law on customs tariff, the Law on excise tax and the Law on value-added tax, customs tariff regulation has been implemented in the country.

Customs tariff is used as an export and import tax on exported and imported goods. Both taxes are used in our country, but the export tax is used relatively little. In developed countries the export tax is used very rarely. Actually, in some ways, export tax influences negatively economy of the country. That is why it is possible to use a license, a quota system and voluntary limitation of the export as instruments of export regulation.

Import tariff has an important role in establishing a proper import structure, making a real impact on national industry and social issues, in protecting national economy from foreign competition, in concluding agreement to sell national products to foreign countries, in using it as basic instrument in negotiation for a free trade zone, or establishment of a customs association, in establishing effective ratio of import and export, and in decreasing trade balance deficit. Mongolia aims to use effectively these roles of the customs tariff and gets some benefit from them.

The following three types of customs tax calculation are used in combination in our country.

1. Customs tax ad valor or a form of calculation based on price of goods
2. Special or a form of calculation based on certain price of real measurements such as established weight, capacity, volume and number

3. Combined or imposing ad valor and special tax at the same time
Mongolia has developed customs tariff regulation by using abovementioned three methods in combination to impose foreign trade customs tax. Customs tariff regulation plays an important role in generating state budget income. Along with direct regulation Customs tariff fulfills such duties as a financial /budget income generation/, protection of national industry and indirect influence on trade policy of other countries. At present time about 40 percent of state budget income comes from the customs. The customs fulfills the duties of budget income generation very well.

In 1990-1997 the customs tax on all imported goods was 15 percent and it was directed to budget income generation. But in order to provide for budget income from July 1st, 1999 a 5 percent customs tax was added on all kinds of imported goods except nine kinds of the goods to be imported "with 0 percent tax' as a result of negotiation with WTO in 1996. In general, customs tariffs have been changed every year in order to provide for budget income. The customs tariff policy of Mongolia is in great measure regulated by international legal norms, first of all by WTO, and GATT norms.

Customs tariffs of member countries of the WTO, including Mongolia, are divided into two groups, reflected in the fall list or not reflected in the fall list.

Since Mongolia took up a responsibility according to international agreements, it can not raise the first group tariffs arbitrarily (by its own will). It is possible to change the second group of tariffs, because it is in the given country's power. Concluding from present situation there are some shortcomings in customs tariff policy and regulation in Mongolia.

1. The common tariff is not used in activities of calculating the customs tax.
2. The customs tariff structure is aimed at income generating and can not fulfill other important duties
3. An effective breakdown of customs tariff is not made. It is necessary to make a detailed research and calculation of production costs and other economic factors.
4. A methodology of determining, calculating a customs tariff of Mongolia is not developed. Developing a basis of methodology to determine an economically well-founded tariff is important for turning tariff regulation into a main instrument of implementing the foreign trade policy.
5. Measures to use non-tariff regulation methods (such as quota, license, monopoly, technical sanctions, voluntary limitation of export) effectively are not taken.

Ways to develop the foreign trade policy and regulation

It is important to increase efficiency of foreign trade policy by the way of its upgrading to provide for development growth of Mongolian economy.

Issues of upgrading foreign trade regulation are discussed here in two ways, first, in the frame of customs-tariff instruments, second, in the frame of non-tariff ways.

Customs tariff regulation is used widely all around the world and has an important role. Legal tariff regulation according to related laws and agreements has been used widely in Mongolia and practical effective measures have been taken to increase the volume of export and import, to provide favorable conditions for trade with neighboring countries, to improve quality of imported goods, to encourage domestic production, to meet demand and needs of the domestic market and to maintain economic security.

However, it is right to take following steps to develop further customs tariff regulation:

1. To establish appropriate, different customs tariff. By imposing different tariff for each kind of goods, it is possible to resolve economic development growth, investment, loan and financial issues in connection. Customs and economic practice shows that non-differentiated tariff, implemented at present, is ineffective.

2. To determine correctly customs data on foreign trade, process research data and use it widely in customs practice. The GAMAS system used at present is effective, but some kinds of goods and services are not registered in this data network. Especially, goods in an amount worth less than 1000$, are not registered. Meanwhile, thousands of small traders pass through border several times a month, which is not reflected in customs statistics.

3. Methodological issues of calculating customs duties. At present a method of processing foreign trade customs statistics and data is used in Mongolia. However, a consolidated methodology of collecting information related to production costs and productivity, price of goods, wages in the frame of the sector or a region, of analysing it, computing well-founded customs duties has not yet been developed. It is important without delay to develop a methodology of determining customs tariff rates in Mongolia for implementation of the customs tariff policy and regulation.

4. Employing professional, capable human resources that are the main condition for implementing customs tariff and trade policy and decreasing customs risks is essential. So a set of training and services issues should be resolved in succession, including revision of present curricula at the Customs and Economics college, training and of customs workers in highly developed countries and upgrading their skills and qualifications.

5. Our research shows that foreign trade structure in Mongolia, especially that of import is extremely insufficient. It is important to increase customs duties on some kinds of goods and decrease duties on other in order to establish an effective foreign trade goods structure. It can not be denied that on the purpose of promoting national production it is necessary to increase the import duty on some goods and raw materials. However, customs duties imposed on luxury consumer goods /gold and silver jewelry, vehicles/ and petrol can be increased.

It is necessary to reduce customs duties on machinery, equipment and its spare parts with the purpose of supporting some leading sectors of national industry.
We should resolve following issues in the frame of non-tariff instruments:
1. It is necessary to establish an incoming and outgoing flow of some goods by the way of determining an appropriate quota which is a basic means of non-tariff regulation. We should use a combination of tariff and non-tariff regulation in order to ensure people's safety, support national production and encourage investment.
2. We should establish proper Para-tariff taxes and fees. A situation when the volume of customs clearance of goods and vehicles depended on the number of customs declarations should be changed and coordinated with customs service charges. At present a value-added tax and a special tax is imposed on imported goods. We include the customs duty and a special tax into the base of value-added tax for import products. This inappropriate system should be changed in some aspects.
3. To establish properly the license control. A flow of certain kinds of goods can be coordinated by the way of using licenses. However, licenses should not be used as means of prohibition.
4. To organize effectively technical control in order to follow strictly safety standards for product quality.
It is necessary to develop separate rules of currency transaction on the purpose of regulating foreign trade. Thanks to successive steps taken since 1990 by the way of utilizing basic instruments of foreign trade, total volume of foreign trade increased and its structure and location have changed. Results of analysis of foreign trade development show it clearly. An issue of developing a methodology of analysis of foreign trade activities emerges from the new market new structure.

8.2 FOREIGN INVESTMENT

Judging from the global trends, foreign direct investment increased rapidly in recent 20 years from 1980, and its growth rate exceeded the global GDP and export growth. For instance, while in 1980-1997 foreign direct investment increased by in average 13% at the global level, export increased by 7 percent and a global GDP grew even less than that.[1] Not only foreign direct investment increased, but also geographical location expanded and covered all regions and countries in the world. Foreign investment is an important source of financing for developing countries. While investment such as private bank loans aims to gain profit in short term and is influenced by numerous factors such as loan interest, foreign direct investment aims to gain long-term sustainable profit from production and services activities. Foreign direct investment not only increases assets and resources of the recipient country, but also introduces production technology, skills, capacity, institutional and management best practices. Moreover, it provides an opportunity for companies of the given country to join the international marketing system via foreign direct investment.

In view of these and other advantages, countries became interested in attracting foreign investment into own country in order to accelerate economic growth and take different policy and regulation measures to encourage investors and influence their choice of geographical location for foreign investment. Furthermore, regions and countries started competing between themselves to attract foreign investment.

In these conditions let us examine the situation with foreign direct investment in Mongolia, its further trends and the state policy of attracting foreign investment.

Since Mongolia made a transition from a centrally planned economy to market economy in 1990s, enterprises with foreign investment have been established and their number and the scope have expanded every year. The Government of Mongolia have taken many measures to support foreign investment. For instance, the Law on foreign investment was approved by the Great Ih Hural first in 1993. Several provisions on providing favorable conditions for foreign investors were reflected in the package of Tax laws and the Law on mineral resources. It can be viewed that favorable legal environment influenced increase in foreign investment.

---

[1] Padma Mallampally and Karl P. Sauyant, 1999, "FDI in developing countries ", Journal of Finance and Development

Figure 8.5 Foreign direct investment /million, US dollars/ 1990-2005

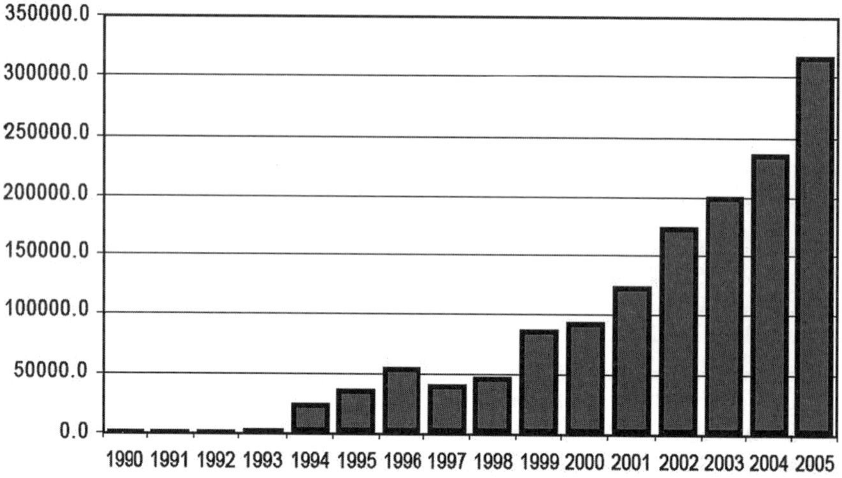

The volume of foreign direct investment in Mongolia grew from 965 thousand dollars in 1990 to 36.4 million dollars in 1995 and reached 317.3 million dollars in 2005, which is nearly ten times greater against 1995.

If foreign investment is examined by countries, in total 86 countries made investment in our country since 1990.

Figure 8.6 Foreign direct investment structure /by countries/

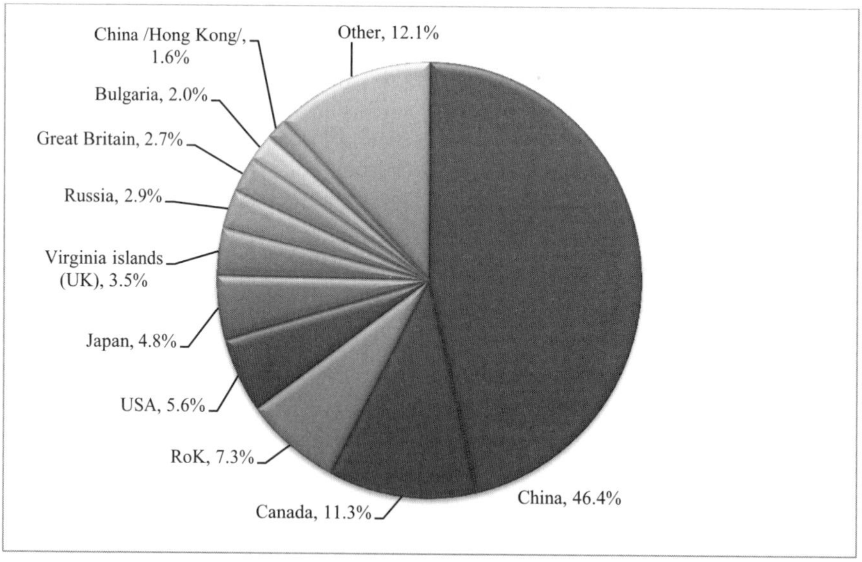

Nearly half or 46.4 percent /730.8 million dollars/ is investment made by the People's Republic of China, our southern neighbor. Of total foreign direct investment 11.3 percent comes from Canada, 7.3 percent - from Republic of Korea, 5.6 percent - from the USA, 4.8 percent - from Japan and 2.9 percent from the Russian Federation. Along with big countries such as Great Britain, Australia, Germany, Italy, France some small countries including Marshall Islands, Minor Outline Islands, and Saint the Helen Island made investment in our country.

Foreign direct investment made in our country since 1990 can be divided generally into 2 parts, namely, investment in mining and that in other sectors. In total foreign investment worth 1 billion 576.7 million dollars was made in our country from 1990 to 2005. As a result, 5789 companies with foreign investment were established.

Foreign direct investment in mining sector

Of total foreign direct investment 43.8 percent or 690 million dollars is in mining sector.

Foreign direct investment in mining sector is directed towards geological survey, exploration and mining and no investment has been made in processing of raw materials, construction and operation of plants with high technologies and high added value.

The majority of foreign direct investment in mining sector or over 50 percent was used in Oyu Tolgoi deposit prospecting and survey. It is investment of Ivanhoe Mines Mongolia company with Canadian investment. The company made in total investment worth about 400 million dollars in the last 6 years. At present exploration and survey work is almost completed and a project on mining and exporting copper and gold concentrate is ready for implementation. It is estimated that further 2 billion dollars investment will be made in the project, so with beginning of this project conditions for dramatic increase of foreign investment in Mongolia will emerge.

Foreign investment in mining sector is also directed towards gold prospecting and mining. As gold prices at the world market have been increasing in last years, foreign investment in this sector shows a trend for increase. In direct connection with foreign investment growth, gold mining has been growing every year. For instance, if in our country 1.8 ton gold was mined in 1994, it grew to 11.8 ton in 2000 and 24.1 ton in 2005.

Foreign direct investment structure /by sector/

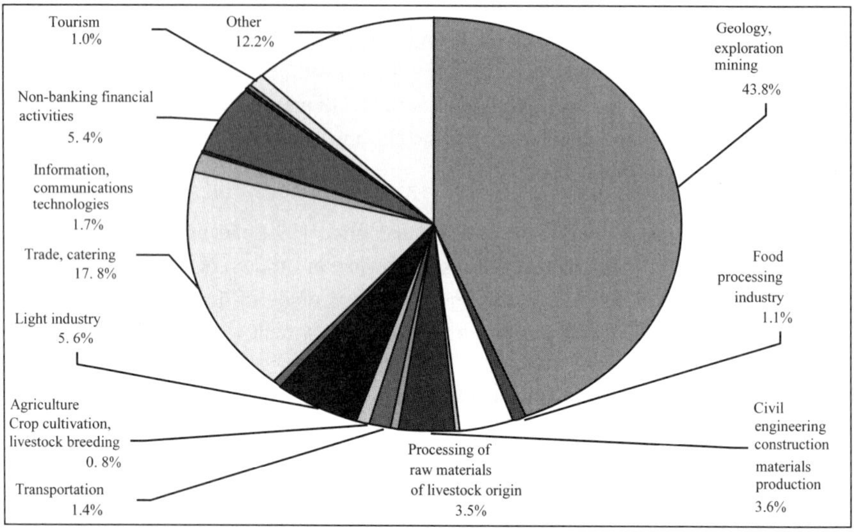

Since 1990 considerable foreign investment was made in and mining the SOKO, USA since 1993, the Donshen, China, since 1994 and Stromkat, Canada, since 2004 made investment in petroleum prospecting and mining. From 1993 to 2004 in total 165.5 million dollars worth foreign direct investment was made in petroleum prospecting and mining, of which 96.2 million dollars was invested by SOKO and 68.5 million dollars was invested by Donshen. As a result, a small quantity of petroleum is mined in Tamsagbulag and raw oil is exported.

In the last years companies with foreign investment carry out activities including mining and exporting zinc, iron ore and fluorspar. Investment is made in geological survey and prospecting of other minerals and non-ferrous metals.

It can be observed that foreign investment in mining sector is directed towards making a quick profit by mining of natural mineral resources in a short term and exporting them without much additional processing. In other words, our country is not able to implement strategic objectives of gaining advantages by the means of foreign investment, such as introducing new technologies to improve its level of technological development, establishing a basis for manufacturing of products with high added value and joining the international marketing system.

Foreign direct investment in other sectors

When foreign direct investment is examined by structure, investment in trade and service sectors along with mining sector occupies the largest percentage. For example, statistical data from 1990 to September 2006 show that 17.8 percent of total foreign investment went to the trade and catering establishment sector, 5.6 percent - to light industry, 5.4 percent- to the banking and financial sector, 3.6 percent- to the civil engineering, construction and construction materials production sector, 3.5 percent - to livestock breeding and 1 percent - to tourism sector.

Although favorable tax conditions for foreign investors and other incentive mechanisms to attract foreign investment into industrial sector have been implemented, the volume of investment is lower than in other sectors.

It can be said that no investment was made in the science and technology sector that has an important role for further development of the country. Meanwhile, the USA, Japan, European Union countries and other developed countries started competing strongly for foreign investment in this sector.

Foreign investment policy and strategy

By attracting foreign investment the country enjoys following benefits:

- Attainment of a source of foreign financing for a country with little domestic accumulation like Mongolia
- an introduction of latest technology and know-how
- an impetus on development and structural reform of enterprises
- complete international economic integration
- intensification of business competition
- strengthening of human resources capacity

Although our country is far from the global market, has a little market and scarce human resources, its rich natural resources is an important factor in attracting foreign investors.

Of total investment made from 1990 to September 2006, 44% was invested since 2004. It shows that foreign investment has been increasing rapidly in the last years, but most of the investment is directed towards utilization of natural resources. The right of our country to enter the US and European Union markets on preferential conditions also attracts an interest of investors in our country.

Mongolia pays much attention to provision of favorable tax conditions for foreign investors and has taken steps towards concluding long-term investment agreements by providing a "tax holiday", tax relief, stable tax environment in laws on regulating taxation, mineral resources and foreign investment relations. Sometimes such tax incentives are not useful for the society. For example, most countries rejected the "tax holiday".

On the other hand, at present, when our country has entered a new stage of development, we should work actively to attract foreign investment that can take responsibility for risks without putting a debt burden on the country, because the level of domestic accumulation is low and we are not able to finance investment and provide for rapid economic growth with domestic resources alone.

It is clear that in the next 5-10 years a large amount of foreign direct investment will be made in the mining sector to finance some big projects. An economic policy, directed towards protection from different kinds of risks that might affect negatively trade conditions and macro-economic stability such as foreign currency rate fluctuations, strengthening of the national currency, should be implemented.

It is necessary to follow a policy of attracting foreign investment in line with development policy and strategies of the country in sectors such as industry, processing of raw materials in mining and agriculture, manufacturing of end products with added value sector.

An OECD research[2] shows that following issues are the most important factors that investors take into consideration when they make a decision about investment in the country.

1. A predictable and non-discriminatory regulatory environment and an absence of undue administrative impediments to business more generally.
2. A stable macroeconomic environment, including access to engaging in international trade.
3. Sufficient and accessible resources, including the presence of relevant infrastructure and human capital.

The most effective action by host country authorities to meet investors' expectations were defined as follows:

- Safeguarding public sector transparency, including an impartial system of courts and law enforcement.

---

[2] OECD, http://www.oecd.org/dataoecd/45/21/2506900.pdf

- Ensuring that rules and their implementation rest on the principle of non-discrimination between foreign and domestic enterprises and are in accordance with international law.
- Providing the right of free transfers related to an investment and protecting against arbitrary expropriation.
- Putting in place adequate frameworks for a healthy competitive environment in the domestic business sector.
- Removing obstacles to international trade.
- Ensuring that public spending is adequate and relevant.
- Redress those aspects of the tax system that constitute barriers to FDI.

In a survey carried out by the Japan Bank of International Cooperation Institute[3] in 2005 following factors were considered as having main influence on making investment. The most important factor was sustainable economic growth of the country and its market capacity. Cheap labor and capacity of human resources also influenced the decision of investors.

In order to encourage investment in the last years countries have implemented actively a "brand country" policy that attracts investment to and stimulates promotion of the country. It is a concept of a comprehensive stimulation policy including effective distribution of information, attracting investment and providing services to potential investors.

With regard to the above research from international organizations and taking into account unique characteristics of our own country, long and short term development objectives, external and internal factors, our country needs to develop an independent, well-arranged policy to attract and regulate foreign investment.

Finally, when implementing a policy to attract foreign investment, attention should be paid to following issues: the influence of an incentive mechanism and measures to attract investment on the state budget, on economy and society, as well as its efficiency should be calculated accurately. In other words, such incentives should not be ineffective, unprofitable, they should not make a negative impact on competition and cause environmental degradation.

[3] JBIC institute, Survey: Outlook for Japanese FDI, 2006

8.3 DEVELOPMENT ASSISTANCE AND FOREIGN LOANS

Donor's aid and loans, their role

By 1990 Mongolia had an economic structure in accordance with division of labor between former socialist countries and became dependent on their markets, loans and assistance from them for production and consumption. Export to former socialist countries made up 95 percent of total export in Mongolia and loans and assistance equal to 30 percent of the budget income was received from these countries. Such assistance was received by Mongolia for many years.

That is why collapse of the socialist system made an extremely negative impact on Mongolia. Only in 1990 to 1993 the GDP production fell by 20 percent and foreign trade turnover decreased 2.5 times. The inflation rate reached 325.5 percent in 1992[4]. Demand for foreign aid and loans were more important than ever to compensate for budget and balance of payments deficit. However, it was impossible to get assistance from former partners because of the economic crisis faced by the Soviet Union and Eastern European countries.

In order to overcome difficulties, the Mongolian government started implementing measures directed towards immediate reform of an old economic system and structure and transition to the market economy. In the frame of economic reform policy, following measures were taken: abolishment of the state monopoly of foreign trade, privatization of state property, price liberalization and transition to a two-tiered banking structure. A strict financial policy was followed to halt the soaring inflation. However, along with economic changes and reforms implemented with "shock therapy methods" decline of living standards, unemployment, poverty became widespread. Mongolia did not have a capacity to overcome emerging difficulties on its own and implement the abovementioned changes consistently. Donors' aid was necessary.

That is why Mongolia became a member of several large international banking and financial organizations in February 1991 including the International Monetary Fund, the World Bank, International Development Agency, the International financial corporation and the Asian Development Bank. As a result of membership in several international financial organizations, Mongolia started receiving an Official Development Assistance/ODA/ from 1991.

Such international financial organizations as the World Bank and IMF granted loans with the purpose of supporting the balance of payment. Although the loans were provided on condition of repayment, it should be noticed that in general they had qualities

[4] Mongolia at the market, statistical bulletin, UB 2004

of aid because they were on preferential conditions: long-term, with low interest rates and long term to start repayment.

Efforts of Mongolian, who chose a development way towards market economy and democratic society in the beginning of the 1990s and started to implementing rapidly democratic political and economic changes, drew attention of some Western countries to Mongolia. Some developed countries viewed that "supporting economic and social development of Mongolia by the way of rendering aid and loans means providing support for democratic development of other developing countries, which are making the same effort"[5].

While in the beginning of the transition period, Mongolia got aid and loans only from international organizations, the frame of aid and loans expanded gradually and some large countries as the USA and Japan started providing financial and economic support to our country.

In the beginning loans and aid granted by such countries as the USA and Japan aimed to "soften" transition difficulties. The Government of Japan claimed that "they provided aid aimed at meeting urgent demand emerging from turmoil of the transition period"[6]. The USA also implemented the same policy and started implementing food aid programs in Mongolia from the first years of transition. Humanitarian aid of the donors in difficult years of crisis was received with gratitude from Mongolian society.

In middle of 1990 donors' aid gradually became more focused on specific goals. For instance, the biggest donor, Japan, started rendering aid in 4 basic directions including "developing human resources required for transition to market economy", "developing an economic infrastructure required to support economic sectors development", "developing animal husbandry and agricultural production" and" improving living environment of people"[7].

Aid and loans from the Asian Development bank focused on 6 basic sectors including agriculture, finance, public services, social sector reform, urban development and road construction. Its aid and loans programs aimed to strengthen good governance and increase economic growth based on private enterprises. The Asian Development Bank is the second largest donor, which implemented in total technical assistance programs worth 54 million dollars in 1991-2003 and granted loans and provided assistance in amount of 570 million dollars[8].

---

[5] JICA "Japan's country assistance program for Mongolia" November 2004 p22
[6] JICA "Japan's country assistance program for Mongolia" November 2004 p22
[7] JICA "Japan's country assistance program for Mongolia" November 2004
[8] http://www.adb.org

Assistance programs implemented by the World Bank in Mongolia were directed towards 4 major issues including "strengthening of democratic process, providing and securing political and economic freedom", "stabilizing economy, preventing collapse of production and protecting population from difficulties of early transition period", "maintaining the human development level and supporting vulnerable groups in the transition period" and "establishing organizations to provide sustainable development in market economy and developing policies"[9]. The third biggest donor, the World Bank, rendered assistance ands loans in amount of 300 million dollars in 1991-2003, of which half went to infrastructure development, 1/4 - to strengthening of the banking and financial sector, 1/8 - to poverty alleviation and 8 percent each - to private sector support and governance[10].

The IMF started implementing a 4-stage program to support economic structure reform, stabilize macro economy and improve the balance of payment[11].

As we mentioned before, aid and loans from donor countries to Mongolia first aimed at "softening" difficulties in transition period, but gradually were directed towards resolution of specific problems such as stabilization of economy, recovery of infrastructure, implementation of structural changes and strengthening of market institutions. Specific goals and directions of assistance and loans started producing appropriate results.

As a result of economic stabilization policy, implemented from beginning of 1990s and foreign assistance and loans, in the first half of the 1990s Mongolia could overcome economic decline and positive growth trends have prevailed in economy in recent years.

While during 1995-2002 the Mongolian economy grew by 2.7 percent a year in average, the average growth leaped to 6.1 percent in 2002-2006[12]. Based on changes in economic structure and positive growth trends in economy, some international organizations made a conclusion that Mongolia overcame the transition period. Although this growth that emerged in Mongolian economy in the last years seems more successful compared to other transition economies in Central Asia, which were in similar conditions, in fact, the general level of economic development did not step far from that of 1990. The GDP and GDP per capita reached the level attained before the transition period only in 2001 and 2004 respectively[13].

---

[9] http://worldbank.org
[10] http://worldbank.org
[11] http://imf.org
[12] Calculations based on statistical yearbooks of related years
[13] Calculations based on statistical yearbooks of related years

While in the beginning of 1990s assistance and loans played an important role in Mongolian economy, in the last years their role tends to decrease slowly compared to the previous period due to foreign direct investment and increasing amounts of remittance from Mongolian working abroad. On the other hand, assistance and loans in transition period had been granted mainly in infrastructure and transportation sector that have little economic effectiveness and recover investment expenses in the long term. That is why there is a critical approach to effectiveness of the donor's assistance and loans. Moreover, many sectors that received assistance and loans still have unresolved problems.

However, it is appropriate to evaluate the overall impact of donors' assistance and loans in difficult years of transition period as positive, since assistance and loans were the main basis of economic growth in recent years. Assistance provided by donors should not be measured with money alone. It is difficult to imagine at what level development of our country would be today without knowledge and technical assistance provided by donors.

Main donors and leading directions of assistance

Mongolia is one of countries that managed to draw attention of donors to its development issues. Although duration of Official Development Assistance was relatively short, Mongolia has been successful in attracting aid and loans from donors. In 1991 to 2000 Mongolia received in total assistance in amount of 1897.1 mln US dollars, of which 903.1 mln dollars was loans and 994.0 dollars was aid[14].

As mentioned in the "Global human development report 2006" aid and loans in our country accounted for 16.2 percent of GDP, which put Mongolia at the 19th position in the world by this indicator. It proved that although income per capita in Mongolia is low, it has high capacity of absorbing aid and loans.

Even though donors developed and implemented independently their own assistance programs, in recent years, in order to increase efficiency of aid and loans, they have tried to join forces in resolving specific development problems.

On 19th-20th of November, 2003, a tenth Consultative Group meeting of donors on Mongolia was held in Tokyo, Japan. Such issues as evaluation of assistance activities in the past years, analysis of economic situation and pressing problems in Mongolia, forms of assistance in the frame of Economic Growth Support and Poverty Reduction Strategy and further assistance and loans from donors were discussed.

[14] MoFE data

During the meeting donors determined that further assistance and loans programs in the frame of long-term development policy should be directed towards support of growth of economic sectors and generation of new workplaces.

They emphasized that in order to provide sustainable economic growth investment in private sector should be increased; to generate new workplaces the investment environment and management of private enterprises should be strengthened; and a legal environment supporting private sector-led development should be created. Furthermore, an importance of improving productivity and efficiency of the social service sector, streamlining the public administration structure and organization, provision of transparency of budget implementation, raising duties and responsibilities of the state officials and developing governance was highlighted.

At the meeting they discussed also poverty alleviation, rural development in order to achieve Millennium Development Goals, importance of social services improvement, rapid urbanization and a need to take measures on fighting urban poverty.

The chief donors that rendered assistance and loans in the past period, are Japan, the Asian Development Bank, and the World Bank. These donors understand clearly difficulties faced by Mongolia, and have developed medium-term assistance programs to be implemented in Mongolia in the future in line with decisions of the donors meeting.

Japan is leading among other donors by amount of aid to Mongolia in the transition period. In 1991-2003 Japan rendered grant aid worth 68.8 billion Yen, provided loans in amount of 36.1 billion yen, implemented technical cooperation program with 23.3 billion yen financing and in total rendered assistance in amount of 128.3 billion yen. It accounts for 70 percent of total foreign aid and loans granted to Mongolia through bilateral cooperation[15]. While aid occupies 95-100 percent of ODA provided by other donors, the percentage of grant aid in Japanese assistance to Mongolia is relatively low.

The government of Japan developed further assistance directions in line with "Economic Growth Support and Poverty Reduction Strategy" approved by the Mongolian government in 2004. They selected the following four priority areas:

- Support for institution building and human resource development necessary for promoting a market economy
- Support for rural development
- Support for environmental protection

[15] In 2003 FY aid of 3 billion 85 million yen and technical assistance of 1 billion 526 million yen, in total 4 billion 611 million was provided

- Support for development of infrastructure to promote economic activity

The second largest donor after Japan is ADB that granted loans in amount of 570 million US dollars and technical assistance in amount of 54 million dollars in 1991-2003 for recovery of agricultural, financial, public service, social sectors, urban development and road construction work[16].

The ADB developed a new strategy and a country program for Mongolia in September 2005. In 2006-2008 the program aims to focus its attention on two basic issues: first, to support sustainable economic growth in a wide frame, especially development of new sectors and balanced development of regions; second, to increase income of poor population and enhance public participation in social development by the way of improving the quality of public services. In December 2004 the ADB approved implementation of 34 projects with 605.8 million dollars financing[17].

The third biggest donor is the World Bank that rendered in total 373.0 million dollars assistance to Mongolia and implemented 12 projects, which cost 207.7 million dollars. As of August, 2006 the World Bank was implementing 9 projects worth 136.5 million dollars and decided to implement 3 other projects, worth 26.0 million dollars[18]. In the past period aid and loans from the World Bank were utilized to develop infrastructure, reform the banking and financial sector, alleviate poverty, support private sector and strengthen governance. In 2006 49 percent of the assistance rendered was in the infrastructure sector, 29 percent - in financial and private sector development, 11 percent- in poverty reduction and 11 percent- in social service improvement[19].

The Council of Directors of the World Bank approved an assistance program to Mongolia in April, 2004 in line with Economic Growth Support and Poverty Reduction Strategy.

Since Mongolia joined the IMF, the fund has implemented a 4-stage loan program as a direct financial aid and granted loans in amount of 73.1 million SDR until September 2006[20]. The objective of the first two stages was to support the balance of payment, the third stage aimed to stabilize macro economy, to strengthen structural reform, the fourth stage had such objectives as poverty reduction and provision of economic growth. The IMF will render further assistance and loans in the frame of EGSPRS.

---

[16] JICA:http://www.jica.org
[17] http://www.adb.org
[18] WB data
[19] WB data
[20] IMF data

Since 1990 the UN rendered assistance in amount of about 60 million dollars in different sectors. The organization developed its 2007-2011 country assistance program in accordance with National Millennium Development Goals and EGSPRS[21]. While the USA limited its Official Development Assistance only food aid and technical assistance until 2003, in September 2003 a 2004-2008 country assistance program was developed. It aims to support sustainable economic development in Mongolia by the way of developing private sector and to make effort to enhance governance. The USA announced 63 countries that met assistance criteria of the "Millennium Challenge Fund" and of Southeast Asian countries only Mongolia is to be involved in the program.

In this way main donors developed their assistance programs to meet development needs of the country and focus their efforts in order to resolve the major development problems of Mongolia.

In recent years our neighboring countries proved by their activities that they are interested in rendering official development assistance to Mongolia.

Even though the People's Republic of China is not a major donor, it is the biggest partner of Mongolia in investment field. The People's Republic of China provided assistance in the form of loans and aid in construction and mining. When Hu Jin Tao, the president of the People's Republic China, made an official visit to Mongolia in June, 2003, he promised to provide a 300 million dollars loan. Since at the Consultative Group meeting the same year the Mongolian government expressed an interest in getting future loans only on preferential conditions, negotiations to provide the loan on preferential conditions began.

The Russian Federation is not a major donor, but after resolution of the issue of the Mongolian debt to Russia, opportunities to develop economic cooperation between 2 countries have emerged. Mongolia established the Altanbulag free trade zone to expand trade relations with Russia and the Russian government announced that in the next years there was a possibility of making a 10 billion dollars investment in Mongolia, which proves that there is a trend for improvement of bilateral relations in the near future.

In this part about donors to Mongolia loans and assistance from foreign non-government organizations should not be left unmentioned. During the transition period foreign non-government organization rendered a considerable amount of loans and assistance. Such non-government organizations as the "World Vision", "ADRA" and

[21] UN country office in Mongolia: UNDAF 2007-2011

"Save the Children" have been carrying out its activities especially in education and health sectors.

The aid and loans policy

As of 2004 the foreign debt of Mongolia reached 1517.0 million dollars, an amount equal to 94.7 percent of its GNP and some international organizations started expressing concern about foreign debt of Mongolia[22]. In 2006 a long-term, 26.5 million dollars loan was repaid, but it is lower than 2 percent of the remainder of the total loan debt[23]. Meanwhile, the loan interest is growing every year.

Judging from it, the foreign debt is one of complicated development problems for Mongolia. Since foreign loan and interest repayment reached its peak, donors observe carefully how Mongolia is going to repay its debt.

In 2003 the Mongolian government finalized a decision to pay off a large debt owed to the former Soviet Union before 1990. According to a preliminary agreement between governments of both countries, Mongolia paid off 250 million dollars, which equaled 2.2 percent of the total debt that was 10 times greater than the GDP of Mongolia, and the Russian government cancelled 97.8 percent of the debt[24].

As a result of resolving that debt repayment issue, Mongolia managed to improve its reputation in the aspect of debt repayment at the international arena. However, the 250 million dollars payment affected negatively the budget balance and a large part of the above payment became an internal debt, which should not be left without attention.

A fact that there exists an imbalance between the foreign debt from loans and assistance and the scope of problems to be resolved in the future became an issue of concern to many people. There are still many important issues to be resolved in Mongolia in order to achieve its goals of providing sustainable macro-economic growth and poverty reduction.

Although further assistance of the donors indisputably plays an important role in development of Mongolia, we need to take into consideration that economic development history of other countries in the world shows that it is impossible to develop by relying only on loans and assistance. As mentioned in the " Global Human Development Report" published by UNFPA in 2006, of 154 countries that received some

---

[22] ADB. Key indicators of Developing Asian and Pacific countries p 273
[23] Bank of Mongolia Annual Report 2006
[24] The Government news

amount of aid and loans the GDP of 34 countries went down from the 1990 level and that of 37 countries was lower than the 1975 level[25].

With regard to the abovementioned conditions and economic growth prospects in the last years, it is necessary to limit the amount of loans and assistance and spend them effectively. In the frame of aid and loans policy special attention should be paid to, first, increasing the percentage of aid in total assistance, second, improving its effectiveness, third, utilization of loans as investment sources rather than in consumption purposes.

There are many issues with special significance for providing further sustainable macro-economic growth that are still unresolved. In the course of changes in economic structure of the country, the gap between the poor and the rich, disparities between regions have increased. Whether Mongolia steps on the road towards sustainable development depends on whether it can eliminate the rural backwardness and reduce widespread poverty of the population. In resolving these issues, especially to improve economic basis of Mongolia, a need for substantial resources will arise inevitably.

Donor assistance and loans is needed like air and water at this time when Mongolia arrived at the crossroad of development ways. However, in meeting this demand for resources we need to rely not only on loans and assistance, but make an effort to attract foreign investment.

A conclusion is often made that when the recipient country knows what it needs assistance for and has a healthy policy for developing its economy in the right direction, loans and assistance are effective. In order to raise assistance effectiveness in the policy frame, in development planning there is a need to take into consideration such problems as improving leadership of own country, strengthening national capacity, receiving aid meeting demand of your own country, as mentioned in the Paris declaration. Moreover, it is important to receive assistance not in a form of specific project financing, but in a form of budget or economic sector financing.

Conclusions, suggestions

Results of research by our researchers prove that innovative changes and progress was made in economic, social, and political situation of our country in the period after transition of Mongolia to market economy.

Our study clearly shows that foreign economic relations of Mongolia have expanded and their effectiveness has improved. Following general conclusions are made:

---

[25] UNDP HDR 2006 p 331-334, 344-346

1. As Mongolia joined WTO, several innovative steps have been taken to develop foreign trade policy and regulation. Total turnover of the foreign trade increased continuously and innovative changes have taken place in export structure. A conclusion can be made that it is related to improved opportunities to trade on favorable conditions with many countries of the world.
2. Our country paid attention to providing favorable conditions for foreign investors and took comprehensive measures to encourage foreign investment by improving laws regulating taxation, mining and foreign investment, which gave good results. In 1990-2005 the volume of foreign investment rose continuously, and 43.8% of direct investment was in mining sector. Foreign investment in mining sector is directed towards making a quick profit by mining of natural minerals in a short term and exporting them without much additional processing. This situation might lead to inability to influence introduction of new technologies to improve its level of technological development.
3. Aid and loans from donor countries to Mongolia first aimed at "softening" difficulties in transition period, but gradually were directed towards resolution of specific problems such as stabilization of economy, recovery of infrastructure, implementation of structural changes and strengthening of market institutions.

Along with growing volume of aid and loans from foreign countries to Mongolia the volume of foreign debt grows every year. It is obvious that Mongolia can not follow a development strategy of only relying on loans and aid. That is why a state policy and regulation on improving effectiveness of aid and loans utilization is needed to be upgraded.

CHAPTER NINE

DEVELOPMENT PERSPECTIVES OF MONGOLIAN ECONOMY

9.1 DEVELOPMENT PERSPECTIVES AND ECONOMIC TRENDS

Due to the actions, taken to stabilize economy, the growth of foreign and domestic investment, loans and grants of donor countries in 2004 GDP per person in Mongolia overtook the period before the transition after all 14 years of collapse and restoration.

Since the middle of 1990s the measures, taken to stabilize and restore economy, which faced the crisis, such as: actions to cut down welfare and social service expenses for decreasing budget deficit; to limit the growth of salaries and wages for stabilizing inflation and to privatize state-owned enterprises for increasing the efficiency played prominent roles.

However, the real amount of GDP in the 1990s was not exceeded than previous years, in the last period Mongolia was able to demolish the old system and improper relations of the economy, inherited from the previous system and survived the serious crisis of the beginning of transitional period and stabilized the economy. Due to the successive actions of privatization and encouraging private sector, market economy system was created, based on the free competition and different kinds of properties and the main structural changes to stabilize further economic growth were done.

"...The first years of the transitional period or 1990-1993 GDP decreased on average by 7,3% in a year, however, this decline was weakened and even in the last 4 years it was increased by 7,5% respectively..." /1/ Over the last years the economic growth was the growth, which was based on the competitive abilities of national economy in the condition of market and free competition and followed by this growth some positive changes were made in social sector. Although the growth reached high level, its benefits were accumulated unequally between cities, rural areas, regions and social groups. There have been many problems to be solved such as: unemployment, poverty and regional underdevelopment, related to the unequal income accumulation. For instance, the statistics, which tell that 36,1% of total population are poor gives the conclusion of Mongolian broadened poverty phenomena. Thus, developing and implementing the strategy, directed to decreasing poverty, becomes the inevitable developmental issue for Mongolia.

During the period of transition due to the implementation of policies to liberalize economy, the market became more open and competitive level of market increased substantially. Following this, enormous changes started in the economic structure. Large national enterprises, which worked inefficiently, went bankrupt because of the inability to compete with low-priced imports and the trends created, when capital and labour force in the free competitive condition concentrated in the sectors with privilege of country's industry , which were able to conduct their activities in the long-run.

Capital began to accumulate in the mining sector and not small part of labour force started concentrating in the agricultural sector. 1990- 2005 the number of employees in the agricultural sector increased from 258,8 thousands to 386,2 thousands or by 49,2%; the number of herdsmen went up from 147,5 thousands to 364,3 thousands or by 147,0% respectively. There was a tendency that parts of labour force concentrated in the service sector, which requires less initial assets and less possibility for foreigners to enter. In the beginning of1990s the economy, which faced deep crisis and steep decline began changing, adjusted to the new environment.

As a result of this, positions of processing industry, light and food industry, wholesaling and retail sailing, governmental service, which took main positions in non-agricultural sector before 1990s were replaced now by wholesaling and retail sailing, repair service of electric home appliance, mining and exploration industry, transportation and warehouse, processing industry, financial intermediary service and construction. In 1991-2005 real amount of GDP increased almost by 30,0%, whilst service went up by 56,6% respectively.

By centralizing industrial factors into more beneficial sectors there is a possibility of increasing competitiveness and efficiency of foreign trade, however, fluctuation and vulnerability of economy tends to occur related to the world market price of a few kinds of exporting raw materials.

Another important achievement, made during transitional period was sufficient investment amount increase, required to develop economy more efficient and more competitive. In 1990 the amount of national accumulation of Mongolia equaled to 1,4 per cent of GDP and investments were done by taking a great number of loans and grants from foreign countries, however, national accumulation increased to level of 16,8% of GDP in 2005./3/ Due to economic recession investment amount, which decreased to the level of 11,2% of GDP reached to the level, equalled to 24,6 of GDP as of 2005 and investment tends to relate more with external resources.

However, investment concentrated heavily in the capital city Ulaanbaatar, where there is more developed infrastructure and market, but it has not influenced on developments of other regions.

As a result of insufficient population and underdeveloped infrastructure investment has not been done in rural areas. As a large amount of population in rural areas is engaged in agriculture and run low-efficient business, poverty has spread even among people with jobs. Currently, unemployment, poverty and underdevelopment in the countryside become one of the most vulnerable issues of Mongolia.

Underdevelopment in rural areas is directly related to the regional market. For certain product existence of its demands and needs is not the condition of effective development of the market and the market needs to be sufficient enough to make profit for running business. The market in rural areas is not able to meet many requirements, thus, it becomes one of the reasons of the underdevelopment in the regions.

In 1990-2005 more than half of foreign investment, done in Mongolia was allotted to the mining and processing industry. Industrial growth of the sector, which has more capacity, has played important roles in the growth of GDP; however, it was not able to increase sufficient work places. Along with the expansion of mining sector development, the issues of environmental crisis and its restoration have been put for public attention.

During the transitional period to extend foreign trade Mongolia expanded its partner's scope not only with former socialist countries, but also other countries, which was global- sized achievement. It was the important step of our country for changing its economic system, which was fully dependent on a few countries.

As Mongolia encouraged direct foreign investment and successfully implemented the policy of open economy, we could increase export amount in GDP by nearly two times than the socialist period. Although mining and agricultural raw materials play important roles in export structure, foreign trade of Mongolia began was based relatively on benefits of national economy, but not on allowance with artificial features and the economy was able to compete on free market.

To sum up, there are several problems to be solved promptly in current economy of Mongolia. Along with the social-economic changes, made during transitional period, inequality among cities, rural areas and social groups and poverty reached high level. Although over the last years there has been a tendency of economic expansion, certain solutions have not been reached to solve how to direct economic growth to the issues of decreasing the inequality and poverty.

Prompt changes in current economic structure, where production of raw materials and processing industry are dominated, play important roles to increase employment and labour efficiency; to create national accumulation; to decrease risky and vulnerable economic condition and to create the sustained economic development. Moreover, it is required to implement policies to attract investment, concentrated in labour force surplus, supply of agricultural sector and mining sector into other sectors.

9.2 LONG-TERM ECONOMIC DEVELOPMENT STRATEGY

We Mongolians of beginning of the XXI century live in wonderful era. As a result of globalization, trade and investment amount has been increased and competitiveness level has gone up. Production and investment have not been limited by domestic demands and supply and there has been a tendency of the increase of technique and technology innovation. Political system, peoples' knowledge and intellectual valuables are changing. Thus, it is important to evaluate the time we were and the time we are in and determine properly further objectives.

As Joseph E. Stiglitz stated: "Progress is the understanding of changing traditional relationships, methods of old understanding, traditional forms of educational and health systems and industries. " /4/ However, reforms are not the goal but it is the changes, made for solving certain problem.

Currently economic growth, i.e. GDP growth is not considered as the final goal, but as the requirement for resolving other development issues. In the frame of development policy, the objectives, which involve more broad scopes such as: democratization, sustained development, improvements in living condition is put in forward. The strategy of Mongolian economy needs of implementing the above problems put in the frame of national economy.

The development problems, confronted country's economic development need to be focused on the Strategic Guidance of economic development and to implement it, it is required to determine the goals and objectives, not adjusted to the completion of previous period and current circumstances, but to direct the implementation of most important issues.

Such a strategic policy involves economic development priority, the scopes, regulated by strategic policy and implementation methods and it needs of focusing on the complex issues of state and private sector; society and community; families and individuals. Moreover, it is required for the strategic policy to direct of efficient utilizing and appropriate material resources such as: assets, capital, natural resources, and external development resources: such as management, knowledge, a social capital " human capital", cooperation, loans and grants, trade, investment. Development strategy needs of involving issues of regional territory for geographical location and issues of developing economic sectors for action direction. In other words, the strategy is responsible for developing the country's progress with less complicated methods.

Macroeconomic policy and strategy

Economic development policy and strategy is directed to creating high economic growth or alleviating poverty. Nowadays, the debates on economic development policies are conducted to connect the issues of economic growth and maintain equality.

Currently large international organizations such as World Bank, International Monetary Fund hope economic development strategy to be directed to decreasing poverty.

The macroeconomic policies, directed to poverty alleviation depend not only on the positions in economy, the effects of economic growth on peoples' income, the progress, occurred in income allocation, the compliance between macroeconomic policy of certain country and practical conditions (Kahn.A 2006), but also requires broadened macroeconomic policy and regulations.(K.Pashe, T.McKenly). Currently the ideology that development strategy of poverty alleviation needs to be based on the employment policy tends to dominate.

To implement strategy of poverty alleviation it is required that the policies of strengthening citizens and supporting people with development incapability should be implemented through the complex policies of social basic service, social welfare in the frame of budget policy. Moreover, it is required to implement certain steps directed to creating work places. To achieve this, investment needs to be done directed to creating work places in the regions, where there is unemployment and poverty and the actions should be taken to encourage investment by taxation and investment policies. However, we should not forget that the more expenditure in social sector, the more tax is collected and it will limit the investment and the growth of work places.

Thus, along with the poverty alleviation goals, the objectives in the frame of long-term development strategy are moving from raw material industry, which is considered as low-efficient to high-efficient sectors, from exploration industry to the industry with final products. To do so it is important to determine efficient development strategy of economic sectors.

Main ingredient of development strategy policy, directed to alleviating poverty is in terms of income, high level of employment and in terms of expenditure low level of inflation. However, theoretically it is not possible to maintain the conditions of increasing employees' wages and salaries and stabilizing living conditions at the same time.

In the frame of monetary policy, the actions, directed to stabilizing currency rate and decreasing inflation limit, export growth and influences negatively on the payment balance, which changes into budget deficit later and limits investment. Such a policy, which limits investment influences negatively on employment. However, on the other hand, people's living becomes more stable when inflation is low. Therefore, there is a need of choosing unemployment or inflation, which are the long-term alternatives on the Fillips curve.

In the frame of monetary policy, loan interest decrease creates favorable environment for investment, thus, it creates work places and work place demand and through it income and salary of people increase.

In the frame of employment it is required to develop sectors with high labour expenditures and small and mid- enterprises and to encourage investment in the regions where there is high level of unemployment and poverty. Our next chapter will discuss it.

Strategic policy alternatives of developing economic sectors

During the transitional period many important changes, directed to creating market relations were implemented in Mongolia. These changes were different in every sector, besides they had different results.

Looking at the agricultural sector, large state-owned enterprises such as cooperatives and agricultural farms were dismissed and livestock, which were public property were privatized and along with these changes, the price was freed and trade was liberalized. Following that many important changes were made in the agricultural sector. In the agricultural sector private sector began dominating and along with the livestock privatization, animal husbandry moved to household level. The interesting change is in economy of the countries the percentage of the agricultural sector has decreased and there has been a tendency to declining employees' number in the sector. However, in Mongolia there has been reverse.

Due to the dismiss of cooperatives and agricultural farms, movement of animal husbandry to household level, increase of the employees in this sector and the dominance of nomadic way of animal husbandry methods and technology, labour efficiency in this sector is at relatively low level. As a result of low efficiency, poverty, dominated agricultural sector is high and unemployment is excessive. Therefore, any strategy, directed to developing the sector should be guided to intensify agriculture more. This strategy needs of increasing employment by creating new job places in the agricultural sector, improving efficiency and quality of employment.

In order to increase the efficiency of agricultural sector it is required to increase the knowledge and skills of the employees in the sector to manage enterprises, to change the methods of employment, to decrease the risks in the agricultural sector and to improve the possibilities to utilize production expansion.

Knowledge and skills of the employees in the sector and methods to manage enterprises do not meet current requirements. The number of livestock tends to increase extensively during certain period, while there is a tendency to facing livestock loses in severe weather conditions: draughts and "zud" / severe winter/. Due to loss of the irrigation system, built during the socialist period, crop production in the agricultural sector reduced.

By dismissing cooperatives and agricultural farms, main service, offered to herdsmen and farmers deteriorated and the increase of efficiency in animal husbandry sector was destroyed. Previously herdsmen looked after their livestock in groups, some members of agricultural farms helped to harvest, to dig wells and to mend herdsmen's fences; however, nowadays herdsmen do the all tasks only by their own efforts. Thus, by fulfilling all tasks small households of herdsmen are in need of fodder in winter and they face other difficulties such as livestock diseases, shortage of assets and money and reaching the market. Due to the labour deficit many families are not available to maintain winter preparation and to be protected from natural disasters.

As stated in the previous part, labour force surplus is one of the main factors, which influence on efficiency of agricultural sector. By our estimation in 1990 in the work place, where worked one person; however, now there are more than two people in that job. /5/ In order to improve efficiency in this sector there is a need of moving the labour force to another sector.

However, investment is scarce in rural areas and there is no improvement of employees in the agricultural sector to move to different sectors, because of the lack of required knowledge and skills.

Any policy and strategy, directed to encouraging regional development and decreasing unemployment and poverty needs to take into consideration the following specific features:

- In regional economy agricultural sector dominates and poverty level is relatively high in rural areas;
- Due to the scattered and low density population, market is small and its capacity is negligible;
- Although labour force participation in rural areas is at high level, its efficiency is minor and incomplete employment is high;

- Production depends on nature and weather conditions and it is seasonal with high risks and along with these, income and consumption is related with seasonal conditions;
- Demands on ready raw materials are low in the domestic market and raw materials are not sold with high price because the transportation cost is relatively high;
- Infrastructure is underdeveloped, there is no possibility of attracting investment; financial service is not developed well and possibility of taking loans is poor.

Considering all these, in order to create effective labor, it is necessary to pay attention to developing small and mid- processing enterprises of agricultural raw material; encouraging cooperative business and investment; training skilled herdsmen and farmers; developing business infrastructure in rural areas and encouraging investment and trade with neighboring countries.

Another important issue here is that there is need of encouraging the market in current conditions and a system, capable of replacing the economic tasks, which were done by former cooperatives. Moreover, it is important to clear up the form and structure of the system in the frame of regional development strategy.

In the current situation it is required to establish cooperatives not as public-owned and use totalitarian methods as in the socialist era, but to set up the cooperatives, suited to individual's property ship rights; local self-governance, democratic principles and regional development objectives. To achieve this, it would be more effective if the firmest and most sustainable community of individuals such as governance, regional community and "khot, ail" / a group of households/ should be established. Such a collective organization might play a role not only to weaken decentralization, but also to attract herdsmen and farmers to social and market relations.

In order to create highly-effective employment in the agricultural sector it is necessary to improve knowledge and skills of herdsmen and farmers. To create work places in rural areas; to do technical and technological innovation in the agricultural sector and to develop small and mid- processing enterprises of agricultural raw material, it is necessary to implement policies and projects, which encourage investment in the regions. In order to attract investment, business infrastructure, attractive for effective investment needs to be developed. This is not only the issue of roads and transportation and communication, but also the issue of creating all conditions, required to run a business.

In terms of other economic sectors, the situation of industries and industrial services is different.

The measures, implemented in the beginning of the 1990s to liberalize prices, to dismiss monopoly of foreign trade and to decrease the subsidies, given to other agricultural sectors from the state affected greatly and due to the actions the production and employment were not stabilized.

In the first years of the transitional period or in 1991-1993 as a result of the serious economic crisis in many non-agricultural sectors both production and employment tended to decrease, however, since the middle of 1990s the situation stabilized and there was a growth in some sectors. Due to the actions, taken to stabilize the growth of foreign and domestic investment and economy, since the middle of 1990s the economy of Mongolia started to improve and non-agricultural sectors played prominent roles in the growth. The amount of production of non-agricultural sectors and the percentage in GDP both exceeded the levels of previous transitional period and over the last decade the percentage in GDP increased from 62,0% to 78,3%, the percentage in the total labour force went up from 53,5% to 60,1% respectively.

To emphasize in the transitional periods the important changes were made in non-agricultural sectors to stabilize further economic growth. For instance, by shifting to the market system most ineffective enterprises went bankrupt or went into serious financial situation and in the replacement of them small and mid-enterprises, capable of competitiveness were established. Enterprises started paying more attention to improving competitiveness. Big changes were made in the structure of economic sectors, especially mining and service sectors, capable of influencing on future economic development of the country were being developed rapidly.

In the frame of economic development strategy, it is important to develop the economic sectors, capable of developing sustainable for a long- run and giving a stimulus in the economic development. In current market and free competitive condition the sectors, based on the benefits of industry are able to create long-term sustained employment. Therefore, it is available to create effective work places by developing industrial sectors, relied upon agricultural industry with relatively benefits and mining industries. The sectors are processing industries of agricultural raw material and industries of final processing in mining production.

The sectors of processing industries, based on agricultural raw materials can be named manufacture of textile, leather, wool and cashmere and food industries, producing milk and milk products. To process raw materials and produce highly effective and quality products, capable to compete on domestic and international market is the main structure of long-term development strategy.

Among them cashmere industry is recognized as a strategically important sector for its scope, because Mongolia is the second biggest importer of cashmere products in the world market and 15% of crude cashmere, imported the world is produced in Mongolia. 75% of the imported cashmere in the world market is produced in China and the remaining is produced in Iran, Afghanistan and other countries.

The quota discount of European Union, offering to Mongolian textile industry, which takes prominent percentage in the industry of GDP, will be dismissed in 2015. Thus, work places in this sector are capable of preserving by shifting the textile manufacture, which plays great roles in the employment to the industry with high competitive capabilities, based on domestic raw materials.

In the frame of long-term strategic policies to encourage employment and decrease poverty, another sector, which we have to pay more attention to, is metal industry. One of the main ways to create mid-term effective employment is to process metal ore such as copper, gold and silver and produce finished products.

In terms of production cost, since Mongolia is non-sea crossing country and distant form transportation network the transportation cost, required to freight export raw materials of mining industry is relatively high. It is clear to coincide with the policy, which encourages the development of the sector and interests of large companies to decrease the expenses and increase the efficiency.

Substantial investment is needed to develop the industrial sectors, based on benefits and infrastructure, required to those sectors.

The statistics, which show that more than a half of labour force is engaged in the service sector, prove the needs of creating high productive employment in this sector. it is necessary fulfill the following tasks : <u>firstly:</u> to set up more hotels, catering service and banking and financial sectors, capable of making high income and concerned with international market; <u>secondly:</u> to implement highly productive advanced techniques and technology in some service sectors, such as construction, banking, financial etc., <u>thirdly:</u> to implement advanced action methods in other service industries.

In current condition, when economic capacity of the country is weak and high level of poverty, it is available to increase labour demand and efficiency and to improve living conditions of many individuals by developing industries with high capability of competitiveness, based on relatively beneficial sectors. Although mining and agricultural sectors take the highest percentage in the industries of GDP, both above two sectors are not able to determine the country's development and create sustainable work places for people, because natural resources are limited and nomadic way of animal husbandry depends highly on weather conditions and it is highly risky.

However, we should not underestimate the future contributions of mining sector in the development of the country. Although relating of high capital expenditure the sector is not able to create more work places it is possible to develop economy by utilizing the income, earned in this sector as investment resources in other sectors. Mining industry will be the stimulus for the economic growth and employment of other sectors and it will play a role of maintaining investment resources and encouraging demands. There is a need of developing consolidated strategy in Mongolia for developing balanced economic sectors and in this frame it is necessary to consider the ways of connecting developments of mining and other sectors. This is the important issues to be implemented.

Policies of developing private sector and business

Due to the policies, implemented to privatize property and liberalize economy since the beginning of the 1990s private sector was created completely newly and it played important roles in the economy, the competitiveness in the foreign and domestic market was still weak. Especially, due to poor competitiveness of business environment there has been a lack of job places and income and high -priced import products have been utilized.

However, private sector, which takes 3/4 per cent in the GDP industry to implement development goals and objectives and speed up the economic growth of the country, has to play prominent roles. Especially, for Mongolia, the country with market system, poor economy and high poverty, it is inevitable for the private sector to increase citizens' employment and income and decrease poverty and inequality.

The government policy to encourage private sector and improve business environment becomes presumable to be implemented when it is based on market methods, but not on administrative methods. The government policy to develop economy and improve citizens' living conditions contributes greatly to implementing general development goals and objectives when it is suited to the income making interests of private sector and its business activities create favorable salaries and highly productive work places.

There are 3 main objectives of private sector in business development strategy. <u>First:</u> business development strategy of private sector needs to be related with the economic development strategy of the country; second: business development strategy of private sector needs to be related with the economic development policy of economic sectors; third: it needs to be related with the regional balanced development policy.

To achieve this it is required to encourage the initiatives, directed to increasing the productivity of private sector, to expand enterprises, to invest, to create new entities and new job places by taxation, investment and other policy instruments.

However, in the regions, where there is poor conditions to create such relations, in other words, the regions with much unemployment and poverty and sum and provinces there is a poor possibility of turning private sector into powerful, efficient sector.

High distance in rural areas and possibilities of market capacity and investment show the importance of developing small and mid- enterprises in the countryside. United Nations Industrial Development Organization (UNIDO) stated in its report that"...compared to the big companies, the prices of products and services and wages and salaries of small and mid-enterprises are more suitable to the conditions..."

Compared with big companies, small and mid-enterprises, which produce the products, which require more labor and expenses, are capable of allocating income equally, so it is required to pay more consideration to the issues of developing the industries for protecting from decline of living standards and poverty. Small and mid-enterprises create industrial network, connected with each other and since they are small in size these entities can be set up in rural areas and they are able to play important roles to demolish differences between urban and rural areas.

Small and mid-enterprises create more work places and provide social low-income groups such as: poor households and women with work places. When small and mid-enterprises, which produce the products, based on local raw materials and sell them in local markets are developed it will influence positively on living standards of the people and the increase local employment.

On the other hand, it is necessary to pay attention to connecting the development policy of private sector with economic development policies and developing economic priority sectors, which will play important roles in future development of the country, especially, processing industry sectors, based on the relatively beneficial industry.

The policy of developing and establishing powerful, competitive, sustainable and effective private sector requires upgrading legislation environment; creating appropriative governmental regulations; encouraging competitiveness; developing infrastructure; maintaining macroeconomic sustainability and forming sustained effective financial system.

In order to encourage private sector many problems are needed to be solved such as maintaining social, political and macroeconomic sustainability; creating the financial system, capable of transforming deposits into effective investment; decreasing loan interest rates; creating fair and equal conditions for market competitiveness and upgrading legislation regulations. In the condition, where government is not capable of doing the required investment completely for private sector development, it is necessary to create sufficient and inevitable conditions for foreign investors in this sector.

Any assistance and grants, provided to private sectors and investment affect directly and non-directly not only on the increase of the supply of domestic products and service, decrease in price and extension of the selection possibility of citizens' products and services, but also on regional balanced development and peoples' migration and settlement.

There is a lack of innovative ideology, knowledgeable managers and skilled employees in the private sector. Highly developed information network, cooperation of government and private sector and underdevelopment of organizations to encourage private sector are the directions that require prompt consideration. To conclude, there are possibilities in the direction of improving conditions for private sector to work effectively.

Regional development policy

The regions, provinces and cities of Mongolia differ greatly in terms of economic and social development, since the 1990s, when the country started shifting to the market economy, the difference has deepened and along with that, inequality, unemployment and poverty have created. Thus, the problems have turned into the most difficult ones.

Along with economic and social transitional processes, enormous economic, social changes were carried out, especially in rural areas. Due to the crisis of beginning of the transitional period, the light industry sector, which played important roles in the economy of provinces suffered from downfall and since that time it has not been able to be recovered yet. Tasks of agricultural sectors have increased.

After the economic deterioration in the beginning of the transitions we have seen some economic recovery. Over the last years there has been a tendency of rapid increase; however, it has differed in regions. Economic conditions have recovered rapidly in the capital city Ulaanbaatar and in Orkhon province, where there is a concentration of capital and labour force and relatively good development of market, industry and infrastructure, however, in terms of other provinces, economic development is in standing position and recovery is prolonged.

Ulaanbaatar city and Orkhon province, where 39,5% of total population live, are producing 67,8% of GDP of the country, whilst other 20 provinces, where there are 60,5% of total population manufacture only 32,8 of GDP respectively. /7/ Without lowering these differences it is impossible to maintain sustainable development of the country.

Especially, due to poor living conditions of people in remote rural areas, poverty and migration is at the highest level. As a result of these circumstances in the last 16 years the percentage of people from rural areas in the total population of the country decreased from 72,8% to 62,3% and in Ulaanbaatar the increase is from 27,2% to 37,7% respectively.

Unemployment and poverty level, compared with other regions, is the highest in the remote areas of western regions. According to the survey, conducted by the National Statistical Agency, World Bank and UNDP in 2002-2003, 51% of the population of western regions live in poverty and the index is high, compared with the capital city with its 27% of the poor./8/ Due to small amount of domestic and foreign investment in rural areas and a lack of high productive work places, unemployment and poverty among citizens have not decreased.

Along with privatization and private sector growth, private sector is engaged main position in the regional economy, however, there is underdevelopment of market and lower level of competitiveness. This relates with small number of population and incapability of market development.

The insufficient regional development resources, the scarcity of local self-governance rights and postponement of reforms are regarded as the main reasons of underdevelopment in rural areas. The process of social transition and market conditions has also affected.

One of the ways to lower regional development differences is independent development capability. During the transitional period Mongolian Government has attempted to speed up regional development by maintaining independent development of the regions, providing rights of local self-governance and weakening the decentralization.

In 1992 "Law on Administrative and Territorial Units, and Their Governance" was enacted by The State Great Hural in 2001, which determines the structure and tasks of administrative and territorial units of regions. Moreover, the Government of Mongolia issued the resolution "Mongolian State policy on reforming government processes and the general system of structure", dated in 1996, states:".. In the future it is crucial for the Government, ministries and agencies whilst decentralizing and transferring functions to local administrations to consider whether the required financial potential and managerial capacities exist locally to be able to assume these functions. If not, to consider and decide on the mechanisms for creating these potentials and capacities based on the views and wishes of local administrations…"

"Guidance of Regional Development", which was issued by the State Great Hural in 2001 was another alternative of decentralizing by setting up bigger administrative units.

Implementation of decentralization policy in Mongolian condition requires local self-financing, high skilled staff of local governance and capability of conducting tasks independently.

In the future ability of independent regional economic development will depend on the regional economic basis. The conditions of regions whether to develop or not in terms of the size, income and structure depend on two factors: firstly: on the demand growth of the products, manufactured in the region, in broad terms, on the growth of external resources of local income; secondly: on the input supply growth to be utilized in the local industry.

In order to increase income resources of rural areas, where agricultural industry is dominated, it is important to expand demands of local raw materials and to encourage the exports of agricultural products by developing national industry and limiting import consumption. To increase input supply to be used in the local industry encouragement of investment is essential.

Regional development depends not only on environmental situation, natural resources, remote position from market, infrastructure development, but also on the policy decisions and social environment factors.

To solve the problems a great deal of asset is required. The questions such as: how and where to find those assets, how to develop the regions, how to provide labor-aged population with work places, followed by the population growth; how to utilize local resources effectively and what policies should be implemented are waiting for prompt replies.

Developing the country regionally by expanding administrative units can be available exit to decrease development differences of regions and maintain development equality. Setting up more extended administrative units offers favorable conditions for earning capital and population decentralization in rural areas, investment and development of production and infrastructure. Moreover, it gives possibilities of strengthening local governance capacity and effective budget asset utilization.

The strategy of sustained development

Previous parts of the chapter reveal that environmental and resource hazardous sectors such as mining, electricity, agriculture is in dominance in the near future. On the other hand, increase in migration, population centralization in the capital city and its surroundings and high level of poverty will influence negatively on environmental situation. Thus, in the process of implementing development goals and objectives of the country the issues of reaching the goals and creating preliminary economic, social and cultural conditions put forward.

Preliminary estimation of environmental destruction of exploration industries such as gold, copper to the environment and developing action proposals to protect environment is required. In the future electricity utilization of processing industry tend to be increased, which means the needs of proper use of electricity and considering the ways of producing non-hazardous and effective electricity. Since the increase of utilization of non-recoverable environmental resources will affect negatively, it is required to implement the policies, which encourage the sectors, producing finished goods, but not the processing industries of non-recoverable environmental resources in the frame of trade, investment and taxation policy.

Poverty in Mongolia is recognized as one of the problematic environmental issues. A shortage of money of the poor affects on environment negatively. In the condition, where land is state-owned, high level of poverty in Mongolia, especially in rural areas becomes the reason of forest resource decrease and biological species reduction. Thus, successful implementation of development strategy, directed to poverty alleviation is beneficial for environment.

Over the last years internal population migration creates the centralization of population in Ulaanbaatar and surrounding areas, which influences hazardously on environment. Due to overcrowding, air pollution in the capital city exceeded above norms and affects negatively on citizen's health. Overcrowded population and livestock create overgrazing in urban areas. Although short and mid-term implementation of policies to reduce air pollution; planting trees and grass and developing intensified animal husbandry might be the exit, however, further it is required to solve the problems, neutralizing the population migration by developing balanced regions in the country in the long-run.

Environmental issue is not governmental issue only and citizen's participation and initiatives on the issue is essential. It is important to consider of directing market mechanism to the environmental issue.

In the frame of sustained environment strategy the following actions should be taken:

- To activate the economic activities, directed to preserving natural resources and creating the taxation and tariff system, directed to reducing environmental burden, along with the financial and human resource increase;
- To encourage voluntary and market initiatives, directed to reassuring products and industries of maintaining environmental sustainability and utilization of environmentally-friendly products;
- To encourage environmentally- friendly technology and production mechanism;
- To improve the assurance of citizens on environment protection and encourage public initiatives and their participation in the issue.

Due to the location of the exploration industries of natural non-recoverable resources in rural areas, overgrazing, desertification and high level of poverty prove the importance of responsibilities of local self-governance on environmental conservation. Therefore in the frame of decentralization environmental monitoring and supervision activities at the local level is essential. However, it is available of maintaining sustained development of environment by granting authority to local governance.

AFTERWORD

These 15 years of transition from the planned economy to the market economy have been for our country a time of achievements and errors. In this period of reform of both political and economic systems common problems faced by transition economies were tackled by our country. Establishment of basic institutions of the market economic system was not straightforward. For instance, industrial collapse of the early years of transition, unemployment, growth of prices, decline of livelihood, poverty, increasing foreign trade deficit, loss of external and internal economic balance were clear examples of it.

In this period following policy measures were implemented:

- A system of free prices and rates was established
- Privatization of agricultural and industrial sectors was conducted
- A new financial system was set up
- Foreign trade liberalization was implemented
- Basic laws of market economy to coordinate economic relations were passed
- Mid-term programs on economic stabilization and structural reform were developed on the basis of agreement with donor countries and international organizations and their implementation started.

These measures were directed towards reform of economic management system and its mechanisms on the basis of reform in property relations, creating a legal basis for the new system, establishing a market structure, improving management at macro level.

Approval and implementation of the package of laws on taxation, laws on budget, on ban of unfair competition, on foreign investment, on currency, on statistics, accounting, on social insurance, which are the main instruments of regulation of market relations by the state, became an important step in formation of market relations.

Policies and measures implemented in the field of budget and financing in the past period were directed towards establishment and strengthening of macroeconomic stabilization. Activities, directed towards provision of sustainability and transparency of the budget, repayment of accumulated debt, improvement of the budget balance, budget and financial reform, improvement of budget planning, implementation and control were taken in the frame of measures providing macroeconomic stabilization.

As Mongolian economy became open, foreign economic relations started expanding in our country. By the way of foreign trade liberalization, a strategic objective of improving the level of security of national economy, which was strongly dependent on one or a group of countries, was implemented.

As a result of economic and social reform, a private sector was established by the way of privatization of state property, which was predominant in economy. As a result of intensive privatization of state property, relations between the state and private sectors have changed fundamentally and private enterprises emerged anew, which provided basic conditions for structural changes in Mongolian economy.

Thus, due to privatization people acquired their own property, and conditions for autonomous, free activities, not dependent in economic aspect from the state, were established, thus giving way to reforms and changes in all parts of the society. Privatization in our country played a historic role in development of multilateral property relations, development of private sector, its growing role and position in economy.

In 1990-2000 as a result of measures, taken by the Government of Mongolia, international banking and financial organizations and donor countries to stabilize macro economy, to intensify structural reforms, to restructure the public sector, to support the private sector, positive trends emerged in the macro economic condition. For instance, basic conditions for economic recovery were established in Mongolia, activities of some industries picked up, for the first time since the beginning of transition the economy grew, the current budget balance became profitable, the foreign trade deficit decreased and the volume of export and import increased.

Although some positive trends were observed in macro economy, not much progress was made in improving the livelihood of population. The real income of population reduced, unemployment went up and poverty became widespread. Results of the 1995 survey, conducted together with international organizations, led to a conclusion that poverty in Mongolia became a real phenomenon and 36% of total population live in poverty. The indicator of income per capita still drags backward the position of Mongolia in human development. Even though in the last 10 years the amount of real income per capita in Mongolia grew by 1/4, it is still 10.3 times lower than the global average.

Numerous important demographic changes have taken place in Mongolia in the years of transition. Deep changes in the living environment of people affected demographic indicators and external and internal migration of population.

A secure life of population was disrupted and rural-urban migration as well as migration from cities to foreign countries has intensified. As a result of internal migration of population, trends for reduction of population in remote aimags and growth of population in the capital city and aimags close to the city, were observed. Results of the last population census show that ¼ f total population in Mongolia participated in migration. External and internal migration of people in search of better opportunities for livelihood show that living environment in urban as well as rural areas is unsatisfactory.

Although the economy grew in a sustainable way in the last decade, the share of population with income lower than the minimal livelihood standard has not reduced significantly.

In our country with a low level of economic development, a low GDP per capita, where 36% of population live in poverty, unemployment is high and urban rural disparities are large, we face an objective of improving living standards of population and providing economic growth by the way of supporting development of main economic sectors by utilizing regulation mechanisms. In order to achieve these objectives the state needs to implement following activities:

- For the state to support development of main economic sectors;
- To support national industry and to provide sustainable growth of the private sector;
- To reduce the amount of social insurance paid by the population and enterprises, to change the present social insurance system;
- To reduce the loan interest rates, to make the loan terms longer, to increase the amount of loans on preferential conditions in order to develop SME;
- To increase foreign investment, to improve legal environment for it;
- To develop infrastructure, to create a favorable business environment in rural areas and regions, to develop SME in rural areas by implementing a differentiated regional policy ;
- To provide population with sustainable workplaces by developing export-oriented SME based on unique features and local resources of regions, to increase real income of population, to reduce unemployment and poverty.

In order to provide economic growth it is necessary to create an optimal structure of economic sectors, to implement well-thought measures to accelerate development of main sectors, to increase the role of sectors in economy, to develop and implement a best policy for improving participation of the private sector in each of the sectors, for increasing its position and role, to make serious changes and achieve real progress.

Especially, state support in development of export-oriented processing SME based on local resources of rural areas and regions, infrastructure development in order to create a favorable business environment, increasing investment will undoubtedly make an important contribution in generating work places, increasing real income and reducing unemployment and poverty.

One of factors making an important impact on development of private sector is investment, financial sources. However, at present investment and financial sources, necessary for private sector development, are limited, so private enterprises are not able to expand their business, increase their profit and create savings. Today the majority of private enterprises have scarce opportunities for attracting investment and finding financial sources, the loan interest rates have not declined significantly, the loan repayment terms are short and many enterprises lack assets for loan collateral, which increases the loan risks, limits investment and affects negatively economic growth.

From the beginning of 1990s production, services, financial and production capital at the global market became more international or globalized. This short transition was also important for developing countries, and their economic relations with industrialized countries have changed fundamentally. In the present globalization era production activities of small underdeveloped countries are included in the common global production network. The flow of human capital and assets has become free and with regard to a need to maintain an ecological balance, to keep the living environment clean, all countries in the world accepted the model of sustainable development in the 21st century and the Millennium Development Goals were put forward.

Now we came to the onset of intensive development with use of the market economy system. A consolidated state policy and development concept are important to lead development in the optimal way. If the economic structure is examined, in the last 15 years primary sectors based on raw materials, such as agriculture and mining played a major role in GDP. It illustrates that the economic basis of our country is highly dependent on the weather conditions and price fluctuations of the global market and has a fragile structure. In the frame of the long-term development strategy policy, the mining sector is not the one with a promising future since natural resources are exhaustible and the sector often causes an ecological instability. Moreover, mining is capital intensive, and it does not produce an added value since raw materials are not processed to final products. Due to that the mining sector does not affect total employment at the national level. Therefore, in the policy frame income generated in the mining sector should be directed towards sectors that can create more workplaces and sectors that determine the future development of the country.

The next stage of transition is transition from the economy based on the primary natural raw materials towards production economy, which creates added value. That is why Mongolia needs to implement successive policies to change its economic structure in order to develop intensively.

AUTHORS

Chapter I.

- P. Luvsandorj, Academician, member of Mongolian Academy of Sciences, Director of Economics Institute, SES

Chapter II.

- B. Suvd, Ph.D, professor in Economics, SES, NUM
- N. Sodnomdorj, Ph.D, professor in Management
- Solongo, Ph.D, head of PTRC, SES, NUM

Chapter III.

- Ts. Ayurzana, Sc.D, professor in Finance, SES, NUM
- D. Tserenpil, Sc.D, professor in Finance, SES, NUM

Chapter IY.

- Ts. Tserendorj, Ph.D, professor in Statistics, SES, NUM
- Ts. Tseveen, Ph.D, professor in Management, SES, NUM
- A. Demberel, Ph.D, professor in Economics
- D. Chimgee, Ph.D, professor in Computer Science, SES, NUM
- P. Oyunbileg, Ph.D, professor in Computer Science, SES, NUM
- S. Handsuren, Ph.D, professor in Statistics, SES, NUM
- B. Davaasuren, Ph.D, professor and head of Marketing department, SES, NUM
- Ts. Tsagaach, Ph.D candidate, head of Statistics department, SES, NUM

Chapter Y.

- D. Dagvadorj, Sc.D, professor in Marketing, SES, NUM
- L. Tsedendamba, Ph.D
- Ya. Otgonsuren, Ph.D, professor in Marketing, SES, NUM

Chapter YI.

- T. Dorj, Academician, member of Mongolian Academy of Sciences, professor in Management, SES, NUM

Chapter YII.

- B. Sainjargal, Ph.D, professor and head of Accounting department, SES, NUM
- T. Jaavaa, Sc.D, professor in Accounting, SES, NUM
- L. Munkh-Ochir, Ph.D, professor in Accounting, SES, NUM
- L. Oyuntsetseg, Ph.D candidate, lecturer in Accounting, SES, NUM
- S. Erdenebileg, Ph.D candidate

Chapter YIII.

- E. Gurgemjav, PhD, professor in ITrade, head of Academic Affairs, SES,NUM
- N. Batnasan, Ph.D, professor in ITrade, Academic Secretary, SES, NUM

Chapter IX.

- Ch. Hashchuluun, Ph.D, professor in Economics, Dean of SES, NUM
- N. Batnasan, Ph.D, professor in ITrade, Academic Secretary, SES, NUM

Afterword.

- B. Bat, Ph.D, professor in Economics, Vice dean of SES, NUM